OKLAHOMA

A Guide to The Sooner State

OKLAHOMA

A GUIDE TO THE SOONER STATE

Compiled by Workers of the Writers' Program
of the Work Projects Administration
in the State of Oklahoma

AMERICAN GUIDE SERIES

ILLUSTRATED

Sponsored by the University of Oklahoma

NORMAN

UNIVERSITY OF OKLAHOMA PRESS

MCMXLI

THE UNIVERSITY OF OKLAHOMA

STATE-WIDE SPONSOR OF THE OKLAHOMA WRITERS' PROGRAM

FEDERAL WORKS AGENCY

WORK PROJECTS ADMINISTRATION

HOWARD O. HUNTER, *Commissioner*

FLORENCE KERR, *Assistant Commissioner*

RON STEPHENS, *State Administrator*

PRINTED IN THE U.S.A. BY THE UNIVERSITY OF OKLAHOMA PRESS

Foreword

OKLAHOMA is a land of timbered mountains, treeless plains, mesquite and sage brush, cypress and pine, massive buildings and small homes, of pioneer newness and old tradition. Within its boundaries is found nearly everything that we think of as genuinely American.

Here are clear fishing streams, beautiful lakes, and rugged mountain scenery. Level plains, where fields of grain bear witness to the rich soil; remote ranch houses and great herds of cattle grazing on the prairies; oil-field derricks symbolizing the state's rich resources in petroleum; cities with skyscrapers, interesting towns —all these reveal the widespread enterprise, contentment, and hospitality of the men and women whose achievements constitute the substance of this *Guide*.

There are people now living in Oklahoma whose memories encompass the whole history of the state. Some of the pioneers who drove the first stakes in the prairies to plat the sites of our cities, farms, and ranches have watched the remarkable progress of Oklahoma since they first arrived. Many men who sat in the constitutional convention and created the state's educational and welfare institutions are still living, as are members of the Five Civilized Tribes who helped to govern small Indian republics as distinct and individual as city states of ancient Greece. In many communities are children of prairie Indians who hunted the buffalo and moved their tepee villages across the plains. United States marshals, cowboys, missionaries, and pioneer educators have been a part of Oklahoma life through the years. Fortunately, some of them survive to recount the story of territorial days as well as the moving events that have occurred since statehood.

In one sense, Oklahoma is new, but in another real sense it is old. The first church was organized in 1830, the first public school law was enacted in 1832, the first printing press was set up in 1835, and the first newspaper began publication in 1844. All these agencies of civilization and culture were established by and for the Indian population; and the state's present economic, social, political, and religious structures were based on these early foundations.

This volume is a serious attempt to present a rounded story of Oklahoma; in its pages both Oklahomans and visitors in the state will find much that is useful and interesting.

W. B. Bizzell

May 15, 1941

Preface

WHILE WORKING OVER the material compiled and written by the Oklahoma Writers' Program for *Oklahoma: A Guide to the Sooner State,* the staff has at times suspected that it was putting together the most comprehensive history of Oklahoma thus far published. Even though the suspicion is probably not justified, it is hoped that the persevering reader will lay down the book convinced that he knows and understands the backgrounds of this interesting state and has at least a speaking acquaintance with its present.

The obvious purpose of a state guide, of course, is to direct. The tours and the section on the principal cities, especially, try to tell accurately what every nook and corner of Oklahoma has of interest to its citizens and to visitors. From almost innumerable sources—books, newspaper files, and above all Oklahomans themselves—the Oklahoma Writers' Program has recorded the state's history, pictured its varied topography, summarized its natural resources and its cultural and industrial development. Beyond the search for facts, however, the staff has sought such material as would add color to Oklahoma's story. It has also kept in mind the need to make clear the complicated and significant story of the close human and political contacts between the Indians and the whites in the century and a quarter since the two races first met in Oklahoma.

It is not possible to list by name the many organizations and persons who helped in the preparation of this book. To all of them we make grateful acknowledgment.

ANGIE DEBO
JOHN M. OSKISON } *Editors*

Contents

PART III. Tours

PART IV. Appendices

Illustrations

Maps

General Information

Railroads: The Rock Island System (Rock Island); St. Louis–San Francisco Ry. (Frisco); The Atchison, Topeka & Santa Fe Ry. (Santa Fe); Missouri-Kansas-Texas R.R. (Katy); Kansas, Oklahoma & Gulf Ry. (KO&G); Midland Valley R.R. (MV); Missouri Pacific R.R. (MP or MOP); The Kansas City Southern Ry. (KCS); Oklahoma City-Ada-Atoka Ry. (OCAA); Texas, Oklahoma & Eastern R.R. (TO&E); Gulf, Colorado & Santa Fe Ry. (GC&SF); Beaver, Meade & Englewood R.R. (BM&E); Panhandle & Santa Fe Ry. (PH&SF); Oklahoma & Rich Mountain R.R. (O&RM); Arkansas Western Ry. (KAW); Wichita Valley Ry. (WV); Wichita Falls & Southern Ry. (WF&S); Ft. Smith & Van Buren Ry. (FT.S&VB); Osage Ry. (OR); Okmulgee Northern Ry. (ON). Many of these lines were organized and constructed under other names but are now (1941) operated under the names given above.

Highways: 21 Federal highways, 9 of them transcontinental or with transcontinental connections. State covered by a network of state and county roads.

Traffic Regulations (digest): Maximum speed determined by safety. Driver's license required after residence is established. Drivers from states that have no drivers' license law (Louisiana and North Dakota, 1941) must secure drivers' licenses in Oklahoma within 30 days. Each town and city has own traffic regulations. State has a uniformed highway patrol of 155 officers. Filling stations every few miles on state and Federal highways; gasoline tax (including Federal) 7 cents. No inspection of passenger cars. *Prohibited:* Operating without headlights and taillights at night. Stopping any part of car on pavement. Using spotlight. Driving while under influence of liquor. *Rules of the Road:* Uniform with those of all other states.

Air Lines: Braniff Airways (Chicago to Brownsville, Texas), stop at Ponca City and Oklahoma City; Mid-Continent Airlines (Minneapolis to Tulsa) has its southern terminus at Tulsa; American Airlines (Transcontinental) stops at Tulsa and Oklahoma City. State has 53 airports and landing fields.

Climate and Travel Equipment: Temperature ranges from zero to 85° F., Sept. 15 to July 1. Heaviest annual rainfall (42 in.) in southeastern section. Changes occur suddenly; occasional dust storms in western half of state in spring and summer. Topcoats seldom necessary before October or after April 1.
Prohibition: Illegal to sell or possess spirituous liquors, or to sell malt liquors containing more than 3.2 per cent alcohol.

Poisonous Snakes and Plants: Rattlesnakes found in all sections of the state; cottonmouth moccasins along streams in swamp areas; copperheads in eastern part of state. Poison ivy common in all wooded areas; can be distinguished by its cluster of three leaves, all other ivy vines having five-leaf clusters. Poison ivy is not always a vine but may grow as a weed in meadows or among rocks.

Recreational Areas: Wichita Mountains Wildlife Refuge, 61,480 acres (*see Tour 3A*); Osage Hills State Park, 740 acres (*see Tour 4*); Roman Nose State Park, 520 acres (*see Tour 5*); Robbers Cave State Park, 8,400 acres (*see Tour 5);* Boiling Springs State Park, 820 acres *(see Tour 12);* Ouachita Mountains *(see Tours 7-15-15A);* Grand River Dam, 54,000 acres *(see Tour 1);* Platt National Park, 848 acres (*see Tour 10A*); Turner Falls Park, 848 acres (*see Tour 10);* Lake Murray State Park, 18,350 acres *(see Tour 10);* Quartz Mountain State Park, 3,000 acres *(see Tour 13);* Spavinaw Hills Park, 1,600 acres *(see Tour 15);* Beavers Bend State Park, 1,300 acres *(see Tour 15A);* Salt Plains, 20,480 acres (now a reservoir), made a Federal Wildlife Refuge in 1930 *(see Tour 2);* Cookson Hills Playground (soil conservation project); Greenleaf Lake, 950 acres, playground of 27,000 acres.

Fish and Game Laws (digest): Licenses issued in drug and sporting goods stores, and by fish and game wardens.
Fishing: All nonresidents over 16 years of age must have a license to fish in Oklahoma with any kind of bait; seasonal license, $5; a 10-day permit, $1.25. Resident fishing license, $1.25; 60 days residence necessary for resident license.
Hunting: Season for migrating birds determined by Federal government and changed from year to year. Quail, Nov. 20–Jan. 2, on Tuesdays, Thursdays, and Saturdays. Squirrel, May 15 to Dec. 31. Other game animals may not be hunted except on specified dates.
Limits: Ten bass or channel catfish, or 25 game fish of all kinds, in one day.

Bass and channel cat must be 8 inches or longer, trout 7 inches, and crappie 5 inches. Ten quail in one day, or 50 in one season; 10 squirrels in one day; 10 wild ducks in one day, or 50 in one season; 4 wild geese in a day, or 12 in a season.

Prohibited: To dynamite, poison, or capture fish in any manner except with baited hook or artificial lures, either on line and rod or trotline containing not more than 100 hooks. To sell plumes, skins, or feathers of wild birds enumerated in the Oklahoma statutes. To hunt between a half-hour after sunset to a half-hour before sunrise. To use guns of larger bore than 10-gauge. To hunt, fish, or trap on land of another without consent of owner. To disturb meetings at churches or schoolhouses by shooting in the immediate vicinity. To shoot at animals or birds from, or across, a public highway. It is unlawful to sell or offer for sale any game animal, bird, or fish. Possession of any game animals, birds, or parts thereof, during closed season shall be evidence that they were taken or killed during such closed season.

Calendar of Annual Events

JANUARY

Third or fourth week	at Oklahoma City	State Bowling Tournament
No fixed date	at McAlester	Calico Ball

FEBRUARY

Second week	at Oklahoma City	Golden Gloves Boxing Tournament
No fixed date	at Edmond, Central State College	Invitation High School Basketball Tournament

MARCH

Third or fourth week	Vicinity of Norman	Cornbread Dance of the Big Jim Band of Absentee Shawnees
Fourth week	at Oklahoma City	Livestock (Fat Stock) Show
No fixed date	at Enid	Industrial Exposition
No fixed date	at Tulsa	Magic Empire Junior Livestock Show

MARCH OR APRIL

Easter Morning	at Lawton	Easter Pageant

APRIL

Second week	at Sulphur	Redbud Pilgrimage
Third week	at Enid	Tri-State Band Festival
Third week	at Watonga	Rattlesnake Hunt
Twenty-second	at Guthrie	Eighty-Niners' Celebration
Twenty-second	at El Reno	Chisholm Trail and Pioneer Day Celebration
No fixed date	at Marshall	Little Town High School Band Festival

MAY

Second	at Guymon	Pioneer Day Celebration
First week	at Norman, University of Oklahoma	High School Interscholastic Meet
Second week (even years only)	at Tulsa	International Petroleum Exposition
Decoration Day	at Barber	Cherokee Indian Decoration Day Ceremony
No fixed date	at Chickasha	Horse Show

JUNE

First week	at Stilwell	Green Corn Shoot of the Cherokees
Second week	at Edmond, Central State College	Annual Folk Festival
Second week	at Seminole	Rodeo
Twenty-seventh	at Broken Bow	Tomato Festival
No fixed date	Vicinity of Drumright	"Busks" of the Creek Indians

JULY

Second–fourth	at Cache, Craterville Park	Indian Fair and Rodeo
Third–fourth	at Drumright	American Legion Rodeo
Fourth	at Lake Holdenville	Free Buffalo Meat Barbecue
Fourth	at Anadarko	Old Settlers' Reunion
Fourth	at Sulphur, Platt National Park	Boy Scout Jamboree; July Fourth Celebration
Fourth	Vicinity of Quapaw	Quapaw Indian Powwow
Thirteenth	Vicinity of Kellyville	Indian Stick Ball Game
Nineteenth	Vicinity of Gore	Sacred Fire Ceremony of the Kee-Too-Wah Society of the Cherokee Indians
Twenty-sixth–twenty-eighth	at Atoka	Rodeo
Fourth week	Vicinity of Holdenville	Green Corn Feasts and Stomp Dances of the Creek Indians
No fixed date	Vicinity of Kellyville	Green Corn Dances of the Creeks and Euchees
No fixed date	Vicinity of Henryetta	Green Corn Dances of the Creeks

AUGUST

First Thursday	at Blackburn	Reunion of Drought Survivors of 1901
Sixth	at Lawton	Pioneer Day
First week	at Hinton	Kiwanis Rodeo
Second week	at Quapaw	Seneca-Cayuga Green Corn Feasts and Dances
Second week	at Boley	Negro Masonic Grand Lodge Celebration
Twentieth (usually)	Vicinity of Norman	War Dance of the Big Jim Band of Absentee Shawnees
Third week	at Seminole	Rodeo
Third week	at Anadarko	All-Indian Fair and Exposition
Fifteenth–nineteenth	at Ponca City	Annual Powwow of the Ponca Indians
Twenty-Fourth–Twenty-fifth	at Okmulgee	Pioneer Powwow and Indian Festival
Fourth week	at Covington	Knox-Mulhall Rodeo
No fixed date	Vicinity of Canton	Dances of the Cheyennes and Arapahoes
No fixed date	Vicinity of Shawnee	Grand Medicine Lodge Gathering and Dance of the Sac and Fox Indians
No fixed date	at Sperry	War Dance of the Creeks and Euchees
No fixed date	at Stillwater, Agricultural and Mechanical College	Farmers' Week and 4-H Club Roundup

SEPTEMBER

First week	at Vinita	Will Rogers Memorial Rodeo
Labor Day	at Guymon	Old Settlers' Reunion
Sixteenth	at Enid; Ponca City; Perry	Cherokee Strip Opening Celebration
Second week	at Ardmore	Southern Oklahoma Free Fair
Twenty-first–twenty-fifth	at Perkins	Old Settlers' Celebration and Iowa Indian Dances
Third week	at Tulsa	Tulsa State Fair
Fourth week	at Lamont	Watermelon Festival
Fourth week	at Pawhuska	Osage Indian Removal Dances
Fourth week	at Woodward	Rodeo
Fourth week	at Oklahoma City	Oklahoma State Fair

OCTOBER

First week	at Muskogee	Oklahoma Free State Fair
First week	at Oklahoma City	State-wide Flower Show
Twelfth	at Pawhuska	Feast of Peace Dance of the Osage Indians
Second week (usually)	at Tulsa	American Indian Exposition
No fixed date	at Wynona	Southwestern Fox and Wolf Hunters' Association Wolf Hunt

NOVEMBER

Eleventh	at Pawhuska	Armistice Day Celebration of the Osage Indians
Fifteenth	at Vinita	Southwestern Field Trials
Second week	at Tahlequah	Eastern Oklahoma Folk Festival
Second Saturday	at Boley	Negro Fair and Barbecue
No fixed date	at Atoka; Antlers	Fox Hunts

DECEMBER

No fixed date	Vicinity of Barber	Quarterly Meeting of the Cherokee Indians
No fixed date	at Oklahoma City	All College Invitation Basketball Tournament

PART I

The General Background

The Spirit of Oklahoma

By EDWARD EVERETT DALE

THAT "the child is father to the man" is as true of a state or a nation as it is of an individual. Largely, we are what our past has made us. Behind ideas and ideals, no less than back of institutions social, economic, and political, always lie certain vital forces which have called them into life and which shape their progress. Such being the case, it is clear that any attempt to analyze or explain that intangible thing which we call the spirit of a state must be made in the light of its history.

The most significant thing in the romantic and colorful history of Oklahoma is the former Indian occupation of this region. A century ago the pressure of land-hungry whites drove the Five Civilized Tribes westward to Oklahoma, and virtually all of the present state except the Panhandle was granted to them for "as long as grass grows and the waters run." It was as though a wall has been erected about Oklahoma by governmental decree. It was an intangible barrier, of course, and yet none the less real because of that. Denied entrance into this "Indian Territory," white settlers crept slowly westward occupying lands on either side of it; but the wall held firm.

Because of this long Indian occupation, Oklahoma presented for generations the picture of an area of arrested development. The last American frontier, it lies in point of time very near to pioneer society, but it has made greater material progress in a single generation than has any other area of comparable size in the United States.

That this long Indian era has profoundly affected present-day Oklahoma is readily apparent. The Five Civilized Tribes in their old homes east of the Mississippi occupied what might be described as a "strategic region," between Spain in Florida, France in Louisiana, and England in the Carolinas and Georgia. The Indians were quick to realize the advantages of their position and with rare ability began to play one nation off against the other.

This long training, to which was added the experience of administering the affairs of their tribal governments after reaching Oklahoma, gave the Indians of the Five Civilized Tribes a knowledge of diplomacy and politics equal to that of any people in the world. Oklahoma's constitutional convention was largely dominated by that group of Indian Territory statesmen trained in the hard school of tribal politics. Many of the outstanding political figures of the state have either had Indian blood or been intermarried citizens of one of the Five Civilized Tribes. Among these may be listed two governors, a United States senator, several members of the lower house of Congress, at least two speakers of the Oklahoma legislature, and many other prominent state officials.

Indians have given Oklahoma not only able statesmen but soldiers, artists, literary men, and civic leaders as well, while the two men the state has honored with statues in the national Capitol, Sequoyah and Will Rogers, were both of Indian blood. Perhaps most important of all, the Indian race has given to Oklahoma many thousands of good citizens who in a more humble capacity have done much for the advancement of their own communities and of the state.

Steadily there is being woven into the fabric of Oklahoma's citizenship this red thread of the Indian. Through intermarriage, Indian blood in Oklahoma is becoming more widely diffused. The time may come when an Indian recognizable as such will be hard to find within the state, but perhaps through wider dissemination the influences of Indian blood may be greater in the future than they have ever been in the past.

Important as has been the influence of the Indian in the formation of the spirit of Oklahoma, that of the pioneer white settler was no less significant. Much of western Oklahoma was opened to settlement by the so-called "Runs." In these it was literally true that "the race was to the swift, the battle to the strong." The first of these, that of the "Unassigned Lands," was at high noon, April 22, 1889. When the President's proclamation, issued thirty days earlier, fixed the date of this opening, it also provided that anyone entering upon these lands prior to that date should forfeit all claim to any part of them as a homestead.

Before the day fixed for the opening many thousand eager young men had gathered along the border of this new Promised Land impatiently waiting for the hour when they would be free to cross the line and choose a claim. Some of these had for years been urging, or "booming," the opening of these lands to settlement and were, in consequence, known as "Boomers."

It is not surprising that some of them should grow weary of waiting and under the cover of darkness cross into the forbidden area too soon. Here they chose choice tracts and either occupied them or lay in concealment near by ready to dash out and assert their claims when the hour of opening had come.

These men, known as "Sooners" because they had entered the territory too soon, had not technically committed any crime for which they could be punished by law. Yet they could not legally secure any of these lands by homestead or acquire a right to any part of them. In the language of sport, they were merely put out of the game for a violation of the rules.

For a long time the term "Sooner" was one of reproach, but with the passing of the years the word began to lose its original connotation. As its origin was gradually forgotten, it eventually came to mean merely one who is alert, ambitious, and enterprising, or one who gets up earlier than others, always takes the lead, and strives to triumph over obstacles.

The first great Run was followed by others. Each of these brought to Oklahoma a fresh influx of aggressive, eager young people to choose lands, build homes, open up farms and establish towns and cities. Regions as large as one of the smaller states of the Union were settled within a single day and developed with amazing rapidity. Then, about the time that the free lands of western Oklahoma were all gone, came the beginning of the marvelous oil development of the eastern portion of the state. Here the opening of each new oil field brought a new "run" of youthful, adventurous people, not for homesteads but for leases, royalties, concessions, and business opportunities. In this fashion Oklahoma was peopled by a hardy, vigorous population strong in their youth and often counting material advancement as the true standard of success.

In the lean years before the coming of oil the pioneer life of Oklahoma was hard, as many people yet living can abundantly testify. But in spite of hardships due to hot winds, crop failures, and lack of material comforts, the pioneer homesteader looked into the future and saw there wonderful things. Like Christian, he had caught a glimpse far off of a celestial city, and he worked early and late to make his dreams come true.

If in his eager seeking after the things of the flesh he should neglect somewhat the things of the spirit, that too was inevitable. With his family housed in a dugout, sod house, or rude cabin, the pioneer would have been somewhat more, or less, than human to give too much attention to music, art, and literature before he had made better provisions for the physical welfare of his family.

Yet even from the first there were always to be found certain elements who kept alive the spark of cultural and intellectual progress and who strove earnestly to fan it into flame. Foremost among these were the pioneer women who planted flowers, beautified the simple home, and urged that churches, schools, and Sunday Schools be established in order that the children might not grow up in want of the finer things of life. Added to their efforts were those of frontier bishops, the presidents and faculties of the struggling little colleges, and those who worked in a far more humble capacity, the rural teachers, circuit riders, and country pastors, to all of whom Oklahoma owes a deep debt of gratitude for their contribution to the spirit of the state.

It was not long before the earnest efforts of these early pioneers began to bear fruit. The dugout or sod house gave place to an attractive farm home. The trail over which the covered wagons rolled west widened to a broad highway. The tiny villages grew to thriving towns. Churches, schools, and colleges multiplied and became comparable with those of older states. Oklahoma was rapidly coming of age.

It is obvious that such a historical heritage should give to Oklahoma a remarkable and distinctive spirit. It is a spirit of youth, of optimism, and high faith in the future. It is a pioneering spirit, eagerly reaching out for things new in economic and social experimentation, or government. In the lean pioneer years, Oklahoma had to depend largely upon borrowed capital for its economic advancement and upon borrowed culture for its intellectual and educational progress. More recently it has developed not only locally produced capital but locally produced culture as well; strong financial figures as well as nationally known writers, artists, and musicians.

In recent years Oklahoma, in common with other states, has felt keenly the pinch of economic depression. This has brought to a few people a feeling of pessimism and discouragement, but only to a few. The pioneer spirit, compounded of courage, optimism, and faith, is still strong among a people so close to the frontier of yesterday.

Natural Setting

The map of Oklahoma suggests in its outline a butcher's cleaver, the Panhandle of the west representing the handle, the north line its straight back edge, the east line its square-cut end, the Red River on the south its irregular cutting edge. Lying slightly south of the geographic center of the United States, it is a part of the Great Plains region, and its surface has a gradual upward slope toward the Rocky Mountains. The lowest point, 324 feet, is in the southeastern corner; the highest is in the Panhandle, 4,978 feet. The average elevation is 1,300 feet.

Oklahoma has an area of 70,057 square miles. It is bounded on the north by Kansas and Colorado; on the east by Missouri and Arkansas; on the south by Texas; and on the west by Texas and New Mexico. Its main rivers flow in a southeasterly direction, and the entire drainage is carried to the Mississippi by the Arkansas and Red rivers. The Arkansas enters the state from Kansas about the middle of the northern border. The Salt Fork (Neecatunga), Cimarron, Grand, Verdigris, and Canadian rivers all flow into the Arkansas within the borders of Oklahoma. The North Canadian flows nearly across the state before joining its companion stream, the Canadian. The Washita and a number of lesser streams in the southern part of the state feed Red River.

In the northeast, the Ozark Plateau extends into Oklahoma. It is a region of moderate hills with deep, narrow valleys and numerous clear streams. The base of the plateau is a great limestone formation known as the Boone Chert; and steep, picturesque bluffs have been formed where the streams have cut it deeply. Timbered with oak, ash, hickory, elm, walnut, pecan, hard maple, and sycamore, this is a region of great beauty, especially in autumn, when the forests are clothed in rich and varied colors.

South of the Ozark region, occupying most of the southeastern corner of the state, the Ouachita (Wah-she-tah) Mountain area, much of which is included in a national forest, consists of parallel ridges formed by the faulting of thick layers of sandstone. Many of the valleys are narrow, and each has its spring-fed stream. This area contains the pine forests of Oklahoma, as well as many hardwoods.

In the south central part of the state are the Arbuckle Mountains, covering an area of about sixty by twenty miles. These old mountains, worn down to a height of only seven hundred feet above the surrounding plains, present a remarkable variety of geological formations—limestone, sandstone, shale, and granite. The limestone is grass-covered, while most of the others are timbered. Many streams and attractive camping places make this one of the popular recreation areas of the state.

South of the Arbuckles and Ouachitas to the Red River, is a strip of sandy plain cut by streams flowing to the river. This is classed as a part of the Gulf and Coastal Plains.

Seventy miles northwest of the Arbuckles, the rough granite peaks of the Wichita Mountains *(See Tour 3B),* break abruptly from the surrounding plains and, with some outlying peaks, extend some sixty miles in a northwesterly direction. Like the Arbuckles, they are the tops of buried mountains, and part of a range of mountains known to geologists as the Amarillo Range. Erosion has left little except the bare granite outcroppings, and there are few trees. The scenery, however, is interesting, and the region worth visiting.

Most of the eastern end of the state not included in the Ozark, Ouachita, Arbuckle, and Red River areas is known to geologists as the sandstone hills region, the rocks being hard sandstones and limestones alternating with softer shales. The hills are low and flat, the fertile valleys wide, accounting for much of the state's best farm land. Native oak and hickory have nearly disappeared before the ax, and there remains little timber besides the nearly worthless blackjack oak on the sandy hills and slopes. In such places erosion has been severe.

Interesting, and important in the history of Oklahoma, is a north- and south-trending strip of rough country known as the Cross Timbers, varying from five to thirty miles in width across the central part of the state. From Washington Irving's *A Tour on the Prairies* on through the accounts of such trail-makers as Randolph B. Marcy, escorting gold-seekers to California over the southern route in 1849, this belt of matted, tangled undergrowth, stiff-branched blackjacks, shinnery, briars, and scions of fire-killed larger trees made a deep and unfavorable impression. It was a region of tumbled rocks and thin soil, gashed by ravines, difficult to cross; and it marked roughly the dividing line between the bluestem prairies of the eastern half of the state and the buffalo grass plains of the western section. On a government map of 1834, the Cross Timbers is designated as the "western boundary of habitable land."

The sandstone hills region merges gradually on the west with the Permian region, one of the most extensive formations of its type known. The red beds extend from the Kansas border to Red River, from almost the center of the state to within forty miles of the west line. They are composed of shales and soft sandstones twelve hundred to sixteen hundred feet in thickness and get their color from ferric (iron) oxide. Some of the state's most fertile farm land lies within this gently rolling region.

The western part of the Red Beds contains several ledges of gypsum; and here, particularly along the Cimarron River, the red and white combination makes striking scenery. The numerous gypsum strata differ in thickness and composition, some being nearly pure and hard, others softer and interbedded with shale. The hard layers topping the buttes of the Blaine Escarpment render these low mesas impressive, because of both their color and location upon otherwise flat plains. One form of gypsum, selenite, is crystalline and breaks into pieces resembling fragments of glass or mica. The Glass, or Gloss, Mountains *(see Tour 4)*, an outlier of the Blaine Escarpment, are so called because their sides are littered with flakes of selenite which glisten in the sun. The gypsum area makes a rough triangle, its base a wide arc north of the Wichita Mountains and its apex at the Kansas border. Wheat, corn, sorghums, and livestock are the principal farming products of the "gyp hills" region.

The Great Salt Plains near Cherokee *(see Tour 2)* and other salt plains in that region have been formed by springs of salt water that, saturated from a deep-lying stratum, seeps through the Red Beds and gypsum formations. Of little commercial importance, these salt deposits are striking in appearance.

The northwestern counties and the Panhandle, included in the High Plains region, are level grassland, treeless except for elms, cottonwoods, and willows along the streams. They are thinly settled, and much of the land is still in native pasture grass. During the first World War, demand for wheat caused the development of great wheat farms in the Panhandle, and for several years Texas County was the banner wheat-producing county of the nation. Sorghums are also an important crop. Because of continued drought, this area became for a time part of the Dust Bowl. Some of it is now regarded as submarginal and should be restored to grass, although frequent rains and a concerted effort to restore the balance of plant life have resulted in a remarkable improvement of the entire area.

GEOLOGY

The Oklahoma region for ages has been in the process of constant geological change. Seas have covered it and receded, leaving swamps, and in the swamps of the Pennsylvanian period, coal formations were laid down. Extensive upheavals, folding, and faulting at the close of this period formed the Arbuckle and Wichita Mountains. An idea of the time required in the geologic process may be gained from the fact that some of the formations laid down at that time are more than a mile thick.

Sandstone and limestone formations that are exposed in the Arbuckle and sandstone hills are important oil-producing strata. From about the middle of the state, northward from a point between Norman and Oklahoma City, and into Nemaha County, Kansas, a buried mountain range of granite, known as the Nemaha Mountains, can be traced in subsurface by means of wells drilled for oil and gas. Along this buried range are found some of the most productive oil pools in both states.

In the Jurassic period this area was swampy, with many lakes and cut-off seas; and at that time dinosaurs from two to eighty feet in length were the characteristic animal life. Fossils of these creatures have been found in many places in the state. During the Lower Cretaceous period, after the time of the dinosaurs, the last submergence occurred.

In the later Pleistocene period, as fossil remains show, the Oklahoma region was overrun by horses, some no larger than a fox; camels, large and small; rhinoceroses, mastodons, mammoths, musk oxen, saber-toothed tigers, and immense herds of elephants of several species.

CLIMATE

Oklahoma lies on the border of distinctive north-and-south and east-and-west climatic zones. Rainfall varies from an average of forty-two inches annually in the extreme southeast to fifteen inches in the western Panhandle; average for the state is between twenty-five and thirty inches. Killing frost comes from the last week in September in the north, to mid-November farther south. Winters are usually mild, with occasional cold waves in January, February, and March.

In the eastern half of the state light to moderate east-to-southeast winds prevail. In the western half, winds of higher velocity blow almost constantly from south or north; and a daytime temperature above 100° F. may be expected in July and August. Nights are usually cool.

PLANT AND ANIMAL LIFE

One hundred and thirty-three varieties of trees are native to Oklahoma. The southern, or longleaf, pine, various species of oak, elm, ash, hickory, pecan, walnut, cottonwood, willow, and some magnolia and cypress are characteristic. In the western part, among the canyons of the Red Beds and

Gypsum Hills, red cedar, or juniper, is abundant. Sagebrush is found in the west, and mesquite in the southwest.

The redbud (Judas tree) and dogwood, which bloom in the early spring, show masses of bright pink and creamy white along the streams and hillsides throughout the eastern, central, and most of the southern parts. Violets, including the dogtooth variety, primrose, anemone, petunia, spiderwort, verbena, gaillardia, phlox, the showy wild indigo in blue and cream varieties, poppy mallow, goldenrod, sunflower, and ageratum are commonly seen. The trumpet flower, though not native, grows well. Roses thrive, as do many other garden flowers. Cape jasmine does well in the southern counties, and crape myrtle is a favorite shrub in the north to middle part of the state.

Wild grapes and many varieties of wild plums are found in nearly every part of the state. In the Wichita Mountains wild currants are common. Pecan, walnut, and some hickory nut trees grow in the east and south. Peaches, apples, cherries, and pears are produced in Oklahoma, though there are few commercial orchards.

Coyotes, cottontails, jackrabbits, and prairie dogs are fairly common on the plains; mink, otter, opossum, gray and fox squirrels, and raccoons are found in the timbered sections. Black bears, numerous in early days, had almost disappeared by the time of settlement. There are deer, though not plentiful, and no buffaloes outside of zoos and game preserves.

The chief species of birds are the mockingbird, meadow lark, swallow, dove, woodpecker, robin, bluejay, and English sparrow. Crows are so numerous that crow-killing campaigns are carried on every winter. In the early fall, immense flocks of blackbirds (grackle) gather and are a striking sight when they settle in feedlots. Recently (1936–37) flights of English starlings have migrated into the state. Redbirds, bluejays, and bobwhites remain the year round. Prairie chickens are sometimes seen in the western counties and are strictly protected. Mallard, teal, and other varieties of duck, and wild geese, fly over in spring and fall. Wild turkeys, found in great abundance by the early hunters, became almost extinct, but they are being successfully restocked in forest regions.

There are few poisonous snakes. The copperhead and cottonmouth, or water moccasin, are most common; rattlesnakes are becoming more and more scarce. Centipedes are found, as well as horned toads and other varieties of harmless lizards.

CONSERVATION

By 1937, twelve permanent agencies were at work in Oklahoma for the conservation of natural resources and the preservation and propagation of wild life. Of this number, five were Federal; the others were controlled by the state.

Oklahoma's Wildlife Council is a federation of all agencies, state or otherwise, concerned with the preservation of wild life. Its program has been adopted by the American Wildlife Institute, which is striving to organize all states on the Oklahoma plan.

Earliest efforts at conservation were hampered by lack of public interest and shortage of funds. The first game department, set up shortly after statehood, consisted of a few men whose duties were mainly to fight the widespread practice of market hunting of deer, prairie chickens, turkeys, and quail. At that time professional hunters were numerous, and records reveal that enforcement officers sometimes captured entire trains of wild game billed to eastern markets. It was not until 1925 that the State Game and Fish Commission was created, and the work of replenishing the rapidly vanishing stock of wild game began. This commission now maintains fish and bird hatcheries, regulates hunting and fishing, and to an extent controls predatory animals.

At the end of the tribal period (1907), great forests of virgin pine still covered much of the Choctaw country; and the Secretary of the Interior worked out a plan for setting them aside as a forest reserve. The project, however, was never authorized by Congress, and the woodland was allotted along with the rest of the tribal lands to individual Indians, who sold the trees to lumbermen. As a result, nearly all of the marketable timber has been cleared from the Choctaw lands.

Forest conservation efforts of the United States in Oklahoma are represented by the control of 140,000 acres of timber in LeFlore County, known as the Ouachita National Forest; the Wichita Mountains Wildlife Refuge; and the Shelterbelt Project, which is planting trees in the western counties in order to stop soil erosion.

When the State Forestry Department was set up in 1925, Oklahoma's timber areas had been so badly slashed that 1,300,000 acres had to be put under fire protection, and 1,630,000 acres into a restocking area. This department, working with the United States Forest Service, established a nursery on the grounds of the Agricultural and Mechanical College at Stillwater for growing stock suitable for reforestation purposes and for woodlot and windbreak planting. More than 650,000 small trees grown here have been sold in one year for fall and spring planting on Oklahoma farms.

Need for the selection of park sites in time for the state to use Civilian Conservation Corps workers brought the first legislative appropriation in 1935 for a park commission. Prior to that date, all state-owned parks were administered by the State Game and Fish Commission. The State Park Commission operates under the Oklahoma Planning and Resources Board, in close liaison with the National Park Service. The Planning and Resources Board also directs the work of the former Conservation Commission and has charge of state forestry projects.

The Conservation Commission and the State Planning Board were set up in 1935. The latter is interested in all forms of conservation, but has advisory powers only. The Conservation Commission, which has functioned under other names or departments since 1907, is concerned chiefly with water projects—dams, lakes, irrigation, and flood control. The State Corporation Commission, though not primarily a conservation body, acts for the oil and gas industry in this capacity. It regulates the drilling of wells and oil production and works to prevent land spoilage and stream pollution.

Federal conservation agencies in Oklahoma are the National Park Service, National Forest Service, Soil Conservation Service, and the Fish and Wildlife Service. The National Forest Service administers the Kiamichi Division of the Ouachita National Forest, co-operates with the state in maintaining fire protection and in distributing planting stock, and supervises the forest activities of the CCC. The National Park Service supervises Platt National Park, protecting the wild game and preserving plant life from insects, disease, and fire. The Fish and Wildlife Service engages in research related to birds and wild animals. Its activities are confined mainly to the Wichita Mountains Wildlife Refuge and Game Preserve and the Great Salt Plains Wild Fowl Refuge. In co-operation with owners, the Soil Conservation Service supervises actual soil conservation work on the land.

Tree planting in the Oklahoma sector of the Shelter Belt (a "temporary" Federal project) began in 1935 in Woodward County and extended through sixteen counties from the northern line to Tillman County. There are completed sections north of Buffalo, twenty strips near Erick in Beckham County, several strips north of Reydon, in Roger Mills County, eighteen near Willow, more than forty near Mangum, thirty-four sections near Cordell, and twelve strips near Moore. The project, although still in its infancy, has measurably decreased erosion losses, and its program has provided work for drought-stricken farmers of the area.

Early Oklahomans

ALTHOUGH it will never be fully known what strange races of men built their long-dead hearth fires in the sheltered eastern woods and along the shallow streams of western Oklahoma, there is evidence of six main prehistoric cultures.

The Folsom Culture. Archeologists generally recognize the "Folsom Man" as the earliest known inhabitant of America, but even the approximate age of this culture has not yet been determined. Traces, however, in the form of the distinctive Folsom and Yuma projectile points, have been found in the Oklahoma Panhandle.

The Basket Makers' Culture. Remains of the Basket Makers have also been uncovered in small rock caves in the extreme northwestern part of the Panhandle, apparently an eastern extension of their main settlements in New Mexico and Arizona. They were a primitive people, unfamiliar with the bow and arrow or the making of pottery, but the baskets, mats, and cradles they fashioned were elaborate; and their small fields were planted in corn, beans, squashes, and pumpkins. Their occupancy probably dates back from fifteen hundred to two thousand years.

The Ozark Bluff Dwellers Culture. At about the same time, the Ozark Bluff Dwellers occupied the limestone caves along the streams of the northeastern part of the state. Like the Basket Makers, they had not discovered the bow and arrow and made no pottery, but they were skilled in basketry, practiced a rude agriculture, and used the dart and throw stick as weapons.

The Ozark Top-Layer Culture. Overlying the Bluff Dwellers sites are remains of what is generally known as the Ozark Top-Layer Culture. This culture, though still crude, represents an advance over that of the true Bluff Dwellers; for these people possessed the bow and arrow, made a greater variety of bone and stone implements, and fashioned crude pottery. Their date has not yet been determined.

The Slab-House Culture. Evidences of this culture, dating from 1000 to 1400 A.D., have also been discovered in the Panhandle. The slab-house people lived in pit dwellings, lined with flat stones set on edge, roofed with rafters supported by central posts, and thatched with reeds, which were covered with earth. They practiced a rude agriculture; made pottery; used the lance, the bow and arrow; and shaped a variety of stone implements.

The Lower Mound Builder Culture. Remains of this culture may also be seen in eastern Oklahoma. It is distinguished by earthen mounds, shaped like cones or flat-topped pyramids, constructed along the banks of the streams. In these mounds is found evidence of a high development of the ceramic art; etchings and carvings on stone, bone, and shell serve further to identify them. These people lived, it is believed, from 500 to 1500 A.D. and were part of a general cultural group that occupied most of the present southern states.

Archeological study in Oklahoma has barely begun; hence the relation between the different prehistoric races and their connection with the Indian tribes living in Oklahoma at the coming of the white man has not yet been determined. Among the most important sites are the mounds east of Wagoner *(see Tour 8)*, the mounds northeast of Spiro *(see Tour 7)*, and the caves southeast of Kenton *(see Tour 2)*. The Spiro Mound has been carefully excavated as a WPA project under the supervision of Dr. Forrest E. Clements, of the University of Oklahoma. A great number of artifacts have been taken from the mound and placed on exhibition at the University; it is hoped that they will materially assist in reconstructing the life of the state's prehistoric peoples, and in placing them in their true cultures.

Among the aboriginal tribes, and those that came into the Oklahoma area in early historic times, six linguistic divisions occurred: the Caddoan, Siouan, Athapascan, Shoshonean, Tanoan, and (a rather late arrival, 1868) the Algonquian. The Athapascan peoples were the Apaches and Kiowa-Apaches; the Siouan stock is represented by the Osages; the Shoshonean by the Comanches; the Tanoan by the Kiowas; and the Algonquian by the Cheyennes and Araphaoes, so closely related that they are usually spoken of together.

Indians of the Caddoan linguistic stock seem to have been most widely distributed in Oklahoma when the region was first visited by white men. The Caddoes proper were settled mainly on the lower Red River in Louisiana, but remains of their culture are numerous in eastern Oklahoma. They made a distinctive and beautiful pottery, used copper in their arts and crafts, and practiced agriculture. The Wichitas, also a Caddoan people, at one time occupied an extensive area between the Arkansas River in Kansas and the Brazos in Texas, but they settled eventually in southwestern Oklahoma. They built a peculiar dome-shaped house over a framework of cedar poles lashed together at the top and covered with shingle-like layers of matted grass.

Sedentary, industrious, and peaceable, they grew corn not only for their own use but for trade with their neighbors. The hardy, far-ranging Pawnees, another Caddoan tribe, were at home in Nebraska, but they hunted buffalo on the plains of western Oklahoma and became adept at stealing horses from Spanish owners in New Mexico. Their houses were substantially constructed of sod over a circular framework of poles. They developed a mythology remarkably rich in symbolism and poetic fancy, and elaborate religious ceremonials connected with the worship of cosmic forces and the heavenly bodies.

In northeastern Oklahoma, the Osages built their tepee villages, rode out to hunt the buffalo and fight with Pawnees on the western plains. They were a southern branch of the great Siouan linguistic stock, and during historic times they occupied a large area in Missouri, Kansas, and Oklahoma. Their mythology and ceremonial observances show that the one factor overshadowing all others in its influence on their lives was the buffalo. Their songs celebrated its habits and characteristics and glorified the prowess of the hunter. Their legends tell how great massed herds came up every year from the distant caves of the Sunset Lands. Their mythological enemies were wicked beings who held the buffalo captive, and their legendary heroes were demigods who dared all magic spells and cunning to bring them back to the hungry people. Next to the buffalo, the sun dominated their imagination, and each morning they poured out their song to the sunrise. The Osages were divided into two groups—the Peace People and the War People—and the two had distinctive functions in the ceremonial observances of the tribe.

More restless and fierce even than the Osages were the Comanches, who set up their tepees along the streams of western Oklahoma, and from these bases set out on raiding and horse-stealing expeditions against the Texas frontier and the distant settlements of Old Mexico. Members of the Shoshonean linguistic stock, they were a recent offshoot of the Shoshones, Utes, and Bannocks of Wyoming, coming to the southwestern plains region at the beginning of the nineteenth century. Breeding horses, first obtained from the Spaniards, and stealing from the Mexicans, they became the most skilled, fearless riders of the plains. The Comanche brave's importance in camp and council was measured largely by the number of his ponies; horse racing was a passion, and betting an exciting tonic. Early explorers marveled at the skill with which the yelling, shield-protected Comanche warrior clung to the side of his mount in battle. Hated and feared by the Texas frontiersmen for the stealth and swiftness of their raids, they were a kindly and hospitable people in the happy, turbulent life of their camps. Their speech became the lingua franca of the southwestern Indians, and they were the most proficient of all the tribes in the use of the sign language of the plains. They practiced no agriculture and depended upon the buffalo herds for food, clothing, and shelter.

Closely allied with the Comanches were the Kiowas, a distinct linguistic stock, who came to the Southwest during the first half of the nineteenth century. With them came a small band of Apaches, an Athapascan people that had become separated from their kinsmen in the North and formed an integral part of the Kiowas' tribal organization. Like the Comanches, the Kiowas set their life to the rhythm of the chase. As soon as the grass on the prairie was green enough to fatten their ponies, they formed small hunting parties and organized raiding expeditions that extended sometimes as far as Durango, in Mexico. In the fall the whole tribe engaged in a great buffalo hunt, the men killing and the women drying the meat and packing it in skin containers, and stretching the green hides to dry. At the end of this busy season they established winter camps in sheltered places on the upper tributaries of the Red River. Here the men chipped out flint weapons, made buffalo-hide shields, repaired saddles, and perfected their marksmanship, while their ponies cropped dried grass or nibbled cottonwood twigs. The women's winter work was to dress skins and make clothing and tepee coverings. The Kiowas, more than any other hunting tribe, had a sense of historic sequence. They kept a calendar on which they recorded, by a crude system of pictographs, the most impressive of each year's events.

In northwestern Oklahoma, western Kansas, and eastern Colorado, ranged the Cheyennes and Arapahoes. These two closely related tribes belong to the great Algonquian stock, which at one time comprised most of the Indians in the northeastern part of the United States. The Oklahoma bands were an agricultural people who came from the northern plains as a consequence of intertribal warfare. About 1840, they made peace with the Kiowas and Comanches, joining in their raids and observing an amicable division of the buffalo range. They became a purely hunting tribe, living in skin tepees, using horses, and following the buffalo herds. The Sun Dance, in which they practiced an elaborate ritual of self-torture, was their great tribal ceremony.

Although the Plains Indians differed widely in language, ceremonials, and traditions, they employed the same economic techniques. Their food was almost exclusively meat, but they learned to prepare it in ways to protect them from nutritional diseases. Their skin tepees could be dismantled, packed on travois poles, and moved to new locations with surprising rapidity. Their women wore beautifully dressed and elaborately decorated skins; and the details of their costumes were so distinctive that even today their civilized descendants adhere rigidly to them. All their activities depended on the horse. Except for this fact, their living techniques were similar to those of other tribes that had preceded them on the plains. In speaking of these earlier people in 1541, Coronado described their characteristics and their dependence upon the buffalo ("cows") in terms that apply equally well to the later Plains tribes:

"And after seventeen days' march I came across a settlement of Indians who travel around with these cows, . . . who do not plant, and who eat the raw flesh and drink the blood of the cows they kill, and they tan the skins of the cows, with which all the people of this country dress themselves here. They have little field tents made of the hides of the cows, tanned and greased, very well made, in which they live as they travel around near the cows, changing with these. They have dogs which they load, which carry their tents and poles and small things. These are the best formed people that I have seen in the Indies."

Certain other generalizations may, with some hesitancy, be advanced concerning the aboriginal and adopted tribes and their historic cultures. The predominant political organization was the village, or band; the civil chief was supreme in authority, except when he was supplanted by the war chief for the duration of raids or expeditions against enemies. Most southern Plains Indians traced descent through the male line; parents controlled marriages; polygamy was permitted when the man could afford to keep more than one wife; and marriages between men and women of different but related tribes was encouraged in order to strengthen informal but real alliances among them.

Such were the aboriginal inhabitants of Oklahoma. But the phase of Indian history that gives the present state its unique character resulted from the plan of the Federal government to set it aside as the permanent home of the Indian race. In furtherance of this project, tribes from the southeastern states were removed from the path of advancing white settlements and sent west with the more-or-less clearly defined purpose of creating an Indian commonwealth *(see History).*

Five advanced agricultural groups from the region between Tennessee and the Gulf and from the Carolinas to the Mississippi became the first modern Indian occupants of Oklahoma; the Cherokees, a populous tribe separated at an early time from the Iroquoian group of western New York; and the Choctaws, Chickasaws, Creeks, and Seminoles—all members of the Muskhogean stock of the Southeast. All brought with them the institutions and customs of civilization; and their development and achievements form an integral part of the history of the state. Later, other tribes and fragments of tribes were brought from the East and North as the white frontier continued to advance upon their homes. Among these were the Delawares,

Shawnees, Sacs and Foxes, the Quapaws—a Siouan tribe of peaceable habits, crowded out of their homes in Arkansas—and the Kaws, another fragment of a Siouan tribe from Kansas.

Members of these tribes now constitute a considerable portion of the citizenship of Oklahoma and have intermarried with the whites until they are no longer appreciably Indian—though they cherish the tradition of their Indian ancestry. In the state are about ninety-two thousand representatives of more than thirty tribes who show pronounced Indian characteristics. They have the same privileges as other citizens of the state, except that some of those with the highest quantum of Indian blood—varying in amount from tribe to tribe—still (1941) hold their individual allotments of land under title which prevents them from selling. These restricted Indians are under the guardianship of seven Federal agencies, which exercise a certain supervision over their land and assist them in acquiring the white man's economic techniques. Most of the children attend the public schools, but twelve boarding schools are also maintained by the United States government for special vocational training. Many young Indians are enrolled in Oklahoma colleges.

A few conservative fullblood settlements exist in remote communities, though most of the Indians are distributed through the general farming population or are engaged in ordinary occupations in the towns and cities.

In fullblood communities the Indians still retain their own social life with tribal dances and ceremonies, but little remains of their native mode of living. The picturesque native of feathers, paint, blanket, and breechcloth is never seen, except at Indian fairs and exhibitions, which are held in many places throughout the state.

History

THE CHRONICLE of Oklahoma is as old as the expedition of Coronado, pushing east in search of gold from Tiguez, New Mexico, in 1541, and as new as the completion of the mile-long Grand River Dam, the greatest multiple-arch dam in the world, in the fall of 1940. If it seems overweighted by happenings before there was a state of Oklahoma, it must be remembered that statehood came as late as 1907—in the youth of men and women now (1941) hardly past their middle age.

A succession of Spanish adventurers were the first recorded explorers of the territory that became Oklahoma. Coming from the east in the winter of 1540–41, Hernando de Soto is supposed to have missed meeting Coronado within Oklahoma's border by not so many leagues. Then, fifty years later, Captain Francisco Leiva Bonilla's expedition probably crossed the Panhandle, to be followed in 1601 by that of Governor Juan de Oñate, from Santa Fe, and that of Diego de Castillo, searching for gold and silver, in 1650.

Beyond some traces of prospecting for gold in the Wichita Mountains, the Spaniards left no impression on the region; they carried back the report that it was peopled only by a few bands of poor Indians, and that its prairies furnished grazing for myriads of strange "crooked-back cows"—buffaloes.

Next to enter the territory out of which Oklahoma was carved was René Robert Cavelier, Sieur de la Salle, who came down the Mississippi and thence west in 1682 and claimed for the French all the lands drained by the great river; some of his followers came up the Red River and pushed north across the eastern quarter of the present state, leaving evidence of their passing in the names of such rivers as the Poteau and the Verdigris.

At long intervals before the purchase of Louisiana Territory by the United States in 1803, traces of French contacts in the Oklahoma area are found: traders out of the post established in 1715 by Juchereau de St. Denis at Natchitoches, on the Red River; Bernard de la Harpe's expedition from Red River to the present town of Haskell *(see Tour 2);* Charles Claude de Tisné's visit in 1719 to the Pawnees in the vicinity of the present town of

Chelsea *(see Tour 1)*; the traders Pierre and Paul Mallet's descent of the Arkansas River in canoes in 1740; and the 1741 winter camp of Fabré de la Bruyère on the Canadian at the mouth of Little River.

Then, in 1762, that part of Louisiana Province which contained present Oklahoma was given back to Spain; and some thirty years later, with the canceling of permits to French traders in the Osage and Missouri River regions, the Spanish attempted to exploit the area. In 1800, however, Louisiana Province was regained by France, and in 1803 it was purchased by the United States. The next year the District of Louisiana was divided, the Oklahoma region becoming part of the Territory of Indiana, and receiving its first code of laws from Vincennes. The arrival from St. Louis in 1822 of Auguste Pierre Chouteau, who established at Grand Saline (Salina; *see Tour 8*) the first permanent white settlement in Oklahoma, marked the beginning of white infiltration through the influence of this great French trading family of Missouri.

Two other early dates are significant, the inclusion of the Oklahoma region in the Territory of Missouri in 1812, and its transfer to the Territory of Arkansas in 1819, when the United States offered a home west of the Mississippi for all Cherokees who would consent to emigrate from Georgia and Tennessee. Incidentally, this arrangement, as the Osages claimed, arbitrarily took land from them and gave it to the Cherokees without their sanction, and led to extended warfare between the tribes after the coming of the Cherokees.

In 1819, by the treaty with Spain which named the Red River as far west as the one-hundredth meridian as the boundary between Arkansas Territory and the Spanish Southwest, the southern and western limits of Oklahoma were fixed. In this same year, 1819, the English naturalist Thomas Nuttall made his trip up the Arkansas through the Cherokee lands, and the Reverend Epaphras Chapman came to open Union Mission on Grand River to the Osages. In 1822, Cephas Washburn, another devoted friend of the Indians, followed the Cherokees who had voluntarily removed to the Arkansas Territory and founded Dwight Mission for their comfort and education. In 1824, in anticipation of the coming of the Five Civilized Tribes, Fort Gibson and Fort Towson were laid out.

Except for a few Osages east of Grand River, small bands of Indians of Caddoan stock, such as the Wichitas and some nomadic Comanches and Kiowas in the west—probably the bands seen by Coronado, Bonilla, and de Oñate—the Indian Territory which was to become Oklahoma was a vacant land when President Jackson began applying so much pressure on the Five Civilized Tribes that they could no longer resist. From 1828 to 1846

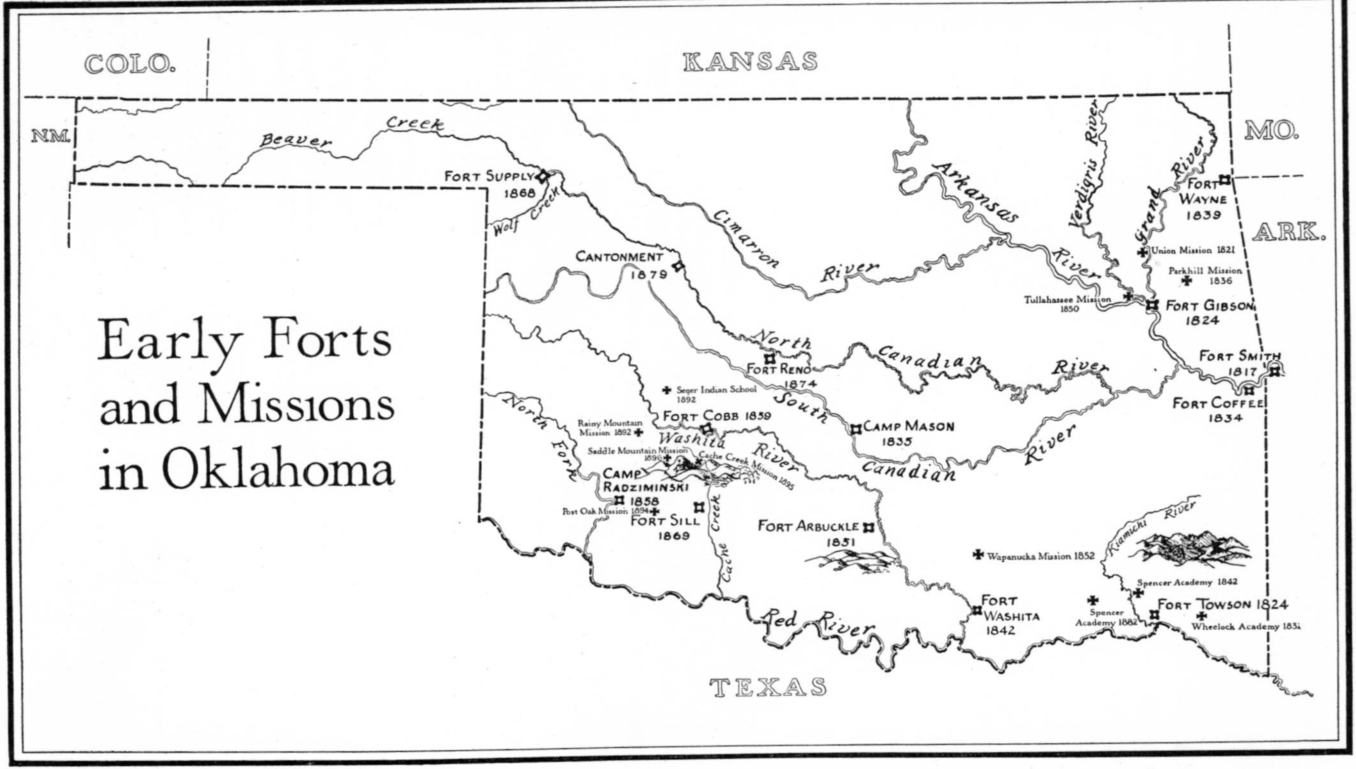
Early Forts
and Missions
in Oklahoma
COLO.
KANSAS
N.M.
MO.
ARK.
TEXAS
Beaver Creek
Fort Supply 1868
Wolf Creek
Cimarron River
Arkansas River
Verdigris River
Grand River
Fort Wayne 1839
Union Mission 1821
Parkhill Mission 1836
Tullahassee Mission 1850
Fort Gibson 1824
Fort Smith 1817
Fort Coffee 1834
Cantonment 1879
North Canadian River
Fort Reno 1874
Seger Indian School 1892
South Canadian River
Camp Mason 1835
Fort Cobb 1859
Rainy Mountain Mission 1892
Washita River
Saddle Mountain Mission 1896
Cache Creek Mission 1895
North Fork
Camp Radziminski 1858
Post Oak Mission 1894
Fort Sill 1869
Cache Creek
Fort Arbuckle 1851
Red River
Fort Washita 1842
Wapanucka Mission 1852
Kiamichi River
Spencer Academy 1842
Spencer Academy 1882
Fort Towson 1824
Wheelock Academy 1832

the long and doleful procession of exiled Cherokees, Creeks, Chickasaws, Choctaws, and Seminoles ended among the timbered hills and on the little open prairies of the eastern end of the present state.

These Indians, distinguished by the title of "The Five Civilized Tribes," had lived in close contact with the whites for more than a century; had adopted many of the white man's habits and customs; were farmers, stockmen, millwrights; had schools and mission churches; and were slaveholders. Some had become wealthy from plantations of the old southern type, though, of course, most lived in simple cabins. All had been at peace with the whites since 1812.

After conflicting boundary claims had been adjusted, the immigrant Indians held title to all of the present state of Oklahoma except the Panhandle; and though their settlements were confined to the eastern half, they made periodic buffalo-hunting expeditions to the western limits of their holdings. Each of the Five Civilized Tribes was organized into a "nation," which maintained a separate existence as a protectorate of the United States under treaties which guaranteed that its tenure should be perpetual, "as long as grass shall grow and waters run." Each nation had its own laws, tried offenders, decided civil suits and probate matters in its own courts; and built capitols in the wilderness, where Indian legislators conducted smoothly-running parliamentary assemblies, and able chiefs prepared state papers and dealt with intricate problems of administration.

Survivors of the forced Removal, after the hard years of pioneering, began to prosper. They cleared land, laid out farms, accumulated livestock, built schoolhouses and churches, and entered into friendly diplomatic relations with each other and with the "wild" nomadic tribes at, and beyond, the western border of Indian Territory. Protected from intrusion by treaties and the Indian Intercourse Acts, for a time they lived apart from the whites.

But the Civil War interrupted their material progress and destroyed their isolation. Naturally, the slaveholding Five Civilized Tribes, coming as they had from the Gulf states, Tennessee, and North Carolina, were in sympathy with the Confederates. Almost to a man the United States agents to the various tribes were Southern sympathizers also; and they, together with delegations from Arkansas and Texas that alternately urged and threatened, persuaded the Indians to joi the South. During 1861 all of the Five Civilized Tribes accordingly made alliances with the Confederacy, and many of the Plains Indians followed their example. But in spite of this official action, there was a strong Union element among the Cherokees, Creeks, and Seminoles; and these tribes were torn by miniature civil wars of their own, the more deadly and devastating because of the close ties binding their citizens.

In the case of the Cherokees, the struggle was so violent that Chief John Ross, who attempted to maintain neutrality for the tribe, was compelled to leave the nation and Stand Watie, made a brigadier general by the Confederacy, claimed the office.

No important battle was fought in the Indian Territory, but guerrilla bands ravaged the country, and Union and Confederate partisans killed each other on sight; refugees left their homes and fled, Union sympathizers to Kansas, and adherents of the Confederacy to the Red River region. While they endured exile, illness, and starvation, thieves looted and burned their abandoned homes and barns and sold their stock to army contractors.

After the war the Federal government contended that the Five Civilized Tribes, by their "rebellion," had forfeited all their lands and treaty guarantees, and it was proposed to open their country to white settlement. Yielding in part to the Indians' strong protests, the United States took only a part of their western lands as a home for other Indian tribes, allowing them to retain the eastern portion under previous treaty status. All were required to liberate their former slaves; and some tribes were induced to adopt their freedmen as citizens with full property rights. Provision was also made for a united territorial government, which it was hoped would in time absorb the separate Indian nationalities and lead to the establishment of a state. At the suggestion of Allen Wright, a Choctaw delegate who once served as principal chief of his tribe, one of the treaties referred to this hoped-for commonwealth as *Okla̱homa,* the Choctaw word for "red people."

Indians living in Kansas and other states were removed to the Indian Territory and settled on the ceded land. The "wild" Plains tribes also went through the form of accepting reservations there, though they continued to hunt in Kansas, Texas, and Colorado until the buffalo herds, which they regarded as their special property, were gone; they then began raiding white settlements. To protect the whites, forts were established at strategic points on the frontier. In the present state of Oklahoma were Fort Supply (1868) on the North Canadian, near the western boundary; Fort Sill (1869), at the eastern edge of the Wichita Mountains; and Fort Reno (1874), also on the North Canadian, in the heart of the ceded territory. By 1875, the "hostiles" were reduced to the status of reservation Indians.

Meanwhile, leaders among the Five Civilized Tribes met at the Creek capital, Okmulgee, in 1871, with the purpose of forming a confederated Indian Territory, to be administered by Indians. They urged it, along with better education and farming practices, as a measure vital to their survival. Other meetings were held in the following four years, at all of which representatives of the hostile Plains tribes listened attentively to talks about the necessity for adopting the white man's civilization; but before their principal aim could be accomplished the Federal government acted to prevent it, and no more meetings could be held.

As though conditioned by adversity, the Indians of the Five Civilized Tribes made a quick recovery from the desolation caused by the Civil War. Farms and plantations once more came under cultivation, and the rich ranges supported herds of Indian-owned cattle. Schoolhouses were rebuilt; the tribes financed the expansion of both neighborhood elementary schools, with educated Indian teachers in charge, and higher grade boarding schools, mainly staffed by white college graduates.

The Indians' problem—how to keep the Territory for their exclusive use and occupation—was complicated by the rapid growth of white population on its northern, eastern, and southern borders; and when the first railroad crossed it (1870–72), any effort to find an answer became hopeless. As other railroads built into, and across, the Territory, white men came in to lay out towns and open farms, some as employees or tenants of the Indians, others as plain intruders, defiant alike of the tribal governments and the Federal Intercourse Acts. In 1890, when the first Federal census was made of the Five Civilized Tribes, there was a population of 109,393 whites and 18,636 Negroes, as compared with a total of 50,055 Indians.

These noncitizens, outside the authority of the Indian governments, were without civil law, and in criminal matters they were under the long-distance jurisdiction of the Federal court at Fort Smith, Arkansas. Their towns were built upon lands to which they could obtain no title, and their children were denied access to tribal schools; naturally, therefore, they were eager for the extinguishment of the Indian land tenure and the creation of a government in which they could participate.

White cattlemen, too, coveted the lush ranges of the Indians. At first, the Indians' grass only helped to fatten the big moving herds which began to cross the Territory from Texas to Kansas railheads soon after the Civil War, and trample deep and wide such trails as the Western, the Chisholm, the East Shawnee, and the West Shawnee. Between five and six million longhorns used these trails. Then Texas cattle-owners thought to secure grazing rights, either leasing great areas from tribal authorities or arranging sham "sales" to citizens of the Territory, then hiring themselves and their cowboys to the Indian "owners" to care for and market the cattle.

Most extensive and richest of the Indians' ranges was the Cherokee "Outlet," or "Strip," some six and one-half million acres of grassland south of the southern border of Kansas, and west of the tribal lands granted by the Cherokees to the Osages. Here for a time the Cherokee national government collected grazing fees from individual cattlemen, then leased the whole area to the Cherokee Strip Livestock Association.

Looking over the border at this cattleman's "fair and happy land," white farmers of Kansas, Missouri, and sections even more remote began the long-continued agitation for throwing open for settlement the fertile acres which were not used and occupied by their Indian owners. Bills were repeatedly introduced in Congress for the liquidation of tribal governments, allotment of reservation land held in common, and making the surplus land available for homesteading.

Beginning about 1879, extensive publicity was given to the fact that no Indian tribes had ever been settled on a tract in the heart of the Indian Territory ceded by the Creeks and Seminoles at the close of the Civil War; and newspapers throughout the West contended that these "Unassigned Lands" —soon to be popularly designated as "Oklahoma Lands"—were subject to homestead entry.

Homeseekers known as "Boomers" gathered at the Kansas border and made repeated and systematic attempts to colonize this tract, but the Federal government, holding that the land had been ceded only for Indian occupation, removed the invaders. They returned in increasing numbers; cattlemen came in without legal sanction, divided the range, built fences and corrals, and grazed their cattle over its rich prairies; and in 1886–87, the Atchison, Topeka and Santa Fe Railroad was built across the region, and stations were established along its right of way.

Finally the United States purchased title to the land from the Creeks and Seminoles; the tract was laid out in 160-acre homesteads; and on April 22, 1889, it was opened to white settlement in the "Run" for farms and town lots which has become one of the most dramatized episodes in western history.

As the hour for the opening approached, great crowds waited on the border, while mounted soldiers stood on guard to turn back intruders. At noon bugles sounded, then guns were fired as a signal that the land was open. Men raced in on horseback, on foot, in covered wagons, hanging to every available hold on the slowly moving trains, all trying to outstrip their fellows in the scramble for "claims." When a homeseeker found a tract of land to his liking, he drove a stake as evidence of possession and held it as best he could against other claimants. On the same day lots were staked in the townsites, and men engaged in feverish promotion.

The weeks following that first Run of homesteaders were busy ones on this newest of American frontiers. In the towns, stores were opened, banks and newspapers were established, doctors and lawyers set up offices. Some of the most substantial business firms in Oklahoma point to this time as the date of their founding; and many elderly couples are now living on well-improved farms which they staked on that historic day.

For thirteen months, the settlers were without any organized government, yet good order prevailed. Frontier living conditions were too rigorous, and money was too scarce, to attract outlaws. In May, 1890, Congress passed the Organic Act, providing for a territorial government, with executive and judicial officers appointed by the President, and a legislature to be elected by the people. The active new town of Guthrie *(see Tour 10)* was designated as the capital, and in spite of the bitter rivalry of its ambitious neighbor, Oklahoma City, it remained the seat of government throughout the territorial period.

The new Territory of Oklahoma increased rapidly in area as well as in population. The Organic Act provided that the Panhandle *(see Tour 2)* should be included within its jurisdiction. This narrow strip of land had had a curious history. Included in the Spanish domain by the treaty of 1819, it had passed by successive revolutions into the possession first of Mexico, and then of Texas. Separated from Texas by the Compromise of 1850 because it lay north of the slavery line, and lying south of the Kansas-Colorado boundary, it had become appropriately known as "No Man's Land." After the subjugation of the Plains Indians and the extinction of the buffalo, homesteaders and ranchers had filtered in and had been completely ignored by the Federal government. In 1887, they met at Beaver City and attempted to create a government for the "Territory of Cimarron," but their action never received official recognition. Now this strip of forgotten frontier was added to Oklahoma.

As different Indian tribes accepted allotment of reservations, their surplus lands were opened to settlement and joined to Oklahoma. The wild scenes of the first Run were re-enacted, and the same building activity followed. The Sac and Fox, Iowa, and Shawnee-Potawatomi reservations to the east of "Old Oklahoma" were opened in 1891, and the Cheyenne-Arapaho lands to the west in 1892. The greatest Run of all occurred when the United States purchased the Cherokee Outlet and opened it, with the Tonkawa and Pawnee reservations, in the fall of 1893. This was followed by the opening of the small Kickapoo Reservation in 1895. Greer County, an area between the north and south forks of the Red River, which later became Jackson, Harmon, Greer, and (in part) Beckham counties, had long been claimed by Texas and settled largely by Texans, many of them cattlemen. In 1896, it was awarded to Oklahoma by the United States Supreme Court; each resident was allowed to retain 160 acres and to purchase an additional 160 acres at $1.25 an acre.

The surplus land of the Kiowas and Comanches and the Wichitas and

Affiliated Tribes was opened for settlement August 6, 1901, this time by lottery instead of a run.

About 1904, four small tribes—Poncas, Otoes, Missouris, and Kaws—divided all their land among their members, except small tracts which they retained for tribal purposes; and the Osages' land also was divided among the citizens without leaving a surplus for white homesteaders. Each Osage received 659.52 acres, but the mineral rights were retained under communal tenure, a fact that was to have great significance to the tribe when the reservation became one of the great producing oil fields of the world. Their allotments were finally completed about 1908, and the land was attached to the Territory of Oklahoma for governmental purposes.

After 1890, the map showed "Twin Territories," the Indian Territory with a population of 178,084, comprising the Cherokee, Choctaw, Chickasaw, Creek, and Seminole nations, and a small corner in the northeast settled by fragments of other tribes; and Oklahoma, with its population of 61,834 white pioneers and allotted Indians, organized under a territorial government with its capital at Guthrie.

The creation of Oklahoma Territory on their border foretold the end of the Five Civilized Tribes as independent nations. David A. Harvey, the Territory's delegate in Congress, joined representatives of surrounding states in demanding the extinction of the Indian governments and abolition of tribal land tenure. Homeseekers who failed to secure land in the runs and lotteries moved over into the Indian Territory, laid out farms, speculated in town lots, and formed ambitious plans for the development of its mineral rights, all looking to a future dominated by the white man's enterprise. In response to this growing demand, Congress in 1893 created the Dawes Commission and authorized it to negotiate with the Five Civilized Tribes for termination of their existence as nations. The Indians steadfastly refused to treat, yet Congress had their land surveyed and rolls made of their citizens as a preparation for allotment. Under such coercion they were finally induced to negotiate; and partly by voluntary surrender and partly through Congressional mandate their governments were liquidated and their estates divided among the citizens.

First, the townsites were segregated and platted; town governments were organized, bonds voted, school systems created, and waterworks and electric light plants established. The Dawes Commission then divided the remainder of the land equally among the tribal citizens. Each allotee received his share under a restricted tenure; his land was inalienable and tax exempt for a term of years, during which he was supposed to gain experience in individual ownership.

By 1906 the work undertaken by the Dawes Commission was approaching completion. Federal officials believed that the Indian Territory was ready for statehood. Leaders of the Five Civilized Tribes, meanwhile, had taken the initiative by meeting, with a few white sympathizers, at Muskogee, in the Creek Nation in 1905, to draw up a constitution to govern all the inhabitants of the Indian Territory. The new state was to be named Sequoyah *(see Literature)* in honor of the revered Cherokee who had taught his people to read and write their language. Constitution and name were submitted to the people, both white and Indian, and overwhelmingly adopted; but they were never accepted by Congress.

The people of Oklahoma had been clamoring for statehood since the first stakes were driven into its prairies, and it seemed desirable to the lawmakers at Washington to unite the Twin Territories as one state. Under the Enabling Act, passed by Congress in 1906, delegates from both sections met at Guthrie to write the constitution.

The voluminous charter framed for the new state showed the influence of Bryan Democracy. The initiative, referendum, and recall weapons were placed in the hands of the people, while the fear that a strong executive might prove too powerful explained the proviso that no governor can succeed himself. Many state offices were made elective. A corporation commission—a new idea—was created to regulate public service corporations operating within the state; passenger fares were expressly limited to two cents per mile; a moderate homestead tax exemption was assured; child labor was restricted; the contracting of convict labor was prohibited; and an eight-hour working day was decreed for mine and governmental employees.

Various groups had brought pressure to bear upon the constitution-makers—the Farmer's Union through William H. Murray, and the mine workers through Peter Hanraty, president and vice-president respectively of the convention. The liquor interests were extremely active. Oklahoma Territory had saloons, but the Enabling Act required prohibition of intoxicants in the Indian country for twenty-one years after statehood. Women lobbyists flocked to the convention to meet defeat in the fight for woman suffrage and for the eligibility of women for the office of governor. They succeeded, however, in securing limitations on the employment of women and children in work injurious to health or morals, and the establishment of a Department of Charities and Corrections for the protection of orphans and inmates of all charitable and penal institutions. One concession won by the women at the time was a provision that the Commissioner of Charities and Corrections "may be of either sex." Kate Barnard, a militant social worker, was elected to that position in 1907, and re-elected in 1910. Except for two terms (1914–

22), the office has been held by two women, Miss Barnard, and Mabel Bassett (1923–41).

State-wide prohibition was adopted at the election which ratified the constitution.

Born at the crisis of the 1907 "money panic," the state was (to quote from the *Organization and Administration of Oklahoma,* a Brookings Institution report made in 1935) "the kind of community that, a hundred years ago, was placing its stamp on our political institutions and governmental practices. Such a community, vigorous, individualistic, and self-confident, was typical of the Jacksonian era, characterized by intense partisanship; loyalty to personalities; localism; territorial decentralization in administration; attachment to local self-government; checks and balances; legislative control of administration; distrust of the executive; numerous elective offices; rotation in office; the spoils system."

State officers were installed on November 16, 1907, including the first governor, Charles N. Haskell. As United States senators Oklahoma's legislature sent to Washington a blind white man, Thomas P. Gore, and a Cherokee citizen, Robert L. Owen. To the House of Representatives were elected Bird S. McGuire, former Territorial Delegate; Elmer L. Fulton; James S. Davenport; Charles D. Carter, of both Cherokee and Choctaw blood; and Scott Ferris.

At statehood, Oklahoma had a population of 1,414,177, of which only 5.3 per cent were Indians. Restless, and critical of the established order, dubbed radicals by outsiders, they had proposed to create a commonwealth for the poor man. Ironically, the first great surge of oil development in Oklahoma occurred just before statehood and called for the investment of enormous amounts of capital in leases, drilling, storage, gathering lines, shipping facilities, and refining. Taxes paid by oil saved the state from bankruptcy in the period when no real estate taxes could be collected from the restricted lands in the Indian half of Oklahoma. Other mineral resources, in the development of which capital was required, also became more and more important: coal, mined as early as 1872 in the McAlester region; lead and zinc, in the northeastern corner; gypsum in the west, and asphalt in the southern part of the state.

What seemed to be happening beneath the surface of the disturbed waters of radical political and economic agitations was the rapid transformation of a Bryanesque commonwealth, controlled by farmers and small business men, to a modern industrial state, dominated by the "big money" which the pioneers had so greatly feared.

At Haskell's inauguration, the state had seen five thousand oil wells drilled, the price of crude had dropped to twenty-five cents per barrel, and the powerful Mid-Continent Oil and Gas Association had been formed. "Standard Oil" was a political battle cry, and the Socialist Party was gathering strength.

The race question was raised by Democrats from the beginning of statehood, and Oklahoma's Jim Crow Law was one of the first adopted. The Grandfather Clause, which would have deprived the Negroes of suffrage, was adopted in 1910. It was declared unconstitutional by the Federal District Court, and the decision was sustained by the United States Supreme Court in 1915. An attempt to initiate a literacy test as a substitute was defeated by popular vote in 1916.

The location of the capital at Oklahoma City in 1910 followed attempts to establish a new city in the geographic center of the state—the "New Jerusalem" plan—which failed, as did Guthrie's attempt to retain the capital after the election in which Oklahoma City was chosen.

Haskell and his successor as governor, Lee Cruce, both faced bitter political opposition. Cruce was embroiled in controversy that brought a threat of impeachment which never materialized. Legislative scandals and the growth of the Socialist Party held down the 1912 Oklahoma vote for Woodrow Wilson to 119,000.

The 1914 Democratic primary was spiced by the vigorous candidacy of Al Jennings, former train-robber, for governor. He received 21,732 votes and ran third. Robert L. Williams was nominated with 33,605 votes. Socialists joined Republicans in an attack on Governor Williams, charging that his election was stolen. At the election, Williams won, polling 100,597 votes to 95,904 by his Republican opponent, who was hampered because the Progressives put a candidate into the field who polled 4,189 votes. The Socialists, who had polled 9,740 votes at statehood, cast 52,703 votes for their gubernatorial candidate; five Socialist members were elected to the state House of Representatives and one to the state Senate. National economic stress contributed to the growth of Socialism; the lack of a cotton market, the decreasing value of all farm products, and the rapid growth of farm tenancy throughout the state aggravated social unrest that was stilled only by the entrance of the United States into the World War.

The First Regiment of Oklahoma's National Guard, which had seen service in Mexico in the short campaign against Pancho Villa, merged with a Texas regiment to form the One Hundred and Forty-second Regiment. This was incorporated in the Thirty-sixth Division and sent overseas. Among the 90,378 Oklahomans who went into the service were more than five thousand Negroes; and Company E of the One Hundred and Forty-second Infantry was made up almost entirely of Indians. A brigade of Oklahoma troops saw action at St. Mihiel and in the final offensive of the Meuse-Argonne. Casualties were 1,046 killed in battle, 502 missing, 710 dead of disease, and 4,154 wounded.

Even before the first World War, Oklahoma's war record was as varied as the character of its people. In the Civil War, there had been Indian regiments on both sides, and in the Spanish-American War, Theodore Roosevelt's regiment of "Rough Riders" had been largely recruited from the Twin Territories.

The Socialist party steadily declined in the state during the war years and fell into disrepute because of opposition expressed by a minority of its members to participation in the war. By 1922, the party was able to muster only 3,941 votes, and in 1924, it was denied a place on the state ballot.

The campaign of 1920 brought the first Republican victory to Oklahoma. That party's representative, J. W. Harreld, was elected to the United States Senate, and five of the state's eight members of the national House of Representatives were Republicans. The majority of the state House of Representatives were also of that party. Governor J. B. A. Robertson, a holdover from the election of 1918, was a Democrat and found himself unable to push legislation through the lower house, which showed its political hostility by voting impeachment charges against Lieutenant Governor M. E. Trapp and failed by only one vote to prefer similar charges against Robertson.

The Red Scare that swept the country after the war stirred into action such secret organizations as the Ku Klux Klan, which gained numerous members in all sections of the state. It elected or controlled many municipal and county officials. During the last two years of Robertson's administration the Klan became such an issue that he forbade officers of the National Guard to join.

Unrest caused by the Klan, growing dissatisfaction among farmers and workmen with post-war depression conditions, and the Socialist remnants in the state—all threatened the dominance of the Democratic party in the election of 1922. In September, 1921, a large convention had been held of delegates from the State Federation of Labor, the railroad Brotherhoods, and the Farmer's Union. These groups formed the Farmer-Labor Reconstruction League, advocating state operation of a number of industries with the elimination of private profits, aid to home building and labor, and free school textbooks. In the following February a more comprehensive platform was adopted and candidates were nominated for state offices; J. C. Walton, mayor of Oklahoma City, was the nominee for governor.

In the primary, R. H. Wilson, Superintendent of Public Instruction, and

Thomas H. Owen, Justice of the Supreme Court, opposed Walton. The Klan endorsed Wilson; this turned the support of Catholics, Jews, Negroes, and citizens of foreign lineage, who had suffered from the persecution of the Klan, to the support of Walton. Governor Robertson used administrative pressure against the Klan, and Patrick S. Nagle, head of the old Socialist party, led most of its adherents into the Walton camp. Walton was nominated and elected despite the bolt of a group of Democrats to the support of the Republican nominee.

Walton began his administration by inviting all his constituents to attend an inaugural barbecue. Thousands gathered in Oklahoma City and many remained as office seekers; the Governor felt obligated to award his friends by overstaffing offices and creating new positions. He encountered opposition from more conservative members of the Democratic party and at the same time lost the confidence of leaders of the Reconstruction League. The Ku Klux Klan remained in opposition. After eleven months of strife, the legislature impeached and removed Walton and M. E. Trapp, lieutenant governor, succeeded him.

In the Trapp administration the State Game and Fish Department was organized, the first legislation was passed for the conservation of natural resources, and the State Highway Department speeded the construction of all-weather roads.

Henry S. Johnston was elected governor in 1926 for the next four-year term, but he immediately broke with some of his closest advisers. The legislature, after one abortive attempt, impeached him on ten charges, the tenth being general incompetency. Acquitted on the other nine charges, he was convicted on the tenth. In March, 1929, William J. Holloway, lieutenant governor, became the eighth governor of Oklahoma.

In 1930, William H. Murray, returned from a five-year colonizing venture in Bolivia, entered, with eight others, the primary contest for governor. He conducted a spectacular campaign by being driven from place to place in an ancient "model-T," and dining publicly, between speeches, on cheese and crackers. Dressed like the popular conception of a sharecropper, he promised relief to the unemployed and the debt-ridden farmers. A prolonged drouth a few weeks before the primary election, causing millions of dollars of damage to the farmers and stock men of the state, reacted favorably to the Murray candidacy. In the regular primary, he lacked fewer than five thousand votes of doubling the vote given his nearest opponent.

Murray soon attracted nationwide attention by his insistence upon the sovereignty of the state; by his use of the National Guard as police; by his verbal blasts at Federal District Courts which he called inferior; by his abolishment of toll bridges, including those spanning Red River, and by his campaign for the presidential nomination. However, a great advance in state administration was made by the creation of the Oklahoma Tax Commission, a body which has varied in membership and personnel but nevertheless has become a powerful adjunct to efficient government. Murray also helped to stabilize the oil industry when he ordered the shutdown of 3,108 flowing wells for three months after crude oil had fallen in price below twenty cents a barrel. Through the temporary shutdown of oil wells and the proration of the greater producing areas the price of oil was forced upward to nearly one dollar a barrel. From these early steps toward proration succeeding administrations formed oil control compacts with all other states of the mid-continent area. Murray, likewise, tried to help the farmers of Oklahoma, and both the thirteenth and fourteenth legislatures provided free seed for applicants and relief to the needy. However, fearing Federal encroachment of power and the entrenchment of bureaucratic control over social and economic problems, he failed to co-operate with the national administration in all its recovery and relief programs.

His successor, Ernest W. Marland, who had built and lost a great fortune in the oil industry, was elected in 1934. Though comparatively new to politics, he had served the previous two years in Congress as a supporter of administration measures and took his election as a mandate for the fullest possible co-operation with the national administration.

Despite his lack of dominant executive leadership, Marland persuaded the legislature to adopt many of the proposals suggested by organized citizen committees who had made studies of the problems and functions of administration. Planning, flood control, employment, housing, public welfare, new industries, and conservation boards were created; an initiative measure providing for homestead tax exemption and another that provided for assistance to the needy, aged, and dependent were passed. Much work was done in soil conservation and flood control by the construction of farm ponds. Work on the $22,500,000 Grand River Dam was begun in February, 1938. Through Federal-state co-operation, state parks were developed by the CCC, more National Guard armories were constructed in Oklahoma than in the rest of the United States by WPA assistance, and PWA and WPA combined in the construction of new courthouses, schoolhouses, swimming pools, stadiums, and recreation centers throughout the state. Highway improvement continued at a rapid rate. Out of earnings from oil wells drilled on the state capitol grounds, the state's modern million-dollar office building was erected; and Marland provided from his own Ponca City home much of the shrubbery that was used to beautify the rather arid landscape about the capitol.

In the primary election of 1938, Leon C. Phillips, a former speaker of the Oklahoma House of Representatives, William S. Key, wealthy oil man and former state administrator of WPA, and William H. Murray, former governor, were the leading Democratic candidates. Indications pointed to a Murray victory, but Phillips polled 179,139 votes to Key's 176,034, and Murray's 148,395.

In line with a recently established tradition that elections ought to be fun, the usual number of "name" candidates was offered for lesser offices: Joe E. Brown placed third in the primary contest for Secretary of State; Oliver Cromwell did nearly as well as candidate for Commissioner of Insurance; Mae West, an Oklahoma City switchboard operator, polled 67,607 votes in the race for Commissioner of Charities and Corrections; Sam Houston III placed fifth among nine candidates for president of the State Board of Agriculture. Second in this race was a farmer, Josh Lee, who capitalized on the name of Oklahoma's popular junior senator and polled 127,940 votes to the successful incumbent's 129,580. Huey Long placed second, and Daniel Boone third for Clerk of Supreme Court to the incumbent Andy Payne, whose political ads in 1934 informed prospective voters that he was the winner of a California to New York footrace, C. C. Pyle's Bunion Derby! These hopefuls had been encouraged by the success of an unknown schoolteacher in capitalizing on the name Will Rogers in winning an election for Congressman-at-large in 1932 in a race against twenty-four other candidates. In the primary of 1938, the political Will Rogers had to face opposition from another William Rogers, as well as from Brigham Young. Others among his opponents have been Robert E. Lee (1934) and William Cullen Bryant (1936).

Inaugurated in January, 1939, Governor Phillips urged a drastic reduction in state expenditure and abandoned many of the experiments in government begun under his predecessor. The sixteenth legislature had appropriated an all-time high of $61,484,154.12 for the biennium 1937–39. This was reduced by the seventeenth legislature for the period 1938–39 to $47,657,465. Phillips has been the first governor of the state to dominate the legislature through both its regular sessions. The eighteenth legislature (1941) continued his retrenchment program, and the voters who have since statehood seen more than two hundred initiative measures proposed and almost one hundred measures referred acted favorably on his proposals for a budget balancing amendment to the constitution, the establishment of a co-ordinating board for higher education, and an amendment pledging state co-operation with the Federal government in its social security program. The Governor, however, resisted the Federal Red River Denison Dam project and resented the influence exercised by Federal agencies within the state.

Generally, the state's unemployment problem has paralleled the national crisis. According to an estimate by the Bureau of Business Research of the University of Oklahoma, there was an increase from under fourteen thousand unemployed in the autumn of 1930 to more than 310,000 during 1932 and the first five months of 1933. With the inauguration of various New Deal measures, the figure dropped sharply to 177,000 in 1935. In 1939, 108,000 heads of families were registered for relief employment, with only a little more than one-half that number receiving it.

The Panhandle, northwestern, and southeastern sections of the state have received the highest per capita relief expenditures. The first two named sections have shown improvement in agricultural and employment conditions, but the problem in the southeastern area has become increasingly severe. A tenant-landlord commission was established during the administration of Governor E. W. Marland, to deal with the crisis in the cotton-growing sections; but its powers were so limited that results were negligible, and it was abolished early in 1939.

Oklahoma's industry has not been materially accelerated by the National Defense Program, but the selection of Tulsa and Oklahoma City as sites for defense factories and airports, the establishment of schools of aeronautics at several points, and the increased activity at Fort Sill have contributed somewhat to the betterment of business conditions.

The Setting

WHITE : WPA

ELDON VALLEY, NEAR TAHLEQUAH

GLASS MOUNTAIN, NEAR FAIRVIEW

EVERETT M. SWAN

DIVISION OF STATE PARKS

QUARTZ MOUNTAIN STATE PARK, NEAR MANGUM

SAND DUNES, NEAR WAYNOKA

EVERETT M. SWAN

LAKE BUFORD, WICHITA MOUNTAINS WILDLIFE REFUGE

NATURAL BRIDGE AT CEDAR CANYON PARK, NEAR FREEDOM

WHITE : WPA

"HE" MOUNTAIN, MCCURTAIN COUNTY

LAKE CLAYTON, PUSHMATAHA COUNTY

DIVISION OF STATE PARKS

IVISION OF STATE PARKS

DRIVE TO OSAGE HILLS STATE PARK, NEAR PAWHUSKA

"TOMBSTONE" WEATHERING OF TILTED ROCK STRATA
ARBUCKLE MOUNTAINS

KLAHOMA GEOLOGICAL SURVEY

DIVISION OF STATE PARKS

BUFFALO HERD IN WICHITA MOUNTAINS WILDLIFE REFUGE

BLACK MESA VALLEY, NEAR KENTON

WHITE : WPA

EE : FSA

ARKANSAS RIVER VALLEY, MUSKOGEE COUNTY

WILDCAT CURVE, NORTH OF GUTHRIE

HITE : WPA

DIVISION OF STATE PARK

KIAMICHI MOUNTAINS, SOUTHEASTERN OKLAHOMA

TURNER FALLS, ARBUCKLE MOUNTAINS

DIVISION OF STATE PARK

Industry and Labor

OKLAHOMA is not a one-industry state, but the business of oil production, handling, and refining overshadows all other industries. Only the output of the state's 179,687 farms—crops, livestock, and livestock products—comes measurably near to approaching oil in value; and where the farmers' income is some $160,000,000 a year, the normal yearly value of crude oil is about $180,000,000—and twice that amount when turned into gasoline and other salable by-products.

Potentially, however, the state is far from being dependent on oil for its reputation as a treasure house of natural resources. Statements which seem to be extravagant concerning its little-exploited minerals are nevertheless justified by reconnaissance. Within its borders are, literally, mountains of building stone—granite, marble, limestone, sandstone; enormous deposits of brick clay, asphalt, glass sand, tripoli, volcanic ash, gravel; and, to quote an Oklahoma Geological Survey pamphlet, "enough limestone and clay . . . to make Portland cement to supply the United States for ten thousand years."

In manufacturing, only a start has been made, but it is expected that when—probably in 1941—the Grand River lake is filled and ready to produce its rated two hundred million kilowatt hours of cheap electric energy annually, new industries will be attracted to the region; and as other planned flood control and power projects are completed on the Red River and elsewhere additional impetus will be given to factory expansion.

Already, important glass-making plants are operating at Okmulgee, Henryetta, Sand Springs, Sapulpa, Blackwell, and Poteau; a subsidiary of one of the big nationally known steel companies and a cotton mill are at Sand Springs; and in the Tulsa area are a number of plants making oil-field equipment. Such regional industries as grain elevators, flour mills, alfalfa mills, creameries, cotton ginning and compress plants, cottonseed mills, brick and tile, lime and rock-wool plants, stockyards and meat packing plants are located at strategic points.

Historically, industry had its birth in the Oklahoma area when the Chouteaus began making salt at their trading post at Salina *(see Tour 8)* about 1819. In a small way, too, lumbering had its beginning in the period during which the Five Civilized Tribes settled in Indian Territory, roughly from 1829 to 1840, and building materials were required; and some coal had been stripped (mined after the removal of the rock overburden) from surface outcroppings. But, in effect, the natural resources of Oklahoma, including lumbering and mining, had hardly been touched as late as the end of the Civil War.

Mining in Oklahoma was not commercially important until after the railroads came in 1872, when J. J. McAlester, founder of the city which bears his name, began to develop a four-foot vein of coal in the Choctaw Nation. In the same year, in the forests of the Ouachitas, an old millman put up a sawmill and produced rough "boxing-boards." The market for this lumber, which he called "boxum," was good, and others began to operate in the same field with small "groundhog" mills that could easily be moved from place to place. Lead and zinc mining, which had to wait for both fuel and transportation, started in Ottawa County in 1890. With the establishment of towns there developed a need for cement and building stone, and the trades associated with these products began to develop.

Long before the first white oil man appeared, Indians in the Kansas-Oklahoma area had discovered seepage oil. Drilling began in Kansas in 1881, and the first practical discovery was made there a year later. In 1884, prospectors extended their "wildcatting"—that is, drilling in unproved territory—into the region that is now Oklahoma. An oil lease was made by the Cherokee Nation to Edward Byrd in 1886; and three years later the first shallow well—thirty-six feet deep—was completed near Chelsea *(see Tour 1)*. In 1891, eleven wells in this region produced thirty barrels of crude for market.

In 1897, the Cudahy Oil Company, founded by Eugene Cudahy, of Kansas City, completed a well in what is today the city park of Bartlesville which is still producing.

The Curtis Act of June 28, 1898, providing for individual instead of collective ownership of Indian lands, made it impossible to obtain leases until the membership roll of the Indian nations could be completed and the land allotted. Thus, although the Red Fork–Tulsa field was opened in 1901, furnishing the first important commercial production of oil in Oklahoma, there was no major activity until 1904, after the tribal lands had been divided. In that year, more than one hundred wells were drilled in the Bartlesville, Alluwe, Coody's Bluff, and Cleveland fields. Nearly every year since has seen the opening of new fields or new pools.

In the Glenn Pool, twelve miles south of Tulsa, opened in 1905, the third well drilled had a daily production of two thousand barrels and attracted national attention to the oil resources of Oklahoma. By June, 1907, this field had reached a peak of 117,000 barrels a day. In 1906–10 new fields were opened in Okmulgee and Osage counties; and in 1912 the Cushing field was brought in, attaining a gross production in 1915 of 305,000 barrels a day. Several smaller pools were also proved during this period.

Ruthless exploitation, unavoidable in the development of a natural resource of such proportions, marked the beginnings of the oil industry in Oklahoma, as an early court decision suggests:

> . . . every landowner or his lessee may locate his wells wherever he pleases, regardless of the interest of others. He may distribute them over the whole farm, or locate them only on one part of it. He may crowd the adjoining farms so as to enable him to draw the oil and gas from them. What then can the neighbor do? . . . Nothing; only go and do likewise.

This was common law, for at that time no specific oil legislation had been enacted. No attempt was made at conservation; billions of cubic feet of natural gas and millions of barrels of oil were wasted, and the life of every important field appreciably shortened by this profligacy.

Much waste was due to inadequate pipe-line facilities; and though transportation of oil is still a problem whenever a new and large field is opened, the continuous building of trunk pipe lines has largely resolved the difficulty *(see Transportation)*.

During the first eighteen years of the oil industry in Oklahoma, little use was made of scientific methods in prospecting. Discovery followed discovery, despite the crude methods of the day. No co-ordination of activities of different producers existed, and the advancement of the industry depended more upon luck and persistence than planned activity. Superstition and ignorance played a considerable part in the exploration for oil, and there are still old-timers who ridicule modern scientific methods. "Doodlebugs"—sometimes the tools of confidence men, but more often the brain children of well-meaning cranks—appeared in every field.

In territory where no wells have been drilled, and in certain producing fields, it is still true that "the only way to find oil is to drill for it." Modern geological methods have, however, greatly reduced the expense of opening new fields. This is clearly indicated by the fact that, as early as 1926, of thirty-one new fields opened during the year, twenty-one, or nearly 68 per cent, were so located. Fear of an oil famine during and immediately after the World War brought in the scientific era in the oil industry. Aided by oil companies, the schools of Geology and Petroleum Engineering of the University of Oklahoma have assumed leadership in the fields of petroleum geology and engineering. The College of Petroleum Engineering of the University of Tulsa, likewise, attracts students from all over the nation.

Tools first used were merely elaborations of the spring-pole machinery employed in drilling water wells. Underreamers, which permit the casing to follow the drill bit down the well, thus preventing cave-ins, were unknown; as were "fishing tools" for retrieving drill bits lost in the well. To a degree, it was up to the driller to create the tools he needed as an emergency arose; and drilling was a long and arduous process.

Two types of drilling machines are used—cable tools and rotary rigs. Cable tools were used in drilling the first wells in Oklahoma and were so much more common than rotaries, for a long time, that they were called "standard." In cable-tool drilling, the bit is lifted and dropped, literally pounding a hole through the soil and rock. Cable tools are not now used to any great extent, though they are still preferred where there is a scarcity of water and where—when the depth of a producing sand or lime is unknown—there is danger of drilling through oil pools and into salt water.

Most drilling is done by the rotary method. A cutting tool is attached to a length of pipe, and power to rotate the pipe is applied at the surface. New lengths of pipe are added as the well deepens. When it is necessary to change the cutting tool, the "string" of pipe is drawn out of the well, dismantled joint by joint as it is brought up, and then reassembled as it is replaced in the hole.

Both the rotary and the cable-tool methods of drilling have their distinct advantages and disadvantages. With the former, the weight on the bit becomes greater as the hole deepens and thus drilling proceeds more rapidly as the work progresses. In cable-tool drilling there is no weight on the tools; the cable by which they are raised and dropped becomes less manageable as the hole deepens, and at a depth below four thousand feet it is an expert driller, indeed, who can give the bit the necessary motion to "make hole." There is still another side to the story, however. Since rotary rigs depend on weight for drilling efficiency, they can make little progress where extremely hard formations are encountered close to the surface of the earth. Generally, a small cable-tool machine called a "spudder" is used to start the hole for a rotary so that drilling can begin with several joints of pipe. In fields where formations change frequently from soft to hard, combination rotary-cable-tool drilling machines are used.

Many erroneous ideas about the location of the earth's petroleum stores have been prevalent. Prospectuses of certain oil companies have referred to "lakes and rivers of oil," which have no existence outside the writer's imagination. Oil is contained in tiny openings between grains of sand, in the pores and crevices of a crystalline limestone, or, as in the largest wells, in the comparatively small openings of a very porous rock. It is generally agreed that oil has migrated to the places where it is now found. Lighter than the water with which the rock formations are saturated, oil and gas have a tendency to rise until stopped by a rock. An oil pool, then, lies under a convex stratum of impermeable rock known as an anticline and has the shape of an inverted saucer. Natural gas is always present with petroleum, separated or in solution. The normal pattern of an oil pool is gas just below the cap rock, then oil, then water.

Oklahoma's prominence in the oil industry has been due to the discovery of a succession of huge pools as the result of persistent "wildcatting." These pools were generally opened by individuals; the large corporations have bought in later. This is in contrast to California usage, where initial development has been a big-company activity.

While the belief that a major part of Oklahoma's population has been made wealthy by oil has no foundation, the Indians and farmers of certain localities have become enriched by the discovery of petroleum on their lands. The Osage Indians, the richest race of people per capita in the world, have received as high as $1,600,000 for a single lease. In June, 1921, fourteen Osage leases brought $3,256,000, while at the December sale in the same year a group of eighteen leases sold for $6,258,000. In addition to the immense prices paid as bonuses for the right to drill, the Osages receive a royalty of one-sixth of the oil on leases producing less than one hundred barrels a day, and one-fifth on wells yielding more than one hundred barrels a day. The usual royalty payment is one-eighth of production.

Gushers in the Seminole field broke the market for crude oil in 1927; and the first efforts at production control in Oklahoma were made when the oil operators signed voluntary agreements to limit production. The agreements were reasonably effective until 1931. In that year, however, the opening of the East Texas oil fields in the midst of the general financial depression drove the price of Oklahoma crude down from $1.57 a barrel to as low as ten cents, and the state, with its gross-production tax alarmingly reduced by the drop, assumed control. On August 5, 1931, Governor William H. Murray ordered 3,106 wells in twenty-seven Oklahoma fields shut down. An oil umpire was appointed, and proration was enforced by the National Guard. Within two months, offers from the major refiners had gone as high as seventy cents a barrel, and on October 3 the wells were allowed to run part of their oil.

With sharp limitations on production, there developed a widespread traffic in "hot oil," or oil produced in excess of a well's quota and smuggled to market without paying the state tax. For a time, this traffic was as difficult to eradicate as the bootlegging of alcoholic liquor.

Since the drilling of the Chelsea well, more than one hundred thousand producing oil wells have been sunk in Oklahoma. Total production has been approximately three billion barrels, valued at more than four billion dollars. Allowable production under proration now averages about four hundred thousand barrels daily. In many years Oklahoma has headed the list of oil producing states, and in still more years—because of the high quality of the oil—the sum paid for Oklahoma crude has been greater than the oil revenue of any other state. Proration has reasonably stabilized the price, and the tremendous waste of past years has been greatly reduced; and through improved drilling methods and equipment, fire hazards have been cut to a minimum.

No one can do more than estimate the extent of Oklahoma's unexplored oil resources. At various times it has been said that they would be exhausted in a few years, and under the old methods of production these estimates might have proved correct. However, with increasing attention to the conservation of this natural resource and with newly developed methods of reclaiming oil from old fields, the industry will continue to be a major factor in the economic life of Oklahoma for decades to come.

When J. J. McAlester began mining coal in the Choctaw Nation in 1872, the railroads were burning wood and he had little difficulty in selling his coal. Demand exceeded supply; and in 1875 the Osage Coal and Mining Company began large-scale developments from deeper veins, paying a small royalty to the national agent of the Choctaws. Individual Indian citizens protested this payment and won their case in the courts. A compromise resulted and royalties were thereafter divided between the tribal treasury and individual citizens.

In 1899, when the Dawes Commission made the Choctaw-Chickasaw allotments, approximately five hundred thousand acres of coal land were set apart as communal tribal property. The area was offered for sale in 1906, but all bids were rejected; then the land was leased to mine operators who paid the Indians a royalty of eight cents per ton.

Annual coal output increased steadily from 1880 until 1903, then slumped until 1910, when more than 2,500,000 tons were mined. From 1910 to 1920 production again took an upward trend, attaining a figure of 4,848,288 tons in 1920, the peak year of the industry, and employing some 8,500 workers.

Because of the thinness of the veins and the sharp tilting of the coal beds, the cost of mining coal in Oklahoma has always been relatively high. Following the serious strikes of 1910 and 1919, many mines closed and others were abandoned; and neighboring coal-producing states, with fewer labor disputes and easier mining, made serious inroads on the Oklahoma market. The World War boomed almost every industry, and the unhealthy condition of coal mining was not apparent until after 1920. Then, through the rapid development of the enormous oil and gas resources of the state, which provided fuel at only a fraction of the cost of coal, coal mining started on a decline from which it has only slightly recovered. The smokeless fuel ordinance of St. Louis, Missouri, however, and the favorable freight rates that were obtained for shipping eastern Oklahoma and western Arkansas low volatile coal has stimulated production in LeFlore County.

From the peak, coal production declined steadily to a low of 986,904 tons in 1933. Since then, however, output has increased, and amounted to 1,352,495 tons in 1938. Broken Arrow *(see Tour 6)* and Catoosa *(see Tour 1)*, where strip mining is practiced, are now (1941) the largest producers. In 1933, Oklahoma miners worked only 93 days; in 1939, 120 days. The working day was shortened from eight to seven hours in 1934. Wages rose from the low of $2.50 a day in 1932–33 to $4.35 a day in 1939.

Coal reserves in Oklahoma have been estimated by the United States Geological Survey at nearly fifty-five billion tons, and the workable coal area covers approximately ten thousand square miles. The state's tremendous store of coal will probably be seriously depleted only when the supply of cheaper gas and oil products is exhausted.

Zinc and lead mining began in Ottawa County in 1890, but Oklahoma lagged behind other states producing these minerals for almost twenty-five years. Production began to climb in 1907 with the opening of the Miami mines; yet in 1914, at the outbreak of the first World War, Missouri was still producing 90 per cent of the zinc of the Tri-State Mining District, embracing adjacent areas in Oklahoma, Kansas, and Missouri, which yields more than half of the zinc mined in the United States.

The tremendous rise in zinc prices occasioned by the war led to an increase in prospecting, and new deposits were uncovered in Oklahoma. The period which followed was like the boom era in a newly discovered oil field. The older and less profitable mines in Missouri were abandoned for these richer and more easily mined deposits. Miners swarmed into the state. By 1920, there were hundreds of mines and mills, and a number of new towns, where before there had been nothing but open prairies.

Lead is produced as a secondary product of the zinc industry. It is found in small pockets, as a rule, although rich pockets of the ore are occasionally encountered. Lead production rises and falls with zinc production, as does its price.

Oklahoma's asphalt reserves, concentrated in the southern portion of the state, are greater than those of any other state in the Union. Asphalt has been mined since 1903, but the industry has attained no great importance since petroleum asphalt is much cheaper than the natural product and comprises more than 90 per cent of the output used in the state.

Oklahoma's extensive gypsum and clay deposits have been exploited hardly at all. Limestone, granite, and other building stones are found in large quantities in central, southern, and western Oklahoma, and production has increased steadily under the impetus of government building projects. Today the state ranks eighteenth in cut-stone production. Two big plants in Oklahoma manufacture Portland cement; the larger with a daily capacity of six thousand barrels, is at Ada; the other is at Dewey. In many towns there are small plants for making cement products for sale locally. There also are a few factories for making cement pipe; the larger plants of this type are at Oklahoma City and Tulsa.

Salt is no longer mined in Oklahoma, and the small amount produced is recovered through a process of evaporation from salt springs or salt-water wells.

Oklahoma produces about one-third of the total natural gasoline output of the United States. This industry had its beginning in 1911 and reached its peak year in 1928, with the production of approximately 620 million gallons valued at more than forty-three million dollars. Since 1936 the annual production has been approximately 419 million gallons, but owing to low prices the yearly cash return has been only about one-third of the 1928 figure. Some two hundred natural gasoline plants are in operation throughout the oil and gas fields of the state. Natural gasoline is obtained from the gas accompanying the flow of crude oil from the wells, and is separated from the gas but not refined. It is blended with most motor fuels and because of its lightness and high volatility is especially adapted to aviation needs. A by-product of natural gasoline plants is "liquid gas"—gas compressed in cylinders in liquid form; when released the liquid vaporizes, furnishing a fuel similar to natural gas.

The manufacture of carbon black is one of the state's newer industries, and there are three plants for making this product in Oklahoma. Derived from natural gas, carbon black is used in manufacturing rubber and as a pigment in making inks and paints.

Petroleum refining is the principal manufacturing industry in Oklahoma, both in the number of wage earners and in the value of the finished products. Although there were small "skimming plants" before that time, the first complete refinery was built about 1907 in West Tulsa. By 1917, so rapidly had the industry grown, there were sixty-six refineries in the state with an annual output worth approximately 150 million dollars. Since 1919 the trend has been toward fewer but larger and more complete plants; and today, the bulk of the state's crude oil is handled by forty refineries in ten cities. Some of these plants distill gasoline, kerosene, and fuel oils; some turn out lubricating oils; and a few manufacture a complete line of oil products—motor fuels and lubricating oils, paraffin wax, petroleum, coke, asphalt, naphtha, and others. The largest refineries in the state are at Tulsa and Ponca City; one plant, at Ponca City, is capable of handling more than fifty thousand barrels of crude daily and is said to be the largest refinery in the world. Oklahoma's position in the refining industry is indicated by the fact that more than three-fourths of the gasoline produced in the state is exported.

Large-scale lumber production began about 1910; and ruthless exploitation of the timber belt followed. Sawmills were small at first, but by 1924, output of the five largest was ninety million board feet per year; and one hundred small mills sawed eighty million board feet. In 1925, the State Forestry Department was set up and with the Federal government began forest conservation work. Since then, more than 1,300,000 acres have been placed under fire protection, and 1,630,000 acres in a restocking area. Also, the Federal government has established the Washita National Forest of 140,000 acres in the southeastern part of the state, and the Wichita Wildlife Refuge in the southwestern part.

At peak production, about 1928, there were seventy-five sawmills operating in the state, turning out lumber (mostly yellow pine) at the rate of 157 million board feet a year. Narrow-gauge railroads carried the timber to the large stationary mills, while small, portable mills followed the loggers. A considerable number of "free lance" forest workers were engaged in cutting railway ties and fence posts. On a much reduced scale, the picture is the same today (1941).

Only factories required for the preparation of raw materials for shipment, such as meat packing and cotton processing plants, and oil refining obtained an early foothold in Oklahoma; and the practice of exporting raw commodities and importing finished products has prevailed.

Saturation of the oil and agricultural markets gave some impetus to general manufacturing, as did the supply of cheap labor which was made available by the depression; but, generally, the manufacturing structure of the state today differs only in size from that of the 1920's.

LABOR

Labor organization began in 1882, when two coal miners from Illinois—Dill Carroll and Frank Murphy—established in the McAlester area the first union in Indian Territory, a local assembly of the Knights of Labor. Unionization was slow and difficult, owing mainly to distrust by mine owners, but by 1894 there were four local assemblies of the Knights of Labor, with an aggregate membership of about fifteen hundred. Three of the locals were mixed assemblies, while the fourth was made up exclusively of miners.

As a rule wages in the Oklahoma coal mines were higher than in the East, and employment was stable, but the advantage of regular work was offset by the hazards under which the labor was performed, and the impositions of the company-town system. Indian Territory mines were rated the most dangerous in the world—fatal explosions were frequent occurrences; often the miners worked in water up to their knees; almost all the mines were badly ventilated.

Soon after union organization started, the Knights of Labor demanded and received a reduction in working hours and an increase in wages. But the real test of unionism came in 1894, when the first major strike was called. Early in March the mine owners, claiming they had lost some of their markets, announced a 25 per cent wage reduction, to a scale of something less than two dollars a day. The miners refused to accept the cut, and one by one various mines were struck.

Almost immediately the tribal government of the Choctaw Nation, where practically all the mines were located, entered the struggle. With the mines closed, the nation was losing its revenues from royalties and from the fees of one dollar a month (which the operators had been paying) required of miners for working in the Indian Territory. At the instance of Wilson N. Jones, principal chief of the Choctaws, D. M. Wisdom, United States Indian Agent for the territory, requested and received aid from Federal troops to deport striking miners.

Accompanied by Indian police to point out the strikers ("intruders"), whose permits to remain in the nation no longer were being paid, the soldiers rounded up several hundred strikers and their families, loaded them into boxcars, and deported them to Arkansas.

Many of the miners caught the first train back to Indian Territory; others (foreigners) lodged protests with the consuls of the various nations of which they were citizens. Within a few months practically all were back in the territory, and no further effort was made to deport them. On July 31, a settlement between the miners and the operators was reached, providing for a 20 per cent reduction in wages, or only 5 per cent less than the proposed reduction which had led to the strike, but giving the miners concessions in the matters of house rent, shooting powder, and fuel.

By 1898, the Knights of Labor organization was practically nonexistent in Oklahoma, and a new union, the United Mine Workers of America, dominated the coal fields. Late in the winter of 1898 the UMWA began calling strikes in various mine localities for better working conditions and wages, and within a year virtually every mine was closed or operating on a curtailed schedule. The strike dragged on for four years, until August 1, 1903, when the operators capitulated. Among other things, the miners were granted recognition of the union, an eight-hour day, payment of wages twice a month, and most important of all, perhaps, to the union the checkoff (deduction of union dues from the miners' wages by employers).

Carpenters, painters, plasterers, and hod carriers began active organization during the late 1890's, as did the typographical workers and the building trades workers. By 1903 almost every trade carried on in Oklahoma was represented by a union. Among the largest of these were the Railroad Brotherhoods.

The first successful attempt to unite all labor unions in the two territories into a coherent working body came in 1903, when J. Harvey Lynch, a plasterer from Lawton, issued a call for a convention which resulted in the formation of the Twin-Territorial Federation of Labor. Known as the Oklahoma State Federation of Labor since 1906, it was organized—largely by the coal miners—at Lawton on March 28, 1903, and received its charter from the American Federation of Labor on February 15, 1904. It claimed to represent approximately twelve thousand organized workers in the two territories.

In 1906, with statehood imminent, there was need for concerted action on the part of labor, and a convention of the Twin-Territorial Federation opened at Shawnee on August 20. At the same time the federation was in session, two other organizations—the State Farmers Union *(see Agriculture)* and the Railroad Brotherhoods—were holding their conventions in the city. Representatives from each convention were selected to form a joint board of ten members which met at Shawnee on September 10 and prepared for submission to the constitutional convention a comprehensive list of twenty-four labor measures which were placed before every candidate for delegate to the convention. So vigorously did labor press its proposals that 75 per cent of the elected delegates approved the program in its entirety, while an additional 15 per cent approved a portion of it.

In 1907 the State Federation established a legislative committee which was credited with securing the creation of the Department of Charities and Corrections; the establishment of eight hours as a maximum working day on public works; the child labor law, prohibiting the employment of children under sixteen in any occupation injurious to health or morals, or especially hazardous to life or limb; factory and boiler inspection laws; laws prohibiting employers from bringing strikebreakers into the state by using false statements as to conditions of employment, and requirement of employers to state in advertisements where there is a strike in progress; prohibition of blacklisting of employees; and the Workmen's Compensation Law. An outstanding achievement is the so-called Labor's Bill of Rights, forestalling any attempt to declare a union illegal.

The Federation's legislative committee also fought the passage of acts such as the Industrial Court Bill, the Conspiracy Bill, the Anti-picketing Bill and the proposal to extend the working day on public works.

From 1907 to 1911, inclusive, the number of unions in the state increased from 303 to 415, with a total membership of twenty-five thousand. But the same period saw the decline of the once powerful Farmers' Union—largely because of a court ruling which admitted outsiders to the farmer co-operatives—and increasing unrest in the agrarian population.

In the latter part of 1914 a militant secret organization known as the Working Class Union sprang up in Arkansas and spread into Oklahoma. It advocated principally the abolition of rent, interest, and profit-taking; and government ownership of public utilities—and proposed revolution as the means to the end. In the spring of 1917 the union had about thirty-four thousand members, most of them in eastern Oklahoma and Arkansas; and with the coming of the Draft Act, the violence which the organization had so often preached was put into practice. Telephone wires were cut, pipe lines destroyed, water mains and sewers dynamited. Several "armies" were organized and sent into the field, subsisting on barbecued beeves and wagonloads of roasting ears. This "Green Corn Rebellion," staged by some two thousand farmers, including Negroes and Seminole Indians, collapsed early in August, when 450 "rebels" were arrested by citizen-police. Strikes were outlawed either by agreement or statute during the first World War, but in the years immediately following, they broke out in almost every industry and were, almost without exception, lost by the strikers. Controversies in which the largest number of workers were involved were the packing-house strike at Oklahoma City, which lasted from December, 1921, to February, 1922; and the Railway Shopmen's strike, from July, 1922, to June, 1923.

In the early post-war years, the Farmer Labor Reconstruction League attained its greatest influence, drawing its membership from the Farmers' Union—which had been revived by a law favorable to farm co-operatives in 1917—the Railroad Brotherhoods, and the State Federation of Labor. Union of the farmers and industrial workers in political action was its purpose; and the League named candidates for entry into the 1922 Democratic primary and began a vigorous campaign for their election. Buttressed by a $3.50 membership fee from an estimated forty thousand members and with a sizable contribution from the Railroad Brotherhoods, the organization sent out speakers and distributed literature. As a result, its candidate for governor, Jack Walton *(see History)*, received a plurality of approximately thirty-five thousand votes over his nearest opponent. Walton went into office on a landslide, and other League-endorsed candidates also were victorious. Walton's impeachment and removal from office meant the downfall of the Farmer Labor Reconstruction League.

The program of labor organization in Oklahoma during the next decade approximated the national curve, losing ground during the middle and late twenties and picking up sharply after 1930. The most important mass movement during the depression years was the Unemployed (Unemployment) Councils, which attained a membership in the state of approximately thirty thousand. After the arrest of their leaders in 1934, the Councils largely disintegrated, and most of their membership was taken over by the Workers Alliance and the Veterans of Industry of America, which had much the same aims but exercised better control over their adherents.

The CIO appeared in Oklahoma in 1937, when on June 1 of that year a charter was given to the Oklahoma-Arkansas Industrial Council. David Fowler became president of the Council, then composed of 7,500 coal miners, 8,000 oil field and refinery workers, 2,000 glass workers, 3,000 metal miners and smelter workers, and 200 journeyman tailors. For a time several thousand members of the Oklahoma branch of the Southern Tenant Farmer's Union were included in the CIO organization as an affiliate of the United Cannery, Agricultural Packing, and Allied Workers. In March, 1939, they were suspended in a controversy involving distribution of dues payments, and in April they returned to the fold as a semiautonomous body. Backed by the CIO, a strike in the big Tulsa refinery of the Mid-Continent Oil Company was called late in 1938 by the Oil Workers' International Union and came to an indecisive end more than a year later. The issue was, nominally, hours and pay and seniority, but in reality it was a test of strength in the oil industry by the CIO.

As to the actual relative strength of the A. F. of L. and CIO locals within the state, no estimate can be made. Two of the largest CIO bodies—the cannery workers and the oil-field workers—have a highly transient membership, subject to severe fluctuations. Many of the A. F. of L. locals are affiliated directly with their nationals, and not with the Oklahoma federation.

Union organization has progressed rapidly in Oklahoma, but has to reckon with the essentially individualistic psychology of a state that is close in time to its pioneer period.

Transportation

From travois to airplane, the story of transportation in Oklahoma follows the pattern worked out by experience for the settlement of the plains region. In its earliest stages, transport was of necessity adapted to passage over broken, hilly stretches; through difficult, desolate areas like the Cross Timbers; and across prairie flats that became almost bottomless bogs in the rainy seasons of spring and late fall.

Burden-bearing dogs, used by the Indians before the Spaniards brought horses into their country, were succeeded by pack horses. Then some experimental tribesmen thought to increase the horse's capacity beyond what it was able to carry on its back by attaching two poles to the packsaddle, allowing the butt-ends to drag along the ground. Between the poles, a carrier—usually a crude, strong basket—was fixed, in which could be placed anything from a supply of corn to a tired child or a grandmother too feeble to ride on the horse's back. French explorers saw the device and dubbed it a travois.

The earliest trappers and traders among the Osages and more western tribes used saddle and pack horses as well. The first trail breakers across Oklahoma moving westward from the neighborhood of Fort Smith, Arkansas, found that wagons drawn by oxen and small-hoofed mules were less satisfactory than pack trains.

Pioneers of Oklahoma, the Indians for whom the region was set aside—the Five Civilized Tribes removed from the North Carolina, Tennessee, Georgia, Alabama, and Mississippi lands, beginning about 1832—first came into their new homes by Arkansas River steamboats; and many of these shallow-draft vessels (which, legend says, could navigate a western stream after a heavy dew!) steamed as far as Fort Gibson, on the Grand River, and as far as the original western Creek Agency on the Verdigris. Later, the same type of paddlewheel boat plied the Red River.

River transportation however, proved to be impracticable because of frequent stages of low water; moreover, it was inadequate to handle the thousands of exiled Indians who, with many of their belongings, were being driven to the Indian Territory. Wagon trains took their place, each capable of supplying the needs of a thousand or more emigrants; and they broke new roads into Oklahoma. During the next seventy-five years, the area that was finally incorporated into the state was criss-crossed and rutted by high-wheeled wagons that changed in character from the ponderous prairie schooner to a much lighter type of farm and general utility wagon.

In the course of the Civil War, the Indian nations that lived in the eastern third of Oklahoma were overrun at different times by Union, then by Confederate, forces. The difficulties met in transporting soldiers and necessary supplies brought forcibly to the attention of the Federal government the need for railroads. After the war, Congress undertook to stimulate the building of railroads across the Indian Territory by authorizing land grants—which were later invalidated—along the right of way, to the first north-south, and the first east-west, road to reach the border. The winner from the north was the Missouri, Kansas and Texas line (the Katy). Its tracks touched Indian Territory soil at the Kansas line on June 6, 1870, and its first southbound passenger train crossed the bridge over Red River into Texas on Christmas Day, 1872.

In the summer of 1871, the Atlantic and Pacific, which became the St. Louis and San Francisco (Frisco), built to Vinita *(see Tour 1),* a station on the Katy, thus winning the east-west franchise. By the summer of 1882 it was in operation to Tulsa; and by 1886 it had bridged the Arkansas River and established its western terminal at Sapulpa *(see Tour 1).*

The Atchison, Topeka and Santa Fe began grading its line south from Wichita, Kansas, in 1886, the ultimate destination being Galveston, Texas. Trains were running across what became Oklahoma Territory two years before the first opening to white settlement—that of unassigned Indian lands in April, 1889.

The Chicago, Rock Island and Pacific built down from Kansas to the border of the Chickasaw Nation in 1890, and in the same year the Choctaw Coal and Railway Company completed a line to link the Rock Island with the Santa Fe at the newly established settlement of Oklahoma City.

Later railroad development consisted largely of local projects—spurs and connecting lines—meant to serve definite industrial needs; and when these proved their economic worth they were taken over by the main-line systems—the Frisco, Katy, Santa Fe, and Rock Island.

The opening to the whites of the Indians' unoccupied western holdings, and the influx of homesteaders to vacant land overnight, necessitated much rapid railroad construction. In 1907, at the beginning of statehood, Oklahoma contained a third of all the railroad mileage built in the United States since the turn of the century.

Meanwhile, in the Indian Territory portion of Oklahoma, the exploitation of coal resources centering at McAlester, the enormous expansion of oil production, and the multiplication of lumber mills brought much new business *(see Industry and Labor)* and stimulated the laying of branch railway tracks.

Oil transportation could be handled by railway tank cars while production was limited to wells in the shallow fields making only a few barrels a day each, but when the gusher fields—Glenn Pool (end of 1905) and Cushing (end of 1912)—came in, pipe lines to connect the wells with refineries (some as far away as the Atlantic seaboard, and others at Gulf of Mexico ports) became an urgent need. Until they were sufficiently extended to handle the load, enormous stores of crude oil were kept in great, round, mushroom-like tanks, each holding fifty thousand or more barrels, grouped —sometimes fifty and more together—on vast "tank farms."

The first local pipe lines, from wells to storage, were laid down in 1905, the year the Glenn Pool gusher field was opened; but the one available line reached only the limited storage and refinery facilities at Bartlesville, some seventy miles away. In the following year, however, there was pipe-line transportation from Kansas to the Gulf of Mexico. By 1909, construction had so extended that facilities equaled demand. With the opening of the Cushing and Healdton pools, around 1912, however, pipe lines and railroads were both swamped. Since then, more than twenty-five thousand miles of trunk and branch lines have grid-patterned the state. A much later extension has been the pipe lines for conducting Oklahoma natural gas from the wells to markets as far away as Chicago. The state's pipe-line investment was $400,-000,000 in 1940.

As general carriers, of course, the railroads with nineteen steam, and six electric, lines in operation (1941) are most important. Trucks and busses, however, have claimed more and more of both short-haul and long-haul traffic as the main highways were hard surfaced and gasoline motors became more powerful and dependable. Operating out of Oklahoma City and Tulsa, two motor truck express fleets, first put into service to speed up newspaper delivery, undertook to cover the small towns and extensive country areas surrounding these cities as quickly and completely as the United States mail. Fifty-seven passenger and express bus lines operate on Oklahoma highways and more than sixty thousand trucks are in use.

Oklahoma is perhaps as air minded as any state in the Union. Development of airplanes and the state's great oil fields were contemporaneous, and some of the first practicable planes were flown by oil company executives. The number of private planes has increased with the lowering of their cost, and the increase of airports and landing fields, which now (1941) number fifty-three. An Oklahoma City–owned line, organized in 1928, maintains service between Chicago and Brownsville, Texas, with stops at Oklahoma City and Ponca City. One transcontinental line stops at Tulsa and Oklahoma City, and a Minneapolis-to-Tulsa line has its southern terminus at Tulsa. Increased activity in this field is resulting from the greatly enlarged government pilot training program in the state.

Transportation in Oklahoma is regulated by the Corporation Commission, which issues licenses to carriers, controls operation, and regulates fares and charges on intrastate business.

Agriculture

PREDOMINANTLY agricultural, with nearly thirty-five million acres of its total area of some forty-four million acres in farms, Oklahoma produces almost every crop grown in the United States. Its various soils —alluvial, sandy loam, black waxy, granitic, prairie limestone, clay hardpan —are adapted generally to such staples as cotton, wheat, corn, oats, and hay; and in selected regions valuable crops of potatoes, alfalfa, sorghum, cane, broomcorn, peanuts, and pecans help to swell the annual value of farm crops and livestock to approximately $160,000,000.

Wheat has replaced cotton as Oklahoma's principal crop, having risen from a 1930 production of some 51,000,000 bushels to more than 58,000,000 in 1940. In the same period, the acreage in cotton was reduced two-thirds, and the output fell from 1,130,415 to 520,591 bales, though the yield per acre went up slightly. Diversified farming, by contrast, has shown a large and steady increase. Evidence of this is the mounting value of such items as forage crops, dairy products, and alfalfa seed. The state ranks first (1941) in production of alfalfa seed.

Oklahoma has suffered, along with most of the farming areas of the Middle West, from abnormally low prices for its products, while the value of farm land has correspondingly declined. From an average valuation, as census figures showed, of $11.33 an acre in 1890, Oklahoma farm land rose to $51.97 in 1920, declining again to a 1940 value of $23.88. In the decade 1930–40, the total value of the state's farms decreased almost a third, while the number of farms shrank 11.9 per cent from 203,866 to 179,687; average acreage per farm, however, rose 14.5 per cent from 165 to 193 acres.

In this period of readjustment, the long-time trend toward increase of farm tenancy in Oklahoma was reversed. The 1940 census showed 81,866 farms operated by owners, part owners, and managers against 78,537 in 1930, an increase of slightly over 4 per cent; the decrease in nonowner operators in the 1930–40 decade was nearly 30 per cent, the total number of tenants falling off from 125,329 to 97,821, and of croppers from 21,055 to 4,954.

Stabilization of farm crop values; the work of county agents; and governmental assistance, national and state, in various types of farm, pasture, water, and woods conservation—all are combining to lighten the picture. Such widespread efforts toward improvement as are made by the Future Farmers of America and the 4-H clubs are especially effective.

Like nearly everything else in Oklahoma, agriculture's beginning traces back to the Indians. The first scratching of its soil is credited to those seminomadic aboriginal tribes who grew limited supplies of corn, beans, melons, and tobacco.

With the arrival of the Five Civilized Tribes from the region between the Cumberland and the Gulf and North Carolina and the Mississippi River, in the period 1829–40, agriculture really began. These Indians brought with them a thorough knowledge of farming and some farming tools, and of necessity undertook with vigor to subdue the new land to the plow and the hoe.

They settled at first in the forested, spring-fed highlands of the eastern section, where fish and game were to be had, gradually moving farther west to wide belts of prairie between the streams. On their selected farms they prospered; certain of the mixed bloods who had brought their slaves established plantations and ranches in the valleys of the Arkansas, Canadian, and Red rivers, where they built sturdy homes with spreading verandas and lived in patriarchal plenty. Such plantations produced the food and clothing needed for its dependents; and surpluses of corn, cotton, and cattle were shipped down the Arkansas and Red rivers to distant markets. Fullblood Indians built their cabins along the streams; planted fruit trees, gardens, and small patches of corn; raised a little cotton, from which the women made their clothing; and let their hogs, cattle, and ponies run on the open range. For a time, the Creeks, more conservative than their neighbors, used the town system of agriculture they had practiced in Alabama, all the men of a settlement working together to till a communal farm. Eventually they, too, adopted individual farming methods, and each family established its cabin in the midst of its own fields.

Driven from their farms during the Civil War, with the return of peace the Indians replanted their orchards, reclaimed their weed-grown fields, and accumulated new herds of cattle. Freed slaves settled in the neighborhood of the old plantations and farmed in a careless fashion; and former plantation owners carried on by leasing their land to white men who by this time were drifting into the country. Most of the full bloods remained in the eastern hills, but the Creeks and Seminoles moved westward to the rough, blackjack-covered sandstone hills. When other Indians were given reservations west of the Five Civilized Tribes, some of them also settled in this region, but most went to the prairies in the western half of the Territory, to become stock-raisers rather than farmers.

In this period the Indian Territory, with or without the consent of its owners, became a cattle country. Even in the Five Civilized Tribes area the Indian population's agricultural needs were so limited that only a small part of the arable land was cultivated. Good grass covered the timbered hills; in the valleys rank bluestem grew as high as the head of a man on horseback; and the Indians fenced their little fields against ranging herds.

West of the Five Civilized Tribes region, the prairies remained unbroken by the plow. At their eastern margin grew the rank bluestem, while their rising levels to the west were covered with the short, dense buffalo grass. Great herds of longhorns were brought in each spring from Texas, fattened on the range during the summer, and in the fall driven for shipment to the railheads of Kansas.

The range cattle industry began to decline in the late eighties, when the surplus lands of the western tribes were opened to white settlement. In the course of these dramatic openings *(see History)*, each homesteader took 160 acres, on a creek if possible, where wood and water could be obtained, and where the most productive "bottom land" lay. His second choice was a level prairie tract, easy to cultivate. Many quarter sections of rugged land, entirely unsuited to agriculture, were taken by less fortunate homesteaders; and in the struggle to make a living from such quarter sections, soil that should have remained in grass was soon worn out.

Usually, the new farmer's first job was to plow a number of furrows around his quarter section as protection against destructive prairie fires. Often this fireguard was planted to peach trees or, if peach seeds were lacking, to watermelons. The next task was breaking the prairie and planting such crops as he had grown before coming to this new country.

Meanwhile the Five Civilized Tribes area was coming predominantly under the white man's plow. In the Indian region, white farmers, either intruders or lessees, came in increasing numbers to settle on tribal land. When the Dawes Commission allotted it, each Indian received from forty to 320 acres of average land. In most cases, the combined holdings of his family formed a larger agricultural unit than he, with his simple farming methods, could cultivate; and while allotments were protected for a varying number of years against alienation, leasing to white farmers was permitted.

At statehood, virtually all of Oklahoma's arable land was under cultivation—the western half, still in 160-acre tracts, was held by the original homesteaders or their successors, except for the small amount comprised in Indian allotments; the eastern half was owned by Indian allotees.

Since that time tenant farming increased steadily, until the last few years, though it was not by any means uniform throughout the state. It has ranged in percentage from 35.1 per cent in the Panhandle county of Beaver, a grain and livestock region, to 78.3 per cent in McIntosh County, where staple crops are corn, potatoes, peanuts, and cotton. Taking the state as a whole, the percentage of tenant farmers increased in the ten years from 1925 to 1935 from 58.6 to 61.2, and the number of tenants from 125,329 to 130,661. In the five years from 1935 to 1940 the reduction in farm tenancy has been over 25 per cent.

Farm tenancy in the western part of the state is explained largely by the failure of homesteaders to survive hard years with only 160 acres as a grain-growing unit. In the eastern half of Oklahoma, most of the allotted land passed out of the hands of Indian owners as soon as it ceased to be restricted. Bought by land speculators, it was rented to white farmers who seldom became owners.

Roughly, the period of land cultivation in Oklahoma dates from 1890. In the brief time since, in the western part of the state particularly, there have been serious losses from soil erosion. Climate, the thin, light character of the soil, the topography of the region, and the exigencies of "quarter section" farming have all combined to hasten the destructive process.

A problem since early territorial days, erosion has been studied intensively at Oklahoma's Agricultural and Mechanical College, and at other farm schools. Paul B. Sears *(see Literature)*, while a teacher at the University of Oklahoma, brought it into national prominence with his book, *Deserts on the March* (1935). At first, efforts by public agencies to check erosion were almost wholly educational, all the practical work being undertaken by the farmers at their own expense. But in 1933 the Federal government began demonstrating methods of erosion control, co-operating with the farmers in supervising actual work on the land. Almost one-half of the land area of the state is now (1941) organized into fifty-six soil conservancy districts.

Varied soil, contrasting topography, and the difference in average annual rainfall—twenty inches in the northwest to more than forty in the southeast—have made possible great diversity in agricultural methods and products. On the level prairies of the northwest central portion, wheat does well and is grown usually in big, tractor-farmed holdings. Farther west and northwest, including the more arid Panhandle area, broomcorn and sorghum crops are surer; the southwestern prairies are planted to cotton, with sorghum providing an alternative crop in the drier sections. A broad belt stretching north and south across the central portion of the state, a region of more abundant rainfall, is occupied with diversified farming, producing a good yield of almost every product grown in other sections. The arable land of the east is planted largely to corn and oats, with an increasing acreage of potatoes and garden products for canning; fruit and pecan orchards flourish in the rich valleys.

The tendency to develop special regional crops in especially suitable soil is illustrated by the growing of potatoes in the Muskogee region, peanuts near Bristow and Okmulgee, and alfalfa in the Washita River valley, centering at Pauls Valley.

The size of Oklahoma's farms is gradually changing from the uniformity of an Indian allotment or a homesteader's quarter section. With increasing use of expensive power machinery—tractors and combines—in the wheat-growing sections, and the restricted production per acre of the semiarid region, farms have grown larger in the western part of the state, while the eastern farm, with more intensive cultivation, has decreased in size. The appearance of farm buildings differs widely in different sections—there is the little mountain cabin surrounded by its Indian peach, and other fruit trees; the prosperous farmstead in the central region with big barns and silos; the clean, bare aloofness of the wheat-farmer's dwelling; and the unpainted shack standing alone with its windmill on the arid plains. But to visitors, especially from the north, Oklahoma farms regardless of location seem poor in buildings. This is due mainly to a climate so mild that shelter for livestock is not required.

Though cotton production has declined to second place in importance, the average annual value of the crop in Oklahoma over the last fifteen years has been in excess of $70,000,000. Corn follows cotton in importance, with a 1940 crop of more than twenty-five million bushels and an average annual production of some forty million bushels over a ten-year span. The state ranked first in broomcorn from 1930 to 1940, except in 1936, supplying approximately half of the national total; it is second in yield of pecan nuts (1940); it is third (1940) in acreage and harvest of sorghum crops; and in dairy products Oklahoma stands twelfth in 1941.

As to livestock, 1940 statistics show an increase over 1930 of nearly 25 per cent in cattle, nearly 15 per cent in swine, and almost 250 per cent in sheep and lambs. With bigger farm units and greater use of tractors, the count of horses and mules fell from 811,669 in 1930 to 491,669 in 1940. The state's chicken census went down from 11,470,000 in 1930 to 9,047,000 in 1940.

While the big-ranch cattle business has almost ceased to exist in Oklahoma, improved strains of livestock on the farms, and livestock products, the development of which is stressed in the training of Future Farmers and 4-H Club youth, account for more than 48 per cent of the income received directly from the state's 179,687 farms.

Farming in Oklahoma is becoming increasingly scientific; leadership in this movement is held by the state Agricultural and Mechanical College and the Agricultural Experiment Station at Stillwater; this work is supported jointly by state and Federal appropriations. Here young men are trained in agricultural methods, and young women in homemaking. They graduate into farm homes, vocational teaching, or the extension service of the college, work which was inaugurated in 1904 and has continued to grow in extent and importance. County farm agents and home demonstration agents directed by this branch of the college reach the agricultural population of all sections.

The Colored Agricultural and Normal University at Langston *(see Tour 2A)* trains young Negroes in scientific farming and homemaking, and a number of its graduates are working as field agents among their people, under the supervision of the Extension Service at Stillwater. These agents, both colored and white, give individual assistance to farmers and their families, but most of their work is carried on through voluntary local associations of farm people.

The most effective Oklahoma farm-aid groups are: the Master Farmers of America and Home Demonstration Clubs, for adults; the Future Farmers of America, for boys studying vocational agriculture in high school; and the 4-H Clubs, for boys and girls participating in agricultural and homemaking activities. Oklahoma Future Farmers and 4-H Clubs for boys and girls have won recognition in national, even in international, competitions. The state produced its first 4-H Club world champion in 1924, the boy of most outstanding achievements; repeated in 1925 with a girls' world champion; and has continued to win more national and international honors than any other five states combined. Some 275,000 farm boys and girls have received training through this organization. Incidentally, the winner of the first world championship and the next year's winner married and established a home at Stillwater. Oklahoma's Future Farmers of America have also won high honors in national contests. In 1926, at the first national meeting of the students of vocational agriculture, Oklahoma boys took first place in stock judging over competing teams from twenty-two states; they repeated this victory the next year over a still larger number of contestants; and since that time they have won nearly a dozen major national titles in this field.

Fred Groff, whose farm is near Guthrie, deserves the title of Oklahoma Burbank for his work in plant breeding. According to the American Society for the Advancement of Agriculture, eleven of the one hundred important recent developments in horticulture have been credited to him. Among his achievements are a freeze-proof lemon tree, giant cucumbers and peas, and an evergreen pea.

Besides the farm clubs sponsored by the extension department of the State Agricultural and Mechanical College, Oklahoma farmers have developed, on their own initiative, a number of co-operative marketing associations. The first were formed by white farmers in the Indian Territory as a part of a widespread agrarian movement that was sweeping the agricultural states in the eighties; farmers' alliances and agricultural wheels were formed in many communities; one newspaper, the *Alliance Courier,* was founded at Ardmore in the Chickasaw Nation, in 1888; and a number of cooperative stores, cotton gins, and gristmills were established in railroad towns. When Oklahoma was thrown open to white settlement, similar organizations sprang up there. The Farmers' Union was established in Oklahoma Territory shortly before 1900 and began to operate stores, gins, grain elevators, and warehouses. The first year after statehood this society had a membership of 8,120, which had increased to 20,703 by 1939. At the present time the Oklahoma Grain Growers Association, the Oklahoma Cotton Growers Association, and the Farmers' Co-operative Grain Dealers Association are active and have important marketing achievements to their credit. The Cotton Growers Association has handled as much as 30 per cent of the state's production, and the importance of co-operative marketing in the wheat sections is dramatically shown by the many farmer-owned grain elevators that tower above the little towns in the northwest. Another society, known as the Oklahoma Crop Improvement Association, attempts through close co-operation with the state Agricultural and Mechanical College to produce and certify superior seed and sell it at an attractively low price.

Sports and Recreation

IN THE HUNDREDS of public and private recreational parks and playgrounds, along the stocked streams, and in the woods-and-pasture areas of Oklahoma, all outdoor enthusiasts—sports lovers, vacationists, bird hunters, fishermen, Boy Scouts, Girl Scouts, and Camp Fire Girls—will find a wide choice of activities.

Game and fish are most plentiful in the eastern section, although quail are found nearly everywhere. Almost every town has its swimming pool, natural or artificial, its municipal or private-club tennis courts and golf course; bicycles can be rented; and bowling alleys are numerous. High class hotels generally provide golf facilities for their guests. Football and basketball are popular in the schools—high schools, junior colleges, and universities; baseball, however, has almost ceased to be a school sport and is largely confined to the town sandlotters. Oklahoma City and Tulsa are on wrestling wheels and boxing circuits, and Tulsa has an ice hockey league team which plays in the beautiful, modern Coliseum. Over the waters of Grand Lake, Lake Murray, Spavinaw, Tulsa's Mohawk Lake and Oklahoma City's Lake Overholser, motor boat racers bounce and sail boats spread their wings.

Recreational facilities for Negroes are provided by the state, the counties, towns, school authorities, and semipublic and private agencies in the regions where the Negro population is greatest. A 1940 survey of thirty-three counties showed ninety-six such areas for their exclusive use.

More than a century ago, Washington Irving described that portion of present Oklahoma covered in his *Tour on the Prairies* (roughly, a great oval, the ends at Fort Gibson and Norman) as "hill and dale, brush and brake, tangled thicket and open prairie." Little remains in that primitive state, but twelve million acres are still well forested, and four mountainous areas in the east and south have been opened to the motorist by the building of adequate roads. Despite the fact that the pioneers and the Indians used dynamite, poisonous herbs, seines, and spears for taking fish, the streams and lakes are well stocked, and there is no closed season for fishermen. The mountain streams supply sport for the fly caster, and such rivers as the Grand, Kiamichi, Black Fork, Poteau, and Little give up catfish weighing as much as fifty pounds to the bamboo pole angler. All fishing waters are being continuously restocked from state and Federal hatcheries.

In 1935, the last open season on deer, between two and three thousand were reported. Short open seasons are fixed by state regulations. In all forested areas, and along the wooded streams of the state, squirrels are plentiful. The best quail shooting is in the northeast corner of the state, and in the Panhandle *(see Tour 2),* where blue (or Mexican) quail and prairie chicken —especially in Ellis County—are fairly plentiful. In other prairie sections wild chickens have all but disappeared—killed out by market hunters and farmers—but they have been strictly protected in late years, and it is hoped that they will again become a common state game bird.

Duck hunting is good along Red River and fair on the many lakes and ponds throughout the state. One may not kill a fox in Oklahoma, but it is permissible to organize hunts; the chase is popular in Atoka County and in the Kiamichi valley.

As a wildlife conservation project, the Oklahoma Game and Fish Commission in 1938 began quail restocking and has established 199 refuges, totaling 99,118 acres, on which some seven thousand quail from the state farm at El Reno *(see Tour 1)* were liberated by 1940. Three hundred more of these refuges, of about one section (640 acres) each, will be checkerboarded over all suitable areas of the state, and twenty thousand more birds placed thereon to breed and spread to surrounding farms and pastures.

Roughly, four scenic regions attract the sportsman and vacationist—the Ozark slope in the northeastern part of the state; the Ouachita National Forest, embracing most of the mountainous Kiamichi country in the southeast; the Arbuckle mountains in the south central region; and the Wichita Mountains Wildlife Refuge in the southwest.

Within Oklahoma's borders, 25,724 acres of recreational parks have been developed; and in addition, there are about five thousand acres of state-controlled and municipal lakes. By far the largest body of water open to public use and enjoyment is Grand Lake, a $22,750,000 Federal flood control and power project on Grand River seventeen miles southeast of Vinita *(see Tour 1),* which covers an area of fifty-four thousand acres, and has a shore line of thirteen hundred miles. The dam was finished in the summer of 1940, and by the end of 1941 the lake was full. Though its development as a recreation center has only begun, the possibilities are almost unlimited for yachting, motor boating, aquaplaning, bathing, fishing, and camping.

Other large completed Federal lake projects are on the Salt Fork, in

Alfalfa County, east of Cherokee *(see Tour 2)*, and northwest of Woodward on Wolf Creek *(see Tour 5)*.

Construction of the dam to impound the Red River flood control and power reservoir, about twelve miles southwest of Durant *(see Tour 6)*, is under way; and when this Federal job is completed an interstate body of water several times larger than Grand Lake will be available to the water-sports lovers of Oklahoma and Texas.

Lake Murray State Park, almost touching the city of Ardmore *(see Tour 10)* on the southeast, is designed to be the most complete recreational plant in Oklahoma when its seventeen thousand acres are developed and the lake, which will cover 6,100 acres, is filled. At the end of 1940, the dam had been finished, and more than 2,500 acres covered with water.

Boiling Springs State Park, six miles east of Woodward *(see Tour 5)*, is notable as the only native tree growth within 120 miles. In this semiarid tract of nine hundred acres, a number of large springs supply a four-acre swimming pool. It has a bathhouse with modern facilities for three hundred bathers. Beavers Bend State Park, in McCurtain County nine miles north of Broken Bow *(see Tour 15A)*, is in a very rough and picturesque setting; and through its sixteen hundred acres runs Mountain Fork River, offering some of the best fishing in the state.

Lake Altus, at Lugert *(see Tour 13)*, has twelve miles of shore line, and lakes at Okmulgee *(see Tour 3)* and McAlester *(see Tour 5)* each have twenty-four miles; Lake Lawtonka *(see Tour 3B)* covers 1,408 acres; Spavinaw Lake *(see Tour 15)*, the source of Tulsa's water supply, is seven miles long and at places two miles wide. Lake Carl Blackwell, west of Stillwater, is one of the latest (1941) recreation spots to be developed. Recreational facilities and tourist accommodations are available at all these lakes.

Trails for hiking have been built in some of the state parks. Especially good are those in Platt National Park *(see Tour 10A)*, the Wichita Mountains Wildlife Refuge *(see Tour 3B)*, and in the Arbuckle Mountains near Turner Falls *(see Tour 10)*.

Oklahoma's parks and lakes, generally, are at their best during the spring, summer, and early fall months; but because of its abundant mineral springs Platt National Park, near the town suggestively named Sulphur, is a popular all-season resort.

The cosmopolitan character of Oklahoma is indicated by its sports—the former Terrapin Derby, for example. It originated in 1928 at the 101 Ranch *(see Tour 10)* as a community joke and proved popular; by 1935 there were 7,100 entries and $3,000 went to the owner of the winning terrapin. Rodeos, usually held in the fall, draw visitors to a number of towns where the cattle business either still flourishes, under fence, or is a fairly recent memory. Some important rodeos are staged at Ada, Dewey, Woodward *(see Tour 5)*, Covington *(see Tour 2)*, Craterville Park *(see Tour 3)*, Gene Autry (formerly Berwyn), and Vinita *(see Tour 1)*. This last is one of the several memorials to the memory of Oklahoma's beloved humorist Will Rogers. Unique is the experiment of holding a rodeo within the grounds of the state penitentiary at McAlester to bolster the morale of the inmates.

The state is noted for its high school and college football teams. The University of Oklahoma's 1938 team, a member of the "Big Six" conference —Oklahoma, Missouri, Nebraska, Kansas, Kansas State, and Iowa State— played Tennessee at the Miami Orange Bowl in an intersectional after-season game. A. and M. at Stillwater has been a member of the Missouri Valley conference since 1924 and is the strongest state rival of the University in athletics. The former's wrestling teams have been among the best in the United States in recent years. Professional football clubs have recruited a number of Oklahoma college graduate football players.

The national amateur tennis champion of 1940, Don McNeill, is a product of Oklahoma City's courts. In golf, the low handicap players of the state rank with the best.

Polo is not a popular sport, though there are twelve teams in Oklahoma, of which five are at Fort Sill. The University of Oklahoma polo team stands high among the college teams. Basketball, everywhere a popular fall and winter sport among the schools, colleges, and Y's, has taken such firm hold on the people at El Reno—adults and youth alike—that the city is known as the basketball capital of the state. Tulsa's ice hockey team, called the Ice Oilers, is a member of the American Hockey Association.

A surprising development in sport in a state so near in time to the rugged pioneer era is softball. Not only in the cities, where teams are maintained that rate high nationally, but in practically every small town and consolidated country school there are at least two teams of boys, young men, and girls; and formal and informal intersectional league contests draw summer crowds to parks that can be lighted for night games. Softball has all but superseded baseball, though such colleges as the University of Oklahoma and A. and M. develop teams from which professional baseball clubs frequently draw recruits. At Oklahoma City and Tulsa, baseball teams of the Texas League play a regular summer schedule of 154 games.

Education

LIKE OTHER PHASES of Oklahoma's story, that of education reaches much farther back than statehood or even the coming of the white pioneer. It originated with the Five Civilized Tribes in their homes east of the Mississippi. The impact of white civilization, pressure from Washington for repeated cessions of tribal lands for homesteaders, the hard necessity of dealing with those who were crowding them into narrower and narrower limits —all these experiences convinced the tribal leaders that only by acquiring the white man's education could they cope with him in the struggle for survival.

The Cherokees took the lead in 1800 when they invited Moravian missionaries to their country. In 1817 the American Board of Commissioners for Foreign Missions founded a school near Chattanooga, Tennessee, where the great Samuel Austin Worcester entered upon a work that was to engage the efforts of this remarkable family for three generations.

But the greatest incentive to Cherokee education came from the invention of the Cherokee syllabary *(see Literature)* by the half-blood Sequoyah, who had gone to the West with an advance Removal contingent in 1818. In 1821 he returned to the East and submitted his alphabet to the chiefs and headmen of his tribe, and the next year he carried a written message from their kinsmen to the Cherokees on the western frontier. From that time until the removal of the eastern Cherokees in 1838-39 the two sections of the severed nation were able to carry on a written correspondence. In 1832 the western Cherokees passed the first school law enacted in the present state of Oklahoma; they provided for the opening of five schools and employed Sequoyah to supervise the teaching of his syllabary to the whole colony. The formal schools established by the missionaries, and later by the Cherokee Nation, carried on their instruction in English, but as long as the Cherokees maintained their tribal existence it was common for parents to teach their children to read and write the native characters before undertaking their regular education.

Soon after the missionaries of the American Board began to work among the Cherokees, the Choctaws invited them to their country; Cyrus Kingsbury was accordingly sent from the Cherokee Mission and established a school among the Choctaws in Mississippi in 1818. Even at this early period the Choctaws contributed to the support of their schools by donations of cattle and money, and a general council of the nation appropriated for education the annuities which they received from the United States for land cessions. By 1830—the year the main body of Choctaws consented to leave their native forests and remove to the present state of Oklahoma—they had eleven schools with an attendance of 260 children who were learning English; 250 adults had been taught to read the native language; and eighty-nine boys, who were to become the future leaders of the tribe, were enrolled in a boarding school established by Richard Mentor Johnson in Kentucky.

The Creeks had more strongly marked native traits than the Choctaws and Cherokees; hence they were more reluctant to admit their need for education. But with the continued pressure of the frontier upon their homes and the increasing demands for land cessions, they learned to depend upon Cherokees to defend them from the white man's tricks of literacy; and they began to feel the need of mastering his useful arts. In 1822 they reluctantly consented to the establishment of two schools in their country, by Methodist and Baptist missionaries. By this time they subscribed in theory to the Cherokee-Choctaw principle that only through education could they hope for the survival of their race. Even so, they were more advanced than the Seminoles and the Chickasaws, who did not yet feel the need of the white man's skills.

The Indians' educational progress was interrupted by the sufferings of Removal and the hardships of pioneering in the West, but some of their devoted missionaries shared their exile and opened schools in the new land. The American Board had established Union Mission, west of the Grand River in northeast Oklahoma, for the Osages in 1821; and when the Creeks and Cherokees began to arrive in that vicinity a number of their more promising young people were enrolled there. Missionaries working in the Creek country reduced the native language to writing, and an illustrated child's primer was printed at Union in 1835—a date significant to present-day Oklahomans, who honored it in a state-wide centennial celebration. The Creeks, however, were so resentful at their expulsion from their homes that the next year they closed their borders against missionaries and all educational efforts. Meanwhile several schools were opened among the Cherokees and Choctaws, two of which—Dwight, in the Cherokee hills, and Wheelock, near Red River—are still (1941) in existence.

After the Removal, the tribes began to develop comprehensive school systems. In 1841, the Cherokees adopted a plan of general education under the supervision of a tribal superintendent, and nine years later established two seminaries—one for young men and one for young women—which were the first public, nonsectarian schools for higher education in the West. The Choctaws' tribal legislature, in 1842, authorized general education under a system of native language schools for adults; neighborhood, or day schools; boarding schools for more advanced instruction conducted by missionaries but supported by the tribe; and college training for selected young men and women who were sent to eastern states.

The Creeks soon lifted their ban on missionary effort and entered into contracts with the Presbyterian and Methodist churches for the establishment of boarding schools, under an arrangement similar to that of the Choctaws. The greatest of these schools was Tullahassee, on the Arkansas, a few miles northwest of present Muskogee. Robert M. Loughridge, a young Princeton graduate from Alabama, and W. S. Robertson, who married a daughter of Worcester, gave devoted service to this school; Loughridge and Mrs. Robertson published readers, tracts, and portions of the Bible in the native language for the use of their Creek-speaking converts. In 1856 the tribal legislature passed a comprehensive school law. A superintendent was appointed for each of the two districts comprising the Creek Nation, and rural schools—in many cases taught by Tullahassee graduates—were opened in the different neighborhoods.

The Chickasaws, although an able people, were slower to respond to educational influences, probably because in their eastern home they had not been so seriously crowded by whites. But in 1848 they decided upon the establishment of two boarding schools. The Chickasaw Academy, for boys, was accordingly constructed with tribal funds and operated by the Methodists; and Wapanucka Institute, for girls, was built by the tribe and conducted by the Presbyterians. The Chickasaws also established six neighborhood schools, most of which were taught by educated Indians. The unfortunate Seminoles were so distracted by war and the sufferings of their forced removal that for several years they were indifferent to education. A few schools were opened in their country by missionaries after 1849.

Every school in the Indian country was shut down at the outbreak of the Civil War. The Cherokees made some attempt to provide educational training for their children in the refugee camps on the Red River, but this seems to have been the sole educational effort during the whole period of the war. As soon as the Indians returned to their devastated country and began to rebuild their ruined homes, each tribe took active steps to place its schools on a permanent basis. The Chickasaws and Seminoles, who had previously lagged behind the other tribes, now established complete school systems. Some of the tribes had compulsory attendance laws. The Chickasaws even compensated the parents under a law passed in 1876, providing an allowance of eight dollars a month for the board of every child attending the neighborhood schools, and fifteen dollars a month to defray the expenses of those parents who preferred to send their children to school in the surrounding states. The tribes that adopted their freedmen also established separate neighborhood and boarding schools for Negro children.

By the end of the century, the Cherokees, Choctaws, and Chickasaws had a higher proportion of educated people than had the neighboring states. Probably half of the Indians of the Five Civilized Tribes were able to speak and read English, and literacy in the native languages was general. All the tribes regarded their schools as their highest creative achievement and freely appropriated money for their support. In the course of their forced land cessions, each tribe had accumulated a considerable capital investment for which it received interest. This income was supplemented by taxes on goods introduced by white traders, permit fees paid for the employment of noncitizen laborers, grazing taxes paid by cattlemen, and royalties paid for the use of coal, timber, and other natural resources.

When the Plains Indians accepted reservations in what is now western Oklahoma, the government established agencies among them and attempted to conduct schools; and courageous missionaries, mainly Quakers and Mennonites, tried to induce the untamed savages to engage in manual labor and submit to the discipline of the three R's. But the proud owners of the prairies were contemptuous alike of the white man's painfully acquired learning and his grubbing economic techniques. It was only when their spirit was broken by military defeats and the loss of the buffalo herds that they turned in desperation to this untried way of life. Even then they would not listen to the white man, but over and over in intertribal councils they appealed to the civilized Indians for help and guidance, and from them they accepted the oft-reiterated advice to till the soil and educate their children. Gradually their schools filled up. They even consented to send a few of their young people to the nonreservation boarding schools maintained by the government at Carlisle, in Pennsylvania; Haskell at Lawrence, Kansas; and Chilocco, in northern Indian Territory.

At the same time, schools were being established for the Indians removed from other states to the land ceded by the Five Civilized Tribes at the close of the Civil War. Some of these immigrants already had imposing educational achievements, and they went bravely to work amid the hardships of pioneering to establish schools in their new homes. Others, broken and beaten by the aggressions that had driven them into exile, were too impoverished to take the initiative, but they responded to the efforts of the government and the missionaries. Some, like the Osages, were indifferent; and some, especially the Kickapoos, were so resentful over their forced removal that they rejected all overtures from the race that had exploited them. But these immigrants also came under the influence of the Five Civilized Tribes and began conscientiously to follow their example. Thus, through a combination of tribal initiative, government paternalism, and missionary devotion, schools were eventually established on all these reservations, and children from these tribes also began to accept training at Carlisle, Haskell, and Chilocco. The most successful missionary effort was carried on by the Quakers among the Shawnees, and the Roman Catholics among the Potawatomis and Osages.

When these tribes began to accept allotments under the Dawes Act, and their surplus land was thrown open to the white man *(see History)*, a few of their children began to attend the public schools established in the area formerly constituting their reservations. Some of the government and missionary schools continued to function, but the general education of the Indians came under the supervision of the Territory of Oklahoma.

The white settlers in the new Territory of Oklahoma had a serious educational problem of their own, but they undertook it with characteristic energy and determination. The homeseekers who arrived on that first day in April, 1889, were too busy breaking prairie, building towns, and providing shelter for their families to think immediately of education; but the following fall, although they were entirely without organized government or public funds, they opened a few schools by private subscription. Their boys and girls, accustomed to living in dugouts, thought nothing of riding their ponies many miles over the prairie to a sod schoolhouse where they sat on boxes or homemade benches and studied from assorted textbooks brought from distant states.

The next spring the Organic Act was passed. The first territorial legislature, which met under its provisions the following fall, made courageous provision for education. The country was divided into districts, embracing four square miles (sixteen homesteads), for the organization of rural schools, and an elective superintendent in each county was entrusted with the duty of supervision; towns of more than 2,500 population were authorized to organize as independent districts; and three territorial colleges were established. Provision was also made for uniform textbooks and the training and certification of teachers; and the office of territorial superintendent of public instruction was created.

The pioneers encountered almost insuperable difficulties in maintaining the public schools established under this act. By the provisions of the Homestead Law, each settler was allowed five years to live on his "claim" before "proving up" and receiving a deed. This meant that very little of the land was on the tax rolls, and so great was the poverty of the pioneers that the amount of personal property subject to taxation was almost negligible. School terms lasted three months or less, the buildings were roughly constructed shacks, and most of the teachers had only grade school education. The purchase of textbooks called for real sacrifice on the part of the parents; a school reader or a slate and pencil was an acceptable Christmas present for a child. But the settlers valued their meager educational opportunities; present-day Oklahomans who spent their formative years under these hard conditions are seldom well educated, but very few are entirely illiterate.

The colleges authorized by the first legislature were established after much trading of votes between the ambitious little towns that had sprung up so recently. A territorial university was located at Norman on the wind-swept prairie bordering the South Canadian; an Agricultural and Mechanical College was situated at Stillwater on the hillside overlooking Stillwater Creek; and a Normal school for the training of teachers was built in the tangle of blackjacks and sand that surrounded the town of Edmond *(see Tour 1)*. The last two schools opened their sessions in churches in the fall of 1891 with enrollments of forty-five and twenty-three respectively. The university opened a year later, and the first building was ready for occupancy in September, 1893. Most of the instruction at these struggling little colleges was of high-school rank, but their faculties felt a deep sense of responsibility for the future and they labored to create a literate leadership for the new Territory.

The legislature had provided that the voters of each county should decide about the establishment of separate schools for Negro children. Some irregular provision was made for them, but their educational opportunities were even more meager than those of the whites. The first institution for the higher training of Negroes was the Colored Agricultural and Normal University, created by an act of the territorial legislature in 1897. It was located at Langston *(see Tour 2A)*, an all-Negro town that had been laid out on a tract of high rolling prairie east of Guthrie the year after the Run.

As the area of Oklahoma was increased by subsequent openings, the new settlements were placed under the same school law and school administration. In each was the same difficult beginning, with nontaxable land, poverty, and inadequate instruction; hence for a few years these sections lagged behind "Old Oklahoma" in educational development. In an attempt to equalize this disadvantage, the territorial legislature established several colleges in the newer areas—a normal school at Alva, in the Cherokee Strip; and another at Weatherford, in the Cheyenne and Arapaho country.

While this provision was being made for the children of Oklahoma, thousands of white people who were living as legal residents or intruders in the Five Civilized Tribes area were entirely without educational privileges. The Federal government therefore undertook to create a uniform school system for the Indian Territory. Under a law passed by Congress in 1898, the Secretary of the Interior assumed the management of the tribal finances and took over the administration of the Indians' schools. The boarding schools, now under the control of Federal officials, were still maintained for Indian children; but the rural schools were opened to white children upon the payment of tuition, first by their parents, and later by a Congressional appropriation. During the same period, as the townsites were platted and sold, the newly organized municipal governments began to establish city school systems supported by a local property tax.

When the "Twin Territories" were united to form the state of Oklahoma in 1907, the rural schools of the Five Civilized Tribes became a part of the state school system; and in order to compensate the state for the non-taxable Indian land, the Federal government paid tuition to these public schools for the attendance of Indian children. The state endeavored to equalize the opportunities for higher education throughout its extended jurisdiction by establishing a number of colleges on the "East Side"; the most important of these were the normal schools at Tahlequah *(see Tour 3),* Ada *(see Tour 14),* and Durant *(see Tour 6),* and the Oklahoma College for Women at Chickasha *(see Tour 3).*

Most of the great historic schools established by the Five Civilized Tribes eventually passed out of existence. In most cases the land was sold, and the buildings were torn down. The commodious Female Seminary building erected at Tahlequah by the Cherokees was purchased by the state of Oklahoma for the normal school established there; it still dominates the campus of the Northeastern State College, an object of peculiar interest to visitors and of pride to the Cherokees.

Six of the schools formerly conducted by the Five Civilized Tribes are still in operation as Indian boarding schools, but the United States now bears the cost of maintenance. Six other boarding schools are maintained by the government for Oklahoma Indians, and others are conducted by religious organizations. Most of these were established for the western tribes, and they have been helpful in assisting the Plains Indians to learn the hard lessons of civilization. The graduates of these schools sometimes return to the Indian neighborhoods, but more often they are merged in the general citizenship of the state. Most Oklahoma Indian children, like their white playmates, attend the regular schools in their communities; in 1940 out of a total of 19,971 young people from six to eighteen years old of one-fourth or more

Indian blood, 15,028 were enrolled in the public schools. The Federal government pays the local district a small tuition fee for the attendance of each child.

Except for Indian education, the school system of Oklahoma resembles that of other states. Consolidation of districts and transportation of children by bus is becoming more and more common, and high-school courses are generally available throughout the state. The most important development, after 1925, was the creation of junior colleges in a number of towns and cities as a part of the public school system; enrollment in these in the school year 1939–40 was 1,772.

Total enrollment in Oklahoma public schools, kindergarten to twelfth grade inclusive, was (1939–40) 611,818, a decrease of 17,210 from the previous year due to the declining birth rate and emigration from the more arid sections.

The University of Oklahoma and the Oklahoma Agricultural and Mechanical College, both of which offer courses extending through the doctorate, are at the top of the educational system. There are, in addition, eighteen state colleges, of which six give normal training; and twenty-eight municipal junior colleges.

An amendment to the constitution was adopted in 1941 providing for a board to co-ordinate the work of all state-supported colleges. It is expected that it will eliminate much duplication and further reduce the disproportionate emphasis on normal instruction which was pointed out in the 1935 Brookings Institution's survey of education in Oklahoma.

The Colored Agricultural and Normal University, at Langston, continues its leadership in the higher education and training of Negroes. Separate schools have been compulsory since statehood; enrollment in 501 Negro schools in the year 1939–40 was 47,579.

WPA contributions to education in Oklahoma have included adult training; correspondence study; projects for instruction in music, museum service, recreation, library service, and art; and the provision of school lunches. These have been made available to both whites and Negroes. From 1935 to the middle of 1940, the WPA has provided 598 new school buildings for whites and twenty-three for Negroes, and has added to, or renovated, 1,925 buildings for whites and eighty-two for Negroes.

As yet (1941), school libraries in Oklahoma are in the formative stage. The minimum requirements for a small high school, for example, are an approved encyclopedia, a dictionary, thirty books for each English course, ten for each history course, and ten each for courses in science, industrial arts, home economics, languages, agriculture, and problems in American democracy. For elementary grade schools the requirement is merely "suitable reference books, supplementary readers, and children's books."

Oklahoma's public schools are supported by taxation, except for a considerable endowment furnished by the Federal government: When the western half of the state was opened for settlement, certain sections in each township were exempt from homestead entry and set aside for the support of education, and when the Indian Territory was joined with Oklahoma, the United States made a cash grant of $5,000,000 in lieu of such school lands in that part of the state.

Because of the initiative taken by the state in creating public institutions of higher education, denominational and privately supported colleges have never been as important in Oklahoma as in other states. Such colleges do exist, however, the most important ones being the University of Tulsa, established by the Presbyterians, but now supported by endowment; Oklahoma City University, controlled by the Methodist Church; Phillips University, maintained by the Disciples of Christ at Enid; Oklahoma Baptist University and St. Gregory's Catholic (junior) College, both at Shawnee; the Catholic College of Oklahoma, for women, at Guthrie *(see Tour 10);* and Bethany Peniel College, maintained by the Nazarene Church at Bethany *(see Tour 1).* Bacone College, near Muskogee *(see Tour 8),* is maintained by the Baptist Church for the education of Indian youths, the only institution of its kind in the United States.

Newspapers

NEWSPAPER PUBLICATION in Oklahoma stemmed from a tribal enterprise of the Cherokee Nation, before the removal from Georgia and Tennessee, when the *Cherokee Phoenix* was founded (1828) to stimulate opposition to encroachments of whites on Indian lands.

This first paper was made possible by the invention by Sequoyah of the Cherokee syllabary and the help of the devoted missionary, Samuel Austin Worcester. In 1827 the tribal council made an appropriation for the establishment of a printing press; and Elias Boudinot, a young Cherokee educated at the Moravian mission in the Cherokee country and the Foreign Mission School at Cornwall, Connecticut, was placed in charge of the printing office which was set up in a log building at New Echota, Georgia, the Cherokee capital, and appointed editor of the tribal newspaper.

This official publication, called *Tsa-la-ge Tsi-le-hi-sa-ni-hi,* or the *Cherokee Phœnix,* first appeared on February 21, 1828. It was a weekly, containing columns in both English and Cherokee, and attracted international attention. Incomplete files are preserved in the British Museum, the Library of Congress, and the Oklahoma State Historical Society. After about six years, the printing plant was seized by the authorities of Georgia in the campaign to force the Indians out of the state. The Cherokees were driven to the West in 1838–39, and almost as soon as they had established themselves in their new home they revived their tribal newspaper.

Their new periodical, the bilingual *Cherokee Advocate,* was established under tribal law, enacted October 25, 1843, to disseminate useful knowledge among the Cherokee people, and "send abroad correct information of their condition, and of passing events generally among the different Indian tribes." An editor, elected for a four-year term by the National Council, was directed to "support and defend the National Rights of the Cherokees, and those recognized in all acknowledged treaties with the United States, and such measures as will in his opinion conduce to their best interests, in a moral and civil point of view."

William P. Ross, an able mixed-blood Cherokee and a graduate of Princeton, was the first editor. A translator from English into Cherokee and two printers were also employed.

The first issue appeared on September 26, 1844, at Tahlequah *(see Tour 3)*. Except for gaps due to the Civil War, a disastrous fire that destroyed the plant, and the exigencies of tribal finances, publication was continuous until the dissolution of the Cherokee government in 1906. When the Cherokees surrendered their tribal autonomy, their printing establishment was sold. Some of the Cherokee type was deposited with the Smithsonian Institution; the rest passed into private hands and has been lost.

The influence of the *Cherokee Advocate* extended to educated Indians throughout the Territory and it was probably this influence that convinced the Creek leaders of the need for an intertribal newspaper to defend the cause of all Indians against hostile propaganda.

In 1875 the Creek delegates presented this plan at the last meeting of the Intertribal Council at Okmulgee and argued earnestly for its adoption. When the other delegates failed to approve, the Creeks then undertook to carry it on as a tribal project. A franchise was issued to a corporation, the International Printing Company, composed of the chiefs of the Five Tribes. William P. Ross was employed as editor, and Dr. Myron P. Roberts, a white man from the north, was in charge of publication.

The first number of the paper, the *Indian Journal,* appeared at Muskogee in May, 1876. Columns in both English and Creek were printed for a time, but the latter section eventually lapsed through lack of popular demand. Under Ross's direction, the paper undertook the active defense of all Indians in the United States and exposed the personal and interested motives of their opponents; but it never exerted a strong influence upon the conservative elements of the Creek population. It was subsidized for a time by the tribal government; then it passed into private hands and gradually lost its Indian character. It is now published at Eufaula and is the oldest surviving newspaper in Oklahoma.

In 1883, the Choctaw Council made an appropriation for a tribal newspaper, the *Indian Champion,* and employed Roberts' two sons, who had become the proprietors of the *Indian Journal,* as editor and publisher. Allen Wright, a brilliant and educated Choctaw who had served as chief, was placed in charge of the native language section. The publication began at Atoka in February, 1884, and continued for a little more than a year.

The denominational press reinforced the efforts of Indian leaders to create an informed public opinion. After Worcester helped to launch the *Cherokee Advocate,* missionaries ceased to have any connection with the tribal newspaper and confined their efforts to religious periodicals. Though most of them were short-lived, they made a vital contribution to Indian Territory journalism.

The first issue of the *Cherokee Messenger,* published at the Baptist Mission, appeared in August, 1844, antedating the *Cherokee Advocate* about a month; hence it holds the distinction of being the first periodical published in the present state. The *Indian Missionary,* a monthly also published by the Baptists, was one of the most important of its successors. Similar in character, *Our Brother in Red,* a Methodist publication with Cherokee and Creek sections, began publication at Muskogee in 1882 as a monthly journal and changed to a weekly in 1887. At one time it reported a circulation of 1,820.

Other periodicals were issued from time to time by the faculties and students of the boarding schools, most of which were under missionary auspices. *Our Monthly,* published at Tullahassee from 1873 to about 1876 by the Robertson family and their Creek assistants and supported by the Creek Council, was distributed free. In one sense, therefore, it was a tribal news bulletin and a forerunner of the *Indian Journal.*

The publications of the Cherokee seminaries show a student participation as lively as that of any modern college periodical. At Park Hill, cultural center of the Cherokees, students of the Female Seminary began in 1854 to publish a magazine known as *Cherokee Rose Buds.* Here, in the sentimental language affected by "females" in that far-off time, one may catch glimpses of genuine girlish idealism, innocent gaiety, and a devoted patriotism. These lines are characteristic:

> Like roses bright we hope to grow,
> And o'er our home such beauty throw
> In future years—that all may see
> Loveliest of lands,—the Cherokee.

Another young writer, under the caption, "View from our Seminary," describes Park Hill as "peeping from among the trees. . . . Instead of the rudely constructed *wigwams* of our forefathers . . . elegant white dwellings are seen. Everything around denotes taste, refinement, and progress of civilization among our people." At the Male Seminary was issued a small weekly newspaper, the *Sequoyah Memorial.* Its motto was "Truth, Justice, Freedom of Speech and Cherokee Improvement," and it printed both seminary and outside news. One of the editors was Joel B. Mayes, who afterwards served the nation as principal chief.

The development of the religious and public press was paralleled by private newspaper enterprise. At least four such papers appeared before the

Civil War—the *Choctaw Telegraph,* founded in 1848 at Doaksville; the *Choctaw Intelligencer,* started in 1850 by a white man and a native preacher; the *Chickasaw Intelligencer,* issued in the Chickasaw Nation; and the *Chickasaw and Choctaw Herald,* published during 1858 and 1859 at Tishomingo, the Chickasaw capital.

All were short-lived. The few extant copies present an interesting picture of everyday happenings among the whites and mixed bloods of that period. Their advertisements show the business that was carried on in the vicinity of the trading posts; one merchant, for example, was willing to sell for "CASH, Hides, Pecans, Corn, Dressed Skins or Buffalo Robes," and several offered "Choctaw and Chickasaw Stripes" among their important dry goods items.

The Civil War halted newspaper development, but in the period following new impetus was given to publication by increasing white immigration. Most of the papers were "Booster Sheets," hostile to the Indian regime and clamoring for the opening of the country to white settlement; it is certain that at least one of them was operated by a man in the pay of the railroads. These foreign publications usually deemed it expedient to carry articles in the local Indian language.

After 1880, newspapers multiplied rapidly as the country filled with white settlers. During the late eighties and early nineties several periodicals were established upon a stable and permanent basis. *The Muskogee Phoenix,* founded in 1888 by Dr. Leo E. Bennett, an able young white man who had married a Creek citizen, became a semiweekly in 1895, and a daily in 1901. While friendly to the Indians and their institutions, it recorded news events from the white man's point of view. From the first it set a high editorial standard, and it is still (1941) one of the influential newspapers of the state. The *Indian Citizen,* successor to the *Atoka Independent,* was established in 1889. Owned and edited by James S. Standley, an able mixed-blood Choctaw, his daughter, Norma, and his white son-in-law, Butler S. Smiser, it was the most completely Indian in its news content and editorial policy of any paper ever published in the Indian Territory.

Two similar newspapers were published in the Cherokee Nation. The *Indian Chieftain,* started at Vinita in 1882, was edited at different times by the Cherokees Robert L. Owen—one of the first United States senators from Oklahoma—William P. Ross and John L. Adair. Devoted at first to Cherokee news and political issues, it passed into the control of white men in 1891 and became an exponent of the white man's point of view. The *Indian Arrow* was founded at Fort Gibson in 1888 by a Cherokee stock company, with William P. Ross as editor; in 1894 it was consolidated with the *Tahle-*

quah Telephone, a paper launched in 1887 and published irregularly by a succession of white and Cherokee editors.

The *Tahlequah Telephone* attempted a daily in 1889, but the first real daily in the Territory, the *Daily Chieftain,* was launched at Ardmore in 1892, and the *Ardmoreite* was started the next year. Both these papers recorded the growth of the Chickasaw country as a rapidly developing white frontier. The *Ardmoreite,* owned and managed by Sidney Suggs, soon became one of the leading newspapers of the Indian Territory and is still (1941) one of the state's influential journals. The first daily paper in Muskogee, published in 1896, was the *Morning Times.* It also was a white man's newspaper, but it was edited for a time by the gifted mixed-blood Creek writer, Alex Posey. It was merged with another periodical, the *Muskogee Democrat,* and under the name *Times-Democrat* it continues—as a contemporary of the *Muskogee Phoenix*—to serve the readers of a large section of Oklahoma.

Against this background of newspaper activity, the Indian Territory Press Association came into being at Muskogee, March 19, 1888, and in the early 1900's it became merged with a similar society representing the newspapers of Oklahoma Territory.

Three periodicals were launched in the Indian reservations that comprised Oklahoma Territory before the coming of the white man. The first was probably the *Indian Herald,* published during 1875–78 at Pawhuska, the seat of the Osage Agency. Edited by William McKay Dugan, the Agency physician, it reflected the Quaker influence that at that time dominated the administration of Indian affairs. It gave a sympathetic account of daily happenings among the Osages, their painful agricultural progress, their last buffalo hunting expedition to the West, the development of mission and agency schools in their country, and the doings of their chiefs and leaders.

At Darlington, the Cheyenne and Arapaho Agency, the *Cheyenne Transporter* first appeared on December 5, 1879, and was continued until 1886. Started as the voice of missionary enterprise to inform eastern philanthropists of the progress made in civilizing the Plains tribes, it soon passed into private hands, but it continued to support the educational work carried on by the government and the religious societies. Supporting the Indians and the cattlemen in opposing the opening of the country to white settlement, it printed caustic articles about the Boomers.

The Boomers had a newspaper of their own, the *Oklahoma War Chief* or the *Oklahoma Chief,* official organ of David L. Payne, Boomer leader, and it was published precariously from 1883 to 1886 at various places along the Kansas border. For a short time in 1884—June 14 to August 7—it was printed on the forbidden land within the present limits of Oklahoma, on the Chikaskia River twenty-five miles northwest of Ponca City. Here several hundred Boomers had established a settlement of tents and rough plank houses, which they named Rock Falls. On the door of the shack used as the printing office was defiantly tacked a government warning that any person attempting to publish a newspaper in the "Cherokee Strip" would be guilty of trespass and subject to fine and imprisonment.

Payne managed to secure printers willing to take the risk, and the papers sold as fast as printed at ten cents a copy, until soldiers arrested Payne and the other leaders, set fire to the printing office, and escorted the Boomers to the Kansas line.

An entirely different type of publication was developing at the same time among the settlers in the far western section known as "No Man's Land." The first paper in this region, the *Beaver City Pioneer,* began its brief career June 19, 1886, with the slogan, "Westward the Star of Empire Takes its Way." The next year a second publication, the *Territorial Advocate,* was started at Beaver City, and a third, the *Benton County Banner,* was launched at Benton in 1888. The fourth paper, the *Hardesty Times*—soon changed to the *Hardesty Herald*—began publication in October, 1890, in a sod house that served as the combination home and office of the editor.

After "No Man's Land" was joined to the Territory of Oklahoma in 1890 as Beaver County, newspapers multiplied. Among the able editors of these papers were Richard Briggs (Dick) Quinn and Maude O. Thomas. Quinn, the editor of the *Hardesty Herald,* nursed the ambitious little settlement of Hardesty from its beginning as a station on a cattle trail, through railroad booms and townsite exploitation, and saw it become a ghost town. Quinn then assisted in organizing the company which established the townsite of Guymon at a switch on the railroad nineteen miles to the northwest, and the *Hardesty Herald* became the *Guymon Herald.* Maude Thomas came to "No Man's Land" in early childhood, grew up at Beaver City, and became the editor and publisher of the *Beaver Herald* in 1902. When the Beaver County Editorial Association was organized at Guymon in 1905, Quinn was elected president, and Miss Thomas secretary and treasurer. H. H. Hubbart took over the paper in 1928, at which time it became the *Herald Democrat.*

The *Guthrie Getup* was probably the pioneer newspaper actually published in the new Oklahoma Territory. Its first number appeared a week after the Run of April 22, 1889. Its salutatory, typical of pioneer Oklahoma, began, "The *Guthrie Getup* prances into the promised land at the head of the procession. . . . Praise God all ye good people, and let these prairies resound to the measured strokes of our job press. Ah, there is the rub, if you do not give us job work we will have to go back to our wife's folks. This would place us in a h—— of a fix, as we are not married. Our last statement is especially directed to single ladies who hold corner lots. . . ."

This paper ran only a few weeks until it was absorbed by a competitor. The same fate overtook several other newspapers started in Guthrie that first year. But three dailies survived from these ambitious ventures, and all three were influential in shaping and recording the development of the Territory.

The *State Capital,* established by Frank Hilton Greer, was first printed at Winfield, Kansas, three weeks before the Opening. It was soon moved to Guthrie, where at first, like many another ambitious business enterprise, it was established in a tent. It ran both a daily and a weekly edition, and its influence extended with the years throughout the increasing area of the Territory.

The *Daily News* also began publication within a few weeks of the Run. It purchased a number of the ephemeral publications that sprang up at that time and entered upon a stable career of daily and weekly service. The *Daily Leader* was the successor of one of the short-lived newspapers of the Territory, and it still serves a large area in central Oklahoma.

The number of society and other special publications established at Guthrie during its first ten years illustrates the vigor of early Oklahoma Territory life. The list includes three religious periodicals, two farm papers, three lodge organs, one medical journal, an official teachers' journal, one foreign language publication, one Negro newspaper, and four populist publications.

Newspaper enterprise in Guthrie was closely paralleled by the development in the enterprising rival settlement of Oklahoma City. Four dailies were launched there the first year. The *Oklahoma City Times* was started even before the Run, when "Oklahoma City" was only a railroad siding. Written on the spot, the copy was sent to Wichita, Kansas, for printing. The first issue appeared December 29, 1888. The novelty of a newspaper bearing an "Oklahoma City" date line appealed to eastern readers and subscriptions came from all parts of the United States and even from foreign countries. But its editor was ejected by soldiers from Fort Reno. Publication was continued irregularly at Wichita, or at Purcell, a border town in the Chickasaw Nation just across the South Canadian River from the "Oklahoma Lands." It became a daily on June 30, 1889.

The first paper actually printed in Oklahoma City, beginning on May 9, 1889, was the *Oklahoma Times,* published by Winfield W. and Angelo C. Scott. Housed in a tent and a partially constructed building, the printing was done to the sound of hammers that marked the growth of the rapidly rising town. Because of the confusion of names with the *Oklahoma City Times,* the second issue bore the title *Oklahoma Journal.* The daily edition started on June 3. Before the end of the year it bought out its rival, and became the *Oklahoma City Times-Journal.* Through various changes of ownership and management it has continued to the present day and appears as the *Oklahoma City Times,* Oklahoma City's evening newspaper.

The *Daily Oklahoman* and the *Evening Gazette* were also established in 1889. The *Oklahoman* eventually absorbed its competitor and increased in influence and circulation until it became one of the most prominent newspapers of the Territory. Since statehood, it has continued, as Oklahoma City's morning paper, to grow in prestige and importance.

As Oklahoma Territory was enlarged by successive openings, newspapers appeared in each new area. Some, like the *Enid Eagle* established by Omer K. Benedict and Charles E. Hunter five days after the opening of the Cherokee Outlet, have survived as important dailies. Of the country newspapers, the *Watonga Republican,* owned and edited by Thompson D. Ferguson and his wife, has achieved prominence. Mrs. Ferguson in *They Carried the Torch* (1937), has written an unforgettable description of the journey from Sedan, Kansas, with the press and type packed in one covered wagon and the editor's wife, with a baby on her lap and a small boy by her side, driving another that contained the camp equipment. They arrived at the little new town of Watonga in the fall of 1892, about six months after the opening of the Cheyenne and Arapaho country, and set up a combination printing office and home in an unpainted wooden building. Their newspaper soon became a power in Republican politics and a stabilizing influence on that raw frontier. In 1901, Ferguson was appointed by President Roosevelt as governor of Oklahoma Territory. Mrs. Ferguson's career—pictured in a different and imaginary setting—was used by Edna Ferber in her novel, *Cimarron.*

The Oklahoma Territory Press Association was formed soon after the first opening. In turn, it founded the Oklahoma Historical Society in 1893 at Kingfisher and began a systematic preservation of newspapers and other documents recording the development of the territories. Out of this far-sighted action has grown the extensive collection of newspaper files now preserved in the Historical Society building in Oklahoma City.

Newspapers multiplied rapidly in the Twin Territories between 1900 and the advent of statehood. The discovery of oil brought a new and dramatic feature into Indian Territory journalism at this period. In 1902, as Bartlesville began its growth from a typical Cherokee trading post to an oil center, the *Bartlesville Magnet* advertised itself as "The Only Newspaper Published in the Natural Gas and Petroleum Region of the Indian Territory." In the same year the boom town of Red Fork launched two newspapers, the *Derrick* and the *Illuminator.* Tulsa, which had been developing gradually from a cow town on the Frisco to a community trading center, was headlined as the oil capital of the region, and eventually as the "Oil Capital of the World"; and its struggling weekly newspapers blossomed into metropolitan dailies. The most notable of these were the *Tulsa World,* which is now one of Oklahoma's leading papers, and the *Tulsa Democrat,* predecessor to the present *Tulsa Tribune.* The importance of oil development was indicated by the growth of the *Oil and Gas Journal,* founded by the Petroleum Publishing Company in 1902; this publication has increased in importance and is read by oil men throughout the world. The interest in approaching statehood was reflected in Tulsa by the launching of such publications as the *Oklahoma Constitution,* founded as a weekly in 1904 and changed to a daily in 1906; the *New State Farm and Home,* started about 1905; and *Sturm's Statehood Magazine,* established in 1905. The *Oklahoma News,* Oklahoma City, was established about this time and operated as a Scripps-Howard paper until its demise in 1939.

During the session of 1905–06 it became certain that Congress would authorize the Twin Territories to enter the Union as one state. On May 18, a month before the Enabling Act was actually passed, newspaper men of the two territories met at Shawnee, Oklahoma Territory, and arranged for covering the news of the proposed constitutional convention and the future state legislature. Although a certain division of "East Side" and "West Side" interests persisted for a few years after statehood, journalism in the new state developed harmoniously.

At present (1941) there are in Oklahoma sixty dailies and 230 weekly or semiweekly newspapers. Circulation ranges from the 101,154 subscribers of the *Oklahoman* to the small list of the struggling country weekly. Besides the regular newspapers there are a number of special news journals. The *American Guardian,* a Socialist weekly of Oklahoma City edited by Oscar Ameringer, has an international circulation. The *Black Dispatch,* the most widely circulated of a long succession of Negro publications, presents local and general news from an alert and intelligent racial point of view.

All these publications are received regularly by the State Historical Society, which has 18,134 bound volumes in its newspaper stacks. These record a period of change from an unsettled region to the complex social and industrial institutions of modern American life. A fitting recognition of this achievement took place in 1935, when the University of Oklahoma Press sponsored a state-wide celebration of the Centennial of Printing and published early in 1936 Carolyn Thomas Foreman's *Oklahoma Imprints,* a comprehensive history of newspaper development in the two territories that formed the state.

Land of the Indians

BUREAU OF AMERICAN ETHNOLOGY

CHOCTAW INDIAN BALL PLAYER : CATLIN

CHOCTAW BOYS PLAYING BALL AT TUSKAHOMA

HITE : WPA

PHILLIPS COLLECTION, UNIVERSITY OF OKLAHO

PONCA INDIANS (ABOUT 1900)

CHEYENNE CAMP (ABOUT 1900)

PHILLIPS COLLECTION, UNIVERSITY OF OKLAHO

L'S STUDIO, LAWTON

GERONIMO, APACHE CHIEF

SEQUOYAH, INVENTOR OF THE CHEROKEE SYLLABARY

CHOCTAW INDIAN FARM WOMAN

LEE : FSA

AN INDIAN MATRON
CHEYENNE-ARAPAHO AGENCY

U. S. INDIAN SERVICE

W

FRED LOOKOUT, CHIEF OF THE OSAGE, WITH WIFE AND GRANDCHILD

CHEYENNE-ARAPAHO SCHOOL CHILDREN IN CHRISTMAS PLAY

U. S. INDIAN SERVI

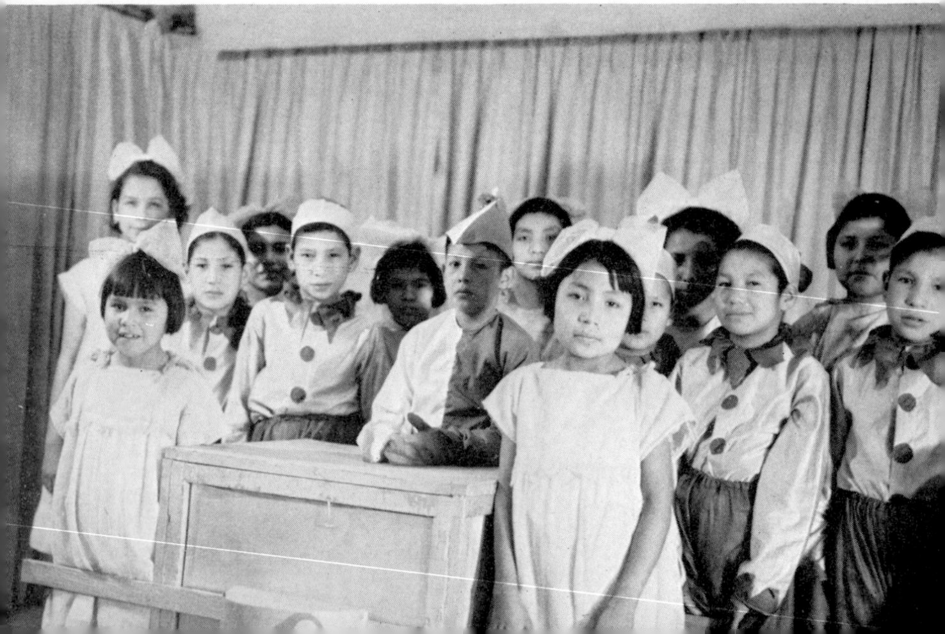

OY YOUNG

INDIAN DANCERS AT ANADARKO

INDIAN DRUMMERS

NNIS C. HELM

WHITE : WP

SEQUOYAH SHRINE, ENCLOSING HIS OLD CABIN, NORTH OF SALLISAW

LOG WATER PIPE, LAID BY INDIANS MORE THAN A CENTURY AGO

WHITE : WP

BUREAU OF AMERICAN ETHNOLOGY

CHOCTAW BALL PLAY DANCE : CATLIN

INDIAN ARTISTS OF TODAY

U. S. INDIAN SERVICE

LEE : F

A NATIVE SCHOOLBOY GRASPS AN OPPORTUNITY
TO LEARN BY DOING

Literature

By KENNETH C. KAUFMAN

LITERATURE in Oklahoma is as new as a baby's first tooth, and yet it antedates the landing of the Pilgrims by almost a century. For there were white men in Oklahoma long before Plymouth Rock served as the world's most famous stepping stone; and one of them was writing a book. His name was Castañada and he was the historian of the famous expedition of Coronado, who passed through a part of what is now Oklahoma in search of the Seven Cities of Cibola. To be sure the line of succession was sadly interrupted, as it has been several times since, and it was a long time after this first writing before literature began in earnest. But whether the reason is to be found in the air or the soil or the sweep of the landscape, something there is in Oklahoma which impels the sojourner of a few days as well as the long-time resident to express himself on paper. Washington Irving, who was, admittedly, a connoisseur of places to write about, had been in Oklahoma only a few weeks when he began his *Tour on the Prairies.* That was a hundred years ago. A dozen years before, the naturalist Nuttall was writing a book on Oklahoma wild life which is today a highly prized collector's item.

Irving had scarcely left the prairies before the Indians themselves were not only doing considerable writing but publishing books. Before they were driven out of their ancient homes in Georgia, Alabama, Florida, North Carolina, Tennessee, and Mississippi by Andrew Jackson, backed by the United States Army, they were actually on a cultural level superior to that of the whites who dispossessed them.

The amazing intellectual advance of the Cherokees was due in large measure to the invention of a Cherokee syllabary by Sequoyah (George Gist), who, although his father was supposed to have been a white man, was unacquainted with English, and totally illiterate. He was, however, an artist (a silversmith by trade) and a thinker. Intrigued by the white man's "talking leaves," he began to study the possibility of an Indian alphabet. A process of trial and error showed him that there are eighty-five possible syllables in the Cherokee language; he invented symbols for those sounds. (Some of them he copied from an English newspaper; however, he could not understand them and merely borrowed them for convenience.) His system was so logical and so simple that any intelligent Cherokee could master the syllabary in three days and so begin immediately to read. Thus the whole nation became literate almost overnight. The achievement of Sequoyah was one of the greatest triumphs of the human intellect in any age among any people.

In 1835, Samuel Austin Worcester, a missionary who came with the Cherokees from their old home, set up at Union Mission *(see Tour 8),* in northeastern Oklahoma, a printing press and almost at once proceeded to publish a book, a sort of primer—not in Cherokee, however, but in the Creek language. Only two or three copies are known to exist. Book publication in Oklahoma, therefore, is seventy-two years older than the state. This press, soon removed to Park Hill *(see Tour 3),* began publication of an Almanac; it poured out books, pamphlets, and tracts by the millions of impressions, even a number of pieces of fictional writing by native authors, some of whom had been well educated in the North. These were, ordinarily, stories designed to teach the Christian way of life, either by setting forth the triumph of the faithful or the horrible fate of sinners. Today they are rare and eagerly sought after.

Indeed, most of the writings done by the Indians of the Five Civilized Tribes and their missionaries and other white friends concerned religion or tribal politics and so have no place in an account of literature as such. Shortly before the Civil War, however, a young Cherokee named John Rollin Ridge was writing poetry. His poems are conventional and in their melancholy and tenderness reflect the prevailing taste of their day. But they compare favorably with the work of white poets of the period.

The Civil War disrupted the peaceful progress of the Cherokees as well as of the other Civilized Tribes and put a stop to what might have become a truly indigenous literature, so that the writings of Oklahomans of Indian blood are no longer in general distinguishable from those of the Anglo-Americans.

It must not be supposed that there was no writing worthy of mention from the Civil War to the era of statehood; army officers and missionaries, cattlemen and Indian agents often believed their experiences worth putting into print, and such volumes as Thomas C. Battey's *A Quaker Among the Indians* (1875) and Mrs. Byer's *Fort Reno* (1896) are today valuable as historical records, if not as literature. Then, when the Unassigned Lands were opened to settlement in the first Run, 1889, this newly-settled country, known today as Old Oklahoma, fairly blossomed into print; there were newspapers in every county seat, and in many other towns. Their columns were flooded with verse; apparently there was something about being in at the beginning of a tremendous undertaking that called forth rhyme irresistibly. Most of this verse seems pretty awful—until it is compared with the newspaper verse of the day in older states. Of it all only the poems of Alex Posey, a Creek Indian, are remembered both for their intrinsic worth and for the light they shed on Indian psychology and ways of life. Posey was also a satirist, aiming his darts in the "Fixico Papers" chiefly at white politicians. There was even a novel in those days; Thompson B. Ferguson, a pioneer newspaper man of Watonga *(see Tour 5),* afterward appointed territorial governor by President Theodore Roosevelt, wrote a story called *The Jayhawkers; A Tale of the Border War* (1892).

But the real flowering of literature in the new state began shortly after the first World War. A group of young poets, most of them connected with the University of Oklahoma, began to place work in such national magazines as *Smart Set, Century, American Mercury, Poetry: A Magazine of Verse, The Bookman,* and so on. Among these were John McClure, Muna Lee, Lynn Riggs, and Stanley Vestal. Their work appealed to Mr. Henry Louis Mencken, who is not unduly given to enthusiasms, so much that he devoted a sizable section of one issue of the *American Mercury* to them, and in his comment used the phrase, "The Oklahoma manner in Poetry."

In the late 1920's, writing in Oklahoma underwent something of a boom. The University of Oklahoma Press, under the direction of Joseph A. Brandt, recently head of Princeton University Press, and more recently (1940) elected president of the University of Oklahoma, was favorably disposed toward regional productions and offered an outlet for a considerable amount of work. B. A. Botkin, a young University English instructor, began publication in 1928 of a regional annual called *Folk-Say,* which instantly earned favorable comment from critics. Many writers, among them Paul Horgan, Mari Sandoz, and N. L. Davis, from outside the state, as well as a number of Oklahomans, notably George Milburn, first attracted attention through their work in *Folk-Say.* Four volumes of the annual were brought out.

In 1927 the University Press began publication of a quarterly magazine called *Books Abroad,* edited by Roy Temple House and devoted to reviews of books in languages other than English. It appears to be the only publication of its kind anywhere in the world, and its fourteen published volumes, totaling some seven thousand pages, constitute the largest single body of information on current foreign literatures to be found anywhere.

At about the same time, Oklahoma's two most distinguished biographers, Marquis James and Stanley Vestal (W. S. Campbell), began the researches for their best works. Marquis James while a boy in Oklahoma knew and admired Temple Houston, son of the Liberator of Texas; and this interest led him, in 1926, to undertake a life of Sam Houston. He expected to finish it in six months; it took him four years. But when it finally appeared it won the Pulitzer Prize for biography. His work on Houston naturally led him on to Jackson, and his two-volume life of Old Hickory, the first in 1934, the second in 1938, again brought him the Pulitzer award. James is also the author of a collection of short stories based on dramatic episodes from American history, *They Had Their Hour,* and, in collaboration with his wife, of juvenile lives of Houston and Jackson.

Stanley Vestal, whose father had been a field worker for H. H. Bancroft, had been interested all his life in Kit Carson and, naturally, also in Indians. When he approached the writing of biography, he went, like a sensible man, to the only living eye-witnesses of many of the events he wished to describe—older members of the Plains Indian tribes. The result is that his works on western history have a unique viewpoint as well as a unique flavor. In 1928 his *Kit Carson: The Happy Warrior of the Old West* appeared, no doubt the definitive life of the old scout. In close succession followed two more biographies, *Sitting Bull: Champion of the Sioux,* and *Warpath,* a life of Sitting Bull's nephew, White Bull.

It is somewhat difficult to define an "Oklahoma Writer." The state is so young that it is hard to find a native of middle age—excepting, of course, the Indians. Then, too, Oklahomans are a restless breed; the lure of green pastures brought them to the state, and many have moved on. In general, an Oklahoma writer is one who was born in the state, or who has lived in the state long enough to have become identified with it. Thus Marquis James, born in Missouri and now (1941) residing in New York, spent the formative years of his life in the Cherokee Strip. Paul B. Sears, native of Ohio, lived in Oklahoma during the years which saw his greatest development and activity as a writer; and he wrote his best-known book, *Deserts on the March,* in Oklahoma and on a subject for which the state offered the most satisfactory workshop.

As might be expected, in view of the dramatic and romantic history of the state, a great deal of the published work of Oklahomans has consisted of history and biography. Oklahomans have been, almost from the beginnings of white settlement, keenly alive to the value of their history as such, and also as the raw materials of pure literature. In 1890, one year after the Opening, the first attempt at a comprehensive history, *The Illustrated History of Okla-*

homa, by Marion Tuttle Rook, was published; and histories of the state, large and small, of every degree of excellence, have been issued ever since.

The Oklahoma Historical Society was founded by the Oklahoma Press Association in 1893, and from that date has taken the lead in collection and preservation of historical material. Its library contains some ten thousand volumes; and since 1921 it has published *The Chronicles of Oklahoma,* a quarterly whose files are a repository of priceless information. In 1927 Mr. Frank Phillips of Bartlesville made a gift of $10,000 (since doubled) to the University of Oklahoma; this sum, under the supervision of Dr. E. E. Dale, has been used in the acquisition of some four thousand volumes of historical material, three thousand photographs, two thousand pamphlets, three thousand photostats, and at least fifty thousand documents. Within the last few years the historical consciousness has developed to such an extent that civic and other organizations in various localities have been publishing (usually on a subscription basis) collections of the memoirs of old settlers. This history at the grass roots is frequently sadly lacking in literary quality, but it is of unique value as the basic material of which both history and literature are made; and the movement comes in time, for most of it will have passed away within a decade.

Probably the dean of historians in Oklahoma was J. B. Thoburn, author of a comprehensive history of the state, which has appeared in two editions, the second prepared in collaboration with Miss Muriel Wright, granddaughter of a principal chief of the Choctaw Nation. Mr. Thoburn served for many years on the governing board of the Historical Society; both Mr. Thoburn and Miss Wright have contributed extensively to magazines and newspapers and have prepared textbooks dealing with Oklahoma and Indian history.

A notable contributor to the history of the Cherokees was Emmett Starr, a member of the Cherokee tribe, whose genealogical histories are invaluable in any study of the nation. Important books on various phases of Oklahoma history are those of W. B. Morrison, who specializes in early forts and military posts; of Roy Gittinger, who has written on the constitutional history and the formation of the state government; of George Rainey, who has studied the Cherokee Strip and No Man's Land; of Morris L. Wardell, whose *Political History of the Cherokee Nation* records one of the world's most astonishing experiments in democracy; of A. B. Thomas and Lillian Estelle Fisher, who have delved extensively into the history of Spain in southwestern America.

Angie Debo produced in 1934 *The Rise and Fall of the Choctaw Republic,* which won for her the John H. Dunning prize for the most notable contribution to American history at the 1935 meeting of the American Historical

Society. Her *And Still the Waters Run* (1940) is an authoritative, unsparing indictment of the processes by which the Indians of Oklahoma have been defrauded. Her *The Road to Disappearance,* a history of the Creek Nation, was published in 1941.

Anna Lewis, in her study of early explorations in the Indian country, *Along the Arkansas,* has made a valuable addition to the history of Oklahoma.

Edward Everett Dale, of the University of Oklahoma, is editor, poet, and fiction writer as well as historian. Probably his best-known work is the history of *The Range Cattle Industry.* His other works include the *Lafayette Letters* and *Tales of the Teepee,* as well as textbooks. He has also edited *The Journal of James Aiken, Jr.,* Evan G. Barnard's *Rider of the Cherokee Strip,* and Frank M. Canton's *Frontier Trails.* He is joint-editor, with Gaston Litton, of *Cherokee Cavaliers.*

Paul I. Wellman, native Oklahoman, has written two historical books on the western Indians, *Death on the Prairie* and *Death in the Desert.* Carl Coke Rister, in addition to *The Southwestern Frontier* and *The Greater Southwest* (with R. N. Richardson), has won favorable comment with his social history of the southwest plains, *Southern Plainsmen. Carbine and Lance,* by Captain W. S. Nye, is the vivid and authentic story of old Fort Sill *(see Tour 3A).*

The most productive of all Oklahoma historians is Grant Foreman, former employee of the Dawes Commission, and retired lawyer, whose books on the history of the Five Civilized Tribes will be indispensable sources for the study not only of Oklahoma but of the whole of the South so far as Indian affairs are concerned. Most of his work is based on unpublished material, for which he has ransacked the libraries of Europe and America. His *Indians and Pioneers, Indian Removal, Advancing the Frontier, The Five Civilized Tribes,* among others, are models of scholarly precision and patient search for truth in history.

In general nonfiction writing a number of Oklahomans have been outstanding. The works of A. B. Adams *(Trend of Business, Our Economic Revolution,* and *National Economic Security)* and of Elgin Groseclose *(Money: The Human Conflict)* have attracted nationwide attention. Groseclose is a former editor of *Fortune Magazine.* Jerome Dowd is a prolific writer on sociological questions, and his books on the Negro in America have made him one of the foremost authorities. W. B. Bizzell has written a number of valuable books on the philosophy of education, on social philosophy and economics. In this connection should also be mentioned Royden J. Dangerfield, Cortez A. M. Ewing, and Frederick Lynne Ryan. Gustav Mueller has a dozen or more books on philosophical subjects to his credit. Howard O. Eaton and

Charles M. Perry have also made important contributions to philosophical literature. Paul B. Sears, author of *Deserts on the March,* pioneer of a considerable list of books on soil erosion and the waste of natural resources, and *This Is Our World,* is a scientist who writes more charmingly than most novelists.

Will Rogers was most famous as a humorist and, in his own words "ambassador of good will" to all the world. Yet he was the author of seven books of homely philosophy and sound common sense, which have a style and an appeal all their own. Since his death have appeared David N. Milsten's *Cherokee Kid,* Spi M. Trent's *My Cousin Will Rogers,* Harold Keith's *A Boy's Life of Will Rogers,* and the authentic biography by his widow, Betty Blake Rogers.

Two of the nation's outstanding women newspaper columnists are Oklahomans, Edith Johnson and Mrs. Walter Ferguson. And an Oklahoman, George B. (Deak) Parker won the Pulitzer Prize for editorial writing in 1936. Vernon M. Parrington's *Main Currents in American Thought* is a classic in the field of literary criticism. Incidentally, book reviews by Oklahomans appear regularly in such publications as the *New York Herald Tribune, New York Times, Saturday Review of Literature,* the *Christian Science Monitor, New Masses,* and *The Nation.* The most spectacular of all Oklahoma critics, and discoverer of new writers, is without doubt the cyclonic Burton Rascoe. Starting out as literary critic of the *Chicago Tribune,* he went on to New York, to *McCall's Magazine,* then successively to the New York *Tribune, Arts and Decorations, The Bookman,* and *Plain Talk.* He has been on the board of the Literary Guild for years, has been until recently general editorial advisor to Doubleday Doran, served as literary critic of *Esquire,* 1933–38, and has written a weekly book review for *News Week* since 1938. His published books include *Titans of Literature, Prometheans,* and a book of memoirs, *Before I Forget.* Another autobiography of merit, which appeared in 1940, was Oscar Ameringer's *If You Don't Weaken,* the story of a radical Oklahoma editor.

After the biographical works of Marquis James and Stanley Vestal should be placed the remarkable *Wah'Kon-Tah* by John Joseph Mathews, a member of the Osage Indian tribe; after them, because it is difficult to classify. Ostensibly, it is the life of Major Laban J. Miles, agent to the Osages; in reality it is a long prose poem in praise of the noblest qualities of two picturesque breeds—the American pioneer and the American Indian. It was a Book-of-the-Month Club selection in 1932, the only book from this part of the Southwest ever to receive such distinction, and the only book thus far (1941) published by a university press anywhere in the United States chosen by a major book club. Mathews is also the author of a poignant novel of Indian life, *Sundown,* and is (1941) working (on a Guggenheim Memorial Fellowship) on a study of the contrasting life outlook of the Anglo-American and the Indian. Another important biography is Althea Bass's *Cherokee Messenger,* a scholarly and readable study of Samuel Austin Worcester. Richmond Croom Beatty, native Oklahoman, is the author of two biographies of importance, *Bayard Taylor: Laureate of the Gilded Age,* and *Macaulay: Victorian Liberal.*

Two Oklahoma dramatists have reached Broadway—Lynn Riggs and Mary McDougal Axelson. Riggs has written a dozen or so plays, all of high literary quality and some successful as stage presentations, notable among them *Knives from Syria, A Lantern to See By, Borned in Texas,* and *Green Grow the Lilacs.* These plays deal with a remembered frontier environment, superficially raw and barren; actually informed with a tender love and freshness, with an undercurrent of romantic tragedy, and silvered over with the magic of nostalgia. His *Cherokee Night* treats the tragedy of the dispossessed Indian; *Russet Mantle,* prominently mentioned for the Pulitzer Prize in 1936, is Riggs' only play on a contemporary subject. His plays as well as his poems (collected in *The Iron Dish*) show a fairylike quality and a kind of Chopinesque transparency. Mrs. Axelson's play, *Life Begins,* had a New York presentation in 1932, and has since been shown as a film in nearly every country on the globe—the last two to permit its exhibition being Siam and Great Britain.

Fiction in Oklahoma has been sporadic and of very uneven quality, although respectable in both quantity and quality. Every genre is represented, from the wild western and the detective story to the novel of domestic bliss and of hard-boiled realism in the lives of tenant farmers. Oklahoma, having been first an Indian, afterwards a cattle, country, offers an especial stimulus to the writer of adventure fiction; so that the magazine stories of Foster Harris and Jesse E. Grinstead, running, literally, into the hundreds, and the published books of Vingie E. Roe (a score or more, in addition to magazine publications), are not surprising. It does seem a bit out of the ordinary for Oklahomans to excel in the detective novel, the most artificial and highly developed, technically, of all forms of writing. Yet Todd Downing, a Choctaw Indian, is the author of eight such novels; Dorothy Cameron Disney, of two books of detective fiction plus a great deal more in the magazines. Newton Gayle (the nom de plume of a well-known Oklahoma poet) has written five, and Stanley Vestal one. All of these have had their day with the thrill hunters, and their popular following appears to be growing. A number of younger writers contribute constantly to popular detective story magazines.

The novel proper is represented by the stories of Dora Aydelotte, who specializes in the problems of farm women, her story of the Cherokee Strip, *Trumpets Calling,* having been a best seller; of Nola Henderson, *This Much Is Mine,* the story of an Oklahoma farm girl; of Isabel Campbell, who specializes in middle-class family life. William Cunningham has written two realistic novels, each with an Oklahoma setting, *Green Corn Rebellion* and *Pretty Boy,* the latter an overly sympathetic fictional account of the outlaw "Pretty Boy" Floyd. Edward Donahoe's *Madness in the Heart* is a dramatic re-creation of the life of a boom oil town, and its social and financial leeches. Since 1939, Alice Lent Covert has been writing realistic and honest Oklahoma fiction with a sympathetic treatment. Many of her short stories have appeared in the magazines, and her two novels, *Return to Dust* and *The Months of Rain,* are vivid and powerful fictional accounts of rural conditions in the Southwest and the Middle West.

John Milton Oskison, Cherokee Indian, has contributed to many magazines and is the author of several novels of the old Indian Territory, the latest, *Brothers Three,* having been a best seller for many weeks. He has written, also, two biographies, one (fictionized) of Sam Houston, *A Texas Titan,* the other *Tecumseh and His Times.* Stanley Vestal is the author of two novels of the Old West, *'Dobe Walls* and *Revolt on the Border.* In this field of fiction are also the novels of the historian of the Indians, Paul I. Wellman, *Broncho Apache* and the best selling *Jubal Troop,* and Ross Taylor's *Brazos.*

All of these novelists also write short stories, but Demma Ray Oldham, Jennie Harris Oliver, Fleta Campbell Springer, and George Milburn may be said to specialize in short stories. Mrs. Oldham's stories of Ozark mountain people have been starred in the O'Brien and O. Henry Memorial anthologies. Mrs. Oliver has contributed a great many short stories to the magazines and has two published books of short stories. Fleta Campbell Springer is the author of a life of Mary Baker Eddy, *According to the Flesh,* several novels, and a play, but she is best known for her more than two hundred short stories. These have appeared in leading magazines and in O'Brien's collections of "the year's best short stories." George Milburn, adherent to the hard-boiled school of realism, who first attracted attention through his work in *Folk-Say,* has published stories of small-town life in Oklahoma in such magazines as *Esquire, Collier's, American Mercury,* and others. His two volumes of short stories, *Oklahoma Town* and *No More Trumpets,* and his novel, *Catalogue,* give him a secure place among the fiction writers of his day. Allen McGinnis and Robert Whitehand are two young writers whose short stories have attracted considerable attention. Edward O'Brien dedicated one of his recent collections to Robert Whitehand.

Poetry seems to be the preferred mode of expression for Oklahomans. From Indian times on, verse from Oklahoma poets has seeped or swirled into print. Vanity publishing has been, and is, rampant. Yet the work of Oklahoma poets appears also in every standard publication and in the better anthologies, while books of poems published on a legitimate royalty basis are frequent. In 1918, fifty years after the *Poems of John Rollin Ridge,* came the Villon-like *Airs and Ballads* of John McClure. Other poets whose work has appeared between boards are Stanley Vestal, with *Fandango,* a book of ballads based on the adventures of trappers, scouts, and Indian warriors, Muna Lee, Lena Whittaker Blakeney, Althea Bass, Katherine Shepard Hayden, Violet McDougal and Mary McDougal Axelson, Lexie Dean Robertson, Zoe A. Tilghman, Mark Turbyfill, Jennie Harris Oliver, and Kenneth Kaufman. Others whose poems have seen the light in magazines are B. A. Botkin, Robert Brittain, Isabel Campbell, Henry T. Chambers, May Frank Rhodes, Maurine Halliburton, Welborn Hope, Anne Dinsmore McClure, Paul Thompson, and Leo C. Turner.

The most spectacularly successful of all Oklahoma poets is no doubt Don Blanding. His books, among them *Paradise Loot, Leaves from a Grass House, Memory Room, The Rest of the Road,* and *Vagabond's House,* all illustrated with exotic line drawings by the author, go through edition after edition, *Vagabond's House* being now (1941) beyond its twenty-fifth. Blanding is, as the titles of his books indicate, an incurable wanderer, but of late his verse has been turning more and more frequently to themes taken from his native prairies and the desert country of the Southwest.

But while poetry in Oklahoma has been prolific, and while individual poets and poems have attracted rather extravagant praise from readers and critics (John Cooper Powys once said Jennie Harris Oliver's "Noon Trail" was the finest poem that ever came out of America), the situation is a bit disappointing. Oklahoma has not produced a single first-line poet; poets who have started out with every evidence of developing into greatness have stopped writing all too soon, either because of a change in philosophical viewpoint or in taste, or for economic reasons; and poetry in Oklahoma has never crystallized into a movement. This may be due to the fact that Oklahoma poets are a cosmopolitan breed, as likely to write on a theme native to New England or Old England or Alaska as to the short-grass country. But the vitality is there, and the native themes cry for an indigenous poetry.

The literary picture as a whole is encouraging. Every year more young people turn to writing as a profession. Recently the state's largest school, the University of Oklahoma, has been offering courses in professional writing.

No state has a richer historical, social, and ethnological background.

While America as a whole has foreshortened the ages of man's progress into a century and a half, Oklahoma has telescoped that century and a half into fifty years. The state was born in drama, and the clash of Anglo-American against Indian, or Yankee against Southerner, or the product of great universities against the rankest of the illiterate, produces strain and tension in real life, which, translated into words, must mean drama, conflict, color.

Architecture and Art

In Oklahoma, architecture has achieved interesting and often distinctive qualities through the adaptation of borrowed designs to local conditions. The first log houses of the Indians, pioneers, and traders in what is now eastern Oklahoma were patterned rather closely after the same types of building in other regions. Because of different climatic conditions and structural materials, however, changes in the construction of these types were soon made. Thus small, clay fireplaces superseded the former huge, stone affairs, and builders used split, rather than whole, logs.

As the buildings were erected hastily, the timber was seldom seasoned; when it shrank the crevices were chinked with clay and in the course of time the structure appeared to be half log and half clay. Generally, the timbers were nailed together, rather than notched. Heavy rains made substantial roofs necessary, and care was taken in the cutting and fitting of "shakes" (homemade shingles) for this purpose. Window shutters, made of split sticks nailed to cross pieces and sometimes faced with cloth or skins, were propped open in warm weather and kept closed during the winter months. For door, a sheet, blanket, or hide might suffice; or an actual door might be brought in by wagon from Texas or Arkansas. Additions were made by cutting a doorway in one end of the cabin and continuing the plan in an elongated pattern. More popular, however, was the lean-to, formed by extending a section of the roof downward and walling up the open sides.

After the first small "groundhog" sawmills were set up, boxing-board shacks became common, but they did not entirely replace log buildings. Plank additions, frequently built on to the cabins, formed a hybrid type still found in the eastern part of the state. Most of the frame houses through this section were of the "shotgun" type—one room divided by a partition; porchless, paintless, and shake-roofed. In appearance and comfort they were hardly an improvement upon the log cabin. Cold in winter, hot in summer, their one advantage was cheapness of construction.

In the western part of the state, where timber was scarce, the dugout was the most common habitation among the first settlers. Since the land was generally level, the dugout could not be built into a hillside as in other regions. Usually it consisted of low sod walls enclosing a cellar, with the above-ground structure varying in height according to the depth of the excavation. To enter the house it was necessary to stoop under a low doorway and descend several steps. In some instances, the dugout had a shingle roof; more frequently, it was thatched over with branches covered with sod. As the region became more thickly settled, box houses began to dot the prairie. These were just what the name implied, square or rectangular box-like structures, often with single slope roofs, and the inside papered with newspapers; the wide cracks that developed as the boards shrank were pasted over with strips of old cloth. Intended as makeshifts, a few of these box houses are still in use today (1941).

Houses in the south and southwest were perhaps better in construction and design than those of other sections. Sturdily built homes were erected by prosperous Indian leaders among the Choctaws and other tribes, and later by white cattlemen with an eye to permanence and comfort rather than economy. These residences combined the best features of the ranch and plantation types farther south. To obtain the maximum exposure, the house was frequently planned in the form of a "T." High ceilings were characteristic, as were wide windows and broad-roofed porches. These dwellings varied in size from eight to fifteen rooms.

Kansans and Iowans who staked out the excellent farms in north central Oklahoma lived in shanties during the early years, but as prosperity came they first built big barns and then big houses. The farmer was judged by the size of his barn, and his wife by the size of her house. Except for an occasional "curlicue" and the almost universal fancy lightning rod, there were few attempts at embellishment; and when agriculture slumped in the 1920's there was little money for repairs or painting. Thus today there are in this section many huge, prematurely aged but still stern-appearing houses remaining to tell the story of pioneer success and pride.

As far as the builders' skill and the materials at hand would permit, the first houses in the cities followed contemporary architectural types in other states. No attempt was made at conformity, and a dozen different kinds of houses might be found in a single block. Later, as the business districts spread out, these houses were either torn down or included in the slums and Negro sections.

As he prospered, the Oklahoman was quick to adopt foreign types of architecture and mix one with another. Imitations of Spanish villas, French chateaux, and English cottages were built side by side. The eclectic period reached its height during the first World War, when the shortage of other building materials made the use of stucco patriotic, even necessary. Plaster, which could be tinted any color the owner desired, was sprayed over a network of chicken wire. Fortunately, from an aesthetic standpoint, stucco and wire parted company after a few years, and the houses had to be torn down or remodeled.

Generally, good architecture and construction were more common in the smaller towns than in the cities. The townsman usually planned the type of house he wanted while he was saving the money to build it, and he was also on hand to supervise the building. Aware that the residence would have to serve as an indication of his good sense and importance for years, he was not easily influenced by architectural fads. The city-dweller, on the other hand, usually acquired a home as a speculation, because it was the "right thing" to be a home-owner, or because he had heard that it was cheaper than paying rent. He was often obliged to accept what the realtor or building contractor had to offer, and trusted to luck to receive value. In many cases, the only permanent thing about these city houses was the mortgage.

Fortunately, development of the oil industry, and the consequent creation of many newly rich families, did not result in a plague of architectural monstrosities. Oil men generally hired the best architects available and saw to it that when the pinch of adversity came (oil is uncertain) they had something that would bear up under a heavy loan. Considerable oil money was spent on apartment houses, and these, too, were usually built with an eye to negotiability. Typically of brick construction, not more than four stories high, they are often divided into "efficiency" apartments, many consisting of one room, bath, and kitchenette. Simply designed, and entirely without decoration, they are built primarily as investments.

The most common modern types of dwellings in both cities and towns are the Oklahoma bungalow, a four- to six-room, hip-roofed, box-like structure with a small porch in front; the California bungalow, differing from the Oklahoma bungalow by having a broad, low roof; the airplane bungalow, with a one- or two-room upper story mostly of windows, an adaptation of the upstairs sleeping porch to the one-story house; the English-type home, a roomy, two-story dwelling of frame or brick, often built lengthwise on a lot; and the Colonial-type house, a severe two-story structure, with shuttered windows and without a porch. Especially Oklahoman are the increasingly popular double purpose brick, stone, and frame apartments built for rental over garages at the back of spacious residence lots.

The most forthright departure from conventional design in private house building in Oklahoma, and one of the best examples of modern residential architecture in America, is "Westhope," Tulsa home of Richard Lloyd Jones, designed by Frank Lloyd Wright, his cousin. Comments of passers-by, attracted by the thousand after the house was finished, varied from "What's it supposed to be?" to the more or less contemptuous, "A pickle factory!" With the growth of its surrounding planting (a part of the design), however, its great beauty and livability are apparent.

The first nonresidential buildings in the state, as might be expected, were of little or no architectural interest and often structurally unsound. The first state architect with enough training to inspire confidence in his architectural knowledge was J. A. Foquart, a Frenchman. His design followed the Norman French, or chateau Gothic style, with circular bays, round turrets, curved windows, bastions, and embattled towers. The Old Central Building and the Biology Building on the campus of the Oklahoma Agricultural and Mechanical College *(see Stillwater)* and the City Hall at Guthrie *(see Tour 10)* are typical examples of Foquart's work.

Fireproof construction was not used for public and commercial buildings in Oklahoma until 1905, and fire caused many losses. The W. J. Pettee Hardware Building, erected about 1906, was one of the first reinforced concrete structures in Oklahoma City. Other good examples of the city's early fireproof buildings are the Western Newspaper Union Building and the Pioneer Telephone Building.

Oklahoma has kept pace with modern developments in the use of architectural concrete, and with that material has obtained buildings excellent in design and permanent in construction. Among the most notable of these is the high school at Bartlesville, designed by John Duncan Forsythe, and the city hall at Chickasha, by Paul Harris. An unusual and practical application of this method of construction may be found in a barn at the Cameron Agricultural College at Lawton, also by Harris. Other commendable reinforced concrete structures are the Fairview City Hall, by John C. Hope; the Buffalo School, by Parr; Stillwater City Hall, by Sorey, Hill, and Sorey; and Altus City Hall, by Moore and Hudgins. These structures are all modern in manner and make use of modern material to good effect.

With the development of oil, local headquarters for the big companies became necessary, and impressive new office buildings were erected. These were not only improvements on existing buildings in Oklahoma at that time, but were often more modern than contemporary structures in other states. The Colcord Building, Oklahoma City, was designed by Carl Wells in the tradition of Louis Sullivan, "father of American architecture." Erected in 1910, it is still one of the best arranged and equipped office buildings in the state. Later, the two tallest buildings of Oklahoma City—the First National Building and the Ramsey Tower—raised their roofs to the sky. The Phil-tower, and National Bank of Tulsa Building in Tulsa, are examples of the new and striking business structures in the "Oil Capital" of Oklahoma.

Many school buildings, churches, and civic structures did not fare so well as business buildings. Too often they were barnlike, of poor design. The old county courthouse at Oklahoma City, for example, was out of date architecturally ten years after it was erected, and it was by no means an isolated example.

There were exceptions, of course. The Administration Building of the University of Oklahoma, at Norman, designed by Shepley, Rutan, and Coolidge, is noteworthy for its chaste decoration and well-studied proportions in a pure collegiate Gothic style. Built in the same manner, the Library Building is considered one of the most successful designs in the state; its main reading room is spacious and well lighted. Other buildings of interest architecturally on the University of Oklahoma campus are the Business Administration and the Biological Sciences buildings, designed by the director of the university's School of Architecture, Joe Smay. They are examples of the application of collegiate Gothic to modern building, made to harmonize with other structures on the campus. The designer has succeeded in securing exceptionally well-lighted rooms. Interesting also is the use of symbolism in the carved ornament, depicting business on one building and the evolution of life over the portals of the other.

Notable examples of perpendicular Gothic ecclesiastical architecture are the Trinity Episcopal Church in Tulsa, George Winkler, architect; the Wesley Methodist in Oklahoma City, and the Post Chapel at Fort Sill, designed by Leonard Bailey. The Boston Avenue Methodist Church in Tulsa was one of the first so-called "modernistic" churches. Especially meritorious are the main portals, where careful design forms a focal point leading to the interior. Supplanting the usual pinnacle and turreted tower, terminal motifs resemble darts that have been dropped from on high. Its architects were Adah Robinson and Bruce Goff. Capitol Hill High School, Oklahoma City, a three-story brick structure of collegiate Gothic style designed by Layton, Hicks, and Forsyth, was when built the best-equipped school building in the state.

The largest and most expensive building in Oklahoma (1941), the First National Building in Oklahoma City, designed by Weary and Alford, is a striking example of restrained modern American skyscraper architecture. At the time of its erection, in 1931, it was said that more aluminum was used in this building—above the main entrance, in spandrels, and in its flood-lighted roof—than in any other in the world. Its Bedford limestone veneer, however, seems somewhat insecure, as bits have dropped off from time to time. Another outstanding building of the skyscraper type is Oklahoma City's

33-story Ramsey Tower, designed by Walter Ahlschlager, of Chicago, and erected in 1931.

Public buildings, constructed with the aid of Federal funds, have been a leaven to architecture throughout the state. Typical of the structures of this kind is the neoclassic group of the Civic Center, Oklahoma City, which includes a county courthouse, a municipal building, auditorium, and jail. The auditorium, designed by Joseph Overton Parr, was selected as one of America's outstanding architectural masterpieces by a committee of the American Institute of Architects. The well-planned city hall, designed by the Allied Architects of Oklahoma City, is characterized by rich aluminum grills that adorn the principal windows.

Scattered over the state are many WPA-built National Guard armories, usually constructed of local stone; they are uniformly of sound design and workmanship and have afforded excellent opportunities for apprentice stonemasons to learn their craft. Bryan Nolen was the architect of most of them.

Outstanding architecturally are the air-conditioned tourist courts in Norman designed by architect W. C. Lightfoot. Not only do they form a pleasingly white housing group, but they pioneer in the extensive use of impervious bituminous binding of earthern materials that keep the interiors surprisingly cool. Such material lends itself to long, low masses and may set a precedent for extensive use of "Oklahoma Adobe."

ART

In purpose, the first painter to work in Oklahoma and the state's latest developed Indian artist are brothers. George Catlin, who came to the Wichita Mountains region in 1834 with the Leavenworth-Dodge expedition, undertook to record the types and customs of a people who, he thought, were dying out. In 1941, Stephen Mopope, university-trained Kiowa Indian artist, was painting murals for the walls of the Interior Department in Washington which he designed for the same purpose. Catlin, remembering the tales told in his home by explorers and hunters when he was a boy, abandoned the law for art, showed his numerous paintings in the East and in Europe in 1840 (they are now in the National Museum in Washington), and in 1841 published his best-known book, *Manners, Customs, and Conditions of the North American Indians,* with three hundred engravings. Nearly one hundred years later, Acee Blue Eagle, a young Ponca-Creek Indian, was invited to show his vivid water colors (and his skill as a symbolic dancer) at Oxford University in England.

Next in the succession to Catlin as a recorder of the early Oklahoma scene was John Mix Stanley (1814–72), a much-traveled artist educated in

Italy. In 1843 he attended an intertribal council at Tahlequah as the guest of Chief John Ross of the Cherokees and remained for a year to paint portraits and make daguerreotypes of the Indians at Tahlequah and Webbers Falls, and of army officers at Fort Gibson *(see Tours 2 and 3)*. Most of this work was destroyed when the Smithsonian Institution at Washington was burned in 1865, but a number of portraits, including one of Will Rogers' mother at the age of eight, are in Oklahoma.

Frederic Remington (1861–1918) was an illustrator, painter, and sculptor, as well as a writer. He came down the Chisholm Trail in 1882, stayed at Fort Reno and the Darlington Indian Agency to paint Indians and army men, gather material for *Crooked Trails,* and jot down his low opinion of the politician type of Indian Agent. His interpretations of frontier life with clean, sharp lines caught the spirit of blanket Indians, blue-clad soldiers, bow-necked bronchos, long-legged and long-horned steers; and his statuettes are vigorous and full of character. Like Catlin, Remington was not a first-rate artist, but his illustrations were excellent; and as authentic records of an all but vanished West his work is in demand by collectors and museums.

Elbridge Ayer Burbank, born in 1858 and trained at the Chicago Academy of Design and in Munich, worked at and near Fort Sill in Oklahoma Territory in 1896–97. He painted some 125 notable portraits of Kiowa and Comanche Indians, and three of the famous Apache captive, Geronimo. Many of these hang in the Field Museum and Newberry Library, Chicago, and in the Smithsonian Institution; only a few are in Oklahoma. A portfolio of reproductions in color of his Indian portraits was published in Chicago in 1899.

John Noble (1874–1934) son of a Wichita, Kansas, cattleman and a cowboy in his early years, made the Run into the Cherokee Outlet in 1893, and secured a claim which he could not hold on account of his youth. Later he went abroad to study art at Julian's in Paris, in Brussels, and London, and remained in France for twenty-one years. His picture, *The Run,* painted from memory, though not one of his best was acquired for its historical value by Frank Phillips for his Woolaroc Museum *(see Tour 4),* then given by him to the state. It hangs in the Blue Room of the capitol at Oklahoma City. One of Noble's portraits, executed for the state capitol collection, is of Thompson B. Ferguson, sixth territorial governor.

Howell Lewis, an army man, some of whose pictures hang in the capitol, and Nellie Shepherd, who died in 1920, painted Oklahoma scenes, the first notable for the size of his canvases and the second for the warm, impressionistic style learned in France and used to depict the hills and prairies of the state.

After the subsidence of interest in the pioneer phase by visiting artists, native Oklahoma art was mainly an activity of more or less amateur practitioners among the house painters, "cafe muralists," and small-town art teachers with more enterprise than talent.

In the surge of development of the state's resources before the first World War, the artist group in Oklahoma became larger and its interests broader. Men made wealthy by oil, ranching, and other industries encouraged art by buying the work of painters developed in the state. In 1916, the Association of Oklahoma Artists was formed and instituted an annual exhibit at the Oklahoma Historical Society Museum; they also exhibited at stores and residences in Oklahoma City.

The influence of the Art School of the University of Oklahoma, headed by Oscar B. Jacobson, an artist of high rank and an enthusiastic teacher, became predominant in this period; and a number of painters and sculptors who emerged into public notice were among his faculty and students—Edith Mahier, Joseph Taylor, Dorothy Kirk, Doel Reed, Leonard Good, Olinka Hrdy, Harold Smith, and others. Nan Sheets, of Oklahoma City, produced paintings of merit and became a leader among the serious workers; her home was loaned for exhibitions not only by Oklahoma Artists but also by those more widely known. May Todd Aaron, Glenn and Treva Wheete, Olive Nuhfer, John O'Neill, Dorothea Stevenson, M. McFarland, and Eugene Kingman, now (1941) director of the Philbrook Museum at Tulsa, are among the contemporary Oklahoma artists developed in this period.

Most notable, interesting, and significant of the University Art School's achievements has been the development of Indian painting in Oklahoma. The encouragement and guidance given here—particularly by Jacobson, who from the first insisted that these Indian students should use Indian themes and a style based on the Indians' historical pictorial art adapted to modern materials—have produced more than thirty worth-while artists of ten different tribes.

Pioneers among the talented tribesmen who have come under Jacobson's teaching and inspiration since 1928 were five Kiowas—Stephen Mopope, Monroe Tsatoke, James Auchiah, Jack Hokeah, and Spencer Asah. Except for Tsatoke, who died of tuberculosis in 1937, these artists have continued to lead in spreading an ever deeper appreciation of Indian art by their work as painters and muralists. Close behind, if not abreast of them, are Blue Eagle, Woodrow Crumbo, a Potawatomi who is (1941) head of the art department of Bacone Indian College *(see Tour 8);* Allan Houser, Oklahoma Apache and grandson of Geronimo; Cecil Dick and Franklin Gritts, Cherokees; Walker Boone, Oneida; Solomon McCombs, Creek; Cecil Murdock, Kickapoo; Paul Goodbear, Richard West, and Archie Blackowl, Cheyennes;

Frank Overton Colbert, Choctaw; and the Cherokee sculptor, Joseph Sequiche Morris.

A portfolio of exquisitely colored reproductions of the work of the five Kiowa painters, edited by Jacobson and printed in France in 1930, attracted much favorable notice both in the United States and abroad. Exhibitions abroad of the Indians' original work were held in a number of countries before the second World War.

Two Indian women, Lois Smokey, a Kiowa, and Marian Terasaz, a Comanche, have shown more than average talent in painting. The first is now (1941) married and no longer paints, but the second has gone on, at Bacone, to portray the traditional life of the women and children of her tribe.

Oklahoma's Indian artists have, almost exclusively, gone to the past tribal culture for their subjects: legends, dances, games, medicine men rites, hunts, and other characteristic phases of the old life. Their visual memory is remarkably detailed and accurate.

Most important of the murals done by them in public buildings are at Tahlequah (Northeastern State College), Muskogee, Edmond (Central State College), Oklahoma City (Historical Society), Anadarko (Agency and School), Lawton (Government Indian School), and the Department of the Interior, Washington. Blue Eagle's work is on the walls of the officers' mess room of the battleship *Oklahoma.*

Predecessors of these modern Indian artists, whose work hardly went beyond the experimental stage, were Carl Sweezy, Arapaho; Spybuck, Shawnee; and Silver Horn.

Aside from its Art School, with ten teachers and an enrollment (1941) of three hundred students, the University of Oklahoma has the most important art collection in the state. The museum contains numerous pieces of oriental art—paintings, bronzes, statuary, pottery, and other objects from China, Nepal, and India. It has a small collection of European masters, and many American Indian paintings, fine baskets, and examples of other tribal crafts. Because of lack of exhibition space, the greater part of its treasures is not on public view. The museum sponsors exhibitions of paintings from other states; from sixteen to eighteen are held each year in the limited space available.

The museum assembled by Father Gerrer at St. Gregory's College at Shawnee *(see Tour 5)* includes some good Italian primitives. At Kaw City *(see Tour 10),* the Laura A. Clubb Art Collection, exhibited in the public rooms of the Clubb Hotel, contains canvases, laces, and rare books.

Except for notices in newspapers, little has been published about Oklahoma art; nothing of its history. In 1928 the *Sooner Magazine* at the University of Oklahoma published a series of critical biographies of painters connected with the school; and in 1930 the University of Oklahoma Press issued a memorial booklet on the work of Laurence Williams, associate professor of art. In 1930, Ethel Gray, at Chickasha, began to issue a monthly called *Interstate Art News,* dealing with painting and minor arts in the Southwest, but it was soon abandoned for lack of support. There is also, in the University Library, a volume of Masters' theses written by students in the School of Art that contains much material about the state's artists and their work. Nan Sheets and Maurice A De Vinna, Jr. have for some years written weekly newspaper departments concerning the state's art activities for the *Sunday Oklahoman* of Oklahoma City, and the Tulsa *Sunday World,* respectively.

Philbrook Art Museum in Tulsa, opened in October, 1939, in the spacious private residence given to the Southwestern Art Association of Tulsa by Waite Phillips, stages traveling exhibits, one-man shows, regional exhibitions, and architectural displays which tell the story of American building. A special effort is being made to fill the Indian rooms with material illustrating the history, and the comparative importance, of native arts and crafts. A full program of shows, classes, lectures, and concerts is promoted at the Museum.

Set up in 1936, and sponsored by the University of Oklahoma and the Oklahoma Council of Art, the Oklahoma Art Project of the Work Projects Administration has done much to stimulate general interest in art, as well as to provide work for needy artists. Galleries, free art classes, and lecture courses, first established in Oklahoma City, Tulsa, and Claremore, have been extended to Shawnee, Okmulgee, Stillwater, Edmond, Sapulpa, Bristow, Skiatook, Clinton, and Marlow. As of 1941, the project occupies five galleries on the fifth floor of the Oklahoma City Municipal Auditorium.

Constructive work has been undertaken with the grade and high schools of the state; and the galleries furnish exhibit pieces, which are changed from time to time, for study.

Another state-wide WPA project, sponsored by the U.S. Indian Service, began in February, 1939, to co-ordinate the arts and crafts work done by Oklahoma Indians and find markets for their products. The supervisor, Mrs. Eula A. Looney, a member of the Chickasaw tribe, in co-operation with some 350 other persons of Indian blood representing twenty-three tribes throughout the state, has encouraged Indian artists and craftsmen through exhibitions and displays of their work, education, the provision of working quarters, and research. Indian arts and crafts, displayed at many places in Oklahoma, have been in such media as tempera painting, sculpture, wood carving, basketry, weaving, jewelry and metal work, costuming, ribbon and feather work.

Music

As in every other phase—industrial, educational, cultural—Oklahoma's development in the field of music is still in its youth. But it has a rich background of folk music upon which to create an indigenous motif. The purposeful native Indian chant and rhythm; the tunes of the Five Civilized Tribes and the staid hymns of the early-day missionaries fused together by propinquity; the plaintive, yet indefinably joyous, spirituals of the transplanted Negro; the boasting, gay, courageous ballads of the cowboy, who sang to ward away his loneliness; and the rollicking, un-pretty songs of the pioneer homemaker, who worked prodigiously in the daytime and forgot, at night, his calloused hands and rude clothes while he raised his voice in a spontaneous outpouring—all may eventually be welded together into a characteristic Oklahoma theme. Thus Oklahoma folk music cannot properly be called native, for each successive immigrant to the state brought the dust of another locale on his feet and the lilt of another people's song on his lips.

The music of the Indian tribes who ranged this region before their more civilized brothers came was not just an adjunct to their daily life, but a vital part of it; nearly every physical act and mental emotion was accompanied by a song, and the most common means of communication with the Great Spirit was through melody. Although each individual Indian exercised his creative instinct at will, the majority of the chants were those which had stood the test of time to become traditionally appropriate as a fitting accompaniment for the act at hand. The ceremonial and historical songs in particular were patiently transmitted as a sacred duty to each new generation. Since these simple people recorded melodies only in their minds, much of their music is lost to the world forever; and the disintegration of their pure race has introduced blood strains foreign to their peculiar, melodic spontaneity. No diatonic scale can catch or interpret the fullness or the beauty of the themes, and proper rendition of Indian music requires congeniality of mind and a mystical union with nature.

The pronounced thinness (to the white ear) of Indian music is due mostly to the scarcity of instruments—they used only the drum for rhythm, a flute-like reed for obbligato, and a rattling gourd for an occasional interpolation, to accompany the vocal melody. Any attempt at harmonization of Indian music loses the true quality and charm, for the melody and rhythm are often at complete variance. Recording of Indian music is the only real means of preserving it, and even that lacks the fullness which would be immediately apparent if one could see the supple body movements attending it.

The Oklahoma Music Program is one of the few in the nation to conduct research on folk music; in the course of this work, recordings were made of Cheyenne, Kiowa, Sac and Fox, Apache, Pawnee, Ottawa, and Osage music. A special portable recording unit was made so that the work might be done on reservations and in the remote homes of full bloods. The records, which include some two hundred songs of war, ceremonials, medicine, animals, love, lullabies, dances, and games, will be preserved in the Library of Congress in Washington, D.C., at the University of Oklahoma in Norman, and at the central office of the Oklahoma Music Program when final transcriptions are made.

One of the recordings is a perfect example of a composite musical entity. It is sung by John Loco, or *Thinc-ah-e-sitten,* an Apache, who when a boy was taken prisoner by Geronimo *(see Tour 3A)* and was subsequently imprisoned in Florida by the United States when that warrior and his band were captured. Probably during this period of confinement, John was influenced by missionaries of the Dutch Reformed Church, and now he sings in his native language a song which he created as a result of these several contacts: "I was lost, but Jesus found out and gave me way. I came back. Now I am happy in Jesus." This illustration is also typical of the Five Civilized Tribes music, which was, by the time they emigrated to their new home in Oklahoma, already deeply influenced by the hymns of the various white denominations whose missionaries had worked among them.

With this earliest Oklahoma music must be included the contribution of the Negroes, who were brought along as slaves by the emigrating Indians. The childlike faith and the intense religious fervor of their spirituals was expressed by the rhythmical syncopation common to the bulk of Negroes and by the plaintive quality resulting from the frequent use of the five-tone scale. Three Negro spirituals, well known and loved today, are said to have been composed in the 1840's by "Uncle" Wallace Willis, a slave on a large plantation near Doaksville in the Choctaw Nation. The actual authorship and origin of spirituals can seldom actually be credited to individuals, but it is a matter of record that "Uncle" Willis sang "Swing Low, Sweet Chariot," "Steal

Away to Jesus," and "I'm A Rollin'" as he worked in the cotton fields of Reverend Alexander Reid, superintendent of a Choctaw boarding school. The story is that Reid wrote down the words and music and sent the transcriptions to the Jubilee Singers of Fisk University. The group sang the numbers on a tour of the United States and Europe; one, "Steal Away to Jesus," is said to have particularly pleased Queen Victoria.

As the plantations declined after the Civil War and many more white people drifted into Indian Territory and No Man's Land, another kind of folk music began to be heard—the nasal, lonely ballads of the cowboy and the fiddlin' rhythms of the pioneer farmer. The mushroom settlements and towns fostered two types of music—inside the homes and churches, voices were raised with fervor in hymnal praise of God, while from the brightly-lighted saloons and dance halls came the rousing tunes of early-day swing music. Percussion instruments were almost unheard of, but the fiddler could be counted upon at almost any time.

The peculiar technique of the fiddler is foreign to the schooled violinist, for many of the effects are produced by tricks not included in the formal study of the violin. One trick, frequently employed to produce a distinctive twangy vibration, is to tune the G string a whole tone higher and then use only the other three; others are the accenting of the last of tied notes, and the playing of a double note on the same pitch. Such idioms are impossible to reproduce on any other than stringed instruments and, as the fiddler maintains, almost impossible for the conventionally-trained violinist to play effectively. Deviations from the violinist's technique include supporting the weight of the instrument in the left hand rather than with the chin; playing entirely in the first position, usually holding the bow nearer the middle than the end; and bowing in quick, sawing motions. These methods of playing allow conveniences the trained violinist is denied—the fiddler's head is left free for nodding and emphasizing the music, and for smoking, chewing, and expectoration. It is said that the fiddler needs only his battered instrument, a chunk of rosin, a chair with a rawhide seat, and a dash of Old Nick to produce a concert.

Texans, who settled in Greer County, brought a tune which has been traced to Illinois, Missouri, and Indiana, where it was known as "Old Lady Tucker," but the Greer County settlers called it "Love Somebody" and set their own words to its melody. Colorado miners came to the new land and brought the nostalgic "Cripple Creek"; "Little Dutch Girl" came by way of Missouri; and "Liza Jane," "Number Nine," "Bonaparte's Retreat, "Lost Indian," "Sweet Child," "Cotton-Eyed Joe," "Grandma Blair," "Five Miles From Town," "Tom and Jerry," "Idy Red," "Cluckin' Hen," "Custer's

Last Charge," and the favorite love plaint, "Little Girl with Her Hair All down Behind," entered Oklahoma by devious ways and from many locales.

The stanzas of many of the early ballads and songs were not merely doggerel—as they may sound today—but correctly interpreted some phase of life to their singer or originator. Cowboys quieted herds of wild and uneasy longhorns with "Old Paint," "The Stampede," "Beans for Breakfast," "Ropin'," "Brandin'," "Old Chisholm Trail," and at the same time consoled themselves with the anticipatory "Little Home to Go to." Missouri immigrants are said to have introduced the fearful

> Oh good Indian, don't kill me,
> For I've a wife and family.

Nearly everyone sang the popular

> Had a piece of pie, had a piece of puddin',
> Gave it all away to see Sally Gooden.

In addition to the research and recording of authentic Indian melodies, the folk music division of the Oklahoma Music Program has transcribed and classified some four hundred of these popular folk songs of early Oklahoma, including 125 fiddle tunes; plans are being made for their publication. Among those which have been fairly generally established as originating in Oklahoma are "Verdigris Bottom," a dance tune; "Oklahoma Run," (also known as "Old Purcell"); "Red Bird"; the "Oklahoma Waltz"; and the "Tulsey Waltz," the last two drippingly sentimental. Two popular tunes originated with their performers at Indian Territory dances—one, "Uncle Paul," was composed on the spot by Paul Toupin, a favorite territorial fiddler; and the other, "Slaton's Waltz," was the brain child of Tom Slaton, playing for a dance near Mangum.

The play-party, the square dance *(see Folklore and Folkways)*, and the singing school furnished other means of musical life to the pioneer. At the "sings" he could rock the rafters with the familiar songs and feel no embarrassment, since everyone joined in lustily. Religious songs, the old faithfuls such as "Darling Nellie Gray," "Tumble-down Log Shanty on the Claim," and "Red Wing," and running of the scales filled the evening till the time came to join in on "Oh the Singin' Schule" for the finale.

Within the last few years, the singing society has again become popular in Oklahoma, and organizations have been formed in many towns and communities; all-day "sings" are frequently held.

After statehood, the erection of gilt-decorated opera houses in the fast-growing towns began to bring classical music—usually executed with a piano and violin, dignified by the term orchestra—to Oklahomans. Lyceum and chautauqua courses introduced soloists with extensive repertoires; bands were formed in towns of any size, and the Sunday afternoon concert in the public square became an established custom. With the coming of statehood and the drafting of the school curriculum, the teaching of music was authorized by law. In some instances, local school boards made provision for the office of a music teacher or supervisor.

Most Oklahoma primary schools introduce some music in the day's activities, more often by phonograph in the field of music appreciation; all accredited junior and senior high schools require music teachers to hold special certificates in addition to their general teaching qualifications; and in the secondary bracket, too, curricular music is stressed as much as extra-curricular activity in the subject. Music appreciation and history are taught in addition to the more technical studies of theory, and instrumental and vocal training. Various musical organizations of the Oklahoma public schools have won many honors in national and regional competition, particularly in the band section—for most schools in the state support their brilliantly costumed marching groups as enthusiastically as their football teams.

Excellent music departments have been established in the state universities and colleges, where instruction is offered in all instruments and voice, and in the more technical fields of theory and composition. The department of music at the University of Oklahoma, at the Oklahoma Agricultural and Mechanical College, at the University of Tulsa, and at Phillips University all support full-size symphony orchestras. Most of the smaller institutions have symphonic or chamber music groups. Bacone Indian College *(see Tour 8)* has an outstanding choral organization which makes extensive tours annually; the school's music department is striving to keep native Indian music from extinction. The *a cappella* choir of Northwestern State College *(see Tour 2)* is a vested group of fifty voices which has become well known in the Southwest, since it makes annual concert tours through several states. The choir, organized in 1928, has a repertoire which includes chorales, masses, madrigals, liturgical music, spirituals, and sacred and secular songs. The two most discerning national music sororities are represented in Oklahoma: Mu Phi Epsilon with an active chapter at the University of Oklahoma and several alumnae groups; and Sigma Alpha Iota with units at the universities in Oklahoma City, Tulsa, Shawnee, and Norman.

Outside the schools, though always working indirectly with them and sometimes in actual collaboration, are various musical organizations throughout the state. The Oklahoma Federation of Music Clubs is the most far-reaching and prominent; there are 212 senior, student, and junior affiliated clubs with a total membership of 4,737 in the state's nine districts. The federation sponsors the state's part in the National Federation's competition for solo and group work and composition, and has also organized an all-state chorus and orchestra which meets to rehearse and perform at the annual convention.

Enid is noted as a particularly music-minded city, for the schools, civic groups, and Phillips University join in sponsoring the annual Tri-State Band Festival and the Cimarron Opera Company. Oklahoma, Kansas, and Texas send bands to the festival, held during the second week in April, where they are judged by nationally prominent band conductors and join, as the finale of the event, for a massed band concert and parade. The meet is open to all bands and is not primarily competitive; it is rather designed for the purpose of inculcating musical standards. The opera company is a civic organization which presents each June in the Glenwood Amphitheater four operas, for which well-known singers are often imported to sing the lead roles; a symphony made up of citizen musicians and university players interprets the score. Tulsa, for a time, supported a symphony, and is the home of two outstanding musical organizations—the Tulsans, one of the state's first male choral groups, and the Hyechka Club, first organized in 1904 and still active with a membership of three hundred. The name is said to mean "music" in the Creek language. The State Organists' Guild is represented by chapters in Tulsa and in Oklahoma City.

Oklahoma City boasts a number of prominent and active musical organizations in which are included the famous Kiltie band, an unusual marching society that has represented the city throughout the state and in most of the important metropolises of the country during the last fifteen years. There is a constant waiting list for the perpetual membership of fifty girls, some 750 girls having worn the bright plaid kilts, the highlander cap, and the fur purse since the start of the band. The minimum age for entrance is sixteen years; rigid moral standards are required; membership pays nothing except trip expenses; and the only musical knowledge necessary is the ability to read music, for instruction in the playing of the bagpipe and the drums is given by the conductor of the band.

The Oklahoma Symphonic Choir, sponsored by the First Christian Church of Oklahoma City, has made enviable progress since it was founded in 1937. It has no denominational restrictions, only a high vocal standard and a limited membership. Mastery of a large repertoire of unusual choral music was responsible for the group's being invited to sing at the New York World's Fair in 1939 and with the famous Westminster Choir at the Westminster College of Music at Princeton, New Jersey, in the same year. Another Oklahoma City music group is the twenty-year-old chapter of the MacDowell Club, represented elsewhere in Oklahoma at only two other cities, Ada and Anadarko. The Oklahoma City group has a constant membership of approximately five hundred and has undertaken the responsibility of sending Oklahoma artists to the MacDowell summer colony at Peterboro, New Hampshire. Musicians who have been given the privilege are Spencer Norton, Lemuel Childers, and Charles B. Macklin. The Ladies' Music Club, established at the turn of the century and listing a membership of five hundred, presents three artist concerts each year, open to members and guests. The Apollo Club is an old and active men's choral group.

The Oklahoma Music Teachers' Association, affiliated with the national organization, has headquarters in Oklahoma City. The state's one hundred members must be accredited by examination before the State Board of Education and possess the necessary college degrees. The association's purpose is primarily to give recognition to the private music teacher by licensing, thus allowing him to give instruction which will accord public school credit to the pupil.

The Flatfoot Four, composed of Oklahoma City policemen, has proved itself a championship quartet in "barbershop" vocalizing, for it was declared winner in the nationwide contest conducted at the New York World's Fair in 1940. A quartet from Bartlesville won second place in the same competition.

The most important state musical movement in recent years is that created by the Oklahoma Music Program, a unit of the Work Projects Administration, with headquarters in the Municipal Auditorium in Oklahoma City. The 75-piece Oklahoma Symphony Orchestra made its debut in January, 1938, with pianist Guy Maier as soloist. Each winter a tour is made—by the end of 1940 seventeen state cities had heard the symphony in thirty-three school concerts, attended by 35,368 children, and in twenty-four public performances, attended by 15,695. School busses travel as far as seventy-five miles to bring children from the rural districts to the place of concert for the afternoon performance, always primarily a music appreciation program preceded by school study on the concert numbers. Oklahoma City school students hear the group regularly. The orchestra presents a series of formal concerts at Oklahoma City in the winter and lighter symphonic revues in the city's Taft Stadium in the summer; artists of national caliber who have appeared with the group are Harold Bauer, Alec Templeton, Albert Spalding, Donald Dickson, Charles Wakefield Cadman, Dalies Frantz, the San Francisco Opera Ballet, and the Littlefield Ballet. Works of thirteen state composers have been presented, and a junior symphony of sixty-five students is sponsored.

The young conductor, Victor Alessandro, is a graduate of the Eastman School of Music at Rochester, New York, the American winner of the Salzburg and Prix de Rome fellowship in 1937, and has appeared as guest conductor of the New York Civic Symphony, the Rochester Civic and Philharmonic Symphonies, and the Eastman Symphony.

The future of the orchestra is being assured through the organization of the Oklahoma State Symphony Society, a nonprofit organization which sponsors the concerts and assures the necessary backing; by the official sponsorship of the University of Oklahoma; and by the Oklahoma City Chamber of Commerce, which for two successive years (1939–40) chose the orchestra as one of its thirteen major activities. The Oklahoma Music Program also has a widespread Music Education unit employing seventy-seven teachers.

Native Oklahomans who have become well known in the concert and operatic field are Giuseppe Bentonelli (Joseph Benton), who was born in Kansas City, Missouri, but was brought to Sayre as an infant, and who is (1941) a leading tenor with the Metropolitan Opera Company; Lushanya (Tessie Mobley), born near Ardmore of Chickasaw parentage, a mezzo-soprano engaged with the Chicago Civic Opera and a concert artist of fame both here and abroad, where she sang before England's King George and Queen Mary and Italy's Premier Mussolini; Princess Pakanli (Mrs. Edwin Underwood), born also in Ardmore of mixed Indian blood, a soloist with the Chicago Civic Opera Company in 1935, and later on the concert stage; Kathleen Kersting, born near Enid, who sang for two seasons with the Chicago Civic Opera, at Bayreuth in the Wagnerian Festival in 1931, with the Berlin Opera Company, and with various other organizations abroad; Ruth Alexander Young, another native of Ardmore, who appeared with the Denver Opera Company and the Denver Symphony Orchestra in 1936–37 and taught earlier at the Conservatory of Music at Manila, Philippine Islands; and Annette Burford, of Oklahoma City, who was the 1940 winner of the Chicago Civic Opera auditions and who is appearing regularly in their productions. Mack Harreld, 1939 baritone winner of the Metropolitan Opera Company auditions, is a native Texan who lived in Oklahoma City for several years.

Dr. Melvin G. Riggs, professor of psychology at the Oklahoma Agricultural and Mechanical College, is making a contribution in the field of music as associate editor of the *Journal of Musicology,* a music research magazine published at Greenfield, Ohio. A number of his articles on experimental psychology in relation to music have appeared in various publications;

one formed the basis for a chapter in Deems Taylor's *The Well-Tempered Listener.*

Oklahoma lays claim to a number of recognized composers, some native to the state and others transplanted citizens. Roy Harris, prominent musician and well-known composer, was born near Chandler *(see Tour 1).* His honors include a Guggenheim fellowship and appointments to head the composition department of the Westminster Choir of Princeton, New Jersey, and the Princeton Festival of American Music. His music, including the *First, Second,* and *Third Symphonies;* the *Time Suite,* commissioned by the Columbia Broadcasting System; "Johnny Comes Marching Home," commissioned by Victor Records; and a number of other works, has been played widely by such orchestras as the New York Philharmonic, the Boston, Washington, D.C., and Seattle symphonies, and by groups in Mexico and Italy. Other native Oklahomans who have achieved a measure of fame are Spencer Norton, University of Oklahoma professor, who wrote *Aeschylus* for orchestra while at the MacDowell summer camp, and who has had several piano compositions published; Wynn York, whose "Silhouettes" has been played by the Chicago Symphony Orchestra; and Albert Kirkpatrick, composer of a number of published concert songs, using the lyrics of the English poet, A. E. Housman.

Native Indian themes have been incorporated in the music written by Lemuel Childers, an Osage born in Pawhuska, and the composer of "Hiawatha," "Peace Pipe," "Warriors," "Laughing Water," and "Sand Dance," all for symphony orchestra; Fred Cardin, born on the Quapaw Reservation *(see Tour 1),* whose "Cree War Dance" for violin and piano has been published; Ingram Cleveland, born in the Cherokee Hills of Cherokee Indian parentage and composer of "Spavinaw Moonlight" for violin, which has been performed in Chicago and has also been orchestrated and performed by the Oklahoma Symphony Orchestra; and Jack Kilpatrick, Cherokee Indian born near Stilwell and a graduate of Bacone College, who has written "Saturday Night on Echota Hill," "Wovoka," and "Cherokee Suite" for orchestra in addition to vocal and instrumental works.

Adopted Oklahomans who are well known for accomplishments in the music world include Claude Lapham, of Oklahoma City, who has received acclaim for his oriental music, including the Japanese opera, *Sokura,* performed in Tokyo and at the Hollywood Bowl in 1933; Edwin Vaile McIntyre (died 1934), of Oklahoma City, a prolific and well-known composer of teaching pieces for piano, many of which are published; Paul Thomas (died 1940), of Oklahoma City, composer of the orchestra number based on Edwin Markham's famous poem, "Man With The Hoe"; Samuel A.

McReynolds, of Oklahoma City, whose *Southwest* was performed by the New York Symphony in 1937, and whose more recent work, *Grand River Suite,* for string orchestra, descriptive of the eastern Oklahoma river, was presented in 1939 by the Oklahoma Symphony Orchestra; Charles B. Macklin, of Seminole, who has five published books of teaching pieces for piano, violin, and voice; Bohumil Makovsky, head of the music department at the Oklahoma Agricultural and Mechanical College, the composer of the *180th Infantry March;* Paolo Conte, dean of music at Oklahoma Baptist University, composer of more than two hundred works including the well-known *The Old Love Story* and *Canzone Triste,* written for piano but later orchestrated; Father Ignatius Groll, former instructor of music at St. Gregory's College, noted for the prelude, *Snow Angel;* Oscar J. Lehrer, of the University of Oklahoma faculty, writer of sixty published anthems and the noted cantata, *King of Alcohol;* Galen Holcomb, of Oklahoma City, whose native African dance, *Poro,* has been performed by the Illinois Symphony Orchestra, the Chicago Women's Symphony, and the Oklahoma Symphony Orchestra, and whose *Capriccio for Tympani and Orchestra,* performed by the Illinois and Oklahoma Symphonies, has received notice for its unusual choice of solo instrument; Marie M. Hine, of Tulsa, who is the composer of two hundred published anthems and six cantatas, among them *The Redemption;* and Mayme Rabinovitz-Travis, of Tulsa, who has written many compositions for voice and violin, including the well-known "Indian Dance" and "O Wonderful Mother of Mine."

In the field of poular music, Oklahoma is represented by Truman (Pinky) Tomlin, of Durant, composer of "Object of My Affections"; Phil Grogan, of Oklahoma City, composer of "Especially for You"; and Helen Myers, of Oklahoma City, a mezzo-soprano well known as a night club singer and a recording artist.

Folklore and Folkways

ACCORDING to an imaginative early historian, a pioneer settler in Oklahoma ran amuck on a visit to town and, in the course of a few minutes, killed a representative of each of five races. The historian adds that it was possible because they were found within the space of a city block. Considering the diversity of sources from which the state's population was drawn, the story is not so farfetched as it might sound. It would be more illuminating, however, if the victims had been identified specifically as an Iowa farmer, a Texas ranchman, a Missouri lead miner, a Pennsylvania oilman, and an Arkansas fruit grower.

Although guns play no part in present-day Oklahoma life, they hold an important place in its folklore. This is particularly true in the western part of the state, where almost any stripling can spin a yarn that, for shooting exploits, would shame Annie Oakley. The narrator may start off with the solemn assertion that he and a rival decided to test their skill by shooting the barbs from a wire fence over a mile stretch. As each was equally successful in the contest, a further test was necessary. So, loading their guns with charges of glue, barbs, and powder, they galloped back over their course, shooting the barbs back on the fence.

"An' if you don't believe that," the tale-teller says, "I'll take you out an' show you the fence where it happened!"

The tall tale is usually not merely a highly improbable piece of fiction, but a method of "codding" a naïve youngster or newcomer. The story starts innocently enough, and if the victim remains credulous it explodes into utter absurdity.

The cyclone is a common subject for such stories. The "codder" begins with a series of events, credible enough, which he claims to have witnessed: his house was blown away, but the cookstove was left undisturbed with fire going and the teakettle steaming. All of his listeners who are aware of what is going on pretend to be not at all interested. The conclusion of the story may be that a sack of meal had been hanging on a neighbor's porch and the wind blew the sack away, leaving the meal hanging there!

The story of Paul Bunyan's great gray wolf—a blood cousin of the blue ox—is an oil-field classic. The wolf, "derrick-high and slushpit wide," became associated with Paul on one of his transatlantic swims. Bunyan met the animal in mid-ocean, swimming for shore with a whale in his jaws. They "spelled" each other with the burden and became fast friends.

Bunyan hitched the wolf to a buckboard and established the first mail line into Oklahoma, making daily trips between this state and Pennsylvania. He finally gave up the mail line to take the agency for a remarkable salve. Paul commonly began its demonstration by cutting off an arm or leg and sticking it back again. Paul and the wolf became rich; but the railroads had always been jealous of the pair. The wolf, who was a guileless animal, accepted a challenge from the Santa Fe to race from Oklahoma City to Ardmore and was just about to win when the engineer threw a crowbar out of the window, slicing the beast in two from nose to tail. Paul rushed to the scene with a satchel full of salve and stuck the wolf together again, but in his haste the two halves were not properly arranged. Two legs were on the ground, the other two pointed to the sky. This proved to be an advantage, however, for, when the wolf grew tired of running on one side, Paul would turn him over and let him run on the other. The wolf finally died of iron poisoning after eating 182 miles of Santa Fe track.

Tall-tale telling is essentially a country diversion, although in the towns and cities of Oklahoma the Negroes are fond of the Paul Bunyan, or John Henry, variety. One of these tells how old John Henry drifted into Oklahoma without either cottonseed or planting tools and found that none of the Indians would sell him any land. But he wasn't discouraged; he just up and drank all the water out of the Canadian River, then took and put his two hands together and drug 'em along the sandy bed of the river, plowing it up with his fingers. Then he reached into the sky to get him cotton plants from the big patches up there that some folks call clouds . . . Was this John Henry a big man? Well, I never seen him till he was four hundred and sixty years old, and by then he was kind of shriveled, not more than seventeen hoe-handles between his eyes.

On the farms, where there is leisure for "codding," almost every dwelling will have some opening that can be pointed out as a "crowbar hole." The town innocent, inquiring into the purpose of the opening, will learn that it is to test the wind velocity. If the crowbar merely bends when thrust through the hole, it is safe to go out. However, if the bar is broken off, it is better to stay in the house.

There is a very real basis for the stories of Oklahoma outlaws, or the outlaws who occasionally made Oklahoma their stamping ground. No one will deny that the Daltons and Doolins were all handy with rifle or six-shooter, or that Belle Starr was able to tell the butt of a gun from the barrel. But the story of the outlaw who lined his family up against a barn door and traced their silhouettes with six-guns can be characterized only as a tall-tale.

A number of stories of bad men have defied exaggeration from the time they were first told. This is the case with the tale of a Panhandle cowboy who was captured by outlaws about 1870. The hard-hearted villains cooped the cowboy up in a barrel and rolled him out on the prairie to die of thirst and starvation. Several hours later a herd of buffaloes passed that way and one came close to sniff curiously at the barrel. As it turned away, its tail slipped through the bunghole and the cowboy seized it. The frightened animal began to run and, the cowboy guiding him by instinct, they reached a town where the barrel was opened and the man released.

There were notable gun-shots in early Oklahoma, of course, and the time probably bred more fearless and daring men than any other period. Life was indeed real and earnest, and the one safe place for a dreamer was his bed. Some of the officers were reformed outlaws, and some of the outlaws had been officers; there was understanding between the two classes even though there was no compromise. There was romance in outlawry, and a broad streak of humor which not even lynching or legal execution could completely extinguish. This light-hearted disregard of life and death is evident in the following song:

A friend of mine once stole a horse,
'T was in a place out West.
The horse just left his owner
Cause he liked my friend the best.
My friend had lots of trouble
When the owner came on deck,
When he found the horse had had
A string around his neck.

Chorus: A little piece of string, it seems a tiny thing,
But strong enough to keep the horse in check.
When my friend I last did see, he was hanging from a tree
With a little piece of string around his neck.

On the great cattle ranches that spread across western Oklahoma after the Civil War, folk songs were almost inevitably popular. During the long, idle winters, a battered accordion or banjo was a god-send in more than one lonely bunkhouse. The balladry of this period is illustrated in these lines:

"Come alive you fellers," hear the foreman shout.
"Drop your books and banjos, fetch your saddles out . . .
"Shake that squeaky fiddle, Red, go and get your hoss,
"Dutch, ain't you got duties, as the chuck-wagon boss?

"Range is gettin' grassy, winter draws its claws,
"Calves are fat an' sassy, teasin' of their maws,
"Loafin' days are over, dreamin' time is gone,
"No more life in clover, fer the round-up's on."

In rural sections, the square dance is still popular. Except during the busy summer season, every community has its weekly "shindig" in some farm home. Only in those districts where big barns are common are these affairs "barn dances." In most cases barns are too small and rickety, or haymows are too full to be used for such purposes. As a rule, the square dance is a social affair, but occasionally one is held to raise money for some charitable cause.

The square dance fiddler's first concern is to carry a tune, but he must carry it loud enough to be heard over the noise of stamping feet, the cries of the "caller," and the shouts of the dancers. When he fiddles, he "fiddles all over"; feet, hands, knees, head, and eyes are all busy. He is usually supported by a "second," whose performance on the piano, guitar, banjo, organ, or another fiddle, gives the music additional resonance and depth.

The "caller" at the square dance is as important as the fiddler or his second. He tells the dancers what to do, but his directions are so enhanced by his poetical fervor, his humor, and his vocalizing that a visitor, unfamiliar with square-dance calls, can hardly understand the words, let alone translate them into commands. The caller is necessarily well acquainted with his audience and is apt to incorporate in his chants well-known bits of family history. He may also make observations upon love-smitten couples, the perils of store teeth at taffy pullings, or hint gently that his own art is a thirsty business.

Dance calls are fairly uniform throughout the state, but each caller puts his own stamp upon them. The result is a rich body of rustic rhymes.

The following verses are typical:

Break trail home
In Indian style;
Swing the gal behind you
Once in a while
Now grab your partner
And go hog-wild!

Two little sisters
Form a ring,
Now you're born
Now you swing!
(A play on the expression "born to be hung.")

Panthers scream
Bobcats squall
House cat jumps
Through a hole in the wall.

Eat ice cream,
  Drink soda water;
Some old man
  Gonna lose his daughter.

Ladies lead off
  In the cowboy style;
Stop and rope one
  Every little while.

Same ol' boys
  An' the same ol' trail;
An' watch the same ol' 'possum
  Walk the same ol' rail.

Walk the Huckleberry shuffle
  And Chinese cling;
Elbow twist and
  The grapevine swing!

Swing your partners one and all,
Swing that lady in the checkered shawl,
Gents, hands in your pockets, back to the wall,
Take a chaw of terbacker and balance all.
Quit that hugging, ain't you a-shamed,
Promenade, Oh Promenade!

In communities where dancing is frowned upon the play-party is popular. It resembles the dance in figures and tunes, but substitutes vocal for instrumental accompaniment. A favorite old play-party song is this:

Rise you up my dearest dear
And present to me your hand,
And we'll go in pursuit
Of some far and better land
Where the hawk 'll chase the buzzard,
And the buzzard 'll chase the crow,
And we'll rally 'round the cane brake
And chase the buffalo.

"Skip To My Lou," another popular play-party song, contains more than a hundred verses. The following is typical:

Red birds singin', two by two,
Red birds singin', two by two,
Red birds singin', two by two,
Skip to m' Lou, my darlin'.

The first line of another verse pictures

Rats in the buttermilk, two by two.

Another early-day expression of social life was the "singin' school." The singing teacher, whose status in the community might range from that of a member of the church choir to an itinerant whisky tenor, was usually paid a dollar for each man; women and children were admitted free, and whole families attended.

Songs shook the one-room schoolhouse rafters on the sharp winter nights when the singin' school "took up," blending with the roaring of red-bellied heating stove and the sad, distant tinkle of harness. Many of the tunes were nameless and of unknown origin, such as this:

I married me a wife in the month of June—
Nickle te, nackle te, now, now, now,
I took her home by the light of the moon,
With a wree-wrah-wraddle,
And a Jack straw straddle
And a little brown bridle come under the broom.

Scales were sung, and some attempt was made to group the different voices, but the people were too intent on fun to submit to any great amount of discipline.

'Coon and 'possum hunts, held in the fall and winter, are the most common outdoor recreations in the hills and wooded sections. The essentials, other than a party of men or boys, are hound dogs and a supply of corn liquor. The dogs "tree" the quarry and stand guard until the hunters arrive. The whisky helps to kill the poison in the night air.

It is in the hills of eastern Oklahoma that the beliefs and customs of another century are best preserved; but in every section of the state there are cures that no doctor would recommend, methods of planting that the Department of Agriculture would not encourage, and modes of speech that grammarians would frown upon. Some of the most interesting superstitions are:

To cure a snake bite, kill the snake, cut it open, and apply the warm flesh to the wound.

To cure the sting of a bee, chew up three kinds of leaves and grass and apply to the wound.

Don't marry in a dotted dress. If you do, you will have as many children as there are dots.

Don't sweep under a sick person's bed lest he die.

A child suffering from "fits" can be cured by putting its feet into the open body of a freshly killed chicken.

Boils can be prevented from recurring by swallowing shot, one shot for each boil the patient may have had.

To remove a wart, loop a thread around it, then remove the thread and throw it away in the woods. When it decays, the wart will have vanished. Another method is to put a kernel of corn on a wart, then feed the corn to a rooster; or the wart may be removed by touching it lightly with a drop of blood from the armpit of an enemy.

Never let a woman be the first to enter your home on Monday morning; let it be a man, even if you must invite him in.

If a cock crows three times at your door, on the porch, or on the back doorstep, a stranger will arrive at your home soon.

If you plan to move to a new house, burn five tallow candles in the new residence in the shape of a cross for good luck; one at each end of the house, one at each side, and one in the center. Let them burn until consumed.

Negroes say that if a man tries to steal your girl or wife, you should first warn him. Then if he fails to take heed, place a miniature coffin, with a drawing of a skeleton therein, under his doorstep. The curse can be removed by having a voodoo doctor burn the coffin. If a person for whom it was not intended steps over it, he must wash his hands in "pine" whisky and either destroy the casket or let the voodoo doctor destroy it.

The following beliefs are typical of the lore of the Five Civilized Tribes, which reflects their long association with whites and Negroes:

Earache should be treated with fire coals. The sizzling coal is momentarily dipped into water, wrapped in a woolen cloth, and applied to the ear.

To cure a headache, the medicine man takes a mouthful of water from a mountain spring and sprays it upon the head of the sufferer.

Medicine kept in a house where death has occurred loses its potency.

Trash should not be swept out of doors on Sunday mornings, or bad luck will follow.

Ashes should be removed from a stove only in the morning. If they are taken out in the afternoon, some member of the family will become ill.

Storms can be avoided by sticking an axe handle in the ground, burning a pinch of tobacco in the fireplace, burning the shell of a turtle or terrapin, or placing a flatiron on top of a griddle in the exact center of the room.

A mourner must not enter a garden, or the plants will wither and die.

Babies must not have their hair cut until after they are a year old, or they will never walk.

If a child is left alone in a room, a Bible or a pair of scissors is placed near it to frighten away witches.

The mother of a baby should scratch the bare hips of her young one with the feet of a live chicken to ensure that her influence over the baby will continue during its life.

The average Oklahoman, of course, is far more literate than he is pictured by some western-story writers. Men do not habitually call one another "pardner," and few children address their mothers as "mammy." However, there are interesting peculiarities of speech in certain sections.

Hill folk are apt to say "et" for "ate" and follow the cockney English custom of dropping or adding the aspirate "h." "You'ns," "they'uns," and "nary'uns" are in general use, as are "I taken," and "I done." The Elizabethan "quote" is often a substitute for "echo"; "sorry" means inferior; and "evenin'" is any time between noon and dusk. In the Arbuckle mountains, the Spanish influence is evident in the use of such words as *loco, hombre,* and "savvy." The southwestern Indians picked up the expression *no sabe* from the Spaniards, pronouncing it "no savvy." The term came to mean, among both whites and Indians, "I do not know." Along the Red River, the slurred "r" is more the rule than the exception, and "h" is carelessly handled. Former Texans also say "putt" for "put," "awn" for "on," and "hone" for "horn." "Gallery" is a synonym for "porch," and a small body of water is a "tank." A common practice is to pronounce "e" like "i," turning the word "men," for example, into "min." In the western part of the state there is a tendency toward Zane Grey vocabularies, which may or may not have a connection with the popularity of his books in that region. Such westernisms are most pronounced in the very young or very simple and either, in moments of excitement, is likely to forget his cowboy-story lingo.

Oil-field workers use strange hybrid words and phrases, some technically sound, some acutely suggestive, some that come from the hobo and criminal lingoes. In general use in the oil-field world are the following expressions:

Bindle—(Bundle) Usually containing cooking utensils as well as clothing.
Bindlestiff—A migratory worker who carries a bindle.
Bronze John—The sun.
Boweevil—(Boll Weevil) A worthless fellow, or a novice at oil-field work.
Button—To end. "We put the button on the job."
Cake—Bread.
Christmas Tree—The collection of valves and fittings at the top of a well controlling oil and gas flow.
Cherries—Beans.
Crumb—Infringing upon the work or rights of others. "Stop crumbing on me." Also an animal parasite.
Crumb Boss—A man who has charge of tents or bunkhouses. Derived from the humorous supposition that he is able to command the crumbs which (may) infest the beds.
Doodlebug—An unscientific device used in attempts to locate oil and other minerals.

Dope—Creosote; used to coat pipe.

Drag-up—To draw one's pay and quit.

Fire, or fire in the hole—"Get out of the way! Explosion due!"

Four-foot gas—Wood cut in four-foot lengths.

Mr. Gluckenheimer—A "wise guy."

High-pressure—The boss. Adjective—"The high-pressure tent."

Hold—To possess money. "What are you holding?"

Jamoke—Coffee. A merging of java and mocha.

Knowledge bench—A three-tiered stool belonging to the driller.

Lazy board—A board above the derrick floor, from which pipe is stabbed into the well. The stabber works spasmodically, hence the name.

Mormon board—A broad board with two handles, used for filling in a ditch.

Mud hog—A rotary driller. Also, a pump.

Rope-choker—A cable-tool driller.

Snake—A West Virginian. This is probably derived from the "treachery" of the West Virginians in siding with the North during the Civil War.

Slush-pit—A hole approximately fifty by one hundred feet, and four feet in depth, where thin mud that circulates about the drill-stem and flushes out the cuttings is stored.

Stroke—A minor foreman. "He is (or has) the stroke on the dope gang."

Swamper—A truck driver's helper.

Tool pusher—The supervisor in direct charge of several drilling wells.

Tower—(for "Tour"), the daily stint of a driller.

Wildcat—A well in unproved territory.

Wildcatter—One who drills in unproved territory.

PART II

Principal Cities

Ardmore

Railroad Stations: 217 E. Main St. for Santa Fe; Broadway and A St. for Frisco.
Bus Stations: 300 W. Main St. for Oklahoma Transportation Co.; 10 E. Main St. for Jordan Bus Line.
Airport: Ardmore Field, 9.6 m. N. on US 77.
City Busses: Terminal, 201 S. Washington St., fare 5c.
Taxis: fare 15c,

Accommodations: 5 hotels; rooming houses; tourists camps.

Information Service: Chamber of Commerce, 100 W. Main St.

Radio Station: KVSO (1240 kc.).
Motion Picture Theaters: 6; 1 for Negroes.
Athletics: Walker Stadium, S St. and McLish Ave., S.W.
Golf: Dornick Hills, 2 m. N. on US 77, greens fee $1; Municipal Golf Club, 2.5 m. N. on US 77, greens fee, 25c weekdays, 35c Sundays and holidays.
Swimming and Wading Pools: for children, Whittington City Park, 800 4th Ave., S.E., free; Lake Murray State Park, 3.9 m. S. on Washington St.
Boating: Lake Murray.
Tennis: City courts, B and 9th Sts., N.W. F St. and 3d Ave., N.E., free.

Annual Event: Southern Oklahoma Free Fair and Exposition, Whittington City Park, 2d week in Sept.

ARDMORE (896 alt., 16,886 pop.), seat of Carter County, is the largest city between Oklahoma City, 104 miles north, and Fort Worth, Texas, 107 miles south. It came into being on the Roff Brothers' "700 Ranch" in the Indian Territory when, in 1887, the Atchison, Topeka and Santa Fe railroad was built through the site.

The growth of this self-styled "capital of south central Oklahoma" from a cattle-loading point in the middle of a big ranch to the wide-spreading metropolis of an area rich in farming land, pastures, oil, asphaltum, and recreational resources, has been steady but unspectacular.

In general, the city has a spaced, comfortable appearance that suggests the predominant southern population. The broad, tree-shaded streets of the section first laid out by Ardmore's pioneers were not made truly north and south and east and west, but were oriented to the Santa Fe railway tracks. Later additions, therefore, laid out by compass, do not jibe with them. Noticeable are the number of fine old native hackberry trees that arch over the sidewalks.

Ardmore's Negroes, who make up approximately 13 per cent of the population, live east of the Santa Fe tracks, north and south of East Main street. They are mainly from the Negro families that were drawn to the cotton fields of the region after it became possible for non-Indians to obtain leases and develop the good cotton-growing farms of the surrounding region.

When Ardmore was founded it was named by an official of the railroad in honor of the Philadelphia suburb he had known, though the young settlement had little of the beauty of its namesake. Two years after it had become a station on the Santa Fe, a pioneer settler from Texas pictured it in these words:

"Father met us at the depot, and on the way to our new home we saw the public well and watering trough in the middle of Main Street.... I remember how my sister and I gazed at the cowboys standing at the well with their ten-gallon white hats, black-and-white checked shirts, and slant-heeled boots. The spot seemed to be attractive to the town's hogs, also, as they had made a wallowing ground around the trough. Before reaching home we saw our first rattlesnake and prairie chickens.

"The first winter we were visited by a fierce, mangy herd of wild horses that stayed near our house for quite a while, snorting and pitching and making it unsafe for us children to venture outside."

There is also the tale of the retired town marshal, drafted to help capture a mountain man charged with attempted homicide, who went alone and unarmed to take him, stayed to dinner, and drove back to the courthouse on the friendliest possible terms with him. Such stories as these are told by Ardmoreites who can say, "I was there and saw it."

In its early days, Ardmore was a trading point for farmers and ranchmen of the Chickasaw Nation and an important primary market for cotton. Five years after the coming of the railroad, it was claimed that more than fifty thousand bales were sold on its streets by growers in the season.

The even progress of the city's growth was stimulated by the discovery of oil near by in 1913; it is perhaps this factor which has determined its regional prominence. In contrast to the history of most Oklahoma oil-boom towns, the subsidence of the gusher phase of the Healdton and other fields in the region did not mean partial paralysis of Ardmore. Under the rule of limited output imposed by proration, the thousands of wells settled into production which as yet shows few signs of exhaustion in the Healdton, Ringling, Wirt, Fox, Hewitt, and other, lesser, fields of the same general area.

As early as 1901, when the first oil developments in Oklahoma were exciting the farmers and ranchers of the Tulsa–Red Fork region, a group of Ardmore citizens, together with investors from Missouri and South Dakota, formed a company to explore the Red Beds for oil. They had seen crude oil on the surface of water flowing from springs, and despite the expert judgment of such men as John D. Archbold, of the Standard Oil Company, who declared he would drink all the oil found in the Red Beds, they persisted in their explorations and found oil at four hundred feet.

But it was not until after Roy Johnson came to start a newspaper at Ardmore in 1907 that a persistent effort to develop the field was made. Johnson was obsessed by the conviction that there must be oil near the extensive beds of asphaltum which had been mapped near Ardmore. The city's streets were being paved with rock asphalt at the time; and Johnson, after examining it, believed that this material had once been saturated with oil, that the light oil had drained away, and that asphaltum had been formed from the residue. He took on as a partner in the venture a young man who could give all his time to securing leases, while he himself undertook to finance the enterprise. When their funds ran out, Johnson negotiated a loan of $2,000, paying a commission of 2 per cent, promising to pay interest at the rate of 10 per cent a year, and giving as security his newspaper publishing plant. When the money was spent, he borrowed more from the young schoolma'am, Odessa Otey, with whom he was keeping company and whom he later married.

Ten years after he and his group had brought in the first well in 1913, Johnson recalled the story of oil in the Ardmore region and suggested that Archbold would have drunk a big mouthful of oil had he made good on his promise—up to that time the Red Beds had yielded some 167,000,000 barrels!

More striking, though perhaps no more important to the oil history of Ardmore than Roy Johnson, were John Ringling, circus man, and Jake Hamon, Republican politician. It was Ringling, who, annoyed by the poor roads between his wells and Ardmore, built twenty miles of railway to a point named Ringling, with a six-mile branch to Healdton, which was later extended. Hamon was so prominent in the campaign which resulted in the election of Harding as President that before his untimely death he was said to be slated for a cabinet post. John W. Harreld, an Ardmoreite living in Oklahoma City, was elected to the United States Senate in the Harding landslide of 1920. He and W. B. Pine *(see Okmulgee)*, who defeated Jack Walton in 1924 *(see History)*, are the only Republicans (up to 1941) ever elected from Oklahoma to a term in the United States Senate. Lee Cruce, of Ardmore, an intermarried member of the Chickasaw tribe, was the second governor of Oklahoma (1913-17).

Ardmore's first newspaper, the *Alliance Courier*, a weekly, was started in 1888, when there was no municipal government, when the city's fire department was a volunteer bucket brigade and its water supply came from cisterns dug beside their stores by the merchants of Main Street, and the only police force was a deputy marshal from the Federal court. Under Jules Soule, this paper served as mouthpiece for the Farmers' Alliance, a radical agrarian movement that was widespread in Kansas and other drought-affected areas, and was brought into Indian Territory by leasers and tenant farmers. Soule acquired the *Ardmore Chronicle* in 1890 and also printed the *Wind Bag.*

Two Negro newspapers, the *Ardmore Sun* (1901) and the *Baptist Rival* (1902), were the next of a number of weekly journals to be born and have a life in the town. The *Chickasaw Chieftain,* which Rezin McAdam established in 1890 to campaign for the breaking up of tribal governments, allotment of Indian lands, and their opening to white settlement, became an evening daily in 1892. In the following year, Sidney Suggs, a picturesque figure who made himself a leader in Oklahoma journalism, bought for $600 the new and struggling *Daily Ardmoreite.* It is the only survivor (1941) of the half-dozen dailies that have tried their wings in the city—Roy Johnson's *Statesman,* the *Daily Citizen,* the *Chronicle,* the *Ardmore Appeal,* the *Bulletin,* and the *Morning Democrat.* The *Ardmoreite* management also prints the *Democrat,* a weekly.

A dramatic highlight in Ardmore's history was the explosion, on September 27, 1915, of a tank car containing highly volatile casing-head gasoline. So terrific was the concussion that the Santa Fe station, most of the business houses, and many residences were wrecked; and some fifty persons lost their lives. It was said that horses eight miles away were knocked to their knees.

From the first traditional one-room schoolhouse, Ardmore's educational plant has multiplied to a modern accredited high school, a junior high school, and four elementary schools which enroll more than 4,400 students. A high school and an elementary school, with twenty teachers, take care of some six hundred Negro students. Twenty-seven churches are supported by the white people of the city, while the Negroes have twelve churches.

As Ardmore grew, park spaces were generously provided. Today (1941) there are ten municipal parks, one of which is in the Negro district. Within an hour's driving distance lie twelve lakes and other attractive recreational features which draw tourists and vacationists to the clear, fish-stocked streams and lakes of the Arbuckle Mountains region.

Among the seventy-three industrial enterprises that have plants in the city are an automobile tire manufacturing plant, oil refineries, cotton oil and flour mills, cotton gins and compresses, manufacturers of guns, cigars, stoves, and pecan-cracking machinery. In all, says Ardmore's Chamber of Commerce, the city's industries have (1941) an annual pay roll of $685,000, and their sales amount to $6,000,000.

Early Settlement

(c) MORTON HARVEY

PIONEER WOMAN, BY BRYANT BAKER; PONCA CITY

OKLAHOMA HISTORICAL SOCIE

WAITING FOR THE RUN, CHEROKEE STRIP, 1893

THE RUN, CHEROKEE STRIP, 1893

OKLAHOMA HISTORICAL SOCIE

GUTHRIE, APRIL 22, 1889

OKLAHOMA CITY, APRIL 24, 1889

OKLAHOMA HISTORICAL SOCIE

SOD HOUSE, CHEROKEE STRIP

SAM HOUSTON HOME, WAGONER COUNTY

HISTORIC AMERICAN BUILDING SURV

WHITE : WPA

SPRING HOUSE AT SALINA; OLDEST WHITE SETTLEMENT
BUILDING STILL STANDING

OLD MILLSTONES
AT DWIGHT MISSION, NEAR SALLISAW

WHITE : WPA

OKLAHOMA HISTORICAL SOCIET

SEMINOLE COUNCIL HOUSE, WEWOKA, 1870

CREEK CAPITOL, OKMULGEE, TODAY

WHITE : WP

OKLAHOMA HISTORICAL SOCIETY

CHICKASAW CAPITOL AT TISHOMINGO

OLD CHEROKEE FEMALE SEMINARY BUILDING
(NOW PART OF NORTHEASTERN STATE COLLEGE, TAHLEQUAH)

WHITE : WPA

OLD CORRAL
FORT SILL

WHITE : WP

OLD CANNON AT FORT GIBSON

FORT GIBSON, RESTORED

Ardmore operates under a city manager. Incorporated as a municipality of the first class in 1899, with a mayor and aldermen, it changed to the commission form of government in 1909. It was the second city in Oklahoma to make this change, Tulsa being the first.

POINTS OF INTEREST

The CARNEGIE LIBRARY, 502 Stanley Ave., a two-story gray stone building, is the successor to a reading room for young men provided in 1895 out of funds collected by a committee of citizens. It has now (1941) more than 26,000 books in its stacks.

In 1904, Mrs. Hosea Townsend started the movement for a library and wrote to Andrew Carnegie stating Ardmore's need. He gave $15,000, and work on the present library was started. The building was opened in 1906, its first accessions being 350 books begged and bought by the women of the Orio Club. Not until 1919 did the city appropriate sufficient funds to increase materially the collection by purchase, but within two years thereafter there were 12,500 books on the shelves. Funds for additional improvements to the library were provided in 1941. A MUSEUM *(free)*, on the first floor of the library, has on display a small collection of documents and relics of historic interest relating to southern Oklahoma history, and also geological and biological specimens.

ST. PHILLIPS CHURCH *(open to visitors)*, E St. and McLish Ave., built in 1927, is an interesting adaptation of the Gothic design of Merton College, Oxford University, England. Built of Missouri limestone, it is a small church seating only 250 worshipers. The stained glass windows—over the altar, in the west end wall, and in the side walls—tell the story of the ascension of Christ: Christ as the Good Shepherd, Saint Paul before Agrippa, and the Angel with the Faithful Women before Christ's empty tomb.

In the belfry of the Gothic type FIRST PRESBYTERIAN CHURCH, C St. and Broadway, is a chime of 11 bells, said to be the first to be installed in Oklahoma. The largest of the bells, weighing 2,500 pounds, can be rung independently.

The YMCA BUILDING, A St. and Broadway, dedicated in 1938, is a small structure of cream brick, beautifully proportioned, modernistic in design and decoration. There are no rooms for rent, and no classes are conducted in the building; the interior—drawing room, two small parlors, banquet room–auditorium in the basement, and kitchenette—is finished and furnished like a club. The building was made possible by a generous contribution by Mrs. Edward T. Noble, supplemented by those of other citizens of Ardmore.

The CARTER COUNTY COURTHOUSE, 1st Ave. between A and B Sts., S.W., is a solid, square building of gray limestone, adorned with tall, massive pillars in front, topped by a dome which is one of the first objects to attract the eye as one approaches Ardmore.

The CITY HALL, South Washington St. at 1st Ave., S.W., is a buff brick structure of modern design.

The FEDERAL BUILDING, 100 N. Washington St., typical of the strictly utilitarian structures built in the 1920's, is of plain brown brick with white trim. It houses the Federal District Court and the post office.

The AMERICAN LEGION HUT, 3d Ave. and Washington St., is the former station of the Ardmore-Ringling railroad, which was taken over by the Santa Fe. Abandoned by the railroad, the property reverted to the city and was turned over to the George R. Anderson post of the Legion on a long-term, dollar-a-year lease in 1940. The renovated building is used as a clubhouse by the war veterans, and also provides quarters for the county draft board and the Red Cross.

The DOUGLAS HIGH SCHOOL (for Negroes), at the eastern edge of the city, a brown brick structure with white trim built in 1917, occupies a site that overlooks the city. Native oak trees, trimmed to fit into the landscaping, give dignity to the school grounds.

The OLD 700 RANCH HOUSE, G St. and 2d Ave., S.E., the first building on the site of Ardmore and the first in the county, has been so altered through the years that only a small part of it remains in its original state. As built, it was a double log house, with a breezeway between the two sections. Old-time Ardmoreites remember when it was headquarters of the ranch on which the city was built, with corrals and outbuildings back of it on the small creek to the south, and with bluestem grass growing near by "as high as a man on horseback." The house, now in the Negro section, is occupied by a Negro family.

POINTS OF INTEREST IN ENVIRONS

Oak Hill Farm, *9.6 m.;* Oil Springs, *25 m. (see Tour 6);* Lake Murray State Park, *3.9 m.;* Turner Falls Park, *14.1 m.;* Price's Falls, *22.2 m.* (*see Tour 10*).

Bartlesville

Railroad Station: Union Depot, 200 W. 2d St., for Atchison, Topeka & Santa Fe Ry. and Missouri-Kansas-Texas R.R.
Bus Station: Union Terminal, 406 Dewey St.
Airport: Commercial, 3.5 m. E. on Tuxedo Rd. (county highway); Phillips Petroleum Field, 1.2 m. W. on US 60.
City Bus Lines: Fare 10c, two for 15c.
Taxis: Fare 15c.

Accommodations: 4 hotels; rooming houses; tourist camps.

Information Service: Chamber of Commerce, 121 W. 3d St.

Newspapers: Morning Examiner and *Bartlesville Enterprise,* evening.
Motion Picture Houses: 3.
Athletics: Baseball, softball, football at Municipal Stadium, 1st St. and Dewey Ave.; seating capacity 3,000.
Wrestling: "The Bowl," 305 Short St., Friday evenings in winter.
Swimming: Sanipool, 120 N. Seneca St., fee 15c for children, 25c for adults.
Golf: Osage Hills, 2 m. W., greens fee 50c; Sunset Course, 3 m. N.W., greens fee 50c.
Tennis: Municipal courts, 1st St. at Osage Ave.; S. edge of city; free.

BARTLESVILLE (694 alt., 16,267 pop.), seat of Washington County, is the center of a productive agricultural region and headquarters for important oil interests. The city claims a greater percentage of college graduates among its inhabitants than any other city in Oklahoma. Though this is not susceptible of proof from available statistics, it is true that university men have been drawn to Bartlesville in large numbers by the U.S. Bureau of Mines experimental station and laboratory, with sixty workers; the Phillips Petroleum Company's research laboratories, employing 190 persons; the head offices of four important major oil companies; and the office and factory of a company that supplies unique oil well equipment.

One other distinction claimed by Bartlesville is that it leads the state in percentage of income tax payers, having one taxable income for every fifteen inhabitants. The explanation is that a large number of its people are executives of companies that produce more than 10 per cent of all the oil brought to the surface in the United States; and much wealth has been drawn into the city by the six thousand wells of the shallow field early developed in Washington County.

Bartlesville is a spreading, tree-shaded city of wide streets, with an air of newness and prosperity. Its eastern end occupies a loop of the Caney River, a section that is sometimes flooded, but the main part of the city lies on high ground to the west. Its skyline is broken by three business buildings that rise well above the half-dozen blocks of stores and offices at the center. Beyond, westward, industrial plants and workmen's homes have reached out to the edge of the blackjack hills of the Osage country. At the city's southern edge is a river shelf on which have been built many fine homes, and a high school plant that is (1941) the finest and most modern in the state. Below this bench are the Caney River bottoms, where in the fall pecans from native trees drop in the backyards.

Founder, and for a considerable time chief owner, a trader named Jake Bartles was the third white man to move into Coo-wee-scoo-wee District of the old Cherokee Nation. The town, named for him, had its birth in 1877 when Bartles quit his original store location at Silver Lake, six miles to the southeast, at that time the site of the Osage Indian Agency, and built the first flour mill in Indian Territory on the bank of the Caney River in what is now the northeastern quarter of the city.

An enterprising pioneer, Bartles had married the daughter of Charles Journeycake, a consecrated native preacher and chief of one remnant of the Delaware tribe of Indians that had been granted equal rights in the Cherokee Nation. This had given him, as an "adopted" citizen, the right to live and trade among the Cherokees. Then, in order to catch the trade of the Osage Indians, to whom a reservation (carved out of Cherokee lands) had been given five years before, he removed to what he thought was the edge of that reservation. It turned out, later, that the border was several miles to the west, but Bartles stuck to his mill and store on the Caney, and within a year he had hauled in a dynamo and was producing the first electric light to glow in Oklahoma.

Bartles prospered. When, in 1880, Jim French and his two stepsons drove down from Kansas with wagons and four-mule teams to establish the first freight line in that section of Indian Territory, the store and camp had become a town.

Another pioneer, Nelson Carr, a white man from Kansas who married into the Cherokee tribe, had preceded Bartles on the Caney and had constructed a small gristmill for grinding corn in 1868. But he sold out to Bartles and disappeared from local history.

Two other early comers are given almost equal credit with Bartles for fanning the town's life spark into a steady blaze; William Johnstone and George B. Keeler, partners, opened a store across the river from Bartles in 1884 and became vigorous rivals of the founder for the Indian trade. Keeler, though a young man, had had experience with the old Chouteau trading dynasty, was an expert in the sign language, and spoke Osage fluently; and for a time he had served as clerk in Bartles' store. Keeler's partner, Johnstone, had also married into the Journeycake family and had also clerked in Bartles' store. Before the coming of oil, the partners were occupied with storekeeping, cattle, and sawmills; walnut lumber from the Caney and Verdigris river bottoms was turned out by the mills and had a good market. After the town began to grow they erected buildings for rental. The first telephone line, linking the two stores with Caney, Kansas, was built in 1897.

After it became possible, in 1898, for townsites to be platted and lots sold, legally, these pioneers reincorporated the settlement, which they had previously organized under Arkansas law. It was not until 1898 that a railroad (the Santa Fe) came; it built in on the grade surveyed and leveled from Caney, Kansas, twenty miles to the north, by Bartles' men. When the tracks went down, the inveterate town-building Bartles moved north four miles to establish the town of Dewey *(see Tour 9)* in honor of the hero of Manila Bay. To that site he hauled his original store and residence at Silver Lake, and also the newer two-story residence he had built near his mill on the Caney.

A second railroad, the Missouri-Kansas-Texas, came to Bartlesville in 1903. By this time the extensive shallow oil field had become important from the eastern Osage border to, and beyond, the Verdigris River. Then the first deep oil-bearing stratum in the Mid-Continent field was discovered and called the Bartlesville sand. In 1901, H. V. Foster established the Indian Territory Illuminating Oil Company, which, under the more familiar title ITIO, twenty-seven years later brought in the discovery well at Oklahoma City and developed into one of the major companies maintaining its chief offices at Bartlesville.

Natural gas, incident to the production of oil, became available and its cheapness as fuel was the deciding factor in bringing a zinc smelter to the southwestern edge of town in 1906. Two more smelters were built, and then a pottery for making the retorts used in the zinc smelting process. Uncertainty in the market for zinc, however, has caused many partial or complete shutdowns of these smelters, and they have seldom run to capacity.

Bartlesville has twelve modern schools with a total enrollment of more than four thousand, a church membership of 7,500, and a large Sunday School enrollment. There is a Town Hall discussion club with a membership of three hundred, a Little Theater Guild, and a Co-operative Concert Association, which brings three outstanding musical attractions to the city each season.

POINTS OF INTEREST

The CIVIC CENTER, Johnstone Ave. between 6th and 7th Sts., was built in 1922 as a memorial to the Bartlesville men who lost their lives in the first World War. Under its spacious roof are quarters for city officials, the American Legion (James H. Teel Post No. 105), the Red Cross, an auditorium with seats for 2,000 persons, and the Public Library. This library is one of the oldest in the state, having been established in 1913. More than 60 per cent of the city's population are borrowers from its stock of 25,000 books; and more than 50 per cent of the readers choose nonfiction.

PHILLIPS PETROLEUM COMPANY RESEARCH LABORATORY *(no visitors),* Jennings Ave. at 6th St., is a windowless glass-brick structure, where the 190 employees are engaged in the study of hydrocarbons in petroleum, and in the working out of problems which arise in connection with such varied oil production as that from the old "stripper" fields adjacent to Bartlesville (where a water repressuring method to stimulate oil flow when natural gas pressure no longer exists has been found feasible) and the deep wells of the Oklahoma City and south Texas fields. In some aspects, its work is similar to that of the Bureau of Mines state laboratory, and in others it is supplementary.

WASHINGTON COUNTY MEMORIAL HOSPITAL, at the eastern end of 3d St., was erected in 1921 at a cost of $225,000. It is thoroughly modern in equipment and personnel.

SENIOR HIGH–JUNIOR COLLEGE, 18th St. on Hillcrest Drive, with a 1940 enrollment of 492 in Senior High and 104 in Junior College, is one of the newest and most modern and complete small-city school plants in the country. The two buildings are strikingly modern in plan and fenestration. The white façade, curved in design, with low windows and rounded corners, is ornamented only by the name of the school prominently carved across the front. Here can be seen in operation in classroom and shops the "6-4-4" city plan of education. That is, six years in the elementary school, four years in junior high (7th to 10th grades inclusive), and four years in senior high and junior college (grades 11 to 14 inclusive).

The school was erected at a cost of $500,000, the Federal government contributing $225,000, the city an equal amount, and the other $50,000 being given by Frank Phillips, head of the Phillips Petroleum Company. With the opening of this school in 1940, the older Bartlesville Central High School, at 9th St. and Cherokee Ave., became the junior high school, with an attendance of 1,270.

The MUNICIPAL STADIUM, Dewey Ave. and 1st St., is a complete athletic plant with baseball and softball diamonds, cinder track and field equipment, and a football gridiron, where high school football games are played. Constructed in 1930 at a cost of $40,000, its concrete stands have a seating capacity of 3,000.

JOHNSTONE PARK, through which the Caney River makes an almost perfect horseshoe loop, is Bartlesville's largest and most accessible picnic area and playground, its 80 acres lying at the northern edge of the city. In the development of the park, the fine old native trees were made the main feature, and further planting was designed to retain the appearance of a natural forest. A shelter house, surrounded by a landscaped and flower-planted area, is near the largest of the picnic spaces. DISCOVERY WELL, in the park, was drilled as the result of talk of oil that had persisted in the neighborhood since George Keeler found a seepage in 1875. The drill rig was hauled from an abandoned location between Red Fork and Tulsa. It took two weeks to get it over the 70 miles of muddy winter roads—"fourteen days with fourteen teams," as oil historians have put it. Drilling began late in January, 1897; gas was found at 1,252–1,275 feet, and the Bartlesville oil sand was first tapped at 1,303 feet. At 1,320 feet, on April 15, the well was shot with nitroglycerin and came in with an initial flow of more than 30 barrels a day. Because of lack of transportation facilities, it was shut in for a time.

Later the well was deepened to 1,345 feet, shot again, and began producing at the rate of 30 barrels a day. In 1932, it was found that the original pipe had corroded and was letting so much water into the well that it was flooded out. With new pipe, it again became a producer. Now (1941), more than four decades after it was drilled, its yield is somewhat less than a barrel a day.

The PETROLEUM EXPERIMENT STATION *(not open to visitors),* Virginia and Cudahy Aves., was opened in 1918 as a joint undertaking of the U.S. Bureau of Mines and the state of Oklahoma. Its purpose is to secure increased efficiency and safety "in the production, refining, and handling of petroleum, natural gas and their products," and to conserve such natural resources "by developing and promoting methods for eliminating unnecessary waste in the petroleum industry." With its 60 experts and administrative personnel, it is the largest of six similar stations in the United States. Its technical library contains more than 4,600 volumes.

POINTS OF INTEREST IN ENVIRONS

Round Mountain, *1.8 m.;* Osage Hills State Park, *11.4 m.;* Frank Phillips Ranch, *12 m.* (*see Tour 4*); Bar Dew Lake, *5 m.;* Silver Lake Agency, *5.1 m.* (*see Tour 9*).

Enid

Railroad Stations: 728 N. Independence Ave. for St. Louis–San Francisco RY.; 722 N. Independence Ave. for Atchison, Topeka & Santa Fe Ry.; 115 E. Market Ave. for Chicago, Rock Island & Pacific Ry.
Bus Stations: 119 W. Maple Ave. for Kansas & Oklahoma Trailways and Panhandle Stages; 124 E. Maple Ave. for Red Ball Bus Lines.
Airport: Woodring Airport, 3 m. E. on US 64; no scheduled service.
City Busses: Junction for all routes at Public Square, fare 5c.
Traffic Regulations: Traffic lights in business section, see signs for turns permitted and parking limits.

Accommodations: 6 hotels; tourist camps on every highway.

Information Service: Hotel Youngblood, N.W. Independence Ave. and Maple Ave.

Radio Station: KCRC (1390 kc.).
Motion Picture Houses: 5.
Baseball: Semiprofessional, Champlin Stadium, 1 m. W. of city; softball, baseball, night games, at Phillips University Fields E. edge of city on US 64.
Swimming: Government Park, 501 E. Oklahoma Ave., fee 25c; Lake Hellums, 6 m. N.W. on US 81, fee 15c.
Golf: University Lake Golf Course, 400 S. 22d St., 9 holes, greens fee 25c; Country Club, 2 m. S. of City on US 81, 9 holes, greens fee 25c.
Tennis: Free courts at all city parks.

Annual Events: County Fair, fall; Industrial Fair, spring; Tri-State Band Tournament, spring; Celebration of Opening of Cherokee Strip, Sept. 16 and week following.

ENID (1,246 alt., 28,081 pop.), the largest city of north central Oklahoma, ranking fourth in size in the state and third in industry, is in the old Cherokee Outlet. It is the center of the state's wheat growing, processing, and marketing industry; the seat of Phillips University and the Southwestern Bible College. Serving three minor oil fields, it is also the home of refineries with a capacity of more than twenty-one thousand barrels of crude oil daily, and of oil-well supply and equipment companies. An Army Air Corps basic flying school was completed at Enid at the end of 1941 as a unit in the national defense program. Built at a cost of $2,870,000, it provides for a personnel of 2,600.

Enid has grown from the tent city which sprang out of the prairie dust on the day of the Strip opening, September 16, 1893, to a typically prosperous, self-contained municipality. Its business section lies on a gently shelving hill, from which the clean and spacious residential streets stretch out. A fourteen-story hotel and two office buildings, eleven and fifteen stories high, modern and utilitarian in design, give the business section a big-city appearance. Fronting the public square are the older business structures, while the newer buildings are spread around in every direction. Fifty-four church organizations occupy forty-one buildings, of which six are for Negro worshipers; and the city's schools have an enrollment of nearly six thousand students.

This "Queen City of the Cherokee Strip" and seat of Garfield County's government began life some time before the historic day of the opening as a watering place for nomadic Indians and stagecoach teams. It successfully avoided having the name Skeleton thrust upon it (from its proximity to the head of Skeleton Creek) and acquired its real name from an official of the Rock Island Railroad who was fond of Tennyson's "Idylls of the King" and felt that Geraint's wife ought to be honored by having a city named for her.

Enid had been chosen as the site of a government land office in the Cherokee Strip in advance of the opening, and government surveyors and troops moved in approximately a year before in order to run section lines and plat townsites.

On that opening day in 1893, it was discovered that certain enterprising Cherokee Indians, with profit in mind, had chosen allotments within the area planned for the town. Discovery of the scheme caused Secretary of the Interior Hoke Smith to order the townsite located three miles south of the original settlement around the railroad station. Consequently, with the government land office, the county courthouse, and the post office separated from the depot, rivalry between the north and south sections developed into a feud. Each claimed the name of Enid, and the other (depending upon which faction one belonged to) was tagged a suburb, North or South Enid. The Rock Island had refused to recognize the government's ruling, continuing to run its trains through South Enid without stopping, when on July 13, 1894, a freight train went off the tracks into a ditch near South Enid. Investigation brought about the discovery that the bridge supports had been weakened by sawing. Rock Island officials announced that while the company would respect any law the government might enact, it would not surrender to mob action. Secretary Smith's decision was upheld, however, by a presidential proclamation, and on September 16, 1894, a freight and ticket office was established in South Enid, which became the present city. A six-foot hatchet, symbol of strife, was later buried with due and proper ceremony by members of both factions.

One of the many escapades told of the rivalry between the towns concerned a massive, three-hundred-pound bell which citizens of South Enid bought and installed to warn the bucket brigade of fires endangering the town's wooden buildings. The arrival one afternoon of a finely-dressed liveryman who extolled the virtues of North Enid caused a loud clanging of the bell. This time the men who responded were also secretly organized into an "egg committee," supplied with ample overripe ammunition, and the North Enidian was turned back by a well-aimed barrage.

Enid's first celebration of the founding of the town and the opening of the Cherokee Strip was staged just one year after the actual event. Fifteen thousand were there to watch an authentic re-enactment of the race, and 150 Cheyenne Indians entertained with tribal dances and ceremonies. This same year proved unfortunate for crops, little grain being raised because of drought. Free seed wheat was supplied by the Rock Island in 1894, but this crop was a failure, as were those of 1895 and 1896, and many of the settlers moved away. In 1897, however, rains were plentiful, the harvest was good, and wheat prices shot up to $1 a bushel. To furnish entertainment for a general celebration of this turn in the community's fortunes, the Ringling Brothers' circus came to town on September 25. On that occasion, the largest crowd ever to be assembled under the Ringling "big tent," up to that time, overflowed its twenty thousand capacity to a record of thirty thousand paid admissions.

Another incident of Enid's early history which is told with gusto by its pioneers occurred in 1899 when a cakewalk contest was staged between the Negro citizens of Kingfisher and those of Enid. Bad feeling, spawned by high betting and previous athletic rivalry, broke into the open when Kingfisher was awarded the prize. Gunfire and general confusion followed, many leaping from the second-story windows of the feed store, where the event was being held. Derogatory criticism of this and other typically "Wild West" incidents brought about a determined campaign against lawlessness which shortly made a quiet, model town of Enid.

Between 1897 and 1903, two railroads, the Santa Fe and Frisco, in addition to the already existing Rock Island, were connected with Enid, laying the foundation for what it later became—the wheat and milling center for northwestern Oklahoma. The town's population rose from 3,444 in 1900 to 13,799 in 1910, a tremendous gain for this sparsely settled section.

Until the 1920's, Enid depended commercially on agriculture, trade, and shipping; then, with the discovery of the famous Tonkawa district in 1921 and the Crescent pool in 1926, both underlying the previously exploited shallow Garber pool, oil began to play an important part in the industrial life of the city. Two refineries were erected, along with the usual influx of oil supply houses, foundries, and machine shops. Flour mills and elevators in 1928 had storage facilities for fifteen million bushels of wheat. The Pillsbury Mill, largest in Oklahoma, was erected in that year.

Five days after the opening of the Cherokee Outlet to settlement, Omer K. Benedict and Charles E. Hunter, pioneer newspaper men, established Enid's first weekly, the *Eagle*. Changed to a daily, it continues as the city's evening paper. Also published in Enid are the *Morning News,* and two weeklies, *Enid Events* and *Garfield County News*.

In addition to grain and oil, poultry feed and eggs are important to Enid, representing an annual turnover of more than $8,000,000. Three packing plants in the industrial section turn out such varied products as meat, butter, canned eggs, dried buttermilk, and cheese. The stockyards do an annual business of $1,000,000; and here is one of the state's best markets for horses and mules. As a division point, the Frisco Railroad maintains at Enid large machine and car repair shops.

POINTS OF INTEREST

The new GARFIELD COUNTY COURTHOUSE, dominating the public square, is a three-story white Texas sandstone building with an additional story in the central section. Modern and functional in design, its utter simplicity makes it one of the most notable architectural achievements in the state.

A half-million dollar FEDERAL BUILDING and POST OFFICE of white marble, south of the county courthouse in the public square, was dedicated in 1941.

The ENID PROFESSIONAL ARTISTS' LEAGUE GALLERY *(free),* 105½ Independence Ave., South, shows and sells the work of its members, including architects, photographers, cartoonists, and window decorators; it also brings exhibits of worth-while art from out of town. The three regular exhibits during the year are opened by talks on art.

The CARNEGIE LIBRARY, with more than 30,000 volumes, is the only city-county library in the state. It has outgrown the building erected with a gift of $25,000 from Andrew Carnegie and dedicated in 1910; plans for a new one are now (1941) being considered. The library had its origin in the Enid Study Club, organized in 1899 to establish a reading room. Its first quarters were in a room over a drugstore, where, with money raised from a "book social," a collection of 150 books was made available for readers. Five years later, the founders' offer to turn this nucleus of a library over to the municipality was rejected because, in the opinion of the city fathers, the Study Club was a "silk stockinged" group. However, it was taken over in 1905 and efforts to obtain a grant from Carnegie were begun. Mr. Carnegie's first offer of $10,000 was rejected as too small, but when he raised it to $25,000 the present site was purchased.

Among the library's special collections are the Southard shelves of rare books, a D.A.R. historical and genealogical niche, and a large amount of Oklahoma material, including more than 700 volumes by the state's authors and thousands of clippings from newspapers and other sources. There is a branch library in the Booker T. Washington School for Negroes.

PILLSBURY FLOUR MILL *(open 10–11:30 daily; guides)*, 515 E. Spruce St., has a capacity of 4,000 barrels of flour per day. Built in 1928, it has operated almost continuously since that date on a 24-hour schedule. Visitors are taken to the top by elevator, then they walk back through the various departments and levels to the ground floor.

GOVERNMENT SPRINGS PARK, Broadway and Market Sts., was perhaps the most noted stopping place on the Chisholm Trail. The springs did not furnish enough water for stock but there was usually an ample supply in Skeleton Creek, two miles east, and the trail drivers grazed the cattle to the creek while they themselves rested at the springs. The park received its name when government surveyors camped there while surveying the townsite and section lines.

The old drinking hole has been cleaned out and walled in, and today the springs supply a small lake with water. North of the lake are picnic grounds with all accommodations, and across the street from the lake are the Sunken Gardens, planted with all varieties of native flowers. The park contains a munipical swimming pool and bathhouse.

PHILLIPS UNIVERSITY, coeducational, east of Government Springs Park at the eastern edge of the city, was chartered October 11, 1906, as Oklahoma Christian University. Seven years later, after the death of T. W. Phillips, of Butler, Pennsylvania, whose generosity made possible the founding of the school, its name was changed to honor him. It is controlled by the Christian Church (Disciples of Christ) and dedicated to Christian education, but proclaims itself nonsectarian. Of its more than 700 students some 300 are enrolled in the Bible School; the faculty numbers 44.

The campus embraces 36 landscaped acres planted with growing trees and shrubbery. There are seven college buildings, including a recently erected women's dormitory, and a stadium seating 2,000.

Within the university, and planned to promote educational activities beyond the regular day schedule, New College offers evening classes and short courses and provides for "interest groups" and conferences. New College courses and conferences are designed for high school graduates unable to attend day classes at the university, adults who wish to continue their education, groups of young people seeking trade and professional training, and persons interested in practical arts and crafts and in mechanical and manual skills.

Music is emphasized at the university, where musical organizations include the band *(see Music),* the String Ensemble, Women's Trio, Men's Quartet, Glee Club, Woodwind Quintet, Brass Quartet, Saxophone Sextet, and Convocation Choir. In the Main Building, third floor, is an extensive INDIAN COLLECTION, a zoological collection of insects, snakes, mounted birds, and shells; cases here are filled with botanical specimens from Oklahoma, New Mexico, Arizona, Colorado, Nevada, and California.

LAKE VIEW ASSEMBLY GROUNDS *(picnicking, bathing, fishing, golf),* lying just south of the Phillips University Stadium, is a tract of 77 acres containing a spring-fed lake encircled by a golf course. Enid's annual Easter morning service is held here. To the south lies the 160-acre farm given to the university in 1919 by Harry H. Rogers.

NORTHERN OKLAHOMA HOSPITAL *(open 1–4 weekdays),* N.E. edge of the city on 26th St., founded in 1910, is the state's only institution for the care of feeble-minded children. The thousand and more patients are housed in 21 buildings on a 687-acre tract. Regular school instruction and training in the crafts are given by the hospital's staff of 98. The large dairy herd is under the management of a graduate of the Oklahoma Agricultural and Mechanical College.

POINTS OF INTEREST IN ENVIRONS

Wild Fowl Hunting Grounds, *8.1 m.;* Meno, largest Mennonite community in Oklahoma, *18.2 m.* (*see Tour 4*).

Lawton

Railroad Stations: Railroad and C Ave. for Chicago, Rock Island & Pacific Ry.; 4th St. and F Ave. for St. Louis–San Francisco Ry.
Bus Stations: Oklahoma Transportation Co., 428 C Ave.; Santa Fe Trailways, 421 C Ave.; Lawton–Fort Sill Bus Co., 202 C Ave.
Airport: 2100 S. 6th St.
Taxis: 10c first 10 blocks; 5c each 10 blocks thereafter.
Traffic Regulations: Parking meters in downtown section.

Accommodations: 6 hotels; rooming houses; tourist camps.

Information Service: Chamber of Commerce, Warren Hotel, 302 C Ave.

Radio Station: KSWO (1150 kc.).

Newspapers: *Lawton Constitution,* daily, evening; *Press,* daily, morning; *News Review,* weekly.
Motion Picture Houses: 5.
Athletics: High School (Roosevelt) Stadium, Bell Ave. and 14th St., for football.
Swimming: Stephens Pool, 804 S. 2d St.; Meadows Pool, 2 Lee Blvd.; Lost Bridge Pool, 2 m. S. of city. Fees at all: adults 25c, children 10c.
Golf: Lawton Golf and Country Club, 2 m. N. on Ft. Sill Blvd., greens fee 35c.
Tennis: Lincoln and Union Parks, 5th to 8th Sts. at I Ave.; Mattie Beal Park, between 9th and 11th Sts. and I and Park Ave.; Harmon Park between 13th and 14th Sts. and Lake and Bell, all free.

Annual Events: Pioneer Day, Aug. 6; Easter morning sunrise services, Wichita Mountain Wildlife Refuge 17.4 m. N.W. (*see Tour 3B*).

LAWTON (1,116 alt., 18,055 pop.), seat of Comanche County, known as the "Post City" from its nearness to Fort Sill *(see Tour 3A),* was named in honor of Major General Henry W. Lawton, who was killed in the Philippines in 1900. It came into being on August 6, 1901, six days after the opening by lottery of the three-million-acre Kiowa-Comanche Indian reservation to white settlers. The site had been designated by the United States Land Office as one of the three county seats to be established; Hobart *(see Tour 12)* in Kiowa County and Anadarko *(see Tour 3)* in Caddo County were the others. Lawton drew an overnight population of ten thousand. Mostly it was made up of men, with their families, who had failed to secure 160-acre homesteads in the lottery of August 1 and came to the townsite in the hope of bidding successfully at the sale of lots.

By August 3, in anticipation of the sale, four hundred temporary business structures, nearly all tents, had been raised; a newspaper, The *Lawton State Democrat,* was being printed; and three streets had been laid out.

The sale of the lots platted on the 320-acre townsite realized $414,845, of which some $125,000 was turned over by the government to meet the expenses of the new town. By the first of March, 1902, five banks were in operation, with deposits of $635,000; a railroad was building in from the north; and although some of the 1,119 inhabitants were still sleeping out of doors, in general the town was adequately "housed, fed and watered."

In brief, Lawton telescoped into a period of months the pioneer phase of a western town which usually extended over years. Until 1930 its progress was steady but not spectacular. Then, largely owing to the expansion of Fort Sill as the principal Artillery School of Fire for the army, a rapid growth began. Between 1930 and 1940 the percentage of population increase—49 per cent—was greater than that of any other Oklahoma city, and its numerical increase—5,934—was exceeded only by Oklahoma City's 19,128. With some 8,300 permanently located active and service troops at Fort Sill and additional consignments sent there for training under the new defense program, there has been an increasingly heavy demand for houses and the incidentals of living from officer-instructors and noncommissioned officers who choose to live in Lawton.

The older part of Lawton is on the second bench of land that rises from the western bank of Cache Creek. In its growth, the city has pushed higher up the slope, toward the north and northwest. Its business section consists of blocks of low brick buildings, and the people seen on its downtown streets represent a true cross section of Oklahoma—white farmers, Indians (some women wearing shawls), Negroes, clerks, professional men. The one different note are the soldiers, on leave from near-by Fort Sill. In the variety of residences, ranging from the shacks of Negroes (who make up approximately 10 per cent of the population) in the south end to expensive homes along Fort Sill Boulevard, the city is typical of Oklahoma, too. Lawton has the arid, clean-swept look of western municipalities, though trees are plentiful in some of the older sections.

The city's initial and permanent growth was helped by the fact that it lay under the shadow of Fort Sill and became a sort of civic center for that important army post. It is also the metropolis of an extensive farming area (there are 2,826 farms in Comanche County), with cotton the principal crop. Among its fifteen industrial plants is one of the big cottonseed-oil mills of the state. To serve the region, the city has forty-five wholesale and 326 retail businesses; at its western edge is Cameron State Agricultural College, the largest junior college in Oklahoma, and within an hour's drive lie many of the finest scenic spots in the state.

Also contributing to Lawton's growth has been the development of near-by profitable deposits of asphalt, and mountains of granite and other building stone. It is said that out of the Lawton neighborhood could be taken enough road building material to pave every road in the state—with a lot left over.

The senior high school is undertaking an interesting experiment in co-operation with Lawton business men; industrial apprentice training is given to a selected group of students who attend classes in the morning and work at jobs which pay $2.00 and $3.00 a week in the afternoons. Each is assigned to a "trainer," who directs his education.

Last of Oklahoma cities to be born, overnight, out of the dust and clamor of an Indian reservation opening, Lawton had among its first settlers many who were aware of the color and drama of its birth and first days. Don Blanding, a poet of recognized talent, wrote in "Prairie Days":

> Lawton, the new town, sprang from the prairie land,
> Grew as a mushroom grows . . .
> All night long the hammers sounded . . .
> Houses grew in the flare of kerosene torches.

As the men streamed in looking for shade, with rolls of currency to pay for town lots in sweat-drenched pants pockets, they saw the lone oak tree on the site; they saw F. M. English's bank—a one-room frame shack—poised on rollers, ready to be wheeled to the lot he meant to buy at the sale; they saw an enterprising citizen take in $500 in dimes for registering intended bidders for lots at ten cents apiece; they heard over and over the cry of "stop thief!" from men and women whose purses were snatched, and the more ominous mutterings of men whose teams were stolen; and they were half choked in the dust raised by water haulers who brought clear, tepid water from Cache Creek and retailed it at five cents a cup until competition forced the price down to fifty cents, then twenty-five cents a barrel.

In the volume called *Neath August Sun,* initiated and assembled by Lawton's business and professional women (not dated), is the picture of that August 6 lot sale in the words of scores of persons who were there. The government auctioneer stood on a dry-goods box beside a big tent and hour after hour and day after day cried the lots beginning at the northern limits of the platted townsite. When he shouted "Sold!" a soldier escorted the successful bidder between lines of other soldiers and into the tent. There, he was given title to his lot if he paid down the amount of its purchase price in cash. In case he did not have the whole amount with him, he could pay $25 to hold the property for thirty minutes.

That provision was to allow him time to reach one of the two banks —Mr. English's and another—which had undertaken to receive and safeguard money, but it sometimes happened that thirty minutes was not time enough for a lot-buyer to work his way down the line of men waiting to withdraw deposits. In that case, the $25 was forfeited to the government, and the lot was resold. In the collection of stories is one of a man who bought a lot for $850, paid his $25, then ran to the bank for the rest. Luckily, after seeing it was hopeless to wait in line, he spotted a good friend inside the chicken-wire cage where four men were working to record withdrawals and hand out currency. To him he appealed, and presently $1,000 in bills was made into a package and tossed over the fence. The first lot sold brought $420, and the top price was $4,555, for the lot opposite the land office.

It is told, too, how a man named Woods, number one in the reservation land lottery, selected a homestead in a strip a mile long and a quarter of a mile wide alongside the Lawton townsite, instead of taking the usual half-mile square. Thus he shut off from the townsite frontage Mattie Beal, the young lady who had drawn number two, and was promptly nicknamed "Hog" Woods. In spite of this deprivation due to Woods' lack of gallantry, Miss Beal received in a space of weeks five hundred proposals of marriage from all parts of the United States, so widely had the news of her second most valuable homestead drawing been published. She finally chose as her husband Charles Payne, a young businessman who had openly professed to having no interest whatever either in Miss Beal or her 160 acres.

There was a "ragtown" Lawton with a "ragtown" restaurant named the Goo-Goo (later Smith's Dining Room), after the avenue of the same name. That was the summer when young men learned from a woman singer with a wagon show the words of "When you make dem goo-goo eyes at me!" And at the Goo-Goo restaurant, if a client dared to order a moderate priced steak, the waiter called back to the kitchen, "One for the dog!" Another sign, put up in a saloon, served to recall the famous crusader of the day, "All nations welcome here except CARRIE."

Described as a "rollicking, hilarious tent and shack city," Lawton had eighty-six saloons—one for every one hundred inhabitants—in November, 1901. Gambling joints grew so numerous that a volunteer committee of citizens swept them out. The first serious fire, threatening to destroy the town, was held in check by hundreds of men and women with wetted quilts and blankets, backed by a bucket brigade supplied by frantically galloping water haulers; and the first big town celebration—a slightly delayed first birthday fete—was a bull fight, with authentic Spanish toreador costumes, plus an Apache Indian dance, in costume too, staged by the distinguished prisoner at Fort Sill, old Geronimo.

For a time the nearest railroad station was Marlow, on the Rock Island; and initiated travelers to Lawton used to leave the cars by the windows in order to rush out and engage a wagon and team to haul their goods and themselves across the prairie to the new town. Many ambitious businessmen from the East, compelled to camp out overnight, trembled at the coyotes' crazy combination of howling and barking.

Among the town's first settlers were two men who became United States senators, Thomas P. Gore and Elmer Thomas; Scott Ferris, who served in the United States House of Representatives; and Jake L. Hamon, the city's first attorney, who wrote his name large in the story of oil development in southern Oklahoma, and was for a time Oklahoma Republican National Committeeman. It has also been recorded that Heck Thomas, the first town peace officer and a well-known outlaw-catcher, once chased Lon Chaney (then a Lawton photographer) for speeding—on horseback!

POINTS OF INTEREST

The CARNEGIE LIBRARY, 5th St. and C. Ave., is a small, neat building of buff brick erected in 1921 with $30,000 from the Carnegie fund for library construction.

In 1903, the second year of the town's existence, a library committee of the City Federation of Women's Clubs was appointed and a fund started for the purchase of books. The merchants of Lawton offered 178 books as a prize to the organization having the greatest number of votes—one vote being allowed for each ten-cent purchase; then another group raised the award to 372 books given under the same condition. With these as a nucleus and an additional sixty-five volumes secured at a book reception by the women, the library came into being and was given to Lawton on condition that if the town failed to maintain it the books would revert to the City Federation. Two rooms on the second floor of the city hall were set aside for the library. When it was removed to its present building in 1922 it had four thousand volumes; the collection has grown (1941) to fifteen thousand.

COMANCHE COUNTY COURTHOUSE, 5th St. and C. Ave., a strikingly modern building erected with the help of WPA, was dedicated in 1939. It is a chaste, solid, three-story structure of buff sandstone, trimmed with chromium steel.

LAWTON HIGH SCHOOL BUILDING, 8th St. and E Ave., housing the senior and junior high schools, is an immense red-brick building, with white Ionic columns and a dome that attracts the eye from afar off. Architecturally, it dominates the city. A large, buff-brick annex, with additional classrooms, a gymnasium, and the school's offices, was completed in 1940.

CAMERON STATE AGRICULTURAL COLLEGE, at the western edge of the city, with an enrollment of more than 700 boys and girls and an annual budget of nearly $80,000, is Oklahoma's largest junior college. Set in the midst of 350 acres of fenced and terraced farm land are three classroom and laboratory buildings; an auditorium with seats for 1,200; a gymnasium; three dormitories for boys, two for girls, and one for married students. A modern poultry plant and a horse and dairy barn are also on the campus. The college farm supports a herd of 20 registered Holstein and Jersey cows, a drove of registered hogs, and a flock of chickens representing all the well-known breeds.

The college, named in honor of the first State Superintendent of Schools, was founded in 1909 as one of six district agricultural high schools offering work beginning with the seventh grade and extending through the twelfth. For the first two years, regular high school subjects were taught, followed by work in agriculture and home economics. The institution was raised to junior college rank in 1927.

Boxing is a favorite sport among the boys; the Cameron Aggie teams have been outstandingly successful in the State Golden Gloves boxing tournaments.

POINTS OF INTEREST IN ENVIRONS

Fort Sill Indian School, *0.8 m.;* Craterville Park, *19.6 m.;* Home of Quanah Parker, *20.6 m.* (*see Tour 3*); Fort Sill Military Reservation, *6.5 m.* (*see Tour 3A*); Medicine Park, *12.1 m.;* Wichita Mountains Wildlife Refuge, *17.4 m. (see Tour 3B).*

Muskogee

Railroad Stations: Intersection of Broadway and tracks for Missouri-Kansas-Texas R.R.; 2d and Elgin Sts. for St. Louis–San Francisco Ry. and Midland Valley R.R.
Bus Station: 201 S. 5th St. for Santa Fe Trail System and Southern Kansas Stage Lines.
Airport: Hatbox Field, 40th St. and Arline Rd.; private and chartered planes only.
City Bus Service: Fare 5c.
Taxis: 10c and upward, according to distance and number of passengers.
Traffic Regulations: Standard traffic signals in business section; parking limits and turns permitted designated by signs.

Information Service: Hotel Severs, 215 State St.

Accommodations: 9 hotels, 2 for Negroes; rooming houses and tourist cottages.

Radio Station: KBIX (1490 kc.).
Motion Picture Houses: 5, 1 for Negroes.
Baseball: Athletic Park, Boston Ave. and 5th St.
Swimming: Municipal Swimming Pool, Honor Heights Park, 40th St. and Park Blvd.; Spaulding Park, E. Okmulgee Ave. and E. Side Blvd., fees 10c.
Golf: Muskogee Town and Country Club, Club Blvd. 2.5 m. N.E. on US 62, 18 holes, greens fee $1.12; Meadowbrook Golf Club, 1.5 m. S.W. on US 64–62, 18 holes, greens fee 50c Mon.–Fri., 75c Sat. and Sun.; Grandview, 2 m. E. on Callahan Ave., 9 holes, greens fee 25c Mon.–Fri., 50c Sat. and Sun.
Tennis: Free municipal courts Spaulding Park.

Annual Events: Muskogee Free Fair, first week in Oct.; Flower Show, spring and fall.

MUSKOGEE (617 alt., 32,332 pop.), third largest city of Oklahoma, was named for the Muskogee (Creek) Indians and lies just south of the confluence of the Verdigris, Grand, and Arkansas rivers. It is surrounded by low, gently sloping hills, blending into a rich, flat-to-rolling farming section. The tracks of the Missouri-Kansas-Texas Railroad pass squarely through the town from north to south, dividing it into almost equal parts. Streets are wide and bordered by trees, and old fashioned two- and three-story houses are set far back in well-kept lawns. Many small parcels of land, such as are ordinarily eyesores in most cities, are here developed into flower gardens and parks.

Thomas Nuttall, widely traveled English naturalist and later curator of the botanical gardens of Harvard University, on a journey up the Arkansas in 1819, predicted that "if the confluence of the Verdigris, Arkansas, and Neosho [Grand] rivers shall ever become of importance as a settlement—which the great and irresistible tide of western emigration promises—a town will probably be founded here at the junction of these streams." Earlier (1805), Meriwether Lewis had recommended to President Jefferson this site for a trading point; and in 1806 James B. Wilkinson advised the government to establish a factory there, and also "a garrison of troops."

It was natural for Nuttall and others to assume that river traffic would determine the location of the town. But the importance of river transportation and river trading posts hardly increased after Nuttall's visit and became negligible as soon as railroads were built into the territory.

Before Nuttall wrote about the region, the "Three Forks" had become a center of trade and a rallying point for buyers and sellers of furs. There the traders Hugh Glenn, Nathaniel Pryor, French and Rutherford, Thompson and Drennan; Jesse B. Turley, the Creek Benjamin Hawkins, and—best known of all—Auguste P. Chouteau trafficked with the Osages who came down the Grand River from the North and the nomadic tribes that brought their peltries down the Salt Fork, the Deep Fork, and the Arkansas rivers and across the comparatively short stretch of country between "Three Forks" and the Canadian.

By 1829, emigration of Creeks from Alabama in response to United States government pressure was well under way, and some twelve hundred were located near the mouth of the Verdigris on land which turned out to be part of the Cherokee Nation. The Creeks were then moved south of the Arkansas, and their agency was established in the vicinity of Fern Mountain, some three miles northwest of Muskogee.

It was at this agency that the first settlement in the Muskogee region started. Not until 1872, when the Missouri-Kansas-Texas railroad crossed the Arkansas, and their agency was established in the vicinity of Fern Mountain, did the town itself come into being. Its first white inhabitants were those hopeful and adventurous fortune seekers who had waited in camp on the north bank of the river for the completion of the bridge; they rode the first train over, got off at the station, and began to build stores and residences on both sides of the track.

Across the site of the new town ran the old Texas Road, over which thousands of settlers had traveled southward by wagon and over which many herds of Texas cattle had been driven northward. In the neighborhood lived a few Creek Indians, but the population was predominantly Negro—Creek freedmen who had chosen the neighborhood as especially suited to their agricultural needs and knowledge.

For a considerable time after the town was established, the Creeks, officially, refused to consider it as an Indian settlement. Appealed to for protection against certain swaggering outlaw Cherokee half bloods and bad men from Texas intent on putting the Negroes "in their place," the Creek chief once instructed the head of the nation's lighthorse (police) force to assist in maintaining order in Muskogee. That officer answered that since it was a purely Negro town he could not appropriately assign any of his men to the task.

Old-timers in Muskogee are apt to point with pride to the city's steady and vigorous growth, its solid and law-abiding people, then cast back in memory to the early days, when hogs rooted and wallowed in the streets and Bradley Collins, bootlegger and bad man, amused himself by shooting them. They will tell of the time one of Bradley's shots winged a United States marshal, and how he was acquitted of blame because "it was a private quarrel and both men had sworn to shoot on sight."

Another memory of Muskogee's early days centers on the old Federal jail, the first to be erected in the Indian Territory. It stood at what is now the corner of Dennison and Third Streets and consisted of a number of wooden buildings surrounded by a twelve-foot stockade. For walls, the jail had two by six inch boards covered with sheet iron. Sometimes, before a Federal court was established at Muskogee in 1889, as many as 350 prisoners were held there at one time; and it is recorded that a number of women remained behind the board walls for two years before being removed for trial by the nearest Federal court, at Fort Smith, Arkansas.

When Muskogee was made a railroad division point the town's permanence was assured, and its importance as a business center was further enhanced by the establishment in 1874 of the Union Agency for the Five Civilized Tribes. Eufaula *(see Tour 8)* had also made a bid for the agency, and an inspector was sent from Washington to determine which of the two towns was better fitted to care for employees. On the night before his arrival, it is said that a resident of Muskogee emptied a barrel of salt into the town well at Eufaula; the inspector, after one taste of the water, decided that Muskogee should be the administrative headquarters of Indian Territory.

In contrast to this phase of Muskogee's history was the organization in 1877, when the town was still hardly more than a huddle of shacks and tents, of the International Indian Fair for the encouragement of farming and stock-growing especially among the more backward Indians of the Five Tribes and of the western Plains tribes. In a call to the people to come to the eleventh fair, F. B. Severs, a Muskogee pioneer, as president, and Joshua Ross, a Cherokee and one of the first settlers, as secretary, said those who came "must bring corn, wheat, cotton, potatoes, fruits and flowers, livestock, and works of art. In all the departments there will be lively contests for prizes, and especially in the musical department."

This annual gathering of Indians, intent on maintaining their Indian character, reached its peak of importance in the fall of 1879 when the threat of "Boomer" invasion of their unoccupied western lands had become serious. A visitor to the Fair, Secretary of the Interior Carl Schurz, inspected the exhibits, saw sales at good prices of baskets and beadwork wrought by the Plains Indians to members of the Five Civilized Tribes, and sat with them in councils in the big barn-like pavilion in which their products were shown. The Osages came to ask for the same self-governing status as the Five Civilized Tribes enjoyed; and from the far-off Chippewas came messages of encouragement.

With the amalgamation of Oklahoma's Indian and white populations, and the Indians' complete adoption of white methods, the need for such a fair passed, and it was dropped. The idea was adopted by the United States Indian Bureau for the more backward tribes living on reservations in other western states.

Climatic conditions in the Muskogee area are favorable to diversified agriculture, and many farmers drifted into the neighborhood, but tribal ownership of the land retarded development. Then, in 1894, the Dawes Commission, formed the year before to allot land to individual Indians, established headquarters in Muskogee, and the town grew rapidly. It was incorporated under the Arkansas statutes in 1898, and its first public school was attended by 235 pupils. Impetus to expansion was added by the opening of oil and gas fields in 1904. Traces of oil had been found and wells drilled within the town's limits, as far back as 1894, but until the Dawes Commission completed its work it was impossible for the white promoters to obtain valid titles to land, so development was halted.

As soon as it became possible to secure titles to land in the Indian Territory, so many white men flocked in that the supremacy of the Indians was seriously threatened. There then began a belated attempt to form the territory into an Indian state. A convention of the chiefs of the various tribes was called to meet at Muskogee in 1905, form a constitution, and complete plans for a new state which was to be called Sequoyah after the inventor of the Cherokee alphabet. However, the vision of an Indian state vanished when the Enabling Act was passed in 1906, joining Indian Territory with Oklahoma Territory to form one state *(see History)*.

In the eleven years, 1889–1900, the population of Muskogee increased from 2,500 to 4,254. Between 1900 and 1907, because of oil development, the number of inhabitants more than tripled, and by 1910, when the city charter was granted, it stood at 25,278. In that year Muskogee was larger than Tulsa by some six thousand persons, and the second city in the state in size. In the next twenty years, census figures rose only to 32,025, because of the shifting of oil interests from Muskogee westward to Tulsa; and in the decade 1930–40 there was a population gain of only 306.

Throughout Muskogee's history the Negro population has been large; at present (1941) it amounts to almost 24 per cent of the total. On South Second Street, the center of the Negro business district, are the plants of three Negro newspapers—the *Muskogee Lantern*, the *Muskogee Parrot,* and the *Oklahoma Independent*—and the main office of the state's largest Negro insurance company. Negroes are largely employed in domestic service, as workers in near-by cotton fields, and in certain minor industries. They have provided for themselves schools, churches, amusement places, apartment houses, and clubs.

During the 1900's, three important oil fields were opened in the Muskogee area; the town gained three new railroads—the Frisco, the Midland Valley, and the Kansas, Oklahoma & Gulf—and farming greatly expanded in the surrounding territory. On the Arkansas River bottom lands truck gardening has increasingly flourished, and canning is an important industry. This area is also noted for potato growing *(see Agriculture)*.

In 1917 a small iron works with only a few employees was established. The plant expanded rapidly and now manufactures derricks, transmission towers, transformer racks, road-building equipment, and steel framework. In addition to the one opened in 1917, another turns out winches, hoists, and various kinds of machinery and equipment. There are two oil refineries with a total capacity of six thousand barrels a day. Other manufacturing plants include a brick factory, a truck-body works, and railroad shops. There are a dozen wholesale supply houses. Excellent low-cost fuel, and good transportation facilities, including nine rail outlets, have given Muskogee an advantageous position for manufacturing.

As an agricultural trading center the city serves all the Arkansas River valley except those areas past midway points toward Tulsa and Fort Smith. The city ranks among the three leading cotton centers of the state, with a cottonseed-oil mill, gins, and a compress. There are also two flour mills, six produce houses, and a meat packing plant.

At the foot of Agency Hill, west of the city, is the airport, where the commercial shops and private ships are being supplemented by the United States Army's expanding program of pilot training.

Under a city manager form of government since 1920, Muskogee owns its water supply system; and the city's light and power comes from a modern plant on the Arkansas River.

Two ably edited daily newspapers, the *Phoenix* and the *Times-Democrat,* are the successors of an interesting line that runs back to 1876, when the *Indian Journal* was proposed as an instrument of the Intertribal Council. When that proposal was vetoed, the paper was started as a private enterprise under the editorship of William P. Ross, a Princeton-educated Cherokee. Its purpose was to champion the cause of all Indians and to expose the designs and personal and interested motives of those who sought to secure their land. The paper was later moved to Eufaula.

In 1882, *Our Brother in Red,* a Methodist missionary monthly, was started at Muskogee, and in 1887 it became a weekly. Like the *Indian Journal,* it had at first both English and Creek language sections; and at one time it reported a circulation of 1,820. It too regarded itself as an instrument of justice for the Indians.

The *Phoenix* was founded in 1888 by Leo E. Bennett, a young white man who had married a Creek citizen. Always friendly to the Indians, it changed from a weekly to semiweekly in 1895, and to a daily in 1901. The first daily, however, was the *Morning Times,* started in 1896, and edited for a time by a talented mixed-blood Creek poet and essayist in the vernacular, Alex Posey. Merged with an evening rival, it became the *Times-Democrat.* The next development was the consolidation under the ownership of Tams Bixby of the two surviving dailies *(see Newspapers).*

POINTS OF INTEREST

MUSKOGEE PUBLIC LIBRARY *(open 9–9 weekdays),* D St. and E. Broadway, is a two-story-and-basement structure, modified Georgian in design, of red tapestry brick and white stone trim. Erected in 1909 with the gift of $60,000 from Andrew Carnegie, the library was designed by Henry D. Whitefield, Mr. Carnegie's son-in-law. Besides its 56,000 and more books, it houses a MUSEUM OF INDIAN RELICS on the second floor; exhibits include a rare double-weave Cherokee basket, medicine man rattles, moccasins, drums, clubs, knives, arrowheads, primitive chairs, and other curios. On the same floor is an art collection; and on the library walls hang paintings, including *French War* by J. Baker, *Grand Canyon* by M. Dupree, and *After the Rain* by George F. Shultz.

The MUNICIPAL BUILDING, 3d St. and Okmulgee Ave., a three-story red-brick structure, its façade broken by five tall columns, covers a block near the business center. Besides housing the city offices, it provides a convention hall with a seating capacity of 3,500; here, in the winter season, weekly wrestling meets are held. On the first floor is a small MUSEUM of historical relics, photographs, and documents.

The million-dollar FEDERAL BUILDING, 5th St. and Broadway, is a many-windowed, four-story building of limestone that fills the block frontage on 5th St. It contains the post office, courtroom, and offices of the United States Court for the Eastern District of Oklahoma. It also houses the offices of the United States Union Agency for the Five Civilized Tribes.

Modern, with simple lines, is the COUNTY COURTHOUSE, 216 State St., a three-story, block-like structure of granite and limestone.

MUSKOGEE MUNICIPAL JUNIOR COLLEGE, 420 Dayton St., established in 1921, was the first institution of its kind in the state. It shares quarters with the old CENTRAL HIGH SCHOOL.

The ALICE ROBERTSON JUNIOR HIGH SCHOOL, S St. and Callahan Ave., is one of the most spacious and modern secondary schools in the state. Named for a member of a famous missionary family and the only woman who has represented Oklahoma in Congress, it was opened for use in 1940. It is a wide-spreading white building of two stories, square-cut in design, with its rows of wide windows broken by flat engaged columns. With its football stadium, east of the building, seating 6,500 spectators, the school occupies almost four blocks. Its erection, at a cost of $368,000, relieved the increasing pressure for space on the Central High School plant.

HONOR HEIGHTS PARK (old Agency Hill Park), 40th St. and Park Blvd., has been developed as a memorial to veterans of the first World War. Covering 20 acres of the 50 which constitute the grounds known as Agency Hill, this beautiful landscaped and watered park tumbles down the hillside in terraces, cascades, pools, flowered borders, and grassy plots to the large lake and public swimming pool at the foot of the hill. Somewhere in its colorful area, nearly every flower and shrub native to Oklahoma is planted and flourishing; and besides evergreens in profusion there are oak trees, maples, redbud, dogwood, hackberry, native and Chinese elms, plum and peach and cherry trees, which succeed the redbud and dogwood as splashes of bloom in the spring. In 1935 this park was awarded a prize of $1,000 for the most beautiful rock garden in a contest sponsored by *Better Homes and Gardens*. UNION AGENCY BUILDING, in the park, is a dignified and beautiful stone structure that was used for a time as headquarters for the government's business with the Five Tribes, and then for a school for freedmen by the Creeks. It is vacant now (1941). Near by is the site of the Alice Robertson home, "Sawokla."

UNITED STATES VETERANS' FACILITY *(open 2–4 daily)*, established as a veterans' hospital in 1923 and as a combined facility of the United States Veterans' administration in 1938, lies just south of Honor Heights Park. Its 17 buildings are set in an attractively landscaped area of 16 acres that overlook the city and the hills that rise toward the western edge of the

Ozarks. The main building, U-shaped in plan and classical in design, rises four stories above a basement; like the other principal structures, it is built of brick, terra cotta, and artificial stone.

POINTS OF INTEREST IN ENVIRONS

Japanese Garden, *5.2 m (see Tour 2);* site of old Steamboat Landing, *9.4 m.;* Fort Gibson National Cemetery, *13.1 m. (see Tour 3);* Bacone Indian College, *2.3 m.;* Three Forks Monument, *7.2 m. (see Tour 8);* New Army Air Field, *5.5 m.*

Norman

Railroad Stations: Intersection of Comanche St. and Oklahoma Ave. for Atchison, Topeka & Santa Fe Ry.; 105 W. Main St. for Oklahoma Ry. (Interurban).
Bus Station: Main St. and Santa Fe for Oklahoma Transportation Co., Santa Fe Trailways, and Greyhound.
Taxis: 15c upward, depending on distance traveled and number of passengers.

Accommodations: 2 hotels; tourist camps on highway.

Information Service: Chamber of Commerce, 132½ E. Main St.

Radio Station: WNAD (640 kc.).
Motion Picture Houses: 5.
Airport: Max Westheimer Flying Field (owned by the University of Oklahoma) 1.5 m. N.W. on State 74.
Golf: University Golf Course, E. of University, grass greens, 50c; Cedar Crest Golf Course, 2 m. S. of south city limits and 1 m. E. of US 77, sand greens, 25c; Norman Country Club, 1.5 m. E. of the city limit, sand greens, 50c.
Swimming: Crystal Lake, 1 m. N. on US 77, fees 20c for adults, 15c for children.
Annual Events: High School Field Meet, April or May. Homecoming Week, usually begins Nov. 14.

NORMAN (1,160 alt., 11,429 pop.) occupies a plateau overlooking the valley of the South Canadian River, the bed of which is about four miles southwest of the town. The surrounding land is gently rolling, most of it cultivated, with some in pasture, and there are a few trees. The city is divided in a northwest-southeast direction by the Santa Fe Railway, and this orientation has been turned to advantage. The streets of the central part of the town run northwest-southeast and southwest-northeast, and form an approximate square. Outlying streets were laid out straight with the compass. This varies the customary pattern of smaller cities, somewhat mitigates the assault of winter winds, and, to a degree, lessens the fire hazard. Fortunately there has been little effort to put as much of the town as possible upon the main highway, US 77.

Except for those that serve the population, there are practically no industries in Norman. The business life of the town is dependent upon the university and the surrounding country-trade area. The greater part of the business district, along Main Street, consists largely of establishments that cater to farmers. It differs little from the main street of any small municipality in an agricultural community; students doing their after-class shopping leave the rural pattern unaltered.

Near the university, however, a different atmosphere prevails. Here, the restaurants and other business houses subsist almost entirely on the patronage of the faculty and students.

Although the townsite originally had almost no trees, its streets today are shaded by many varieties—elm, maple, oak, locust, ash, sycamore, walnut, pecan, and other trees indigenous to Oklahoma. This is largely due to David Ross Boyd, first president of the university, a tree enthusiast, who planted thousands of saplings in spite of the popular belief that trees would not grow there, and established a nursery of his own on the campus. From this beginning the city of Norman and the grounds of the university have become notable for their shaded streets and parked spaces.

"It is not claimed for this city," said the *Norman Transcript* in 1893, "that she will ever be a great metropolis, but it is a city of homes, and one of the most desirable places of residence of which the mind can conceive." Lacking industries, the town has attracted residents through civic improvements and cultural advantages. Schools are excellent, and churches numerous.

The city owns its own water plant and has an abundant supply of deep-well water 99.6 per cent pure. In 1919 the commission form of government was adopted, and a city manager chosen. The five city commissioners serve without pay. In the years 1928–34 there was no tax levy for general government expenses as the city used revenue from its water plant, fines, licenses, and other sources; there has been no deficit in operating funds, and since 1934 the tax rate has not been above 1.25 mills.

Norman was named for a government engineer who pitched camp about eighteen miles south of the present site of Oklahoma City in 1872. Little is known of him beyond the fact that when the Atchison, Topeka and Santa Fe Railroad built through the Territory several years later, a boxcar was set out near the spot where he had camped and designated "Norman Switch." It was all that there was on the site of the present city when the Territory was opened for settlement on April 22, 1889.

The population of Norman Switch, or of Norman as it came to be called, jumped from zero on the dawn of opening day to five hundred at nightfall. On January 25, 1890, the *Norman Transcript* boasted that the community already had "two newspapers, four churches, and twenty-nine business houses of importance."

The Indian Mission Annual Conference of the Southern Methodist Church, in April, 1890, ordained that a college be established within the bounds of the newly created Oklahoma Territory; and the board of trustees was instructed to negotiate with towns interested in such a school and "to accept the bid that seemed the most advantageous."

Norman was selected, and on September 18, 1890, High Gate Female College opened its doors with an enrollment of 130. Stringent rules were laid down for the students. They were not allowed to attend places of amusement, and all correspondence with persons outside the school was subject to examination. Even a code governing the conduct of faculty members was promulgated, one rule requiring that male members, when appearing on the streets, should wear a silk tie and a Prince Albert coat. In 1892, with the opening of the university, the enrollment at High Gate decreased rapidly, and in the following year its buildings were sold to the Oklahoma Sanitarium Company. This company, which had secured a contract from Oklahoma Territory for the care of insane persons, in turn sold its property to the state in 1915. The institution, renamed the Central State Hospital, provides Norman with its second largest pay roll.

THE UNIVERSITY OF OKLAHOMA

THE UNIVERSITY OF OKLAHOMA, between Lindsay and Boyd streets, and Elm and Jenkins Avenues, occupies a grassy, tree-grown campus of 217 acres. The School of Medicine, University Hospital, and Crippled Children's Hospital are in Oklahoma City *(see Oklahoma City);* on the Norman campus there are forty-one buildings, seventeen of which are used for class work. Collegiate Gothic architecture predominates and the plant is one of the show spots of the state. Enrollment for 1940–41 in the regular sessions was 7,054; in the summer sessions, 2,497; and in the correspondence courses and service classes, 2,059. In the academic year 1939–40 a total of 12,690 persons registered for forty-four institutes and short courses of a few days. The attendance at fifty-one institutes and short courses in 1940–41 was approximately 19,500.

The university is a part of the educational system of the state *(see Education)* and is supported by legislative appropriations made biennially. It is a constituent member of the Oklahoma State System of Higher Education, supervised by the Oklahoma State Regents for Higher Education, an appointive board of nine members. Immediate supervision of the university is in charge of the University of Oklahoma Board of Regents, consisting of seven members appointed by the governor, who is also an ex officio member of the board. Sound scholarship, good citizenship, and the duties of the individual to the community and the state—briefly, these are the points emphasized in the university's teaching. Currently, its annual budget totals some $1,555,000, more than $1,250,000 of which is spent in salaries for the faculty of 301 and others employed to maintain the plant. Part of the university's annual income—an average of $80,000—is received from land endowment and the sale of school land.

In September, 1892, the university opened in a rented store building in Norman, with David Ross Boyd as its first president; the faculty consisted of four teachers; the curriculum provided for preparatory courses and two years of college work. Since there were no high schools in the Territory, it was necessary to maintain the preparatory department for fifteen years, until adequate local school systems had been built up. The first group of students numbered fifty-seven, all in the preparatory school. In 1893 a three-story-and-basement brick structure with a small tower was completed, looming starkly out of an expanse of level prairie that was still scored by the paths of game and cattle. Until destroyed by fire in 1903, this building housed the university.

Living expenses at the school were low, but not many students had the small amount of money needed. President Boyd encouraged ambitious young men and women to come anyway, and to work their way through at such jobs as were available. Few business houses in Norman could give employment, and part-time work in early years generally consisted of chores for men and housework for girls. With the growth of the city and the school, more jobs for students became available, and today about one-third of the student body is self-supporting.

The university's School of Geology, established in 1900, has graduated a number of well-known geologists. Many have played important parts in the oil industry in Oklahoma and other oil-producing states. The organizer of the school, Dr. Charles N. Gould, was for some years also head of the State Geological Survey, which operates under the Board of Regents and the president of the university. The School of Government, with a faculty of ten (1941), trains an ever-increasing number of men who take an active part in government. The first degrees from the School of Law were given in 1912 and today (1941) about half of the members of the state bar are university alumni. The School of Petroleum Engineering attracts students from all parts of the world.

The name "Sooners," applied to Oklahomans generally, is given to the athletic teams of the university, and to its publications.

As a land-grant college, the university maintains a military unit of the Reserve Officers Training Corps. The first two years of training are required; the last two, or advanced course, are elective. Between the junior and senior years, advanced students are given a six-weeks course in active service, usually at Fort Sill. In the fall of 1940, a unit of the Naval Reserve Officers' Training Corps was installed at the university.

One of the most colorful events of the year is the annual High School Field Meet, in April or May, a series of athletic, musical, and curricular contests. This event draws an attendance of thousands of high school students, who in this way become acquainted with the university.

CAMPUS TOUR

The buildings are listed in order of their location from the main entrance, University Blvd. and Boyd St. Unless otherwise stated, the buildings are open during school hours.

The PRESIDENT'S HOME is a two-story frame house of classic revival design.

HOLMBERG HALL (the Fine Arts Building), a three-story structure of concrete, brick, and stone, completed in 1918, was named for Frederik Holmberg, professor of music and dean of the College of Fine Arts.

ADMINISTRATION HALL, a collegiate Gothic, three-story structure at the head of the North Oval, is notable for its chaste decoration and fine proportions. The building contains the general administrative offices of the university, the Graduate School, the College of Arts and Sciences, and the offices, classrooms, and laboratories of the department of mathematics, philosophy, physics, and psychology.

The four-story EDUCATION BUILDING was erected in 1904 as the Carnegie Library; in 1920 it was remodeled for the College of Education and now contains the offices and classrooms of that college and the university demonstration schools.

MONNET HALL, known as the "Law Barn," is a three-story structure of white Bedford stone. It contains the offices, lecture rooms, courtroom, and library of the School of Law, the offices and library of the department of government, and the offices and museum of the department of anthropology. In the basement *(open 9–4, Mon.-Fri.)* a great many objects of archeological interest, taken from the Indian mounds near Spiro *(see Tour 7)*, are on display.

The ART BUILDING, a concrete, brick, and Algonite stone structure, was erected in 1920 as the Library Building; in 1930 it was remodeled and now houses the offices, studios, classrooms, and exhibition rooms of the School of Art. Paintings, etchings, sculpture, and items of industrial arts are on display; the exhibits are loans, for the most part, and are changed every two weeks. In this building is the MATZENE COLLECTION OF ORIENTAL ART *(open 12–5, Mon., Wed., Fri.)*, valued at more than $100,000 and including Chinese, Manchurian, Japanese, East Indian, and Persian objects of art. Indian graduates of the School of Art have attracted national attention with their authentic paintings of Indian life.

In addition to the space occupied by the department of geology, the

GEOLOGY BUILDING contains the offices, laboratories, and publication rooms of the Oklahoma Geological Survey, and the MUSEUM OF PALEONTOLOGY *(open 9–5, Mon.-Fri.)*. On display are scale models of plant and animal life of the Devonian and Jurassic periods, prepared as WPA projects by university students; archeological remains excavated from all sections of Oklahoma; and minerals and rocks from many other states.

The OKLAHOMA (STUDENT) UNION BUILDING was completed in 1928 and a tower was added in 1936. Donations from students, alumni, faculty, and friends of the university paid for the building and its furnishings; and fees paid by the students at the time of their registration support it. It contains the quarters of the University of Oklahoma Association, the Men's Council, the Independent Men's Association, the University Christian Associations, the student centers of several religious groups, the offices and studio of the department of speech, the Book Exchange, a recreation hall, a cafeteria, dining rooms, a lounge, a ballroom, meeting rooms, and living apartments for several members of the faculty. In the tower are the offices, studios, and rehearsal rooms of WNAD, "The Voice of Soonerland," the university broadcasting station.

The PETROLEUM ENGINEERING LABORATORY contains laboratories and research rooms of the School of Petroleum Engineering. Immediately north of the building is an oil refinery, consisting of a 96-tube bubble tower and a tube still with a capacity of 250 barrels of crude oil a day. A brick building near by, completed in 1936, houses an experimental lubricating-oil plant.

The School of Journalism is in the UNIVERSITY PRESS BUILDING. Here is published *The Oklahoma Daily,* student newspaper; and here also is the University Press, publishing division of the university, organized in 1929. Besides departmental bulletins, the Press prints *Books Abroad,* a quarterly which has earned an international reputation for scholarly criticism, and has published a widely varied list of books. Among these are *Wah'Kon-Tah,* a Book-of-the-Month Club selection; four volumes of *Folk-Say: a Regional Miscellany;* 22 volumes of a series called "Civilization of the American Indian"; and seven volumes in a new "American Exploration and Travel" series.

BUCHANAN HALL (formerly known as the Liberal Arts Building) is occupied by the English, history, and classical and modern languages and literatures departments. Walls in the classrooms of the Latin and Greek departments are lined with bas-relief—casts of the Elgin marbles. Other classroom walls in the building are covered with symbolic murals, the work of former art students in the University. The building was named in honor of James Shannon Buchanan, a former professor of history, acting president and president of the university.

The PHYSICAL EDUCATION BUILDING (locally called the Field House), a three-story structure, contains a large gymnasium, with balconies seating 3,500 and main-floor seats for 2,000, the quarters of the department of physical education, and the offices of the Intercollegiate Athletic Council. A frame structure adjacent to the building houses the men's swimming pool. The spring graduation exercises are held in the gymnasium.

MEMORIAL STADIUM, consisting of two wings each 400 feet long and 57 feet high, with 62 rows of seats affording a total seating capacity of 32,000 persons, was erected as a World War memorial. Intercollegiate football games are played here, and track meets are held on its quarter-mile cinder oval and 220-yard straightaway. In the space beneath the seats are classrooms, facilities for the student athletes, and the living quarters of members of the student co-operative dormitory. Here, too, student assistants and graduate workers, employed by NYA and WPA, clean and mount animal skeletons for paleontological exhibits. Thousands of fossil bones are stored here, but they must remain in packing cases until funds are appropriated for an exhibit building.

The BUSINESS ADMINISTRATION BUILDING is designed in the collegiate Gothic style, in harmony with most of the other buildings on the campus. Topping the pylons at each side of the main entrance are statues representing Industry and Commerce, and surmounting the octagonal bay is a horizontal frieze of the famous coins of history. The stone gable is ornamented with conventionalized carvings of Oklahoma agricultural products—cotton, corn, and kaffir. Panels on the first floor represent Oklahoma's four major sources of income—oil, mining, agriculture, and commerce; and in recessed niches are other murals that depict all phases of state industries. Grotesque corbel-heads, symbolic of the inhabitants of the Oklahoma plains and their relation to history, adorn the auditorium on the second floor in a vertical design. Libraries, classrooms, and laboratories provide adequate facilities for students in the School of Business Administration.

The BIOLOGICAL SCIENCES BUILDING is decorated with a series of conventionalized carvings of animal types, executed in stone by Joseph R. Taylor, of the art faculty. In the building are laboratories, classrooms, libraries, a herbarium of Oklahoma plants, and a large and interesting ZOOLOGY MUSEUM, which contains specimens from many parts of the United States. The AMPHIBIAN COLLECTION *(permit from the zoology department)*, in the basement, contains thousands of specimens of amphibia common to Oklahoma waters.

The LIBRARY is perhaps the most impressive building on the University of Oklahoma campus. Its collegiate Gothic architecture is similar to that of Administration Hall, with which it will ultimately be joined. The reading room (second floor) extends east and west across the entire length of the building. The PHILLIPS COLLECTION OF SOUTHWESTERN LITERARY MATERIAL *(open by permit from History Department)* is on the first floor. The TREASURE ROOM *(permit from Librarian)*, on the same floor, contains many rare books and valuable manuscripts. In the basement are seminar and research rooms.

Additional buildings on the campus are the Faculty Club, Debarr Hall (Chemistry Building), Science Hall, Engineering Building, Engineering Laboratory, the Armory, the Women's Building, Pharmacy Building, Physics Laboratories, the Infirmary, and the Military Science Buildings.

OTHER POINTS OF INTEREST

McFARLIN MEMORIAL CHURCH (Methodist), University Blvd. and Apache St., was built by Robert M. McFarlin as a memorial to his son, at a cost of more than $1,000,000. The church, rising above the surrounding tree-shaded residences, seems impressive in its plain white stone simplicity. It is neo-Gothic in design; the interior is richly ornamented, with hand-carved walnut woodwork and other decorative features.

During the 1930's the 16 acre CITY PARK was made into a notable recreation center, as a WPA project, with an ampitheatre that seats 2,200, more than 600 trees and thousands of shrubs, athletic grounds, and game equipment. In 1940, attendance at the park exceeded 198,000. A handicraft and recreational program, also sponsored by the WPA, is carried on there throughout the year. It had an average daily attendance of 40 boys and girls in 1940.

CENTRAL STATE HOSPITAL *(visitors by appointment)*, 6 blocks E. of junction of US 77 and Main St., is the state's largest institution for the treatment of mental disorders. Representing an investment of more than $4,000,000, it has 820 acres of land and 111 buildings, mostly plain two-and-three-story structures of red brick. There are approximately 300 employees and 2,500 patients. The institution operates its own farm, dairy, canning plants, laundry, and mattress and furniture factories. Recreational facilities consist of moving pictures, ball games, square dances, and indoor games such as bridge, checkers, and dominoes.

POINTS OF INTEREST IN ENVIRONS

Washington Irving Marker, Moore, *9.2 m* *(see Tour 10)*.

Oklahoma City

Railroad Stations: Union Station, 300 W. Choctaw St. for St. Louis–San Francisco Ry. (Frisco), and Chicago, Rock Island & Pacific Ry. (Rock Island); Santa Fe Station, Santa Fe Ave. and California St., for Atchison, Topeka & Santa Fe Ry. (Santa Fe); Katy Station, 200 E. Reno St., for Missouri-Kansas-Texas R.R. (Katy) and Oklahoma City Ada-Atoka Ry.
Bus Stations: Union Bus Station, Grand Ave. and Walker St., for Oklahoma Transportation Co., Greyhound Lines, Santa Fe Trailways, Southwestern Trailways, Panhandle Trailways, Missouri-Kansas-Oklahoma Coach Lines, Red Ball Bus Line; 15 W. Grand Ave., for All-American Bus Line.
Airports: Municipal Airport (N.W edge of Bethany), 6.9 m. W. on US 66, for Braniff Airways, Mid-Continent Airlines, and American Airlines; Wiley Post Field, N. May Ave., 4 m. N. on US 66 (no scheduled service).
Taxis: 15c and upwards according to distance and number of passengers.
Streetcars and City Busses: Intracity rate 10c or two for 15c; interurban electric lines to Norman, El Reno, Guthrie, and intermediate points, terminal Grand Ave. between Hudson and Harvey Sts.
Traffic Regulations: Parking limit varies with street. Parking meters, which originated in Oklahoma City, on most downtown streets; 5c dropped in slot allows motorist to park for time shown on meter. No charge between 6 P.M. and 7A.M. No all-night parking.

Accommodations: 19 hotels, 2 for Negroes; 2 tourist hotels; residential hotels; rooming houses; many tourist camps; no seasonal rate.

Information Service: Oklahoma Auto Club, Biltmore Hotel, Grand Ave. and Harvey St.

Radio Stations: KOCY (1,340 kc.), KOMA (1,520 kc.), WKY (930 kc.), KTOK (1,400 kc.).
Theaters and Motion Picture Houses: Municipal Auditorium, Walker Ave. between 1st and 2d Sts.; and Shrine Auditorium, 6th St. and Robinson Ave., for local and touring stage productions; 18 motion picture houses, several with stage shows, 2 for Negroes.
Swimming: Lincoln Park Pool, Grand Blvd. and N. Eastern Ave., free, accessories for rent; Rotary Park Pool, Westwood Blvd. and S.W. 15th St., free.
Golf: Two municipal courses, Lincoln Park, Grand Blvd. and N. Eastern Ave., and S. W. 29th St. and May Ave., greens fee 25c, Sat. and Sun. 40c. Other courses: Woodlawn, 3401 Lincoln, 18 holes, greens fee 50c; Capitol Hill, 501 S.W. 44th St., 9 holes, greens fee 30c; Fairview, 2602 N. Eastern, 18 holes, greens fee 30c; Shepherd, N.W. 23rd and Grand Blvd., 9 holes, greens fee 30c; Rowlett, 3000 S.W. 29th St., 9 holes, greens fee, weekdays 25c, Sat., Sun., & holidays 40c.
Tennis: Municipal courts at N.W. 25th St. and Robinson Ave., N.W. 35th St. and Western Ave., N.W. 20th and Broadway Sts., 23d and Glen Ellyn Sts., N.W. 4th St. and Pennsylvania Ave., 12th St. and May Ave., S.W. 29th and Broadway Sts., S.W. 15th and Blackwelder Sts., S.W. 10th and Shartel Sts., 18th and Miramer Sts., 6th St. and Eastern Ave., and 12th and McKinley Sts.: free during day, 40c an hour at night.
Baseball: Texas League Park, 1837 N.W. 4th St., Texas League (Class A).
Wrestling: Each Wednesday night (winter) at the Municipal Auditorium, Civic Center.
Boating and Fishing: Lake Overholser, W. from city on 39th St.

Annual Events: State Fair, Fair Grounds, Eastern Ave. and 7th St., last week in Sept.; Flower Show (state-wide), Municipal Auditorium, 1st and Dewey Sts., first week in Oct.; Golden Gloves amateur boxing tournament, Municipal auditorium, in Feb.; Livestock Show, Stockyards Coliseum, last week in March.

OKLAHOMA CITY (1,194 alt., 204,424 pop.) is not only the largest municipality in the state, and the capital, but is also the most representative of all phases of Oklahoma life—with one important exception—it has no trace of the Indian character which still gives color to the major part of the state. It has no Indian history, for it began as a pioneer town. Here, on the undulant acres north and south of the sandy, nearly always dry, bed of the North Canadian River, the city takes in skyscrapers, two of the nation's finest hotels, a fabulously rich oil field with drill-rigs reaching up out of the back yards of many fine homes, scores of parks and parkways, an excellent medical school, a sectarian university, a splendid new Civic Center, packing, manufacturing, and wholesale districts, and wide areas of homes that, whatever their cost and pretentiousness, are as Oklahoman as the rows of native elms which shade the streets. Characteristically, too, the city's slum section is a "Stringtown" of picturesque, makeshift shacks along the river bank occupied not only by victims of poverty but also by nomads who know quite well how to contrive for themselves.

Downtown, on the streets, in the stores, and in lodging places that range from twenty-five cents a night to the luxury of fine hotel suites, fur coats and overalls, oil-field workers and clerks, farmers and their families and sophisticates who know Europe and South America as well as they know the playgrounds of the United States—all these mingle and make Oklahoma City a true American metropolis.

At the edge of the high plains country that rises gradually to the Rockies, the city gives an impression of altitude not justified by the figures. Viewed from a distance, it strengthens that impression by a skyline broken by tall buildings. In climate and clarity of air, too, Oklahoma City suggests a mountain-slope city rather than one in the Mississippi Valley.

Roughly, the city falls into four fairly equal sections, bisected from east to west by Grand Avenue and from north to south by Broadway. Mounting to the observation tower on top of the thirty-two-story First National Building in the heart of the business district, you may look north to the domeless capitol and the governor's official home, on 23d Street, overtopped by the clean-cut, spidery steel towers of oil wells that go down six thousand feet and more to tap four richly yielding oil-bearing strata. As your eyes swing eastward they pass over a section of ten blocks of new and beautiful homes, where, as in other newly developed sections, there are no sidewalks—a car in every family (almost literally true), and no one thinks of walking! Then, below 13th Street, you see older homes, of the architectural styles of the 1890's and 1900's, bowered in trees, with sidewalks in front.

Next, extending south to California Street, beyond the wide webbing of railroad tracks almost directly east of you, the largest Negro section, housing most of the city's twenty thousand Negroes, unrolls across a low ridge, once covered by blackjack oaks, from the Santa Fe tracks eastward to, and beyond, the State Fair Grounds.

Shifting your eyes to the southeastern quarter of the city, south of the river, you realize what is meant by the familiar oil-field description, a "forest of derricks." Literally, they crowd, row on close-set row, a whole quarter of the city until the few residences left in that oil-soaked area are all but invisible. Nine hundred and more of them, they lead the eye southward to the city limits six miles away where the discovery well was brought in on December 4, 1928.

Now you're facing south, looking along the line of the Santa Fe, and that of the interurban line which will carry you in forty minutes to the university city of Norman. Under your eyes as they swing a bit westward is Capitol Hill, a section of modest homes set close together facing wide streets, dominated by one of the largest and best high schools in the state. Beyond lie productive farms, on which suburban developments are impinging; and still farther on is the distant line of timber that marks the South Canadian (five times as wide, and as sandy and waterless as Oklahoma City's North Canadian). In that quarter, too, is the Army's busy Will Rogers flying field.

Look west, and beyond the business district lies Packingtown, the stockyards, and meat processing plants, which make this the principal livestock market in the state. In that area, too, are most of the 266 manufacturing establishments, large and small, which employ nearly five thousand workers, pay out more than $5,000,000 annually in wages, and produce goods worth $68,000,000.

Last, the northwestern quarter of the city spreads fanwise, street after street, mile after mile of residences, occasional apartment houses, schools, Oklahoma City University, hospitals, local business centers, outlying movie houses, and an impressive high school stadium. It is in this sector that you will find at their best homekeeping Oklahomans, from the clerk paying installments on a low-priced car and a five-room bungalow to the oil-enriched millionaire with his elaborate mansion in the Nichols Hills district just beyond the city limits.

Progressively, as your eyes lift from the older residence streets of this quarter to the latest developments five miles away, the shade trees that line the sidewalks of nearer streets, then dot the farther lawns in blocks devoid of walks, are younger and smaller. The lawns, too, are newer and less lush, the ever-present shrubs and flower beds scantier. Everywhere, except in that segment where oil development has marred the yards and streets of the big pie-shaped area which is Oklahoma City, there is breathing green of grass, shrubs, flowers, and trees. The city grew up amid the stiff-limbed blackjack oaks, some of which still survive, and loves shade.

A common description of western towns is that they "sprang up overnight." In the case of Oklahoma City, the literal truth is that it came into being between noon and sunset of April 22, 1889; and certain cynical historians insist that a considerable population had appeared on the site fifteen minutes after the noon signal for the "run" had been given to those lined up more than thirty miles away. Three years later, Richard Harding Davis (in his *West From a Car Window)* said that "men of the Seminole Land and Town Company were dragging steel chains up the street on a run" at 12:15 P.M. that day. In any case, ten thousand settlers had camped by nightfall over the wide expanse east and west of the Santa Fe's single-track boxcar station, where land had been set aside for a townsite.

For thirteen months the community had no legal municipal existence; only with the setting up of Oklahoma Territory on May 2, 1890, came authority to organize one. However, the settlers formed a provisional city government on May 23, 1889, a month after the Run, choosing first a committee of fourteen, then a mayor and council.

The first provisional mayor was William L. Couch, who had succeeded David L. Payne as leader of the "Boomers" *(see History)*. He and the makeshift council were chosen at a mass meeting "on their looks," for when a man was named for a place he stood up on a dry-goods box to be appraised by the crowd. One candidate who failed of election because he did not please the people was James B. Weaver, once a candidate for President of the United States on the Populist ticket; and Mayor Couch held office only briefly before he died in an "argument" over title to land which is now the center of the city.

Another "argument," which fortunately did not reach the gun-arbitration stage, arose between two townsite companies. One, working north of Grand Avenue, made its survey west from the Santa Fe track, while the one platting south of Grand Avenue took as its eastern base a true north and south line; and when the surveys met there the streets failed to jibe. Neither company would yield to the other, hence the apparently inexplicable jog at Grand Avenue of the streets that run north and south.

At times during the months of provisional city government, United States deputy marshals were called in to enforce Federal law, and on one occasion at least—when an enterprising citizen took possession of the only pump in town and began selling water—troops were required to prevent bloodshed. On the whole, however, Oklahoma City's first settlers succeeded in governing themselves admirably.

The second phase of the city's history, from its formal organization as a municipality on May 23, 1890, to 1910, when the capital was voted away from Guthrie and removed to Oklahoma City, was that of vigorous growth as the trade center of an expanding new territory. In those twenty years, the population grew from 10,037 to 66,408; and it had become by far the largest city in the state. Four other railroads had reached in to help the wholesale merchants extend their trade areas; to serve the farmers, flour mills and cottonseed-oil mills grew in size and numbers; and in 1910–11 two meat-packing plants were established. When the capital was moved from Guthrie, many state employees came to Oklahoma City and remained after their political employment ceased. With the development of the state's natural resources of oil, coal, and metals the city became a financial and manufacturing center. Population growth was again greatly stimulated by the high wages of the World War period. In 1920 the population of Oklahoma City was 98,317, increasing almost without interruption from that time to the 1940 figure of 204,424.

After the first World War, wholesalers intensified their activities; manufacturing became less bound up with agriculture and expanded into new fields; and then a gusher oil field was found to lie within the city's limits. As it grew industrially, Oklahoma City added iron and steel plants, potteries, factories for making furniture, clothing, and electrical equipment. Various large utility companies and brokerage and commission concerns established their headquarters downtown.

Of the approximately sixty thousand workers in Oklahoma City, about sixteen thousand are organized. The Oil Workers' Union, with a membership in the state of eight thousand, has many members in the city. The building trades, too, are largely organized. The Amalgamated Meat Cutters, once a strong union, has, however, almost completely disintegrated. The Oklahoma City Central Trades and Labor Council is one of the most progressive labor bodies in the state.

Though, as has been said, the principal Negro district lies east of the city's main business section, there are two other growing centers, the so-called western block west of Shartel Avenue, and the Walnut Grove Community in the Southeastern quarter between Stiles and Eastern Avenues. Except for a poor district bordering the river, the Negro quarters compare favorably with the average residential and suburban business districts occupied by the whites; and there are a few homes costing from $20,000 to $30,000 each. One Negro, W. J. Edwards, has amassed a fortune as a wholesale junk dealer, and there is a gradual seepage of Negroes into other than the usual service industries.

On the cultural side, Oklahoma City Negroes have provided themselves two movie houses, churches, lodge and dance halls; Tolan Park, on the west side, is for their enjoyment; they maintain a little theater, opened in 1935, and some of its productions have been attended by more than a thousand; their own weekly newspaper, the *Black Dispatch,* established in 1916, has not only a state-wide circulation but many subscribers in other states. Well made up and printed, it carries local and world news, book and motion picture reviews, and a department of news and comment on Negro music and musicians. It is claimed that their high school has the only Negro girls' drum and bugle corps in the United States.

The educational picture for present-day Oklahoma City shows sixty-five public schools, including five senior and eight junior high schools; Oklahoma City University, the University of Oklahoma Medical School, and the Carnegie Library, with its eleven branches and 116,000 volumes. The schools enroll some forty-six thousand students and employ twelve hundred teachers.

The city's growing interest in the arts is expressed through its musical organizations, which offer their own programs and instruction to members and make possible the appearance of nationally known artists; by the increasingly competent Oklahoma Symphony Orchestra of the WPA Music Program; by the fine arts department of Oklahoma City University, and the type of musical instruction given in the schools; and by the Art League and the vigorous activities of the WPA Art Center at the Municipal Auditorium.

The city is headquarters for the Oklahoma State Writers' Club, with a membership of about three hundred; a considerable number of these fulfill the requirement for active membership, selling something at least once a year. The writers have no fixed meeting place, but they get together once a month. The Club's quarterly contests stir Oklahoma poets, playwrights, essayists, and short story writers to action. A half dozen of the city's writers have books to their credit. Nine retail and secondhand bookshops serve the city's readers.

Four daily newspapers were started in the first year of Oklahoma City's existence—one of them, in fact, the *Oklahoma City Times,* before the opening of the land to settlement. Prior to his ejection as a trespasser, its editor wrote the copy on the site of the future capital and sent it to Wichita, Kansas, where the paper was printed. The first newspaper printed in Oklahoma City, issued from a tent, was called the *Oklahoma Times;* its name was changed to the *Oklahoma Journal;* then it was combined with its rival as the *Oklahoma City Times-Journal.* After dropping the *Journal* out of its title, it has continued as the city's principal, and now (1941), only evening paper. The *Daily Oklahoman* and the *Evening Gazette* were also established in 1889. The *Oklahoman* absorbed the *Gazette* and became the only morning paper. Both daily newspapers are (1941) under the same management.

As part of the national defense program, the War Department, in September, 1940, designated the Oklahoma City municipal air terminal as the Thirty-seventh Army Air Corps base, and also the base of the new forty-eighth light bombardment group. The expansion will mean the detail of some 350 officers, and 4,200 enlisted men. It will also involve a $1,400,000 building program to provide barracks, mess halls, stores, administration buildings, and shop. Also, at the southeastern edge of the city, is the War Department's Mid-West Air Depot, a fifteen-million-dollar plant for conditioning and repairing bomber planes.

The development of the Oklahoma City oil field, beginning in 1928, is one of the highlights in the dramatic story of the oil industry in the Middle West. It attracted national attention because of the amazing potential production of its wells—at times exceeding sixty thousand barrels a day from a single well; the enormous rock pressure, and gas flows, resulting in such spectacular fires in the midst of the city's residences as the industry had never before known; and the then unprecedented depth (from four thousand to seven thousand feet) to which the drill bits were sent. Small in area as it is, this pool is one of the richest ever developed.

For several years before the discovery well came in on December 4, 1928, geologists had believed that oil might be found under this area, but probably only at such depths as to make exploration impracticable; its exploitation had to wait until drilling equipment was developed to a point that would make such deep wells profitable.

After drilling started, it was learned that the main part of the pool lay under the southeastern sector of the city, and a legion of derricks came advancing toward the city limits. Then in March, 1930, the Mary Sudik, blowing in, got out of control. For eleven days it ran wild, spouting nearly thirty-five thousand barrels a day in a roaring brown-black geyser that sent spray as far as the town of Norman, fifteen miles to the south. The fire hazard was so great that the other wells were closed down and the area was put under police control.

As drilling operations pushed on toward the north and west, there arose a controversy over drilling within the city limits. One faction argued that the wells outside were drawing oil from under the city and demanded the right to share in the profits by sinking wells, if necessary, in their back yards. Another, remembering the danger of a disastrous conflagration during the wild run of the Mary Sudik, demanded that the derricks stay out of town.

In July, 1930, the city council, in an effort to please both sides, enacted two ordinances, one to establish safety regulations, and the other allowing drilling in the southeast corner of town. Shortly the derricks were towering above the homes in that residential district. Additional ordinances setting more strict rules for safety and providing a system of permits and rigid inspection were enacted.

Demands for extending the drilling zone forced the city council to call a special election in the spring of 1935, with the result that the derricks moved north along the east side of town. Then in the spring of 1936 another election was held and the drilling zone was further enlarged to the vicinity of the state capitol. Governor E. W. Marland demanded that production be allowed on state-owned land around the capitol so that the state would receive a share of the revenue; and when the city council refused to include it in the area voted upon, he put the lands under martial law and issued drilling permits in defiance of the city government. Twenty-four wells went down immediately, some within a few yards of the capitol and of the governor's mansion.

The full extent of the field has not been determined. It is believed that the area of four hundred acres directly beneath the business section of downtown Oklahoma City would yield as richly as any part of the pool thus far developed. Production has been from four different horizons, one at a depth of more than seven thousand feet. Up to January 1, 1938, there were thirteen hundred wells in the field, only nineteen of which had come in as "dry holes." Nine hundred and forty-nine of the wells are still producing (1941).

Oklahoma City is out-of-doors and sports-minded. Among its seventy-one parks are four of considerable size situated at the four "corners of the city" and connected by an outer drive called Grand Boulevard. The city contributed the 1940 amateur tennis champion of the United States *(see Sports and Recreation)* and has sent many fine golfers to national tournaments. At 640-acre Lincoln Park is a zoo containing 350 animals, birds, and reptiles, and a lake which is a resort for wild fowl. There is a smaller zoo at Wiley Post Park. Everywhere in the parks, small or large, picnic grounds are provided; and on summer evenings literally thousands of the city's families take advantage of these facilities.

Oklahoma City has a city manager and city council form of government.

POINTS OF INTEREST

1. The STATE CAPITOL, Lincoln Blvd., between 21st and 23d Sts., an example of neoclassic architecture, was designed by S. A. Layton, of Oklahoma City. Erection of the building was begun in 1914 and finished in 1917. The original design called for a dome on the central tower, but it was not built for reasons of economy. The matter was at one time a political issue.

The massive five-story edifice is in the form of a cross with projecting central pedimented pavilions at the front and rear. A low central tower, over the crossing, is the base of the proposed dome. The east and west section is 434 feet in length and 136 feet in width; the north and south division 304 feet long, and 88 feet wide. The exterior of the building is of granite to the second-floor level, and the superstructure is of Indiana limestone. Entrances are provided on all four sides of the building, with the main entrance on the south. Because of crowded conditions, the west entrance has been closed to permit the use of the west corridor for offices. Before the south entrance stands a STATUE OF A COWBOY on a wild pony, executed by Constance Whitney Warren. The statue has been much criticized by old-timers, who insist that "it don't look much like the real thing." There are replicas in Texas and Colorado. The north and south façades have Corinthian porticoes, and the east and west have Corinthian pilasters.

The interior is decorated with classic features in harmony with the exterior—lobby floors, stairs, and balustrades are of light-colored marble; columns, pilasters, painted beams, lunettes, and Italian elliptical vaulted ceilings adorn the various offices. The second and the fourth floors are the most elaborate in the building.

The governor's office and reception room are on the second floor, as are the courtrooms and offices of the two appellate courts, the state supreme court, and the criminal court of appeals. On the fourth floor are the two chambers of the state legislature. Over the grand stairway, on the south wall of the corridor of the fourth floor, are three World War memorial murals, painted by Gilbert White and presented to the state by Frank Phillips, wealthy oil man. The artist, a painter in the conservative French tradition, combined classic allegory with realistic portraiture to memorialize Oklahoma's part in the World War.

2. The CAPITOL OFFICE BUILDING (ANNEX) *(open during office hours),* Lincoln Blvd., S. and W. of the capitol, a severely plain neoclassic six-story white limestone structure, was built to relieve congestion in the capitol. Chromium steel is used for the light standards at the north and east entrances and for the decorations under the wide windows between the first and fourth floors; there are low-relief sculptures over the east entrance and on the walls of the first-floor lobby. The architect was J. Duncan Forsythe, Tulsa.

3. The STATE HISTORICAL SOCIETY BUILDING *(open 8:30–5 Mon.-Fri., 8–12 Sat.),* Lincoln Blvd., S. and E. of the capitol, is a three-story neoclassic structure, with massive façade pillars, designed by Layton, Hicks, and Forsyth, of Oklahoma City. Completed in 1930 at a cost of $500,000, it

has a Georgia granite base and Indiana limestone superstructure. The building houses the society's museum and library, and quarters of veterans' organizations. The interior arrangement is simple, affording appropriate background for many exhibits. The corridor walls are decorated with life-size figure paintings of Indian dances by Steve Mopope and Monroe Tsa-to-ke, Kiowa Indian artists.

The Oklahoma Historical Society was organized at Kingfisher, in 1893, and was housed in a tiny room of the courthouse. Later it was moved to the state university at Norman, and then to the basement of the Capitol Building, where it remained until 1930. Membership in the society is open to anyone upon the payment of one dollar a year. Money for the salaries of employees and the upkeep of the building and museum is appropriated by the legislature; there are no endowments.

The museum has many valuable and interesting relics not only of Oklahoma and the Southwest, but of Indians elsewhere—for example, the pipe used by the Delawares when they made their treaty with William Penn in 1683. There are also many large pictures of famous Indian leaders, including all modern chiefs of the Choctaw Nation, Pleasant Porter of the Creeks, Bacon Rind of the Osages, and John Ross of the Cherokees, Greenwood LeFlore, Quanah Parker, Pawhuska, and Mrs. Alice Davis, who served as chief of the Seminoles.

In the museum's cases are objects illustrating life among the Indians who were removed from various sections of the United States to the territory that became Oklahoma: Chief Joseph's war bonnet, worn when that great Nez Percé leader was forced to leave his Oregon home and remain for a time as prisoner in Oklahoma; highly decorative headdresses of Cheyennes, Kiowas, Iowas, Osages, Delawares, and others; a collection of ceremonial and everyday fans made from the feathers of the eagle, hawk, magpie, turkey, and (rarest) the scissorbill bird used in the peyote ceremony; a Choctaw version of the Lord's Prayer worked in needlepoint; an Apache pictograph representing the Devil's Dance; a Cheyenne ceremonial shirt decorated with long wisps of hair from enemy scalps; a Kiowa child's chest; Kickapoo and Potawatomi rugs made of dyed reeds and cattails; the land grant to the Choctaws and Chickasaws in 1842 signed by President Tyler.

There are mortars and pestles used in crushing corn; and two millstones, given to the Choctaws by Andrew Jackson before the removal of the tribe to Indian Territory; a stagecoach used in Oklahoma in the early days; a covered wagon, minus the wagon sheet, used in the Run of 1889 and the Cherokee Strip Opening of 1893; and a one-cylinder Cadillac of the vintage of 1900, one of the first cars in Oklahoma.

In the museum are also several Lincoln mementos; a desk used in his Illinois law office, a bedspread that he used as a shawl on a trip from Springfield to Decatur, Illinois, and a number of letters in his handwriting.

The LAURA A. CLUBB FAN COLLECTION of 86 fans includes one of handmade lace and mother-of-pearl, inlaid with gold, once owned by Sarah Bernhardt; another presented by Queen Victoria to Jenny Lind; a seventeenth century carved opera glass fan; and a "kingfisher" fan used by an emperor of Japan.

The NEWSPAPER FILES in the basement contain nearly 20,000 bound volumes of newspapers, some more than 100 years old, and many dating from, and carrying accounts of, the first attempts to open Oklahoma Territory to settlement. Bound volumes of every newspaper in the state published in a town of 1,500 or more are in this room.

4. The GOVERNOR'S MANSION, 700 E. 23d St., a 19-room, three-story building of concrete faced with Bedford limestone, was designed in the Dutch Colonial manner by Layton, Hicks, and Forsyth, and built in 1928. The oil well east of the mansion is "whipstocked," that is, drilled at a slant so that it will take oil from directly beneath the building.

5. The UNIVERSITY OF OKLAHOMA MEDICAL SCHOOL, 801 E. 13th St., a five-story buff brick building, is used exclusively for classrooms, while most of the clinical laboratories are in the University Hospital on the opposite side of 13th St. The legislative act creating the Medical School made the Hospital and the Crippled Children's Hospital, to the east, both state institutions, a part of the school.

6. The FIRST NATIONAL BUILDING, 120 N. Robinson St., 32 stories (447 feet) high, is the largest bank-office structure in the state. It occupies an area of 140 by 200 feet for the first 13 stories, then rises 19 additional stories as an approximately square tower. Of functional modern design, its exterior facing is polished black granite to the second-floor windows, and Bedford limestone above. The trim is made up of aluminum cast panels, grilles and ornaments, aluminum sand-blasted spandrels, and polished extruded aluminum window jambs. More aluminum was used in the building than in any other in the United States up to the time it was erected.

The 32d story is an enclosed observation platform, from which rises an aluminum-sheathed airplane beacon tower in which a light of two million candle power can be seen by flyers from a distance of 75 miles. On occasions, the exterior of the main tower building is illuminated at night by floodlights.

The main banking room of the FIRST NATIONAL BANK, on the second floor, is elaborately designed, with a pavement of Italian marble. On the walls are enlarged reproductions of ancient coins, among them a silver coin minted

In the Cities

NGE : FSA

ENTRANCE TO STATE CAPITOL, OKLAHOMA CITY

OKLAHOMA CITY CIVIC CENTER

DOWNTOWN OKLAHOMA CITY

THE SKYLINE

TULSA

BOSTON AVENUE
METHODIST CHURCH

WHITE : WPA

WOODWARD PARK

HARRIS STUDIO, MUSKOG

OLD UNION AGENCY BUILDING, MUSKOGEE

SENIOR HIGH—JUNIOR COLLEGE, BARTLESVILLE

KLAHOMA HISTORICAL SOCIETY

GUTHRIE; ARCHITECTURE OF 1889–90

PONCA CITY MUNICIPAL BUILDING

IORTON HARVEY

UNIVERSITY OF OKLAHOMA

ADMINISTRATION BUILDING, UNIVERSITY OF OKLAHOMA, NORMAN

"OLD CENTRAL"
OKLAHOMA A. & M.
COLLEGE, STILLWATER

OKLAHOMA A. & M. COLLEGE

OSAGE
TRIBAL MUSEUM
PAWHUSKA

AGE AGENCY

WHITE : W

CARTER ACADEMY (FEMALE INDIAN SCHOOL) ARDMORE

WHEAT ELEVATORS AND FLOUR MILL AT ENID

MC CONKAY STUDIO, E

at Antioch between 83 and 69 B.C., a Byzantine coin minted at Constantinople between 857 and 867 A.D., and a coin of Macedonia minted, probably, about 150 B.C. This room also has four large murals by Edgar Spier Cameron, of Chicago, two of which depict the Run of 1889, another the Louisiana Purchase, and the fourth the Cherokee tribe coming to Oklahoma. The last named was first entitled *The Trail of Sorrow,* but when someone noticed that it was over the door of the loan department of the bank the title was changed to *Sunset Trail.* The murals are painstakingly executed, and figures hardly visible from the floor are said to be draped in the authentic costumes of the period—except that the Cherokee Indians are represented as wearing war bonnets of the Plains tribes.

7. The CIVIC CENTER occupies the old right of way of the Frisco and Rock Island railways through the center of the city. The group of city and county buildings is between Harvey Ave. and Shartel Ave. on the east and west, and between 1st and 2d Sts. on the north and south.

The old city hall at Broadway and Grand Ave., and the old courthouse at Main St. and Dewey Ave. had become inadequate for housing these offices. Taking advantage of the offer of a WPA grant, the taxpayers of the county and city voted a bond issue for the construction of the new buildings in 1935; and they were completed, at a cost of more than $10,000,000, in 1936–37.

The COUNTY BUILDING, between Harvey and Hudson Aves., is the chief structure of this group. Designed by S. A. Layton and George Forsyth, it is a successful adaptation in Bedford limestone of the classic style. Over the broad main entrance on 1st St. is a sculptured group in deep bas-relief representing Indians, cowboys, early settlers and, at either extremity, Lincoln and Washington.

In the lobby, with its terrazzo floor and walls of rose-colored marble broken by flat fluted columns of black marble, is a frieze of separate squares depicting such appropriate symbols as the lamp of truth, the scales of justice, the book of knowledge, and the Roman fasces. Doors, window frames, and ornaments are of aluminum.

The first six floors provide for five district courtrooms, two common pleas courts, and the county court, as well as the necessary jury rooms and other offices. On the seventh and eighth floors is a modern jail.

The MUNICIPAL BUILDING, between Walker and Hudson Aves., was designed by the Allied Architects of Oklahoma City in harmony with the courthouse and the auditorium both in the use of Bedford limestone for exterior facing and in its modified Romanesque architectural motif. Set, like the other buildings of the group, in the center of a smoothly landscaped square, this three-story-and-basement structure consists of a main section, with

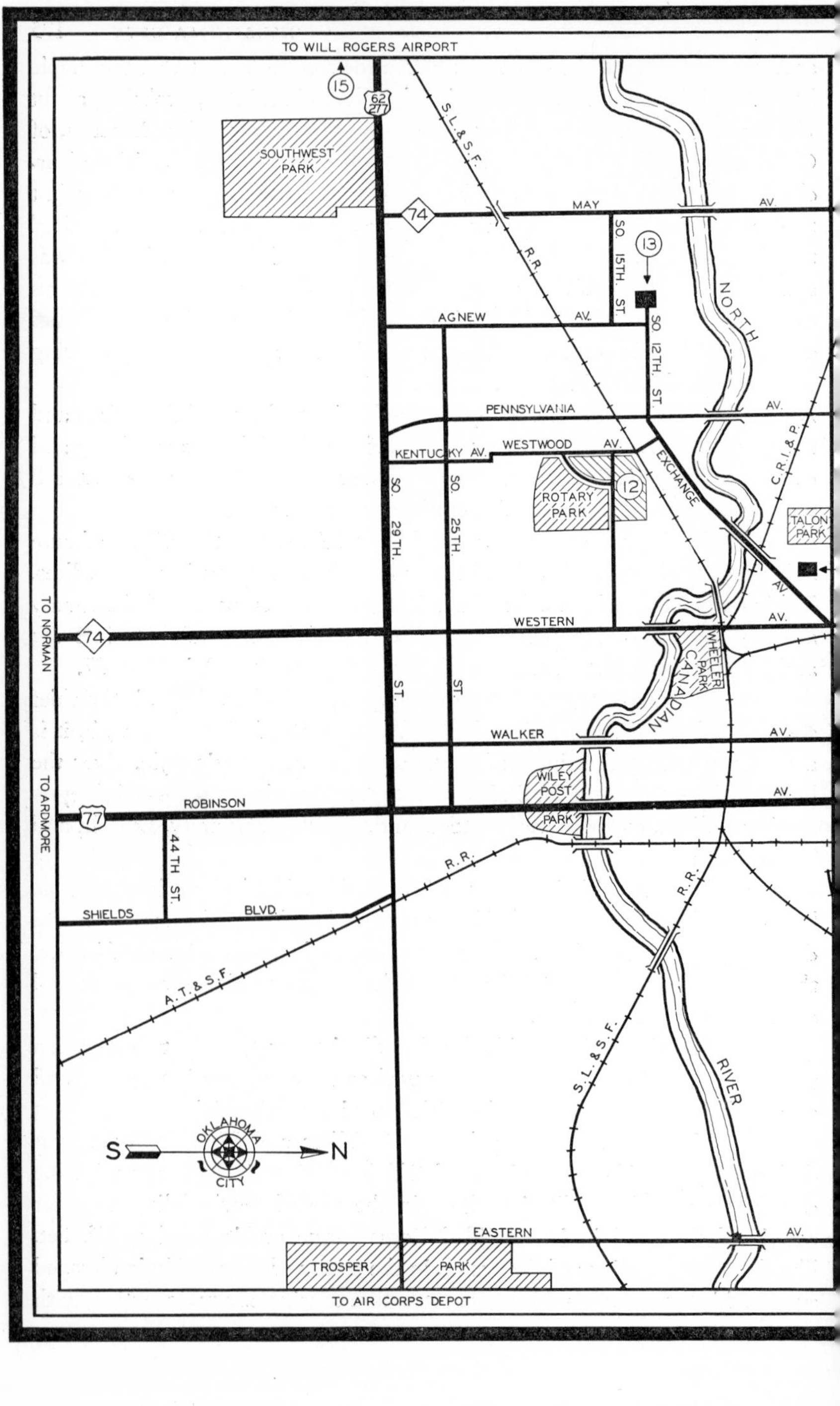

TO WILL ROGERS AIRPORT
15
62
277
SOUTHWEST PARK
S.L.&S.F. R.R.
MAY AV.
74
SO. 15TH. ST.
13
NORTH
AGNEW AV.
SO. 12TH. ST.
PENNSYLVANIA AV.
C.R.I.&P.
KENTUCKY AV.
WESTWOOD AV.
EXCHANGE AV.
ROTARY PARK
12
TALON PARK
SO. 29TH. ST.
SO. 25TH. ST.
WESTERN AV.
TO NORMAN
74
WHEELER PARK
CANADIAN
WALKER AV.
WILEY POST PARK
TO ARDMORE
ROBINSON AV.
77
44TH ST.
R.R.
SHIELDS BLVD.
R.R.
A.T.&S.F.
S.L.&S.F.
RIVER
S
OKLAHOMA CITY
N
EASTERN AV.
TROSPER PARK
TO AIR CORPS DEPOT

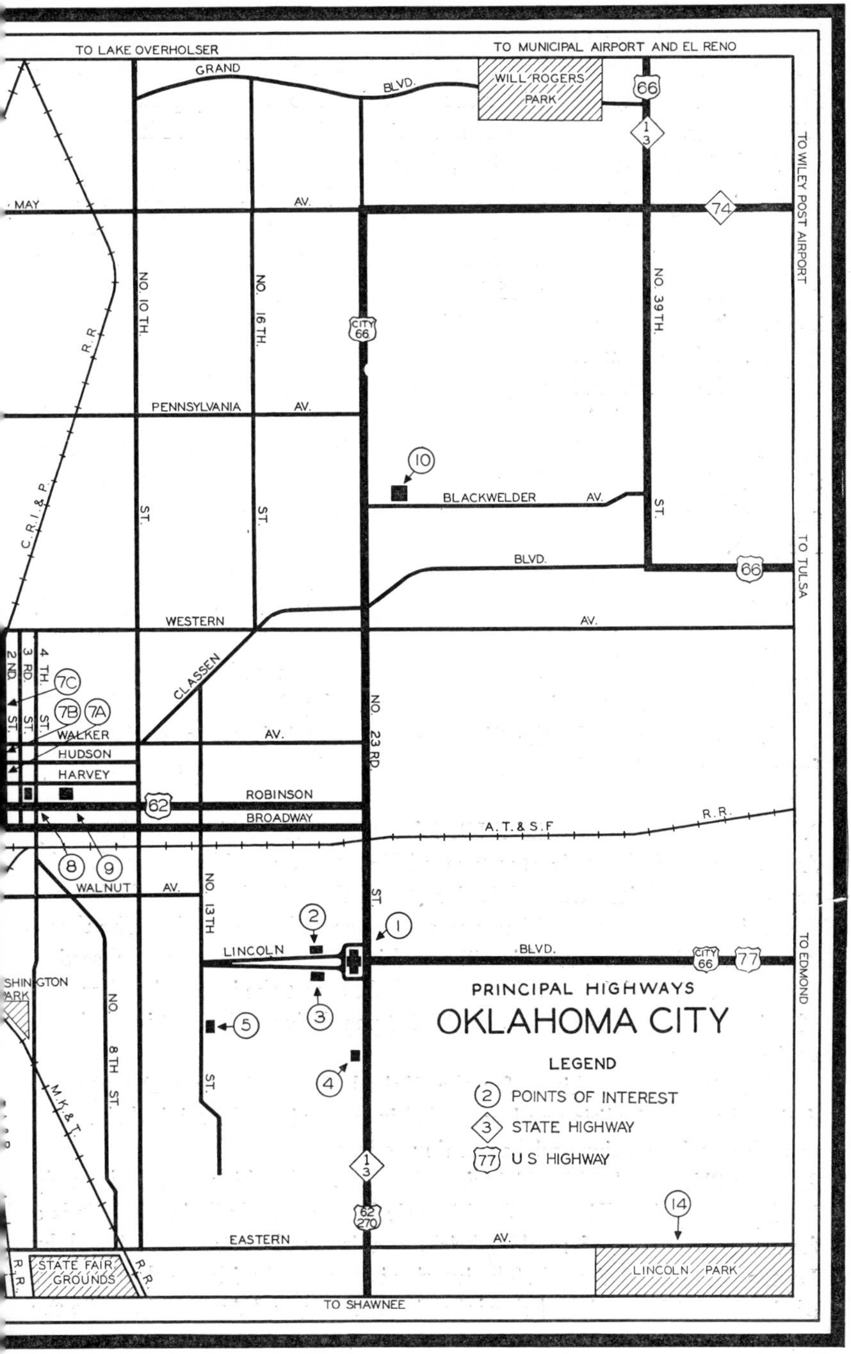
TO LAKE OVERHOLSER
TO MUNICIPAL AIRPORT AND EL RENO
GRAND
BLVD.
WILL ROGERS PARK
66
13
MAY
AV.
74
TO WILEY POST AIRPORT
NO. 10 TH. ST.
NO. 16 TH. ST.
NO. 39 TH. ST.
CITY 66
R.R.
C.R.I. & P.
PENNSYLVANIA
AV.
10
BLACKWELDER
AV.
BLVD.
66
TO TULSA
WESTERN
AV.
CLASSEN
2 ND. ST.
3 RD. ST.
4 TH. ST.
7C
7B
7A
WALKER
AV.
HUDSON
HARVEY
NO. 23 RD. ST.
62
ROBINSON
BROADWAY
A. T. & S. F
R. R.
8
9
WALNUT
AV.
NO. 13TH ST.
2
1
LINCOLN
BLVD.
CITY 66
77
TO EDMOND
SHINGTON PARK
NO. 8TH ST.
3
5
4
M.K.&T.
PRINCIPAL HIGHWAYS
OKLAHOMA CITY
LEGEND
2 POINTS OF INTEREST
3 STATE HIGHWAY
77 U S HIGHWAY
13
62 270
14
EASTERN
AV.
R.R.
STATE FAIR GROUNDS
R.R.
LINCOLN PARK
TO SHAWNEE

six flat fluted columns that rise from the broad steps leading to the first-floor lobby to the capitals under the roof, and two perfectly plain attached office sections. In front of the eastward-facing main entrance on Hudson Ave. is a fountain dedicated to the 89'ers, the city's first settlers.

The MUNICIPAL AUDITORIUM, *between* Lee and Dewey Aves., is an all-purpose community meeting house that fills almost the entire block. Its main hall has seats for 6,000, a convention hall seats 900, and a small theater can take care of an audience of 400. There are five galleries for art exhibits, 22 committee rooms, and an exhibition hall with 38,000 square feet of floor space. Within the auditorium are staged such varied diversions as the annual Golden Gloves amateur boxing tournament, the programs of noted musicians, the concerts of the city's own symphony orchestra, wrestling bouts, basketball and ice hockey games, indoor tennis and track events, little theater productions, religious revivals, and automobile shows. Among the activities carried on here is the work of the Oklahoma WPA Art Center and the WPA Music Program.

Designed by J. O. Parr, of Parr, Frye and Aderhold, of Oklahoma City, the building is described as modern classic, with the accent on the practical. The exterior is faced with Bedford limestone. The main entrance, to the east, has five wide doorways at the top of a broad, shallow flight of steps; above the doorways five great windows dominate the façade.

The power plant for the Civic Center group is in the next block west from the auditorium, between Lee and Shartel Aves. The same building also contains the city jail.

8. The FEDERAL BUILDING, 3d St. between Robinson and Harvey Aves., a modified classic structure of limestone, provides space for the postoffice, the United States District Court, the Circuit Court of Appeals, the United States Veterans' Bureau, and other Federal agencies. The three-story east section was erected in 1912, and in 1934 a nine-story central section and a west wing of three stories were added to meet the imperative demands of a city that had grown from some 80,000 population to 200,000 in the intervening 22 years.

M. F. Foster, architect for the United States Treasury Department, designed the 1934 edition and succeeded in fitting it to the original structure to make an impressive and harmonious effect.

9. The SHRINE TEMPLE *(private)*, 6th St. and Robinson Ave., formerly headquarters of Oklahoma City Masonic bodies, was built in 1922. It is a four-story structure of marble, brick, granite, and concrete, designed by Layton, Hicks, and Forsyth. The interior is decorated with the classic orders of Greece and Rome. The hall of the Eastern Star, and Amaranth, while the

simplest of all the rooms, is thought by many to be the most beautiful. It is modeled after one of the early Christian churches; the massive low arches, heavy columns, simple decoration, and chaste ceiling supported by great crude beams are in keeping with early Romanesque traditions. The commandery room is decorated in the manner of the Inner Temple of London. To the left of the vestibule, with its Doric marble columns, is a small auditorium that seats 750 persons. The murals in the main auditorium were painted by G. A. Fush and tell, in part, the story of Freemasonry. The main auditorium, used as a theater and convention hall, has a seating capacity of 2,062.

10. OKLAHOMA CITY UNIVERSITY, N. Blackwelder Ave. and 24th St., a nonsectarian school under the jurisdiction of the Methodist Church, includes a College of Liberal Arts and a College of Fine Arts. In 1940 it had a student enrollment of 1,500 and a faculty of 65.

The school was founded in 1904 at Oklahoma City as Epworth University. In 1911, it was removed to Guthrie, where it was known as the Methodist University of Oklahoma; in 1919 it was established at its present site under the name of Oklahoma City University.

ADMINISTRATION HALL, planned to dominate a quadrangular group of buildings, is a large brick and stone structure of collegiate Gothic design. On the top floor is the University LIBRARY *(open 8–9 weekdays, 8–12 Sat.)*. The FINE ARTS BUILDING, erected in 1928 directly north of Administration Hall, contains 18 classrooms for painting and sculpture, commercial design, and crafts; studios, quarters for dramatic art work, and an auditorium. The Journalism Building, University Press Building, Hinderlin Training School, and cafeteria are east of the campus entrance. Adjoining the Gymnasium are the football and other outdoor fields.

11. The PUBLIC MARKET, 1201 Exchange Ave., built in 1928, comprises a main building, occupying the center of a block, and sheds. The two-story main building, finished in three-tone buff stucco with terra-cotta colored trim, was designed by Gaylord B. Noftager in the modified Spanish style. It has an auditorium on the second floor, used for athletic events, and shops on the ground floor. Surrounding the block on three sides are steel and concrete sheds, where Oklahoma County truck gardeners have their market stalls and dealers handle vegetables shipped in from the Rio Grande Valley.

12. WILL ROGERS COURTS *(visitors invited)*, 1620 Heyman St., an extensive housing project for low-income tenants covering 37 acres in the southwestern section of the city near "Packingtown," is under the direction of the U.S. Housing Authority. Here, in an attractively landscaped area, units are provided for 354 families with maximum incomes of $25 a week and

(with some exceptions) minimum incomes of $9.00 a week. Rent for the two-to-five-room modern apartments ranges from $13.25 to $17.50 per month. The 85 oblong red-brick buildings with flat roofs are nearly all one story in height; a few are two stories high.

Begun early in 1936 and completed in 1937 as a WPA project with an appropriation of $2,000,000, the Will Rogers Courts were taken over in 1939 by the Housing Authority. Apartments are supplied with gas ranges, refrigerators, and shades; and the management maintains for the tenants a library, a kindergarten, "Toy-land," and other play facilities for children. There is an active women's club. Donald Gordon was the architect, and the landscaping was done under the supervision of the city's park department.

13. STOCKYARDS AND PACKING PLANTS *(conducted tours 10:30–1:30 daily except Sat. and Mon.)*, Exchange and Agnew Aves., is one of the largest livestock centers in the Southwest. Armour and Company and Wilson and Company have plants here.

The morning is generally the best time to visit the plants as most of the butchering is done at this time. Visitors are permitted to see every phase of the packing industry, from sheep being led to the killing pens by a goat, with no other duties than to encourage them to follow his nonchalant lead, to the canning of eggs in five-gallon lots for the baking trade.

The two packing plants were located at Oklahoma City in 1910 on payment of bonuses by businessmen; the stockyards came as a natural adjunct to these plants. Prior to the development of the city's oil fields, the packing industry was the city's largest employer of labor. Approximately 1,000,000 head of livestock, aside from horses and mules, pass through the stockyards each year.

POINTS OF INTEREST IN ENVIRONS

Bethany Peniel College, *6.9 m.;* Lake Overholser, *9.1 m. (see Tour 1);* Lincoln Park, *4.5 m.;* Home of the Poor Prophet, *4.6 m.;* Municipal Airport, *7 m.;* Bombardment Training School and Base, *8.4 m.;* Horseshoe Lake, *21.1 m. (see Tour 3);* Memorial Park, *10.1 m. (see Tour 10).*

Okmulgee

Railroad Stations: E. 5th St. and tracks, for St. Louis–San Francisco Ry.; 723 W. 6th St. for Okmulgee Northern Ry. (no passenger service).)
Bus Stations: 112 E. 7th St., for Southwest Greyhound Lines; 220 W. 7th, for Santa Fe Trail System.
Airport: Municipal Airport, 3 m. E. on US 62.
City Transportation: Busses, fare 5c; taxis, fare 15c.
Traffic Regulations: 25 m. city speed limit; 2-hour parking.

Accommodations: 6 hotels, 1 for Negroes; rooming houses, 2 for Negroes; tourist camps.

Information Service: Chamber of Commerce, 5th St. and Grand Ave. (McCulloch Bldg.).

Radio Station: KHBG (1240 kc.).
Motion Picture Houses: 4; balcony in 1 for Negroes.
Athletics: Harmon Stadium, 12th St. and Creek Ave.; Hospital Park, N. Okmulgee Ave., Melrose to Belmont Aves., for baseball, softball.
Wrestling: Armory, 2d St. and Alabama Ave.
Boating: Lake Okmulgee (*see Tour 3*), 7 m. W. on State 27; Douglas Park, 400 E. 8th St.
Swimming: Douglas Park; Greenwood Lake, adjoining city on S.E.
Golf: Country Club, on Mission Rd., adjoining city on S.E. Greens fee, 35c weekdays; 50c Sundays and holidays.
Tennis: Hospital Park (6 city-owned courts).

Annual Events: Regional Tennis Carnival, June; Creek Indian Stomp Dance, mid-July, at nearby Henryetta (*see Tour 3*); Pioneer Powwow and Indian Festival, Aug. 24–26.

OKMULGEE (670 alt., 16,051 pop.), seat of Okmulgee County, and capital of the Creek Nation from 1868 until the tribal government was extinguished by the coming of statehood in 1907, emphasizes both its Indian past and its industrial present. It retains its annual Indian powwow and also uses as its slogan, "Where oil flows, gas blows, and glass glows," to point its varied modern qualities.

The city is set in a wide valley between low, timber-covered hills. Its spruce business section has spread over the lowland; its residences, parks, and playgrounds are spotted on the view-giving slopes on the northwest, west, and south. To the north and east, the city fades into fertile, level farms.

It is said that in choosing Okmulgee as the site of their capital the Creek Indians assured themselves immunity from cyclones. In justification of their choice, the people who live in the two or three square miles of comfortable homes with porches and shade trees have never yet (1941) been visited by a cyclone, though "twisters" have skirted the region.

Oil was discovered within a half mile of the old Creek Council House, in 1904, and three years later had become a leading factor in the town's growth. Five glassmaking plants have been built during Okmulgee's history, though glassmaking has turned out to be an uncertain business. More stable are its packing plants, cotton processing industries, oil refining business, and market for peanuts and pecans. Nuts from the world's largest native pecan orchard, twenty-five miles west on the Deep Fork of the Canadian River, are marketed in Okmulgee.

The city's period of swiftest growth was what it calls its "golden decade," 1907 to 1918, when oil development reached its peak. By 1930 the population had reached 17,097; the decrease of 6.1 per cent between that date and 1940 may perhaps be accounted for by the waning importance of oil and allied industries, and the shutting down of glass plants which have had troubled industrial careers.

Since 1912, when a new charter was adopted, Okmulgee has had a commission form of government. Its water supply is municipally owned. In the county are ample supplies of fuel oil, natural gas, and coal.

The story of Okmulgee goes far back in the history of the Creek Indians and begins long before their removal to what is now Oklahoma. According to tribal tradition, these Indians originated somewhere in the western part of America, and in the course of time migrated to the Alabama-Georgia region, where the white men first found them. Arriving there, the Indians sought as a site for their principal (capital) town a never-failing spring; and having found it they called it Okmulgee, which means "bubbling water." It was there, they say, that the powerful confederation of the tribes of Muskhogean stock was formed to resist the encroachment of whites on Indian lands. In course of time, the white name for one of the tribes—the Creeks—became fixed upon it, although it is still sometimes called Muskogee.

From the time of their enforced exile from the east, 1829–36, when twenty thousand were settled in the new Indian Territory, to the building of their Council House at Okmulgee in 1868, the tribal meeting place was at High Springs, near Council Hill, some twenty miles southeast. Factional strife and the almost complete destruction of property in the Civil War led to the selection of the new site, and the name which was sacred to all.

Their first capitol was a two-story log structure, with a roofed-over breezeway separating the meeting places of the two branches of the Council, the House of Kings, anciently concerned with civil administration, and the House of Warriors. There, encouraged at first by the United States government, met not only the Creek lawmakers but also the important Intertribal Council composed of the head men of the Five Tribes and, in the later years, delegates from the so-called wild western tribes, Comanches, Kiowas, Caddoes, Cheyennes, and Arapahoes. Others that came in the years from 1870 to 1875 included the Sacs and Foxes, Osages, Shawnees, Ottawas, Wyandottes, Quapaws, and Peorias—mainly remnants of once powerful tribes east of the Mississippi and north of the Ohio River. At the last meeting, twenty-nine tribes were represented.

This council was discontinued when the United States government refused to finance it further because the delegates had reached the point of proposing to form an Indian Territory according to their own conception and writing out a constitution for its government. When it became certain that Washington would insist upon retaining the veto power on any legislation enacted by this Territory's legislature, there no longer existed a reason for the Council, and the 1875 meeting was the last.

Silas Smith, a blacksmith, was the first white resident of Okmulgee. He was sent there by the Federal government to help the Creeks secure and keep in order the tools necessary for their farming operations.

By 1878, Okmulgee had become an active Indian trade center; the Creeks had recovered from the ravages of war; the people of the farms and ranches were prosperous; the tribal schools were flourishing; and it was decided that the old log Council House must go. It was torn down, and on the site a square two-story-and-cupola stone structure was erected. The new capitol, set in the town square and dominating the fringe of stores around it, served also as a community meeting place and schoolhouse.

In 1894, when the question of alloting Creek lands and coming under a territorial government which would soon be dominated by the whites had been hotly debated in the grounds of the Council House between Indian leaders and representatives of the Federal government, Chief Legus C. Perryman called for a vote. He asked all who opposed allotment to move to the west side of the grounds, and those who favored it to the east. All save one moved west; Moty Tiger alone stepped east and turned to face the three thousand who opposed allotment. When called upon to explain his stand, he said that whatever the Indians did the whites would overwhelm them, and that it would be best to accede to the Federal government's desires and obtain whatever favors they could from the white man's government. Five years later, allotment was accepted and Moty Tiger's stand vindicated.

As a modern city, Okmulgee's history began after the Creek tribal lands, in 1899, ceased to be held in communal ownership and were allotted to individuals. That change meant the coming of whites and a great stimulus of trade and commerce. The first bank was opened in 1900, and in the same year train service was begun.

Okmulgee's growth from a trading point with a population of some two hundred to an incorporated municipality, with a mayor and four aldermen, with telephone service to Muskogee, and a determination to dominate the region, was swift after allotment. By the end of 1905, thanks to oil discoveries near by, the city's population had risen to four thousand.

Okmulgee citizens call 1907 their year of years. It brought statehood and the first of the gusher oil fields to be opened in its territory. In April a well was brought in that produced five hundred barrels a day; in June a thousand-barrel well blew in; and the rush of drillers, lease hounds, speculators, and the platoons of men and women who always follow the developers of an oil field soon boosted the population to six thousand.

By 1910 the surrounding oil region was so well established that a refinery was built; and it is still (1941) the largest employer of labor in Okmulgee, with 325 workers on its pay roll.

Until 1916, the old Creek Council House served more or less adequately as the Okmulgee County Courthouse. Then the need for more space became pressing, and a $125,000 bond issue was voted for the construction of a new one. When these bonds were offered for sale, the white guardian of an illiterate Creek woman, Katie Fixico, who had been adjudged by the County Court an incompetent, used $133,379 of her money to buy them. Her wealth had, of course, come out of oil wells drilled on her allotment.

The city's roll of honor is truly varied: General Hugh Johnson; Katie Fixico; W. B. Pine, a wealthy oilman, hog rancher (with three droves of purebred Hampshires totaling eight thousand), and Republican U.S. Senator (1924–30); Dr. L. S. Skelton, who established the first glass manufacturing plant at Okmulgee and contributed to many other enterprises; Captain F. B. Severs, an early-day trader and the city's first dealer in nuts from Okmulgee County's 125,000 pecan trees; Enos Wilson, said to be the richest Indian since the death of Jackson Barnett; E. H. Moore, who could not quit the oil business after making as much of a fortune as he wanted, but after selling out went into it again and added to his wealth; and Dr. R. M. Isham, an oil chemist and researcher of national reputation.

Negroes, who make up approximately 12 per cent of the city's population, live in a district by themselves, provide their own amusements, have fourteen churches for the use of their worshipers, a hospital (city owned), and a branch of the Okmulgee Public Library.

The city shares with Muskogee, to the northeast, and McAlester, to the southeast *(see Tour 5),* the trade of the eastern section of the state. It is also the trade center of the county, in which lie more than 3,500 farms, with some 160,000 acres of land in cultivation. Cotton is a million-dollar-a-year crop;

nearly five million pounds of pecans are harvested from Okmulgee County's groves—mostly of wild trees, but some in which the big papershell species have been grafted on native trees. Truck farming, poultry breeding, and dairying also contribute largely to its business.

Newspaper history in Okmulgee began when E. P. Gupton started the *Record,* printed at Muskogee, on April 3, 1900. It lasted only a few weeks. Then Valdo Smith, on August 23, 1900, established the weekly *Democrat,* which after various changes of ownership has continued. On September 3, 1901, George Wood put out the first issue of his *Creek Chieftain,* which became the *Times* in 1918 and began publication as a daily. Since 1925, both the *Times* and the *Democrat* have been issued by the same management; and the *Democrat* has changed from an afternoon daily to a weekly.

POINTS OF INTEREST

The CREEK INDIAN NATIONAL COUNCIL HOUSE *(free; open 9–4:30),* 6th and Morton Sts., at the center of the city, is set in a square shaded by enormous maple trees. It is a source of pride to the city, though at one time the mayor made every effort to have it removed as an old and ugly blot on the fair face of Okmulgee. He wished to have a new and expensive Federal Building on this central site.

The council house is a plain four-square, two-story structure of brown stone, with a cupola rising from the center, suggesting in its simplicity and excellent proportions the best of New England Colonial architecture. On the first floor, its four spacious rooms house a growing Museum of Creek History. Upstairs, where the House of Kings and the House of Warriors used to meet in two rooms when Council was in session, a WPA art project and a kitchen and dining room for the YWCA are (1941) carrying on the tradition of service to a community. The building, acquired by Okmulgee from the Creeks when the tribal government went out of existence, is in the care of the Creek Indian Memorial Association, whose purpose is to gather for exhibition "all data relating to the history, traditions, folklore, relics, handicraft, art, music, and all that is finest and best in the life of the Creek tribe of Indians, and the preservation of the...Council House." What has already been collected constitutes one of the most interesting tribal exhibits in the state.

The OKMULGEE PUBLIC LIBRARY, 218 Okmulgee Ave., is a commodious one-story brick building trimmed with white stone. The library developed from a tiny club reading room equipped with a secondhand Bible and 80 other books contributed at a "pink tea and book shower" given by the Civic Club in May, 1907. First quartered in a business building, the library moved to two rooms in the old Creek Council House in 1910.

When the Council House rooms became overcrowded, the city asked the Carnegie Corporation for funds with which to build a library. The offer of $15,000 was deemed inadequate, so the municipality voted $75,000 in bonds and later added $25,000 for furniture and equipment. Today (1941) the Okmulgee library has more than 38,000 volumes and ranks as one of the best in the state. In certain ways, it also serves as a community center, for here the Okmulgee Law School, university extension classes, and the Okmulgee Little Theater hold their meetings. Its Dunbar Branch, for Negroes, has more than 5,000 books. In 1923 the library acquired a considerable collection of books belonging to William H. ("Alfalfa Bill") Murray, who later became governor *(see History)*.

The FEDERAL BUILDING, at 4th St. and Grand Ave., a modern three-story, block-like structure of granite and limestone, might well be the answer to the prayer of the mayor who wanted to banish the old Council House to a farm site. Its cost, $350,000, suggests its size but not the effectiveness of its tall, square-pillared façade or the beauty of the interior where the Federal District Court meets and the city post office is housed.

Of a different type of architecture—red brick with interesting white limestone trimming—the HIGH SCHOOL BUILDING, Okmulgee Ave. and 2d St., and the near-by OKMULGEE JUNIOR COLLEGE, the second largest municipal college in the state, top an educational system that comprises also ten elementary schools for white students and three for Negroes, a Negro high school, and two parochial schools.

HARMON STADIUM, 600 E. 12th St., is a modern concrete amphitheater, enclosing a softball field, capable of seating 5,000 spectators; it is also used for track meets.

HOSPITAL PARK, Okmulgee Ave. and Belmont St., a landscaped area six blocks in extent, is the principal recreation ground within the city. In this spot is also an NYA training school. Among the facilities are picnic grounds, baseball and softball diamonds, wading pools, and six concrete-surface tennis courts, city owned, where the annual district summer tennis carnival is held. Four smaller parks are included in Okmulgee's park system.

BALL BROTHERS GLASS PLANT on S. Madison St., and the SOUTHWESTERN SHEET GLASS COMPANY on W. 20th St. *(both open to visitors in working hours)*, on the outskirts of the city, illustrate one important phase of the city's industrial activity.

POINTS OF INTEREST IN ENVIRONS

Lake Okmulgee, *7 m.;* Rifle Range, *7 m.;* Nuyaka, *16 m.; (see Tour 3);* Fidelity Laboratories, *4.1 m. (see Tour 9)*.

Ponca City

Railroad Stations: 1st St. and W. Oklahoma Ave. for Atchison, Topeka & Santa Fe Ry.; 700 S. 3d St. for Chicago, Rock Island & Pacific Ry.
Bus Stations: 114 N. 4th St. for Missouri-Kansas-Oklahoma; 201 N. 2d St. for Santa Fe Trail Transportation Co.; and 1st St. and Grand Ave. for Turner Transportation Co.
Airport: Municipal Airport, 1.5 m. N.W.
City Transportation: Busses, fare 5c; taxis, fare, 10c first 15 blocks; 5c each additional 5 blocks.
Traffic Regulations: 20 m.p.h. in business district, 30 m.p.h. elsewhere.

Accommodations: 6 hotels; rooming houses; 3 tourist camps.

Information Service: Chamber of Commerce, Community Bldg. N. 3d St.

Radio Station: WBBZ (1230 kc.).
Newspaper: Ponca City News, daily.
Theaters: 4 motion picture houses, Municipal Auditorium.
Athletics: Blaine Park Stadium, Brookfield Ave. and 6th St.; Conoco Ball Park, S.W. edge of city (9 blocks W. on South Ave. from 5th St.), reached by US 60.
Golf: Marland Course, 9 holes, between E. Grand and Highland Aves. at N. 10th St.
Swimming: Wentz Pool, 5.5 m. N.E. (children 15c, others 25c); municipal pools (free), Ponca Ave. and S. 6th St. and W. Chestnut and Palm Sts.
Boating: Lake Ponca, 4 m. N.E. of city, via Cann Blvd.
Tennis: Municipal free courts, N. 7th St. between Highland and Overbrook Aves.; N. 7th St. between Grand and Cleveland Aves.; W. Otoe Ave. and S. Oak St.

Annual Events: Ponca Indian Powwow, 3d week in Aug.; Wentz Bathing Beauty Revue (for girls under 5; also those under 12 years of age), Sunday before Labor Day; Cherokee Strip Opening celebration, Sept. 16.

PONCA CITY (1,003 alt., 16,794 pop.), "built on oil, soil and toil," as its people say, lies nearly in the center of a triangle at the points of which, roughly one hundred miles away, are the cities of Wichita, Kansas, Tulsa, and Oklahoma City. It is the chief city in Kay County, which borders on Kansas. There are no city taxes, since the municipality, under the city manager form of government, is supported from the earnings of its municipal light plant and waterworks.

Ponca City impresses one as a clean, somewhat bare, city set in a prairie landscape. It is built on a tableland, rolling slightly toward the east where its outskirts approach a belt of scrub oak. Here the streets of widely spaced homes suggest comfort and well-being, rarely luxury or ostentation. Most of the city's growth was in the two and one-half decades from 1915 to 1940, an era of prosperity largely due to oil, when buildings, paving, parks, and other public conveniences were planned and executed in a generous mood. In that era, too, came the inspiration to depart from the usual semiclassic Greek type of public buildings in favor of warmer Spanish models.

Oil was responsible for Ponca City's 129 per cent increase in population from 1920 to 1930, as compared with a growth of only 4 per cent in the following decade, when oil production in the region had become stabilized. While oil more than doubled the population, the city is also the trading center of a good farming and stock-raising area; and abundant supply of natural gas for fuel has attracted twenty-four manufacturing establishments (not including oil refineries and allied works) employing 2,400 workers, with an annual pay roll of more than $4,000,000; there are now (1941) some 320 wholesale, retail, and service organizations, with nine hundred employees who draw around $786,000 annually as wages and salaries.

Like Enid, another northern Oklahoma metropolis, Ponca City came into existence in an afternoon, and for the same reason. At noon of September 16, 1893, its site was raw prairie, a part of the six million and more acres of the Cherokee Outlet, which the United States opened to white settlement that day. By nightfall, thousands of homeseekers had covered the twenty miles from the Kansas border by wagon and buggy, on horseback, and by train—some of the overflow clinging to the steps or riding the Santa Fe engine cowcatcher—and three thousand were camped on the spot where, according to the government's map, a town named Cross was to be laid out three miles north of the present Ponca City. But a group of men headed by B. S. Barnes decided that a more logical location would be near the border of the Ponca Indian reservation. Inside the reservation was a Santa Fe station called White Eagle by the government, and Ponca by the railroad, so Barnes and his associates dubbed their location New Ponca, and in the spirit of pioneer town-builders undertook to "wipe Cross off the map."

One handicap in their fight was that the railroad did not recognize New Ponca and would not stop the trains there, maintaining speed between Cross, two miles to the north, and White Eagle, seven miles to the south. However, the town's hopeful citizens finally secured a railroad station and the order to halt trains there. Old-timers tell how a crowd of elated citizens rode down from Cross on the first train to stop at New Ponca, distributing cigars to men passengers, flowers to the women, and to all a card reading, "The train stops at New Ponca the same as Chicago." In time, Ponca City grew far enough north to absorb Cross.

A pioneer woman of Ponca City has recalled that sixty days after the opening of the Outlet the first one-room school building, erected by public subscription, was completed. To celebrate, excursion trains came from Guthrie, Perry, Orlando, and Arkansas City, Kansas. In all, thousands made of the occasion a holiday; to feed them, beeves were slaughtered and barbecued over huge firepits by Ponca Indians from the reservation a few miles south. Since that time nearly $2,000,000 has been spent for plants to provide public education.

Oil production, in fields developed in the Ponca Indian reservation south of the city, and in the Osage holdings to the east, began before 1909, when wildcatting brought showings on the big Miller 101 Ranch *(see Tour 10),* leased from the Ponca Indians. But until E. W. Marland, an operator from Pennsylvania, with a "nose for oil and the luck of the devil," plus solid financial backing in New York, got under way the field was small. Then the picture changed. It was said that in the choice of locations to drill Marland couldn't go wrong. Year after year, under his leadership, the Ponca Pool was extended; and presently wildcatters found that the trend was eastward into the Osage country. Upon the opening of the Burbank and Shidler fields, the story developed into a saga which drew national attention.

With an apparently limitless supply of crude oil available, and his luck in bringing in new rich well holdings, Marland began building what is known as an integrated company, that is, one which handles the oil all the way from the well to its delivery as gasoline to the motorist. Ponca City became the site of the largest refinery in the Mid-West field; the name Marland went up on filling stations over an ever-expanding area; and Marland's pipe lines reached out into widening fields to gather the crude from the Marland Company wells.

Wealthy, generous, and with a genuine liking for his fellow men, Marland undertook to make this prairie town, his adopted home, a model; and to make of his own organization a sort of country club. But oil is slippery, and a man's luck in the oil business seldom lasts beyond a brief decade. When Marland's ran out, and his extravagant organization could no longer support itself, eastern financial support was withdrawn. "Wall Street" took over; the Marland Company polo team was disbanded; Marland retired from his baronial mansion on the outskirts of Ponca City to live in the gate lodge of the estate; and apparently finis was written to another epic of oil entitled "From riches to rags."

But after a period of eclipse he entered the oil business again in a small way, then became interested in politics, and was elected to Congress. One term in the House of Representatives and he came back as a strong exponent of President Roosevelt's New Deal policies to capture the Democratic primary in the race for governor; he was elected in 1934 *(see History).*

In a sense, Marland's successor as the dominant figure in the oil business of the Ponca area, and as the generous, public-spirited first citizen of the growing city, is Lew (Lewis Haines) Wentz, another Pennsylvania trained oilman. The best evidence of his interest in the people is the big Wentz Educational Camp *(see Tour 10),* near by. No one has ever said anything about the "Wentz luck," but it seems to be the sort that, though unspectacular, holds. Wentz's selection, in 1940, as Oklahoma member of the Republican National Committee would indicate that he is also following the Marland transition from oil to politics.

Three elevators, capable of handling 540,000 bushels of grain; a packing plant; and a creamery producing all kinds of dairy products provide service for the surrounding farming and stock-raising activities.

Ponca City's recreational facilities include thirteen parks comprising 1,335 acres, fishing and boating on an eight-hundred-acre suburban lake, three supervised playgrounds, ten gymnasiums, and ten auditoriums.

POINTS OF INTEREST

PONCA CITY LIBRARY, Grand Ave. at 5th St., is a one-story white stucco building of modified Spanish design, erected in 1936. Above the three-arch entrance, the central section rises an additional story to a sloping tiled roof. In its stackrooms, which hold more than 18,000 volumes, is a section devoted to the works of Oklahoma writers, practically every book having been autographed by its author. There is also a small but growing exhibit of Indian relics, an auditorium, kitchen, and other facilities for the entertainment of small groups.

The MUNICIPAL BUILDING, Grand Ave. opposite the library, an example of Spanish-Moorish architecture, is said to be one of the most beautiful buildings in the state. Set in well-landscaped grounds, its southwestern mission type tower stands out as a distinctive feature.

In BLAINE PARK, a 10-acre playground between 5th and 7th Sts. on Brookfield Ave., is the flood-lighted PONCA CITY STADIUM, built of native stone, with an enclosed press and broadcasting room at the top of the stand. It has a well-sodded and drained football field, a quarter-mile cinder track around the field, and baseball and softball diamonds; the stadium proper seats 3,000.

The city's SENIOR HIGH SCHOOL, 7th St. and Overbrook Ave., built in 1926, has a feature unique among Oklahoma schools, its radio instruction. One program is broadcast, over facilities provided by Station WBBZ and the city Chamber of Commerce, every morning by the Future Farmers of America; all assembly and special programs are also broadcast; and at intervals broadcasts are sent from every classroom in the three-story building. During the school year every student who cares to take part in these radio demonstrations has the opportunity. The building, Spanish type in design, has a red-tiled roof and truncated towers.

CONOCO REFINERY and CLUB *(club and cafeteria open to public)*, at the southwestern corner of Ponca City, together with the extensive TANK FARM where 10,000,000 barrels of crude oil can be stored, symbolize the oil business of Oklahoma, the state's most important industry. This refinery, capable of converting 50,000 barrels of crude oil daily into gasoline and other marketable products, is the largest in the state and one of the most modern in the world. Taken over, with all its other properties, from the Marland Refining Company by the Continental Oil Company in 1929, it has been constantly enlarged and improved. It employs (1941) some 2,500 workers, the majority of whom own their homes.

Shared by the people of the city are the facilities of the 18-hole golf course laid out by the company, the baseball grounds, swimming pool, the tennis courts; and the big RECREATION BUILDING erected by the Continental Associates for social, educational, and athletic purposes. This building developed out of the need for more office room and the company's wish to provide play space and equipment for its workers, their families, and friends. It is 240 by 165 feet in area, one of its two big wings being devoted to offices, and the other to a gymnasium, cafeteria, and game rooms; amusement facilities are also provided in the connecting wings. Between the main wings, an out-of-doors swimming pool 80 by 38 feet in area is turned over to the children of the city on Saturday mornings in the summer.

POINTS OF INTEREST IN ENVIRONS

Pioneer Woman Statue, *1.5 m.;* Ponca Indian Reservation, *5 m.;* 101 Ranch, *10.2 m.;* White Eagle Monument, *12.2 m.;* Laura A. Clubb Art Collection, *15.8 m. (see Tour 10);* R.A.F. Flying School, *4 m.*

Shawnee

Railroad Stations: Main St. and Minnesota Ave. for Atchison, Topeka & Santa Fe Ry; 225 S. Broadway for Oklahoma City-Ada-Atoka Ry.
Bus Station: Union Station, 123 N. Union Ave., for Oklahoma Transportation Co. and Turner Transportation Co.
Airport: 1 m. W. of city limit on US 270.
City Transportation: Busses, fare 10c; taxis, fare 20c.

Accommodations: 5 hotels; rooming houses; 5 tourist camps.

Information Service: Chamber of Commerce, Aldridge Hotel, 9th St. and Bell Ave.

Radio Station: KGFF (1450 kc.).

Motion Picture Houses: 5.
Athletics: Athletic Park, Burns and Pottenger Aves., for baseball, track, and football.
Basketball and Wrestling: City Auditorium, 400 N. Bell Ave., weekly in winter.
Swimming: Municipal pool, Woodland Park, 401 N. Broadway, fee 45c.
Tennis: 12 free municipal courts, at Woodland Park; Farrell Park, 301 W. Hayes St.; Jefferson School, 800 N. Louisa St.
Boating: Shawnee Lake, 8 m. W., via W. Highland Ave., and unnumbered graveled highway.
Golf: Shawnee Country Club, 2 m. E. on US 270, greens fee $1; Elks Country Club, 5 m. N.W., greens fee $1; Meadow Lark course, 5 m. W. on US 270, greens fee 35c.

SHAWNEE (1,008 alt., 22,053 pop.), seat of Pottawatomie County, at the edge of its own small oil field and near the rich developments of the big Seminole and Earlsboro areas, is built on land that has been claimed at different times by Spain, France, England, the Creek and Seminole Indian nations, and the Sac and Fox tribe. The first settlement was called Shawnee Town, because it was a trading place for the Shawnee Indians, whose reservation lay near by. In 1895, according to a special count, the town had only three hundred inhabitants; the 1940 census showed it to be the fifth city in size in Oklahoma.

Shawnee is still an Indian trading post, as well as the center of perhaps the richest agricultural section of the state. Today, however, ~~in the reassuring~~ words of a Chamber of Commerce writer, "the Sac and Fox, Shawnee, Potawatomi, and Kickapoo tribes live peacefully in and around Shawnee under the protection of the United States Indian Agency, with headquarters at Shawnee."

Set on a broad bench in a jagged horseshoe loop of the North Canadian

River, the city rises toward rolling prairie ridges to the east and north. Its southern edge drops abruptly to a wide basin of farm land that is sometimes inundated by the uncertain river. To the west, its suburbs slope easily outward. Carved out of a thick forest of ash, cottonwood, hickory, and elm, Shawnee has kept many of the fine native trees. They tower above close-clipped lawns and dominate little Woodland Park, the heart of Shawnee. Downtown, the streets are broad, clean, and bordered by two- and three-story buildings, old and new. One hotel, built in oil-boom times, rises well above the low sky line, the only suggestion of skyscraper opulence.

Shawnee's history has been highlighted by a strenuous county seat fight; a flood disaster that cost approximately $1,000,000; a tornado which swept twenty-eight city blocks; a smallpox epidemic; two bank failures; and a serious railroad shopmen's strike. But, paradoxically, during its most troubled days there were fewer business failures in Shawnee than in any other Oklahoma city of its approximate size.

In the late twenties, Shawnee was the principal city in the largest closely grouped area of highly productive oil fields in the world and for five years grew prodigiously, once claiming a population of almost thirty-five thousand. By 1930, however, the census takers found only 23,283; and this number was reduced by 1,244 in the next ten years, owing largely to the decreasing activity of near-by oil fields.

A more reliable, steadier prop for the city's prosperity are the products of Pottawatomie County's 4,400 farms, comprising more than five hundred thousand acres. From these acres are taken the state's best cotton crops and valuable crops of grain sorghums, alfalfa and other types of hay, and pecans, mainly from wild groves. Dairying is important, also; and two nationally known firms maintain cheese factories at Shawnee. The Pottawatomie County Wednesday Community sale, held at the northern edge of the city, attracts thousands of farmers from a wide area.

Shawnee's pioneer memories go back to the opening to white settlement, on September 22, 1891, of the reservations of the Sac and Fox, Iowa, and Shawnee-Potawatomi Indians. It is told that Etta Ray and her sister, young women from Oklahoma City, stood on Kickapoo Indian land with their toes touching the western border of the territory to be opened, and when the opening gun was fired they stepped across and drove their stakes. On the 160-acre claim obtained by Etta the new town began to grow; later, after she married Henry G. Beard and the first railroad sought a right of way eastward from Oklahoma City, one-half of the farm was given on condition that the station should be built there. Today (1941), close by the fine new Municipal Auditorium, the original Beard log cabin still stands.

A sidelight on the manners and morals of the homeseekers who made the Run for land is that the claims of both Etta Ray and her sister were contested—by men. After a long period of litigation, Etta bought off the contestant to her claim for $65, but her sister had to give up half of her land to stop the fight for the whole 160 acres.

In the spring of 1892 a town-building company was formed, trees were cut to open a street, and a sawmill was brought in to save the long and difficult hauling of lumber by ox team from Oklahoma City, forty-five miles away. Another ambitious group attempted to create a town to be called Brockway, but had no luck. When the Beards and their associates had built a store and set up a blacksmith shop, they applied for a post office. To make it simpler, they asked that it be named Shawnee. It was, and Mrs. Beard became the first postmistress. Mail came from the town of Tecumseh, five miles across the river to the south, and the carrier, who supplied his own transportation, was paid $10 a month.

Out of the pioneer past, too, comes the story of the bitter fight between Tecumseh and Shawnee for the county seat of Pottawatomie County, one of the two new counties carved out of the opened reservations. To call attention to its already established importance, Tecumseh's citizens organized an old-time "anvil shoot," and Charlie Miller wrote a parody of "Sweet Marie," which jeered,

Come to me, poor Shawnee,
Poor Shawnee, come to me.
Just because we will not move,
Love, to thee.

When you hear the whistle plain,
And you see the Frisco train,
You will surely lose your brain,
Poor Shawnee!

Because of the nationwide financial depression of 1893, the coming of the first railroad was delayed until the summer of 1895; the arrival at Shawnee of a train of the Choctaw, Oklahoma and Gulf (later absorbed by the Rock Island) was the outstanding feature of that year's Fourth of July celebration. In March, 1902, the Santa Fe railroad reached Shawnee, and two years later the Oklahoma City-Ada-Atoka built in. No doubt to the disappointment of Charlie Miller, the Frisco did not come either to Tecumseh or Shawnee.

About 1910, when it became evident that the state capital was to be removed from Guthrie *(see Tour 10)*, the citizens of Shawnee made an attempt to secure it but could not offer sufficient ground space within the city to make a serious fight against much larger Oklahoma City.

The location at Shawnee of the big Rock Island shops and the shops of the Santa Fe, together employing some nine hundred workers, made the city acutely conscious of the countrywide strike of railroad shopmen against a cut in wages that began July 1, 1922, and continued to October 1. The railroads' property was under heavy guard and on the morning of August 18 a scattering volley of thirty shots was fired into the Rock Island's yards. Over the protest of the city's peace officers, the report went out that conditions at Shawnee were the worst in the United States, and that radical agitators were in control. However, it was said in Shawnee that during the period of the strike mail trains were never delayed and regular service was little affected.

On March 28, 1924, a cyclone swooped upon the northwestern residential section of the city, killed eight persons, and caused damage to property exceeding one-half million dollars. Following tradition, this "twister" leveled buildings, uprooted trees, and "left no living thing in its immediate path."

Shawnee's trial by flood came on April 4, 1928, when a torrential seven-inch rainfall sent the North Canadian River out of its banks and choked the deep and narrow channel of Shawnee Creek, which ran through a populous section of the city. Hundreds of houses were swept from foundations and wrecked by the flood, and the roofs of other hundreds were so seriously damaged by the battering of the terrific hailstorm preceding the deluge that their interiors were ruined. Six persons, unable to move out of the way of the rushing water, were drowned.

A map issued by Shawnee businessmen at the crest of the oil boom in the 1920's listed six richly productive fields within the city's trade area, the most distant only one and one-half hours away by automobile. The thousands of workers, most of them highly paid, and the wealth brought to the men who drilled the ten thousand and more wells gravitated largely to Shawnee; and the city was hard pressed to take care of the newcomers. There were days when the hungry visitor paid a dollar for a sandwich and was lucky to get one. There were nights when this same visitor paid five dollars for a cot in a room with three other sleepers. So rapid was the development in such fields as Earlsboro, Seminole, and Cromwell that for a time it was impossible to supply accommodations for all who rushed in to exploit them. It was during this period that Shawnee was believed to have a population of nearly thirty-five thousand.

The oil rush ended, Shawnee tackled the job which has faced various other Oklahoma cities, that of adjusting itself to the normal growth of an inland city after the subsidence of an oil boom.

Shawnee's first newspaper, named by Editor Phelps the *Shawnee Chief,* appeared for a few weeks in 1892 and was then removed to Tecumseh. Next came the weekly *Shawnee Quill,* in time to record the fire that all but wiped out the business district on December 13, 1895. The *Quill's* estimate of the loss of fifteen buildings and a wagon yard was $26,700. Since then, through various changes, dailies have been established; the morning *News* and the evening *Star,* now (1941) under the same ownership, claim a large circulation throughout a wide territory. There are three weeklies, distributed free in Shawnee—the *County Democrat,* the *Herald,* and the *American.*

A city manager, working with a mayor and council, carries on the business of the municipality; the real estate tax rate (1941) was 33.18 mills on an 80 per cent valuation. Industries have been attracted by low-cost natural gas—ten cents per thousand cubic feet—and by plentiful and cheap fuel oil and coal. The biggest industry, a milling company, has a pay roll of more than $1,000 each working day; and a cotton oil mill which turns out cottonseed meal and cake for cattle feed describes itself as "the connecting link between cotton and livestock."

POINTS OF INTEREST

The MUNICIPAL AUDITORIUM, 400 N. Bell Avenue., in the center of downtown Shawnee, is a modern red-brick structure with a seating capacity of 3,000. Built with a WPA grant of $61,363 and the proceeds of a $75,000 municipal bond issue, it has been a popular meeting place for conventions, because of its size and convenience. The building has complete gymnasium, basketball, indoor tennis, and stage facilities, including projection booths and sound equipment for movie showings. Two low, flat-roofed wings flank the southern entrance.

WOODLAND PARK, four blocks in area, is directly north of the auditorium and is dominated by a big swimming pool, with ample dressing rooms. Concrete tennis courts and picnic facilities under the tall native ash and elm trees add to the park's attractiveness. At its center is the BEARD LOG CABIN *(private),* the first residence in Shawnee.

The POTTAWATOMIE COUNTY COURTHOUSE, in the 300 block on N. Broadway, built in 1934, is a three-story-and-basement building fronting on Broadway, with Woodland Park at its back. Simple and modern in design, it has a base of black Missouri limestone which supports walls of Indiana limestone, trimmed at the corners in terra cotta. Its façade is ornamented with spandrels of aluminum; and above the granite front steps are plaques that picture the Indian, the Pioneer, and Justice. Inside, a wide, two-way branching stairway of warm-tinted marble leads to an elaborate mezzanine; from it opens the high-ceilinged modernistic courtroom with wainscoting of oriental walnut. The architect was A. C. Davis.

The CARNEGIE LIBRARY, just north of the courthouse on N. Broadway, was opened in 1905; later it was seriously damaged by fire and rebuilt. Its book stacks contain (1941) more than 25,000 volumes, and its book circulation exceeds 250,000 a year. The library's facilities are available to the faculty and students of Oklahoma Baptist University as well as the people of Shawnee.

OKLAHOMA BAPTIST UNIVERSITY, coeducational, lying partly within the city at its northwestern corner, had a 1941 enrollment of more than 750 students, and a faculty of 32. Plans for its founding were made in 1906, and its pioneer classes met in September, 1911, in the basement of the First Baptist Church of Shawnee and in Convention Hall.

By 1915, the first building (Shawnee Hall) on the present campus of 60 acres, donated by the city, was ready to receive students; since that time the university plant has expanded to include another classroom building (Montgomery Hall), a publications building, a well-equipped, small observatory, a gymnasium for men, a men's dormitory, a dormitory for women, and other residence facilities for students and faculty. A new dormitory for men is now (1941) under construction.

West of the landscaped quadrangle are the football field, a nine-hole golf course, and the flying field where the O.B.U. School of Aviation trains student flyers.

The university library, housed in Shawnee Hall, contains 15,000 volumes, including the Gillon collection of religious books and denominational records. Its reading room seats 115 and has a "browsing nook" with an open-shelf collection of books for cultural and recreational reading.

ATHLETIC PARK, at the western edge of the city, contains two fields, one for baseball and one for football. The baseball plant, lighted for night games, has seats for 3,000, and the stadium at the football field, with seating capacity of 4,500, is encircled by a cinder track. There is a stone clubhouse with dressing rooms for players.

POINTS OF INTEREST IN ENVIRONS

Shawnee Quaker Mission and Shawnee Indian Sanitorium, *2.5 m.;* St. Gregory's College, *3.3 m.* *(see Tour 5)*.

Stillwater

Railroad Station: Intersection of tracks and E. 9th St. for Atchison, Topeka & Santa Fe Ry.
Bus Stations: 111 W. 7th St. for Turner Transportation Co.; Grand Hotel for Missouri-Kansas-Oklahoma Trailways.
Airport: Searcy Field, 2 m. N. on State 40 and 0.5 m. W.; no scheduled service.
Taxis: 10c upward, according to distance and number of passengers.

Accommodations: 4 hotels; tourist camps.

Information Service: Chamber of Commerce, Municipal Bldg., 8th and Lewis Sts.

Golf: Hillcrest, 1.5 m. N. on State 40, and 0.5 m. W., greens fee 25c; Yost Lake Course, 4 m. N. and 3 m. E. on State 40.
Tennis: Free courts at High School, Duncan St. and 11th Ave.
Swimming and Boating: Yost Lake, 4 m. N. and 3 m. E. on State 40; Stillwater Lake, 1.5 m. N. and 0.5 m. W. on State 40; Lake Carl Blackwell, 7 m. W. on State 51.

Annual Events: Junior Livestock Show, March; Flower and Vegetable Show, late June; Farmer's Week, and 4-H Club Roundup (sponsored by Oklahoma Agricultural and Mechanical College), Aug.; Payne County Fair, 2d week in Sept.; Homecoming Celebration, early Nov.

STILLWATER (886 alt., 10,097 pop.), seat of Payne County and site of Oklahoma Agricultural and Mechanical College, was laid out, legally, immediately after the opening of the original Oklahoma Territory in 1889. Previously, however, the site was known to the "Boomers," those men who contended that this occupied Indian land could be homesteaded, and in January, 1885, a force of six hundred United States troops was sent to oust a settlement of five hundred that had been living in dugouts in "Prairie Dog Town," on the present-day Fair Grounds. Their leader, William L. Couch, defied the soldiers, who instead of firing on the entrenched intruders cut their lines of supply and starved them out.

The present city was located on Stillwater Creek by a group who made the Run together; the majority of them were from Cowley County, Kansas. A 240-acre tract was assembled from their 160-acre claims by five men in honor of whom Lewis, Duck, Husband, Lowry, and Duncan streets were named. The land thus donated, plus eighty acres which it was discovered had not been staked in the Run, was to constitute the townsite, but the man who was chosen to file on the unclaimed eighty and then turn it over to the town's promoters refused to give it up until the matter was settled at a hearing by land-office officials. In the beginning, $6.25 would pay for one business and two residential lots; and until after the passage of the Organic Act of 1890 government of the town was wholly voluntary, without formal authority. Money from the sale of lots went into the town's treasury and was spent for bridges, a well, and street improvements.

The main streets of most Oklahoma towns and cities are laid out east and west, but that of Stillwater runs north and south; and the explanation is an interesting illustration of the practical working of the pioneers' sense of fairness. When it was found that an east-west layout would unduly enhance the value of one man's holdings, its direction was changed.

Eighteen months after Stillwater was laid out the first legislature awarded to it the new college of agriculture; and since then Stillwater's story and that of the college have developed together.

On a slight slope north of Stillwater Creek, bowered in trees, the city spreads up to, and beyond, the campus of Oklahoma Agricultural and Mechanical College, familiarly known throughout the state as A. and M. A big small town in appearance, its business buildings are low, trim, and solid; its residences, set in big yards, large and comfortable.

The town's first boost came when it was designated as a registration point for the opening of the Cherokee Outlet in 1893; and the next big help was the coming of the railroad in 1899. Before that year, the outside world was reached by hack to Wharton (now Perry), twenty-five miles away.

Stillwater describes itself as a business and educational center, measuring up to the dreams of its founders in enterprise, culture, and hospitality. Its population is the familiar Oklahoma college-town mixture of retired farmers; those who serve the surrounding farm region by operating creameries, hatcheries, grain elevators, flour mills, and cotton gins; retail merchants who cater to the student body of A. and M.; the faculty and regular students; and the increasing number who come for short courses and summer sessions.

Under a commission form of government, Stillwater has levied no municipal taxes since 1931; the government is supported by revenues from its utilities. A roomy, modern municipal hospital, a municipal library, and a beautiful municipal building of modern design serve the city.

OKLAHOMA AGRICULTURAL AND MECHANICAL COLLEGE

A. and M. occupies a 120-acre campus at the northwestern border of Stillwater. An outlying farm of twelve hundred acres, west of the city, is used as an experiment station, and the college owns 880 acres of farm land elsewhere. The fifty-five buildings on the campus include thirty used for instruction and administration; nineteen barns and other agricultural structures; and seven residence halls capable of housing 950 women students and 825 men.

One of the two most important institutions of higher education in the state, A. and M. enrolled 6,483 students in its regular courses in 1940–41; in summer sessions, 2,557; and 1,151 in correspondence and extension courses. Attendance at short courses (from four days to two weeks) totaled 7,193.

The teaching staff numbers 306; there are some four hundred additional employees at Stillwater, and 280 workers in the Extension Division distributed over the seventy-seven counties. At the 1940 spring commencement, 749 bachelors' degrees were conferred in all departments. Masters' degrees were also awarded to 219 students.

On Christmas Day, 1890, the act of the territorial legislature establishing the college became effective. The law "required that the county of Payne, or the municipality in or near which the institution might be located, should issue its bonds in the sum of $10,000 . . ." These were to be sold by the territory's secretary "at not less than their par value."

Payne County defeated the bond issue, but the residents of Stillwater, at a municipal election in April, 1891, plumped for the bonds, by 132 votes out of 136. The bonds brought only $8,600; the $1,400 required to bring them up to par was raised by selling city warrants and by a note for $352 made by members of the city council.

By July of that year two hundred acres of prairie land adjoining the town on the northwest had also been donated as a site. It was, said an early catalogue, "untouched by plow or other implements, with the exception of about 16 acres. The work of fencing this land and reducing it to cultivation was at once begun, the first furrow . . . being turned on the 2d day of December, 1891." As a land-grant college, Stillwater was entitled to Federal aid; in its first year, however, this amounted to only $3,000; and in the following year to $750.

Out of these very limited resources, a small laboratory for the chemistry department, a barn, residences for the school head and farm manager were built in 1892, and next year engine and seed houses—small frame structures—were added. Meanwhile, classes were held in the Congregational Church. In June of 1894, Assembly Hall—known now as "Old Central"—was ready for classwork.

Commencement exercises were held at the end of each college year, but it was not until 1896 that there were any graduates to receive degrees. Then six young men qualified. Of the June, 1893, commencement, a Stillwater paper said that the college had "over 150 students under the care of an able and energetic board of regents and faculty. This was a commencement without a graduate, although the sweet girls were there just the same." All graduates up to 1915 had to return for additional work in order to have their degrees recognized.

An integral part of the college, the Agricultural Experiment Station is maintained by funds provided by Congress under successive acts, and its work was started at the same time, in December, 1891, when "most of the good people of Stillwater" turned out to help the first director burn off the tall grass that hid the corner markers of the property; and again when the first furrows were turned. "A pair of mules," once wrote the station's head, "was probably the first property acquired. . . . Tradition has it that one evening Professor Magruder, overseer of the farm, caught a pair of runaway mules and held them until the owner came up in a furious mood and offered to sell them to any man who would offer a price. Magruder got the mules." And, presumably, tamed their wild spirits by hitching them to a sod plow.

On the college's twelve-hundred-acre farm adjoining the campus have been tried varied experiments like the sowing of wheat on the same plot every year since 1892; determination of the minimum vitamin A requirements for dairy cattle; the improvement of hogs through inbreeding; determination of the effect of environmental factors on the composition of vegetables; the effects of different forms of waste from oil wells; insect control; meat laboratory work; and research on diseases of cattle, horses, sheep, hogs, and chickens. The station also carries on, through county agents and home demonstration women aides, a state-wide program of extension work.

Short courses of a week or less bring adults to the college for instruction in many subjects ranging from firemanship to school custodianship, cafeteria, and waterworks management. Special meetings of one or two days deal with stock feeding, agronomy, vocational guidance, "band clinics," choral festivals, editing, and many other topics.

Student activities include the publication of the *O'Collegian,* a campus daily (twice weekly during the summer session), the *Redskin,* the college annual, various departmental periodicals; and seven musical organizations. Because the college is far from any city of considerable size, the student body and faculty rely to an unusual extent upon themselves for extra-curricular interests.

Loosely grouped on land that was level prairie, with little attempt at landscaping and with few trees as yet to add shade and variety to the campus scene, the college's buildings are primarily utilitarian in design. The whole effect is one of bareness, neatness, and the utmost economy in the use of building funds.

CAMPUS TOUR

The buildings are listed in order of location from the corner of Knoblock and College Sts., the most convenient starting point. Ordinarily they are open during school hours.

FIREMANSHIP TRAINING BUILDING is a two-story brick firehouse, with regular fire-fighting equipment below and quarters for students above. The tall octagonal tower at the north end of the building is somewhat suggestive of a New England meeting house. Here is the equivalent of a three-company fire brigade, with classrooms and laboratories. It is the only school department of the kind in the country.

WILLIAMS HALL, in which is housed THE PRAIRIE PLAYHOUSE, is a reconditioned old building where the work of the speech and English departments is carried on. The equipment includes an auditorium, stage, dressing rooms, and drama workrooms.

"OLD CENTRAL," set back from Knoblock St. (L), was the first building erected on the campus for classroom use. A quaint, square, squat, pink-brick little survival, it was described at its dedication in 1894 as "a handsome structure . . . 67 by 67 feet in size, consisting of two stories, and contains 16 rooms." In the minds of loyal students and alumni, "Old Central" has retained at least a sentimental beauty. It is still (1941) commodious enough (a third story has been added) to house the Graduate School, the Department of Agricultural Education, the Geology Department, the Former Students Association and Placement Bureau, a museum, and an auditorium.

The AUDITORIUM, corner of Knoblock and Morrill Sts., is a brick and reinforced concrete structure, equipped with a large stage, dressing rooms, and drama workrooms.

GARDNER HALL, opposite the auditorium on Morrill St., a plain but well-designed four-story red-brick structure with dormer windows, houses the activities of the Extension Division, the women's section of the Department of Health and Physical Education, and a part of the staff of the School of Commerce.

MORRILL HALL, Morrill St., facing toward "Old Central," is a four-story, wide-spreading structure of the older period, built of brick and stone. Here are the departments of commerce, education, foreign languages, and art. The hall was named for United States Senator Justin S. Morrill, who wrote the Federal act establishing land-grant colleges.

Farther along on Knoblock Street, Athletic Avenue (L) marks the southern boundary of an area devoted to sports. Here, flanked by concrete-surfaced tennis courts are the GYMNASIUM 167 by 107 feet; the football STADIUM, with seats for 30,000 spectators; and GALAGHER HALL, the college Field House named for the long-time coach of A. and M.'s wrestling teams. The Field House, a great modernistic block-shaped hall, is used for such indoor sports as wrestling and basketball; and when the school's basketball team plays that of the University of Oklahoma—A. and M.'s traditional rival—all its 7,000 seats are filled.

West of the Stadium is CORDELL HALL, an enormous wide-H-shaped residence hall of red brick trimmed with white stone, with quarters for 525 men students. First used in the school year 1939–40, this "dorm" is one of the largest in the Southwest.

The agriculture school's utilities are west of the athletic area and Cordell Hall. The impressive ANIMAL HUSBANDRY BUILDING is a steel, concrete and brick structure, with rounded roof and tall Ionic columns supporting a lofty porch. Within is an arena 59 by 180 feet, with seats for 2,000.

Farther west on the 1,200-acre experimental farm is the huge BEEF CATTLE BARN, with four commodious wings, flanked at its four corners by enormous brick silos. Other structures in this area are the DAIRY BUILDING, the HOG BARN, the HORSE BARN, the SHEEP BARN, the EXPERIMENTAL SHED, and the POULTRY FARM BUILDING.

The section of the campus on Washington Street, to the west, is given over to women's residence halls. Here, in order from north to south, are FRANCES E. WILLARD HALL (L), a modern four-story red-brick home for 410 students; NORTH HALL (R), with accommodations for 150 women. A covered arcade leads from North Hall to the big MURRAY HALL, housing 410 students, where there is a joint dining room for North and Murray halls.

North of Frances Willard Hall is WHITEHURST HALL, the Agricultural and Administration building. Constructed of brick, stone, and concrete, four stories high, it is typical of A. and M.'s simple, practical architectural style. Similar in design is the LIFE SCIENCES BUILDING, which houses the departments of zoology, bacteriology, physiology, botany, and veterinary science, and the ENGINEERING BUILDING used by the Mechanical Engineering Department.

POINTS OF INTEREST IN ENVIRONS

Boomer Lake, *1.9 m.;* Stillwater Lake, *3.4 m.;* Lake Carl Blackwell, *13 m.;* Midget Cattle Farm, *14.2 m. (see Tour 2).*

Tulsa

Railroad Stations: Union Depot, 3 S. Boston Ave. for Atchison, Topeka & Santa Fe Ry., St. Louis–San Francisco Ry., and Missouri-Kansas-Texas R.R.; Frankford Ave. and 6th St. for Midland Valley Ry.

Interurban: Waiting Room, 27 E. Archer St. for service between Tulsa and Sand Springs.

Bus Stations: Union Bus Station, 319 S. Cincinnati Ave., for Missouri, Kansas & Oklahoma Trailways, Southwestern Greyhound Lines, Southern Kansas Greyhound Lines, Union Transportation Co., Santa Fe Trailways; All-American Bus Station, 215 S. Boulder Ave., for All-American Bus Lines.

Airport: Municipal Airport, E. Apache Ave. and Sheridan Rd. for American Air Lines and Mid-Continent Lines; 30-min. cab service (fare 50c) from Hotel Mayo, Cheyenne Ave. and 5th St.

City Bus Lines: Fare 5c, universal transfers.

Taxis: 15c to 50c, according to number of passengers and distance.

Traffic Regulations: No left turn on or into Main Street between 2d and 5th Sts. inclusive. Parking only at designated places. Obey School Zone signs.

Accommodations: 22 hotels, 8 for Negroes; rooming houses, tourist camps and trailer parks on every highway. Capacity rates during International Petroleum Exposition, 2 weeks in May, even years.

Information Service: Chamber of Commerce, Tulsa Bldg., 3d St. and Cincinnati Ave.; Auto Club of Oklahoma (for members), Adams Hotel, 4th St. and Cheyenne Ave.

Radio Stations: KTUL (1430 kc.); KVOO (1170 kc.); KOME (1340 kc.).

Theaters and Motion Picture Houses: Tulsa Little Theater,1511 S. Delaware Ave., local productions during fall and winter; Convention Hall, 101 W. Brady St.; and Akdar Theater, 4th St. and Denver Ave., local productions, occasional road shows, and concerts; 20 motion picture houses, 2 for Negroes.

Athletics: Texas League Baseball Park (night) 4300 E. 15th St.; Skelly Field (Public High School and University of Tulsa Stadium), 2900 E. 11th St.

Hockey, Wrestling, and Ice Skating (winter and spring): The Coliseum, 501 S. Elgin Ave.

Boating: Mohawk Park Lagoons and Mohawk Lakes *(see Tour 9A).*

Swimming: Newblock Pool (municipal), 20 blocks W. of Main St. on US 64, 15c and 25c; YMCA, 4th St. and Cincinnati Ave., 25c; Crystal City Park, S. of city on US 66, 25c.

Golf: Mohawk Municipal Course, Mohawk Park, 5 m. N., reached by Peoria, Lewis, and Howard Aves., 18 holes; Northridge, N. of city near Mohawk Park; McFarland, Memorial Drive and East Federal, E. of city; Kennedy (sand greens) N.W. of city; Wil-Croft (sand greens) 21st St. and Harvard Ave., greens fees at all 75c.

Tennis: Free municipal courts at 6th St. and Peoria Ave., 11th St. and Peoria Ave., 13th St. and Cincinnati Ave., N. Boston Ave. between Queen and Tecumseh Sts., Edison St. and Quannah Ave., Newblock Park, 2500 S. Quannah Ave., 21st St. and Olympia Ave., 42d St. and Yukon Ave., and Admiral Blvd. and Utica St.

Annual Events: Magic Empire Junior Livestock Show, March; Oil Capital Horse Show, Fair Grounds Pavilion, May; Tulsa State Fair, Fair Grounds, 6 blocks E. of 15th St. and Harvard Ave., Sept.; Mid-Continent Kennel Club Show, Fair Grounds, Poultry Bldg., Nov.

International Petroleum Exposition: Biennial event, in May of even years. Exposition Grounds (adjoining Fair Grounds).

For further information regarding this city see TULSA, *A Guide to the Oil Capital,* American Guide Series, published May, 1938, by the Mid-West Printing Company, Tulsa, Oklahoma.

TULSA (750 alt., 142,157 pop.) is built chiefly on low, rolling hills and on the flat between the hills and the east bank of the Arkansas River. The city has reached out across the river, however, and includes West Tulsa, now (1941) an integral part of it. Stretching away to the south is one of Oklahoma's most fertile farming and fruit-growing sections; toward the north and east the land is broken and better adapted to grazing; and on the northwest are the lower ranges of the Osage Hills, a part of the Osage Indian oil lands.

Tulsa, the second largest city in Oklahoma, is the oil center of the great Mid-Continent area and the state's largest oil refining center, yet it is neither typically Oklahoman nor a typical oil-boom town. It is a city of contrasts, resulting from the transplanting of a metropolitan population to a small settlement of Indians and white pioneers. In certain sections, as north of 3d Street, old Tulsa still exists (1941) with the squat one- and two-story frame, stone, and brick buildings of its earlier days. Generally, however, the city is eastern in the character of its people, in its office buildings on Boston Avenue between 3d and 6th Streets, and in its southern section, where elaborate homes suggest New York or Philadelphia suburbs rather than Oklahoma.

The sections flanking the railroad tracks between 1st Street and Archer Avenue and West Tulsa, across the river, are industrial in character; and beyond Archer to the northeast lies the extensive Negro district.

A dramatic view of Tulsa from the southwest, across the vast refinery plant dominating West Tulsa and the wide sand-carpeted bed of the river, shows tall, smoke-stained stacks giving way, on the skyline, to the taller modern-city group of skyscrapers that serve the office and hotel needs of its hundreds of oil companies. It is a visual summary of the city's description of itself as the oil capital of the world.

More than 98 per cent of Tulsa's population is American born, but it is composed of many elements. The first organized settlement was made by civilized Indians, and the first whites were a mixture of workmen, small-scale merchants, missionaries, and adventurers. After statehood brought the right to buy land, many farmers and ranchmen came from the South and West to settle in the vicinity, and their children built homes in the city. To this already conglomerate citizenry the oil industry added thousands of administrative, technical, and clerical workers from the North and East.

Tulsa has wealthy citizens whose fortunes are generations old and others whose wealth is new. Many of the poor became rich and many of the rich lost their money as the status of oil in the Mid-Continent region fluctuated. Indians and whites intermarried extensively; factory workers drifted in; leisure classes developed; businessmen retired and took up the hobbies of leisure. The city's great middle class, composed of minor oil executives, tradesmen and clerks, mechanics and oil office workers, increased.

There are citizens of all degrees of Indian mixture, but even those of less than one-eighth proudly call themselves Indians. They boast, as did the late Will Rogers, who was a Cherokee member of Tulsa's Akdar Shrine, that their ancestors were not Mayflower passengers, but were on the "reception committee." Tulsa's Indians are not easily identified unless they are of more than one-quarter blood. Their dress, pursuits, and attainments are exactly the same as those of the white population.

About 12 per cent of Tulsa's population is Negroes, who live in a segregated district of which Greenwood Avenue is the principal business street. This district lies to the northeast of the Union Depot, running in a fan shape from a line almost due north to a line approximately northeast, and extending indefinitely to the city's edge. Housing facilities here are generally poor, reflecting the income of a people largely dependent upon work as servants or casual laborers. There are, however, a few fine residences, the homes of successful business and professional men. Within the Greenwood district are the "separate" schools, Negro hotels, a park, places of business and amusement, a municipal hospital, and churches.

Tulsa existed as early as 1879 as a postoffice on the pony mail route through Indian Territory. The office was in the home of a Creek rancher, George Perryman, near what is now 41st Street; the rancher's brother was the first postmaster. Into this primitive section, unknown to any whites except a few cattlemen and those who had married into the tribe, the old Atlantic & Pacific Railroad built in 1882. Originally the builders planned to stop in the Cherokee Nation, about a mile from the river bank, but since the Cherokee laws prohibited commercial transactions by native, intermarried, or adopted Cherokee citizens, the rails were extended into the Creek Nation where whites were permitted to trade by posting a bond. There, on the site of the present Tulsa business section, the railroad established a terminal with a roundhouse and a large loading pen. The vast herds of cattle from the Southwest, formerly driven overland to Vinita *(see Tour 1)*, were now loaded in Tulsa for shipment to the stockyards of St. Louis and Chicago. Trains began making daily trips between the terminus and Vinita, stopping at intervals to let passengers shoot prairie chickens along the way. Traders and an occasional professional man drifted in. The Creek rancher moved his postoffice to the terminal.

The town was first called Tulsey Town, for the Creek Indians who belonged to the Tallassee or Tulsey community. The present Tallassee, Alabama, was the former home of this group before the Indians were removed to Oklahoma.

Isparhecher ('Spa-hich'-se), an insurgent Creek leader, had organized a small army of full bloods and harassed those Creeks loyal to Chief Checotah. Guerilla warfare was rampant throughout the nation in 1882, and the little stores of Tulsa, unable to replenish their stocks for fear of looting, did practically no business all fall and winter. By August, 1883, however, the Creek trouble was settled and the town began to breathe normally. Floored tents were replaced by wooden shacks, and plank-built stores were provided with covered porches. With the coming of summer, 1883, Tulsa had all the earmarks of a "fair little city," as its inhabitants called it, even to a community water well and a Negro barber.

The early settlers of the town felt that one hundred feet was "too far to wade the mud," and main street was made only eighty feet wide. The street was surveyed by a railroad engineer who ran his line at right angles to the railroad, thus causing the downtown district to be built "cattywampus," as the old-timers express it, while the rest of the city is straight with the compass. In writing of this Main Street a pioneer recalls that "whether it was dusty or muddy depended upon the weather. We had to dodge roaming hogs, goats, and cows when crossing, and sometimes wild animals would venture into the middle of town."

Alcoholic liquor was prohibited under Indian Territory law, but thousands of gallons poured into the town. There were no important trading points within a radius of sixty miles, and Tulsa's isolation made it a resort for gamblers and bad men. The only law was that enforced by the Creek Lighthorsemen and the U.S. deputy marshals who paid brief and rare visits; or the "two volumes of common law" that every man carried strapped to his thighs. In spite of this wild-west atmosphere, however, the first organization of any kind was a union Sunday School, formed in 1883 in the tent of a railroad carpenter.

In 1884 the Presbyterian Home Mission Board of New York City erected a small mission school on the summit of a wooded hill at what is now the southeast corner of Fourth Street and Boston Avenue. Here Tulsa's first congregation was organized, one that included many Indians and an elder who used the Cherokee language when called upon to pray. It was near the old cattle trail, and herds of cattle were driven past it almost every day until about 1888. Its site is now (1941) occupied by the Cosden Building.

There were many things to retard the development of Tulsa. First, a long fight with railroad officials who claimed a right of way three hundred feet wide south of the tracks that would have included some of the town's buildings. Then certain of the Indians eyed the site of the little settlement greedily, claiming most of it as their personal allotments after the nation's land, once held in common, had been divided among individual Creek citizens. As a result of these land disputes, residences and business houses were built on the first white cemetery and the Creek burial grounds on the heights overlooking the river. One of the most serious difficulties was the lack of an adequate water supply, which caused the railroad to shift its terminal to Sapulpa. In 1900, at the time of the first government townsite survey, Tulsa, with a population of 1,390—including whites, Negroes and Indians—was merely an unimportant town in Indian Territory.

Then, on June 25, 1901, Tulsa rocketed into national attention. Across the river at Red Fork (now within the city limits) the state's first commercially important oil well was brought in. During the next two years Red Fork and Tulsa both grew rapidly; but since Tulsa was cut off from oil development by the Arkansas River, there was a possibility that she might become a suburb of the other town. A bond issue to build a wagon bridge failed, but three citizens built a toll bridge with their own capital and Tulsa invited the ever-increasing horde of oil men to "come and make your homes in a beautiful little city that is high and dry, peaceful and orderly. Where there are good churches, stores, schools, and banks, and where our ordinances prevent the desolation of our homes and property by oil wells."

The oilmen took Tulsa at its word. By 1910 a building boom was in full swing and brick plants were working at capacity. Pipe lines were opened to the Gulf of Mexico and oil prices were climbing. Hotel and office buildings were erected. Streets were paved. Banks were established. The total value of buildings under construction reached $1,365,000 by late August. Down through the Creek country and up through the lands of the Osages into Kansas went the drillers; but in Tulsa lived the bosses, and here the operating money was banked. The population leaped from 19,500 in 1910 to 76,966 in 1920, and to 141,258 in 1930.

Immediately following the World War, there was increasing racial bitterness due to the influx of both white and Negro laborers seeking employment in the oil fields. After months of unrest and threats of vigilante activity, a minor incident on June 1, 1921, developed into a serious race riot. Armed conflict between whites and Negroes spread to several sections of the city. Vigilantes invaded the Greenwood (Negro) district and laid it waste by fire. It was estimated that more than thirty-six persons were killed in the various clashes. After a night of terror and two days of martial law the whites organized a systematic rehabilitation program for the devastated Negro section and gave generous aid to the Negroes left homeless by the fire. Nationwide publicity of the most lurid sort naturally followed the tragedy, and Tulsa's whites and Negroes joined in an effort to live down the incident by working for a better mutual understanding.

Many of the early settlers were cultured people, and the city's many-sided interest in music has developed from their activities *(see Music)*. One of the first ensembles of one hundred pianos heard in the United States played in Tulsa in 1934 and was broadcast over a portion of the Columbia Broadcasting System's network.

The business life of the town is dominated by oil and the industries allied with oil. Of the latter there are machine shops, tank companies, rig and derrick manufacturers, and a score of the nation's best-known makers of other oil-field tools and equipment. It is estimated that 540 oil companies with headquarters in Tulsa purchase supplies and equipment with a value of approximately $400,000,000. Much of the financing is made possible by the city's banks, which specialize in oil-field enterprises and handle successfully oil promotions that other banks would not consider. As a center for financing such operations, the city is second only to New York.

Petroleum refining is by far the most important industry in Tulsa. One of the largest refineries in the state, with a daily capacity of forty thousand barrels of crude oil, is across the Arkansas River from the business district. Here are also two other refineries with capacities of eleven thousand and six thousand barrels a day; and in the suburb of Sand Springs, seven miles west, there is a fourth refinery that handles eight thousand barrels of crude oil daily.

Cheap fuel and an abundant supply of raw materials account for the city's industrial importance in fields other than those associated with oil. In the Sand Springs district are several glass plants, one of the largest cotton mills west of the Mississippi, chemical works, a furniture factory, steel works, garment and tent factories, automobile body works, brick and tile plants and oxygen making and distributing centers. An aircraft company, with which is connected a school of aeronautics, represents a considerable investment, and its expanding activities are closely tied in with the national air defense program.

With the coming of oil, Tulsa's two struggling weekly newspapers, the *Democrat* and the *World,* blossomed into dailies. In 1920, the *Democrat,* an evening paper, came under new management and the name was changed to the *Tribune.* The *World* became a morning daily and for a short time put out an evening edition also. Published weekly at Tulsa is the *Oil and Gas Journal,* the most important, authoritative oil publication in the country, and one that is read by oilmen all over the world.

The *Oklahoma Constitution,* the *New State Farm and Home, and Sturm's Statehood Magazine,* now only memories, were started in the period 1904–06 to further the movement for statehood.

POINTS OF INTEREST

1. UNION DEPOT, 3 S. Boston Ave., on a site 125 by 155 feet in extent, is at the heart of old Tulsa. The exterior walls of this modern building are formed of alternate blocks of white and very pale gray Bedford limestone, with little decoration except above the windows and along a coping which takes the place of a cornice. The cornice effect is achieved by a carved Greek key motif, broken by conventional shield designs bearing figures of eagles and winged wheels in bas-relief. In the interior, the upper walls are plastered in imitation of travertine marble while the two-tone marble of the wainscoting is laid in a panel design. This, the first Union Depot in Oklahoma, was designed by R. C. Stephens, Frisco Railway architect, and completed in 1931. Because the railway tracks were on a level with the diked banks of the Arkansas River and could not be lowered, the streets in the neighborhood were raised to cross over them. Thus, while the main entrances and waiting room of the depot are at street level, they are 30 feet above the tracks. The outstanding feature of the building is the foyer extending from Cincinnati to Boston Avenues.
2. The SEAMAN OFFICE BUILDING, 14-16 3d St., formerly contained the Elks' clubrooms, in which, in November, 1906, the last passionate protest against white occupancy of the Creek Nation was made by Chitto Harjo, later leader of the Crazy Snake Rebellion. Harjo, speaking before a congressional committee and the chiefs of the Creeks and Cherokees, reminded the government of its treaties and begged that all its promises be kept.
3. The FEDERAL BUILDING, Boulder Ave. between 2d and 3d Sts., is a three-story limestone structure of neoclassic design with a Corinthian colonnade across the front. The southern third of the building was erected under the supervision of James A. Wetmore, acting supervising architect of the Treasury Department, in 1915. Using the same design and structural materials, the building was enlarged to its present size in 1932.
4. The COUNTY COURTHOUSE, N.E. corner 6th St. and Boulder Ave., a four-story limestone structure of modified Greek design, was erected

in 1910-11. On this site in 1886, George Perryman, brother of Legus Perryman, who was a principal chief of the Creek Nation, built a sizable residence, which at that time was considered "way out in the country."

5. CENTRAL SENIOR HIGH SCHOOL, between Cincinnati and Detroit Aves., extending from 6th to 7th Sts., is a red-brick structure trimmed with white stone. The entrances are flanked by towers, Tudor Gothic in feeling. The school was built in two sections—one in 1916, the other in 1921—at a cost of approximately $2,000,000. The south auditorium *(open during school hours)* is equipped with the first pipe organ placed in a public high school in the United States, a gift of the graduating classes from 1925 to 1935 inclusive.

6. The BOSTON AVENUE METHODIST CHURCH, Boston Ave. between 13th St. and 13th Place, is a notable example of modern ecclesiastical architecture. The unusual design was conceived by Miss Adah Robinson, Tulsa artist, and executed by Rush, Endicott, and Goff, Tulsa architects. Construction was completed in 1929.

The massive limestone walls of the main building, four stories high, terminate in cubistic images of praying hands. The same symbolic imagery, in less detail, is carried out in the illuminated tower that rises 290 feet above the doorways with their pointed arches and terra-cotta and bas-relief figures of pioneer characters. The lower floors are occupied by a community hall, gymnasium, kitchen, auditorium, chapel, and educational rooms. Other offices, classrooms, and studios are in the tower. The building of the church attracted international attention, and newspapers and magazines in many parts of the world printed photographs and descriptions of it.

7. The OLD COUNCIL TREE, on the lawn of a private residence at 1730 S. Cheyenne Ave., is marked by a bronze tablet nailed to the trunk. The ground around the tree was the traditional meeting place for the heads of the Creek families composing the Tallassee Lochapokas (town) for their councils or busks. It is supposed to have been used as early as 1836, until the Spanish-American War. The busk was the official town meeting, but included purification and recreation rites as well as business. Several days before the appointed time, a messenger from the town chief would deliver to each family a bundle of sticks. One stick was withdrawn and broken each day until one remained. This last stick was presented at the roll call on the following day. The men purified themselves by drinking an emetic of willow root. Recreation took the form of feasting, dancing, and Indian ball. This game was so important to the Creeks that their general council passed stringent rules governing it.

8. BOULDER PARK, Boulder Ave and 18th St., was a favorite camping

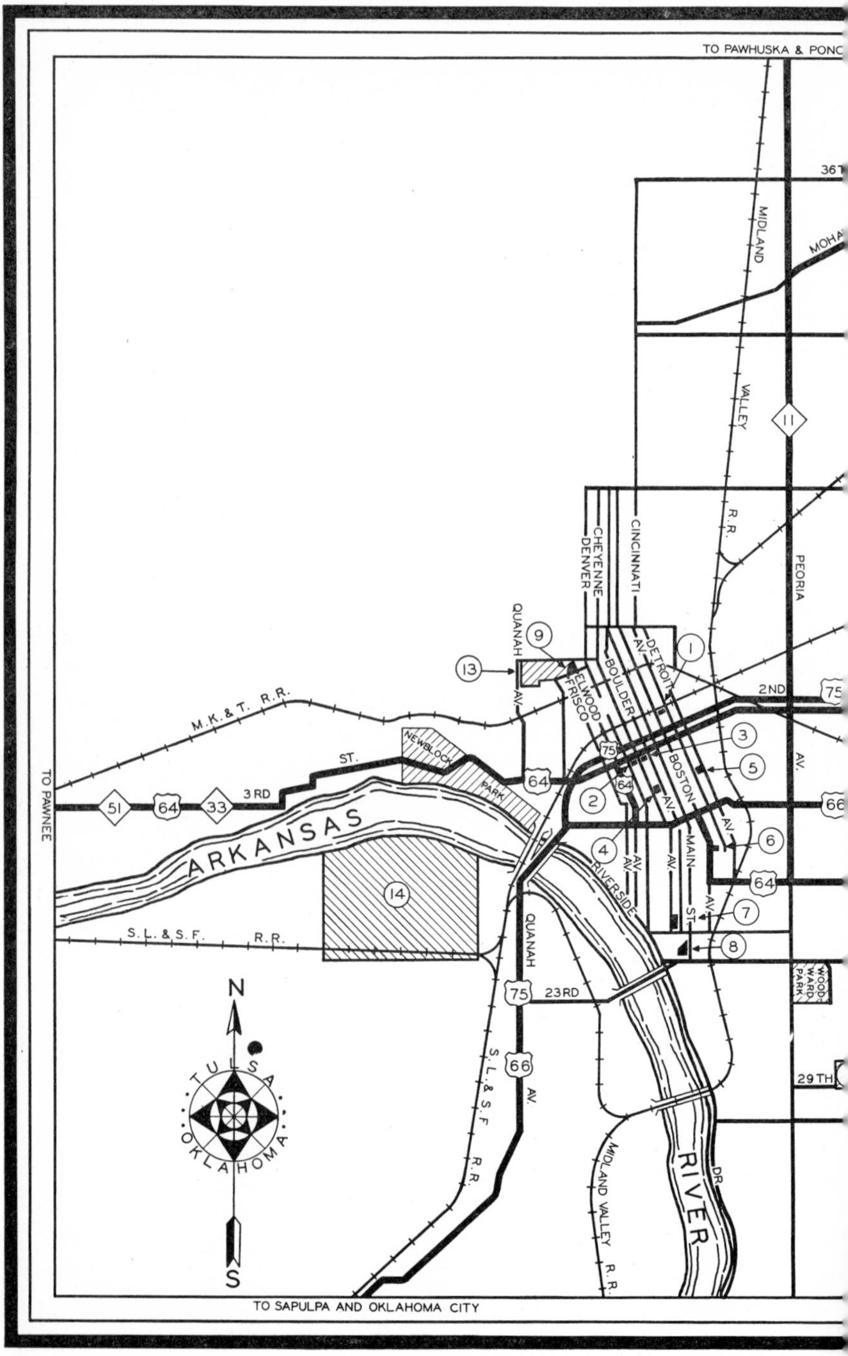

TO PAWHUSKA & PONC
TO PAWNEE
TO SAPULPA AND OKLAHOMA CITY
36T
MOHA
MIDLAND
VALLEY
R.R.
11
PEORIA
AV.
CINCINNATI
CHEYENNE
DENVER
QUANAH
AV.
DETROIT
AV.
BOULDER
ELWOOD
FRISCO
2ND
75
M.K.& T. R.R.
ST.
3 RD
51
64
33
NEWBLOCK
PARK
BOSTON
AV.
MAIN
ST.
66
ARKANSAS
RIVERSIDE
DR.
RIVER
S.L.& S.F.
R.R.
23RD
29TH
WOOD WARD PARK
QUANAH
AV.
S.L.& S.F
R.R.
MIDLAND VALLEY R.R.
N
S
TULSA
OKLAHOMA
1
2
3
4
5
6
7
8
9
13
14

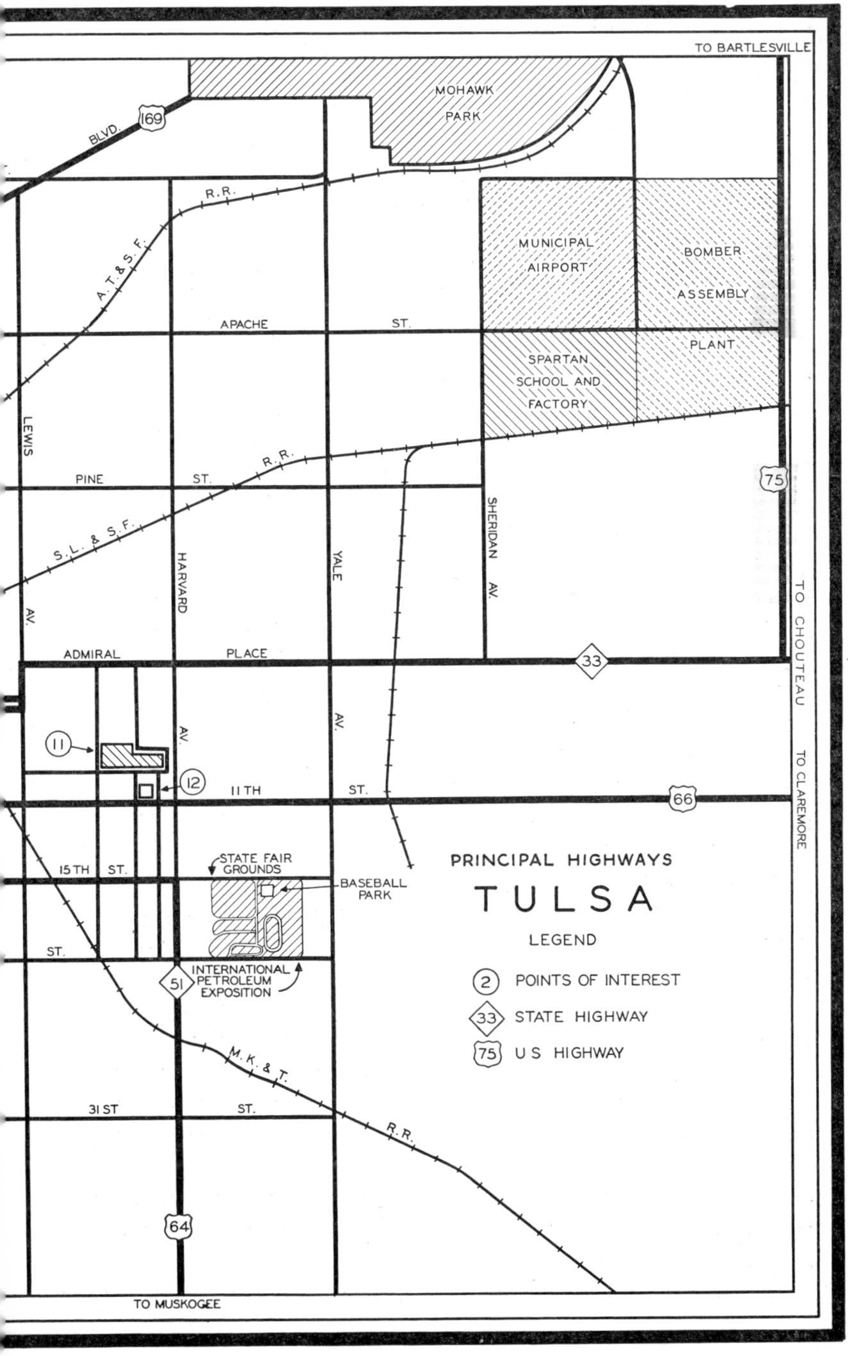

TO BARTLESVILLE
MOHAWK PARK
BLVD.
169
R.R.
A.T.&S.F.
MUNICIPAL AIRPORT
BOMBER ASSEMBLY PLANT
APACHE ST.
SPARTAN SCHOOL AND FACTORY
LEWIS AV.
R.R.
PINE ST.
S.L.&S.F.
75
SHERIDAN AV.
HARVARD AV.
YALE AV.
TO CHOUTEAU
ADMIRAL PLACE
33
11
12
11TH ST.
66
TO CLAREMORE
PRINCIPAL HIGHWAYS
TULSA
LEGEND
2 POINTS OF INTEREST
33 STATE HIGHWAY
75 U S HIGHWAY
15TH ST.
STATE FAIR GROUNDS
BASEBALL PARK
ST.
INTERNATIONAL PETROLEUM EXPOSITION
51
M.K.&T. R.R.
31 ST ST.
64
TO MUSKOGEE

place for the Indians, and the scene of several feuds between the Creeks who were divided in loyalty by the Civil War. Among the park's attractions are a formal flower garden, a softball diamond, and an archery range.

9. INDIAN BOUNDARY SITE, intersection of Frisco and Elwood Aves. and Edison St., is marked by a bronze plate set in the center of the Edison Street paving at the exact corner where the Osage, Cherokee, and Creek nations met before the Cherokee and Creek boundaries were obliterated by statehood. (The Osage Nation, now Osage County, still retains it boundary.)

10. The PHILBROOK ART MUSEUM, *(open 10 A.M. to 6 P.M., except Sun. and Tues., 2 P.M. to 6 P.M. Closed Mon. Admission free Sun. and Thurs., other days 25c),* 2727 S. Rockford Ave., was formerly an elaborate and beautiful private residence. It was given to the city by Mr. and Mrs. Waite Phillips, who also gave the necessary funds to convert it into a home of regional art. The museum opened in October, 1939. Under the direction of the Southwestern Art Association, it houses changing exhibitions of paintings, sculpture, tapestries, and other art forms; and offers lectures and classes in painting, drawing, sculpture, and modeling for children. One of its principal purposes is to emphasize Indian art. On the first Thursday of each month, there are special showings for Negroes, with Negro docents in attendance.

11. Many of the buildings and the grounds of the UNIVERSITY OF TULSA, between 5th and 7th Sts., and Delaware Ave. and Gary Place, are gifts of Tulsa philanthropists. Some of its $1,252,000 endowment, however, came from public subscriptions. The school was moved to Tulsa in 1907 from Muskogee, where it was founded in 1894 as Henry Kendall College. Originally controlled by the Presbyterian Board of Home Missions, it became a nonsectarian school in 1928. The university has an enrollment (1940) of 1,836 students and a faculty of 125.

The principal group of seven buildings is in the center of the campus, the front, or west, half of which is marked by a horseshoe drive. This half of the campus was given to the school in 1929, and College Avenue was closed where it passed through the grounds. The university oval was then laid out, and the Library, Fine Arts, and Petroleum Engineering buildings were erected there. These buildings, of modified Gothic design, are of native limestone, while Kendall Hall and Robertson Hall are of red brick, and the Union building is of stone. Together with the grey-brick Harwell Gymnasium they occupy a thick grove of oaks and elms, planted 30 years ago. Seen from the west, the green of the grove, splotched with the red of the older buildings, Kendall and Robertson Halls, makes a pleasant background for the new stone structures bordering the horseshoe; the shrubs and flower beds, young trees and velvet expanse of the front campus, give delightful depth to the view.

KENDALL HALL, the original brick building from which the university grew, contains the historic bell that rang out the news of statehood to Tulsa citizens in 1907. Other and newer buildings on the 50-acre campus are Robertson Hall, Kemp Lodge, and Tyrell Hall, occupied by the College of Fine Arts and certain administrative offices. MCFARLIN LIBRARY *(open 8-10 weekdays; closed Sat.* P.M. *and during Aug.)* contains more than 55,000 bound volumes. It also houses the Alice M. Robertson Collection of old trinkets and manuscripts of early mission days. The PHILLIPS ENGINEERING BUILDING, seat of the College of Petroleum Engineering, has the largest oil well-sample library in the Mid-Continent oil fields.

12. The PUBLIC SCHOOLS (SKELLY) STADIUM, E. 11th St. and S. Florence Ave., is a steel and concrete structure, with seating capacity of more than 15,000. It is completely equipped with electric scoreboard, public address system, and floodlights for night games. Both the University of Tulsa and the city high schools use the stadium.

13. In OWEN PARK, N.E. corner of W. Edison St. and Quanah Ave., is a limestone MONUMENT on which a bronze plate, upheld by bronze stalks of Indian corn, commemorates the signing of the treaties by which the Cherokee, Creek, and Osage tribes were assigned to their national lands in the Indian Territory. The park is a well-landscaped area, with flower beds, tennis courts, a lake and rustic bridge, a wading pool, and a rest house.

14. MID-CONTINENT PETROLEUM CORPORATION REFINERY *(open 9-3 daily; guides),* 17th St. and Union Ave., W. Tulsa, is the largest refinery in the world operating exclusively on high gravity, 100 per cent paraffin-base crude oils, and is Tulsa's largest industrial plant. Within the ordered chaos of its equipment, covering 800 acres, are massive "crackers" that attain a heat of 1,000 degrees F. and a pressure of 1,000 pounds to the square inch. "Fractionating towers" rise 120 feet above the heating units; 16 stillblocks, one with 100 stills in a row, sprawl across the landscape. The plant has a capacity of 1,680,000 gallons of crude oil daily, operates on a 24-hour schedule, and employs 1,000 workers. Oil comes from the company's own wells in the Mid-Continent field, through the company's 1,400-mile pipe-line system. The refinery opened in October, 1913, with only one battery of stills and a few tanks. Now its storage tanks hold more than 4,000,000 barrels, and the refinery circulates more than 30,000,000 gallons of water per day in making steam.

POINTS OF INTEREST IN THE ENVIRONS

Red Fork, *6.9 m. (see Tour 1);* Tulsa's First Post Office, *5.4 m.;* Sand Springs, *8.2 m.;* Sand Springs Home Interests, *10.3 m. (see Tour 2);* Mashed O Ranch, *7.7 m.;* Mohawk Park, *9.9 m. (see Tour 9A).*

PART III

Tours

Tour 1

(Baxter Springs, Kans.)—Tulsa—Oklahoma City—El Reno—Clinton—Sayre—(Shamrock, Tex.); US 66.
Kansas Line to Texas Line, 386 m.

Frisco Ry. parallels route between the Kansas Line and Oklahoma City; Rock Island Ry. between Oklahoma City and the Texas Line.
Roadbed concrete-paved throughout.
Good accommodations at short intervals.

Known for many things, Grapes of Wrath families, "Cash and Carry" Pyle's Bunion Derby, its popular local titles, "Main Street of America" and the "Will Rogers Highway of America," US 66 runs the gamut of hot and cold, mountains and prairies, beauty and sordid ugliness.

Its path through Oklahoma has evolved from trails and footpaths worn deep in virgin prairies and blazed through blackjack tangles. Jealousy and rivalry played their part in its growth, for the brash new towns of the young state all wanted to be on the highway which connected the east with the rapidly growing center, Amarillo, Texas, to the west. In 1916, the part of US 66 linking Oklahoma City with Amarillo was improved as a postal highway.

US 66 runs southwestward to the center of the state through mining districts and oil and gas fields, thence westward to the Texas Line through farming and stock country. Part of the route traverses the area visited by Washington Irving in 1832, when the land was a virgin wilderness. He related his adventures in *A Tour on the Prairies,* published in 1835.

Toward the western end, as the highway rises gradually to higher elevations, the air seems to become clearer, towns are visible at great distances, and tall office buildings loom mirage-like above the level land. The region is aptly called the country of short grass and high plains.

Section a. KANSAS LINE *to* TULSA, *109.3 m. US 66*

Crossing the KANSAS LINE, 0 *m.,* four miles south of Baxter Springs, Kansas *(see Kansas Guide),* US 66 passes through a district in which are the greatest lead and zinc mines in the world, a section known to Oklahoma, Kansas, and Missouri as the Big Business Corner. For about fourteen miles huge man-made mountains of chat (waste rock) border the highway. The lead and zinc deposits were discovered shortly after the Civil War by adventurers searching for gold.

At 0.8 *m.*, under the highway, is part of an abandoned lead mine which yielded $10,000,000 worth of ore to its first owners. When they ceased operations, they stripped out most of the roof supports and leased the mine site. A slide, caused by the unstable retimbering done by the new owners filled the main shaft with rocks and earth, and the ruined mine was abandoned.

QUAPAW, 4.5 *m.* (840 alt., 1,054 pop.), was built on land once owned by the Quapaw Indians. The tall prairie grass, abundant in the surrounding country, made the town a logical center for hay-shipping at the turn of the century. Cattle-grazing later became important.

Zinc mining, however, which makes this section a hub of industry today (1941), is at present the commercial mainstay of the town. Mining began in this region as early as 1897. By 1907, ores from the Dark Horse Mine, opened in 1904, were being taken out in paying quantities. After the first World War, when the demand for the two metals had lessened, the fast growth of Quapaw was arrested. However, the modern tree-shaded residential section indicates the prosperity which mining leases have brought to the citizens. A large number of Quapaw Indians live in the town; many of them received immense royalties from their allotments during the boom years of 1917–18.

Near Quapaw an Indian Powwow is held annually on July 4, and, during the second week of August, the Seneca-Cayuga Green Corn Feast and Dances are observed. Visitors are welcome to both.

COMMERCE, 10.8 *m.* (805 alt., 2,422 pop.), is a mining town surrounded by large piles of slag and chat that mark the mining leases on all sides. Five types of crystal formation and many kinds of ore specimens are displayed for sale on the main street corners. In the town is the abandoned Turkey Fat Mine (R), the first in the area.

Commerce is at the junction with US 69, which unites southward with US 66 for thirty-nine miles *(see Tour 8)*.

At 13.7 *m.* is a flying school for the training of R.A.F. pilots.

MIAMI, 14.7 *m.* (800 alt., 8,345 pop.), now a financial center of the important Tri-State mining area, was originally a trading post called Jimtown in the sparsely settled region set aside for a number of small Indian tribes. This post, in the vicinity of the present North Miami, was the home of four farmers named Jim; hence the early name. In 1890, mail for the near-by Quapaw Agency had to be brought from Baxter Springs, Kansas. To facilitate delivery of the agency mail, arrangements were made with Jim Palmer (one of the four Jims) to establish a post office. The name chosen for the new office was Miami, in honor of Palmer's wife, who was of Miami Indian blood. A year later the townsite was platted and the first lots sold.

Miami might have followed the usual development from a trading post in Indian Territory to a small town in a farming community had it not been for the discovery of lead and zinc in 1905. Boom excitement caused the population to increase 141 per cent in a brief period.

The principal industry in the surrounding territory, in addition to mining, is cattle-raising and dairy production; purebred cattle have replaced to a large extent the longhorns which formerly grazed over the reservation.

At the eastern edge of the city, on a forty-acre campus, is the NORTHEASTERN OKLAHOMA JUNIOR COLLEGE, established in 1919 by the state legislature as the Miami School of Mines. Naturally, considering its location in a region of high production of lead and zinc, the school at first emphasized scientific mining instruction. Then, as Miami lost importance as a mining center, it became a junior college, and the name was changed. Regular students number from 250 to 300, with another 200 taking special courses, and there are (1941) fourteen teachers. The school plant includes a large modern ADMINISTRATION BUILDING, a combined GYMNASIUM AND AUDITORIUM, a shop building, and two dormitories, one each for men and women students.

At 24.9 *m.* is the junction with US 60 *(see Tour 4),* which unites with US 66–69 for 25.1 miles.

At 28.7 *m.* is the junction with US 59 *(see Tour 15).*

AFTON, 29.7 *m.* (290 alt., 1,261 pop.), a thriving farm center, lies in a level area of rich, black soil near Horse Creek. It is said that it was named for the river Afton made famous by Robert Burns' poem.

At 41.5 *m.* is the junction with a graveled road.

Left on this road to the GRAND RIVER DAM, 15.5 *m.,* a recently completed (1941), tremendous power project belonging to the people of Oklahoma. The idea of harnessing the waters of the Grand River, which is fed by Kansas streams and also by Ozark Mountain springs, was first thought of in 1891. Successive private efforts failed, then the state legislature created the Grand River Dam Authority in 1935. Through a Public Works Administration loan and grant, $22,750,000 was made available for the project; the debt is to be retired by the sale of hydroelectric power.

In August, 1938, construction was started on the 6,565-foot—the longest multiple arch dam in the world (1941)—creating a vast inland sea covering fifty-four thousand acres. It is estimated that the project will develop two hundred million kilowatts of power annually to be distributed through private utilities.

Public grounds bordering the thousand-mile shore line are rapidly being developed for recreational purposes, and the lake is being stocked with fish by the State Game and Fish Commission.

VINITA, 45 *m.* (702 alt., 5,685 pop.), was named by Colonel Elias C. Boudinot, a Cherokee Indian and one of the promoters of the townsite, in honor of Vinnie Ream (1850–1914). Miss Ream, a sculptor, received a Congressional commission to model the life-size statue of Abraham Lincoln which stands in the capitol at Washington, D.C.

Although there was a small settlement, known as Downingville, here in 1870, Vinita was not founded until 1871 when two railroads were extended to this section. Vinita's early history, like that of many frontier villages, was linked with railroad controversies. The Missouri-Kansas-Texas Railroad had planned to make a junction with the Atlantic & Pacific Railroad (now the Frisco) at a point north of Big Cabin *(see Tour 8)* and refused to stop its trains at Vinita. The Atlantic & Pacific, however, stopped at a crossing near Vinita whenever a train from the other road was due to pass by. Eventually, the Missouri-Kansas-Texas capitulated and a station was built at Vinita.

The annual Will Rogers Memorial Rodeo is held here in the first week in September. Rogers had planned to be present at the first event in 1935, but was killed on August 15 of that year. He attended a secondary school here, but in his writing facetiously referred to Vinita as his "college town."

The Eastern Oklahoma Hospital *(visits by appointment)* is a state institution for treatment of mental diseases. It was here that a patient, under the pseudonym, "Inmate Ward 8," wrote the book, *Behind the Door of Delusion* (1932).

At 49 *m.* is the southern junction with US 69 *(see Tour 8).*

At 50 *m.* is the southern junction with US 60 *(see Tour 4).*

CHELSEA, 63.3 *m.* (723 alt., 1,642 pop.), is well known as a town which was frequented by Will Rogers in his boyhood. Mrs. Sallie McSpadden, his sister, lives here (1941) in a home known as Maplewood. A Boy Scout cabin, for which Rogers contributed the money, is located in a near-by park.

The first oil in Indian Territory was discovered west of Chelsea about 1889 by Edward Byrd, who had secured a lease from the Cherokee Nation. The first shallow well was drilled to a depth of thirty-six feet. Prior to the passing of legislation regarding the leasing of Indian land for drilling, development of the known fields was difficult. But after paying quantities of oil were found in the Tulsa and Red Fork districts in 1901, the United States government started the legislative machinery which led, in 1902, to the complete control of the mineral leasing of Indian-owned land by the Department of the Interior. A shallow field including Chelsea, Alluwe, and Coody's Bluff (to the north) was part of the large area quickly developed.

Since discovery of that first well, oil, as a major industry, has been mostly responsible for the town's growth; formerly cattle-raising and prairie-hay shipping were of prime importance.

BUSHYHEAD, 69.7 *m.* (700 alt., 50 pop.), is a small farming community named for Dennis W. Bushyhead, at one time (1879–87) chief of the Cherokee Nation.

At 71 *m.,* the highway passes between waste piles from strip coal mines.

CLAREMORE, 82.3 *m.* (602 alt., 4,134 pop.), is the seat of Rogers County, named in honor of Clem Rogers, father of Will Rogers.

Claremore had its beginning as an Osage Indian town in the early nineteenth century. The name is that of the Osage chief who established the town; it is a variation of the French spelling, *Clermont* or *Clermos.* A famous battle between this settlement of Osages and a party of Cherokees took place in 1817 on Claremore Mound, northwest of the city.

The water at Claremore which attracts people seeking its healing power was discovered in 1903 when a test oil well was drilled; instead of oil, the drill struck a large flow of artesian mineral water at a depth of eleven hundred feet. The United States Indian Hospital, erected in 1928, is supervised by the Department of the Interior.

Claremore has established a Bureau of Information for tourists at the junction of US 66 and State 20. What is said to be the largest individual Collection of Guns in the United States, owned by J. M. Davis, is in the Mason Hotel near by.

Extensive publicity has been given to Claremore by many who erroneously believe it to be the birthplace of Will Rogers. Rogers himself was mainly responsible for the error, since, in his own words, he was born "half-way between Claremore and Oologah *(see Tour 9A)* before there was a town at either place." He referred more to Claremore than Oologah because, he said, "nobody but an Indian could pronounce Oologah."

Oklahoma honored its famous citizen by the erection of the WILL ROGERS MEMORIAL *(open 9–5)*, approximately ten blocks west (R) of US 66. Rogers had owned the original twenty-acre site on the side of the hill for more than twenty-five years, and after his death it was given to the state by his widow. In 1937, the Oklahoma legislature appropriated $200,000 to construct the memorial. The building resembles a low, rambling ranch house of brown stone. The exterior is finished with stone quarried at Catoosa, the interior with silverdale limestone from Kansas, and the floor of the foyer is of split rock from Maine. The Memorial houses four principal galleries—Indian, Pioneer, Historical, and Educational—with a fifth gallery reserved exclusively for the display of keepsakes and mementos of the famous humorist. The statue of Rogers, in the main entrance, is a duplicate of the one by Jo Davidson, well-known sculptor, which stands in the national capitol. The memorial building was dedicated on November 4, 1938, the fifty-ninth birth anniversary of the beloved Will. A crypt on the grounds will be the final resting place for the body, which is now (1941) in California.

Adjoining the memorial grounds on the south is the OKLAHOMA MILITARY ACADEMY, established in 1920 by the state. Its graduates are admitted, on appointment, to West Point and Annapolis academies without the usual entrance examinations.

A farmhouse, 93.4 *m.*, on Spunky Creek (L), is on the SITE OF FORT SPUNKY, a station on the Star Mail Route through this vicinity before the coming of the railroad. It is said that a part of the framework and the stone chimney of the farmhouse are remnants of the original building.

CATOOSA, 94.3 *m.* (618 alt., 405 pop.), was named for "Old Catoos," the rounded hill just west of the town. The name is said to be a derivation of the Cherokee expression, "Gi-tu-zi," meaning "Here live the People of the Light." The story is that the "People of the Light" clan formerly met on the summit of the hill.

As a result of treaties made with the Indians after the close of the Civil War, the railroads made slow but inevitable advances west through Indian Territory, each step tapping a new reservoir of wealth in cattle. For a short time in 1882, Catoosa was the terminus of the St. Louis–San Francisco Railway before that line was extended to Tulsa. During this period, the town was typically frontier—the Saturday-night gathering place of roistering cowboys who had driven cattle here to the stockyards.

On the summit (R) of LOOKOUT MOUNTAIN (914 alt.), 95.5 *m.*, the Indians built a cairn, presumably as a trail-marker.

At 96.5 *m.* is the junction with paved State 33.

Right on State 33 to the junction with Sheridan Road, 8 *m.;* R. here to TULSA MUNICIPAL AIRPORT *(open to visitors)*, SPARTAN AIR SCHOOL AND FACTORY *(not open)*, and U.S. BOMBING PLANE ASSEMBLY PLANT *(not open)*, 10 *m.*

This is one of the two important aviation groups in the state. The airport, stretching north and east of the modernistic Administration Building and the hangars for more than one hundred planes, was at one time (1930) the world's busiest airport, outranking in volume of traffic Le Bourget (Paris), Tempelhof (Berlin), and Croydon (London) fields. It is still (1941) an important station for transcontinental and local planes.

The Spartan Air School and Factory have been much expanded as a result of the increased demands of the national defense program. The new Bombing Plane Assembly Plant is laid out on a thousand-acre tract adjoining the airport on the east. There, $15,000,000 is being spent (1941) to provide facilities for turning out and testing fifty giant four-motored bombers per month; the parts are to be fabricated elsewhere. Though provided by the government, the plant is to be operated by one of the large airplane manufacturing companies.

In TULSA, 109.3 *m.* (700 alt., 142,157 pop.) *(see Tulsa),* are junctions, with US 64 *(see Tour 2),* US 169 *(see Tour 9A),* State 33 *(see Tour 2A),* and US 75 *(see Tour 9),* which unites southward with US 66 for fifteen miles.

Section b. TULSA *to* OKLAHOMA CITY, *120.8 m. US 66*

The country southwest of TULSA, 0 *m.,* is mostly rolling prairie, dotted with clumps of scrubby post oak and blackjack trees. Mistletoe, the official state flower, clings abundantly to the trees in winter. In spring, the creek banks and small ravines are crimson with redbud blooms.

RED FORK, 6.9 *m.,* is an industrial suburb of Tulsa; many of the city's manufacturing plants are located here.

The FRANKHOMA POTTERY PLANT *(visitors welcome; open work days, 8–4),* 12.7 *m.,* manufactures a native clay ware named in honor of its creator, John N. Frank, a former member of the faculty of the University of Oklahoma *(see Norman).*

SAPULPA, 15.2 *m.* (712 alt., 12,249 pop.), a cattle-shipping, cotton-marketing, and manufacturing city, is also in the center of oil and gas fields. Sapulpa's largest field was a part of the rich Glenn Pool (L), which extended to within four miles of the town.

About 1850, Jim Sapulpa, a Creek Indian, came to this point from Alabama and commenced farming on Rock Creek, about a mile southeast of the present site of Sapulpa. Later he started a store in his home, hauling his goods by team and pack horses from Fort Smith.

In 1886 the Frisco Railway built to this point, and for a few years Sapulpa was the rail terminus; this laid the foundation upon which the city later became an important cattle-shipping center.

One of the boarding schools maintained by the Creek Indians as a part of their well-knit educational system was established here in October, 1893. The institution was founded for the Euchees, an alien people who had united with the Creeks in their former eastern home and had consequently been moved here with them. The language of the Euchees was so foreign and unintelligible (even to the Creeks) that all communication between the tribes had to be carried on through interpreters. Cut off as they were from their neighbors by this linguistic wall, the Euchees were particularly observant of customs and traditions. With the passage of the Curtis Act by Congress in 1898, the Creeks lost control of their schools to the Department of the Interior and in 1928 the maintenance was also taken over by the Federal government. Since then, this institution, renamed the EUCHEE INDIAN BOARDING SCHOOL, has offered instruction in the first four grades to Indian boys of all tribes. For higher grades, the boys attended Sapulpa's public schools.

The diversified industries of Sapulpa include a milk-bottle factory, a glass plant which manufactures tableware, a brick and tile plant, and a meat-packing company; all are served by an electric railway connecting with the freight terminals of Tulsa.

PRETTYWATER LAKE *(cabins, swimming, fishing)* north of Sapulpa, is an attractive vacation resort.

At Sapulpa is the southwest junction with US 75 *(see Tour 9)*.

KELLYVILLE, 24.1 *m.* (764 alt., 647 pop.), is an agricultural community; there are shallow oil wells in the surrounding district.

Just west of Kellyville are the DANCE GROUNDS of the Creek and Euchee Indians. Celebrations known as "busks" are usually held here in June and July and last four days—the number "4" being sacred to the Creeks *(adm. 25c a person; cameras by permission)*. On the eve of the first day the celebrants purify their bodies with *Micco Anija* (King of Purgers), the root of the red willow, which produces vomiting. The next day is devoted to Indian ball. An ox or deer skull is nailed to a tall post, a ball of hide is thrown into the air and the players catch it in the cup-shaped ends of their two-foot-long ball-sticks, then fling it at the skull. The women frequently play against the men; they are permitted to throw the ball with their hands while the men must use the sticks. The *Hajo-Banga* (Crazy Dance) climaxes the busk; the dancers literally "go crazy," no restrictions being placed on their enthusiasm.

BRISTOW, 39.3 *m.* (818 alt., 6,050 pop.), followed the pattern of a number of towns in eastern Oklahoma in that it began (1897) as a trading post on Creek land in the Indian Territory.

After Oklahoma Territory was opened, the railroads advanced from the east, building across Indian Territory to reach the new white domain. Scheduled stops for the trains soon grew to settlements and were platted and founded as towns. White civilizations encroached from all sides and each white settlement gave it another firm foothold. The Frisco Railway, with its terminus at Sapulpa for a few years, extended its route, and Bristow, on the line of march, accordingly developed. The town was founded December 23, 1901, and named for J. L. Bristow, then fourth Assistant Postmaster General.

Oil and gas in the area around Bristow dominate its business life, and many large oil companies have plants or offices in or near the city.

STROUD, 56.8 *m.* (905 alt., 1,917 pop.), was founded in 1896, a few years after this part of Oklahoma Territory was opened to white homesteaders. Since it was only two miles from the Indian Territory and was a large shipping point for cattle from the near-by Creek land, it attracted much illicit liquor trade. Whisky, denied to the Indian by the government, was often hidden in supply wagons of groceries and commodities headed for the Territory; and the consumption of liquor by celebrating cowhands who had driven cattle to the loading pens was no small part of the town's business. With the advent of statehood, however, Stroud's nine flourishing saloons were closed, and the place began to develop as a trading center for an agricultural community. Oil is an additional industry.

Stroud is at the junction with State 99 *(see Tour 14)*.

DAVENPORT, 64.3 *m.* (840 alt., 975 pop.), was founded in 1903, when a group of Southern Methodists, wishing to establish a community, purchased a farm and laid out a townsite. In 1924, oil was discovered near by, creating the boom sale of eighty additional acres which were platted as town lots. Shortly after this hasty expansion, the big Seminole field *(see Tour 5)* about thirty-seven miles due south was opened; and several thousand of the newcomers in the area, attracted by greater riches, migrated to Seminole.

Oil activity is still important, however, with two large gasoline plants operating and with the opening of new fields in adjacent areas.

CHANDLER, 71.2 *m.* (865 alt., 2,738 pop.), seat of Lincoln County, was founded in September, 1891. The town was platted on a series of low hills and named for George Chandler, of Kansas, Assistant Secretary of the Interior under President Harrison (1889–93).

Every building in Chandler (with the exception of the Presbyterian Church) was razed and fourteen persons were killed in the terrible cyclone of 1897. When the small group of citizens who had taken shelter in the church emerged, they found that tall trees had been hurled through the air, and houses, barns, and animals had been blown across the town.

Today, Chandler is known as one of the largest pecan-shipping points in the nation. A new pecan-shelling plant, to take care of the fast-growing industry, is being erected (1941). Among the town's other industries is a honey-packing plant.

A moving picture history of the town was begun in 1904 by Bennie Kent, now a veteran newsreel cameraman; the picture is brought up to date each year.

At 104.1 *m.* is the junction with US 77 *(see Tour 10),* which unites southward with US 66 for 21.6 miles.

A large Roadside Park *(picnic facilities),* 107.7 *m.,* nestles (L) in an unspoiled setting of low, rough hills and sharp ravines shaded by blackjack oak trees.

EDMOND, 107.5 *m.* (1,200 alt., 4,002 pop.), was first established as a watering and coaling station when the Santa Fe Railway was extended into the Territory in 1887, and was named for one of the railway officials. It served as a shipping point for cattle and as a concentration point for supplies bound for trading posts on the Kickapoo and Iowa reservations. In the Run of April 22, 1889, the townsite was homesteaded.

Pioneer foresight is apparent in the beauty of the landscaping and natural setting of the town; houses are set on deep lawns where there are tall trees and many flowers. Edmond is a trading center for the surrounding farms, has several small factories, and a towering grain elevator, and is rapidly developing a near-by oil field.

On the east side of town stands Central State College, a coeducational school with an enrollment (1941) of 858 students. It was established here as the Territorial Normal School in October, 1891. North Tower, the oldest of the nine buildings on the campus, was originally built of brick made near the college, but when the structure was enlarged it was covered with native red sandstone. The Library contains approximately thirty thousand volumes. In the rear of the buildings are tennis courts and a stadium. Stately old elms and some twenty other kinds of trees cover the landscaped campus.

At 111 *m.* is MEMORIAL PARK (L) *(see Tour 10)*.

OKLAHOMA CITY, 120.8 *m.* (1,194 alt., 204,424 pop.) *(see Oklahoma City)*, is at the southern junction with US 77 *(see Tour 10)*; US 62 *(see Tour 3)* and the eastern junction with US 270 *(see Tour 5)*.

Section c. OKLAHOMA CITY *to* TEXAS LINE, *155.9 m. US 66*

From Oklahoma City to the Texas Line US 66 passes through a farming region, and though some of it lies within the much publicized "dust bowl," it is in general reasonably productive. With the planting of trees (which has been greatly stimulated by experiences in the shelter-belt zones) and better farm practices, wind erosion and sun-scorching of crops will be greatly lessened.

West of OKLAHOMA CITY, 0 *m.*, US 66 and US 270 *(see Tour 5)* are united for 33.3 miles.

At the western edge of Oklahoma City is the junction with May Avenue, a paved street.

Right on May Avenue to WILEY POST AIRPORT, 3 *m.*, named for the noted flier who was killed in the crash in Alaska in which Will Rogers died. Here, in 1941, was being carried out a program of pilot training under contract with the Civil Aeronautics Authority. Some three hundred students were being trained by sixteen instructors. No passenger service is offered at this airport.

At 4.6 *m.* is a large, gray brick building (R), which until recently was known as the HOME OF THE POOR PROPHET. It was built in 1910 by a real estate company which offered it to the state for use as a capitol before the present building was constructed. The offer was rejected, and a private school leased it. In 1913, Eugene Arnett, an insurance broker, bought the property and named it the Home of the Poor Prophet, placing the cement letters of the title on the front lawn. Arnett lived here and attempted to carry out sociological experiments and reforms; he was considered eccentric and many tales grew up about his queer doings. The building is now (1941) dilapidated and abandoned.

BETHANY, 6.9 *m.* (1,212 alt., 2,590 pop.), is primarily the home of members of the Nazarene religious sect. Under the terms of the town's charter there are no theaters, billiard halls, or beauty parlors; and the sale of tobacco and intoxicants is forbidden. Even billboards advertising these articles are banned.

The BETHANY-PENIEL COLLEGE, with an average enrollment of four hundred and a faculty of nineteen, was founded in Oklahoma City in 1906 and moved to its ten-acre campus at Bethany in 1909. It was given its present name in 1920 when the Peniel College of Peniel, Texas, was incorporated with the original institution. The school specializes in training for the Nazarene ministry; it is, however, nonsectarian and has high school, junior college, and college courses.

Adjoining Bethany on the northwest is the new (1941) Oklahoma City

MUNICIPAL AIRPORT. When the army took over the former Oklahoma City field to enlarge it for a bombardment training school and air base *(see Tour 3)*, this site was acquired and developed into one of the most modern airports in the Middle West. It is used by the Oklahoma-owned Braniff Airways, Mid-Continent Airlines, and the coast to coast American Airlines. The new Airport represents an expenditure of approximately $1,500,000, of which the Federal government contributed some 75 per cent.

At 9.1 *m.*, a steel bridge spans the northern end of LAKE OVERHOLSER *(fishing, boating, picnicking)*. This seventeen-hundred-acre lake with a ten-mile shoreline was created by the damming of the North Canadian River in 1916 to furnish a water supply for Oklahoma City, and named for Ed Overholser, mayor of the city (1915–18).

For about six miles along the east side of the present lake and the Canadian River is the SITE OF CAMP ALICE, established in 1883 by David L. Payne, a Civil War veteran and former member of the Kansas legislature. Twice Payne and his land-hungry band of Boomers had attempted to settle in the territory that is now the state of Oklahoma. United States troops had halted the former invasions, but in April, 1883, Payne, with a caravan of 117 wagons and 516 men and women reached this spot, setting up Camp Alice, also known as Payne's Trading Post. Here the group surveyed and platted a townsite and also laid out the site of a capitol for the proposed state which they were advocating and attempting to create. The colonists staked out farms and began plowing in order to put in crops. In the following month, however, a company of United States infantry destroyed the camp and forced the colonists to return to Kansas. In 1884, Payne led another group to a site near where Blackwell now stands, but again the colonists were removed. Payne died in Wellington, Kansas, November 28, 1884.

Lake Overholser has been approved (1941) as a seaplane base. A float, shelter house, and necessary markers have been provided, and the lake became the first officially designated seaplane base in Oklahoma.

YUKON, 13.9 *m.* (1,298 alt., 1,660 pop.), an agricultural and milling center, was laid out in 1891 by the Spencer brothers, who owned the 160-acre site. Frisco, a small town of one thousand population, had been established near by; but when a railroad was built through Yukon, most of Frisco's people moved there. The large flour mills on the eastern edge of Yukon dominate the town's commercial life as well as its buildings.

At 14.7 *m.* is a junction with a graded dirt road.

Left on this road, 1 *m.*, to a SPRING, once a favorite stopping place for travelers following the old Chisholm Trail *(see Tour 11)*.

At 16.9 *m.* is the junction with a paved road.

Left on this road to the new (1941) privately operated AIR TRAINING SCHOOL, 1 *m.*, where, under a contract with the United States government, men are given primary instruction in flying.

EL RENO, 26.9 *m.* (1,363 alt., 10,078 pop.), the seat of Canadian County, situated not far from the south bank of the North Canadian River, was founded when the Rock Island railroad was routed to the site two months after the Run of April 22, 1889. The town derives its name from Fort Reno near by *(see below)*.

Reno City, with a population of fifteen hundred, was located on the north bank of the North Canadian immediately after the Run and, consequently, expected to have the railway connection. The Rock Island, however, changed its plans when the Reno Cityans refused to pay the high bonus asked for the line. As a result, the residents decided to move to the new town, loading their household goods—even their buildings—on wagons and crude rollers, and crossing the shallow, unbridged river. A three-story hotel building, meeting difficulties, was stranded on the river bed but was operated continuously until its removal to more stable ground.

In July, 1901, El Reno's population increased to approximately 145,000—literally within a day—when the Kiowa-Apache-Comanche reservation was opened by lottery to white settlers, affording the last opportunity to obtain free land in the Territory. Living accommodations were completely inadequate for this sudden influx, but, fortunately, most of those seeking homesteads left as soon as the drawing was completed.

Pioneer Day, celebrated on April 22, is an annual holiday in El Reno. Residents dress in 89'er costumes, place historic relics on display, and hold a parade and rodeo.

Marketing, flour milling, shipping, and transportation are the chief industries. The main lines of the Rock Island Railway meet here, where the railroad maintains district offices and division shops. On the division office grounds stands a geological oddity, a petrified tree stump eight feet high, which grew in a swamp some millions of years ago. It was discovered in 1914 by a Rock Island coal-mining crew while sinking a shaft at Alderson, Oklahoma.

El Reno is at the junction with US 81 *(see Tour 11)*.

At 28.8 *m.* is the UNITED STATES SOUTHWESTERN REFORMATORY *(visitors not admitted)*. This institution (L), built at a cost exceeding $1,000,000 in 1934, houses first offenders against Federal law, short-term prisoners, and convicts under thirty-five years of age. The buildings are erected around a rectangular court in the western section of a thousand-acre tract formerly a part of the Fort Reno Military Reservation.

At 29.1 *m.* is a junction with a graveled road.

Right on this road, 1.8 *m.*, to FORT RENO, the United States Army's largest remount station. The post was originally established to protect the old Darlington Indian Agency on the opposite bank of the North Canadian *(see Tour 11)* from Cheyenne Indian forays. During a Cheyenne uprising in 1874, the Darlington agent sent for help to the Fort Sill Military Reservation *(see Tour 3A)* and to the fort at Leavenworth, Kansas. The Fort Sill troops met hostile Indians near the Wichita Agency at Anadarko and could not reach the agency, but the soldiers from Leavenworth arrived. Fort Reno was established by these troops in July of the same year and named for Union General Jesse L. Reno, who had been killed at the Battle of Antietam in the Civil War. The Indian insurrectionists were finally subdued in March, 1875. Permanent fort buildings were then erected and by 1880 there were three hundred cavalrymen stationed at the garrison to oversee the fifteen hundred Indians camped near by. For the next five years, the troops were kept busy expelling

Boomers from the surrounding region; and, in 1889, they guarded the boundary of the new land to be opened to settlement. Military supervision was necessary in order to keep the Sooners from jumping the line ahead of the starting gun. With the coming of the white settlers and the allotment of Indian lands, need for troops at this point decreased and the fort was abandoned in February, 1908; but, in April of the same year, it was re-established as a remount station, where horses are broken and trained for other military camps.

At 36.5 *m.* on the main route is the western junction with US 270 *(see Tour 5).*

At 52.3 *m.* is a junction with paved US 281– State 8.

Left here is HINTON, 8 *m.* (1,650 alt., 842 pop.), where in the first week in August a colorful rodeo is held at KIWANIS PARK *(free swimming and fishing),* 8.4 *m.* This park is reached by a road blasted out of steep sandstone walls which sometimes rise as high as one hundred feet. A dam forms a lake eight feet deep. Overlooking one bank is a massive rock towering 125 feet above the water. Large springs gush from crevices in the rocks, and trees stud the canyon slopes.

Access to KICKAPOO CANYON *(S.E. of the park)* and WATER CANYON *(N.E. of the park)* is difficult, except in a few places, because of the steep walls. Near the divide between these two canyons, small creeks have cut valleys fifty to one hundred feet wide and several miles long, with level floors about two hundred feet wide. Growing here are more than twenty varieties of trees and many shrubs, herbs, ferns, mosses, lichens, and fungi.

WEATHERFORD, 71.5 *m.* (1,644 alt., 2,504 pop.), is a well-ordered trade center for the surrounding agricultural population. It was founded in 1893 and named for William J. Weatherford, a United States marshal who was stationed here during Territorial days.

In the city is the SOUTHWESTERN STATE COLLEGE OF DIVERSIFIED OCCUPATIONS, founded in 1901 and known until 1939 as Southwestern State Teachers' College. Situated on the brow of a hill (R), it has ten buildings and a large ampitheater on a sixty-five-acre campus. The change of name was brought about by a change in the educational policy of the institution. While the training of teachers is still important, emphasis is placed on the study of trades ranging from mechanics to beauty culture.

Indian powwows are frequently held near Weatherford; a few miles south of town is a "stomp ground" where Indians gather in tribal costume to stage ceremonial dances. Annually, in September, the dancers perform at an Indian fair in the town.

At 85.7 *m.* is the CLINTON INDIAN HOSPITAL (R), an institution opened by the Federal government in 1933 to care for the sick among the Indian population. Most of the thirty beds are occupied by tuberculous patients. The three one-story red-brick buildings stand on an eight-acre tract. The Indians were at first hesitant to accept the benefits of medical care, but now generally welcome the aid offered here.

CLINTON, 86.6 *m.* (1,564 alt., 6,736 pop.), is built on a level plain within a bend of the Washita River. Upon the opening of the Cheyenne-Arapaho Reservation in 1892, the land where Clinton now stands was passed up by many who considered it not worth staking out. The town was founded in 1903, when the Frisco Railway built to the site and named for Federal Judge Clinton F. Irwin.

Clinton has grown to be an important shipping center for the surrounding cattle lands and wheat fields. One of the nine camps established by the Soil Conservation Service of the Department of Agriculture in an effort to check erosion is located here. Because of its high elevation and the dryness of the atmosphere, Clinton has two large private hospitals, caring mostly for tuberculous patients; the WESTERN OKLAHOMA CHARITY HOSPITAL, at the southern city limits, is maintained by the state.

Clinton is at the junction with US 183 *(see Tour 12).*

The STATE TUBERCULOSIS SANITORIUM *(visitors by appointment)* 87.1 *m.,* also state-owned and controlled, was first established at Supply in 1917 but was moved to Clinton in 1919. The large hospital (L) consists of fifty-three buildings on an 810-acre tract of ground. Those who are able to do so pay for their care. Negroes are admitted to the wards, since there is no segragated Negro unit.

At 96.8 *m.* is a junction with a graded dirt road.

Right on this road, 0.5 *m.,* is the CLINTON DAM AND WATERWORKS, which forms a seven-hundred-acre clear-water lake. Around the lake Clinton maintains a landscaped public park *(picnicking and fishing: free).*

Westward, the route crosses over tree-bordered creeks into a section where barren red hills rise suddenly above almost level prairies.

On the eastern edge of CANUTE, 108.1 *m.* (1,910 alt., 374 pop.), is the ROMAN CATHOLIC CEMETERY (R), in which is a replica of the Crucifixion Scene. Surmounting a low hill is a bronze figure of Christ on the cross, with the two Marys kneeling below. In the side of the hill, a glass-enclosed sepulcher holds the waxen image of Christ. The scene was planned by Father Peter Paul Schaeffer, of the Holy Parish; the sanctuary will be the final resting place of Father Schaeffer and Frank Flies, whose financial aid made its erection possible.

Canute has only a small residential and business section, but sheet-metal cotton sheds and gin houses, spread out on both sides of the highway, indicate the town's main industry, cotton ginning. The town was founded in 1902 by an independent townsite company.

West of Canute, the land is rolling and hilly, the soil deep red, and the farms have a prosperous appearance.

At 115.3 *m.* is a Y-junction with State 34, a graveled road. In the center of the plot bounded by the Y is a granite marker, designating 34 as the Chisholm Trail *(see Tour 11).* Actually, however, State 34 marks the old Western or Texas Cattle Trail, a later route.

Right on State 34 is HAMMON, 14.6 *m.* (1,736 alt., 705 pop.), a farming settlement. Right from Hammon on a dirt road to a CHEYENNE INDIAN SETTLEMENT, 16.2 *m.* For a small sum, the Indians will sometimes put on their tribal dress and pose for pictures. The group of boarded-up tents and shacks, clustered under the trees, is the old camp of Whiteshield, former chief of the Southern Cheyennes. In 1871, Whiteshield went to Washington, D.C., as a member of the delegation representing the Cheyenne and Arapaho Indians. There, from President Grant, he received a treaty medal, symbolizing peace, agriculture, education, and Christianity. Upon his return, Whiteshield began to live in accordance with the treaty symbols and became an earnest advocate of civilization, schools, and missions. A white and blue cottage, bordered by a picket fence, northeast of the Cheyenne settlement, was Whiteshield's home in later life and is now occupied by his relatives.

ELK CITY, 116 *m.* (1,926 alt., 5,021 pop.), was originally named Busch, in honor of Adolphus Busch, of St. Louis. Because of the similarity of the name to that of another post office, it was renamed Elk City; Elk Creek skirts the town limits.

One of Oklahoma's first co-operative medical ventures is the COMMUNITY HOSPITAL, located at Elk City, sponsored by the Farmers' Co-operative Hospital Association. Doctor M. Shadid, a Syrian-born physician, was instrumental in establishing the institution in which each stockholder—for $25 a year—receives all necessary medical treatment for himself and his immediate family.

SAYRE, 132.3 *m.* (1,810 alt., 3,037 pop.), seat of Beckham County, was named for Robert H. Sayre, a stockholder in the railroad extended to the city at its founding, September 14, 1901. The North Fork of the Red River flows along the southern outskirts of the town, its sandy banks affording a natural beach for swimming. The area has been developed into a public park.

Sayre is chiefly dependent on the surrounding rich gas fields and serves as a market for broomcorn. It has an oil refinery and a large plant in which 420,000 burners convert natural gas into carbon black. A weekly community sale of livestock and farm utilities is held here.

Jess Willard, former world's champion prize fighter, once ran a rooming house in Sayre. Another famous son, Giuseppi Bentonelli (Joseph Benton), Metropolitan Opera tenor, was brought there as an infant in 1900.

Sayre is at the junction with US 283 *(see Tour 13)*.

Westward for a few miles, there are weed-covered sand dunes and patches of gnarled dwarf trees; then the highway descends into a valley where there is more vegetation, although most of the land is uncultivated.

Prior to 1896, Texas claimed the land south of the North Fork of the Red River, crossed at 133.8 *m.;* in that year the United States Supreme Court ruled that the southern fork of the Red River was the northern boundary line of Texas, and the area between the forks was added to Oklahoma Territory.

ERICK, 148.2 *m.* (2,080 alt., 1,591 pop.), was incorporated in 1902 and named for Beech Erick, a member of the townsite company. US 66 passes between two long rows of widely spaced houses and bisects the eight-block business section. The town is surrounded by rich farming lands, cattle ranches, and a natural-gas field.

Southwest of Erick is an old SALT SPRINGS, nature's gift to early-day cattlemen. As the beeves were driven north from the Texas ranches each spring, many herders made this a stopping-place so that the cattle might lick the salt. The fresh-water springs which flow through COX'S CAVE near by made the spot an ideal camping place in that early period.

Between Erick and the Texas Line, the prairie stretches in shelving levels to the west. Most of the land is under cultivation. The wind-mill-like devices on the roofs of many of the houses are wind generators, a popular means of rural electrification.

TEXOLA, 155.3 *m.* (2,150 alt., 337 pop.), on the Texas-Oklahoma border, combines syllables from the two state names to form its own. The business section still retains the wooden sidewalk awnings—supported at the curb by iron or cement posts—that were in general use during pioneer days.

At 155.9 *m.* US 66 crosses the Texas Line, fourteen miles east of Shamrock, Texas *(see Texas Guide)*.

Tour 2

(Fort Smith, Ark.)—Gore—Muskogee—Tulsa—Enid—Alva—Guymon—Kenton—(Raton, N.M.); US 64.
Arkansas Line to New Mexico Line, 603.9 m.

Roadbed intermittently paved with concrete and asphalt; also graveled.
The Missouri Pacific R.R. roughly parallels route between the Arkansas Line and Muskogee; the Katy, between Muskogee and Cleveland; the Frisco, between Pawnee and Alva; the Santa Fe between Alva and Buffalo; the Katy between Gate and Boise City; and the Santa Fe to the New Mexico Line.
Good accommodations available at short intervals, except west of Cherokee.

Marked by great variety of landscape, climate, and population, US 64 crosses Oklahoma from east to west, the longest highway in the state. Near the Arkansas border it is shadowed by the verdant Cookson Hills; then by the timber along the beautiful Illinois River; then it crosses the Arkansas and Cimarron, rivers that are occasionally turbid floods but more often little more than wide ribbons of blowing sand.

As it continues westward, the route climbs slowly and steadily to higher, more arid country, where trees are scarce and burning summer winds threaten the crops. It edges the Great Salt Plains, now a wildfowl refuge, runs the length of the Panhandle, impressive in its barrenness, and finally passes the high, dry Black Mesa in the extreme west.

Varied, too, are the personalities and appearance of the towns through which the route passes, from the earliest Indian settlements to those that were mushroom camps within the memory of men who are (1941) scarcely past middle age.

For forty miles, roughly from the Arkansas Line to Gore, US 64 follows the Cherokee "Trail of Tears," broken by the exiles from Georgia and Tennessee during the two decades from 1819 to 1839.

Among those who have given character to the region through which the route passes are such diverse figures of history as Washington Irving, the effete traveler who found that he could also rough it; Loughridge, hardy missionary to the Creeks; Sam Houston, pausing for three years between his Tennessee and Texas careers; Kit Carson, who by mistake established a frontier fort within the boundaries of Oklahoma; Dull Knife, the Cheyenne, and Bacon Rind, the Osage, figures out of an almost legendary Indian past; and the Dalton Boys, brothers who made outlawry a life work and train- and bank-robbing a trade.

Section a. ARKANSAS LINE *to* TULSA, *135.6 m. US 64*

Crossing the ARKANSAS LINE, 0 *m.,* at the Arkansas River immediately west of Fort Smith, Arkansas *(see Arkansas Guide),* US 64 approaches the rough Cookson Hills of the Ozark region. There are camp sites along the highway or near small clear streams, and in spring and summer the hills are covered with flowers; the pines furnish greenery throughout the year.

MULDROW, 9.8 *m.* (478 alt., 638 pop.), is a rural community and market center.

At 15.8 *m.* is a junction with a dirt road.

Right on this road to the HOME OF SEQUOYAH, 7.5 *m.,* standing on an elevation a few hundred feet from Skin Bayou Creek. A large two-story stone building, constructed as a WPA project, completely encloses the small log cabin built by Sequoyah himself about 1830 and contains rooms and alcoves in which are exhibited relics and documents related to Sequoyah's life and to the Cherokee Nation. The surrounding ten acres were deeded to the Oklahoma Historical Society, which sponsored the work of preserving the site.

Sequoyah, whose English name was George Gist, was a half-blood Cherokee. A silversmith, soldier, and manufacturer of salt at various times during his life, he is better known throughout America as an influential tribal statesman and an educator who bestowed upon the Cherokees the greatest addition ever made to the culture of a primitive people. When Sequoyah first conceived the idea of his syllabary he was thought to be possessed of evil spirits, and his fellow tribesmen picked a group of warriors to try him. After a week of trial, all of the jury had learned to read and write by Sequoyah's system, and he was vindicated.

As a leading man of the "Old Settler" Cherokees who migrated west before the forced removal, Sequoyah signed the Act of Union with the "Newcomers" on July 12, 1839. He was voted a literary pension by the Cherokee Nation for his invaluable work, but died before he received the first payment. The Cherokee Nation also presented him with a medal, which he wore on a chain around his neck for the rest of his life; it appears in the portrait of him by the artist, Charles Bird King, now in the Smithsonian Institution at Washington, D.C. The giant Sequoia trees of California were also named for him, and his statue, by George Julian Zolnay, stands in Statuary Hall in the national capitol at Washington, D.C. Fittingly, Sequoyah was chosen as one of the world's twelve alphabet inventors to be reproduced in bronze on the great doors of the Library of Congress Annex designed by Lee Lawrie, of New York. It is interesting to note that ten of the other characters chosen are mythological: T'sang Chieh, Nabu, Brahma, Cadmus, Tahmurath, Hermes, Odin, Ogma, Itzamna, and Quetzalcoatl.

SALLISAW, 22.6 *m.* (531 alt., 2,140 pop.), once a trading post and a camping site, is now the center of a rich farming district. French trappers named the place *Salaison,* meaning salt provision or salt meat, because of the large deposits of salt near by.

Near Sallisaw in the Cherokee-Cookson Hills, the many spring-fed streams afford excellent fishing. Sallisaw, Little Sallisaw, Big Skin Bayou, Greasy, and Vian creeks are all easily accessible and contain many kinds of fish, including the Kentucky or spotted bass, a bronze and gray fighter. The State Game and Fish Commission has built a number of low-water dams in this district.

In Sallisaw is the junction with US 59 *(see Tour 15)*.

VIAN, 33.8 *m.* (545 alt., 941 pop.), is an agricultural community nestled in the foothills of the Cookson Hills area.

At 34.9 *m.* on US 64 is a junction with a dirt road.

Right on this road, up a steep slope, is an old SALT SPRING, 3.2 *m.*, once the source of supply for a large salt factory near by. In the vicinity of this spring is a ridge road that overlooks the Illinois River *(see Tour 16)* to the west.

At BOX, 8.2 *m.*, a very small settlement, is a junction with a winding country road. Right on this road to the summit of BLACK GUM MOUNTAIN, 10.5 *m.*, where the Kee-Too-Wah Society of the Cherokee Indians holds its annual Sacred Fire Ceremony on July 19 *(visitors welcome)*. The ceremony expresses what is generally accepted as the original Cherokee myth. The Great Spirit gave the sacred fire to the Cherokees, who were to keep it perpetually burning. The priests or *ku-ta-ni* were to tend the flames, but designing ones among them stole it. For this crime, all priests were executed; thus all primal religious practices were closed to the Cherokees since the tenets had been kept alive only verbally as priest succeeded priest. Some authorities hold the derivation of the name Cherokee is *a-che-la* (fire) and *ah-gi* (he takes).

The Kee-too-Wahs, whose organization is both ancient and secret, brought the sacred fire from Georgia, according to members of their fullblood clan, and have kept it burning in the hills ever since. Their aim is to perpetuate tribal tradition and history. The membership is said to be six thousand.

Scene of the ritual is a broad, two-acre clearing centered by a great pile of ashes, the accumulation of years of ceremonial fires. Seven brush arbors surrounding the ash mound represent the seven original clans of the Cherokees, consolidated after their removal to Indian Territory. Building of the fire, smoking of the peace pipe, and feasting fill the day from dawn to dusk, when all circle the fire in a lively dance.

Just east of the bridge, over the Illinois River, 40 *m.*, stands the FISH CAMP (L), which is flashed on the screen in the movie version of *Grapes of Wrath,* shortly after the Joads started their long trek to California. Tourists will be surprised at the realization that they have just passed through the area named as the locale of the beginning of the *Grapes of Wrath* tale. For there, instead of dust storms and tenant farming, one finds well-wooded hills, an abundance of water, and not much farming.

Near the east bank is the site of the Cherokee town, TAHLONTEESKEE (R), which served as a meeting place for national councils and lawmaking bodies from 1828 to 1838. This was an "Old Settler" council ground, named for a former chief.

At 42 *m.* is the junction with State 10, an improved dirt road.

Right on State 10 through a section dotted with the cabins of an isolated group of Indians. The majority of these people are fullblood Creeks who became members of the Cherokee tribe. While yet in their eastern homes, they opposed removal to the new Indian Territory and fled to the Cherokee Nation. Later, when the Cherokees were also forced to move, these adopted sons and daughters continued to live with them. Scattered among them are a few Natchez, members of a tribe which is usually regarded by ethnologists as extinct.

The Natchez were almost exterminated by the French in Louisiana, but some escaped, found refuge with the eastern Creeks, and were eventually moved to Oklahoma.

At BRAGGS, 13 *m.* (520 alt., 392 pop.), is a junction with the improved earth road; (R) here to the COOKSON HILLS PLAYGROUNDS *(lodge, cabins, bathing, boating)*, 16 *m.*, a thirty-two-thousand-acre recreation area, owned by the Federal government and supervised by the Soil Conservation Service of the Department of Agriculture. The cabins and other buildings are of native stone and comfortably modern; the project was completed late in 1938.

The surrounding wooded hills are an ideal setting for the nine-hundred-acre GREENLEAF LAKE, which is the focal point of the playground. It abounds in fish, since the several mile-long fingers jutting out from the main body of water to curl around the bases of the hills furnish ideal spawning grounds. Near-by GREENLEAF MOUNTAIN has been a favorite ball field for the Cherokees and Creeks for more than a century. The Indian game —which combines features of baseball, basketball, and football—is played with two sticks, with oval netting at one end. The player must catch the ball in the net and pitch it to hit the goal at the top of a forty-foot pole. Among the hundreds of Indian paintings by George Catlin, nineteenth-century artist, there are several of this strenuous game.

GORE, 42.9 *m.* (480 alt., 334 pop.), on the east bank of the Arkansas River, appeared on a map by Guilliaume de Lille, a French explorer, as Mentos or Les Mentous in 1718. A succession of name changes followed when settlement of this district took place. The town was called Campbell when it was a stop on the stage line between Fort Smith and Fort Gibson. When the railroad came through in 1888, the name was changed to Illinois. After statehood, it was called Gore, in honor of one of the United States Senators from Oklahoma.

It was to this Cherokee settlement that Sam Houston came in 1829, after his resignation as governor of Tennessee. By a special act of the Cherokee Council in 1829 at Tahlonteeskee, Houston was formally adopted by the tribe. Houston took an Indian wife and remained in the vicinity several years *(see Tour 8)*.

Right from Gore on a dirt road, to the SITE OF A SALT WORKS, 7 *m.*, on Saline Creek. Bean and Sanders, partners in the business, operated the works here in 1820. From the one hundred huge kettles of salt water kept boiling most of the time, the refined salt was taken to a warehouse just above the falls, where it was stored until keel boats carried it down the river to Arkansas and Louisiana. A few years later, after the Cherokee removal to this part of Indian Territory, Walter Webber, a wealthy mixed-blood Cherokee, acquired this land by evicting the former owners and took over the salt works. A friend of Sam Houston and of the missionaries, he gave land and money to help in the re-establishment of Dwight Mission *(see Tour 15)*.

WEBBERS FALLS, 44.7 *m.* (479 alt., 486 pop.), was named for Webber and for the falls in the Arkansas River which are now hardly more than a riffle across the channel, though they were once several feet high at a normal stage of the river.

In WARNER, 55.9 *m.* (570 alt., 391 pop.), a farming community, is the CONNORS STATE AGRICULTURAL COLLEGE, which was established in 1908 as a preparatory school. In 1927, the curriculum was extended to include junior college courses. The school has a well-equipped 225-acre experimental farm.

Oil

EYERS, OKLAHOMA CITY

OIL WELLS IN FRONT OF STATE CAPITOL
OKLAHOMA CITY

OKLAHOMA STATE CHAMBER OF COMMER

PAPOOSE OIL FIELD, SHOWING OLD STYLE RIGS, NEAR OKEMAH

WELL BLOWING IN, SHOWING MODERN ROTARY RIG

ENNIS C. HEI

OLD STYLE "STANDARD"
WOODEN DRILLING RIG

OLD STYLE PUMP JACK
AND STAR RIG DRILL
FOR SHALLOW WELLS

LEE :

A ROUSTABOUT

BONE AND BLOOD AND SINEW OF
THE OIL INDUSTRY

PAINTING
THE DERRICK

LEE : FSA

OIL REFINERY EQUIPMENT

E : FSA

OIL INDUSTRY
CHEMIST

OIL REFINING STILLS

LEE : FSA

E : FSA

TANK FOR NATURAL GASOLINE

OIL FIELD
MACHINIST

LEE : FSA

ROCK BITS
FOR ROTARY DRILL,
BEFORE AND AFTER

Left from Warner on the graveled State 2 is PORUM, 11 *m.* (583 alt., 502 pop.), once the home of Tom Starr, ardent supporter of the treaty faction during the turbulent days of the establishment of the Cherokee Nation. He was a half-blood, Irish and Cherokee, and had five sons, one of whom became the husband of Belle Starr. Dissension between the "Old Settlers" and "Newcomer" Cherokees, arising from the fact that one party had signed the Removal Treaty with the United States, broke into open warfare with a series of brutal assassinations. Among those of the treaty party who were killed was Tom's father, James Starr. Tom set himself the task of killing as many of the antitreaty faction as possible. The war became so intense that the Cherokee government, not able to capture or kill Tom, made a treaty with him. Provisions of the act gave $100,000 and complete amnesty to Tom to end his bloody activities. This is said to be the only treaty with an individual in the history of the Cherokee Nation. To avoid further trouble, Starr moved to the Canadian River near Briartown, fulfilled his part of the agreement, and became a leader in the community.

Right from Porum on a dirt road to a junction with a second dirt road, 4.5 *m.;* left here to a junction with a third road 8.7 *m.;* right here to BELLE STARR'S GRAVE, 9.7 *m.* The crypt is a small stone mausoleum on the north bank of the broad Canadian River. Though her Missouri parents were respectable and wealthy, Belle became a notorious woman outlaw. In the Civil War she became a Confederate spy, during which time she made the acquaintance of the James and Younger boys. Her first marriage was to Jim Reed, one of Quantrill's men, and after he was killed by officers of the law she married Sam Starr, son of Tom Starr, and settled on a farm on the Canadian River near Eufaula and not far from her future final resting place. Their home became a rendezvous for outlaw friends, and both met violent deaths.

At Warner, US 64 turns sharply north (R).

In MUSKOGEE (Mus-ko′-gee), 77.1 *m.* (617 alt., 32,332 pop.) *(see Muskogee),* are junctions with US 69 *(see Tour 8)* and US 62 *(see Tour 3),* which unites westward with US 64 for 15.4 miles.

Right on a graveled road from the junction of 40th Street and the Kansas-Oklahoma-Gulf tracks, to a V junction with two improved roads, 2 *m.*

Left to the JAPANESE GARDEN *(private: apply to caretaker),* 1.2 *m.,* where Japanese plants and flowers are supplemented by native Oklahoma plants. Gateway, wells, lanterns of stone and wood, temple bells, and bridges combine to create a picturesque reproduction of the Far East.

Right from the V junction to the SITE OF THE TULLAHASSEE SCHOOL, 6 *m.* This, the largest of the three Creek Nation mission schools, was established in 1850 by Rev. R. M. Loughridge, a Presbyterian minister who was under a contract with the tribal government; the other missions were at Bixby and Coweta. The list of graduates from the school in its prime reads like a roll call of the future Creek tribal leaders. The school was damaged during the Civil War when much of the surrounding country was laid waste; but the Creeks repaired the plant and operated it until it was destroyed by fire in 1880. It was then rebuilt and used by the Creeks through the rest of the tribal period for the education of their Negro freedmen.

TAFT, 86.9 *m.* (605 alt., 772 pop.), is an all-Negro community which grew up because of the large number of Negro freedmen who settled near the confluence of the Arkansas and Verdigris rivers shortly after the Civil War. The United States required the Creeks to adopt their former slaves as citizens, and many allotments in this district were given to Negroes, who were thus listed on the rolls of the Creek Nation. The original townsite was platted on sixteen acres, purchased from a freedman, and named in honor of a prominent Negro, W. H. Twine. Later the town was renamed for President William Howard Taft.

At 87.3 *m.* are (R) the STATE DEAF, BLIND AND ORPHANS' HOME FOR NEGRO CHILDREN, founded in 1909; and the STATE TRAINING SCHOOL FOR NEGRO GIRLS. At 87.7 *m.* is the STATE HOSPITAL FOR THE INSANE (L.), opened in 1933. All three organizations were consolidated under one administration in 1935. The $500,000 hospital building has twelve wards accommodating fifty inmates each. The four hundred acres of land belonging to the institution produce a large part of the food supply and provide pasturage for the institution's dairy cattle. Peanut butter, broom, and canning factories are operated on the grounds, adding greatly to the revenue.

At 92.6 *m.,* is the western junction with US 62; US 64 turns northwest.

HASKELL, 97.6 *m.* (620 alt., 1,572 pop.), is an agricultural trade center, named in honor of the first governor of Oklahoma, Charles N. Haskell (1907–11).

Southeast of Haskell is the site of the old Blue Creek Mission of the pre–Civil War days. Chief Pleasant Porter, elected head of the Creeks in 1899, was born in this vicinity. President McKinley once called Porter the greatest living Indian of his time. His beneficent work among his people continued until his death in 1907.

Right from Haskell on graveled State 72 through a historic region of the former Creek Indian Nation. The highway crosses the ARKANSAS RIVER, 8 *m.,* and then follows the course of Coweta Creek, on whose banks the Coweta division of the tribe settled, to COWETA MISSION SITE (R). Here the Reverend Robert M. Loughridge established the first of three missions in 1843; he preached and his wife conducted a boarding school for the children of the near-by Creek families. The mission grew in size and holdings, but its buildings were burned during the Civil War and never replaced. Northeast of the site of the church, Loughridge, his young wife, and their baby, Olivia, are buried in an abandoned hillside cemetery, the headstones long since fallen and covered with debris.

The COWETA CEREMONIAL GROUNDS (L) was the scene of many solemn councils in the nineteenth century. Four brush arbors for the accommodation of spectators and participants surrounded a square where the ceremonial fire was kindled. Near by was a ball ground where men and women played the Indian ball game for recreation, and also (R) the ball-ground reserved for formal, and always strenuous, games between towns.

COWETA, 10.2 *m.* (625 alt., 1,455 pop.), is on the site of the early settlement named by the Creeks for their famous town in Georgia before the removal to Indian Territory. At that time, the Creek Nation was a confederacy formed by the union of semiautonomous towns. Governmental functions were divided into "peace" and "war" activities, with the towns classified as "white" or "red" according to the function. Coweta was the leading "red," or "war," town and the scene of many important treaty councils. When the tribe migrated to the West, members of Coweta Town settled here in the valley of the Arkansas; and the white settlement which gradually supplanted it has perpetuated the ancient name.

The tradition of the towns has never passed from the memory of the Creeks. When they adopted the white man's system of agriculture, they gradually moved out from these compact settlements to individual farms, but they continued to recognize the town organization as a social, ceremonial, and governmental unit. Even though they are scattered throughout Oklahoma at the present time, all Creeks remember their town affiliation.

These tribal traditions and institutions were almost completely wiped out by the domination of the white man and the adoption of the Indians into American citizenry. However, the Oklahoma Indian Welfare Act, passed by Congress in 1936, authorizing groups of Indians to incorporate for the purpose of acquiring land and carrying on collective activities, is sympathetic toward the traditional forms. The ancient Creek town organization formed the basis for the newly created chartered associations.

Near Coweta (L) is the SITE OF THE COWETA DISTRICT COURT, where the Creeks dispensed justice, sentencing and punishing almost simultaneously. Whipping was the most common punishment for all offenses.

At 113.9 *m.* is the junction with an improved county road.

Right to the SITE OF WEALAKA MISSION, 5 *m.*, on the south bank of the Arkansas River. Founded by the Creeks in 1881 with Rev. R. M. Loughridge as superintendent, the mission was built on land once belonging to Chief Pleasant Porter. The chief is buried not far from the site. The mission served as a Creek tribal school during and after Territorial days.

BIXBY, 114.9 *m.* (649 alt., 1,291 pop.), established in 1893, quieted down after an early history of outlawry to become a prosperous agricultural center. It was named for Tams Bixby, chairman of the Dawes Commission, created by Congress in 1893 to close out the affairs of the Five Civilized Tribes.

At 131.3 *m.* is the junction with 41st Street on the southern edge of Tulsa.

Left on 41st Street to TULSA'S FIRST POST OFFICE, 1.1 *m.*, marked by a red granite stone bearing an inscription and the date of establishment, March 25, 1879. The building *(private)* originally was the home of George Perryman and was the headquarters of the Figure-4 Ranch. Lumber and material for its construction were hauled in wagons from Coffeyville, Kansas. Though some changes have been made and some materials replaced, the moss-covered foundation blocks, the brick flues, sills, wainscoting, molding, and six-inch flooring still remain. The sills were hewn by hand, then mortised; the walls covered with canvas, then papered, when the building was first erected.

It was in the spring of 1878 that the Post Office Department decided to extend service from Fort Smith westward to the Sac and Fox Agency. A post road was routed and a post rider delivered mail once a week to the Perryman house. Josiah C. Perryman, a brother of George and one of the most respected citizens of the Creek Nation, was appointed postmaster. When the Frisco Railway came to Tulsa in 1882, the post office was moved from the Perryman home to a store near the tracks.

TULSA, 135.6 *m.* (700 alt., 142,157 pop.) *(see Tulsa),* is at the junction with US 66 *(see Tour 1),* US 75 *(see Tour 9),* and US 169 *(see Tour 9A).*

Section b. TULSA *to* ENID, *126.3 m. US 64*

West of TULSA, 0 *m.*, are many towns which grew from early Indian settlements. The highway follows the Arkansas River for about twenty miles, skirts the southern edge of the Osage reservation, and crosses the Pawnee reservation and the Cherokee Outlet.

SAND SPRINGS, 7.6 *m.* (700 alt., 6,137 pop.), is an industrial city (R) that began as an unusual philanthropic venture.

The business section of Sand Springs, where a Creek settlement was located in 1833 and named Adams Springs, in honor of a prominent Creek family, is six-tenths of a mile (R) from the main highway. The sandy springs in the near-by Osage Hills gave the city its present name.

Washington Irving, in his *Tour on the Prairies,* relates that he first saw the Cimarron River (or, the "Red Fork of the Arkansas River," as he termed it) from a hill called Beattie's Knob, north of present Sand Springs.

In 1907, Charles Page, oil millionaire, bought a 160-acre tract of land, on which he built a home for widows and orphans, and connected it with Tulsa by an electric railway. Industrial interests began locating here and, in 1911, the city of Sand Springs was platted. Today (1941), approximately eighty-five industries operate in the Sand Springs area, making it an important suburb of Tulsa.

PAGE MEMORIAL LIBRARY *(open weekdays: 1–9 P.M.)*, 3d and Main Streets, was built by Mrs. Page as a memorial to her husband, who died in 1926. The $100,000 structure, buff stucco with bronze trim, is modern in design and houses ten thousand volumes. Across the street from the library is TRIANGLE PARK, a small plot of ground in which stands a life-size bronze statue of Page, with smaller figures of orphans looking up to him. The group is the work of Lorado Taft.

Right from Sand Springs on 1st Street to SAND SPRINGS HOME INTERESTS, 2.1 *m.*, founded by Page to provide for orphans and needy widows with children. The property now includes sixteen thousand acres of farm land and a four-story modern building, affording accommodations for one hundred orphans and fifty widows. Many of the city's industries are owned by the Home Interests, income derived from them going toward the support of the institution. The farms supply much of the home's foodstuff.

Right, from the western boundary of the Home Interests, on an oiled asphalt road through a gateway, 0.9 *m.;* left to SHELL CREEK, 3.3 *m.* In the four DALTON CAVES, which line the creek, the Dalton gang is supposed to have hidden after their spectacular bank and train robberies. It is said that they buried some of their loot in or near the caves, but treasure hunters have never found it.

At Sand Springs, US 64 turns left at right angles and crosses the Arkansas River bridge, 8.2 *m.*

At the turn a CREEK BURIAL GROUND (L), more than one hundred years old, has been enclosed by an iron fence and preserved through the philanthropy of Charles Page.

KEYSTONE, 19.6 *m.* (684 alt., 406 pop.), is now a quiet farm community with the usual stores, churches, and schools, showing no traces of its saloon-infested frontier past.

Keystone was first settled on the south bank of the Cimarron River at its confluence with the Arkansas. The Osage reservation was to the north, bordered by the Arkansas, and the Creek reservation lay just to the south. The white man's "firewater," abundant in Keystone, attracted cowboys, farmers, and outlaws, as well as the prohibited Indians.

About 1903, real estate promoters bought two cornfields on the north bank of the Cimarron, just across from Keystone. In typical boom fashion, they laid out the townsite of Appalachia, pictured in alluring colored maps as a busy river port reached by steamboat. The fact that the Cimarron rarely has much water except after heavy rains was apparently ignored, for the new town began to spring up with saloons in abundance. The enterprising promoters and saloon-keepers built a rickety swinging footbridge across the river, and hundreds of vehicles and saddle horses waited on the Keystone side while their owners spent hours in the new town's more attractive saloons. Often, on the return trip, the revelers fell into the chilly waters and many sobered up sufficiently to take the pledge. Appropriately, the footbridge was named for Carry Nation, whose temperance campaign was in full swing in Kansas at the time.

A U.S. marshal arrived to keep order at the height of Appalachia's prosperity; instead, he opened a saloon on the Keystone side. Others followed his example, and Appalachia was soon abandoned.

Keystone is at the junction with State 33 *(see Tour 2A)*.

At 23.4 *m.*, US 64 turns left, closely paralleling the Arkansas River, which here is a wide, sandy stream, bordered by a fringe of timber and low, rugged hills.

On November 19, 1861, Opothle Yahola, leading a band of approximately five thousand Creeks loyal to the Union government, camped at ROUND MOUNTAIN (R). Here Confederate troops caught up with them and attacked, but Opothle Yahola led his band away under cover of darkness. Attempting to reach Kansas and refuge, many died of starvation and disease and, as winter closed in, others froze to death. The survivors reached southern Kansas about the middle of January, 1862, destitute and with greatly depleted ranks.

CLEVELAND, 36.9 *m.* (740 alt., 2,510 pop.), named for President Cleveland, was established by a townsite company shortly after the opening of the Cherokee Strip in 1893. The Osage reservation was near by, and "going to town" for thousands of Osages meant going to Cleveland; the muddy streets were usually lined with their ponies. For some time the bridge across the Arkansas River at Cleveland was the only crossing between the one at Tulsa to the east and the Kansas Line to the northwest, where the river passes out of the state. Cleveland gained the title "Gate City," during this period.

Oil fields in the vicinity have produced great quantities of crude oil for many years and several gasoline companies are in operation here, but Cleveland has never had the boom town appearance.

In Cleveland is the junction with State 99 *(see Tour 14)*, which unites westward with US 64 for six miles.

At 48.9 *m.* is a junction with an improved dirt road.

Right on this road is BLACKBURN, 6.1 *m.* (798 alt., 198 pop.), where the annual reunion of the Drouth Survivors of 1901 is held on the first Thursday in August. In that year, hundreds of people abandoned their farms and homesteads here. Those who stayed banded together into an association, and the group—about two hundred—still meets for a reminiscent get-together.

Left from Blackburn, 5 *m.*, on a dirt road, is SKEDEE (833 alt., 235 pop.), named for the Skidi division of the Pawnee tribe, and once known as the Crystal Creek Campgrounds. An interesting COLLECTION OF INDIAN CURIOS *(open weekdays: 9–4)* is owned by Colonel E. Waters; he was an auctioneer during the period of the million-dollar oil lease sales in Osage County *(see Tour 4)* and participated in many of the fabulous deals. A concrete statue, showing Bacon Rind, an Osage leader, and Colonel Waters shaking hands in a "bond of friendship," stands on the Waters grounds. The sculpture bears little resemblance to Bacon Rind, who was perhaps the most photographed of all American Indians.

PAWNEE, 57.9 *m.* (822 alt., 2,742 pop.), originally a trading post, was made the site of the Pawnee Agency in 1876 when that tribe was removed from their home in Nebraska to new lands in Oklahoma. In 1893, when the Pawnees accepted allotments, the residue of their land was opened for settlement, and the present-day town began to develop.

Pawnee still retains the flavor of its early days, and blanketed Indians are a common sight. On a broad limestone panel above the main entrance of the PAWNEE COUNTY COURTHOUSE, erected in 1933, are carvings depicting scenes of pioneer and Indian life. The courthouse square is the center of activity on Saturdays and on court days in the spring and fall.

Tourists wishing to see "real" Indians are rarely disappointed when visiting the PAWNEE AGENCY on the eastern edge of town. It was from this center that General George A. Custer recruited Indian scouts to aid him in his campaign against the wild Plains tribes *(see Tour 3A)*. On June 10, 1876, Captain Luther North sent a group of scouts from this point to Wyoming to serve under Custer. Some (who had been absent at a hunting party at the time) set out later; within a few days, they returned to the agency, reporting that smoke signals had told them that Custer was dead. Ten days later the Pawnee agent received official word of Custer's death.

Right from Pawnee on asphalt-paved State 18 to LAKE PAWNEE *(swimming, recreational facilities)*, 1 *m.*, which covers 305 acres. Five hundred acres around the lake have been developed by the town into a park and recreation center, with a large, native stone club-house and a fish hatchery.

On BLUE HAWK PEAK, 59.7 *m.*, stands the rambling brick home of Major Gordon W. Little—known as Pawnee Bill—Indian interpreter, frontiersman, scout, and originator of Pawnee Bill's Wild West Circus with which he toured widely for a number of years. Born in Illinois in 1860, Lillie came to Indian Territory in 1882 and joined a cattle outfit in the Cherokee Strip. Shortly after, he became an instructor in the government school at the Pawnee Agency; he was a leader among the Boomers, the group of whites who attempted to settle in Indian Territory before official action by Congress allowed them to do so legally. Pawnee Bill's circus ventures took him abroad to the World's Fair at Antwerp, Belgium, in 1894; on a successful tour of America; and once joined him in partnership with Buffalo Bill (W. F. Cody) in a show called "The Two Bills."

OLD TOWN, 61.4 *m. (no admission)*, is a group of dilapidated buildings representing a typical frontier settlement, erected by Lillie as a commercial enterprise. It includes a central trading post, Pawnee council house, log cabins, and a Hopi Indian pueblo, which was used as a filling station. In the trading post is the old Stag back-bar of solid mahogany, twenty feet long and eleven feet high, used in the Two Johns saloon in Oklahoma City. The council house is a circular, sod-brick structure with a tapered roof. The herd of buffalo that once was quartered here is gone. The depression wrote finis to this venture.

At 73.6 *m.* is the junction with State 40, a paved highway.

Left on State 40 to STILLWATER LAKE, 8.6 *m. (dancing and picnicking facilities; boating, 50c a day; fishing, 25c; hunting, 50c)*, which covers twenty-one acres.

BOOMER LAKE, 10.1 *m. (boating and fishing, 50c)*, is the municipal water supply for Stillwater.

STILLWATER, 12 *m.* (886 alt., 10,097 pop.) *(see Stillwater)*, is at the junction with State 51, an improved dirt road.

Right on State 51 to a junction, 9.9 *m.*, with a graveled road; (R) on this road to LAKE CARL BLACKWELL, 13 *m. (swimming, picnicking, boating, hunting)*.

State 40 continues to the MIDGET CATTLE FARM *(visitors welcome)*, 14.2 *m.* (R), where Otto Gray has developed a small herd of midget milch cows. He started (1931) with a freak Angus cow, the four calves from which (sired by ordinary Hereford and Jersey bulls) were all midgets. The herd in 1941 consisted of nineteen midget cows and the breed has held true for four generations. One of them holds the record of having produced her own weight in milk in eleven days. Others in the herd gave as much as five gallons of milk daily; and the milk tests high in butter fat.

At 21.2 *m.* is the junction with State 33 *(see Tour 2A).*

PERRY, 85.7 *m.* (1,005 alt., 5,045 pop.), is a center for the surrounding agricultural area and seat of Noble County. On the morning of September 16, 1893, the first of the Santa Fe special trains entered the Cherokee Strip, loaded with eager, shouting land-seekers. The first stop was at a station named Wharton, one mile south of the present Perry station. Clambering off, the passengers rushed into the already platted townsite, which had been designed as a land-office town by the Department of Interior and named for a member of the Federal Townsite Commission. They drove their stakes into the ground, and the mushroom town of tents and clapboards was born.

Sooner Land (1929), by George Washington Ogden, a native of Kansas, gives a colorful description of the early days of Perry. It tells of the large number of Sooners, the fourteen saloons, the many gamblers, and their hangers-on which caused the Federal government to send three marshals here until a city government could be organized. The wooden buildings of the old land office still stand in GOVERNMENT SQUARE PARK, but a modern courthouse, a CARNEGIE LIBRARY, and the rows of parked automobiles now bordering the square eclipse them—the rip-roaring early days are forgotten.

Perry is at the junction with US 77 *(see Tour 10),* which unites westward with US 64 for 5.6 miles.

COVINGTON, 103.9 *m.* (1,141 alt., 780 pop.), was named for John Covington, an early settler. When the Arkansas Valley & Western Railroad built a station here, Covington asked the railroad officials to grant him this honor because, having no sons, he wished to perpetuate his name.

The Knox-Mulhall Rodeo is held each fall, usually in September, at the KNOX RANCH, 104 *m.*

West of Covington, wheat fields line the highway and the towers of the grain elevators in and around Enid are visible. This section is the most productive wheat-raising region in the state. An oil field, extending from Covington to Garber *(see Industry),* was discovered with the drilling of the Hoy Well in 1916.

At 110.9 *m.* is the junction with paved State 15.

Straight ahead (north) on State 15 is GARBER, 3 *m.* (1,148 alt., 1,086 pop.), where an annual celebration is held on September 16, commemorating the opening of the Cherokee Strip on that day in 1893. Whiskers are coaxed to grow long in the early-day fashion, and pioneer clothes make their appearance as the whole town "dresses up" for the occasion.

ENID, 126.3 *m.* (1,246 alt., 28,081 pop.), *(see Enid),* is at the southern junction with US 60 *(see Tour 4)* and US 81 *(see Tour 11).*

Section c. ENID *to* NEW MEXICO LINE, *342 m. US 64*

Between Enid and the New Mexico Line, US 64 passes through an agricultural section in which the leading crops are wheat and forage; the land, especially in the far western Panhandle section, is high and arid. Towns are far apart and comparatively small.

North of ENID, 0 *m.*, US 60 and US 81 unite with US 64 to 19 *m.*, where the route turns sharply west.

At 33.7 *m.* is the junction with an improved dirt road.

Right at this point on a series of dirt roads; (R) at 1 *m.;* (L) at 2 *m.;* and (L) again at 6 *m.* to the GREAT SALT PLAINS DAM, 6.5 *m.*, a $2,000,000 structure started in 1938 and scheduled for completion in 1941. The reservoir, created by the dam for flood control and conservation, has a storage capacity of 317,000 acre-feet of water. When completely filled, the lake will extend ten miles up the Salt Fork of the Arkansas River with a maximum width of twelve miles, covering all of the area lying within the Great Salt Plains. Approximately 19,400 acres—69 per cent of the total reservoir bottom—is government owned and has been reserved as a wild-fowl refuge under the jurisdiction of the Department of the Interior. The remaining ground covered has little agricultural value. Construction of the dam reduces the hazard of flood damage in the Salt Fork valley to the south and east as well as in the valley of the Arkansas River. Recreational facilities for northwestern Oklahoma are provided by the project, which will also prove a refuge for migratory birds and other wild life.

Geologists hold conflicting theories as to the formation of the Great Salt Plains. The most commonly accepted explanation is that the area was once covered by a great prehistoric sea which has evaporated, leaving the salt bed. Another, advanced by a University of Oklahoma geologist, is that the Plains were the result of consistent weathering of a soil that does not support enough vegetation to prevent erosion. The soluble salt, laid down in geologic formation fifty million years ago, "sweated up" out of the ground or crystallized about salt springs fed by water that flowed through salt beds not far from the surface. The salt formed a thin, wafer-like crust on the flat surface covering approximately sixty square miles, lower in elevation than the surrounding country. The glistening white crust appeared to migratory fowl as a vast and welcome expanse of water. When it rained, the salt crust dissolved, making it appear an ordinary section of ground; this transformation was dangerous, however, for the clay and sand beneath the surface became quick. Although completely barren, the plains supported four forms of life—two birds, the lestern and the snowy plover, and two insects, the tiger beetle and a sea blite. Climatic conditions in the region are the most extreme outside a desert; ample spring rains are followed by a long and severe drouth when 114° F. is not uncommon. Winter often brings blizzards that force the temperature to 14° below zero. Salt Springs, feeding the Salt Fork (which winds along the north and east edges of the Salt Plains area), flow thousands of gallons of brine daily.

According to available records, the first white men to see the Plains were those in the party of Major George C. Sibley, Indian agent from Fort Osage, Missouri. In 1811, Sans Oreille, an Osage Indian, with others of his tribe, guided them to the spot, which Sibley called the Grand Saline. The Salt Fork of the Arkansas River, flowing around the plain, was known to the Osages as *Nescatunga* (big salt water). Another early explorer to see the Great Salt Plains was Captain Nathan Boone, son of Daniel Boone, who headed a government expedition from Fort Gibson into what is now central Kansas in 1843. Boone described the phenomenon as a "lake of white water."

In drafting the treaty which defined the territory to become the so-called permanent home of the Cherokees in 1828, the United States government withheld the Salt Plains area with the provision that, "The right is reserved to the United States to allow other tribes of red men to get salt on the Great Salt Plains in common with the Cherokee Tribe." Possession of the Plains had probably been the cause of many Indian battles, since its value lay not in its salt alone but in the rich hunting afforded by the animals migrating here for the salt supply. The Great Salt Plains have thus been the scene of many Indian councils both of war and peace. A war council of Plains Indians was called to meet here in 1845 to plan concerted opposition to immigrant Creek Indians, whose reservation lay farther to the east. Creek diplomacy and emotional appeal resulted in peace and, thereafter, the councils held on this spot were usually of a peaceful nature.

The commercial value of the salt was highest during the earliest days of the settlement of the Indian Territory, when transportation to this wild country was difficult; western Kansas and Texas cattlemen sent wagons here to haul away great loads. Near-by farmers used the salt for livestock.

CHEROKEE, 51.8 *m.* (1,181 alt., 2,553 pop.), the seat of Alfalfa County, is a thriving agricultural outlet for the surrounding fertile farm country. Wheat, alfalfa, corn, and sorghum are profitable crops for the area, and milling is an important Cherokee industry.

Mrs. Walter (Lucia Loomis) Ferguson, whose daily syndicated column, *A Woman's Viewpoint,* appears in many newspapers, formerly lived here. With her husband, Walter Ferguson (d. 1937), former state legislator and son of the sixth territorial governor, Thompson B. Ferguson, she published the *Cherokee Republican.*

At 54.9 *m.* is the junction with State 58, a graveled road.

Straight ahead on State 58 to a junction with graded County Highway 15, 4.5 *m.;* (R) here to the DRUMM MONUMENT, 7.7 *m.,* marking the site of the old 150,000-acre U Ranch, which Major Andrew Drumm (1828–1919) established in 1874 after moving here from southern Kansas. The ranch lay at the confluence of the Medicine River and the Salt Fork. Drumm was one of the first cattlemen to turn his herds to graze on the plains of the Cherokee Outlet, dependent entirely on the grass. When the Cherokee Strip Livestock Association *(see History)* was formed, he became the first president. In 1893, the U Ranch, as well as other Cherokee Outlet acres, was opened to settlement. A part of Alfalfa County now covers this once large domain.

STATE FISH HATCHERY No. 5, 12.2 *m.,* was established in 1929 on an eighty-acre tract (L). Eleven artesian wells provide water for the twenty-five culture ponds at an average temperature of 60° F.; trout are being propagated successfully here.

At 70.9 *m.* is the junction with asphalt-paved US 281.

Right at this point to the junction with a dirt road, 9.3 *m.;* (R) on this road to ELM SPRINGS, 14.7 *m. (boating, 25c; swimming, 50c; and fishing 25c).* Springs bubble from both sides of a small canyon, and the stream thus formed has been damned to make a small lake. Early settlers and explorers found Indians camping on this spot; councils of war were held there and, sometimes, the weird and hideous scalp dance.

In 1879, Stith and Walkins, ranchers, established a cow camp at the springs and maintained it for several years. The trail, over which supplies for the army were transported to Fort Supply *(see Tour 12)* from the nearest railroad point (Kiowa, Kansas), passed through Elm Springs. Thus the springs became a favored camping place. Following the Run of 1893, the site of Elm Springs was included in a homestead allotment and has changed ownership several times since then.

At 71.8 *m.* is NORTHWESTERN STATE COLLEGE (L), founded in 1897, the second oldest normal school in the state. The first building, constructed at a cost of $110,000 in 1898, was underwritten by the citizens of near-by Alva, then a town only a few years old. This building, called "The Castle on the Hill," was destroyed by fire in 1935 and sixty thousand volumes, housed there, were also lost. Two buildings, Jesse Dunn Hall and a training school, have since been built. General Hugh S. Johnson, NRA Administrator (1933–34) and well-known columnist, was graduated here in 1901. His father was formerly the Alva postmaster.

In the college LIBRARY is a small brown leather book of forty pages, containing signs and symbols indicating cattle identification brands registered with the Cherokee Strip Livestock Association for the roundup of 1886. The book shows approximately six hundred listings for three hundred ranches. Two methods of branding were used; one, a running brand of letters, figures, or symbols applied with a red-hot poker-like iron, and the other with an iron shaped with the trade mark of the rancher. Among the well-known brands were: Bar-M, Lazy B, 101, Bar-Turkey-Track, and Mule-Shoe.

Right from Northwestern State College, on College Avenue, is the business district of ALVA, 0.5 *m.* (1,351 alt., 5,055 pop.), the seat of Woods County. Alva was designated as one of the four land-office towns at the time of the opening of the Cherokee Strip (1893). Originally a Santa Fe Railway stop, it was named for Alva Adams, attorney for the railroad and later governor of Colorado. The town, built around the courthouse square, serves a large area as a business and community center.

Left from the college on US 281 to WAYNOKA, 25.8 *m.* (1,475 alt., 1,584 pop.), an important division point and the second largest railroad yard in the state, with car and engine repair shop. As many as four hundred refrigerator cars are serviced here daily during the summer months. Waynoka operates its own municipal light and water plants. A park, covering approximately twenty-seven acres, with swimming pool, playground, and picnic grounds, has recently been completed.

Waynoka has grown from a railroad siding, known as Keystone, which was established here in 1886. The present town, platted in 1893, was named Waynoka by a subchief of the Cheyennes, Man-On-Cloud.

South and west of Waynoka erosion has taken its toll; sand dunes, evidence of centuries of shifting of the course of the Cimarron River, extend to the river bed, some six miles south of Waynoka. Some of the dunes are more than one hundred yards wide, with steep slopes of from twenty to fifty feet. In its slow movement, the sand covers all vegetation, even large trees. Near the river, where the sediment has been washed or blown away, roots of trees that sprouted from trunks while they were imbedded in sand are often seen a yard or more above ground. The tops of telephone poles, showing from two to fifteen feet above the dunes, indicate an old line built along a road running here before the present US 281 was surveyed.

Dull Knife, Northern Cheyenne chieftain, camped south of the Cimarron River in 1878 with a small band of followers in flight from Oklahoma to their former home on the northern plains. After the Custer massacre *(see Tour 13)*, when the resistance of the northern Indians had been broken, Dull Knife and his band were brought to the Cheyenne reservation near El Reno, where they were promised subsistence. Later, suffering from homesickness and illness, the group pleaded to be allowed to return to Dakota. When their request was denied, the band of eighty-nine warriors and 246 women and children, led by Dull Knife, set out in flight for the north. A skirmish with Federal troops sixty miles from the reservation resulted in the death of three soldiers. Along the way, several settlers and cowboys were killed, houses were burned, and supplies were confiscated by the desperate Indians. News of the march spread to military outposts and, at one time, some twenty-four companies of cavalry and infantry were pursuing the fleeing Indians. Another engagement with troops near Fort Dodge, Kansas, turned into a rout for the soldiers. Finally, near Fort Robinson, Nebraska, Dull Knife and his group were captured and held during the winter. They broke away again and started northward, with the military in pursuit. Dull Knife's march has been described as a masterly feat of military strategy, although he met defeat finally in Dakota when, surrounded in a snowbound canyon, he and his remaining followers were forced to surrender.

At 97.5 *m.* on the main route is a junction with State 50, an improved dirt road.

Left on State 50 to FREEDOM, 3.1 *m.* (1,521 alt., 364 pop.), a farming settlement.

Right from Freedom on a dirt road, 2.4 *m.*, to the Little SALT PLAIN, also called the Edith Salt Plain, after the settlement a few miles northwest on the Cimarron River. This Plain, three miles wide and extending for twelve miles along the river, is smaller than the saline deposit at Cherokee, but still more barren. Except near its edges, no life whatever exists. From a distance, the Plain looks like a roaring rush of water in time of flood. Gypsum-capped bluffs to the south combine with the Plain to create a huge mine of exposed mineral. Undoubtedly the salt has some commercial value but, to date, ventures to capitalize on it have met with failure. In a faintly salty tributary to the east, two microscopic forms of ocean life have been discovered, supporting the theory that this spot and the Plains at Cherokee once formed the bed of a prehistoric sea.

State 50 crosses the Cimarron River to a junction with a dirt road, 5.2 *m.;* L. here to the main entrance of rugged CEDAR CANYON PARK. The approach is through prairie country, but the park lies in a deep valley between the rough, red-clay walls of a canyon. A spring-fed stream tumbles through the wooded gorge. Knives, arrowheads, and primitive tools of volcanic rock have been found in the region, indicating that it was one of the early-day camping grounds of the Indians.

Just inside the entrance to the park stands a CLUBHOUSE *(meals or kitchen and dining-room facilities, 50c)*. Near by is the (so-called) EXTINCT GEYSER FIELD, where great holes, mistakenly thought to be former geyser domes, dot the hillside. The holes, lined with solid rock, are pitted with pockets probably formed by water percolating to, and dissolving, the gypsum. Geologists believe, however, that these were formed by movement of the deposits of salt and gypsum in the underlying beds. Across a small canyon is a NATURAL BRIDGE, perched at an elevation of nearly nineteen hundred feet above sea level and 150 feet above the canyon floor. The perfect arch, forty feet wide and thirty feet high, carved by ancient rushing waters through a barrier of solid gypsum, gives a splendid view of Cedar Canyon's wonders.

About 250 yards northeast of the clubhouse is the entrance to the ALABASTER CAVERNS *(adm. 75c),* also known locally as the Bat Caves. Inside the entrance, a vestibule, lined with great slabs and masses of stone blasted from the ceiling, is the start of the one and one-half hour trip through the caverns, every foot of which opens upon new scenes of grandeur. During portions of the trip the roar of subterranean waters is heard. The visitor ascends gradually to the upper reaches and emerges at last on a plateau, where there is a panoramic view of the park and the Cimarron River country.

Millions of bats live in the caves, and between sunset and dusk in summer they pour out in a great funnel-shaped black cloud. From the first frost, usually in October, until the warm days of March the bats remain hanging to the walls of the caverns without sustenance, waking to squeek in protest only if plucked from their perch. The brown-coated, flat-headed mammal is of the *Tadaria vulgaris* or common Guano variety.

Large translucent crystals sparkle from the roof of the Milling Chamber, their beauty enhanced by colored electric lights. A corridor (R) leads to the crystal-decked Aladdin Chamber, in which is a tiny lake of clear spring water. In the Encampment Room, once used by the Indians as a meeting place, have been found many arrowheads, lance points, ornaments, and pieces of pottery.

Other features of the caverns are Gun Barrel Tunnel, a round passageway hollowed out by a stream of water through the rock; Pulpit Hall, a room decorated with tiny stalactites; the Bathtub, a concavity in a ledge of solid granite into which a thin stream of water falls from a hole in the ceiling; and the White Way, a section of the passage lined with fantastic formations of alabaster, carved by water action. Cavities resembling geyser vents are lighted by electricity, bringing out the delicate tracings and scroll work.

Blind Fish Cavern is so called because crayfish, washed into the water through the vents and fissures above, become transparent after a short time and many have a growth of skin covering their eye sockets.

The CIMARRON RIVER, crossed at 110.4 *m.,* is almost a mile wide in places and is bordered by extensive sand dunes. The high, dry winds of this section carry the sand out of the river bed and pile it into white mounds on the rolling red prairie.

At 127.1 *m.* is a junction with US 183 *(see Tour 12),* which unites southward briefly with US 64.

West of BUFFALO, 128.5 *m.* (1,791 alt., 1,209 pop.) *(see Tour 12),* the rolling plains are dotted with clumps of sagebrush and cactus; small gullies and ravines break the smooth fields, exposing the red clay, which contrasts sharply with the green and gray of the grass.

At 133.6 *m.* is a junction with an improved dirt road.

Right on this road is DOBY SPRINGS, 0.3 *m.*, named for an early settler, Chris Dobie, who staked his claim on the site during the run for the Cherokee Strip lands. Dobie established a ranch there, and his house, built near the artesian springs and still standing, was one of the first in this part of Oklahoma; dugouts were the most common abode since lumber was difficult to transport. The town of Buffalo acquired the site several years ago, naming it Doby Springs Park. The springs have been dammed to create a small lake which furnishes the town's water supply and is stocked with game fish *(25c fishing fee)*. Prior to 1874, when buffaloes were common, this was a favorite watering place for many herds.

At 144 *m.* is the junction with US 283 *(see Tour 13)*, which is united westward with US 64 for 4.5 miles.

GATE, 153.7 *m.* (2,230 alt., 243 pop.), lies on the western slope of a basin, which perhaps held an ancient lake. Northeast of Gate, extensive deposits of silica (volcanic dust), nine feet deep in places, support the theory that a volcano was once active in this area (probably in the Mt. Capulin region in New Mexico). Approximately one hundred carloads of the mineral are shipped yearly.

North of Gate is Horse Creek, where what is said to be an ancient irrigation canal, about twenty-five feet wide and five feet deep, runs parallel with the stream. In several places all traces have been obliterated by the shifting creek channel. The ditch ends abruptly without an outlet, the method of irrigation evidently having been to allow it to fill and overflow the adjacent cultivated fields. Some authorities believe that the canal was constructed by prehistoric peoples.

US 64 traverses the Panhandle strip where the land is fertile, but crops are at the mercy of the elements. Wheat, broomcorn, and forage yields are large when drouth and winds temper their fury. Many of the acres, particularly the broad plateaus with their terraced canyons, are used as grazing land for cattle. The familiar "short grass" carpets the level tablelands. Between Guymon and the western border, the flat, even terrain creates mirages on a wavering horizon. Inhabitants tell of standing in the open and being able to see towns many miles away. The Spanish explorer, Coronado, who traveled through this section in 1541, spoke with amazement in his report of the "level, smooth country," saying that "one can see the sky between the legs of the buffalo, and if a man lay down on his back, he lost sight of the ground."

Tumbleweeds, which grow profusely here, are blown about by the wind and pile against houses and outbuildings. On especially windy days, sand swirls over the fields, burying seeds and young plants deeply, and justifying the term "dust bowl," with which the Panhandle has been tagged. *Tumbleweeds* (1923), a historical novel by Hal G. Evarts, describes the Cherokee Strip and the Panhandle.

This narrow strip of land was possessed successively by various governments, for awhile ignored and called No Man's Land, and finally added to Oklahoma. Maps of the state which, for economy's sake, show the Panhandle as a separate section tacked on in waste space to the side or bottom are unpopular with the residents; and many of the schools in the section refuse to use them. The people who pioneered in the Panhandle probably suffered and "sweated" more than those who broke the virgin sod in other parts of Oklahoma, for theirs was a constant fight against the elements. The progress of the whole section was measured by inches of advance as each man toiled to make a home. A plaintive verse sung by these pioneers shows both their struggle and the spirit in which they met it:

> Pickin' up bones to keep from starving,
> Pickin' up chips to keep from freezing,
> Pickin' up courage to keep from leaving,
> Way out West in No Man's Land.

In this jingle, "bones" and "chips" are relics of the buffalo.

At 180.6 *m.* is the junction with US 270, a graveled highway. A MONUMENT TO CORONADO (L), a three-ton granite boulder, has been erected here by the Colonial Dames of America.

Left on US 270 to BEAVER, 6.6 *m.* (2,493 alt., 1,166 pop.), the seat of Beaver County and onetime capital of the "Territory of Cimarron." A sod building, erected here in 1879, served as a store for cattlemen driving their herds across Beaver Creek on the way to the markets of Dodge City, Kansas.

The peculiar conditions which left the Panhandle without legal government brought about the formation of the "Territory of Cimarron" in 1887—an earnest effort by the people who had settled there to bring a semblance of law and order to No Man's Land. The convention for its formation was held at Beaver, and this town was named its capital. The Federal government never recognized the territorial organization; the Organic Act of 1890 automatically dissolved it and added the entire section to Oklahoma Territory as Beaver County. When Oklahoma became a state, the Panhandle was divided into three counties, with the eastern one retaining the name of Beaver and Beaver as its county seat. One of the earliest white man's newspapers published in Oklahoma and the first in this section of the state was issued in this town in 1886 as the *Beaver City Pioneer* *(see Newspapers)*.

In 1910, the Wichita Falls & Northwestern Railroad bought options on land six miles north of Beaver with the intention of extending their line to that point and of founding a town at the terminus. This the company did, creating the present town of Forgan; but Beaver citizens, in the meantime, had obtained articles of incorporation to build a railroad to forestall the devastating effect which the prospective town would exert on their business. The proposed road was eventually to connect with Meade and Englewood in Kansas; but its slow construction, carried on with small contributions of both money and labor from practically every Beaver citizen, took many months to cover the six miles to Forgan. During this period the road was offered as a gift several times to the Katy corporation, which had taken over the Wichita Falls & Northwestern, but the offer was refused. Profitable wheat trade during the first World War brought prosperity to the struggling little line, however, and it was extended into Texas and Cimarron counties. The Missouri-Kansas-Texas Railroad shortly afterwards paid more than $2,000,000 for the Beaver, Meade, & Englewood Railroad, a line which had been offered as a gift some fifteen years before.

Beaver is now an important shipping center for the widespread wheat farms to the south.

FORGAN, 181.9 *m.* (2,565 alt., 428 pop.), which looms up on the clear, unbroken prairie from miles away, is a center for the farming section lying between the Cimarron and the North Canadian rivers. Most of the surrounding acres are planted with wheat.

The town was named for James B. Forgan, a Chicago banker who helped finance the Wichita Falls & Northwestern Railway (now operated by the Missouri-Kansas-Texas), the first railroad to enter Beaver County. The townsite was laid out and its sale promoted by the railway company.

TURPIN, 203.9 *m.,* BAKERSBURG, 212.9 *m.,* and HOOKER, 222.9 *m.* (2,984 alt., 1,140 pop.), are farm communities surrounded by miles of level wheat fields and isolated houses.

OPTIMA, 233.9 *m.* (3,090 alt., 69 pop.), is on the site of a prehistoric village representing an ancient culture about which little is known. Within the vicinity are the privately owned ruins of at least six slab-lined pit houses. Considerable study has been given to the largest of these by the department of anthopology of the University of Oklahoma, and a large collection of fossil bones is in the university's Museum of Paleontology.

Texas County's largest individual industry is the GENERAL ATLAS CARBON COMPANY PLANT, 240.1 *m.,* located on the Rock Island Railway, which parallels the highway here. The plant normally produces a carload a day of carbon black, used in the manufacture of rubber and as a pigment in ink and paint.

GUYMON, 242.1 *m.* (3,125 alt., 2,290 pop.), on a flat plain in the approximate center of the Panhandle, serves the surrounding farm country as a trading center. It is the seat of Texas County.

One of the largest and most colorful annual events of this section is the Pioneer Day Celebration held here on May 2, the anniversary of the passage of the Organic Act of 1890, which made the Panhandle a part of the Territory of Oklahoma. Pioneers from the entire region, and many from Kansas and Texas, gather to parade, participate in the rodeo, and eat the barbecued buffalo meat that is served free to all comers.

An erosion control project here under the supervision of the U.S. Soil Conservation Service demonstrates proper methods of soil treatment in the Panhandle.

Left from Guymon on paved US 54 is GOODWELL, 11 *m.* (3,218 alt., 360 pop.), home of the PANHANDLE AGRICULTURAL AND MECHANICAL COLLEGE, established as an agricultural school in 1909. The course of study was later extended to include the regular college schedule. The school owns and maintains 720 acres of land which it uses as an agricultural experiment station. Four main buildings and three dormitories (two more are now under construction) comprise the college plant; 640 additional acres are maintained as a livestock farm, with modern dairy equipment.

In the MUSEUM, in Hughes-Strong Hall, data and collections relating to the history of the Panhandle are displayed. The museum, sponsored by the No Man's Land Historical Society, which took it over in 1934, is operated on a co-operative loan basis; individuals lend and borrow material at will.

At TEXHOMA, 22 *m.* (3,486 alt., 577 pop.), just north of the Texas-Oklahoma Line, a thousand or more of the town's residents and neighboring farmers gather for an annual Rabbit Drive in the third or fourth week of October. Forming a twenty-mile circle, they close in at a set time, corral many rabbits, and shoot a number of wolves and coyotes. A rodeo, barbecue, and a wild-cow milking contest usually close the day's events.

Two prominent structures stand out on the plains as one approaches BOISE CITY, 303.4 *m.* (4,164 alt., 1,144 pop.)—the two-story, red-brick Cimarron County Courthouse in the center of the town square, and a tall, black water tank flanking the residential section.

Westward the level Panhandle land gives way to a rugged terrain, characteristic of New Mexico.

At 304.3 *m.* is the junction with State 3, a graveled road.

Right on State 3 to the intersection with the old SANTA FE TRAIL, 8.7 *m.* Hardy early-day pioneers broke the trail to connect Santa Fe, New Mexico, with Independence, Missouri, the starting point for overland travel to the West.

Impatient at its length, Captain William Becknell set out in 1822 to find a short cut, accompanied by thirty men and a caravan of mules, horses, and "prairie schooners" loaded with merchandise. He was warned of the danger of the Cimarron desert—the stretch between the Arkansas River in southwestern Kansas and the Cimarron River in Oklahoma—which was waterless except in the rainy season, when the shallow creek beds carried their temporary burden to one of the two wide, sandy channels. The party's water supply soon became exhausted after leaving the Arkansas and pointing toward Santa Fe. The men and animals were slowly dying of thirst when Becknell shot a buffalo and on cutting into its stomach found about three gallons of fresh water, indication that the animal had drunk recently. After an hour's ride, the caravan reached the Cimarron, filled their water kegs, and returned to the Arkansas River and the regular route. However, other travelers and wagon trains soon began using the short cut.

The government surveyed the Santa Fe Trail and found that by 1860, the peak year of traffic over it, three thousand wagons, seven thousand men, and sixty thousand mules were using the route annually. Heavy traffic continued until after the Civil War.

Ruts made by wagons, driven three abreast as a defense against possible surprise attack by Indians, are still visible along portions of the old Trail. Near Fort Nichols, three paths—ten feet in depth and twenty feet wide—run side by side, cut by the passage of thousands of heavily laden wagons. In 1875, upon completion of the Santa Fe Railway line through Kansas and Colorado, partially paralleling the trail, use of the route was discontinued. The old Trail is described in *Commerce of the Prairies* (1844), by Josiah Gregg.

At 318.5 *m.* on US 64 is a junction with a graded section line road.

Left on this road to a junction with a second graded road, 1 *m.;* R. here through WHEELESS POST OFFICE, 6 *m.,* an isolated postal station serving the few residents of the surrounding area, to a junction with an unimproved dirt road, 8 *m.;* R. here to the SITE OF FORT NICHOLS, 10.2 *m.,* established by Kit Carson in 1865, by orders of the War Department. Carson was directed to locate the fort in New Mexico near the 103d meridian as a protection for the users of the Santa Fe Trail, but he selected a site (L) on a high knoll, on the banks of Carrizzo Creek, about four miles east of the present Oklahoma–New Mexico boundary. Rocks for the walls and barracks were brought from the creek bed; the stone floor of the barracks building and of the headquarters building are still visible. The rampart wall is also still standing, though it is now (1941) only six feet in height at the highest point, for near-by farmers have carried away many of the smoothed stones for their own use. A pile of rocks outside the eastern wall identifies the sentry tower which commanded a wide sweep of the plains and of the Santa Fe Trail.

At 329.8 *m.* on the main route is a junction with an improved dirt road.

Right on this road *(following signs)* to HALLOCK PARK, *(cabins, dancing, picnicking)* 8.1 *m.,* consisting of ten thousand acres of canyons and mesas, part of which has been developed for recreation purposes. A clear creek has been dammed to form a swimming pool. Of the 120 springs which gush forth here, several are the source of streams, affording abundant water for the campsites. Along the face of a sandstone bluff (six feet high and more than a quarter of a mile long), facing northeast, is a series of PICTOGRAPHS, startling in their color contrast of blue paint against the sandy rock. They depict Indians, in crude fashion, at their various daily activities. There also are many figures of animals; among them, bears, deer, antelope, coyotes, and beavers can easily be discerned.

At 330.7 *m.* is a DINOSAUR QUARRY (R), burial ground of many mighty monsters who roamed the earth during the Jurassic age, more than ten million years ago. Erosion uncovered the spot sufficiently so that workers have been able to remove many fossils intact. A WPA project has been digging, cleaning, and classifying the bones before shipment to the University of Oklahoma *(see Norman)*, where they are reconstructed into skeletons for classwork and display. Four types of the prehistoric animals have been excavated, of which the *Brontosaurus*—measuring seventy feet in length and about sixteen feet in height and weighing some thirty-six tons when alive—is the largest. This species together with the *Stegosaurus,* almost its equal in size, and the *Ornithopoda,* a giant lizard species, were herbiverous, but the *Allosaurus*—the fourth type brought to light—was a flesh-eater. Surmounting the entrance to the quarry is a concrete cast of the six-foot long femur (upper thigh bone) of a *Brontosaurus.*

The SPHINX *or* OLD MAID ROCK, 331.7 *m.,* 200 yards (R), is a curious formation, carved by the elements from the point of a sandstone bluff. A magnificent figure, it stands out boldly against the blue sky above the mesa in the background.

At 334.1 *m.* is a junction with an unimproved dirt road.

Right on this road is the NATURAL ARCH, 3.7 *m.,* in the bottom of a wide canyon north of the Cimarron River. The opening of this white sandstone arch—twenty feet high and eight feet wide—was probably formed by the constant battering of sand and wind. There are no other rocks or ledges of similar color or composition within a radius of eight miles.

At 338.3 *m.,* US 64 crosses the Time Zone Boundary Line, dividing line where travelers going west turn back their watches one hour for Mountain Time while those facing east add an hour for Central Standard Time.

KENTON, 339.5 *m.* (4,349 alt., 250 pop.), nestles in a high valley under the shadow of lava-capped Black Mesa to the northwest. Before statehood, Kenton was a roistering saloon town known as the Cowboy Capital. It was platted and laid out as a townsite in 1892 by a nephew of P. T. Barnum. The name, Kenton, is a variation of Canton (Ohio), for which this settlement was named.

At a filling station here is displayed the so-called SKELETON OF A PREHISTORIC BASKET MAKER, estimated to be more than a thousand years old. The bones were unearthed in a near-by cave, which has since been called the Basket Maker's Cave.

Right from Kenton on an improved dirt road to a junction with a second dirt road 2 *m.;* L. here to BLACK MESA, 3.9 *m.,* a plateau capped by lava deposit from an extinct volcano. The lava cap, underlaid with Dakota sandstone, ranges from twenty to seventy feet in thickness and extends some forty miles into Oklahoma from the New Mexico line. In the center of the mesa is the highest point in Oklahoma, 4,987 feet above sea level, designated by a marker of lava fragments and concrete, and topped with a piece of rose-colored granite from the quarry at Granite *(see Tour 13)*. The summit of this almost mile-high plateau was formerly a camping place for Indians; many arrowheads have been found here.

The old Penrose Trail to Fort Lyon, Colorado, began at Black Mesa and extended northwest into Colorado. In the fall of 1863, General W. H. Penrose surveyed this route for the purpose of transporting a fieldpiece for an assault against a bandit fortification near the Mesa, known as ROBBER'S ROOST. Later the Penrose Trail was used by adventurers, and, in the 1870's, by cattlemen who had settled in the valleys of the Arkansas and Cimarron rivers. This trail and others of its kind did much to facilitate the settlement of the West; along their routes were fresh-water holes and sheltered spots, without which neither man nor beast could have endured the long marches over the untamed and ruthless lands.

At 4 *m.* on the main side route is the DEVIL'S TOMBSTONE, a towering slab of brownish sandstone twenty feet high, eighteen inches thick, and twelve feet wide. A hole, worn by constant battering of the elements, is at the bottom of the huge formation and exactly in the center. Sightseers frequently photograph each other peering through the opening, the finished picture making it appear that the face is imbedded in the rock. The rock is, according to compass findings, set in true directions; the flat sides face north and south.

At 342 *m.,* US 64 crosses the New Mexico Line, ninety-eight miles east of Raton, New Mexico *(see New Mexico Guide).*

Tour 2A

Keystone—Cushing—Langston—Guthrie; 80.3 m., State 33.

Roadbed concrete-paved.
The Frisco Ry. parallels route between Keystone and Mannford; the Santa Fe between Drumright and Guthrie.
Good accommodations at frequent intervals.

State 33 crosses the northwestern corner of the former Creek Nation, traverses for some fifteen miles the old Cushing-Drumright oil field, passes some of the hundreds of huge steel oil storage tanks that make this the largest tank-farm area in Oklahoma. The route passes through a region of low wooded hills for some thirty miles, then climbs to the prairie upland north of the Cimarron River, crosses that river, and rises again to wind through red highland farms and orchards.

State 33 branches southwest from its junction with US 64 *(see Tour 2)* in KEYSTONE, 0 *m.,* (684 alt., 406 pop.) *(see Tour 2).*

Taking its name from Mann's Ford on the Cimarron River, MANNFORD, 6.6 *m.* (740 alt., 403 pop.), was built on land formerly owned by Tom Mann, who established the ford. It is the trading point for a considerable farming community.

The old BERRYHILL FARM, near the southern edge of Mannford, opened up by a citizen of the Creek Nation, was at one time a hide-out for the outlaw Dalton gang; and it is believed locally that large sums of money taken from banks by the Daltons are still buried somewhere on the farm.

A large projecting shelf of rock (R) is known as DALTON CAVE, 7.4 *m.* It was, according to local belief, the place where a half-blood Creek Indian named Tom Bartee hid and fed the Daltons when they were pursued by United States deputy marshals after their raids.

At 21.9 *m.* is the northern junction with State 99 *(see Tour 14),* which unites with State 33 for 10.5 miles.

At DRUMRIGHT, 29.3 *m.* (866 alt., 4,303 pop.) *(see Tour 14),* is the southern junction with State 99; State 33 turns sharply west.

CUSHING, 38.9 *m.* (940 alt., 7,703 pop.), was founded in 1892 on the old Turkey Track Ranch in the northern part of the Sac and Fox territory, and was named for Marshall Cushing, private secretary to John Wanamaker, then Postmaster General of the United States. It was incorporated as a town in 1894, and as a city in 1913.

The discovery of the rich Cushing oil field in 1912 marked the beginning of the town's swift expansion; by the end of 1915 there were 710 wells in this field producing seventy-two million barrels of oil annually. To care for this enormous output, twelve refineries were built at Cushing and near by; on the prairies of the region more than seven hundred huge steel tanks capable of storing nearly thirty-nine million barrels of oil were erected in groups called tank farms. Cushing also became the center of a vast system of pipe lines laid to gather oil from the wells and carry it to distant refineries—some as far away as the Atlantic seaboard.

Cushing's loss of 1,598 in population between 1930 and 1940 was due to the waning importance of oil. Its present (1941) status is that of a supply point for a large farming and ranching area, and an industrial center. Cheap natural gas, an abundant water supply from a three-hundred-acre municipal lake, and a municipal light and power plant are among Cushing's industrial assets.

A high school and seven grade schools, including one for Negroes, and one parochial school; a municipal auditorium seating eighteen hundred; an eighteen-hole golf course; fishing, swimming, and tennis courts; a new flood-lighted athletic field; a modern gymnasium for the Negro school; one daily and two weekly newspapers; and a splendid new public library costing $80,-000—these are in the 1941 picture of Cushing.

As echoes from the roaring boom days in the big Cushing oil field are heard such tales as that of the drunken tool pusher who looked the town over and told the crowd who had gathered around him, "You got new buildin's here; you got new stores an' new churches; an' I'm goin' to start a new graveyard!" But when he attempted to carry out his promise, the hammer of his six-gun caught on his belt and he shot himself in the leg.

At 48.2 *m.* is the junction with a paved road.

Right on this road to RIPLEY, 2.4 *m.* (812 alt., 415 pop.), a farming settlement; R. from Ripley is the ghost town of INGALLS, 3.2 *m.,* named for John J. Ingalls, United States senator from Kansas (1873–91). The few remaining buildings are falling into ruins, and the streets are overgrown with grass. Most noticeable of the decrepit relics is the former TRILBY SALOON, the interior of which is bullet scarred. The Doolin and Dalton gangs of outlaws sometimes retreated to Ingalls after their raids. Following the attempted robbery of two banks at Coffeyville, Kansas, in 1892, when three of the bandits were killed by the citizens of the town, Bill Doolin and Bill Dalton came to Ingalls and then reorganized their forces in a cave near the Cimarron River.

At 54 *m.* on State 33 is the junction with a paved road.

Left on this road to PERKINS, 1 *m.* (829 alt., 728 pop.), serving a farm area. The town was established at the time of the opening of old Oklahoma to settlement in the Run of April 22, 1889. An Old Settlers' Celebration is held here annually, September 22–25, with dances, barbecues, pony races, and bow-and-arrow shoots.

At 2 *m.*, immediately after crossing the Cimarron River, is a junction with an unimproved dirt road; L. here to a junction with a second unimproved road, 6 *m.;* R. to the IOWA INDIAN COMMUNITY HOUSE, 7 *m.*, where the spring and fall green corn dances and other Iowa Indian dances and festivals are held; visitors are admitted.

At 54.9 *m.* is the junction with State 40 *(see Tour 2).*

On the grounds of a country school, 57.9 *m.*, is a WASHINGTON IRVING MARKER (L) placed by citizens of Payne County to commemorate Irving's passage in 1832. An actual camp site of the Irving party, unmarked, is said to be in the middle of what is now (1941) a field of alfalfa about 1.5 miles northwest of the marker near the north bank of Wild Horse Creek.

It was here, as readers of Irving's *Tour on the Prairies* will learn, that the author and his companions had their first exciting experience in capturing wild horses.

State 33 crosses the CIMARRON RIVER, 65.9 *m.*

Once named Iowa City, COYLE, 66.5 *m.* (866 alt., 440 pop.) was first located two miles northwest of its present site, and was moved when the Santa Fe Railway built through in 1900. The principal street of the town is over-arched by fine elm trees. Two cotton gins are supplied by the cotton grown in the good river bottom farms that lie between the town and the river.

On the upland prairie, LANGSTON, 68.1 *m.* (962 alt., 514 pop.), is the all-Negro town founded in 1890 by E. P. McCabe and named for the Negro educator and member of Congress (1890-91), John M. Langston, of Virginia.

As early as 1885, the movement to establish an all-Negro community—possibly a state—was started by S. H. Scott, a Negro lawyer of Fort Smith, Arkansas. After the 1889 Opening, McCabe, who had been State Auditor of Kansas, promoted the town at the present site, and it is said that at one time its population exceeded two thousand. It shrank radically when the Negroes who had been attracted to the town by McCabe's enthusiastic words had exhausted their savings and found it impossible to earn a living here. Many—including McCabe, who became deputy auditor of Oklahoma (1907–08)—moved on to Guthrie, the territorial capital.

LANGSTON UNIVERSITY *(for Negroes; visitors welcome)* was authorized by the Territorial legislature in March, 1897. Supported by the state and by Federal funds under the Morrill Act and the Smith-Hughes Act plus generous grants from the General Education Board and the Rosenwald Fund, the university's biennial budget has ranged from $81,000 to $397,000. Its aggregate enrollment (1940–41) was 1,050 in the college, high school, training (elementary) school, extension and correspondence courses; the faculty numbers seventy-six.

Gradually and steadily, the physical plant of the university has grown and been improved until it compares well with any other in the state. In all, eighteen buildings are used for school work. Trees, which were lacking for a long time, have been planted and are now large enough to remove somewhat the impression of barrenness suggested by the simple red-brick buildings set on a prairie ridge. Besides remodeling and landscaping, recent additions are a SCIENCE AND AGRICULTURE BUILDING, an industrial workshop, two barns, and an addition to one of the two men's dormitories. With the exception of the campus, the four hundred acres owned by the university are all under cultivation.

Dr. G. L. Harrison, who holds a Ph. D. degree from Ohio State University, is now (1941) president. He is successor to other able Negro educators who have built up the university to its position as one of the best Negro institutions in the country.

Langston has consistently carried out the program suggested in the act creating the school: to train teachers, to give instruction in industrial arts, and to teach the boys to be good farmers. Trades and industrial and electrical engineering are emphasized. Military instruction, for which credit in physical education is given, is required during the first two years of the college course.

A library of more than ten thousand volumes is housed in PAGE HALL, a two-story stone and brick building named in honor of Langston's first president. All the usual extra-curricular activities are carried on by the Y's, Greek letter fraternities and sororities, and various clubs; *The Langston Lion,* a monthly, is the student publication.

GUTHRIE, 80.3 *m.* (1,021 alt., 10,018 pop.) *(see Tour 10),* is at the junction with US 77.

Tour 3

(Fayetteville, Ark.)—Muskogee—Oklahoma City—Chickasha—Anadarko —Hollis—(Childress, Tex.), US 62.
Arkansas Line to Texas Line, 418.1 m.

Roadbed alternately concrete- and asphalt-paved and graveled.
Route is roughly paralleled between Westville and Tahlequah by the St. Louis–San Francisco Ry.; between Muskogee and Taft by the Midland Valley R.R.; between Boynton and Henryetta by the Kansas, Oklahoma & Gulf Ry.; Harrah to Oklahoma City by the Rock Island Ry.; between Blanchard and Chickasha by the Santa Fe Ry.; between Chickasha and Lawton by the Rock Island Ry.; between Lawton and Altus, by the St. Louis–San Francisco Ry.; and between Altus and the Texas Line by the Missouri-Kansas-Texas R.R.
Good accommodations available in cities and towns.

No other route across Oklahoma passes through areas settled by so many different nationalities as the twisting path made by US 62. And though racial assimilation has been at work for many years, the essence of those distinctive strains still remains. In the east are the hills where the Cherokees for sixty years maintained a self-governing Indian nation and built a culture of their own. At Fort Gibson, in that nation, was written the military history of eastern Oklahoma from the initial appearance of the Indians of the Five Civilized Tribes, through its contacts with the so-called wild tribes of the western plains, and the turbulent years of the Civil War when the Five Civilized Tribes were split into factions and both Union and Confederate forces at different times occupied the post.

Along this route, too, an aftermath of the Civil War is seen in the Negro settlements made by slaves freed by their Indian owners, for in the final liquidation of the tribal governments these freedmen shared equally with the Indians in the allotment of land.

US 62 crosses the former Creek Nation, passes through its capital, then skirts the northern boundary of the reservation to which the Seminoles came, reluctantly, from Florida.

The route, like most long highways across Oklahoma, taps rich oil fields and fine farm lands. In its western section, before leaving the state at its southwestern corner, US 62 passes through regions of red earth, rock-pitted breaks and canyons, high plains, and short-grass pastures that were once the hunting grounds of the Kiowas, Comanches, Apaches, and Wichitas. Here, if anywhere in Oklahoma, may be seen the Plains Indian not too far removed from his native condition; and here, too, are the evidences of his capacity to adopt the highest type of civilization.

Section a. ARKANSAS LINE *to* OKLAHOMA CITY *215.5 m. US 62*

US 62 crosses the ARKANSAS LINE, 0 *m.,* thirty miles west of Fayetteville, Arkansas *(see Arkansas Guide).*

WESTVILLE, 2 *m.* (1,128 alt., 716 pop.), is on the edge of the heavily wooded area of the Cherokee Hills. Fish abound in the many near-by creeks, but it is advisable to employ a local guide *(50c to $1.50 a day)* to find the best holes. During the early 1900's a considerable variety of wild game was found in this section, and a crusade to preserve the wild life was begun by thirteen local men. In 1922, a chapter of the Izaak Walton League was established here.

Westville is at the junction with US 59 *(see Tour 15),* which unites briefly with US 62.

CHRISTIE, 10.8 *m.* (834 alt., 100 pop.), is a marketing-place for the large crop of strawberries produced on near-by farms. A co-operative association acts as the selling agency; there is no other local government.

PROCTOR, 15.9 *m.* (788 alt., 55 pop.), is a small settlement, named for Ezekial Proctor, a Cherokee.

At the Goingsnake Schoolhouse, which stood on the bank of Baron Fork Creek south of Proctor, Ezekiel Proctor was tried, in May, 1872, in a tribal court for the murder of Polly Chesterton *(see Tour 15).* This trial precipitated the Goingsnake Massacre. Proctor had surrendered after the killing to the sheriff of Goingsnake District of the Cherokee Nation, and Blackhawk Sixkiller had been appointed to try the case. Dissatisfied with the Cherokee system of prosecution, Chesterton, husband of the victim, filed charges against Proctor in the United States court at Fort Smith, Arkansas. Since provisions of the government treaty with the Cherokees had guaranteed to them the right of trial and punishment of their own people, this action was deeply resented. When word was received that Fort Smith officers were coming to arrest Proctor, the Cherokees immediately prepared to defend their treaty rights by force, if necessary. Everyone present at the trial in the schoolhouse—chosen because it could be more easily defended than the courthouse—was armed for attack. Without warning, a posse of Fort Smith marshals charged. Seven officers were killed, the prisoner and the judge were wounded, and the clerk was slain at his desk.

In reprisal, indictments were returned by a Federal grand jury at Fort Smith against twenty Cherokee citizens, who had been at the trial, and all the officers of the tribal court. The Cherokees also issued warrants for a number of their own tribesmen. Later all indictments were dismissed by the United States government. After Proctor recovered from his wounds, he lived a law-abiding life even to the extent of being elected sheriff of the Flint District of the Cherokee Nation, and a member of the Cherokee Council.

East of the ILLINOIS RIVER *(see Tour 16), 29 m.,* the vegetation is thick and green. On the west bank is a cliff called the Point of Pines; its top affords one of the most beautiful views in the state.

TAHLEQUAH, 31.2 *m.* (864 alt., 3,027 pop.), was chosen as the permanent capital of the Cherokee Nation on July 12, 1839, when the East and West Cherokees met at Takotokah, northwest of Tahlequah, and signed the Act of Union. Until 1843, when the present town of Tahlequah was first platted, the capital consisted of a council ground and camping site for the delegates attending the conferences. In that year, three cabins were constructed in which the council, senate, and treasury were housed.

The Intertribal Council of 1843, which was called by the Cherokees and attended by representatives of eighteen tribes, was in session here for four weeks discussing mutual problems arising from the removal of the various tribes from their former homes.

On January 8, 1845, a measure was enacted ordering all houses on the PUBLIC SQUARE to be moved before September 1; on their removal, the main streets were laid out and a brick building was erected for the Cherokee Supreme Court. The *Cherokee Advocate (see Newspapers),* official publication of the Cherokee government, was printed here. During a fire in 1874, the old building was partly gutted but was rebuilt shortly after; the *Advocate* was housed in the Cherokee jail during the interim. Located just across the street from the southeast corner of the public square, the first SUPREME COURT BUILDING still contains part (mostly the outside walls) of the original materials used in its construction in 1845. In the square also stands the old CHEROKEE CAPITOL, completed in 1869. It now serves as the COUNTY COURTHOUSE for Cherokee County. West of the courthouse and on the grounds of the old square are STATUES of W. P. Adair and Stand Watie, prominent in Cherokee politics and war, respectively.

A present-day hotel, across the street (N) from the courthouse square, is on the SITE OF THE NATIONAL HOTEL, erected in 1848 as an inn for the convenience of the representatives attending council sessions. The hotel was built by a Mormon bishop and two of his followers, who arrived here on their way to Texas in 1847. The Mormons were being driven out of the East at that time, but these three men had chosen not to accompany the main body headed for Utah. In Tahlequah, the bishop attempted to carry on his church work but was so deeply resented that he soon left. In another building (immediately across from the north end of the west side of the square), erected in the same year by Mormons, one of the first telephone lines in Oklahoma, from Tahlequah to Fort Gibson, was installed in 1886 by Ed Hicks, a Cherokee who still (1941) lives in Tahlequah.

Down Tahlequah's main thoroughfare, Muskogee Street, in November, 1855, marched the famous Second Cavalry numbering 750 troopers on the way from Jefferson Barracks at St. Louis to Texas, where the regiment was engaged in fighting Indians until the outbreak of the Civil War. In command was Colonel Albert Sidney Johnson. Lieutenant Colonel Robert E. Lee, second in command, had been detained at Leavenworth, Kansas, on court-martial duty and joined the regiment after its arrival in Texas. Among other officers of the regiment were Captain Edmund Kirby Smith, Lieutenant John B. Hood, and Lieutenant J. E. B. Stuart.

In 1851, the Cherokees established two schools of higher learning—one, a Male Seminary just southwest of Tahlequah, and the other, a Female Seminary at Park Hill, approximately four miles south of Tahlequah. Both buildings were destroyed by fire—the school for boys in 1910, and the female institution in 1887. The latter school, relocated at Tahlequah in that year, was purchased in 1909 by the state of Oklahoma to form the nucleus of NORTHEASTERN STATE COLLEGE. The plant comprises six buildings on a campus of much natural beauty.

A separate building on the grounds houses the NORTHEASTERN HISTORICAL MUSEUM, in which numerous Indian relics and documents are preserved. Among these are many volumes of the *Cherokee Advocate,* the national tribal newspaper; leather saddle bags and other effects which belonged to General Stand Watie; a plow and ox yoke brought here by the Cherokees along the Trail of Tears from Georgia; and portraits of Sequoyah and Samuel Houston Mayes, a Cherokee chief. A church bell, reputed to be the oldest in Oklahoma, is also on display.

At 35.3 *m.* on US 62 is a junction with a graveled road.

Left on this road, 0.5 *m.,* to the JANE ROSS MEIGS HOUSE (L), built more than one hundred years ago for the daughter of John Ross, chief of the Cherokees. Jane, unlike her father, had come west with the first migration; when he arrived later, he bought this house, which had been constructed some years before, as a gift for her and her husband.

At 1 *m.* is a junction with a dirt road.

Left on this road to the SITE OF PARK HILL MISSION, 1 *m.,* established in 1836 by the Presbyterians as a religious and educational center for the mission and the schools, homes for missionaries and teachers, a boarding hall, gristmill, shops, stables, and a printing office and book bindery. Samuel Austin Worcester, the first missionary here, brought his printing press from Union Mission *(see Tour 8)* in 1837 and published many works for both Cherokees and whites. Millions of pages of tracts, schoolbooks, and extracts from the Bible (mostly translated into Cherokee by Worcester) came from this press before the Mission was destroyed during the Civil War.

Just north of Park Hill are the ruins of the CHEROKEE FEMALE SEMINARY, which was established by the national council in 1850. A disastrous fire in 1887 left only parts of the walls and the foundation.

Straight ahead on the graveled road to the MURRELL MANSION, 1.2 *m.,* standing in a grove (R) of oaks and catalpas. Though now in disrepair, the stately old building was considered the finest residence in the vicinity in Civil War days. All the lumber and finishing materials were cut from the near-by trees, but most of the furniture was imported from France or bought in New Orleans and shipped up the Arkansas and Illinois rivers by steamboat. George Murrell, the original owner, was a prominent merchant and a member of the Ross faction of the Cherokees. Before, and during, the Civil War, the house was the center of social activities for near-by Fort Gibson; later it passed rapidly from one owner to another, serving at one time as a school. Today (1941) it is occupied at intervals by tenant farmers. The spacious piazzas and the portico are gone, but the sturdy foundation beams of the house are still in place.

Southeast of the Murrell Mansion, a quarter of a mile through a field, is the PARK HILL MISSION CEMETERY, where Samuel and Ann Worcester, founders of the mission, are buried. The old burial ground has long been abandoned; the monuments to the Worcesters, however, are still standing and enclosed by an iron fence. The inscription for Samuel reads, "To his labors, the Cherokees are indebted for their Bible and hymn book."

At 1.5 *m.* on the main side route is the GROVE (L) where the Cherokee Confederate Treaty was signed in 1861.

In the ROSS FAMILY CEMETERY, 2 *m.,* stands the JOHN MCDONALD ROSS MONUMENT (L), enclosed by a three-foot stone wall surmounted by iron pickets. A circular shaft of white marble, broken at the top to represent life interrupted at its prime (he died at the age of twenty-one), marks the grave of a nephew of John Ross, leader of the Union faction of Cherokees, who is also buried here. The story is told that Confederate General Stand Watie, needing ammunition, remembered the lead balls which decorated the iron palings atop the burial wall of the nephew's grave and ordered his men to remove them to make bullets. Thus the lead from a Ross grave was used to bring death to members of the Ross faction. A few of the ornaments which Watie's men overlooked still remain.

The SEQUOYAH INDIAN TRAINING SCHOOL, 36.6 *m.,* is a government-maintained institution for Indian orphans. By an act of the Cherokee council in 1872, the Cherokee Orphans' Home was created and established near Salina *(see Tour 8).* In 1904 it was moved to this site and, in 1914, sold to the Federal government. From the original building and forty acres (which had been occupied by the Cherokee Insane Asylum prior to 1904), the present Sequoyah institution has grown into a well-equipped plant with thirty-seven buildings, 425 acres of land, and an annual appropriation of $100,000 for operating expense.

At 51.1 *m.* is a junction with an improved dirt road.

Right on this road to FORT GIBSON NATIONAL CEMETERY, 1.1 *m.* In the circle of officers' graves is that of Tiana Rogers, Cherokee wife of Sam Houston. The inscription, perpetuating an old error, gives her name as Talihina.

Another woman who lies in the officers' circle—in a grave marked simply "Vivia" —still retains an aura of mystery, for her real story has never been told. The legend—probably true—tells of a teen-age girl in love with a soldier, and of her pursuit of him to his post at Fort Gibson, where she masqueraded as a young lieutenant. Her sex was not known until after her death. It is said that Fort Gibson officials consulted with Washington headquarters as to her disposal and were told, "Bury, and say nothing."

Captain Billy Bowlegs, famous Seminole warrior, lies in this circle of men and women who made frontier history. Montford Stokes, governor of North Carolina (1830–32), chairman of the Indian Commission (1830–34), and the only known Revolutionary War veteran to be buried in Oklahoma, is also interred here.

FORT GIBSON, 52.9 *m.* (542 alt., 1,233 pop.), a rural community on the bank of Grand River, stands on the site of the frontier post, Fort Gibson. This was one of the strongest links in the chain of fortifications stretching from the north to the south borders of the United States. Until 1857 it served as the chief military center for the whole of Indian Territory, and many treaties with the Indians were concluded here.

In October, 1806, Lieutenant James B. Wilkinson, second in command of the Zebulon M. Pike expedition, was detailed to explore the Arkansas River. With five enlisted men, he set out from the site of the present Larned, Kansas, in an attempt to float down the river to its mouth. Freezing-over of the river forced the group to follow the banks on foot. At last the party reached the mouth of the Verdigris River; then, on December 6, they came to an Osage village, situated on the east bank of the Grand River, which joins with the Arkansas and Verdigris at this point. This site, recommended by the lieutenant in his report as suitable for a garrison, was chosen for Fort Gibson in 1824, when a military post was needed to halt Osage depredations and to establish peace along the frontier. Colonel Matthew Arbuckle, who came with a part of his troops by boat while others had traveled overland, was in command of the building of the fort, which was to serve as a communication and transportation link between Fort Leavenworth, Kansas, and Fort Smith, Arkansas.

In 1834 an important intertribal Indian council was held here. The fort was abandoned in 1857, but was reoccupied by Union soldiers during the Civil War. Toward the close of the war, six thousand refugee Creeks encamped here on their return from Kansas, where they had fled to seek haven with the Union forces. The Fort also sheltered some ten thousand other refugees in the immediate neighborhood, most of them Union Cherokees who had been harried by the guerilla tactics of the Confederate Cherokee general, Stand Watie. Watie, master of this type of warfare, took their food and stock, pillaged their homes, and even at one time stripped them of their clothing so that the destitute women and children of his own group might have sustenance and cover.

Fort Gibson was, during its heyday, a busy and active place, frequented by many whose names are now famous. Jefferson Davis, later president of the Confederacy, served here under General Zachary Taylor, who was inaugurated President of the United States in 1849. Washington Irving, accompanying an exploring expedition in 1832, camped here, and it was from this spot that he started the trip described in his book, *A Tour on the Prairies*. The supposed site where his tent was pitched is marked by a slab made from two stones, one said to have come from the original barracks building and the other from the house once occupied by Jefferson Davis.

The old Texas Road, with its constant traffic of cattlemen, emigrants, freighters, and traders, passed near the fort, but the main communication for the troops and the residents of the surrounding country was by means of steamboat navigation on the Arkansas River. French fur traders of the Southwest made it a center for their business transactions, and supplies for a large area were imported and dispersed at this point.

Fort Gibson was finally abandoned in 1890, and the reservation was turned over to the Department of the Interior. Many of the old buildings have since been restored—the four-sided square stockade was rebuilt by the National Fort Stockade Commission and the barracks by the Oklahoma Historical Society. The stone barracks constructed during the Civil War are on a hill overlooking the stockade.

At 53.7 *m.,* the ARKANSAS RIVER is crossed. A few hundred yards south of the bridge is the approximate SITE OF THE OLD STEAMBOAT LANDING. The first river boats here were canoes and pirogues (hollowed-out logs); these were succeeded by keelboats which relied on manpower, pulling from the bank, for motivation. The early steamboats coming up the Arkansas to this region usually stopped at Fort Smith and reshipped their cargoes upstream by keelboat. In 1824, however, the sixty-ton steamboat, *Florence,* carrying one hundred recruits for the new military post, Fort Gibson, ventured this far. Three Forks, as the region was known since it is the confluence of the Grand and Verdigris with the Arkansas, became a busy trading area for the next fifty years owing to the advance of river traffic. Because of many shoals in the river bed, this particular landing was much used since here the water was deeper. In February, 1828, the steamboat *Facility* (117 tons) ascended to this point towing two keelboats laden with 780 emigrant Creek Indians; a new Creek agency had just been established at Three Forks *(see Tour 8).*

River traffic continued to increase, with only a slight interruption during the Civil War, and in February, 1870, a government engineer said in his official report: "Twenty steamboats now ply between Fort Gibson, Fort Smith, Little Rock, and New Orleans, Memphis, St. Louis, and Cincinnati. The amount of the up and down the river trade received and shipped at Fort Gibson is about 25,000 tons annually, exclusive of Government freight. . . . The Government freight received at the same point amounts to about $5,000,000 annually . . . and merchants expect traffic to double in the next eight months." Two years later, however, the Missouri-Kansas-Texas Railroad built tracks to Muskogee and gradually absorbed the traffic which had been carried by the river and the Texas Road.

For years, Muskogee and near-by towns attempted to obtain Federal funds to construct a deeper and more permanent river bed for the Arkansas, and reopen river traffic. The increase of soil erosion in the upper drainage area of the Arkansas, however, together with the utilization of much of the upstream water for irrigation purposes, has so changed the character of the river as to make the plan impracticable.

The OKLAHOMA SCHOOL FOR THE BLIND, 62.5 *m.,* is attractively situated on a campus (L) of ninety-nine acres. A coeducational school with an enrollment (1941) of 144 with 23 teachers, it offers instruction through the twelfth grade, and in singing, piano, and pipe organ. Emphasis is placed on physical and industrial training; and it has been found that students are especially apt at weaving and piano tuning. There is a boys' orchestra.

The school plant of twenty buildings includes the four large cottages, two each for boys and girls, where the students live during the nine months of the school year. A herd of Holstein milch cows belongs to the school, and visitors are invited to watch the milking at 3:30 P.M. In the three months of summer vacation, students not required to stay and maintain the plant are placed in such jobs as they can do throughout the state.

In MUSKOGEE, 63.1 *m.* (617 alt., 32,332 pop.) *(see Muskogee),* are junctions with US 69 *(see Tour 8)* and US 64 *(see Tour 2),* which unite westward with US 62 for 15.4 miles.

TAFT, 73 *m.* (605 alt., 772 pop.) *(see Tour 2).*

At 78.6 *m.,* US 62 turns sharply south (L).

BOYNTON, 86.1 *m.* (620 alt., 842 pop.), was a farming community until oil was found near by in the early 1920's. A refinery and a brickmaking plant, both since dismantled, were the town's largest industries.

In OKMULGEE, 106.8 *m.* (670 alt., 16,051 pop.) *(see Okmulgee),* is the junction with US 75 *(see Tour 9),* which unites southward with US 62 for 22.7 miles.

Right from Okmulgee on paved State 27 to LAKE OKMULGEE, 7 *m.,* the water supply for the city. The lake (L) covers 720 acres and is a beautiful recreational spot.

A RIFLE RANGE (R) was leased by the United States in 1931 to be used for target practice by National Guardsmen and civilians. The range provides a running deer target and facilities for antiaircraft marksmanship and bayonet practice.

At 14 *m.* is a junction with a graveled county road; R. on this to NUYAKA, 16 *m.,* a small settlement where NUYAKA MISSION was established by the Presbyterians in 1884, when the village was a fullblood Creek settlement. Miss Alice Robertson, pioneer state educator, secured funds from church women in the East to build the structure and carry on the religious and educational work. Although the Nuyaka school was sponsored and partly supported by the Creek Nation, it remained under the auspices of the Presbyterian Church until all Indian schools were taken over by the Federal government in 1898. It was later discontinued as an Indian school, and the buildings were sold; one is still standing and is used as a residence.

In 1790, when the Creek Confederation occupied what is now Alabama and a part of Georgia, both Spain and the United States were seeking its friendship and commerce. Spain was planning to use the Creeks as a buffer state between her possessions and the boundary of the United States. President Washington, eager to obtain a treaty and also a cession of land, invited twenty-six Creek dignitaries to New York for a conference. They were so impressed with the city that, after their return to the Creek land, they named a town New Yorker. Since the Creeks soften and scarcely pronounce the consonant "R," the white man transcribed the name as Nuyaka. After the removal to the West and the naming of Nuyaka Mission, the same spelling persisted; it still refers to New York.

Nuyaka's square was the scene of prolonged councils in the fall of 1880 and, in the summer of 1882, insurrection threatened in the Creek Nation, with this the starting point. The administration of justice by the ruling party and the cession of a small tract of land to the Seminoles was the source of friction, with a group composed mostly of fullbloods responsible for the rebellion. Creek soldiers and lighthorsemen, sent to quell the disturbance, were inadequately provided with food and helped themselves liberally to the surrounding peach orchards—hence the name, the Green Peach War. No real battles occurred and, although most of the insurrectionists were finally captured, they were soon freed.

HENRYETTA, 120.6 *m.* (691 alt., 6,905 pop.), surrounded by low hills, was founded in 1900 when the Frisco Railway built to this point. The city's industries include coal mining, smelting, and glass manufacture; the iron foundries, smelters, and coal mines are on the outskirts of the town.

Left from Henryetta on a graveled road, 1.5 *m.*, is the JACK NICHOLS RECREATION PARK, a 640-acre tract which includes a lake *(fishing and swimming)*; fifty acres have been set aside as a national campground for the Creek Indians.

At 129 *m.* is the southern junction with US 75 *(see Tour 9)*.

OKEMAH, 139.6 *m.* (882 alt., 3,811 pop.), was opened to white settlement in 1902, when lots were offered for sale at an auction attended by three thousand people. Since there was no railroad, many people walked long distances while others came in wagons and on horseback to attend the event. Tents were erected, and it was not until several months after the opening that the first building was constructed—a one-story structure of bark and poles built by Indians. Drinking water had to be hauled at twenty-five cents a barrel.

A barbed-wire fence, completely enclosing the town, was erected during these early days as protection from the thousands of longhorn steers on the surrounding broad prairies. Strong, self-closing gates, which the animals could not push open, were placed at the east and west ends of the present Broadway. Today, the former grazing lands have been plowed and planted with pecans, corn, sweet potatoes, and cotton—and Okemah is a modern town deriving its business from agriculture and near-by oil fields.

At 151.6 *m.* is a junction with an improved dirt road.

Left on this road is the STATE TRAINING SCHOOL FOR NEGRO BOYS, 1.2 *m.* Two large brick buildings contain the classrooms and dormitories, while separate brick or frame structures house the cafeteria, gymnasium, stables, and shops for cobblery, tailoring, carpentry, and machine work. The 140 boys in the institution (ages 10–16) make their own clothing and learn trades and farming. Class work is both academic and vocational.

In BOLEY, 154.1 *m.* (859 alt., 942 pop.), (R) is the STATE MASONIC TEMPLE FOR NEGROES. Once a year, in August, Negroes from all parts of the state gather here for a celebration and barbecue. The idea of this all-Negro town was first advanced by the president of the Fort Smith and Western Railway townsite company in 1903, when the railway was being extended westward toward Guthrie. The Fort Smith and Western roadmaster, W. H. Boley, was greatly responsible for carrying out the plan and was honored in the naming of the town. The location of Boley was particularly chosen because much of the surrounding area had been allotted to Negro freedmen listed on the rolls of the Creek tribe at the time of the division of the Indian lands.

PRAGUE, 164.5 *m.* (992 alt., 1,422 pop.), a farming center, was established in the early part of the twentieth century by a group of Bohemians (Czechoslovakians) with the idea of creating a village like those of their homeland.

Though the inhabitants have become completely Americanized in most respects, many Bohemian customs have been retained, largely by members of such organizations as the Sokol Society and the Western Bohemian Association. Prague resembles a "Little Bohemia" when the two societies hold annual celebrations just before Easter, on the sixth of July, and on Thanksgiving Day. Residents appear in their colorful native costumes for a program beginning with a noonday feast. Society meetings follow, and a spirited dance ends the day's festivities. Every two months the societies sponsor plays and musical programs presented in the Czech language and with "old country" settings and costumes. Gymnastics, at which the Bohemians are proficient, are the main activity of the Sokol Society.

Many of the houses here are typically Bohemian—square white or blue structures in a setting of cedar trees which partly obscure the front. Entrance is usually made by way of the back door, since the front opening leads into an ornate and stiff parlor that is rarely used except on such important occasions as weddings, christenings, or funerals.

Prague is at the junction with State 99 *(see Tour 14).*

MEEKER, 177.8 *m.* (874 alt., 502 pop.), is a trading center for the surrounding fertile farm lands, forming the divide between the North Canadian River and its tributary stream to the north, the Deep Fork. Meeker is the home town of Carl Hubbell, well-known (1941) pitcher for the New York Giants baseball club.

HARRAH, 193.5 *m.* (1,080 alt., 620 pop.), a farm village, is the birthplace of Paul and Lloyd Waner, star players (1940) for the Pittsburgh Pirates, National League baseball team. Paul (Big Poison) and Lloyd (Little Poison) received their nicknames because, as heavy hitters, they were "poison" to opposing pitchers.

Harrah is at the junction with US 270 *(see Tour 5),* which unites westward with US 62 for twenty-two miles.

At 195.6 *m.* is a junction with an oil-asphalt road.

Right on this road to HORSESHOE LAKE *(free fishing),* 1.2 *m.,* so-named because of its shape. The lake, in a verdant setting which has been made a State Game Preserve, furnishes water for a large electric generating plant operated by steam.

At 211.2 *m.* is the junction with Eastern Avenue (paved) on the outskirts of Oklahoma City.

Right on Eastern Avenue, to LINCOLN PARK, 0.8 *m.,* Oklahoma City's largest public recreational center *(picnicking and camping facilities; children's playground; hiking and bridle trails; golf fees, 50c).* This park, with its low, tree-covered hills and spring-fed lake, was purchased by the city in 1908 but remained unimproved until 1925, when a zoo was moved here from another city park. The Zoo covers fourteen acres and contains more than five hundred animals. Extensive work on improvements and posting of classifications for the large collection of animals has been done in recent years by CCC and WPA workers. Monkey Island is one of the most popular spots, for its chattering population furnishes entertainment against a background of an old ship's bow projecting above the surface of the ground. The funny little animals perch in the rigging and portholes and promenade on the inclined deck. Other attractions include the alligator swamp, the bird and reptile cages, and the bear pits. As nearly as possible, abodes have been constructed which resemble the natural habitats of the animals.

In OKLAHOMA CITY, 215.5 *m.* (1,194 alt., 204,424 pop.) *(see Oklahoma City),* are the junctions with US 66 *(see Tour 1),* US 77 *(see Tour 10),* and the western junction with US 270 *(see Tour 5).*

Section b. OKLAHOMA CITY *to* TEXAS LINE, *202.6 m. US 62*

Southwest of OKLAHOMA CITY, 0 *m.,* the land is gently rolling and to a large extent cultivated. The farms are well ordered, and, in many instances, the bungalow farmhouse is overshadowed by a commodious hay barn and silo, indicative of the productiveness of the section.

At 8.4 *m.,* on the enlarged grounds of the former Oklahoma City Municipal Airport, is the new (1941) ARMY LIGHT BOMBARDMENT TRAINING SCHOOL AND AIR BASE, built at a cost of $2,000,000. Under the national defense program, this unit will be manned by some 350 officers and 4,200 enlisted men for flying duty and ground personnel. It is one of the three government bases of this kind in the United States.

The nucleus of the base is the old 640-acre flying field and the four stone buildings of Indian pueblo design set in attractively landscaped grounds.

The long NEWCASTLE BRIDGE, 14 *m.,* spans the South Canadian River. Most of the time, the wide, sandy bed is broken only by pools of muddy water or, at best, a very narrow channel, completely belying the river's dangerous character when rushing waters come tumbling down its course. Thick growths of cottonwood trees line the banks and dot the bed.

Southward, the land becomes more hilly and has many trees. Where the highway has cut through a small hill, the banks reveal the rich red soil peculiar to this section of Oklahoma.

BLANCHARD, 28.9 *m.* (1,239 alt., 1,139 pop.), was named for W. G. Blanchard, who assisted in laying out the site at the founding of the town in 1906.

Near the Washita River crossing, 45.8 *m.* is the spot where the old Chisholm Trail crossed the river in the nineteenth century. The Trail is practically paralleled, today, by US 81 *(see Tour 11)*. During the 1870's, a trading post, known as Fred (named for Colonel Frank Fred, who ran a series of such posts) was established here. Later the store was moved farther south on the Trail to a point where a connecting wagon road brought more business.

CHICKASHA, 48.8 *m.* (1,116 alt., 14,111 pop.), seat of Grady County, is a market place for a wide and prosperous farm and ranch region, the home of the largest college for women in the state, and an industrial center, where cotton, grain, and dairy products are processed.

A well-built, spreading municipality, its wide downtown streets are bordered by brick and stone business buildings, old and modern; along the gently upsloping residence streets radiating out to the west and south are trees, some planted in the 1890's. Near by, to the north, the Washita River bottom marks roughly the boundary between the city and farm lands.

Before there was a town, the Rock Island had a train stop here (1892). The site of Chickasha was included in the "Swinging Ring" cattle ranch owned by an intermarried citizen of the Chickasaw Indian Nation, the western boundary of which was within a few miles of the place.

The first considerable industrial development at Chickasha was a cottonseed oil mill, and the next was cattle feeding pens where the residue from the mill, called "cake," was the chief fattening feed for the thousands of steers shipped out every month. At one time, more than ten thousand cattle were in the fattening pens there.

When the new town was only a straggling handful of stores and shacks in the middle of a cornfield, and corner sports bet on whether or not a team would "pull" the slough at the western edge of the field, the *Chickasha Express* began publication as a small, four-page weekly in a leaky shack. Today (1941) it is a daily of wide circulation, housed in its own substantial brick-and-steel building.

Ten years after its founding, Chickasha had a population of 6,370 and became a city of the first class. Its growth was greatly stimulated by the opening to white settlement in 1901 of the Kiowa-Comanche reservation, which adjoined the former Chickasaw Nation on the west. The Rock Island made the city a division point and established shops there. More cotton processing plants—gins, mills, and compress—were located in Chickasha.

After statehood, the growth of the city was steady though census figures show a population gain of but twelve between 1930 and 1940. Only two small oil fields, the Cement and Carter Knox pools with some three hundred oil wells, and the Chickasha gas field with 272 wells have (as of 1941) been developed in the Chickasha area, but the surrounding farms and ranches have continued to maintain the prosperity of the city. The Lindsay neighborhood, some twenty-five miles to the southwest, is known as the world's greatest producer of broomcorn, and much of it is processed and marketed at Chickasha.

Recreation is provided by the city's Shannoan Springs Park, the municipal swimming pool, a softball diamond, tennis courts, picnic and croquet grounds, and public and private golf courses.

The modern three-story-and-basement GRADY COUNTY COURTHOUSE, is a gray limestone building designed along severe lines; and the older FEDERAL BUILDING contrasts with it architecturally. The new SENIOR HIGH SCHOOL is a red-brick structure of modified collegiate Gothic design set in well-landscaped grounds.

The OKLAHOMA COLLEGE FOR WOMEN, at the southwestern edge of Chickasha (S.W. 17th St.), is one of the few state-supported women's colleges in the United States. Founded in 1908 by an act of the first Oklahoma state legislature, the college grants degrees in liberal arts, fine arts, and science. Courses are also given leading to teachers' certificates, and preprofessional courses are offered in medicine, law, nursing, and journalism. A teaching and executive staff of seventy-eight is required for the 959 students enrolled (1941).

Spread over a tree-shaded campus of seventy-five acres on top of a low ridge, the college plant consists of seventeen modern buildings, including the big Administration Hall, 220 by 214 feet; Fine Arts, Austin, and Physical Education Halls, and eight residence halls. Physical Education Hall contains a swimming pool, and close by are six concrete-surfaced tennis courts, two playing fields for outdoor games, and golf practice putting greens. On the college's 140-acre farm an experiment station is maintained by the Department of Biology.

SHANNOAN SPRINGS PARK *(boating, fishing),* also in the southwestern section of the city, is a popular recreational center with a winding lake, where rushes and lilies grow in profusion. In the park, too, is the city's zoo and a museum of pioneer relics, housed in the old Territorial jailhouse.

Chickasha is at the junction with US 81 *(see Tour 11)*.

VERDEN, 58.4 *m.* (1,136 alt., 575 pop.), stands on the site of a cottonwood grove near the Washita River where in May, 1865, an important intertribal council was held. Because a majority of members of the Five Civilized Tribes had sided with the Confederacy, a reckoning had to be made with the Union. Also fresh outbreaks of trouble with white outlaw bands and with groups of wild Plains Indians, bent on following the warpath, made the calling of the council almost a necessity.

The entire present town of Verden was included in the site chosen for the large encampment, called Camp Napoleon. Attending delegates were Confederate-sympathizing members of the Five Civilized Tribes and allied bands of Caddoes, Osages, and Comanches who came to treat with representatives of the Plains Indians—Kiowas, Arapahoes, Cheyennes, and some Comanches, Caddoes, and Anadarkos. The peace pipe was passed, ceremonial tokens were exchanged, and a compact was adopted and signed. What might have been originally intended as a military alliance turned out to be a league of peace, for the Indians present realized that their greatest need was to establish strength and unity within their own race in order to combat further white aggression. Solemnly, in their compact, they recognized their situation; that "our vast and lovely country and beautiful hunting grounds, given to us by the Great Spirit, and knowing no limit but the shores of the Great Waters and the horizon of the heavens, is now, on account of our weakness, being reduced and hemmed in to a small and precarious country that we can scarcely call our own." Finally and inevitably they agreed that if they were to survive, "an Indian shall not spill an Indian's blood."

This event has been commemorated by the MARKER on the Verden school grounds (L) facing on US 62, erected in 1931 by the Oklahoma College for Women; it reads, "Ancient council fires shall be kept kindled and burning."

ANADARKO, 67.5 *m.* (1,190 alt., 5,579 pop.), seat of Caddo County, was named for the Anadarkos, a kindred tribe affiliated with the Wichita Indians.

The city was founded on August 6, 1901, when the surrounding Kiowa-Comanche and Wichita reservations were opened to white settlement. On that day, some twenty thousand people arrived at the previously surveyed townsite to await their chance of occupation of the adjacent lands. At least ten thousand remained for several months after which the population shrank to three thousand. Probably the first business establishment on the townsite was a bank, set up in a tent three weeks before the official land opening. It announced its mission on a large piece of canvas hung in front of the tent on which the names of the directors were painted. Several days before the opening, trainloads of liquor had been shipped into the town on the Rock Island Railway, which had built through while the site was still a reservation. For a time saloons and gambling establishments flourished, but the citizens soon tired of being bilked and the gamblers were chased away. Business then adjusted itself and proceeded normally until the early 1920's when an oil flurry brought about near-by oil-field development and the subsequent growth of Anadarko to almost twice its former size. The present business section has many modern structures contrasting sharply with the older buildings; one of the latter is the red brick CADDO COUNTY COURTHOUSE, Broadway and 2d Street, erected in 1907.

Anadarko is an important trading center for farmers of the Washita valley; alfalfa, cotton, wheat, corn, and watermelons are the chief products; stock-raising, cotton-ginning, and cottonseed-oil milling are main industries.

In 1878, the Kiowa, Apache, and Comanche agencies were consolidated here with the Wichita office, and the combined organization is still maintained as an active INDIAN AGENCY, serving about 4,600 Indians belonging to the four tribes and their affiliates. The agency is now (1941) housed in the FEDERAL BUILDING, 1st Street and Oklahoma Avenue and employs 150 persons to handle business involving approximately $1,000,000 annually. On the walls of the main floor of the buff-brick building are murals of Indian scenes and peoples, drawn in the true Indian spirit by Mopope, a well-known Kiowa artist.

The outstanding annual event is the American Indian Exposition, *(adm. 50c)* usually held the third week in August and attended by a great number of full bloods from many tribes. Dressed in gaudy native costume, representatives of Wichitas, Caddoes, Tawakonis, Keechis, Delawares, Apaches, Comanches, Lipans, Kiowas, and other tribes make the four-day celebration a pageant of color. Pony races, bow-and-arrow shoots, scores of unusual ceremonial dances, a display of arts and crafts, barbecues, and rodeos make up the program.

Right from Anadarko on asphalt-paved US 281, across the Washita River, is the RIVERSIDE INDIAN BOARDING SCHOOL, 1.5 *m.* founded in 1872. About half of the 2,200-acre reserve (L), controlled by the government, is under cultivation by the pupils. In the rear of the four large red-brick buildings on the twenty-acre campus are TWO GRASS HOUSES, typical of those formerly used by the Wichita tribe. The primitive abodes, constructed by students, have a framework of trimmed cedar poles imbedded in the ground at one end and lashed together at the top forming a dome. Dried reeds and grass woven together are used as shingles. The only opening is a low, narrow door. It was the custom for fifteen or twenty people to live in each house.

ST. PATRICK'S MISSION SCHOOL, 69.7 *m.,* for Indian children (R), is managed by Father Aloysius Hitta under the supervision of the Federal government. Father Hitta's home houses a COLLECTION OF INDIAN ART OBJECTS *(shown by appointment only)*. The school was established in 1892, by Father Isidore Ricklin, on a hill overlooking the site of the agency and the future Anadarko. Ricklin, a Belgian, was adopted by the Comanche tribe during that same year. The present three-story brick edifice was erected after the burning of the original frame buildings in 1909. A MEMORIAL CHAPEL, built in memory of Father Rickin, has a series of brilliant murals on its sloping ceiling. The panels, outlining the school's history, were painted by the Kiowa Indian artists Asah, Hokeah, Mopope, and Auchiah, while they were students at the school.

Near the mission and along the Washita River (R) is the area called TONKAWA VALLEY because it was the site of the gruesome massacre of the Tonkawa Indians. In 1862 this tribe was encamped along the river just south of Fort Cobb, the original Wichita Agency situated on the north side of the Washita some seven miles northwest of this point. The other tribes, served by the agency and encamped in the region, abhorred the Tonkawas because they were suspected of cannibalism. After finding the dismembered body of a Caddo child who had wandered away from his tent, they made secret plans to exterminate the Tonkawas.

On the night of October 23, Osages, Shawnees, and Delawares—who had come down from Kansas—together with Caddoes from the agency started on a warpath which ended in the near extermination of the Tonkawas and the complete destruction of Fort Cobb and several of its Confederate officials. Most of the Indians at the agency had remained loyal to the Union and consequently had no compunction against aiding the Kansas Indians in wiping out the Southerners. The whites (except for some who escaped) were first killed, then thrown into the buildings which were set afire. The Tonkawas, who had been alarmed and started to flee that morning, were pursued to their camping place along the Washita (near the present Catholic Mission) and attacked at dawn. Their camp was completely obliterated except for the bones of the massacred that lay blanching in the valley for years. Fort Cobb was never rebuilt—though the site was occupied by General Philip Sheridan and his troops for a short time in 1868 *(see Tour 3 A)*—but a present-day small town near by bears its name.

APACHE, 87.4 *m.* (1,300 alt., 1,047 pop.), is in the center of a rich agricultural community through which Cache Creek flows. The principal crops raised are wheat, corn, alfalfa, and cotton. About 35 per cent of the rural population are Indians. Oklahoma's newest oil field (1941) is being developed near by.

South of Apache the land is rolling prairie, with only a few trees along the creek bottoms, but the blue of the Wichita Mountains dominates the horizon to the southwest.

RICHARDS SPUR, 97.1 *m.* (1,199 alt., 150 pop.), is a company village for the near-by limestone quarry. Small, bluish-gray uniform houses line the highway, and in the distance (R) is a great crusher cutting down a rounded limestone hill, one of the foothills of the Wichitas. Great tilted exposed ledges of limestone indicate the force with which the mountain mass was originally thrust up.

At 100.8 *m.* is the junction with State 49 *(see Tour 3 B)*. Between 101.2 *m.* and 105.4 *m.,* US 62 passes through the FORT SILL MILITARY RESERVATION *(see Tour 3A),* which extends for several miles on both sides of the highway.

At 104.2 *m.* is the junction (R) with the paved Fort Sill Road *(see Tour 3A)*.

A U.S. Agricultural Experiment Station, 106.5 *m.,* is one of the string of similar institutions operated by the Division of Dry Land Agriculture in the Great Plains region. The station (R), established in 1915, consists of several cottages and barns on 160 acres of land, and has the appearance of a private farm. The work done here is primarily for the purpose of finding what crops may be successfully grown, since the region's rainfall is light and uneven; wheat, oats, barley, sorghums, and sweet clover are being grown on the tract.

The FORT SILL INDIAN SCHOOL and the KIOWA INDIAN HOSPITAL, 106.6 *m.,* lie within a thousand-acre tract (L) including both farming and pasture land, utilized for the vocational instruction and the maintenance of both institutions. Established in 1871 under President Grant's "peace policy," the school served as a branch of the Kiowa-Comanche Agency, operated at that time by the Quaker agent, Lawrie Tatum. Since the opening date, the capacity of the school, one of twelve Indian boarding schools in Oklahoma, has been overtaxed; the average enrollment is 250. Primary students are taught in a little red schoolhouse, and other grades through high school are housed in modern brick and native stone pueblo-type buildings, which were erected and are maintained by the Indian Bureau of the government. Murals painted by Kiowa Indian artists decorate the walls of the buildings.

The INDIAN HOSPITAL, north of the school, is a commodious, well-equipped institution; its three red-brick buildings, trimmed in white, are modern and contain a solarium for the use of tuberculous patients.

At 106.9 *m.,* US 62 turns sharply west (R) to CACHE, 121.5 *m.* (1,260 alt., 620 pop.), located in the foothills of the Wichita Mountains.

Right from Cache on an improved dirt road to CRATERVILLE PARK *(camping and recreational facilities, bridle paths, store, hotel)*, 3 *m.,* a large natural amphitheater, enclosed by hills, covered with grass and timber, and watered with clear sparkling springs and a mountain brook.

The All-Indian Fair and Exposition was first organized here in 1924, but it was moved to Anadarko in 1935. Many of the Indians who live in the region still visit Craterville Park in the spring and summer months to hold powwows and dances. While here, they usually construct and live in grass houses and arbors. Footraces among the young braves are often run on a half-mile track. Annually, on July third and fourth, a rodeo is held.

Left from the entrance of Craterville Park to the HOME OF QUANAH PARKER, 1 *m.,* last chief of the Comanches. Quanah was the son of Cynthia Ann Parker, a white woman, and Peta Nokoni, a Comanche chief. Cynthia's story has been told in literature and song; she was kidnaped (1836), when nine years old, by the Comanches who destroyed the Texas frontier fort where her family had settled. Years later Cynthia was identified and urged to return to her own race, but through her marriage and the birth of her half-Indian children she had become a true Comanche at heart. Texas Rangers forcibly returned her to her family, and she died soon after.

Quanah, who had been born about 1845, was of superior intelligence and character. While principal chief of his tribe, he led his warriors in the battle on Adobe Walls in Texas, the last great Plains Indian fight against white buffalo hunters. He rode at the head of his tribe when they surrendered tribal rule at Fort Sill in 1875, marking the close of Indian warfare in the region of southwestern Oklahoma. Quanah was later allotted this tract of land on which he lived with his five wives and built his eight-room home in 1890. On one occasion the old chief was being given advice by Theodore Roosevelt on "how to walk the white man's road." The gist of the counsel was that Quanah should end his bigamous status by relinquishing all his wives except one. The Comanche's concise answer was, "You tell 'em which one I keep!" The old house, in which he lived until his death in 1911, is now occupied (1941) by his daughter, Mrs. Neda Birdsong.

Right (N) from the entrance to Craterville Park is the south gate, 0.5 *m.,* of the WICHITA MOUNTAINS WILDLIFE REFUGE *(see Tour 3B)*.

On the main route is INDIAHOMA, 128.8 *m.* (1,335 alt., 337 pop.), a trading center for Indians and farmers of the surrounding vicinity.

Right from Indiahoma on a dirt road to a junction with a second dirt road, 2 *m.;* L. on this road to the old POST OAK MISSION, 5 *m.,* founded in 1894 by the Mennonite

Brethren Home Mission Society. Lumber for its construction was hauled from Marlow, some sixty miles distant and the nearest railroad station at that time.

In the mission cemetery are the GRAVES OF CYNTHIA AND QUANAH PARKER. Cynthia Ann's body had first been interred at Stevens, Texas, but was removed here for reburial in 1910 at her son's behest. Quanah Parker was buried beside his mother, as was his wish, in 1911; and on May 30, 1930, before a crowd of five thousand people, a seventeen-foot granite monument, purchased with a Congressional appropriation, was raised above the chief's grave.

SNYDER, 140.8 *m.* (1,360 alt. 1,278 pop.), is the center of a diversified farming area. Three years after its founding in 1902, Snyder was almost completely demolished by one of the severest storms ever to occur in this part of the state. The courageous townspeople rebuilt and, today, Snyder is a modern municipality. The terrible destruction of that early-day storm, however, is still vividly remembered; most residents have constructed cyclone cellars in the rear of their homes. Granite, of unusual hardness and distinctive coloration, is quarried and processed near by.

Snyder is at the junction with US 183 *(see Tour 12).*

HEADRICK, 152.3 *m.* (1,361 alt. 174 pop.), is a farm community which remains a busy trading center despite several unfortunate fires and a cyclone, each having almost destroyed the town's buildings.

Just west of Headrick is an unusual rock formation (R) rising abruptly in a near-by level field. The side sloping toward the highway looks like a gigantic hand, the thumb and fingers seeming to grasp the lower end of a rock crescent.

ALTUS, 163.4 *m.* (1,389 alt. 8,593 pop.), an oil and cotton marketing center and seat of Jackson County, was founded in the spring of 1891 at the height of a flood. Near-by Bitter Creek had overflowed suddenly and inundated the surrounding territory. Settlers seized what household possessions they could and rushed up the slope of the hill on which the city now stands. Here they established a camp out of reach of the waters and called it Altus, since one of their number declared the name meant "higher ground." Inured to hardship, they lived in dugouts until lumber could be hauled over the rutted wagon roads and "rustled" wood for their fuel from the Indian reservation across the North Fork of the Red River, some fifteen miles away. Church services were held in the dugouts or under arbors constructed of brush and young saplings laboriously hauled up the creek. School children assembled wherever convenient—once in the livery stable—and the length of the academic term was governed by the length of time in which the settlers could provide a teacher with board, room, and a little cash.

In the city square is a concrete marker designating the spot where the COMMUNITY PUMP once stood. Today (1941) water is supplied by the municipally owned Lake Altus waterworks at Lugert *(see Tour 13)* on the North Fork of the Red River.

Two hundred bales of cotton were ginned here in 1897 by a sixty-saw gin run by a threshing machine engine; in 1937, the number of bales had grown to 110,000 and the quantity is steadily increasing. Jackson County, in which Altus is located, is termed a one-variety cotton region where all the growers obtain a higher price by producing a uniform fiber. Oil development of the surrounding vicinity started when a well was drilled two miles northwest of the town in 1908. Since then production has increased rapidly, and gas has recently been found at a depth of seventeen hundred feet.

Altus is at the junction with US 283 *(see Tour 13)*.

West of Altus, trees are fairly numerous since the route is through the valley formed by the Red River and its forks. The prairie is dotted with graceful, shrub-like growths of mesquite.

At 175.4 *m.* the highway crosses a steel and concrete bridge over a dry, sandy river bed. Westward the prairie is broken by valleys and long curving hills; much of this sandy land is covered with short grass, and is used for pasturage.

DUKE, 177 *m.* (1,417 alt., 412 pop.), is surrounded by cotton fields; approximately 7,500 bales are ginned here annually. A silver-domed water tower overlooks the two-block business district through which the highway passes.

The route proceeds through a rocky area, covered with clumps of brush and cactus.

Just northeast of GOULD, 189.3 *m.* (1,621 alt., 391 pop.), are the base marks from which the one hundredth meridian was located by the United States Geodetic Survey.

The terrain becomes more barren between Gould and Hollis; trees are few, and wind-swept tumbleweeds are packed against the fences in great, bushy walls.

HOLLIS, 197.6 *m.* (1,615 alt., 2,732 pop.), is situated in the extreme western part of old Greer County (now Harmon), the Red River territory which Texas claimed prior to a Supreme Court decision in 1896. Cattle-raising is the chief industry of the area.

At 202.6 *m.* US 62 crosses the Texas Line, twenty-six miles northeast of Childress, Texas *(see Texas Guide)*.

Tour 3A

Junction US 62—Fort Sill—Junction with US 62; 6.2 m., Fort Sill Road.

Roadbed paved throughout.
No accommodations in Fort Sill; available at near-by towns.

A part of the FORT SILL MILITARY RESERVATION is always open to visitors except during times of national emergency. *(Visitors must not photograph armed units in maneuvers; no civilian visitors, except personal guests of officers, allowed anywhere on reservation except at points mentioned below.)*

The reservation proper covers 51,242 acres, varying in topography from rolling open prairie, marked by several abrupt hills on the east, to the rugged, granite peaks of the Wichita Mountains on the west. This tract of ground, set aside for national military purposes, is shaped much like the figure 7, the short arm pointing north. The area is watered by Medicine Bluff and Cache creeks. Medicine Bluff (R) is a granite and porphyry formation about three hundred feet high. Indians once invested it with supernatural powers, often leaving their sick on its top either to recover or die.

The Wichita Indians were the first people known to have inhabited the region; it has been established that a group of them built a village in the latter part of the eighteenth century near the mouth of Medicine Bluff Creek, where it enters into Cache Creek. Some of their grass houses stood where the post polo fields are today. Osage depredations and attacks caused them to move to a site on the North Fork of the Red River west of the Wichita Mountains. It was there that they were found by Colonel Henry Dodge and his regiment of dragoons in 1834. Dodge and his men had been sent out from Fort Gibson *(see Tour 3)* to establish friendly relations with the wild Plains Indians so that Santa Fe Trail travelers might be protected and peace assured to the Five Civilized Tribes following their removal from the East. Treaties with the United States were signed the following year as a result of Dodge's friendly expedition, on which he made successful overtures to the Wichitas and to a band of Comanches who were then occupying the site of the former Wichita village on the western half of the present fort. The Colonel first saw the Comanche village when he and his company topped a hill, later named after him, in the northeastern part of the present Fort Sill area. The dragoons camped on the east side of Cache Creek across from the Comanches, not completely trusting their hosts. Soon after making camp, they were amazed to see the Stars and Stripes raised over the lodge of the Indians' chief.

The only white habitation in this region during this period was the trading post established by an agent of the Chouteau interests in 1837. Nothing is known about it except that it was located on the west bank of Cache Creek a little south of where the present road leading from Post Field joins US 62.

Since the Dodge expedition also established peaceful relations with the warring Osages, the Wichitas were enabled to move back to the site of Fort Sill. Here they lived until 1850 when, because of a malarial infection, they migrated east to near the present site of Rush Springs *(see Tour 11)*. The region of Fort Sill was deserted for several years although, in 1852, the military and exploratory expedition of Captain R. B. Marcy arrived and camped for a few days where the post now stands. Marcy had been told to explore the country north of the Red River, and his company accomplished their task in a systematic manner, making a geological survey, classifying the natural life, marking the meridians, and making a map. The captain noted the desirability of the Fort Sill site for use as a military post, but it was not until 1868 that a fort was established there.

General Philip H. Sheridan, of Civil War fame, was assigned the task of pacifying the Plains Indians and placing them on reservations; in 1868, at the start of his campaign, he established his troops at the site of the burned and abandoned Fort Cobb *(see Tour 3)*, some thirty miles to the north of present Fort Sill. His purpose was also to protect the agency there and to keep the peaceful Indians away from the warring ones so that what had been gained toward final harmony might not be lost. The lack of adequate food and shelter in this camp became so acute that late in 1868 Sheridan sent Colonel Benjamin H. Grierson on a reconnaissance trip to Medicine Bluff to decide on a new camp site. Grierson had explored there before, and now confirmed his former recommendation. When Sheridan arrived in January, 1869, he decided to erect a permanent fort at Camp Wichita, as it was then called.

At first the troops—the Tenth and Seventh (Custer's) Cavalry, and the Nineteenth Kansas Cavalry (Volunteers), lived at various places over the post area in brush-roofed dugouts. Headquarters for the Fort Cobb Indian agency were moved to Camp Wichita, and many of the roaming Indians were brought in to live on the reservation. Sheridan left Camp Wichita in February, eventually to rise to the position of Commander in Chief of the United States Army in 1884. Grierson, the new post commander, aided by the troops left at the fort after Sheridan's departure, began construction of permanent buildings. Logs were cut from the surrounding stand of timber.

On August 1, 1869, the post was officially named Fort Sill by General Sheridan, in memory of Brigadier General Joshua W. Sill, who had been Sheridan's West Point classmate and a fellow officer during the Civil War. By 1870, the building program was well under way. Stone was found in Quarry Hill, southeast of the post, and lime for mortar was prepared in rude ovens along the banks of Cache Creek. Most of the work was done by the soldiers, though some artisans were imported. In early 1871 the quarters were finished and a lookout post, the BLOCKHOUSE *(visible from the highway)*, was erected on Signal Mountain in the western section of the reservation. The remaining construction work was carried on intermittently for the next five years.

The careers of three Kiowa warrior chiefs—Satanta, Satank, and Big Tree—interlaced closely with the development of Fort Sill during this time and for several years after. The quick-witted Satanta, called the "Orator of the Plains," first came in contact with the military when he was arrested in 1868 after the Battle of the Washita. He was released by Sheridan at Camp Wichita in 1869 after promising to keep his followers at peace. In 1871, he played a leading part in the Jacksboro wagon-train massacre in Texas, an event which brought swift reprisal from General W. T. Sherman, who was visiting Fort Sill on an inspection tour at the time. Satanta, whose moral outlook was that of a statesman at war but whose keenness was sometimes exceeded by his vanity, boasted in connection with the massacre, "I did it. If any other Indian claims the honor, he will be lying; for I did it myself," thereby practically placing a rope around his own neck.

Satanta, Satank, and Big Three were arrested and placed in the old guardhouse in which Geronimo later spent many days. The three were loaded into wagons and sent to Texas (where the massacre had occurred) for trial; Satank was killed along the way as he made a desperate attempt to escape. The others were sentenced to hang, later given commutations to life imprisonment, and were finally promised pardons at a conference at Washington, D.C., on condition that their people should fulfill certain peace agreements. Following parole in 1873, after being again lodged at the Fort Sill guardhouse, Satanta immediately reverted to his warrior's role and took part in several raids. Finally he surrendered and was brought to Fort Sill in 1875 in chains, to be confined again in the Huntsville, Texas, prison, from which he had been paroled. When he found that there was no chance of being set free, he committed suicide by plunging head first from his second-story cell—the fulfillment of an early and prophetic utterance made by him, "When I settle down, I grow pale and die."

Indian outbreaks continued, though usually on a much smaller scale than in the days before Sheridan's campaign of dissuasion. The forays finally led to a discontinuance in 1874 of the Quaker Peace Policy *(see Tour 1)* of handling the Indians at Fort Sill. Finally, by use of sterner methods and under military command, Indian resistance was virtually broken in 1875. After 1876, the Fort Sill garrison found it necessary in many instances to protect rather than fight the Indians, for swarms of unscrupulous whites drifted into the section to plunder the subdued foe.

Agriculture had been introduced meanwhile to the Indians camped at Fort Sill. The Wichitas and the Caddoes needed little training in farming for they had been in the habit of raising much of their foodstuff, but the Kiowas and Comanches found it difficult to learn the rudiments of horticulture, though they liked its products. Logically enough, to them, their method of plunder seemed much more convenient than the orthodox routine of growing. The agent once sent a party of Comanches to the agency at Anadarko to drive back eleven head of cattle, to be used for rationing at Fort Sill. On their return, the wily Indians passed a melon field and promptly traded five of the beeves for some of the melons. When the agent took the group to task, the Comanches, both hurt and surprised, explained that they had only been trying to act in the "white man's way" by paying a good price for what they wanted rather than stealing it. The agent perforce exonerated them.

In 1891, when the last Indian disturbance occurred, quartermaster Lieutenant Hugh L. Scott and a faithful Kiowa assistant, I-see-o, managed to keep the Fort Sill Indians from taking the warpath. This near-rebellion—the Ghost Dance or "Messiah Craze"—covered most of the western part of the United States and was in part an outgrowth of the misfortunes which had befallen the Indians. John Wilson, a Piute Indian of Nevada, had fathered the religion which involved a mystic conception of a Messiah who had thrown over the white people for the red, and whose coming would be synonymous with the return of the almost-extinct buffalo. Many self-appointed prophets sprang up and acquired converts and tribute through a type of spiritual mesmerism. The Ghost Dance, the main ceremonial of the faith, began with the believers' forming a circle in which they moved slowly while chanting. The medicine man in the center strove by exhortation to induce a hypnotic trance in which the dancer would fall in a stupor and experience visions of the Utopia to come. An Arapaho named Sitting Bull agitated the craze among the Fort Sill Indians. To deal with a situation that promised to develop into an uprising, Scott kept watch unobtrusively through I-see-o and allowed the obsession to fall of its own weight. Scott later appointed I-see-o a sergeant for life, and the respected old Indian was given military burial with full honors at death.

Fort Sill was a busy and crowded place in 1901 when the surrounding land was thrown open to white occupation. While awaiting the results of the drawing at El Reno, people converged from all directions to camp at the post. Finally in 1909, after the fort had been in danger of abandonment, work was begun on the construction of a new post, northwest of the group of old buildings. A School of Fire for field artillery was established here in 1911, and in 1917 the field artillery unit and its equipment was increased tremendously for the duration of the World War. A field officers' advance course was inaugurated in 1922; since then courses have been given for regular army officers, National Guard, Citizens' Military Training Corps, Reserve officers, and enlisted specialists. In 1930, the fort was made a permanent location of the Field Artillery School, whose maintenance is its main purpose.

The Selective Service Act passed by Congress in September, 1940, as a part of the nationwide defense program, gave renewed importance to Fort Sill. An extensive building program (estimated at $1,500,000) and the addition of some twenty thousand acres to the reservation is now (1941) being carried out to accommodate the men inducted into service for training.

The Fort Sill Road branches right (N.W.) from its junction, 0 *m.,* with US 62 *(see Tour 3),* 16.8 miles south of Apache *(see Tour 3).* The POLO FIELDS (L) are kept smoothly level with velvety, short-cropped grass. New barracks, built hastily at the start of the national defense program, line both sides of the route.

The OLD CORRAL, 0.3 *m.,* is a loopholed, stone-walled structure (R), built by Colonel Grierson in 1870 to protect the fort livestock from the Indians.

The buildings in the square comprising the OLD POST, 0.6 *m.,* are of white stucco and limestone. The OLD CHAPEL, 0.8 *m.,* is a small ivy-covered structure (R) of native stone with six windows and a heavy, iron bell with a pull rope. Built in 1870, the chapel has a fine fireplace and is furnished with dark, wooden pews; a reed organ occupies the choir at the rear. It is now (1941) used by the Catholics of the post.

Between the Old Post and US 62 is the SITE OF THE PRISON in which some one hundred Indians were incarcerated from December, 1874, to March, 1875. These were the captives taken in the last big campaign during which Indian resistance was finally broken. The prisoners were mostly subchiefs and warriors who had taken an active part in the battles. They were moved from here to the St. Augustine, Florida, military prison, from which they were released in 1878. Only the floor of the old structure, later used as an icehouse and a blacksmith shop, is still visible.

A white stone, two-story residence on the north side of the square has been used as the POST COMMANDANT'S QUARTERS since the early days, although new quarters were built in 1936. It was here that an attempt on the life of General W. T. Sherman was made by an Indian named Stumbling Bird.

Opposite the southwest corner of the Old Post Parade ground is the MUSEUM *(open 8-11:30 a.m., 1-4 p.m. weekdays, 1-5 p.m. Sun.),* 1 *m.,* in the old guardhouse, where Geronimo was sometimes confined while at the post. The Apache chief and other prisoners of his band had been sent here in 1894 after being quartered in Florida and Alabama from the time of their capture in 1886. At Fort Sill, Geronimo was subject to military control, but was free to roam at will over the reservation. The old chief, who was addicted to spirits, was of necessity often confined to the guardhouse in an effort to sober him. Fort Sill inhabitants of those days grew familiar with the sight of the notoriously bloodthirsty Indian recovering from a hangover while splitting wood at the rear of the jail. Geronimo was much in demand for traveling fairs and shows; since he liked being stared at, he obtained leave for this purpose as much as possible. He died of pneumonia on February 17, 1909, and was buried in the Apache cemetery near Cache Creek on the post grounds; the other Apaches were returned to Arizona.

The museum was founded in 1934 and contains a comprehensive collection of old carbines, field guns, uniforms, medals, flags of various epochs and units, Indian weapons, dresses, and peace pipes.

The ADMINISTRATION BUILDING, 1.2 *m.,* a large three-story brown stucco structure (R) contains the library, the lecture rooms of the Field Artillery School, and the administrative offices of the post. North of the Administration Building are the STATION HOSPITAL *(visiting hours, 2-4 p.m. and 6-8 p.m.),* NURSES' QUARTERS, OFFICERS' QUARTERS, and the ACADEMIC AREA where the brown stucco officers' quarters line both sides of a wide parked driveway.

At 1.4 *m.* is a junction with a side road.

Right, 0.1 *m.,* to the HORSESHOE RING, where in normal times an annual horse show is held in the late spring or early summer; animals from the post and from outside stables are exhibited.

The route, which follows the four sides of the NEW POST PARADE GROUND, turns right at 1.9 *m.* to parallel the east side.

Used by the Protestants, the NEW CHAPEL, 2 *m.,* is a narrow, brown-brick structure (R) designed in a pseudo-Gothic style; near by is (R) the white stucco LIBERTY THEATER *(civilians not admitted),* with a tile roof.

At 2.2 *m.* Fort Sill Road turns left to parallel the north side of the Parade Ground, with quarters for officers (R). Near Medicine Bluff Creek, to the northeast, is the site on which Custer and the Seventh Cavalry camped at the founding of the fort in January and February, 1869. Depressions marking the sites of their brush-roofed dugouts are still visible.

Turning left again, 2.7 *m.,* the route passes along the west side of the Parade Ground, which is bordered (L) by the cream stucco barracks of a FIELD ARTILLERY REGIMENT, and (R) by the gun sheds and garages of the same unit. The Field Artillery is motorized and equipped with 75 mm. guns; the other outfits use 75 mm.'s and 155 mm. howitzers.

Again turning left, at 2.9 *m.,* the route (here called Randolph Road) runs along the south side of the Parade Ground. On the left are more field artillery barracks. This regiment is equipped with one battalion of truck-drawn 155 mm. howitzers. Additional barracks, the POST EXCHANGE *(only post personnel permitted to trade here)*, the GUARDHOUSE, SIGNAL OFFICE, and QUARTERMASTER'S OFFICE are R. Gun sheds and stables for field artillery units are south of these buildings. Directly across the road from the Guardhouse and on the edge of the Parade Ground is the HEADQUARTERS BUILDING. In front is the FLAGPOLE, 3.2 *m.*, where the retreat ceremony is held daily *(5:15 p.m. winter; 5:00 p.m. summer)*. Bugles sound, the retreat gun is fired; all present stand at attention while giving the hand salute as Old Glory is slowly lowered.

Leaving the Parade Ground, the route, again Fort Sill Road, turns right 3.4 *m.* and passes (L) a quarry, 3.7 *m.*, from which rock is taken for camp construction.

Between the quarry and Post Field is the former summer-camp site of the Oklahoma National Guard (R). The area (approximately a square mile) is now (1941) occupied by units quartered here in connection with the national defense program. An enormous number of barracks and tents stretch row on row.

Fort Sill Road turns left, 4.8 *m.*, and passes through POST FIELD, 5.2 *m.*, the aviation field established in 1917. It was named for Sergeant Henry B. Post, Twenty-fifth Infantry, who was killed in 1914 while attempting to set an altitude record at San Diego, California. An observation "blimp" usually sways some five hundred or a thousand feet above the field; from it officers observe artillery fire. Buff stucco hangars and barracks are on both sides of the road throughout Post Field.

At 6.2 *m.* is the South Gate of the Fort Sill reservation and the junction with US 62 *(see Tour 3)*.

Tour 3B

Junction US 62—Medicine Park—Wichita Mountains Wildlife Refuge—Indiahoma; State 49, Meers Highway, Scenic Highway; 31.8 m.

State 49 asphalt-paved; Scenic Meers Highway graveled.
Good resort accommodations at Medicine Park; tourist camps at East and South gates of Refuge; camping and picnicking facilities within Refuge.

This tour passes through the resort and national forest areas of the Wichita Mountains, a region closely packed with low but rugged mountains, clear streams, and small, oddly-shaped lakes that are easily reached.

State 49, a paved highway, branches west (R), 0 *m.,* from its junction with US 62 *(see Tour 3)* at a point 13.4 miles south of Apache *(see Tour 3).*

At the beginning of the mountainous area is MEDICINE PARK, 6.6 *m.* (1,765 alt., 25 pop.), a popular summer resort. LAKE LAWTONKA *(fishing, swimming, boating),* extending from the northern edge of town, covers approximately fourteen hundred acres. A dam, 60 feet high and 375 feet long, was constructed across Medicine Bluff Creek at the mouth of a steep gorge to form this reservoir for the city of Lawton and the Fort Sill Military Reservation *(see Tour 3A).*

West of Medicine Park, the route crosses a wagon bridge and passes through the East Gate, 7.4 *m.,* of the WICHITA MOUNTAINS WILDLIFE REFUGE *(adm. free; no guides necessary),* an area comprising 61,480 acres. This range of mountains, extending northwest and lying completely within Comanche County, is sixty miles in length and twenty to thirty miles wide. The rounded summits of the granite peaks average 650 to 700 feet in height. According to geologists, these mountains are among the oldest in the United States, and the crumbling rocks and general disintegration of the strange formations bear out this theory to the layman's eye. Interveining of quartz with the prevailing granite results in shadings from purple to red. The water has an alkaline substance, yet is clear and limpid. Scrubby white oak predominates, but the valleys have many leafier trees, such as ash, cottonwood, and willow.

Until the middle of the nineteenth century, the only inhabitants of this area were Indians. The onetime presence here of a tribe of Wichita Indians has been substantiated, and remains of other tribal lodges have been found. In the extreme northwestern section of the Refuge is CUTTHROAT GAP, scene of the hideous massacre of a band of Kiowas by Osages in 1833. The Kiowa camp was occupied on this tragic day only by the young and old, for the warriors were all away hunting. The Osages struck suddenly, first slitting the throats of their victims, then cutting off their heads, which they placed in the convenient buckets of the Kiowas as an offering to their gods. One of these buckets, found standing in the ruins of the village after the disaster, is in the Fort Sill Museum *(see Tour 3A).*

When this section of Indian land was opened for white settlement in 1901, Congress set aside the Wichita Mountains as a forest reserve under the jurisdiction of the Department of the Interior. When it was transferred to the Forest Service of the Department of Agriculture in 1905, along with all national reserves, it was designated a game preserve by proclamation of President Theodore Roosevelt. After several changes of name and jurisdiction, the area was given its present name, the Wichita Mountains Wildlife Refuge in 1935. Five years later it was placed under the jurisdiction of the Fish and Wildlife Service of the Department of the Interior.

The alarmingly rapid disappearance of the buffalo was responsible for the Roosevelt proclamation of 1905. A herd of fifteen buffaloes was donated to the government by the New York Zoological Society, which had been making a determined effort to perpetuate the breed, and Congress appropriated $15,000 to fence eight thousand acres in the Wichitas as a pasture for the animals. By 1940 the original fifteen buffaloes had grown in number to 439, including a record crop of 111 calves in 1939. One of the original herd, weighing 2,800 pounds, was the largest of the breed ever recorded. Since the acreage of the pasture limits the size of the herd, some have been given away; among the recipients were the governments of Mexico and Uruguay. Mesquite, buffalo, and bluestem grass furnish grazing in the area set aside for the bison, and the surrounding rock-capped hills and red granite cliffs afford shelter.

Other wild life being conserved in the Refuge are elk, white-tailed deer, Texas longhorns, wild turkeys, and birds; the elk numbered 200 in 1939; the deer, 750; the longhorns, 123; the turkeys, 400; and there were about 62 different species of birds. The first elk was placed here in 1911 and the turkey brood was started in 1912. The longhorn cattle are descendants of domesticated animals brought to this continent by the Spanish in 1521. By the close of the Civil War, Texas was overrun with this type of cattle that had been allowed to run wild. With settlement of the range and consequent increase in value of land, the longhorns had to give way to improved breeds and were rapidly becoming extinct. Upon the government's initiative, a few were found along the Rio Grande and the Gulf Coast and brought to the Wichita Refuge in 1927, where they have since increased to their present number. An attempt was also made to establish the antelope here, since this is its natural habitat, but the only ones available were from conservation herds at Yellowstone National Park and in Canada. They had become acclimated to those locations, and the sudden change to the variable Oklahoma weather proved fatal to most of them.

Some twelve hundred head of privately owned livestock graze on sections of the Wichita Refuge not needed for the conservation herds; this privilege is granted by government permits.

Oak trees—white, blackjack, and post oak—comprise most of the natural stand of timber in this area, but tree plantings of various other varieties have been made under government auspices. In 1913, juniper, bois d'arc (osage orange), black and honey locust, black walnut, and mulberry trees were set out on the lower slopes of the mountains. These plantings have grown to such an extent that they play a large part in making the Refuge an attractive haven for birds. Those most commonly seen are the cardinal, different types of wrens, titmouse, chickadee, and bluebird. Thirty-three varieties of wild flowers grow here; among them are the colorful yellow coreopsis, calliopsis, and black-eyed Susan, mingling with the purple-shaded larkspur, and verbena.

State 49 passes through the tree-shaded MOUNT SCOTT CAMPGROUNDS *(fire grates and water),* 8.4 *m.* A quarter of a mile south of the camp ground is LAKE THOMAS *(free swimming),* an artificial lake named for Elmer Thomas, who has represented Oklahoma for fourteen years in the United States Senate (1941). Senator Thomas was formerly the owner of the land on which Medicine Park stands and still maintains his home here. A broad driveway leading across the top of the dam offers an excellent view of the lake.

At 9.5 *m.* is the junction with the graveled Mount Scott Scenic Road.

Right on this winding, looping road, 3 *m.,* to the summit of MOUNT SCOTT (2,400 alt. 1,000 ft. above the base), named for General Winfield Scott, of Mexican War fame. Scott also conducted a part of the removal of the Cherokee Indians from the East to their new home in what is now Oklahoma. Construction of the scenic highway, completed in 1935, necessitated blasting through granite walls twenty to sixty feet high. From LOOKOUT POINT on the top there is a wide view of the surrounding country. A foot trail winds over the summit.

The Indians say that the Great Spirit appeared on Mount Scott after a devastating flood; here He called all Indians to Him and provided them with the means to survive. Other legends tell of the gold which Spaniards supposedly mined here in the seventeenth century. An old trail, connecting the Spanish possessions east of the Mississippi with their Southwest holdings, is said to have skirted the base of this mountain. Rusty knives, pieces of armor, and other relics have been found here, giving some credence to the tale.

At 12.1 *m.* is the junction with Meers Highway (graveled).

Right here to MOUNT ROOSEVELT (1,800 alt), 1.1 *m.,* named for President Theodore Roosevelt. On the south flank of the mountain is the Easter Holy City *(see below)*.

A quarry, at the base of MOUNT SHERIDAN (2,000 alt.), 1.6 *m.,* produces and ships a carload of blue-granite slabs each week. On the mountain's northeastern slope, a knob-shaped peak of solid granite juts out to a height of one hundred feet from a perpendicular wall of rock.

At 1.8 *m.* is the junction with a dirt road.

Right here to CEDAR PLANTATION, 0.2 *m.,* a seventeen-acre government nursery from which young fifteen-foot cedar trees are transplanted each year to other parts of the Refuge. After the seasonal thinning, there are usually approximately fifteen thousand trees left in the plantation.

At 2 *m.* is the North Gate to the Refuge.

Left on Meers Highway, now the main route, to the junction with Rush Lake Trail, a graveled road, 12.3 *m.*

Right on the Trail to the EASTER HOLY CITY, 0.8 *m.,* site of the annual Easter Pageant and Passion Play *(3:30 A.M. to dawn; free adm.)*, presented by the citizens of Lawton. On the slope of the small hill is a natural amphitheater which seats an audience of approximately 150,000. Buildings of red sandstone, constructed by WPA workers on the flank of the opposite hill, are used as dressing rooms by the two thousand persons who participate in the pageant. The six-hour program is broadcast over a national radio chain. The Garden of Gethsemane, the Tomb, and the Court of Pilate have all been reproduced out of natural rock as the setting and are an effective background for the floodlighted performance.

At 2.1 *m.* are LAKE RUSH *(fishing)* and BLUE BEAVER DAM.

At 12.5 *m.* on Meers Highway is the junction with a graveled road.

Right here is LAKE JED JOHNSON *(picnicking; no camping)*, 0.2 *m.,* one of the many artificial lakes which have been created in the Refuge.

The route leaves the Refuge, 13.6 *m.,* and re-enters it at 14.9 *m.*

At 15.2 *m.* is the junction with a dirt road.

Left on this road to INDIAN HILL LAKE (locally known as Crater Lake), 0.5 *m.* On a rock butte, which projects from a near-by hill into the water, are traces of rock fortifications said to have been erected by Indian war parties.

At 15.7 *m.* is the "Y" junction with the Scenic Highway.

Left on the Scenic Highway to a junction with a dirt road, 1.7 *m.*

Left here to the PECAN SPRINGS CAMPGROUND AND WADING POOL, 0.2 *m.,* a shallow pool affording safe swimming and wading for children.

Along the Highway

LLEGE STUDIO, TAHLEQUAH

MONUMENT TO GEN. STAND WATIE

WHITE : WPA

HIGHEST POINT IN OKLAHOMA, 4,778 FEET

THE SANTA FE TRAIL, AS SEEN FROM U S HIGHWAY 64

HITE : WPA

DIVISION OF STATE PAI

BEAVERS BEND STATE PARK, NEAR BROKEN BOW

BUFFALO IN WICHITA MOUNTAINS WILDLIFE REFUGE

NEW YORK ZOOLOGICAL PA

VISION OF STATE PARKS

ON THE WAY TO BEAVERS BEND STATE PARK

SCENE ON MOUNTAIN FORK

VISION OF STATE PARKS

H. A. GOTTHO

OIL AND WHEAT, NEAR EDMOND

STATE FISH HATCHERY, NEAR DURANT

STATE GAME AND FISH DEPARTME

E ERHARD : TULSA WORLD

WILL ROGERS MEMORIAL, CLAREMORE

CUSTER'S BATTLEFIELD, TWO MILES WEST OF CHEYENNE

ITE : WPA

ROTHSTEIN : RESETTLEMENT ADMINISTRAT

ZINC MINE AT PICHER

GYPSUM PLANT, NEAR SOUTHARD

WHITE : V

COAL MINE AT HENRYETTA

GRAND RIVER DAM, LOOKING NORTH

KLAHOMA PUBLISHING COMPANY

DIVISION OF STATE PA

TUCKER TOWER, LAKE MURRAY

QUARTZ MOUNTAIN STATE PARK, NEAR MANGUM

DIVISION OF STATE PA

The route passes through the South Gate of the Refuge, 1.9 *m.*, and proceeds to CACHE, 5.4 *m.* (1,260 alt., 620 pop.) *(see Tour 3A)*, at the junction with US 62 *(see Tour 3)*.

Right from the "Y" junction on Scenic Highway, now the main route, to a junction with a graveled road, 16.1 *m.*

Left here to the QUANAH PARKER DAM AND LAKE, 0.8 *m.*, named in honor of the last chief, whose home and grave are not far from here *(see Tour 3)*. The dam, the largest in the Refuge, is semicircular, with a siphon spillway, and measures seventy feet from summit to base. Steps at each end enable visitors to walk across the top; below the spillway is a small auxiliary dam. The lake covers eighty-six acres.

At 16.6 *m.* on the main route is the junction with the Seminole Beach Trail.

Left on this trail to the QUANAH PARKER CAMPGROUNDS, also named for the Comanche chief, and SEMINOLE BEACH, 0.3 *m.* All work on the extensive beach, the one-hundred-foot diving pier, and the surrounding native-stone buildings was done by the CCC. Some of the large, flat slabs of red granite used in the construction of the buildings are ten feet in height; the tawny red of the igneous rock is colorfully highlighted by the velvety green of clinging moss and lichens. The main structure, the COMMUNITY HOUSE, has an arched ceiling of white pine, scorched to reveal the beauty of the grain; the walls are finished with rough plaster, and the huge fireplace carries out the prevailing theme of granite. The fifteen-foot mantel is inlaid with an Indian pictograph of arrowheads and pines. The near-by bathhouses are square stone structures built in Spanish style; their dressing rooms *(no charge)* open into a patio.

A footbridge spans the western arm of Quanah Parker Lake here, and a foot trail leads one mile west over Mount Baldy to LAKE OSAGE. On the eastern shore a large mound of rock rises almost perpendicularly from the water to form a jagged peninsula.

At 19.3 *m.* on Scenic Highway is the junction with the Lost Lake–Boulder Campgrounds Trail.

Left here to LOST LAKE, 1.1 *m.*, which legends say was at one time the site of a natural lake. Once, after an absence of three years, Indian hunters returned to find that the body of water had completely dried—hence, its name. Lawton citizens subscribed funds for the creation of the present artificial lake and campgrounds and dedicated the recreational improvements to the National Forest Service on May 31, 1926. Upstream there is a chain of fish culture dams.

At 2. *m.* is a junction with a foot trail.

Left here over a cement bridge and up a steep hill to BOULDER CANYON VIEW, 0.3 *m.* This point provides a thrilling view of the Narrows, the sheer one-hundred-foot granite walls which imprison West Cache Creek just before it breaks through into the plains. Red-tailed hawks build their nests high on the steep cliffs, and in the morning and evening skim up and down the canyon in their search for food. The rugged, massive walls, reflecting the ever-changing colors caused by the play of light and shadow on the stream below, make the canyon a miniature Garden of the Gods.

CAMP BOULDER *(tables, benches, fire grates)*, 2.5 *m.*, is the scene of an annual course in nature study given by the Wild Life Institute, sponsored by the University of Oklahoma and other organizations interested in biological research.

In PRAIRIE DOG TOWN, 20.5 *m.*, where some four thousand prairie dogs have dug their dens, the little brown animals—about the size of small puppies—whisk in and out of their holes so rapidly that they defy observation. They usually emerge at dusk or early in the morning to seek food, but dodge back into their holes at the slightest sound. They are strictly vegetarians, and because of their proclivity for burrowing and the consequent destruction of crops, farmers regard them as nuisances.

Westward, the EXHIBITION PASTURES (L) cover a large area of gently rolling prairie land surrounded by high, round-topped hills and red granite cliffs and ridges. Small groups of elk, bison, deer, and Texas longhorns are pastured here so that visitors may watch them graze. The majority of the animals making up the vast Refuge herds roam far from the traveled roads, but magnificent specimens may be seen here. The pastures, extending along the route for about a mile, are covered with an abundant growth of mesquite, buffalo grass, and bluestem, and groves of blackjack and post oaks grow at the bases of the hills and cliffs. Visitors are forbidden to enter the exhibition pens, and any molestation of the animals is rated a Federal offense.

At 21.4 *m.* is a "Y" junction with a graveled road.

Straight ahead on this road to REFUGE HEADQUARTERS *(maps and descriptive pamphlets)*, 0.2 *m.*, which comprises the main office, the superintendent's home, and the residences of the other Refuge workers. In the main office *(open to visitors)* is a COLLECTION OF WILDLIFE SPECIMENS: heads of deer, elk, antelope, longhorn steers, water buffalo, and coyote. There are also mounted squirrels and birds; the skins of three enormous rattlesnakes with more than thirty rattles apiece; and a section of a petrified tree. Wild turkeys wander about in the yards of the buildings here; squirrels dart through the trees and even hang to the window screens; glistening, black, fat crows stalk about unafraid; and the deer come in herds at dawn to be fed personally by the superintendent.

At 1.6 *m.* is a junction with a dirt road.

Left on this road is FRENCH'S LAKE, 0.4 *m.*, named for a former superintendent of the Refuge. There is a large spiral fish ladder at the dam, and downstream from the lake proper is a long line of fish culture ponds extending as far as Lost Lake. A hiking trail, beginning on the left side of French's Lake, follows the stream to that point.

Countless bats live in BAT CAVE MOUNTAIN, 3.1 *m.* The mouth of the cave is about thirty feet above the base of the small red granite, moss-covered mountain (R).

The main route turns sharply left (south) to the junction with graveled Treasure Mountain Road, 24.1 *m.*

Right here, 0.2 *m.*, to TREASURE MOUNTAIN, where scores of hunters have dug for gold said to have been cached here in the seventeenth century by the Spaniards. At the mountain is a junction with a dirt road.

Right across Post Oak Creek to TREASURE TREE, 0.2 *m.*, estimated to be more than five hundred years old. Only a few limbs remain, for the seekers of the legendary gold have hacked at the tree in addition to digging many gaping holes at its base. Near the tree is an OLD CABIN, which probably originally served as headquarters for bandits or rustlers. But the wretched hovel is believed by each new treasure-seeker to have been a hiding place for Spanish gold; the floor boards have been ripped up and scattered about.

At 0.3 *m.* on the Treasure Mountain Road is a cement culvert spanning a dry creek bed; L. here to the SPANISH CAVE, 0.5 *m.*, which opens from the side of a canyon wall. Inside, the walls are of yellow stone, spotted with a clinging olive-hued moss. The floor, stained by countless campfires, is a solid ledge of red granite flecked with a blue substance. Forming the other side of the canyon opposite the entrance of the Spanish Cave is a huge, round rock, balanced high on a pile of jagged boulders. The canyon abruptly terminates in a curious formation resembling a gigantic chair.

The POST OAK CAMPGROUNDS *(tables, benches, fire grates)*, 1.4 *m.*, lie on one side of POST OAK LAKE *(swimming permitted, but no facilities)*. A rugged mountain rises above the deep lake on the opposite shore; a siphon spillway dam holds the twenty to forty foot depth of water.

TREASURE LAKE *(diving board and wire depth line; no other facilities)*, 2 *m.*, shares in the tradition of Treasure Mountain and Treasure Tree; fanatical diggers, with so-called ancient treasure maps as standard equipment, are not unusual in this vicinity. One legend of buried gold arose from a story told by Indians some years ago about a band of Comanches who had robbed an army paymaster and buried the stolen money near the lake. Racketeers immediately made and sold more than 250 maps, each one of which was the "original map." According to another tale, a "Catholic pope was killed in Mexico and buried near the lake; in the grave was also buried a golden calf, weighing 100 pounds." Rangers are on the lookout at all times to enlighten the credulous treasure-seeker, appearing with a shovel on his shoulder, a wild gleam in his eye, and the quest of a buried fortune in mind.

The main route passes out of the Refuge at the Southwest Gate, 24.6 *m.*, and proceeds southward to INDIAHOMA, 31.8 *m.* (1,335 alt., 337 pop.) *(see Tour 3)*, at the junction with US 62 *(see Tour 3)*.

Tour 4

(Seneca, Mo.)—Bartlesville—Ponca City—Enid—(Canadian, Tex.); US 60, Missouri Line to Texas Line, 360.1 m.

Alternately concrete and asphalt paved and graveled roadbed between Missouri Line and Fairview; graveled and graded earth between Fairview and Texas Line.
The Frisco Ry. roughly parallels US 60 between Seneca, Mo., and Vinita; the Katy between Bartlesville and Pawhuska; the Rock Island between Ponca City and Tonkawa; and between Pond Creek and Meno; and the Santa Fe between Cleo Springs and Fairview.
Good accommodations between Missouri Line and Enid; at longer intervals between Enid and Texas Line.

Crossing from Missouri, US 60 continues for a short distance among the rocky, wooded ridges and narrow valleys of the northwestern slopes of the Ozark range, a region where in mid-April dogwood blossoms make vivid white splashes against the dark leafless oaks. It then passes through a section of alternate forest and grassland, where the remnants of a number of small Indian tribes live. The route crosses Grand River, then traverses open country fairly evenly divided between farms and pastures.

Westward is the northern portion of the former Cherokee Nation, near the western edge of which scattered wells of the first extensive shallow oil fields developed in Oklahoma are still (1941) producing.

Next the route bisects the Osage Indian reservation, an area of blackjack oak woods and rich upland pastures where gusher oil wells and fine Hereford cattle have brought wealth to these lucky Indians and to the white ranchmen who lease their grazing land.

Beyond the country of the Osages the route touches the lands of the Ponca and Tonkawa Indians. It crosses the richest wheat-growing region of the state east and west of Enid, then a part of the arid, dust-blowing high plains broken by gypsum-crusted formations that suggest, on a giant scale, five-and-ten-cent-store decorations. Near the Texas Line, the desert motif is emphasized by the appearance of the graceful, drought-resistant yucca plants.

Section a. MISSOURI LINE *to* BARTLESVILLE, *89.7 m. US 60*

US 60 crosses the MISSOURI LINE, 0 *m.,* at a point 0.8 miles west of Seneca, Missouri *(see Missouri Guide)* and winds for a few miles through the Oklahoma Ozarks. Numerous streams have cut narrow, V-shaped valleys in the plateau, forming broad, flat-topped hills from six hundred to thirteen hundred feet high. Post oak, hickory, cottonwood, and walnut are abundant in both hills and valleys and, in the spring, the bright redbud and the white, wild plum blossoms splash young blue-green prairie grass with color.

WYANDOTTE, 7.5 *m.* (754 alt., 348 pop.), was named for the Wyandotte Indians, whose reservation included this area after the land was ceded to the United States by the Senecas in 1867. Today (1941), Indians make up the greater part of the population of the village and the vicinity. The heavily wooded country is unsuited to agriculture except along the creek bottoms; most of Wyandotte's activities are dependent on the near-by Seneca Indian School.

Right from Wyandotte on a graveled road to the SENECA INDIAN SCHOOL, 0.5 *m.* *(visitors welcome),* founded by the Quakers. The first building, a log cabin north of the present site, was erected in 1869; now a dozen brick and frame structures comprise the plant, occupying a high bluff overlooking Lost Creek. The institution, which is under government supervision, is open to members of all the northeastern Oklahoma tribes coming under the jurisdiction of the Quapaw Agency, and has an annual enrollment of 275. The school museum contains a collection of Indian relics.

The town of FAIRLAND, 15.6 *m.* (828 alt., 781 pop.), was originally about two and one-half miles east of the present site and was called Prairie City. The first settlement moved to the present spot and changed its name to Fairland when the postmastership was obtained by an early-day storekeeper on this location.

Fairland is in the center of a cattle-raising section, which also produces hay and grain. The large consolidated school, municipally owned water system, and modern business section will aid in making the town, which is within a few miles of the newly created (1941) Grand Lake, a resort center.

Northwest of here are large deposits of tripoli—a rock which is ground into a flour used as an abrasive and a polisher in metal-working trades, for foundry facing, and as a filter. Most of the refining of the raw mineral is done at mills located at Seneca, Missouri.

At 19.7 *m.,* the route unites southwestward with US 66-69 *(see Tours 1 and 8)* for twenty-five miles.

At 22.9 *m.* is the junction with US 59 *(see Tour 15).*

AFTON, 23.9 *m.* (790 alt., 1,261 pop.) *(see Tour 1).*

VINITA, 39.5 *m.* (702 alt., 5,685 pop.) *(see Tour 1).*

At 43.5 *m.* is the western junction with US 69; at 44.5 that with US 66.

At 66.1 *m.* is the junction with an unimproved dirt road.

Left on this road to a DELAWARE CHURCH, 3.2 *m.,* built in 1871 by Rev. Charles Journeycake, the last chief of the Delaware Indians. South of the church is a monument to the old chief.

Near the bridge across the Verdigris River at COODY'S BLUFF, 62.5 *m.* (648 alt., 64 pop.), is a log cabin that has been standing since pioneer days. The town was named for a Cherokee Indian family.

An unusual method of oil extraction has been used in this area since 1937—the use of water pressure in order to produce enough oil from stripper wells to warrant their being operated. Water is forced down a well drilled to the same depth as several surrounding wells; it makes its way through the minute crevices and channels of the oil sands in which pockets of crude have been left in the normal process of drilling and pushes that crude toward the various holes, from which it can easily be retrieved by pumps. This re-pressuring method has brought about a "five-spot" appearance to the fields, since the original wells were fairly regularly spaced, one to every ten acres of drilling land; now a water well usually occupies the center of each forty-acre tract. A central powerhouse and reservoir furnishes water and power for as many as five of the forty-acre divisions. The process was first instituted because geologists estimated that only two thousand barrels had been removed from each potential forty-thousand-barrel acre.

The turreted and spired houses of NOWATA, 68.5 *m.* (707 alt., 3,904 pop.), with their ornamental lattices, carved banisters, and porch posts are typical of the "turn-of-the-century" architecture. In 1868, this area was included in the land sold by the Cherokee Indians to the Kansas Delawares. From the trading post, which was established a short time later, a settlement grew up to become the town of Nowata. When the railroad built through, two company surveyors are said to have named it Noweta at the suggestion of a Cherokee woman who said that the word meant, "We welcome you to come." The spelling was later changed in the records of the Post Office Department.

Nowata is at the junction with US 169 *(see Tour 16).*

At 87.3 *m.* is the junction with US 75 *(see Tour 9).*

BARTLESVILLE, 89.7 *m.* (694 alt., 16,267 pop.) *(see Bartlesville).*

Left from Bartlesville on graveled State 23 to the FRANK PHILLIPS RANCH *(admission only by appointment with Phillips Petroleum Co., Bartlesville),* 12 *m.,* the country home of Frank Phillips, president (1941) and founder of the widespread Phillips Petroleum Company. A rustic arched gateway marks the beginning of the winding drive through the ranch grounds to the WOOLAROC LODGE AND MUSEUM, synthetically named for the words "woods," "lake," and "rock." The ranch, consisting of one thousand acres, is a private game preserve, and has seven lakes stocked with game fish. The entire estate is fenced, enclosing the vast pastures on which numerous species of animal and fowl, both native and foreign to Oklahoma, are kept.

The ranch buildings are situated on a hill overlooking Outlaw Gulch and the largest of the lakes. Steps of native stone lead to the lake's edge where there are bathhouses, bathing beach, picnic grounds, barbecue pits, an Indian tepee, and an old prairie schooner. The Lodge is a rambling, twelve-room, log structure. In the reception room the furnishings carry out the rustic theme; the piano and phonograph are covered with a veneer of bark, and on the walls are stuffed animals, trophies, and many paintings.

The museum was dedicated by Phillips to the Osage Indian tribe, of which he is the only white man to be an honorary member. A native-stone structure, it contains a varied and valuable collection, including the airplane, "Woolaroc," which Phillips furnished Art Goebel for his prize-winning flight to Honolulu in the Dole race of 1927. Fossils, relics, Indian costumes and trophies, shrunken human heads excavated in Central America, and gem-studded saddles are also displayed. Many oil paintings—mostly western and Indian subjects—are hung against backgrounds of animal skins. John Noble's famous painting, "The Run," depicting the Cherokee Strip opening of 1893, is probably the most notable of the collection. A large album lists the approximately seventy-five thousand documents making up the Frank Phillips collection of historical papers at the University of Oklahoma Library *(see Norman).*

Right from Bartlesville on a dirt road to the barren summit of ROUND MOUNTAIN, 1.8 *m.,* from which there is a widespread view of the surrounding countryside. Atop the hill is a beacon for air navigation.

Section b. BARTLESVILLE *to* ENID, *134.3 m. US 60*

Between BARTLESVILLE, 0 *m.,* and Ponca City, US 60 traverses the confines of the old Osage Nation, now Osage County. Indian teepees once dotted the rocky hills but today they have been replaced by "stripper wells" and "pumping jacks." The high-rounded Osage Hills encompass well-watered valleys, both blanketed in the spring and summer with many wild flowers.

In 1872, the Osage Indians were removed from Kansas to Silver Lake *(see Tour 9),* and then to this tract of almost 1,500,000 acres, which they purchased from the Cherokee Nation. They had been paid $9,000,000 by the Federal government for their Kansas land, and since they lived on the interest from their money, they were known as the wealthiest Indians in the country. Their new lands were composed of hills and prairies, which was much to their liking, for they were naturally hunters and fighters rather than farmers. Many leased their lands for pasture; others adopted the white man's way and became ranchers themselves.

The Osage roll, which was approved in 1908, listed 2,230 persons receiving an allotment of 657 acres. All mineral rights were reserved for the benefit of the tribe, each individual headright to receive a pro rata share of the income. The discovery of oil and gas in the southwest corner of the nation in 1903 and the subsequent development of the vast field catapulted the Osages into an even greater luxury. By 1916, each member of the tribe was receiving annual amounts ranging from $2,200 to $15,000, and those who had inherited headrights had a still larger income. Total royalty and lease-bonus payments received by the tribe for their oil by 1934 amounted to some $252,700,000.

On the closing date for enrolling the Osages, some unique names were given to newborn babes, whose arrival might mean another headright for its family. One boy, born at 11:50 on the last night before the closing of the rolls, received the title of Johnny-On-The-Spot; while a luckless girl baby, who came into the world half an hour after midnight, was dubbed Mary-Too-Late.

During the period of luxury for the Osages, it was not unusual to see a blanketed Indian—braids down his back and a Stetson on his head—at the wheel of an expensive automobile, while his wife and family, also colorfully blanketed, occupied the back seat. Today (1941), because of the depression years and a partially depleted oil basin, the value of the Osage headrights is considerably smaller but it is still appreciably larger than the income of the average white citizen. The Osage per capita wealth is now estimated at $4,700.

The OSAGE HILLS STATE PARK *(cabins, picnicking, swimming, and fishing facilities)*, 11.4 *m.*, is a rolling, wooded area of 720 acres which has only recently been developed as a recreational area. Civilian Conservation Corps workers, under the supervision of the National Park Service, have constructed hiking and bridle trails, picnic areas, shelters, a bathhouse, swimming pool, and natural-stone cabins. Sand Creek *(boats 50c per day)*, a clear-water stream winding throughout the park, is stocked with several varieties of game fish. The gorges, glens, and bluffs furnish an ideal sanctuary for the wild game protected here.

The recreation area was originally developed by citizens of the near-by city of Bartlesville, when they contributed money to build cabins for city Boy Scout troops. Now (1941), scouts from eight counties, and other organizations including the YWCA, YMCA, and Girl Reserves use the site as a summer camping ground.

At 23.9 *m.* is the junction with graded County Road No. 7.

Left on this road to PAWHUSKA INDIAN VILLAGE, 0.8 *m.*, home of many members of the "Dwellers-in-the-Thorny-Thickets" *(see Tour 14)* division of the Osage tribe. CHIEF BACON RIND'S HOME is a grey, two-story structure with four gables; it has been allowed to deteriorate since the death of the famous chief in 1932. Bacon Rind, or Wah-she-hah, was born in 1853 of a family long important in the tribal government. His brilliance, fine physique, and ability as an orator in the Osage tongue (though he spoke little English) made him one of the best-liked Indians. After his death, Bacon Rind lay in state in his home, face painted in ceremonial fashion and body clothed in Indian costume. The funeral was a strange mixture of traditional Christian and Indian burial rites; weirdly singing mourners were employed and the guests feasted following the interment. A statue of him has been erected at Skedee *(see Tour 2)*.

A dance to commemorate the removal of the Osages from Kansas is held in the village in the latter part of September *(visitors welcome)*; invitations are sent to neighboring tribes to attend the ceremonies. The dancing continues for four days with rites honoring past chiefs. Other powwows and feasts are held in the arbor here during fair weather, but during rainy seasons the "round house" at Grayhorse is used. One annual dance, around the American flag, celebrates the day *(October 14)* on which the tribe received from President Calvin Coolidge a certificate of thanks for Osage participation in the World War.

The use of peyote, a dried cactus "button," as a sacrament figures largely in the elaborate night-long Osage religious ceremonials. As early as the Spanish conquest, certain Mexican tribes employed peyote in religious rituals, and gradually its use spread northward until the end of the nineteenth century when it became popular among the Indians of Oklahoma. It was introduced on the Osage reservation in 1898 by John Wilson, a Caddo-Delaware. In 1911, a charter for the incorporation of the Native American Church was obtained from the state by Oklahoma Indians—the articles specifying the use of peyote as a sacrament.

The Osages hold their church meetings on Saturday nights in octagonal lodge houses with earthen floors and cement altars. About sixty feet from the church door is a sweat-bath house in which the ceremonial participants purify themselves physically with a buckeye root emetic while taking the bath. After purification, the Indians are led into the cleanswept church by the "Road Man" or leader; all seat themselves on blankets placed on the dirt floor and observe silence while the leader makes and lights a corn-shuck cigarette and prays aloud for the whole world. After the prayer the cigarette is placed on the "Road," and the "Road Man" continues during the night, admonishing, exhorting, and pointing out the right road to the worshipers, who throughout the ritual use the peyote both in its original form as a cactus button and steeped in a tea. The rhythms of a drum and gourd heighten the emotions until the end of the services on Sunday morning when the participants partake of a feast.

The GRAVE OF BACON RIND, 1 *m.*, is located on the hilltop (L) in traditional Osage fashion.

PAWHUSKA, 25.2 m. (885 alt., 5,443 pop.), is the seat of Osage County, the largest county in the state, and the tribal capital. The town, which still has the traditional Indian atmosphere, was named for a famous Osage chief. Pahu-çka, or White Hair, received his name from an incident in the battle known as St. Clair's Defeat, fought during Washington's administration. The Osage, then a youth, wounded an officer wearing a powdered wig. He started to scalp his quarry when, to his amazement, the whole scalp came off and the victim escaped, leaving the Osage standing with a fluffy, white wig grasped in his fingers. Believing that the wig had supernatural powers, the warrior henceforth wore it fastened to his roach.

The original White Hair was chief of the Osage tribe at the beginning of the nineteenth century, a position which he is said to have usurped from the lawful heir, Clermont, through the influence of the Chouteau family *(see Tour 8)*. This action brought about a division of the Osage Nation, Clermont's band separating entirely. Both White Hair and his son, also known as Chief White Hair, were presented with medals by Lieutenant Zebulon M. Pike *(see Tour 3)*.

On the site of the first station here for the disbursing of funds to the Osage tribe is the FLATIRON BUILDING, Ki-he-kah Avenue and Main Street. A hitching rail originally enclosed the area; later, Pawhuska businessmen purchased the triangular plot and erected the modern building. The fabulous oil lease auctions of the Osage lands were held where the KI-HE-KAH THEATER, Ki-he-kah Avenue and Main Street, now stands. The yearly lease sales ranged from one to fourteen million dollars from 1916 to 1928, with the exception of 1926. On one occasion, an opening bid of $500,000 started a series of sales which closed at a total of more than $3,000,000.

Rising above the business district is AGENCY HILL; at its foot is the CITY HALL, Main and Grandview Streets, formerly the Osage Council House. At the top of the hill are the stone and frame buildings of the OSAGE AGENCY, on a 104-acre tract. Here the tribal business is conducted by the superintendent, aided by a council composed of the chief of the Osages, assistant chief, and eight councilmen and a secretary elected by the tribe.

The OSAGE TRIBAL MUSEUM AND AUDITORIUM *(free adm. 1:15 to 4 P.M. workdays; 2 to 5 P.M. Sundays)*, constructed of native sandstone, occupies the site of the first agency building on the hill. Its erection in 1938 was sponsored by the Osage tribal council in order to preserve linguistic and mythological data relating to the Osage Indians. The museum houses several extensive collections, the most outstanding of which are the Chief Bacon Rind and the John Bird accumulations of tribal costumes, paintings, bead and feather artcraft, treaties, and valuable documents. Bacon Rind's collection was willed by him to the Smithsonian Institution at Washington, D.C., but with the building of the Osage Museum the institution loaned the historical objects to the tribe for an indefinite period. There are also old photographs, voice recordings in the tribal language, and other materials necessary to trace a complete history of the tribe.

Pawhuska is the home of Mary Todd Aaron, contemporary Oklahoma artist; Lemuel Jennings Childers (b. 1898), composer of works using authentic Indian themes; and John Joseph Mathews (b. 1895), of Osage blood, whose books have received wide acclaim.

Herbert Hoover, President of the United States (1928–32), spent several boyhood summers here with his uncle, Major Laban J. Miles, who became Osage agent in 1878. Some Pawhuskans remember the interest of the orphaned boy visitor in the rocks of the surrounding Osage Hills—an interest which later blossomed into a mining and engineering career.

In the hills near the city are widespread grazing lands on which as many as four hundred thousand cattle are pastured in one season. Approximately two-thirds of the herds are owned by Osage ranchers; the remaining third is shipped in from Texas and other states, during March and April, to be fattened for July and August markets. Agricultural products of the ranches are corn, cotton, oats, hay, fruit, and berries.

Pawhuska is at the junction with State 99 *(see Tour 14)*.

Right from Pawhuska on the graveled Osage Highway to the BARNARD-CHAPMAN RANCH *(visitors welcome)*, 15.4 *m.*, which covers one hundred thousand acres of rolling, prairie hills on which more than sixteen thousand head of Hereford cattle graze. The ranch house is a sprawling, twelve-room, brick building with a tile roof and many porches. The ranch has its own shipping pens and station located on the main line of the Midland Valley Railroad, which runs through the far-flung acres. When the ranch was first established, cattle were allowed the right of way and gates were put up across the highway so that they might saunter from one side to another at will. There were some thirty-seven gates across roads leading from Tulsa to the Barnard-Chapman Ranch at that time. With increasing travel, however, the gates were removed and notices of the cattle crossings posted, warning the motorist to slow down. In addition to the grass-covered pastures, Sand, Dog, Buck, and Bird creeks cut across the ranch and afford a plentiful supply of water. It is said that there are more grass-fattened cattle shipped from here annually than from any other point in the United States.

Right from Pawhuska on an unimproved dirt road is the CHIEF SAUCY CHIEF HOMESTEAD, 3.6 *m.* Nellie, the daughter of the chief, was the first Osage to be given Christian burial. She contracted pneumonia in 1885 at the Carlisle Indian School in Pennsylvania and was sent home, where she died. Major Laban J. Miles, the Osage Agent at that time, persuaded her parents to conduct the Christian rites rather than their customary procedure of burying the dead in a sitting posture on the summit of a hill. However, the Indians kept their own mourning customs, the chief wearing only a white sheet, moccasins, and breechclout for a three-and-a-half-month period, despite the snow-covered ground. In preparation for the three-day dance which was to end the mourning observance, the funeral party rode out solemnly to capture the scalp of a town merchant who had ingratiatingly decided to submit himself to a mock scalping; he allowed the Indians to cut off his forelock, minus the traditional accompaniment of skin. Major Miles was accorded the honor of leading the group—much to the amazement of Pawhuska citizens, who saw him riding into town holding the scalp-pole with the hair flying from its top. After Saucy Chief had been bathed and dressed in warm blankets, the dance began. Nellie's death had been properly observed, and her spirit sent on its journey with the blessing of both the white and red man's ritual.

At 46.9 *m.* is the western junction with State 18, a graveled road.

Left on State 18 to Fairfax, 9.6 *m.* (841 alt., 2,327 pop.), located in the center of large oil fields.

Left from Fairfax on an improved dirt road to the GRAVE AND STATUE OF CHIEF NE-KA-WA-SHE-TUN-KA, 4.3 *m.,* the last Osage chieftain to receive the complete Osage burial ceremony. This included the killing of his favorite horse and the placing of a human scalp on his grave at the end of the mourning period to allow his spirit to enter the Happy Hunting Ground. The scalp secured in this case was that of a Wichita chief, A-sa-wah, and its taking precipitated an intertribal incident which caused the government to forbid all future scalp-hunting. The Osages finally settled the score by making large payments of money and goods to the Wichitas.

Left from Fairfax on graveled State 20 to a junction with a county road, 3 *m.;* L. on this road to GRAYHORSE, 4.5 *m.,* where the "Dwellers-on-the-Hilltop" division *(see Tour 14)* of the Osage Indians hold tribal dances and gatherings in the "round house" in inclement weather.

State 18 continues south from Fairfax to the SITE OF AN OLD OSAGE RIVER FORD, 15.7 *m.,* on the east bank of the Arkansas River, just across from the small town of RALSTON, 15.9 *m.* When the river at this point divided the Osage and Pawnee Nations, charges of stealing and the raids of scalping parties caused many skirmishes between the two tribes at the ford.

In the early history of Oklahoma, there were many attempts to establish a trade route up the Arkansas River past Fort Gibson *(see Tour 3),* at which point ascending navigation became dangerous. In 1878, one small steamer managed to go as far as the mouth of the Walnut River in Kansas; and in the 1880's, a flour carrier, "Kansas Millers," successfully made the trip from Arkansas City, Kansas, to the Arkansas Line. In 1885, a steamer unloaded merchandise at the Kaw Indian Agency (northwest of this point), and in 1898, the "Minnie" made the last attempt to ascend farther than this landing. Loaded with walnut logs to fill a contract for gunstock lumber, she went aground on a sand bar just southwest of this ford; her cargo was unloaded and hauled to its destination by wagon. In the early 1900's, a small steamboat made several trips between Ralston and Tulsa. Though the ship, using a threshing machine engine for power, was not much more than a flatboat, it provided a means of transporting merchandise to towns having no transportation facilities other than freight wagons and stage coaches.

BURBANK, 49.1 *m.* (935 alt., 329 pop.), until the discovery of oil brought a boom to the town, was primarily an Osage settlement. The near-by bluffs on which cockleburs grow in profusion are said to have furnished the inspiration for the town's name, suggested by railroad men when the Santa Fe established a station here in 1903.

At the opening of the Burbank field in May, 1920, the sale of leases brought less than $10 an acre, but after production was well under way, leases sold for as high as $10,000 an acre. The rush for leases in the Burbank boom brought fabulous prices for land which had sold for as little as $800 a quarter section prior to 1920. In June, 1921, the sale of fourteen leases brought $3,256,000, while in a December sale of that year, eighteen sold for $6,250,000. By 1922, two leases sold for $1,335,000 and $1,160,000, respectively. In addition to the bonuses paid to the Indians for the right to drill, all contracts with them call for a special royalty on the production. The ordinary royalty is one-eighth of the oil and gas produced, but the Osages receive one-sixth on leases producing less than one hundred barrels a day and one-fifth where the yield is more.

At 67.9 *m.* US 60 crosses the Arkansas River.

At 68.5 *m.* is the junction with US 77 *(see Tour 10)*, which unites southwestward with US 60 for 4.2 miles.

PONCA CITY, 69.4 *m.* (1,003 alt., 16,794 pop.) *(see Ponca City)*.

At 80.5 *m.* is the junction with US 177, a paved highway.

Right on this road to BLACKWELL, 11 *m.* (1,020 alt., 8,537 pop.), the second largest municipality in Kay County and the center of a rich farming region. Extending from the southwest bank of the Chikaskia River to and beyond US 177, which is its main north and south street, Blackwell spreads over four square miles of flat land.

This prairie city came into existence at the opening to settlement of the Cherokee Outlet in the Run of September 16, 1893. A. J. Blackwell, an adopted citizen of the Cherokee Nation, who asserted his right to occupy and use land assigned to the tribe as an outlet to hunting grounds, platted the site, set up a provisional town government with himself at the head, and sold lots. A group of families from Winfield, Kansas, were the first permanent residents.

Even before the opening, however, a tent city of some fifteen hundred of Payne's "boomers" *(see History)* was established just across the river from the present city. The trespassing colonists lived there in the summer of 1884, until United States troops drove them out, and published a little newspaper called the *Oklahoma War Chief (see Newspapers)*.

For a considerable time after Blackwell was established, its founder continued his practically one-man government. His despotic attitude caused resentment, and when he undertook to bring in Negro workmen in defiance of the unofficial but strict ban on their residence or employment in town, the tent they occupied was fired upon at night. Some were killed, and others were wounded, and neither Blackwell or anyone else made further attempts in that direction.

As town-builder and boss, Blackwell had a tumultous career. In his role of self-ordained Baptist preacher, he earned the title of "prophet"; as a hot-tempered frontiersman, he twice drew indictments for murder, neither of which resulted in conviction.

With the founder's passing, the town settled into a period of steady growth as the market for a good wheat-growing section. Then, to serve the needs of cattlemen of the Tonkawa and Ponca reservations region to the south and southeast, a packing plant was established, and its products still (1941) find a market in northern Oklahoma and southern Kansas. During the first World War a zinc smelter was built, where for a time 650 workmen treated some seven thousand tons of ore monthly. After being shut down for years, this smelter was reopened in 1941 in response to demands for zinc and lead due to the second World War. Other industries are an oil refinery, a glassmaking factory, a brickmaking and two cabinetmaking plants, a cheese factory, and two that turn out other dairy products.

An excellent public library, in a tile-roofed, red-brick, one-story building, grew out of a small Chautauqua collection of books housed in a single room over a bank in 1903. Among its more than thirteen thousand volumes are many autographed copies of books by Oklahoma writers, a considerable collection of material on the state's history, and thirty pictures by Oklahoma Indian artists donated by Mrs. Laura Clubb, of Kaw City *(see Tour 10)*. In the library is a minature theater for presentation of puppet plays. The building was erected in 1931 at a cost of $35,000 for building and furniture; this sum came from a fund accumulated from a two-mill municipal levy for library purposes imposed in 1921. The library's current annual budget of some $7,700 is provided from a continuing levy.

There is an airport west of the city, and Wheeler-Huston Athletic Park *(lighted; dog racing)* is at its southern edge.

Named for the Tonkawa Indians who once owned the land surrounding it, TONKAWA, 82.6 *m.* (1,003 alt., 3,197 pop.), is today a busy oil city.

Wells in the vicinity have been producing since 1921 and are covering an ever-widening area.

In 1879, Chief Joseph and his band of Nez Percé Indians were brought as prisoners and exiles from their home in Idaho and placed on a reservation located at the Yellow Bull crossing on the Salt Fork of the Arkansas River, just a few hundred yards west of the present main street of Tonkawa. The crossing received its name from the Nez Percé chief, Yellow Bull, who built a log house near by. Here they stayed for several years, always longing to return to their former home, and finally they were allowed to remove.

The Tonkawas, who were few in number, seem to have originated in Texas; but during the Civil War they were encamped on the Washita River near Anadarko *(see Tour 3)* where, because they were suspected of cannibalism, the tribe was almost exterminated. During their wanderings, these so-called "Ishmaels of the Plains" were successively thinned by war, massacre, and disease, before they finally found a home here on the Salt Fork of the Arkansas. It is said that the meaning of the name, Tonkawa, is "They all stay together." They accepted allotments in 1891 and sold the remainder of their land to the United States; it was opened for settlement along with the Cherokee Strip in 1893. At present (1941) the only available count of the Tonkawas lists eighteen persons.

Tonkawa was platted the year after the Run, and in 1901 was chosen as the site for the present TONKAWA UNIVERSITY PREPARATORY SCHOOL AND JUNIOR COLLEGE *(five blocks L. from junction of US 60 and Grand Avenue)*, by the Territorial legislature then in session. The state-owned institution is housed in five buildings in the center of a twenty-acre tract; the oldest structure, ivy-covered Central Hall, contains workshops, the business school, and classrooms. Wilkins Hall, which is the newest of the buildings, has an imposing entrance supported by two massive Corinthian columns. North Hall and the Gymnasium complete the college group.

Since the vicinity was included in the Cherokee Strip opening, Tonkawa citizens join a number of other Oklahomans in the annual celebration of September 16, anniversary of the Run. The day begins with a parade and reproduction of the stirring chase for land, the participants dressing in authentic costumes of 1893. The Old Settlers program in the afternoon includes Indian dances, reels, and fiddling contests.

LAMONT, 97.9 *m.* (997 alt., 577 pop.), named for Daniel Lamont, Secretary of War (1893–97), is near the sandy lowlands of the Salt Fork, where unusually large and delicious watermelons are grown. Annually in September, the residents celebrate their harvest with a Watermelon Festival, when they boast that they serve ten tons of the fruit free to visitors. A huge concrete pit, which was constructed back of the Community House especially for storage of the melons, is the center of the day's events; these include a football game, horseshoe pitching, terrapin derby, dancing, and the coronation of the festival queen.

POND CREEK, 112.4 *m.* (1,050 alt., 1,019 pop.) *(see Tour 11)*, is at the eastern junction with US 81 *(see Tour 11)*, which unites southward with US 60 for twenty-two miles.

At 116.8 *m.* is the junction with US 64, which unites with US 60 and US 81 to Enid.

ENID, 134.3 *m.* (1,246 alt., 28,081 pop.) *(see Enid),* is at the southern junction with US 81 and US 64; US 60 again turns sharply west.

Section c. ENID *to* TEXAS LINE, 136.1 *m. US 60*

West of ENID, 0 *m.,* US 60 passes through wide-stretching wheat fields, where grain elevators occasionally tower like skyscrapers above the level land. In the high, dry country west of the North Canadian River, towns are seen at a great distance because of the clarity of atmosphere. Overgrazing and overcultivation in addition to prolonged years of drouth have caused this section of Oklahoma to suffer in recent years; but a farseeing program of contour farming, reforestation, and planting of soil-binding crops is checking the Dust Bowl encroachment.

At 8.2 *m.* is the junction with an improved dirt road.

Left on this road to DRUMMOND, 8.1 *m.* (1,213 alt., 245 pop.); just west of the town are flats which fill with water during the rainy season in the fall, affording excellent hunting for ducks, geese, and other migratory wild fowl.

The largest community of Mennonites in Oklahoma, and probably of the Southwest, live on farms near MENO, 18.2 *m.* (1,300 alt., 180 pop.), which serves as a trade center. The sect has a church here, with eight hundred members, and a grade school, high school, and college. In accordance with their age-old custom, many of the older men still wearing unclipped beards, and black-capped old ladies wearing picturesque white neckpieces and black shawls, may be seen on the street.

At 22.2 *m.* is the junction with State 58, a graveled highway.

Left on State 58 to RINGWOOD, 1 *m.* (1,307 alt., 288 pop.), named for the ring of woods encircling the town. The site was homesteaded in 1895, and the township platted and lots sold at auction in 1901.

At 33.3 *m.* is the junction with State 8, an improved dirt road.

Right on State 8 to CLEO SPRINGS, 1 *m.* (1,242 alt., 386 pop.), which, according to legend, was named for an Indian maiden and the near-by presence of clear-water springs. There is a large swimming pool *(free),* fed by the limpid spring water, in the town.

The wide, sandy CIMARRON RIVER, 34.3 *m.,* is typical of all river beds in the western part of Oklahoma; shifting sands allow the channel to change course frequently, and gypsum deposits have given the banks a bare and desolate air.

ORIENTA, 36.2 *m.* (1,245 alt., 37 pop.), a farming hamlet, is at the junction with State 15, an improved dirt road.

Right from Orienta on State 15 are the gypsum-covered buttes of the GLASS MOUNTAINS, 5 *m.,* so named because their surface is covered by millions of tiny, sparkling selenite crystals. The abruptly-rising, fancifully-shaped hills are a part of the Blaine Escarpment, a great gypsum formation which extends across most of western Oklahoma. Geologists believe that water, through the centuries, has worn away the softer shales and clays, leaving the resistant gypsum to form a hard, protecting top. Gradual erosion has left strange formations—appearing to be feudal castles, or minarets, or human profiles—carved in solid caps of the gypsum, four to five feet thick. Large quantities of the selenite crystals and bands of satin spar cover the Glass Mountains, which range in height from a few feet to three hundred feet above the valley floor. Chunks of the crystal, clear as processed glass, may be picked up, but will crumble into powder when light pressure is applied.

One towering, crystalline rock, CATHEDRAL MOUNTAIN (300 alt.), 5.8 *m.* stands out from the rest—shaped like a great cathedral, with portals and towers. From a distance its thick layer of gypsum, which has been streaked a gray-green by the weather, gives the appearance of varicolored and mullioned windows. Westward from there, sand dunes have piled up on the edges of the mountains, covering some of the smaller peaks. Because the vicinity is so desert-like, there are few houses; even the perennial filling station has been routed.

US 60 is the main street of FAIRVIEW, 42.8 *m.* (1,302 alt., 1,913 pop.), the seat of Major County. The town is located on a flat plain in an agricultural section, with the Glass Mountains to the northwest and the Cimarron River valley to the east, making a setting of natural beauty. Because of the presence of gypsum in the water underlying the townsite, the city supply is piped from a source northeast of the Cimarron River. The water and electrical systems are both municipally owned.

West of Fairview, many of the farms seen for the first few miles belong to members of a separate sect of the Mennonites. This group, called the Church of God in Christ Mennonites, are descendants of German-Russians who first followed the teaching of Menno Simons (1492–1559), a Catholic priest who discarded the Roman faith to join the Anabaptists and then formed a new sect which eventually took his name. Their emblem is the cedar tree—chosen for its sturdy and resistant qualities—and their homes may be easily distinguished, for the yards are usually dotted with evergreens. The simple life is their creed, and they believe in a doctrine of nonparticipation in civil or military activities. They boast that none of their members has ever registered as a relief client; the financial status of each individual is under supervision of the church at large, its approval being necessary before debt can be incurred.

SEILING, 75.2 *m.* (1,760 alt., 629 pop.), was named for the original homesteader of the townsite. It is located in the fertile valley between the North and South Canadian rivers, with big-scale wheat raising as its main agricultural activity. In the spring and fall, races are held at the near-by Necklace Downs, earning for the town the sobriquet of "The little Louisville of the Southwest."

Amos Chapman, famous army scout in the days of the settlement of Oklahoma, lived at Seiling after his retirement and was buried in the family cemetery east of town. Chapman was the hero of the Buffalo Wallow fight *(see Texas Guide)* when he lost a leg attempting to save a soldier. His wife was a relative of Chief Black Kettle, the Cheyenne chief. General W. T. Sherman's aide-de-camp, Colonel Richard Dodge, said in his book, *Our Wild Indians,* that Amos Chapman was "one of the best and bravest scouts . . . I have ever known."

Seiling was also for a short period the home of the prohibition-crusader, Carry A. Nation. It was probably from here that she started many of her lecture tours and hatchet-wielding forays through the saloon-infested parts of Oklahoma Territory. Later she moved to Guthrie, where in 1905 she began to publish her newspaper, *The Hatchet (see Tour 10)*.

In Seiling are the junctions with US 270 *(see Tour 5)* and US 183 *(see Tour 12)*, which unite with US 60 for two miles. The route continues almost due west from this point to the Texas Line, traversing a high flat country in which timber grows only along the streams. Cattle-raising was once the dominant activity of the section, but agriculture (particularly wheat-raising) has gained ascendancy.

Near VICI, 96.2 *m.* (2,253 alt., 617 pop.), a cattle and farming center, are large quantities of bentonite, a clay used in the manufacture of cosmetics. The substance is also used in refining crude oil.

Westward, the rolling plains are covered with tumbleweed and yucca or soapweed—a sturdy plant of many sword-shaped leaves thrusting skyward abruptly from the earth, and adorned with tall spikes of creamy, drooping, bell-shaped flowers. The yucca withstands the most adverse weather conditions because of its long, tough roots; farmers dig and boil them to make a thick soap, and one commercial soap product is made entirely from the plant. In some places, the highway has been cut through red-clay hills; piles of brush, weighted with logs and stone, line the slopes to prevent dirt slides. Scattered clumps of scrub oak have been left infrequently to serve as windbreaks, but most of the small frame houses have no protection or shade.

At 122.7 *m.* is the eastern junction with US 283 *(see Tour 13)*, which unites westward with US 60 for 6.6 miles.

In the center of the ARNETT 123.2 *m.* (2,460 alt., 529 pop.), town square is the Ellis County Courthouse; also in the square is the public library. Near the town are several large ranches; one, the Berryman Ranch, has a herd of purebred cattle and a wildlife refuge stocked with quail and prairie chicken.

At 124.1 *m.* US 60 crosses the old INDIAN BUFFALO TRAIL, which ran from old Fort Supply *(see Tour 12)* to a huge buffalo wallow northeast of the Antelope Hills *(see Tour 13)* in a bend of the South Canadian River. Many Indian hunting parties once filed along this trail, and General George A. Custer and the Seventh Cavalry marched south on it from Fort Supply to the Washita River when they met the Cheyennes and allied tribes in the Battle of the Washita *(see Tour 13)*.

At 129.3 *m.* is the western junction with US 283.

Left at this point on a series of graded dirt roads; R. at 5.4 *m.*, L. at 6.4 *m.*, R. at 7.5 *m.*, and L. again at 8.3 *m.* to the BURNETT GRISTMILL, 12.8 *m.*, built by W. F. Burnett on his homestead about 1900, and run by the waters of near-by Little Robe Creek. The mill was abandoned in 1925, then used for several years as a canning factory; today (1941), the board walls are warped and peeling, the floor is sagging with the weight of stored baled hay and rusty mill machinery, and the huge paddle wheel is broken. The sturdy axle, which turned the wheel for many years, was originally hewn from a single tree and still is in place.

A story is told of a battle between Texas Rangers and a band of Comanches that supposedly took place near the site of the old mill. In the late spring of 1858, a detachment of Rangers, accompanied by friendly Tonkawa Indian scouts, came up the Red River and attacked a Comanche village which was then on Little Creek. Prohebits Quasho (Iron

Jacket), the band's war chief, rode out to greet the attackers, mounted on an iron-gray horse and wearing a rusty coat of mail—armor which had probably been taken from a Spanish explorer some generations before and handed down to each succeeding Comanche chieftain as an insignia of leadership and invulnerability. Iron Jacket courageously braved the fire of the rangers, the bullets having no effect other than to cause him to swerve back and forth. He passed unscathed through the barrage, warranting—even to some of the Rangers—the Comanches' belief that he bore a charmed life. But the bullet of one of the Tonkawa scouts found its mark in his neck, exposed for a moment as he abruptly turned his horse, and Iron Jacket fell dead. The Comanches were easily routed after the death of their leader.

US 60 crosses the Texas Line at 136.1 *m.,* twenty-seven miles northeast of Canadian, Texas *(see Texas Guide).*

Tour 5

Junction US 271 — McAlester — Oklahoma City — Watonga — Seiling; 299.5 m. US 270.

Roadbed alternately paved and graveled.
The Rock Island Ry. parallels the route between Junction US 271 and Watonga.
Accommodations available chiefly in towns and cities; few tourist camps.

Both in the eastern and western parts of the state, US 270 passes through rugged country—mountainous and wooded, bald and hilly. In the middle section are fertile valleys where busy cities have grown steadily from Territorial villages or shot up abruptly after the discovery of oil.

Constantly changing, too, are the racial strains of the people. At its eastern end, where US 270 tops the northern edge of the peaceful, green Winding Stair mountain range, the Choctaw Indians once established a republic. Earlier, intrepid French explorers had left their stamp in the naming of the Fourche Maline and the Sans Bois foothills. Later, swarthy Italians came to mine the valuable coal deposits of the section. West of McAlester, US 270 passes through land formerly belonging to the unhappy and sometimes turbulent Seminoles, the hospitable Creeks, and the smaller groups of Shawnees, Potawatomis, and the recalcitrant Kickapoos. Here the route crosses one of the greatest oil fields of the state.

Northwest of El Reno are strange formations of bare gypsum hills, through which the North Canadian River cuts a gash to reveal peculiarly beautiful red soil, heightened and contrasted by growths of cedar trees. The Cheyenne and Arapaho Indians once ranged there, and later the abstaining

Amish, Dunkard, and River Brethren flocks made their homes in isolated communities. Calm and unchanged, they adhere to the tenets and customs of their forefathers.

Section a. JUNCTION US 271 *to* McALESTER, *59.9 m. US 270*

US 270 branches west from its junction, 0 *m.,* with US 271 *(see Tour 7)* at a point 14.3 miles southwest of Poteau *(see Tour 7).*

Plans have been drawn for the construction of a dam at the confluence of the Fourche Maline and the Poteau rivers a few miles southeast of this junction, creating a large lake which would parallel the highway. No definite action (1941) has been taken, however.

In the nineteenth century, this wooded and mountainous section was dotted with many Choctaw settlements, but today only scattered piles of stone mark their sites. After the coming of the railroads, coal mining was an important industry, but with the decreased demand for coal and the concerted development of more productive areas, these mines are being worked on only a small scale. Agriculture and tourist trade are the industrial mainstays of the region.

RED OAK, 14.2 *m.* (590 alt., 484 pop.), is a small farming center which was named for a large red oak tree that stood in the center of the town when this region was the Choctaw Nation. The Indians held district court there and used the oak as a whipping post.

The most serious political disturbance in the history of the Choctaw Nation had its finale at Red Oak when Silan Lewis was executed for his part in the Nationalist uprising at Antlers *(see Tour 7),* following the election of 1892. The fullblood Lewis, who had once been sheriff of his own district, upheld the traditional Choctaw honor when he came striding in from his woodland home on the appointed day, November 5, 1894, and quietly sat with back against the tree to await his death from the firing squad.

WILBURTON, 27.1 *m.* (657 alt., 1,925 pop.), was named for Will Burton, a contractor employed in the construction of the Choctaw, Oklahoma, and Gulf Railroad (now Rock Island) through this vicinity in 1890. After completion of the railroad, coal mines were opened near Wilburton and much coal was shipped from here for a number of years; today (1941), mining operations have greatly decreased.

Right from Wilburton on State 2, a graveled highway, is the CHOCTAW INDIAN COMMUNITY SETTLEMENT PROJECT, 1.7 *m.,* established in 1933 as a rehabilitation measure. The settlement, which is operated under the colony plan, was built on 2,200 acres of unsold mineral land belonging to the Choctaws. The community hall and offices are grouped at the south end of the area, and the cottage homes are located on twenty-acre tracts; the construction work was done co-operatively by the Indians, who share their farm implements and other equipment. The project is supervised by the Indian agent at Wilburton.

ROBBER'S CAVE STATE PARK, 4.3 *m.,* a mountainous tract of 8,400 acres, is one of the largest recreation areas owned by the state. The canyons, pine-covered hills, streams, and huge rocks of the Sans Bois range are visible from the winding highway and the many foot trails. Six miles of the sparkling, clear Fourche Maline Creek, running swiftly over rock bottom, are within the park; in places, the stream has cut deep gorges, lofty cliffs, and imposing bluffs. The Fourche Maline has been damned to form Lake Carlton, a fifty-two-acre basin; work on the lake, the grounds, and recreation facilities was done by CCC workers under the direction of the National Park Service. The entire area is enclosed with a seven-foot, all-steel fence because the park has been designated as a game refuge.

In the center of the park is the TOM HALE BOY SCOUT CAMP *(No trespassing; permission to camp may be obtained from caretaker at headquarters building), 7.6 m.,* covering 140 acres adjoining Fourche Maline Creek. The camp was named for Tom Hale, a generous contributor to welfare projects for the young people of southeastern Oklahoma, and has accommodations for 175 boys. The buildings were constructed of native stone at an estimated cost of $50,000.

Just north of the scout camp is ROBBER'S CAVE, for which the park was named. Steps have been carved to the mouth one hundred feet up the side of a sandstone cliff. Within the cave are many chambers, tunnels, and labyrinths supposed to have been used as hiding places by outlaws. Legend has it that loot once cached by early-day robbers and highwaymen is still buried in the cave, and many treasure-seekers visit here yearly. One story is told of "Fiddlin' Jim," an admirer of the notorious Belle Starr *(see Tour 2)* who was slain here by a jealous rival as he sat playing his fiddle at the entrance of the cave. Natives say that a weird melody is heard when the harvest moon shines—"Fiddlin' Jim" is playing again.

At 28.9 *m.* on US 270 is the western junction with State 2.

Left on State 2 to the SPANISH WAR VETERANS' COLONY, 8 *m.,* founded in 1936 and controlled by the Oklahoma group of the United Spanish War Veterans. The 760-acre tract is owned by the organization, which retains the deed to the land although a veteran and his family may, for a $5.00 fee, build a house here and remain for life. More than thirty houses, a large administration building, and a central office building have been constructed of native stone and pine. Individual gardens, a communal orchard, wild fruit and berries, good fishing streams, and free pasturage for their cattle provide the colonists the most needed foodstuff.

The EASTERN OKLAHOMA AGRICULTURAL AND MECHANICAL COLLEGE, 30.1 *m.,* is a state junior college (R), founded in 1909 as a School of Mines and Metallurgy. Wilburton citizens gave sixty acres of land to establish the school, which was a mining engineering institution until it was closed for two years during the first World War. After the war, the Federal government operated it for several years as an industrial training school for disabled veterans. In 1927, the name was changed to the Eastern Oklahoma College, and a general college curriculum was established in addition to vocational secondary work. In 1935, the state legislature authorized the school to care for and educate dependent youths and orphans; many counties are now taking advantage of this benefit and sending deserving youths to the school. The name of the college was changed again in 1939 to conform to the specific courses now being offered in addition to the regular program. A 270-acre farm, well-equipped machine shop, men's and women's dormitories, administration building, and dairy barn comprise the campus unit.

GOWEN, 38.2 *m.* (691 alt., 633 pop.), a coal-mining center, was once the home of the popular Negro screen actor, Stepin Fetchit (Lincoln Perry). The one-mile walk from his home to the school here was "jes too much," so the story goes, and he rarely attended; but he so successfully capitalized his laziness that he rose from a $3-a-week job with a medicine show to his present (1941) status as a well-known movie character actor. His screen name has evolved from the consistent answer he makes to a request for action, "I'll step'n fetchit purty soon."

At 45 *m.* is a junction with a narrow lane.

Right on this lane to the JONES ACADEMY, 0.5 *m.*, an Indian boys' school established by the Choctaw tribe in 1891 as a companion school to the Tuskahoma Female Academy *(see Tour 7)*. The institution was named for Wilson N. Jones, then principal chief of the Choctaws, and became the most important of the tribal boys' schools after the Spencer Academy near Soper *(see Tour 6)* burned in 1896. The Choctaw Indians still own the buildings and grounds, but the academy is at present (1941) supported by Federal appropriations. The course includes vocational and agricultural training.

In this vicinity, Bernard de la Harpe, the French explorer, camped in 1719 during his expedition to the Arkansas River, where he hoped to make treaties with Indian tribes.

HARTSHORNE, 45.4 *m.* (705 alt., 2,596 pop.), and HAILEYVILLE, 47.3 *m.* (612 alt., 1,183 pop.), were both established about 1890 and platted in 1902, and both have coal mining as their principal industry. Hartshorne was named for Dr. Hartshorne, an early settler, and Haileyville for Dr. David Morris Hailey (1841-1919), who emigrated to Oklahoma from Louisiana after the Civil War. Dr. Hailey assisted in sinking the first coal mine shaft in the McAlester district of the large Pittsburg County field. His portrait hangs in the State Confederate Memorial Hall of the Oklahoma Historical Society Building in Oklahoma City.

Since both towns have depended almost entirely on coal mining for livelihood, populations and community wealth have decreased since the cessation of large-scale mining activities. Between Hartshorne and Haileyville, residences and shops line the highway, and an interurban service is maintained for the short distance. Farming, lumbering, and livestock-raising have to a certain extent replaced the mining industry in the district.

A pioneer coal-mining settlement, ALDERSON, 55.3 *m.* (680 alt., 340 pop.), was the scene of an unusual labor situation in 1894. The Choctaw Nation required the mining corporations to pay a small monthly tax for each employee. As the result of a strike by the miners over a 25 per cent wage reduction, the company refused to pay the tax; and the workers thereby automatically became intruders in Indian Territory. The Choctaw Chief then asked that the miners be removed from his nation since the tribe received no royalties when the mines were closed. The appeal passed through the offices of the Commissioner of Indian Affairs, the Secretary of the Interior, and finally to President Cleveland, who approved it. Three companies of infantry and two of cavalry were dispatched to deport the group; Alderson was designated as troop headquarters and all arrested miners were brought here. Approximately two hundred workers and their families were loaded into boxcars and taken to Jenson, Arkansas, the nearest town outside of Indian Territory from this point.

The governor of Arkansas protested against the action, and Italy and Great Britain, since many of the evicted miners were citizens of these countries, also protested through the State Department. But the strike was broken, mines resumed operations shortly, and royalties once more poured into the Choctaw treasury.

KREBS, 58.4 *m.* (715 alt., 1,436 pop.), was built in the midst of coal mines that are now (1941) abandoned, and great piles of waste rock may still be seen throughout the town. Many Italian miners, who first came when the mines were flourishing, are engaged in farming today.

Wide differences in the background of these early settlers and the confusing circumstances of rule by Choctaw law, Federal courts, and the Indian agent gave the town an unsavory reputation during Territorial days. Legal restrictions regarding the importation, sale, and manufacture of liquor differed and allowed so many loopholes for violation that Krebs became known for its production of a drink called Choctaw or "choc" beer, made of hops, tobacco, fishberries, barley, and alcohol. In 1895, Congress enacted a law which was sufficiently comprehensive to override all previous judgments, and "choc" beer was finally made illegal.

A drug store, established here in 1888, is still operating. It has been the scene of many emergency treatments, for in Indian Territory days there were no hospitals, and numerous injuries, gas burns, and explosions occurred in the near-by mines. Vaseline was stocked in five-hundred-pound quantities, raw linseed oil in fifty-barrel lots, and iodoform in ten-pound lots. One particular explosion caused by blackdamp in 1892 kept the store open day and night for two weeks. A story is told about the tattered clothes of an Italian victim of this tragedy; in their haste, rescuers hung the articles on a fence, where they flapped in the wind for days until the brother of the man identified them and, upon examination, found $975 sewed in the ragged jumper.

McALESTER, 59.9 *m.* (718 alt., 12,401 pop.), started as a tent store at the crossroads of two well-traveled Indian Territory roads, the California Trail and the Texas Road. The heavy traffic of the Texas Road, used until 1872 when the Missouri-Kansas-Texas Railroad built tracks almost parallel with it, and the influx of adventurers along the California Trail after the discovery of gold in 1849 made a flourishing business for James J. McAlester, who established the crossroads store in 1870.

McAlester is also given credit for the discovery of coal in Pittsburg County. A geologist's memorandum book, telling of rich deposits of the mineral, had fallen into his hands and this resulted in his coming to Indian Territory. After his arrival, McAlester married a Chickasaw girl and thus became a citizen of the Choctaw Nation, since by the treaties of 1837 and 1855 the two tribes owned their land in common and enjoyed full citizenship rights in either nation. When the coming of the railroad made mining operations possible, he and other Choctaw citizens began extracting the coal under a Choctaw constitutional provision allowing a citizen the right to mine for a mile in every direction any mineral discovered by him. Controversy resulted when the Choctaw government claimed the royalty which McAlester's group began to receive from the lessees. Legality of the transaction was approved by the tribal court, but Chief Coleman Cole expressed his opposition to the mines by sentencing McAlester and three of the co-owners to death. They escaped, however, with the aid of their guard, and a compromise later settled the affair by giving half the royalty to the Choctaw Nation and the other half to the mine owners. McAlester later became lieutenant governor of Oklahoma (1911–15).

The town which grew up around the founder's store is now called North

McAlester; the main part of present-day McAlester developed later when the Rock Island Railway built to a junction with the Missouri-Kansas-Texas line. The city is laid out over a series of hills, with the main business district on one hill. US 270, which becomes Grand Avenue, one of McAlester's important thoroughfares, passes the PITTSBURG COUNTY COURTHOUSE, Grand Avenue and 2d Street, and the chief hotels. The red-brick courthouse is constructed in a U-shape around an elevated concrete court and sits flush with the street.

The OHOYAHOMA CLUBHOUSE, North Main Street and Park Avenue, is an unpretentious frame building with porch, lean-to, and stone chimney. It was built in 1876 and served as the Tobucksy County Courthouse in the days of the Choctaw Nation. After the absorption of the Choctaws into United States citizenry, the building fell into disuse; recently it was purchased and restored by the Ohoyahoma Club, a local organization of Indian women. The club maintains a MUSEUM *(free)* in the building with a large collection of authentic Indian articles on display.

The INDIAN SCOTTISH RITE CONSISTORY, Adams Avenue and 2d Street, one of the two consistories in Oklahoma, is a huge, block-long, cream-colored brick and stone building elaborately decorated with algonite and Carthage stone. A great copper sphere, rising fifty feet above the roof, contains multicolored lenses and when lighted may be seen for several miles. Will Rogers received Scottish Rite degrees here in 1908.

Meat packing, cotton-oil milling, macaroni manufacture, lumbering, and dry gas drilling make up the city's important commerce.

McAlester is at the junction with US 69 *(see Tour 8)*.

Right from McAlester on the graveled Rainbow Highway to the OKLAHOMA STATE PENITENTIARY *(9-11:30 A.M. and 1-3 P.M. Tues. and Fri.; guide provided)*, 1 *m.*, where more than three thousand prisoners are confined in the ten-acre tract enclosed by a fourteen-foot concrete wall. The main structures within the wall spread out fanwise from the large Administration Building facing south. The 1,985-acre farm west of the penitentiary is worked by the inmates. There is a branch of the Central State Hospital for the Insane *(see Norman)* on state-owned land adjoining the penitentiary; only senile dementia cases are treated here. Rainbow Highway parallels the east wall of the penitentiary and curves around a long hill to a gateway, 2.4 *m.*

Right through this gateway to LAKE NO. 1 *(camp sites, fishing)*, 0.2 *m.;* LAKE NO. 2 is separated from it by a small dam.

The main side route continues to a junction with a graveled road, 8 *m.;* L. here a short distance at the top of a steep hill, overlooking Lake McAlester, are the RAINBOW GARDENS *(apply for adm., 319 E. Grand, McAlester)*, on a beautifully landscaped seventy-five-acre estate owned and controlled by the girls' organization, the Order of the Rainbow. This international character-building society for girls from thirteen to twenty years of age was founded in 1922 by Rev. W. Mark Sexson, of McAlester, under the sponsorship of the Order of the Eastern Star. The supreme Office of the Rainbow order is in McAlester; in addition to the United States units, Canada, Australia, Alaska, and the Canal Zone have chapters.

The dining hall, kitchen, sleeping quarters, counselor's home, bathhouses, and the caretaker's cottage are all built of native stone and provide accommodations for fifty girls. The gardens are set in the natural rock formations of the hilly tract, with many transplanted flowers dotting the available spaces of soil between the sloping ledges. From the Temple of Silence, a stone clubhouse in which the floors are painted with a giant rainbow, the Path of Initiation skirts a hill, leads into the heart of a canyon, and then passes over the shoulder of another hill to a place representing (in ritual) the House of Gold. For ten days, while in camp, the initiate spends a portion of her time tracing a symbolic journey along the pathway.

A dirt road *(impassable in wet weather)* starts at LAKE McALESTER DAM, 9.1 *m.,* and encircles the thirty-five mile shore line of LAKE McALESTER *(fishing, 50c a day)*. The road is fringed with cabins, stores, and minnow ponds, and the lake is kept stocked with several varieties of game fish by the city of McAlester, which maintains culture ponds near by. The best fishing is said to be from boats in the center of the 2,500-acre lake.

Section b. McALESTER *to* HARRAH, *112 m. US 270*

From McALESTER, 0 *m.,* US 270 angles to the northwest, passing through widespread oil fields, including the Seminole and Oklahoma City areas, the two largest in the state. Drilling rigs—mostly the slim 130-foot steel derricks—oil-field camps, and tool shops are seen frequently on both sides of the highway.

The huge whitewashed, stone chimney of WHITE CHIMNEY, 16 *m.,* a log house (R) said to have been constructed in 1828, served as a guidepost on an old wagon road through this vicinity. An Indian named Honubby built it, but after he moved away it became a rendezvous for outlaws. Numerous bullet holes are visible in the walls and posts, substantiating the story that many crimes were committed in the house; a recent tenant is said to have unearthed human bones while digging a cellar.

At 31.1 *m.* is the southern junction with US 75 *(see Tour 9),* which unites with US 270 as the route makes an abrupt turn north. At 40.8 *m.,* the northern junction with US 75, US 270 turns sharply westward.

HOLDENVILLE, 49.1 *m.* (866 alt., 6,632 pop.), the seat of Hughes County, is on the eastern edge of the Greater Seminole oil field. Farm trade also contributes to the town's business activities.

A small combination store and post office called Fentress was operated about two miles from the site of the present town when the Choctaw, Oklahoma, and Gulf Railroad (now Rock Island) surveyed the townsite in 1895. When the survey was completed, the Post Office Department designated the new site, Fentress, and so it was called for a short time until the name of Holdenville was approved.

The HUGHES COUNTY COURTHOUSE, a native stone structure, housed a Federal court in Indian Territorial days and has served as the county governmental building since statehood.

Left from Holdenville on asphalt-paved State 68 to LAKE HOLDENVILLE *(fishing, boating),* 4.5 *m.,* a 550-acre body of water (L), with a well-timbered fourteen-mile shore line.

At 6 *m.* is the SITE OF FORT HOLMES (R), on the south bank of the Little River near its confluence with the South Canadian. Fort Holmes or Fort Edwards, as it later came to be known, was established in 1834 under the supervision of Lieutenant Theopolis Hunter Holmes, an officer of the dragoon expedition that had been sent out from Fort Gibson *(see Tour 3)* to meet the Plains Indians and make treaties with them. Fort Holmes was soon abandoned but a firm of traders, Edwards and Shelton, established a trading post just across the river and for years it flourished as Edwards' Settlement and Trading House or Fort Edwards. Jesse Chisholm, half-blood Cherokee and famous guide and scout for whom the well-traveled Chisholm Trail *(see Tour 11)* was named, married Edwards' daughter and lived at the post for a time. It was on the busy California Trail and was also a favorite trading place for many of the southwestern Indian tribes who not only brought furs and pelts to trade but also white prisoners. The Comanche Indians, in particular, trafficked in human beings, usually kidnapping the whites at isolated settlements in Texas and exchanging them for merchandise at trading posts or for ransom at Fort Gibson.

Between Holdenville and Wewoka there are many field camps of the oil companies of the Greater Seminole Field. The comparatively shallow wells are equipped with shorter derricks than those seen in the Oklahoma City Field *(see Oklahoma City)*.

WEWOKA, 60.4 *m.* (788 alt., 10,315 pop.), the seat of Seminole County, was named for one of the former Creek tribal towns in the East; when the Seminole Indians, who were affiliated for a time with the Creek confederacy, branched from the league, they also had an eastern Wewoka town, and transferred the name to this site in Indian Territory at the time of their removal.

A controversy developed in 1845 over the Seminoles' migration to the Territory. They agreed to settle on Creek land and under Creek government; but the comparatively free status of their Negro slaves was distasteful to the Creeks, whose own slaves were held in stricter bondage. The Negroes among the Seminoles had a status similar to that of renters or sharecroppers of today; they lived in separate villages and enjoyed equal liberty, paying a portion of their crops for the use of the Seminole land. They could even own land on which their masters made no claim. When the United States General Thomas S. Jesup was conducting his campaign to subdue the Seminole tribe in Florida, he had promised the Creek Indians that they might have all the Seminole slaves they could capture. But the Federal Attorney General later ruled that all Negroes taken under Jesup's order were to be restored to the Seminoles, and 286 Negroes from Florida were accordingly delivered to a group of Seminole chiefs at Fort Gibson in January, 1849.

The Creek Indians were resentful over the decision and passed a law declaring that no town of free or limited slavery Negroes could exist in their country and also forbidding the possession of arms by slaves. The Negroes had already settled in the vicinity of present Wewoka and, aware of the hostility of the Creeks, had armed themselves. On June 24, 1849, an armed party of Creeks, with some whites and Cherokees, came to Wewoka to seize several Negroes whom they claimed were rightfully their slaves. Many of the Seminole Indians prepared to aid in the defense of the Negro town, but troops from Fort Smith, Arkansas, intervened in time to stop the battle. A council was held, and a few of the Negroes claimed by the Creeks were turned over to them; the threat of a real war between the two tribes subsided.

As an aftermath of the dispute and in accordance with a treaty signed in 1856 by the Creeks, the Seminoles, and the United States, the Seminole tribe was assigned a separate domain. When they purchased their present tract of land in 1866, a mistake was made in surveying the boundary line but it was not discovered until after Wewoka, which straddles the line, had been established as the Seminole capital. The boundary between the Creek and Seminole nations has remained a subject of friction even since allotment, mainly because of public improvements, like schools, which were built by the Seminoles on land found later to belong to the Creeks. Present-day Seminole

Street (one-half block east of Main Street) in Wewoka was the last-named true boundary between the two nations.

The government set up by the Seminoles in their new land in 1866 was the most primitive of those of the Five Civilized Tribes. The principal chief, his assistant, the treasurer, and the superintendent of schools were elected by the people, and a council, composed of fourteen clan chiefs, assumed both the legislative and judicial duties. The only record of law was written in a book kept by the chief. Twenty "lighthorsemen" performed police duty and also officiated at floggings and executions.

The chief and the treasurer personally owned trading posts where they extended credit to enrolled citizens in anticipation of the per capita payments due them.

The railroad through Wewoka was constructed in 1899, and a townsite laid out shortly after, but white settlers did not arrive until 1902. Though oil was first discovered there in 1912, the region of the Greater Seminole Field was not developed until 1926. Wewoka's population doubled within sixty days at that time, and for several years it ranked as one of the principal oil towns of the state.

Seminole County and the immediate vicinity of Wewoka is the foremost corn-growing region of Oklahoma; it has won first prize almost consistently at the State Fair since 1926, when the Oklahoma Silvermine species was first produced in the county. It is estimated that fifteen hundred bushels of Silvermine seed have been shipped to other states and foreign countries since that year; some of the seed corn has sold for as high as $5.00 a bushel.

The COUNTY COURTHOUSE, Wewoka Avenue on Courthouse Square, is a modern, three-story brick building; similar in design is the CITY HALL, 204 South Wewoka Avenue.

An old pecan tree, Courthouse Square, was used as a TRIBAL WHIPPING POST from 1899 until statehood (1907); it replaced the original "execution tree," the stump of which is now (1941) on exhibition in the Oklahoma Historical Society Building *(see Oklahoma City)*.

Right from Wewoka on paved State 56, 1 *m.,* to the last COUNCIL HOUSE OF THE SEMINOLES, now used as a residence on the Youngblood farm. It was built about 1890 and replaced the brush-covered arbor that had previously served as the tribal capitol. Here, too, were the campgrounds and the big spring of the Seminoles.

Right from the former Council House to the old "Line Store," 1 *m.,* built about 1867 by Ard Brothers to serve the traffic on the route westward from Fort Smith to a terminus on the Wichita Indian reservation. Present-day Lawton is on the site of this terminus.

At 62 *m.* is a junction with an improved dirt road.

Right on this road to LAKE WEWOKA *(swimming, fishing, free campgrounds, recreational facilities)*. 1.4 *m.* The lake, three miles long, supplies water for Wewoka.

In the valley midway between the North and South Canadian rivers is SEMINOLE, 72.4 *m.* (863 alt. 11,547 pop.), named for the Seminole Indians, who originally were a branch of the Creek confederation. Their habit of living apart gave them the name Seminole, which means "wild" or, literally, "those who camp at a distance."

When the Mekusukey Mission was built three miles southwest of the site of the present city in 1890, shipments of freight for the mission were billed to a "Mr. Tidmore," and until the Post Office Department officially named it Seminole, the sleepy little settlement was called Tidmore. Cattlemen of the surrounding territory made it a trading center, but from statehood until 1926 Seminole remained just a small agricultural community.

In that year one of the greatest oil pools in the history of the nation was tapped. Overnight the population jumped to several thousand, and the usual meager country town facilities were strained to the utmost to care for the influx of people—many slept under pool tables while the click of balls went on ceaselessly, others slept in motion picture houses, and thousands walked the streets; the water supply was soon depleted and no one bathed, for the precious fluid had to be hauled from a distance and the price was exorbitant; fabulous rentals ranged from $400 a month for a basement and $200 for a barn to $50 for one room in a smokehouse; farm produce was scarce and commanded "Klondike Gold Rush" prices, for farmers had exchanged the plow for the drilling rig.

For six months during 1926, the Rock Island Railway did more than a million dollars worth of business in Seminole; it was claimed that only the great shipping center at Chicago exceeded the town in volume of freight during that period.

Vice and crime became the boom town's biggest problem, since gamblers and riffraff from every section of the country had been lured to Seminole by the plentiful "black gold." W. A. Bishop, an attorney who had lived peacefully in a big house on the edge of town, suddenly found that a suburb called Bishop's Alley had mushroomed at his doorstep—and Bishop's Alley soon became known far and wide for its "49er's Dance Hall," the "Big C," and the "Palace." Bootlegging, dope-peddling, brawls, hijacking—with an occasional mysterious murder—were daily fare along the street. After the killing of a state peace officer, a crusade was started by Seminole citizens, backed by the state press and officials, and the lawless element vanished.

Today (1941), Seminole is a substantial and civic-minded city—the hectic days are over for the oil flow has been steadied by proration, a check on production and price regulation first introduced because of the immense reservoir discovered in this field, and later embodied in a compact between the oil states. Some scars from the roaring twenties still remain—next door to beautiful modern homes stand clapboard shacks, thrown up in a few hours in the housing exigency of 1926. The more than fifteen thousand people who live in company camps within a ten-mile radius of the city make Seminole a busy place. The oil field continues to be the main industry; but agriculture is also important in this fertile region.

The Seminole High School, 501 N. Timmons Street, a large buff building of concrete and stone, also houses the SEMINOLE JUNIOR COLLEGE. This coeducational college has an annual enrollment of approximately eighty and is supported entirely by tuition fees. It is operated in connection with the city public schools and is under the supervision of the city superintendent.

Southwest from Seminole to the SITE OF MEKUSUKEY MISSION, 3 *m.*, built in 1890 by the Seminole Indians as part of their tribal school system and supervised by the Presbyterian

Church until the Federal government took over the Indian schools in 1906. The institution was closed in 1930. The red sandstone brick used in the construction of the buildings was hauled overland by oxen from Muskogee. An unexpected bonus of $35 per capita was paid to each enrolled member of the tribe in 1934 when oil was discovered on the school grounds to which the Seminole tribe still retained the title. The wells are producing today (1941), though on a minor scale.

Seminole is at the junction with State 99 *(see Tour 14)*.
SHAWNEE, 90 *m.* (1,008 alt., 22,053 pop.) *(see Shawnee)*.

Left from Shawnee on paved State 18 to a cluster of buildings, 2.5 *m.*, the SHAWNEE INDIAN SANITORIUM (L), the SHAWNEE INDIAN AGENCY (R,) the old SHAWNEE QUAKER MISSION (L), and the MISSION CEMETERY (R). The entire center started when the Society of Friends built the tiny, white, frame Shawnee Quaker Mission in 1885. Their missionaries had previously held services in log cabins in the Shawnee lands until one of them, Franklin Elliot, completed this single-room church, set facing east on a hill. The lumber was hauled from Independence and Coffeyville, Kansas, over a route that was unbroken much of the way. The heavy iron bell, still hanging in the open belfry, was brought overland in the same manner. After white infiltration into the surrounding vicinity, the two races worshiped in the old mission until it was abandoned in 1924. Since then, it has been opened only once for the wedding of the granddaughter of Anthony Bourbonnais, one of the three Indian men who hauled the original lumber. In co-operation with the Quaker Church, which still retains the title to the accompanying three and one-half acres of land, the Pottawatomie County Historical Society has restored the old landmark and the near-by Mission Cemetery.

A school was conducted as a part of the early work of the old Quaker Mission; the supervision was later transferred to the government, which continued to maintain it as an educational institution until 1918. In 1925, the Department of the Interior decided to utilize the plant as a sanitarium to combat the ever-growing prevalence of tuberculosis among the Indians. Accordingly, the Shawnee Indian Sanitorium was established on the site of the school and the 240 acres of surrounding land. Materials from the old buildings were used in construction of the present plant of fifteen units, centering around a large, modern, fireproof, brick infirmary.

The Shawnee Indian Agency, which ministers to the 1,107 enrolled Indians, was established by the Federal government on government-owned land near by; the white frame structures include an administration building, stores, and living quarters for employees.

At 93 *m.* on US 270 is the junction with a graveled drive.

Right on this drive is ST. GREGORY'S COLLEGE FOR YOUNG MEN, 0.3 *m.*, a large, red-brick and white-stone, five-story structure considered one of the best examples of Tudor Gothic design in the Southwest. Turrets surmount the four corners of the square tower. Part of the hundred-acre campus is cultivated for the institution's food supply.

The school, which offers accredited junior college and high school courses to the approximately one hundred students, is an outgrowth of the work of the Benedictine Fathers of Sacred Heart Abbey *(see Tour 14)* in the southern part of Pottawatomie County. The Abbey, which was established in 1876 on a land grant from the Potawatomi Indians, was burned in 1901; it was rebuilt and is now (1941) used as a home for the fathers in their old age. The early school work of the order was perpetuated in the founding of St. Gregory's here in 1915.

The GERRER MUSEUM AND ART GALLERY *(open to public during school terms, 1-5 P.M. Sun.)* has an outstanding display of paintings and art objects which have been collected over a period of twenty-five years by Rev. Gregory Gerrer. Father Gerrer, who is a distinguished artist, painted the official portrait of Pope Pius X which hangs in the Vatican at Rome. Although he was the youngest of the six famous artists invited to paint the Pope's portrait in 1902, his work was chosen as the finest; it was later exhibited at the Louisiana Purchase Exposition in St. Louis, Missouri, in 1904, and at the Century of Progress World's Fair in Chicago, Illinois, in 1933–34. A replica of the brilliantly colored and expressive likeness is in the art gallery here. Seventy-three of the 176 paintings exhibited in St. Gregory's east and west parlors were executed by Father Gerrer; his other subjects include Indian portraits, landscapes, and still-life pictures done in Oklahoma and during his travels in the United States and abroad.

The gallery has priceless canvases by the Renaissance artists Il Guercino, Raphael, Murillo, Aretino Spinello, Guido Reni, José de Ribera, and others. One is the famous painting, "The Adoration of the Magi," by Giulio Romano, pupil of Raphael. Whistler and Rembrandt are among those represented in the group of etchings; several works by the Kiowa Indian artists—Mopope, Asah, and Auchiah, of Anadarko *(see Tour 3)*—are also on display.

The museum contains a comprehensive and varied collection of four thousand specimens, art objects, and curios gathered from all parts of the world. Egyptian mummies; skulls; strange and ancient seeds and nuts; old copies of newspapers; specimens of minerals (many representative of Oklahoma formations); native and foreign woods, shown in cross section; mounted and classified rare birds, mammals, and reptiles; antique and modern firearms and medieval armor; primitive utensils, Indian handicraft, rare Oriental art works, and antiques of Babylonian, Greek, Roman, Aztec, and Toltec origin are included in the various sections.

DALE, 100 *m.* (1,037 alt., 372 pop.), a farm trade center, was first established in 1889 as King's Post Office since it was located on the allotment of an Indian named John King. In 1890, it was moved two miles east and named Dale, in honor of Judge Frank Dale, a Federal Territorial Judge of Guthrie *(see Tour 10),* noted for his stern treatment of Territorial bad men. When the Choctaw, Oklahoma, and Gulf Railroad (now Rock Island) was built through this vicinity in 1895, Dale was moved to its present location; the buildings were loaded on wagons and moved intact.

On a hilltop about one mile from Dale is said to be the site of a Civil War encampment from which Confederate raiders made forays into Kansas. Well-defined trenches of the earthwork fortification still remain. Cartridge cases have been found near by.

In a rich farming section on the bank of the North Canadian River is McLOUD, 104.4 *m.* (1,058 alt., 616 pop.), established at the time of the extension of the railroad and named for John W. McLoud, railway attorney.

Right from McLoud on an improved dirt road to the junction with a second dirt road, 3 *m.;* R. here to KICKAPOO VILLAGE, 3.5 *m.,* where the Kickapoo Indians hold a ceremonial dance *(small adm. fee)* annually during the latter part of July. This well-defined tribal ritual was formerly a war dance; only elaborately costumed men performers take part.

The Kickapoos, closely related to the Sac and Fox tribe, were driven out of their former home in Illinois to the Southwest by the inexorable advance of the white man about the middle of the nineteenth century; a band of them drifted into Mexico, where they made frequent raids across the border into Texas. In order to solve this international problem, the United States persuaded them to return in 1873 and settled the tribe on a small reservation in this vicinity to become the peaceful neighbors of the Sax and Fox tribe, the Seminoles, the Potawatomis, the Shawnees, and the Iowas. But after the opening of near-by land in 1889, white settlers made a practice of cutting timber on the Kickapoo reservation and driving cattle there to graze, so angering the Indians that they were apparently ready to take to the warpath. Wild rumors reached the citizens of newly founded Oklahoma City to the northwest, and for a few days hurried and frenzied preparations were made for defense of the sodhouse and tent settlement. A Federal order prohibiting white men from encroaching on the Kickapoo reservation checked the rumored revolt, however, and the scare was over. When the government proposed to open their land for settlement in 1895, the tribe strenuously objected—since their treaty had made no provision for such action—and earned the name of the "Kicking Kickapoos." The majority of the remaining tribesmen now live on their allotments on the old reservation.

HARRAH, 112 *m.* (1,080 alt., 620 pop.) *(see Tour 3),* is at the junction with US 62 *(see Tour 3).*

Section c. HARRAH *to* SEILING, *127.6 m. US 270*

West of Harrah, US 270 passes through a well-populated section until it turns northwest into the Gypsum Hills—"Gyp Hills" as they are termed by cattlemen. Where erosion has worn away the top soil, ledges of dead-white gypsum stand out as though drawn with chalk. The hills, with bold, flat-topped knobs rising at intervals, extend for some one hundred miles across Blaine, Dewey, and Woodward counties. The Cheyenne and Arapaho Indians roamed in this section before it was assigned to them as a reservation *(see Tour 1).*

Westward from HARRAH, 0 *m.,* US 270 unites with US 62 to OKLAHOMA CITY, 24.1 *m.* (1,194 alt., 204,424 pop.) *(see Oklahoma City).*

In Oklahoma City is the junction with US 66 *(see Tour 1)* which unites with the route westward for 33.3 miles.

At 57.4 *m.* is the western junction with US 66; US 270 turns abruptly north (R).

CALUMET, 60.3 *m.,* is a small agricultural community in the fertile valley of the North Canadian River.

At 67.2 *m.* is the junction with an unimproved dirt road.

Left on this road is COYOTE BUTTE, 1.5 *m.,* formed by a ledge of white dolomite and affording an excellent view of the North Canadian River valley. Since dolomite is a harder and more resistant substance than sandstone, the butte is striking evidence of erosion through the years. This spot was a favorite meeting place for the Cheyenne and Arapaho Indians, whose present tribal center is only a few miles east at Concho *(see Tour 11).* Many gatherings took place here in 1890 during the "Ghost Dance" or "Messiah" craze *(see Tour 3A).* The fanatical belief of the devotees was that the Indian Messiah was coming, and anticipatory preparations for his arrival needed to be made; consequently the group meeting at this spot placed an iron bedstead, equipped with springs, mattress, and blankets, on the summit of the butte. The Indians' logical explanation of the action was, "When the white man's God came to visit His children, He was a poor man. He had no house. He had no bed. He had no money. The little bird had a nest in the tree, the coyote had a hole under a rock, but white man's God had no place to sleep. We are better than white man. When our God comes He will find that we, His people, have bed ready for Him."

Although named in honor of Ed Guerrier, a pioneer settler, this busy, farm trade center early became known as GEARY, 73.3 *m.* (1,499 alt., 1,634 pop.). The community was first established in 1898 on land which had belonged to the Cheyenne and Arapaho Indians until it was thrown open to settlement on April 19, 1892.

Since this is an important wheat-growing region, the flour mill located here is the prime industry; a cheese factory has also been established in Geary recently. The town has a $25,000 civic recreation park with a large swimming pool, baseball field, tennis and croquet courts. Near by is a Soil Conservation Camp, one of the Oklahoma soil-control units under the supervision of the Soil Conservation Service of the Department of Agriculture.

GREENFIELD, 80.8 *m.* (1,455 alt., 303 pop.), is a farming town named for William Greenfield, an early settler. Many Cheyenne and Arapaho Indians accepted their allotments and have continued to live near by; although their children attend the local public schools, the native tongue is spoken in most of the homes, and the tribal members gather often to hold ceremonials and dances.

Right from Greenfield on a graveled road to a junction with a dirt road, 4.5 *m.;* R. here to a farmhouse, 5.6 *m.;* in the pasture near the house is JESSE CHISHOLM'S GRAVE, on the side of a sloping knoll. Chisholm was the Cherokee half-blood who laid out the famous Chisholm Trail, now followed approximately by US 81 *(see Tour 11)*. His grave is marked by a simple wooden cross on which his name is inscribed.

Between Greenfield and Watonga, the route lies close to the North Canadian River (R) and makes a long curve around the Red Hills, a short outcropping of white dolomite and shale; at 88.4 *m.* the wide, sprawling, lazy river is crossed.

Named for an Arapaho chief, WATONGA, 89.9 *m.* (1,515 alt., 2,828 pop.), the seat of Blaine County, was first established in 1892. Many Cheyenne and Arapaho Indians still live in or near the town; and the older members of the tribes retain their traditional dress, the women in blankets and moccasins and the men with their hair in long black braids interwoven with gaily colored ribbons.

An important feature of the early history of Watonga was the publication of its first newspaper, the *Watonga Republican (see Newspapers)*. Its editor, Thompson B. Ferguson, was appointed by President Theodore Roosevelt as governor of Oklahoma Territory in 1901.

Three cotton gins and three grain elevators make Watonga the commercial center for the chief activity of the region, agriculture.

Right from Watonga on graveled State 8 is ROMAN NOSE STATE PARK *(picnicking, trailer camp, boating, swimming)*, 6.1 *m.*, named for Chief Henry Roman Nose, the last warrior-chief of the Cheyennes. Although the surrounding area is open prairie, the 520 acres comprising the park consists of rolling hills gashed by canyons and streams. The site served as a favorite camping ground for the Cheyenne Indians when they roamed freely through the region, and at the time of allotment Chief Roman Nose chose his 160-acre tract here. Near the dugout in which he lived was the "Spring of Everlasting Water," which today (1941) feeds the four-acre lake and swimming pool. Roman Nose, who had taken part in the Battle of the Washita *(see Tour 13)* as a member of Black Kettle's band, died here about 1917, but his many descendants still live near by.

An old military trail from Fort Reno *(see Tour 1)* to Fort Cantonment, northwest of the park, led through this area, and the sparkling, clear spring was usually chosen as a camping site by the Federal troops. Local legend tells of several Territorial outlaw bands who found the hills and canyons an ideal hiding place both for themselves and their loot.

The park land, marked irregularly by lines of exposed, white gypsum, was bought by the city of Watonga and deeded to the state, which developed the tract as a game sanctuary and recreational ground. The springs have a total flow of eight hundred gallons per minute and provide water for the several small streams, the newly created lake, and the concrete swimming pool. Recent improvements have been made in the area by CCC workers under the supervision of the National Park Service. Many squirrels and opossums inhabit the elms, cottonwoods, and cedars dotting the canyons, and native bushes afford shelter for the wild fowl.

Between Watonga and Seiling, the main route traverses an undulating plain with scattered growths of scrub oak and blackjack. During the winter, snow fences may be seen a short distance from the highway wherever the fields are rolling in character; for although snow is on the ground for only short periods, the intense winds would otherwise pile great drifts on the road. The rust-red fences, not familiar to most Oklahomans, look like grass matting, so closely are the thin, narrow laths placed together; in summer they are easily rolled up for storage.

The route again crosses the North Canadian River, 94.8 *m.,* bordered here by high sand dunes; the district is sparsely settled.

At 99.8 *m.* is the junction with State 33, a graveled highway. US 270 turns sharply northwest here.

Left on State 33 is THOMAS, 12.1 *m.* (1,513 alt., 1,220 pop.), an agricultural town platted in 1902 on land which had been homesteaded by Joseph W. Morris in the Run opening the Cheyenne and Arapaho territory ten years before. Extensive sweet potato fields furnish the town with an unusual industry, for the plants grown are of such excellence that seedlings are shipped from this point to all parts of the United States; a cannery makes the surplus crop marketable. There is also a Farmers' Co-operative grain elevator to handle the large wheat production of the surrounding farm lands.

Near Thomas are the homes and community settlements of three religious groups, the Amish, the Dunkards, and the River Brethren—all similar in general character and purpose with the Mennonites, though only the Amish are an actual branch of that sect.

The Amish, popularly called the "Hook-and-eye Dutch," first came to America from Holland and Switzerland in the seventeenth century, hoping to settle where they might be free from all hindrances in following their customs and institutions. They emigrated to New York and Pennsylvania, where they settled near the Quakers. Later, when the eastern United States began to become heavily settled, some of them came to their present home in Oklahoma. The forefathers of the Amish were among the first persons in America to protest against slavery. The present-day church still uses the German language in its services. Originally, the Amish did not permit private ownership of land, but today it is countenanced; they tend to marry within their sect and meet in their homes in small groups to worship, observing a fixed order of service. They consider color and style in clothing frivolous and unworthy; both men and women wear dull brown or rusty black, often in homespun materials, and all cut by a certain pattern—the women in long, full-skirted, high-necked, long-sleeved dresses and modest poke bonnets of the same color, and the men in straight sack coats, blunt-toed, high-laced shoes, and flat, widebrimmed hats with uncreased crowns. Neckties are never worn, nor are buttons used; the original European Amish began using the traditional hook-and-eye fastener as a protest against what they considered an unfair tax on buttons. The absence of whiskers on the smooth faces of the Amish men, with the exception of the distinctive rim around the chin, also began as a protest against taxation. The children are counterparts of their parents in appearance. Saturday is their market day, and the streets of Thomas are usually crowded with horse-drawn vehicles as whole families come to trade produce for merchandise.

The Dunkards or the Church of the Brethren, as they prefer to be known, are an outgrowth of the widespread church-reform movement in Europe in the early part of the eighteenth century; this sect originated in Germany, vowing to found a new church by baptism, and later the entire group emigrated to the United States. They observe the distinctive ritual of washing one another's feet, commemorating the act of Christ and His Disciples at the Last Supper. Besides the feet-washing ceremony, they observe the kiss of charity and the feast of love and lead a generally austere life, aloof from politics or current world upheavals. The sect is not as strict in matters of dress and custom as are the Amish, but the women observe certain conventions of dress: they use no cosmetics, arrange their hair in tight buns at back or on top of their heads, and wear tiny, plain poke bonnets of black silk or satin perched straight on the top of their heads and held in place by chin straps. The Dunkards are progressive farmers and have accepted many of the conveniences made available by present-day inventions.

The River Brethren (or Brethren in Christ) probably originated in Pennsylvania when the first group began the practice of immersion in the Susquehanna River. Their church tenets suggest a Mennonite origin, although they have no definite creed, merely stressing plain living, spiritual regeneration and sanctification. The Thomas church was founded by a missionary from Indiana who persevered until a church had been built, and several missions in the region and the Jabbok Bible School and Orphanage had been established. The school continued caring for orphans, both Indian and white, until 1925, when this part of the work was dropped; a dairy, run by the students, provides the chief source of revenue.

At 119.5 *m.* on the main route is the junction with State 51, a graveled highway.

Right on State 51 to a junction with a second graveled road, 11.2 *m.*

Left on this road to the CHEYENNE-ARAPAHO SUBAGENCY, 2.8 *m.*, on the site of old Fort Cantonment. The fort was established in the spring of 1879 and troops were billeted here to control the Cheyennes during the Plains Indian campaign *(see Tour 3A)*. The fort was located just sixty miles due northwest of the old Darlington Agency near the present Fort Reno *(see Tour 1)*, which also served the Cheyennes and Arapahoes; but the establishment of Cantonment was considered necessary because of the hostile feeling between the Southern Cheyennes, who were in home territory, and the Northern Cheyennes, who had been brought south from Nebraska and the Dakotas. Not long after the fort had been founded, a number of stone buildings were erected, three of which are still standing. After the dissatisfied Northern Cheyennes returned to their original home, the necessity for Fort Cantonment's existence decreased, and it was abandoned in 1882. The plant was then turned over to the Department of the Interior, which contracted with Mennonite missionaries to open a school for the Plains Indians.

The Mennonites conducted the school for a few years before erecting a private institution, and in 1898 the government took over the supervision of the Cantonment school, which it has maintained until the present time (1941). It is now a day school for children of the Cheyenne and Arapaho tribes.

The subagency was established in 1903, when the jurisdiction of the old Darlington Agency was divided. Ceremonial dances of the two tribes are frequently held here, and the ritual of the Peyote Dance, despite the absence of the forbidden peyote, is often observed.

Straight ahead on State 51 to CANTON, 12.9 *m.* (1,590 alt., 775 pop.), an agricultural and cattle-raising center which came into being as a result of the proximity of the old fort and the Indian school. The many Indians who lived near by trade in Canton and on Saturdays and holidays crowd the narrow streets.

Construction has begun on a $15,000,000 dam across the North Canadian River at a point one mile north of Canton and present (1941) plans call for its completion by 1942. The structure, three miles in length, will span the river at the turn of a sharp bend and will provide flood control, irrigation, and better water supply for the surrounding region.

Right from Canton on State 51, now a graded road, to the UNITED STATES GYPSUM COMPANY PLANT *(guides available)*, 19.2 *m.*, comprising mines and mills which have been operated by the company since 1912. Although totals vary according to business conditions, annual shipments of gypsum are estimated at from four to five thousand barrels; in addition, plaster board, partition tile, stucco plaster, gypsum plaster, and plate glass are manufactured. The entire property embraces one thousand acres of gypsum beds.

SEILING, 127.6 *m.* (1,760 alt., 629 pop.) *(see Tour 4)*, is at the junction with US 60 *(see Tour 4)* and with US 183 *(see Tour 12)*.

Tour 6

(De Queen, Ark.)—Hugo—Durant—Ardmore—(Burkburnett, Tex.); US 70. Arkansas Line to Texas Line, 268.5 m.

Intermittently paved roadbed of various types, also graveled and unimproved stretches. Texas, Oklahoma & Eastern R.R. parallels route between the Arkansas Line and Broken Bow; St. Louis–San Francisco between Idabel and Ardmore; Santa Fe, between Ardmore and Ringling.
Good accommodations in larger towns.

Passing between rich cotton lands to the south and what was once an area heavily timbered with pine and other marketable lumber trees, the route bisects the oldest Choctaw Indian settlements in Oklahoma. It is approximately the trail beaten out by the Choctaws as they pushed westward from their first settlement in the new land to which they were exiled from their Mississippi homes in 1831–33.

Between Idabel and Madill, US 70 roughly parallels the north bank of the Red River, keeping to the high ground above the wide river bottoms that are sometimes inundated at flood stage. West of Durant, the highway crosses the old Chickasaw Nation and completes its course in the southern edge of the former Kiowa-Comanche reservation.

Thus US 70 throughout its course in Oklahoma is reminiscent of Indian history. Along it were established the first schools and churches for the immigrant Choctaws and Chickasaws, their first mills and trading posts, and the few big plantations owned by enterprising mixed bloods. Beside it live the descendants of slaves freed by the Civil War from Indian masters, a considerable Negro population that for the most part cultivates small patches of cotton and corn in the cutover sections of the southern Kiamichi mountain slopes. Along this highway, if anywhere in Oklahoma, can be seen relics of the life lived by the Indians of the Five Civilized Tribes more than a century ago. On inconspicuous roads leading off from the main highway live what are known locally as "pure strain" Indians, full bloods who seem to have lagged a hundred years behind the world and who regret their backward state not at all!

US 70 crosses the ARKANSAS LINE, 0 *m.*, 8 miles west of De Queen, Arkansas *(see Arkansas Guide).*

EAGLETOWN, 6.7 *m.* (400 alt., 300 pop.), was the site chosen by one of the three district chiefs of the Choctaws, on the removal of the tribe to Indian Territory in 1831–33, as the principal town of the Upper Town people. The Choctaw name, Apukshunnubbee, was that of a chief who died just before the removal. The old district courthouse stands on the spot where the exiles' first building was erected; and there, too, is the big tree to which offenders against Choctaw laws were bound and whipped. On July 1, 1834, Eagletown was named a post office, one of the first to be established in Indian Territory, and the missionary Loring S. Williams was made postmaster.

From the first, the town was given added importance as a station on the military road from the East to Fort Towson and Doaksville; much later it was a headquarters for Texas cattlemen; and still later it was known as a rendezvous for outlaws—Indian, Negro, and white.

At 8.5 *m.* is the junction with a country lane.

Right on this lane is a farmhouse, 0.2 *m.;* R. here on foot trail to a CYPRESS TREE, 0.4 *m.,* on the south bank of Mountain Fork River in the midst of pines and sycamores. This ancient cypress is fifty-six feet in circumference and ninety feet high; the trunk is carved with many initials, hearts, flowers, and other devices. A lightning rod has been fixed in its top as protection against electric storms.

West of Eagletown some small pastures and barnyards are enclosed by old zigzag rail (worm) fences, and the dooryards have palings made by splitting six-foot lengths of logs with a mallet and frow, an old-fashioned tool for riving shakes, clapboards, and barrel staves.

At 8.5 *m.* US 70 crosses Mountain Fork River, a well-stocked fishing stream, one of the clearest and most beautiful of the Kiamichi mountain region. It plunges down to Little River over riffles and falls and between rock cliffs overhung by willows and tall gum trees. North of the highway, HOFFMAN'S CAMP *(cabins, boats, fishing gear),* a two-story stone building (R), is a favorite meeting place for sportsmen.

BROKEN BOW, 15.4 *m.* (467 alt., 2,367 pop.), center of the state's largest timbered area, was named by the Dierks Brothers, pioneer lumbermen, for their Nebraska home; the mill they erected still turns out its daily thousands of feet of white pine and hardwood lumber—hickory, walnut, and gum. Throughout the year, the aroma of fresh-cut pine fills the air and mingles with the acrid smell of coal smoke from the mill's tall stacks.

On Saturdays, the wide streets become a parade ground for the farmers of the region, among them overall-clad Choctaws and their families, who come to trade produce for groceries. An annual tomato festival is held here by the growers.

A few hundred feet west of the lumber mill (L) is the tall steel lookout tower of the STATE FORESTRY SERVICE *(open),* where a ranger is constantly on duty.

Broken Bow is at the junction with State 21 *(see Tour 15A).*

Westward, cotton fields lie on both sides of the road; and in the fall families of cotton pickers—Indians, Negroes, and whites—may be seen at work between the white-bolled rows or camped near the scene of their seasonal employment. "Clearin's" or "burnin's," new fields carved out of the forest area, in places border these cotton patches; and high up among the branches of surrounding trees—elm, hickory, gum, and cottonwood—mistletoe grows in such abundance that the farmers make Christmas money gathering and shipping it to markets in northern states.

IDABEL, 27.8 *m.* (504 alt., 3,689 pop.), seat of McCurtain County, on the divide separating the valleys of Little and Red rivers, was at first named Mitchell, then renamed for the daughters, Ida and Belle, of a Choctaw citizen on whose land the town was built. Farming and lumbering are the principal supports of the town; and here is the main office of a big lumber and coal company.

GARVIN, 37 *m.* (500 alt., 170 pop.), was one of the towns laid out when the Frisco railroad was built through this region. The first bank in the county was opened here, and here sat the first U. S. Commissioner's Court in the southeastern section of the state. The little town is supported almost entirely by farming.

MILLERTON, 41.7 *m.* (519 alt., 225 pop.), is one of the first towns established in the Choctaw Nation.

Right from Millerton on a graded road to WHEELOCK ACADEMY, 1.9 *m.*, founded in 1832 for the education of Indian girls by the missionary Alfred Wright, who helped to reduce the Choctaw language to writing. On top of a small hill near the present school are the ruins of one of the original log buildings occupied by the United States soldiers who conducted the first Choctaw exiles from their homes in Mississippi.

The academy was named for Eleazer Wheelock, founder and first president of Dartmouth College, Hanover, New Hampshire. South of the Academy site is the stone WHEELOCK MISSION CHURCH, said to be the oldest church building in the state, erected by Presbyterian missionaries in 1842. Near by is the old missionary cemetery where Wright was buried.

Since its founding Wheelock Academy has been rebuilt, added to, and remodeled. The plain wooden buildings, attractive in their simplicity, house one of the most complete institutions of its kind in Oklahoma—a school for orphan Choctaw girls, maintained by the Federal government. Its centennial celebration, in 1932, included an elaborate pageant illustrating one hundred years of Choctaw history.

At 44.5 *m.* on the main route is the junction with a dirt road.

Left on this road to Valliant's WATERWORKS, 0.5 *m.*, where an old water mill is enclosed by the waterworks building. The mill was installed for grinding corn meal in 1834 by Joel Kemp, a rich plantation owner who had one thousand acres, worked by one hundred slaves. At the time of the Civil War an Indian farmer named Oklabbi got possession of it and installed a turbine in place of the undershot drive; later he turned it into a cotton gin. The crude press was operated by horse power, and seven bales a day was maximum output.

The natural dam near by, connecting with one of concrete to impound the water, is a ledge one hundred feet long formed almost entirely of fossil shells. A swimming pool has been built here.

VALLIANT, 46.3 *m.* (522 alt., 551 pop.), is a center for lumbering and farming.

The ALICE LEE ELLIOTT MEMORIAL SCHOOL (Negro) here was founded as Hill School, then called the Oak Hill Industrial Academy, and finally, about 1902, on receiving a special gift in memory of Alice Lee Elliott, it was given its present name.

In the period from the end of the Civil War to 1885, former slaves of the Choctaws had no legal status in the nation, and the United States government failed to carry out its promise to remove them. It was in this period that missionaries undertook to provide, in whatever meager way they could, for the education of the freedmen's children; and Oak Hill came into existence as a Presbyterian chapel-school. After 1885, freedmen as adopted citizens of the Choctaw Nation were schooled by the tribe.

Right from Valliant on a series of dirt roads; R. to WRIGHT CITY, 12.3 *m.* (520 alt., 573 pop.); R. to a junction, 16.9 *m.;* then L. to ALIKCHI, 21.6 *m.,* where it is said that the last tribal execution of an Indian in McCurtain County took place in 1902. Tried by a jury of fellow Choctaws, he was convicted of murder; then, according to an old custom, was allowed to go home until the day of his execution; and on the appointed day he presented himself to be shot to death.

At 56.2 *m.* on US 70 is the junction with a dirt road.

Right on this road are the RUINS OF THE ORIGINAL FORT TOWSON, 0.5 *m.* The fort was established in 1824 to protect the Choctaws who were induced by the Federal government to emigrate voluntarily from their Mississippi homes both from the raiding western Plains Indians and the outlaws that made their headquarters along the north bank of Red River. Soldiers sent to Fort Towson had little military work to do and were occupied mainly in building roads; and in 1829 the post was abandoned. It was re-established, however, when enforced removal of the Choctaws began in 1831. Abandoned again in 1854, it was used as a Choctaw Indian Agency until the outbreak of the Civil War, when it was taken over by the Confederates. In 1864 the fort was headquarters for General S. B. Maxey; and here in June, 1865, two months after the official ending of the war, the Cherokee Confederate General Stand Watie surrendered.

It is said that Sam Houston met representatives of the Pawnee and Comanche tribes at Fort Towson in December, 1832, to negotiate treaties of peace between them and the tribes then being removed from east of the Mississippi; and that from this meeting Houston went on to begin the four-year campaign that ended with the wresting of the Province of Texas from Mexico.

All that remains of the commodious hewn-log barracks and lathed and plastered officers' quarters, ample for the accommodations of four companies, are scattered stones and traces of the foundations of some of the buildings.

FORT TOWSON, 56.8 *m.* (448 alt., 501 pop.), named for the old military trading post, is a trading place for farmers.

A 970-acre flood control and recreational lake is (1941) under construction just north of Fort Towson; and the site of the old fort will be at the top of a seventy-five foot bluff overlooking the new reservoir.

Right from Fort Towson on a dirt road is the SITE OF DOAKSVILLE, 1 *m.* Established in 1821 by the Doaks brothers, fur traders, the settlement became an important center for trappers and Indian and white settlers as the frontier pushed farther and farther west. Shallow-draft steamboats on Red River and overland freight served the place; in 1833, seventeen boats discharged cargoes for Doaksville of such varied items as powder and shot, churns, and cloth, and loaded peltry and cotton for the return voyages.

By a treaty made at Doaksville in 1837, the Choctaw Nation agreed, for a consideration of $530,000, to grant equal rights in their country to the Chickasaws; and the boundaries of a Chickasaw District were defined. In 1855 the tribes agreed to formal separation, and the Chickasaw District became the Chickasaw Nation. From 1850 to 1863, Doaksville was the Choctaw capital. Its decline and disappearance were due to the war, removal of the capital, discontinuance of river traffic. Nothing remains of the old town but two ruined log buildings and the cemetery which contains many pre–Civil War gravestones.

Near Doaksville, two girls' schools were located; Goodwater, founded in 1837 by the missionary Ebenezer Hotchkin; and Pine Ridge, opened in 1845.

SAWYER, 63.4 *m.,* came into existence about 1900 when the Arkansas and Choctaw Railroad (later the Frisco) built its branch line between Texarkana, Arkansas, and Ardmore to provide an outlet for the lumber and cotton produced in this district.

At 66.6 *m.* is the junction with an improved dirt road.

Left on this road, 1.5 *m.* to the ROSE HILL CEMETERY (R), where Captain Robert M. Jones, perhaps the most notable figure in the history of the neighborhood, is buried. He was a half-blood Choctaw, who established a store here as one of his many enterprises, including stores at Scullyville *(see Tour 7)* and Lukfata, and six plantations with five hundred slaves. One of the plantations, which he called Lake West, consisted of some five thousand acres of rich Red River bottom land planted to cotton; the others, strung along Red River, were called Boggy, Rose Hill, Root Hog, Shawneetown, and Walnut Bayou. To carry his produce to market and bring in stocks for his stores, he also owned and operated two steamboats.

The cemetery is on the site of the old Rose Hill plantation, which was Captain Jones' home in the days when he lived in truly southern opulence. The house was elaborately finished in oak, maple, walnut, and mahogany, furnished largely from France (as was customary among rich ante bellum plantation owners); it burned in 1912, long after it had been abandoned and had fallen into decay. Today, only a small tenant house, some cedar trees, and other plantings remain. Jones was ruined by the Civil War and died at Rose Hill in 1873. The cemetery, with its impressive tombstones, has been enclosed with a rock wall and otherwise restored as a WPA project.

HUGO, 71.1 *m.* (549 alt., 5,909 pop.), seat of Choctaw County, was named by Mrs. W. H. Darrough, whose husband surveyed the original townsite, in honor of Victor Hugo, her favorite author. Its growth was stimulated when the Arkansas and Choctaw Railroad, building westward, crossed the tracks of the Frisco. After that first mild boom and considerable real estate speculation, the town settled down to steady development as the center of a productive farming region. It has a pecan-cracking mill, a peanut butter factory, and one of the largest creosoting plants in the state.

Hugo is at the junction with US 271 *(see Tour 7),* which unites westward with US 70 for 7.2 miles.

SOPER, 83.5 *m.* (551 alt., 481 pop.), is in a productive farming area.

BOSWELL, 94 *m.* (580 alt., 962 pop.), grew up on the site of a much older settlement of Choctaws and the region has remained largely Indian in character. Here in a modified form is still followed the old custom of holding a Funeral Cry twenty-eight days after the burial of a Choctaw. Formerly, on the day of the burial, the surviving head of the family cut twenty-eight small sticks representing the duration of the lunar month, and each morning one stick was taken from the bundle and broken. When only seven sticks remained, he sent invitations to kinsmen and friends to come for the cry on the day the last stick was broken. Each family brought its own provisions of corn meal, flour, beef, and vegetables and camped near the burying ground. The Cry began with the recital by a close relative of the good qualities of the deceased, and as he proceeded the mourners, gathered around the grave with heads covered, started to cry. This ceremony sometimes lasted several days. In bad weather, it was held in the church, lighted at night by candles.

Right from Boswell on a dirt road is the SITE OF MAYHEW COURTHOUSE, 4 *m.,* where the Choctaws held tribal court, generally four sessions each year. The courthouse was a one-room building in which offenders received whipping or death sentences. All that remains is an old picket fence and a four-room house of logs and slabs.

BENNINGTON, 105.2 *m.* (615 alt., 513 pop.), an old Choctaw settlement on a part of the route that coincides with the original road from Doaksville to the west, is the trade center of a rich farming and grazing area. The town grew up around a church, organized in 1848 by the Presbyterian Mission Board. Still standing on the spot known locally as Old Bennington, the church has a burying ground near by.

Best remembered of the old church's ministers was Rev. W. J. B. Lloyd, who preached there after the Civil War. It was Mrs. Lloyd who told the story illustrating early banking practices. One day in the seventies she rode on a visit to the home of Wilson N. Jones, later chief of the Choctaws. As she prepared to return, Jones came out and tied a small, heavy bag to her saddle, saying, "This is $10,000 in gold; take it home and keep it until I come for it. I'm afraid of being robbed here, but no one would think of robbing a preacher!" It is said that Mrs. Lloyd kept the bag of gold, hidden in the foot of a feather bed, for five years before Jones claimed it.

Some Choctaws live in BOKCHITO, 111.9 *m.* (615 alt., 581 pop.), trade center of a farming region.

Right from Bokchito on a dirt road are the ruins of ARMSTRONG ACADEMY, 2.3 *m.* In 1844, two years after the Choctaw Nation had provided for a school system, the academy was built to serve the western portion of the Pushmataha District, placed under the supervision of R. D. Potts, a Baptist missionary, and named for the popular Choctaw agent, William Armstrong.

Instruction for adults was undertaken on week ends; and toward sunset on Friday evenings wagons bearing families began arriving at the campground in the clearing around the school. From Saturday morning to Sunday evening classes for men and women were held in which reading, writing, and arithmetic were taught along with religious instruction.

The academy site, renamed Chata Tamaha (Choctaw Town), served as capital of the Choctaws from 1863 to 1883, when the tribal lawmakers removed it to Tuskahoma *(see Tour 7)*. Closed in the Civil War, Armstrong Academy was reopened in 1882 by the Presbyterians, under contract with the Choctaw Nation, and continued as a school for orphan boys until it was burned in 1921. Some of the old buildings, now ruins, are still standing.

At 119 *m.* US 70 crosses Blue River. On the east bank is PHILADELPHIA *(brotherly love)* CHURCH, erected in 1840, and housing the oldest functioning Baptist congregation in Oklahoma. The minutes of the church for 1850 record the reception and baptism, among others, of a Choctaw named Yokmetubbe, who had been tried for murder and sentenced to death. On his conviction he was placed in charge of an officer of the church and urged to repent and prepare his soul; the record says that "he prayed for forgiveness of his sins—and though compelled to suffer the penalty of the law of his country, we trust he will escape the severe penalty of God's law through mediation of Jesus Christ."

For many years the church had only Choctaw ministers, and the congregation is still almost exclusively Indian. Its male quartette gives concerts throughout southern Oklahoma.

Seat of Bryan County and metropolis of the Red River Valley section of Oklahoma, DURANT, 162.2 *m.* (643 alt., 10,027 pop.), was first settled by the Choctaw family of that name in 1870 and built on the Dixon Durant ranch. The present (1941) principal chief of the tribe is W. A. Durant, also of the same family.

Lying in a region somewhat broken and roughly terraced by nature, Durant has grown to its position of local importance through service to a variety of agricultural needs, and as a seat of two colleges, one maintained by the state and the other—for women—by the Presbyterian denomination.

Cotton is the principal crop to contribute to the city's market activities, though the region is also productive in livestock, grain, potatoes, hay, and peanuts. Two peanut warehouses built in 1940 by the Bryan County growers' co-operative were filled at harvest time with 2,800 tons, to be held for a better market under a Federal government guarantee of a minimum price. The crop of wild pecans is also important—as it was in 1834 when a Choctaw tribal law forbade the cutting of pecan and hickory trees. A pecan cracking and picking plant in the city has sent out in one year forty-eight carloads of the nut kernels to be used in confectionery factories. Two peanut processing plants and a cottonseed-oil mill are evidences of Durant's dependence on the soil.

Unusual among industrial enterprises is the factory established here for utilizing the wood of the bois d'arc (Osage orange), most commonly known as a hedgerow bush and valued in the old days by the Indians as material for bows. It grows abundantly in the Durant area, and the factory has fashioned paving blocks and wagon felloes from the tough and durable wood; has utilized smaller bits for insulator-supports on telegraph and telephone lines; and out of the sawdust and ground-up waste has produced a valuable yellow dye which is sold as far away as eastern Europe

A free County Fair, and Farmers' Sales Day, make for close co-operation between Durant and the surrounding farms.

One daily newspaper, the *Durant Democrat,* is the survivor of ten that have been published there at different times.

Characteristic of Durant's architecture are the galleried residences, with high ceilings and big windows, that reflect the influence of the old southern plantation owners' "town houses."

SOUTHEASTERN STATE COLLEGE, with an enrollment (1941) of 1,064 and a faculty and administrative staff of sixty-three, is one of the six training schools for teachers in Oklahoma. Opened in June, 1909, its plant has grown to include seven buildings devoted to college work, a stadium and athletic field, and an amphitheater capable of seating three thousand persons. These are on a campus of thirty-eight acres at the northern edge of the city. Concrete walks connect the buildings, and the grounds are landscaped and planted to flowers and ornamental shrubs.

Connected with the college is the RUSSELL TRAINING SCHOOL, a laboratory for advanced college students, with elementary department and junior and senior high school courses. There, embryo teachers are given demonstrations in the best teaching practices on each grade level and later permitted to teach under the direction of a supervisor. Music, art, and physical education are among the branches taught in the training school.

On an elevated tableland at the western edge of Durant, the OKLAHOMA PRESBYTERIAN COLLEGE FOR GIRLS occupies a twenty-two-acre campus. Its work is carried on in a three-story brick main building, which also provides dormitory space for seventy-five girls. Another dormitory, modern and well furnished, is connected with the main building by a covered passageway. With a teaching staff of seven and an enrollment (1940) of forty-eight college, and twenty preparatory, students, the school attempts (in the words of its circular) to make of its graduates "well rounded young women, prepared in mind, soul, and body for consecrated leadership in activities properly belonging to women." Approximately half of the students are Indian girls whose expenses are paid by the Federal government. The college has a swimming pool, gymnasium, library, and a pipe organ in the main building.

Nearest city to the site of Denison Dam, Durant has received a new impetus as supply base for the builders; and when the lake comes into existence (probably in 1944), plans will be carried out for making the region around the reservoir an extensive recreation area, with shelters and piers for sailboats and other craft.

In Durant is the junction with US 69 *(see Tour 8)*.

Just west of Durant, US 70 crosses the boundary line between the former Choctaw and Chickasaw nations. When the Denison Dam is completed a section of the highway will be inundated, and it will be necessary to reroute it to Madill.

MADILL, 154.2 *m.* (775 alt., 2,594 pop.), named for an attorney of the Frisco railroad, is the seat of Marshall County. Around it is a farming and livestock growing area, dotted with the pump jacks of the shallow oil field which was opened here in 1907 and is still producing oil of very high gravity. The town, however, has never experienced an oil boom comparable to those at other Oklahoma towns and cities, although a new, productive field is being developed near by. Madill's first bank was known locally as the Cottonwood National, because it was built of boards sawed out of cottonwood trees. School desks, and pecan cracking, shelling, and packing machinery are manufactured here. In Marshall County are many groves of wild and paper-shell pecans.

Madill is at the junction with State 99 *(see Tour 14)*.

At 174.2 *m.* is the junction with graveled State 18.

Right on State 18 to a junction with a graded farm-to-market road, 18 *m.;* R. here to OIL SPRINGS, 22.5 *m.* This is an old resort for swimming, camping, and fishing and was named for the trace of oil found on the water that gushed from the spring. There has been no commercial oil development in the neighborhood, however.

At 175.2 *m.* is the junction with an improved dirt road.

Right on this road to OAK HILL FARM *(visitors admitted)*, 2.5 *m.*, one of the largest establishments in the world for the breeding of show ring horses, especially three-gaited and five-gaited saddle horses; in addition, entries in the fine harness classes are sent to the annual shows throughout the Southwest and at Kansas City, St. Louis, and Louisville.

On the farm's three thousand acres, and in its commodious barns—the largest 324 by 54 feet, with concrete stalls for fifty-four animals—are kept more than fifty registered brood mares; five pedigreed stallions; some Thoroughbreds; some standardbreds; a few Percherons; a small herd of registered Durham cattle; and three hundred Angora goats. About fifty colts a year are foaled here, to be trained for the show ring.

ARDMORE, 182.3 *m.* (872 alt., 16,886 pop.) *(see Ardmore),* is at the junction with US 77 *(see Tour 10).*

RINGLING, 210.5 *m.* (846 alt., 902 pop.), was named for one of the brothers who operated the old Ringling Brothers–Barnum and Bailey circus. The story is that in the early 1900's a young lawyer named Jake L. Hamon boarded the circus train that lay on a siding at Ardmore and presented his card to John Ringling, who said, "I'm afraid we can't do anything for you; our legal business is already taken care of."

Hamon answered, "I don't want your legal business, I want three dollars. Several years ago I worked as a roustabout for this circus, and when I was paid off you beat me out of that amount."

Ringling liked the young man's nerve, invited him to stay for dinner, they became friends; and in 1914 when oil was found on Hamon's leases west of Ardmore he induced Ringling to enter the field and build twenty miles of railroad to their holdings. That road was extended, and at its western terminus is the town named for the circus man.

In 1916, most of the residents of Cornish, a small town one mile south, moved to Ringling, leaving only an orphans' home on the old site.

At 233.2 *m.* is the Y junction with US 81 *(see Tour 11).*

WAURIKA, 234.2 *m.* (873 alt., 2,458 pop.), is a town that in layout resembles a stadium, its residence section spread out and overlooking an arena of business buildings. Like many other Oklahoma towns, it has in its short history changed names. When first laid out in 1892, the railroad station was called Monika. It became the seat of Jefferson County in 1908 after a year's fight with the near-by town of Ryan *(see Tour 11).* Besides farm trade, Waurika is also dependent on the Rock Island shops at the southern edge of town.

West of Waurika are hill pastures covered with nutritious buffalo grass; in the days of the trail drives cattle were allowed to linger here in order to put on fat quickly.

This varied range and farm country was a part of the Kiowa-Comanche reservation, opened to white settlement in 1901. Where once stolen Comanche ponies ranged, graded white-face cattle now (1941) graze. Stretches of flat alkali-whitened land alternate with rolling pastures, wheat fields, and the frayed-thread-like timber borders of small creeks. Farmhouses, with wind chargers whirling above the roofs, indicate by their size and state of repair a wide range of prosperity.

Where the route comes close to the Red River bottoms there are patches of good timber, mesquite, tamarack, irregular windrows of blown sand, some small farms, and one extensive peach orchard, which suggests one of the possibilities of the region.

RANDLETT, 261 *m.* (1,248 alt., 327 pop.), a collection of neat houses extending for a considerable distance along the route, is a farm trading center.

South to Red River is level land, poor soil, buffalo grass, and mesquite. Some wheat, however, is grown in the region.

US 70 crosses over a long bridge spanning a wide expanse of river-bed sand and a narrow stream to the TEXAS LINE, 268.5 *m.,* at a point 2.5 miles northeast of Burkburnett, Texas *(see Texas Guide).*

Tour 7

(Fort Smith, Ark.)—Poteau—Talihina—Antlers—Hugo—(Paris, Tex.); US 271.
Arkansas Line to Texas Line 165 m.

Roadbed graveled throughout.
Kansas City Southern Ry parallels route between Spiro and Poteau; the Frisco Ry. between Poteau and Paris, Tex.
Accommodations limited to the larger towns.

> *Ch ah ta Oḳla i Minḳo sia hash himmaḳa oḳla ḳana hoḳeya, pi yaḳni illappa ietanowvt nine chito micha boḳe oḳa achuḳma, yaḳomi ḳa oḳla pisat itanowa chi ḳa ashliha illappa pit achile hoḳe."*
>
> Translation: "As chief of the Choctaw people, I do hereby extend a welcome and an invitation to all who wish to visit the Indian country and view the mountains and the many beautiful fishing streams."
>
> —W. A. Durant, present (1941) Principal Chief of the Choctaws.

US 271 winds through the rugged hills and narrow valleys that were once the home of the Choctaws. Driven from the East, they labored to re-create the traditional strength of their nation in this area of verdant beauty. Log and brick buildings and forgotten piles of stone, now standing amid the upland forests of pine and oak, testify to tribal decisions that school children of today recite as history.

For a few miles along the most eastern portion of US 271 in Oklahoma the Chickasaws, too, once beat out their Trail of Tears, and not long afterwards there passed over it the turbulent remnant of the fierce Seminoles, who had fought so desperately in Florida to protect their homes against white aggression.

The old Fort Towson Road, along which processions of troops and supplies from Fort Smith were routed to Fort Towson, nearly parallels US 271; deep ruts made by the heavy wagon wheels are still visible in places. Piles of stone, from chimneys long in disuse, indicate the buildings that once were havens of rest and refuge for hardy early-day stagecoach passengers. Across this region from the southeastern corner of the state, up the divide between the Little and Kiamichi rivers, across the latter stream near Tuskahoma, and on to the northwest went Bernard de la Harpe, exploring for the glory of France in 1718.

The highway passes through the beautiful game-stocked region of the Ouachita National Forest and crosses clear, plunging streams in which there is good fishing. Over the Winding Stair and Kiamichi mountains and through the regular rows of the Potato Hills US 271 twists and dips.

US 271 crosses the OKLAHOMA LINE, 0 *m.,* six miles west of Fort Smith, Arkansas *(see Arkansas Guide).*

BRADEN, 7 *m.* (423 alt., 150 pop.), lies in the wooded valley formed by the confluence of the Arkansas and Poteau rivers. Much of the rich bottom land has been cleared to form a fertile farming district.

The almost completely deserted village of SCULLYVILLE, 11.2 *m.,* was established in 1832, when the Choctaws were being removed from their eastern homes. The site was chosen by the Indian agent as a center where annuities due the Choctaws were to be paid—hence the name, derived from the Choctaw word *iskuli,* meaning money. A part of the old AGENCY BUILDING, erected from hand-hewn logs on a four-foot stone foundation, is still standing. Appropriately and succinctly, the Choctaws called it the "pay house."

It was here that Moshulatubbee, important political figure of the Choctaw Nation, lived while serving as chief of the northern district, of which Scullyville was the capital.

Although today (1941) there are only a few buildings left standing in Scullyville, a century ago it was an educational, social, and political center for the Choctaw Nation. The artist, George Catlin, visited there in 1834 and painted his virile canvas, "Tullock-chisk-ko," using as a model the most distinguished ballplayer in the nation; the picture is in the Smithsonian Institution at Washington, D.C. Catlin told of watching a ball game (the subject of another of his famous paintings), on a site southwest of the town, with some three thousand cheering and betting Indians in attendance. The games were usually played between teams of the different districts, with much rivalry and sometimes a riot. The game is still played by Choctaw boys in various Indian schools.

In 1844, New Hope, the most noted of the schools established for Choctaw girls, was located here. The institution was closed during the Civil War, reopened in 1870, and continued in operation until it was burned in 1897. The custom of the Choctaws at the time was to send some of this school's graduates to an eastern college at the expense of the nation. Only fragments of the foundation of this important seminary remain.

When the famous Butterfield Overland mail route was established between St. Louis and San Francisco in 1858, Scullyville was made one of the stations on the line. The nearness of the town to the Arkansas River (some five miles northwest) also made it a busy trading post for river traffic; the Scullyville boat landing served both this settlement and Fort Coffee.

The Choctaw cemetery there is the final resting place of many of the early leaders of the nation, including members of the McCurtain, Folsom, and Ward families. Some lie in unmarked graves and some in graves with half-fallen stones, dating back to 1830.

In 1863, Union forces captured Scullyville and held it until the end of the Civil War, leaving devastated fields and ruined homes behind them and bringing about the early decline of this once important town. One residence, the Tom Ainsworth home, survived the war and is still in good repair.

At 13.5 *m.* is the junction with an improved dirt road.

Right on this road to a junction with a second graded dirt road, 4.3 *m.*

Right here, 1 *m.*, to the SPIRO INDIAN MOUNDS *(200 yds. L)*, the best-known archeological site in Oklahoma. The mounds were leased by the University of Oklahoma in 1934 for excavation, which has been done as a WPA project under the direction of the university's department of anthropology. The workers have dug up ornaments whose carvings indicate Aztec origin; pearls and beads of shell, copper, wood, and stone; vases in the shapes of owls and frogs; ceremonial maces, arrowheads, bone fragments, and woven cloth. The bodies of ancient chiefs had been placed on beds of sand with their ornaments and weapons arranged around them according to the ceremonial burial custom of this ancient civilization. There are three mounds, which had been partially despoiled by souvenir-hunters before the university acquired the excavation privileges. Scientists estimate that the burial mounds antedate the coming of Columbus, and that the builders were members of a southwestern group of Indians. Another archeological theory is that these sites are the traces of a Lower Mississippian Indian civilization which existed about 750 years ago.

At 5 *m.* on the main side route is the junction with a second dirt road; R. here to a farm home, 0.5 *m.*, which has been built (L) on the site of the quadrangle of FORT COFFEE. The post was established in 1834 and named in honor of General Coffee, who was a close friend of President Andrew Jackson and aided in the removal of the Choctaws from the East. Fort Coffee was a busy and important military post during the removal years. It was built on a high bluff on the south bank of Arkansas River, the one-story buildings grouped to form a hollow square in the manner of pioneer fortifications. The barracks were constructed of rough slabs, with battened doors and window shutters, and with a natural stone fireplace and chimney at each end. The post faced in the direction of the river, with a watch tower—commanding a sweeping view of the stream—perched on the tip of a rocky promontory on the bank. The Scullyville boat landing was also located at this strategic point.

After the abandonment of Fort Coffee in 1838, an academy for Choctaw boys was established there in 1844 and remained in operation until the outbreak of the Civil War. Today, nothing remains of the buildings except the large blocks of sandstone which formed the foundation.

SPIRO, 15.2 *m.* (494 alt., 1,041 pop.), was founded about 1895 when the Kansas City Southern Railway was built through this region. At that time, the majority of the few inhabitants still at Scullyville after its devestation during the Civil War moved to this new town. A few years later, the Fort Smith and Western Railway also built to Spiro, making it a shipping point for the adjacent area. Today (1941), four cotton gins are located there and, in addition, Spiro is an important marketing center for potatoes, a crop porticularly suited to the Arkansas River bottom land which surrounds the town.

At 18.3 *m.* is the northern junction with US 59 *(see Tour 15)*, which unites with US 271 for 17.2 miles.

PANAMA, 23.3 *m.* (490 alt., 880 pop.), like Spiro, was established about 1895 as a result of the extension of the Kansas City Southern Railway through this part of the state. The name was chosen because of the interest of the residents in the Panama Canal, the reconstruction of which was being planned at that time.

Panama is primarily a coal-mining town, but farming and stock-raising are additional commercial interests.

SHADY POINT, 25.6 *m.*, is an outgrowth of an early Choctaw settlement about one mile west, known today as "Old Town." A well-known Choctaw politician, Jacob B. Jackson, once made his home there. In Old Town is an early-day Choctaw church with the familiar shingle-and-brush-sheltered graves of its cemetery surrounding it. The ancient tribal burial customs, including the "burial cry" *(see Tour 6)*, are observed here, as in former years, whenever rites are conducted for the older Choctaws.

Near this settlement, in the days of the stagecoach route on the Military Trail to Fort Towson, was a stop called Brazil Station.

POTEAU, 31.5 *m.* (483 alt., 4,020 pop.), seat of LeFlore County, was founded in 1898 and named for the Poteau River near by. The town is located in a valley which lies between the Cavanal and Sugar Loaf mountains, the latter (2,600 alt.) being one of the highest in the Ouachita region. Because of the mountainous terrain, the streets of Poteau wind and dip, paying no particular attention to definite direction. Only one home in the town has the distinction of being in line with a cardinal point of the compass; it faces due west.

Coal-mining was the primary industry of Poteau until production slackened in that field; since then lumbering, cotton-raising, truck gardening, and glass manufacturing have become important.

Within ten miles of the city are more than a dozen large lakes and streams in which bass, bluegill, crappie, channel cat, and bream are plentiful. Fourche Maline and Poteau rivers, which join south of the town to half-circle it to the east, are good fishing spots. A canyon at the foot of Mount Cavanal has become known as a miniature Royal Gorge, for its jagged rock cliffs and tumbling water falls resemble that famous and beautiful site in Colorado.

At 35.5 *m.* is the southern junction with US 59 *(see Tour 15).*

WISTER, 41.3 *m.* (510 alt., 763 pop.), was first known as Wister Junction because two important railroads, the Rock Island and the Frisco, crossed at this point.

At 45.8 *m.* is the junction with US 270 *(see Tour 5).*

Turning sharply southwest, US 271 passes through the region of the Winding Stair Mountains of the Ouachita National Forest, with the contrasting beauty of the dark-green pines and the lighter-hued oaks against a background of red-tinged soil on every side.

At 70.1 *m.* is an old CHOCTAW CEMETERY (R).

TALIHINA, 73.1 *m.* (688 alt., 1,057 pop.), was a small, unnamed missionary settlement in this valley in the Winding Stairs Mountains when, in 1888, the Frisco Railway built across the mountains from Fort Smith, Arkansas, to Paris, Texas. The name Talihina dates back to this event, for in the Choctaw language it means "Iron Road."

As the road crews laid the shining steel rails, the Indians looked on in superstitious wonder. In the diary of one of the missionaries, present at the time, are recorded the words of a chief who had once been on a train: "I have ridden on the railroads east of the Mississippi. They have little houses on wheels which can be shut up and locked. If we allow these railroads to come, the white men will invite all the full bloods to a picnic and get the men to go off and play ball. Then they will get our women to go into the little houses on wheels and lock them up and run off with them into Texas or Missouri. Then what will we do without our women?"

Despite the objections of the Indians, the railroad was completed and the missionary settlement grew into the present town. Until 1919, Talihina remained almost inaccessible except by rail. At that time a highway was built through the near-by forest by convict labor. Since then highways have been constructed through the valley to the west and eastward toward Hot Springs,

Arkansas. Many streams for fishing, and consistent wildlife protection by Federal and state governments have made this section a popular playground for sportsmen. Practically all of the business activity at Talihina is dependent on lumbering. Large oak, pine, and hickory forests surround the town.

Right from Talihina on asphalt-paved State 63 to a V junction, 2 *m.,* with two graveled roads.

Right *(following signs)* to the STATE TUBERCULOSIS SANITORIUM, 1.5 *m.,* built in 1921. Set down among the oaks and pines on the side of a mountain that protects it from north winds, the sanitorium has the appearance of a summer resort, for many of the patients are housed in two-room cottages and the long, white ward building is completely covered on one side with screened-in porches. The ADMINISTRATION BUILDING, constructed of brick in a design of medieval simplicity, contains the dining room, kitchen, operating rooms, and laboratories. The grounds and structures of the institution are enclosed by a rail fence.

Straight ahead *(following signs)* to the CHOCTAW-CHICKASAW TUBERCULOSIS SANITORIUM, 3 *m.* The hospital was first established here in 1916 with $50,000 furnished by the Choctaw and Chickasaw Indian tribes and built under the supervision of the Federal government. Originally only tuberculous patients were admitted, but in 1936 Congress appropriated money to enlarge the hospital so that general medical service might be offered. The present-day $1,000,000 plant includes a huge, rambling building of native stone, built around an open court; nurses' quarters designed in tourist-camp style, four rock residences and five frame, used by doctors and employees. The main building contains air-conditioned X-ray and operating rooms, and corridors decorated in tasteful colors rather than the usual hospital white.

ALBION, 81.9 *m.* (678 alt., 240 pop.), is a lumbering town.

KIAMICHI (Ki′-a mish′-e), 87.0 *m.,* is a small settlement named from the Kiamichi River, which flows near by, paralleling the highway for six miles. In a report made in 1805 by Dr. John Sibley, United States explorer, he speaks of a tributary to the Red River, "which is called by the Indians *Kiomitchie.*" Fishing is excellent in these waters, crappie and catfish being abundant.

At 91. *m.* is the site of SPRINGS STATION, a stop on the old Fort Towson Military Road from Fort Smith, Arkansas, named for John Springs, an influential Choctaw, whose home was there. Near by, in a field, is the unmarked grave of William Bryant, principal chief of the Choctaws from 1870 to 1874.

The present town of TUSKAHOMA, 93 *m.,* came into existence with the coming of the railroad. Long before, however, it was the political capital of the Choctaws. As early as 1838, representatives of that nation first met to legislate for the people in their new home. Today, as citizens of a nation embracing all races, descendants of those same Choctaws live in and around Tuskahoma.

By the Treaty of Dancing Rabbit Creek, made in Mississippi in 1830, the Choctaws were promised many things in return for their land; one provision was that funds would be appropriated for the erection of a new council house in the approximate center of the land that they would henceforth occupy. The site selected was on a mound about one and one-half miles northwest of the present Tuskahoma. This was in 1834, but it was 1838 before the pine-log house was erected and ready for the first council meeting in the new capital, Nunih Wayah; the name had been brought from the East, where a sacred mound, which figured in the legends pertaining to the Choctaw origin, was also named Nunih Wayah.

Because of factional disputes, the seat of government was located at various places until 1883, when the council appropriated funds to erect a building on a permanent site about two and one-half miles northeast of the original capital, Nunih Wayah. The new structure, built of wood from the surrounding forests and of red bricks from native clay, remained the capitol of the nation until tribal government was ended in 1906.

In 1888, the Frisco Railway built through the region, but the Choctaw Council refused to pay the excessive bonus demanded by the company for building a station near the capital. A town gradually grew near the railway stop some two miles south, however, and thus the present Tuskahoma came into being.

Right from Tuskahoma on an improved dirt road to a junction 0.5 *m.,* with a second county road.

Left on this road to the SITE OF NUNIH WAYAH, 1 *m.,* which is unmarked but easily located by the large pile of rocks (L) that was once the chimney of the old log capitol. An early-day CHOCTAW BURIAL GROUND is near by.

At 2 *m.* is the junction with graveled State 2; R. on State 2 to the SITE OF THE TUSKAHOMA FEMALE ACADEMY, 3.3 *m.,* which was established in 1891 to serve as a companion school for the Jones Academy, Choctaw boys' institution at Hartshorne *(see Tour 5).* The main building burned in 1927 and a home (R), built partially of its ruins, now stands on the spot—the residence of Dr. Anna Lewis, a well-known historian of Choctaw blood, who once attended the academy.

At 2 *m.* on the main side-tour road is the CHOCTAW COUNCIL HOUSE (L), a solid rectangular red-brick building of two stories and a mansard garret third story, erected in 1883. In 1934, the Choctaws drafted plans to restore the building and to purchase one thousand acres around it for use as a park and for farm lands, the proceeds from the latter to be used to maintain the historic site permanently. In June, 1938—one hundred years after the first council meeting at Nunih Wayah—the Tuskahoma Council House, last of the Choctaw capitols, was rededicated as a historical and educational institution. Each year, in May or June, a meeting of general tribal interest is held here.

North of the Council House is an old BURYING GROUND, where many well-known Choctaws rest. In this spot are the graves of Jackson McCurtain, who was chief of the nation when the council building was erected; of his wife, Jane, most prominent and capable of the few Choctaw women who took an active part in politics; and of Peter Hudson, brilliant educator and writer, who used his talents to keep alive Choctaw history and tradition. A few feet from the Council House stands the MCCURTAIN HOME, built at about the same time as the capitol, where many prominent tribesmen were entertained while the council was in session.

LAKE CLAYTON, 99.3 *m.* (R), is named for the near-by village of Clayton. The lake, which covers one hundred acres, was completed and stocked in 1936 and affords abundant fishing.

The route continues to wind through the sparsely settled rough slopes of the Kiamichi Mountains, roughly following Cedar Creek, one of the fine fishing streams of the region.

FINLEY, 123.6 *m.,* lies in a fertile valley just south of the Kiamichi mountain range. Stock-raising and lumbering comprise the industry of the town and vicinity.

ANTLERS, 133.8 *m.* (511 alt., 3,254 pop.), was so named because of the Indian custom of fastening a set of antlers to a tree to mark the site of a spring; a large spring near the town had been marked in this way. The chief industry

Agriculture

E : FSA

OKLAHOMA FARM LANDS NEAR MUSKOGEE

WHEAT FARM NEAR HENNESSEY

LAHOMA PUBLISHING COMPANY

OKLAHOMA PUBLISHING COMPA

BEEF CATTLE ON THE RANGE

CORNFIELD, OKLAHOMA COUNTY

EVERETT M. SV

COTTON FIELD, HUGHES COUNTY

PICKING STRING BEANS, MUSKOGEE COUNTY

E : FSA

U. S. FOREST SERVICE

STARTING A SHELTER BELT

A SHELTER BELT IN SERVICE

U. S. FOREST SERVICE

ACK : SOIL CONSERVATION SERVICE

CONTOUR FURROWING FOR PASTURE LAND

CONTOUR PLOWING

B. C. MCLI

CONSERVATION DAM, NEAR KENTON; AT LOW WATER

BROOMCORN HARVEST, LINDSAY

4-H CLUB GIRL

4-H CLUB BOYS

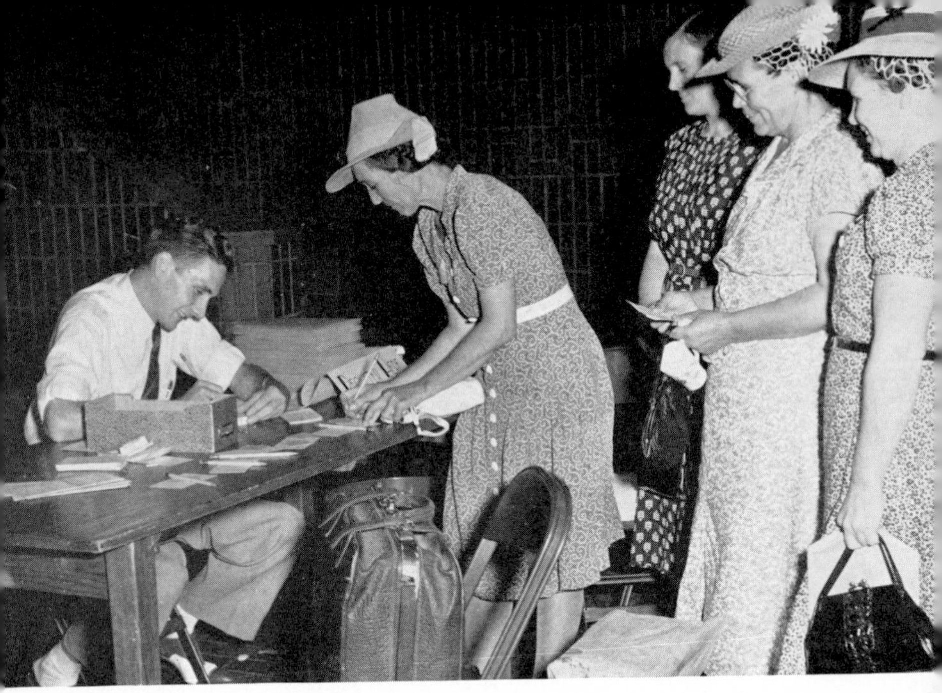

FARM WOMEN REGISTERING FOR FARMERS' WEEK
AT OKLAHOMA A. & M. COLLEGE

WEIGHING AND LOADING

LEE : F

of this district is lumbering, and a large lumber and planing mill is one of the town's most prominent structures.

During the winter of 1892–93, Antlers was the scene of a political insurrection still known locally as the "Locke War." Congress had voted to pay $2,943,050 in settlement of a land claim to the Choctaw Nation, and bitter strife developed between the citizens as to the handling of this money. The question became the main issue in the election of 1892, when the voters were to cast their ballots for principal chief. The two main political parties, Nationalist and Progressive, had as their respective candidates Jacob B. Jackson, an influential full blood who had received a college education and had held numerous tribal offices, and Wilson N. Jones, a wealthy ranchman then serving as chief. The vote was very close, but the party in power, which canvassed the returns, decided in favor of Jones. The Nationalists formed armed bands with the intention of marching against the capitol and seizing the government. Most of them were dispersed with little bloodshed by the tribal militia, but about 150 of the insurrectionists barricaded themselves at Antlers under the leadership of Victor M. Locke, an intermarried white man, and prepared to defy the administration. Chief Jones' militia attacked their stronghold, but few casualties resulted since neither side was willing to engage in a pitched battle. For the first time in the history of the Choctaw people, Federal troops were called in to restore order, and a United States commissioner finally persuaded the leaders of the two factions to make peace. Jones served out his term without further incident, but the log stockade in which the Nationalists had barricaded themselves at Antlers remained standing for many years as a grim reminder of the most serious political disturbance in the history of the Choctaw Republic.

FORNEY, 148.3 *m.* (609 alt., 50 pop.), a small settlement, is at the western junction with US 70 *(see Tour 6),* which unites eastward with US 271 to HUGO, 155 *m.* (549 alt., 5,909 pop.) *(see Tour 6).*

At 156.1 *m.* is the junction with a graveled road.

Right on this road to the GOODLAND SCHOOL, 2.3 *m.* In 1848, the Indian Presbytery was petitioned by the Choctaws living in this vicinity to send a teacher. In 1850, Rev. O. P. Stark and his wife settled at Goodland and established a mission and school in their log cabin home. A church was soon built, and the school was conducted in this building for a number of years. Until 1890, the institution depended largely on the support of the community; this was obtained mostly through the efforts of Mrs. Carrie LeFlore, wife of Basil LeFlore, the chief of the district. In memory of her and her husband, their home has been moved to the campus and dedicated as a MUSEUM *(open to visitors)* of Indian and mission history. The institution is now a public school supported and supervised by the state. A dormitory on the grounds operated by the Presbyterian Church cares for Indian orphans; Hugo social service organizations aid in its upkeep. Eight modern buildings on 430 acres of land comprise the school plant, where regular scholastic courses throughout high school grades are given.

GRANT, 159.7 *m.* (573 alt., 309 pop.), which was established at the time the Frisco Railway built through this region, is a marketing town for the surrounding agricultural lands of the Red River bottom.

ORD, 164.7 *m.* (422 alt., 206 pop.), was named for a town in Nebraska.

At 165 *m.,* US 271 crosses Red River at the Texas Line, fifteen miles north of Paris, Texas *(see Texas Guide).*

Tour 8

(Columbus, Kans.)—Vinita—Muskogee—McAlester—Atoka—Durant—(Denison, Tex.); US 69.
Kansas Line to Texas Line, 272.2 m.

Roadbed intermittently paved with concrete and asphalt; also graveled.
The Missouri-Kansas-Texas R. R. parallels the route throughout.
Good accommodations at short intervals; hotels chiefly in cities; numerous tourist camps.

Probably as significant historically as any route throughout Oklahoma, US 69 follows almost exactly the old Texas Road, over which fur traders, trappers, freighters, emigrants, and pioneer settlers traveled. From the Kansas Line to Muskogee, the Three Forks district, it follows the old Osage Trace, along which the Osage Indians frequently sent hunting parties into the wilderness region. Records have established the trail's use as far back as the opening years of the nineteenth century.

Soon after came the establishment of trading posts, missions, and the military outpost of Fort Gibson; then the Trace developed into a road advancing rapidly toward Texas and other points to the southwest. The heavy traffic that followed left ruts that are still visible today. A count taken in March, 1845, showed that one thousand wagons crossed from what is now Oklahoma over the Red River into Texas in a period of six weeks.

Indians and early pioneers surveyed skillfully, even though they did not have twentieth-century knowledge and equipment; when the inevitable railroad and highway were laid out, they followed the rutted old road very closely.

Many Indians still live along the route, for some of the areas traversed belonged at various times to the Osages, the Cherokees, the Creeks, the Choctaws, the Chickasaws, and the Caddoes. Though Washington Irving's description of the Osages as "... stately fellows, stern and simple in garb and aspect" and the Creeks as "gaily dressed," does not fit the appearance of present-day Indians, much of their former colorful array may still be seen in museums and displays along the way.

Section a. KANSAS LINE *to* MUSKOGEE, *114.2 m. US 69*

US 69 crosses the KANSAS LINE, 0 *m.,* at a point 13.1 miles south of Columbus, Kansas *(see Kansas Guide).*

Here the route passes through the lead and zinc mines of the Tri-State area *(see Tour 1).* The mines are now (1941) operating on a full-time basis adding to the many huge piles of chat that are reminders of the boom days of the first World War. In some places board or stone barricades protect the highway from the encroaching man-made hills.

In PICHER, 1.6 *m.* (820 alt., 5,848 pop.), houses have been located in a hit-and-miss fashion in the spaces about the great shaft openings and the sprawling chat piles. The small houses in which the miners live are built impermanently, for approximately the entire townsite is leased to the mining companies, making the buildings subject to removal when mine operations require it. Picher's business district is composed of a dozen or so one-story brick structures facing the highway.

Mining in the Tri-State area is of the shaft type, the shafts sometimes extending into the earth for almost a quarter of a mile with octopus-like arms branching off in many directions. The miners work by the light of carbide lamps attached to their caps as they follow the veins—drilling, blasting with dynamite, picking, and shoveling the ore into cars drawn by well-trained mules. The animals often spend most of their lives underground drawing the cars from the workings to the elevators that haul the raw ores to the top. The ore is next crushed in huge mills and separated from the accompanying rock; then, as a "concentrate", it is transported to the smelters for refining.

CARDIN, 2.7 *m.* (813 alt., 437 pop.), formerly named Tar River, came into existence as a mining camp in the boom years of this area. It was incorporated in 1918 and named for W. C. Cardin, who laid out the townsite. Some farming is done in the surrounding prairie land, but the chief commercial activity is lead and zinc mining.

The recently built EAGLE-PICHER CENTRAL MILL *(open 8 A.M. to 4 P.M.; visitors must register at office),* 4.2 *m.,* is one of the largest and most modern in the world, milling approximately eight hundred tons of ore daily. In recovering the lead and zinc from the rock, much chert and limestone is extracted, and this substance, called chat when crushed, is used widely as road surfacing material.

COMMERCE, 5.7 *m.* (805 alt., 2,422 pop.) *(see Tour 1),* is at the junction with US 66 *(see Tour 1),* which unites southwestward with US 69 for thirty-nine miles.

At 20.6 *m.* is the eastern junction with US 60 *(see Tour 4),* which unites with the route southwestward for 24.1 miles.

At 23.8 *m.* is the junction with US 59 *(see Tour 15).*

AFTON, 24.8 *m.* (790 alt., 1,261 pop.) *(see Tour 1).*

VINITA, 40.2 *m.* (702 alt., 5,685 pop.) *(see Tour 1).*

At 44.7 *m.* is the western junction with US 66 *(see Tour 1);* US 69 turns sharply south.

BIG CABIN, 50.7 *m.* (720 alt., 270 pop.), is a farm and poultry center named for the frame cabin belonging to the settler who first occupied the site.

Cabin Creek (L), which runs almost parallel with US 69 between Vinita and its confluence with the Grand River near Langley, was the scene of two important Civil War battles. Approximately eight miles east of the highway there, where the old Texas Road crossed Cabin Creek, the Confederates attacked a Union supply train of two hundred wagons on July 1 and 2, 1863.

Food supplies for Fort Gibson *(see Tour 3)*, held during the latter part of the war by Federal troops, were being brought from Fort Scott and Baxter Springs, Kansas, for the many soldiers and Indian refugees who had been existing at the fort on half rations. The Confederates, numbering about fifteen hundred under command of the Cherokee General Stand Watie, were trying to blockade the garrison, but the attack was beaten off and the train reached Fort Gibson safely.

In the battle on the same spot in the following year the Confederate General R. M. Gano and General Stand Watie captured a Federal supply train valued at $1,500,000. The 295 wagons, several ambulances, and 260 men en route from Fort Scott to Fort Gibson and Fort Smith, Arkansas, were attacked by the Confederates at two o'clock in the morning of September 19 by artillery pieces, hidden in the timber. Only 130 wagons were taken away; the others, including ricks carrying some three thousand tons of hay, were destroyed by order of General Gano. In addition to clothing and food, the wagons contained a quantity of whisky on which the Confederate troops are said to have become quite drunk after the fighting was over. Watie stopped the drinking by ordering the remaining whisky poured into the near-by creek.

ADAIR, 60.2 *m.* (682 alt., 407 pop.), was named for the prominent Cherokee Indian Adair family. The town was a center for the surrounding rich grazing lands, which, after allotment, were cut into small farms whose produce and livestock are marketed there today (1941).

In July, 1892, the Dalton gang of outlaws *(see Tour 11)* committed one of their most daring robberies at the Missouri-Kansas-Texas Railroad station in Adair. A shipment of $17,000 in currency was carried by the express due to stop there, but the plans of the Daltons had become known and a posse of deputy marshals was also on the train. Despite the hot gunfire, the gang managed to escape with the money, which they are said to have buried in the Dalton caves near Sand Springs *(see Tour 2)*.

Left from Adair on a graveled road is PENSACOLA, 8.5 *m.* (681 alt., 109 pop.), built on the SITE OF HOPEFIELD MISSION, a branch of the old Union Mission near Chouteau. Hopefield was originally established for the Osage Indians farther south on the Grand River, but the Cherokee-Osage treaty of 1828 placed that site in Cherokee country; hence the mission was moved there, where it remained a busy and helpful organization for several years.

East of Pensacola, at the great bend in the Grand River, is the GRAND RIVER DAM *(see Tour 1)*; highways, railroad right of ways, and even entire townsites were moved as the shore line of the immense new Grand Lake lengthened.

PRYOR, 70.8 *m.* (627 alt., 2,501 pop.), was given its present name in honor of Nathaniel Pryor, who served as a scout with the Lewis and Clark expedition and as a captain in the Battle of New Orleans. In 1819, after honorable discharge from the army, Pryor obtained a license to trade with the Osage Nation and, by 1820, he had established a trading post near the mouth of the Verdigris River. Later, he built a post southeast of Pryor on the creek which was also named for him.

The United States Department of Agriculture has an experiment station here and is sponsoring the construction of diversion ditches and terraces throughout some fifty thousand acres of surrounding farm land. The program also includes reforestation, soil testing, and restoration of worn-out land. Mineral water is plentiful in near-by springs but is not commercially marketed. In Pryor there is a mineral-water SWIMMING POOL *(adm. 25c).*

Left from Pryor on graveled State 20 to SALINA, 11.2 *m.* (618 alt., 687 pop.), a modern town built on the SITE OF THE CHOUTEAU TRADING POST, established in the early nineteenth century by the famous French family that figured in the founding of St. Louis, Missouri.

In the latter part of the eighteenth century the Chouteaus possessed the license to trade with the Osage Indians, then living in the present limits of Missouri, but the Spanish governor cancelled their privilege and granted it to Manuel Lisa, a Spaniard. The Chouteau brothers decided to retain the trading business without official sanction, however, and accordingly Major Jean Pierre Chouteau set out at the close of the century to establish new posts and cement the family's relation with the Indians. The expedition brought him to this ideal location on a wide, navigable river, the Grand, known as the Neosho in Kansas, bounded by well-wooded hills on the east and level lands to the west; near by were both clear-water and salt-water springs. He set up a trading post here (exact date is a matter of controversy), but the establishment was not really active until 1802, when Chouteau persuaded some three thousand Osage Indians with whom he had traded for a number of years to remove to this area. He appointed a new chief for the emigrants—Cashesegra or Big Track—and became a benevolent but firm dictator of his self-made empire. Since the country was rich in furs, fowl, tallow, wild honey, and many other marketable products, he enriched the family coffers.

Auguste Pierre Chouteau, son of Jean Pierre, took charge of the post some twenty years after his father first arrived; he built a pretentious home here, which Washington Irving visited in 1832 and described in his *Tour on the Prairies* as a large, two-story log structure filled with valuable furnishings and surrounded with trees, shrubberies, and flowers. Smaller houses dotted the river bank and the woods. Texas Road travelers found gracious hospitality at this frontier palace, where lived Auguste and his numerous children by his two wives (one, a cousin; the other, an Osage Indian). He also had a large retinue of Indians and Negroes.

Auguste died in 1838 at Fort Gibson while engaged on a government diplomatic mission with the Indians. He was heavily in debt, and his slaves, stock, and merchandise were mostly attached or stolen. John Ross *(see Tour 3),* chief of the Cherokee tribe, and his brother Lewis acquired many of the Chouteau holdings and built a brick mansion on the site now occupied by the Salina High School gymnasium. In one corner of the schoolyard still stands a BLOCKHOUSE, built by Ross, enclosing one of the springs used since the founding of the Chouteau Trading Post.

The settlement then became known as Grand Saline and served as an important point on one of the California trails. A marked depression near the bridge on the west bank of the Grand River is said to have been made by the wagons of the many emigrants who traveled to California in 1849 and later. Traffic became so heavy that a post office was established on June 11, 1849. In 1872, the Lewis Ross home and surrounding farm lands were purchased by the Cherokee Nation for the establishment of the CHEROKEE ORPHAN'S HOME, which operated there until the building was destroyed by fire in 1903 and the institution moved near Tahlequah *(see Tour 3).*

In recognition of the significance of the site, a STONE MARKER has been erected in the center of Salina's main street, commemorating the dates of the trading post, the Cherokee town, and the orphan asylum. The state legislature proclaimed October 10, the birth anniversary of Major Jean Pierre Chouteau, as "Oklahoma Historical Day" and in 1940 the first observance of the date was held at Salina.

Some three miles south of Salina a small creek flows from the east into the Grand River at the foot of a range of rocky bluffs. High on the cliffs is the spot which Cherokee Indian legends say is the home of the "Little People" who have been a part of Cherokee traditional lore since ancient times. When the tribe lived in the East, they believed in the "Little People," who were supposed to be no more than knee-high, but well-formed, handsome, and exceedingly clever. They lived far back in the mountains and were never seen except at dusk or by solitary individuals.

Some Cherokees, at the time of the Removal, still believed in the legendary figures and moved their "Little People" to the new nation and to this site. Tribal members would stop fishing at a certain spot in the Grand River if stones happened to roll down the bluffs into the water, usually with the remark, "Let's move downstream, I see the 'Little People' live here and want the fish for their own use."

State 20 continues to SPAVINAW, 13 *m.* (668 alt., 255 pop.) *(see Tour 15),* and the SPAVINAW HILLS PARK.

WHITAKER STATE ORPHANS' HOME, 71.5 *m.,* was first established in 1879 for the orphans of Indian Territory. In 1908, the state took over the institution, and today (1941) it represents an investment of $500,000, occupies six hundred acres, and provides a home and school for more than three hundred children.

The business district (R) of the town of CHOUTEAU, 79.4 *m.* (627 alt., 400 pop.), which was named for the Chouteau family, is a market center for a considerable farm area; east of the town is the big $80,000,000 powder plant to be built (1941–42) as a part of the national defense program.

At 84.4 *m.* is the junction with an unimproved dirt road.

Left on this road, across railroad tracks, 0.9 *m.;* R. here 3.5 *m.;* then L. to the SITE OF UNION MISSION, 5.2 *m.,* indicated by a stone marker at the top of a wooded hill near the road. All that remains of the twenty buildings formerly comprising the old mission are a few foundation stones placed around the spring (300 yds. S.E. of the marker) about which the buildings were originally grouped.

Epaphras Chapman, a Presbyterian missionary, located the site in 1819 and obtained permission from the American Board of Commissioners for Foreign Missions and the Osage Indian tribe to set up a mission here in the Osage territory. On November 5, 1820, Chapman and his caravan of nineteen men, women, and children (two had died along the way) reached the remote wilderness station after suffering much hardship and sickness on the long journey from New York. They cultivated about one hundred acres of the surrounding land and, in 1821, opened the Union Mission school, which they continued to operate until 1832–33. In addition to the Osages, some twenty Creeks, who were destined to play an important part in tribal life, enrolled in 1830. Presbyterianism spread among the Creek tribe from this start. The Cherokee-Osage treaty of 1828, however, placed Union in Cherokee country and, since the mission had been established primarily for the Osages, the work was necessarily curtailed. This circumstance brought about the founding of the Hopefield Mission near Adair *(see above).*

In 1835 the Presbyterian minister, Rev. Samuel Austin Worcester *(see Literature),* came from Georgia, installing his printing press in Union's vacant buildings. The press had been retrieved once along the way when the boat carrying it sank in the Arkansas River. Worcester printed the first publication issued in what is now Oklahoma, said to be *The Child's Book* or *I stutsi in Naktsokv* (Creek or Muskhogean); it was written by John Fleming, of the American Board of Commissioners for Foreign Missions, and James Perryman, prominent Creek Indian, who together reduced the Creek language to writing. In June, 1837, the press was moved to Park Hill *(see Tour 3),* where many publications in the Cherokee, Creek, and Choctaw languages were printed; several volumes from this press are now preserved in the Library of Congress in Washington, D.C.

A monument here marks this SITE OF OKLAHOMA'S FIRST PRINTING PRESS. Across the road from the marker is the UNION MISSION CEMETERY, where the founder of the mission, Rev. Epaphras Chapman, who died in 1825, is buried. Near by, in a grove of black locust trees, is an old FRENCH CEMETERY where growing crops almost cover the toppled and broken headstones that once marked the graves of early French traders.

A short distance north of Union Mission site is the SALINE SPRING, mentioned in a report made by Major Amos Stoddard in 1806 concerning the natural resources of the Louisiana Territory. Later the Osages came here to make salt, frequently borrowing from the Union missionaries kettles in which to boil the water. Two men, named Campbell and Earhart, acquired the property and built a furnace (one hundred feet long) to quicken the boiling-water process of extracting the salt; many people were employed by them to cut the wood necessary for fuel. The spring is still active, but there are no remains of the old furnace; one of the huge kettles said to have been used then is at present (1941) on display at the Brooks Hotel in Wagoner.

MAZIE *(cabins, camp sites, boats),* 85.1 *m.* (620 alt., 200 pop.), a popular stopping place for sportsmen as the Grand River near by (L), offers exceptionally fine fishing for bass, perch, and channel cat; natives tell of a ninety-pound catfish taken from the Grand in this vicinity.

At 92.6 *m.* is the junction with an unimproved dirt road.

Left here, 3.5 *m.;* then R. to a FISHING CAMP *(cabins),* 3.8 *m.,* on the Grand River. Quail and squirrel hunting is permitted in season.

WAGONER, 95.7 *m.* (588 alt., 3,535 pop.), serving an agricultural area, was established when the Arkansas Valley and Kansas Railroad built to a junction here with the Missouri-Kansas-Texas line in 1886. It is said that the town was named for a popular train dispatcher, "Bigfoot" Wagoner, of Parsons, Kansas.

In the CARNEGIE LIBRARY *(open weekdays: 9 A.M. to 6 P.M.)* is a MUSEUM (free) where relics of the Civil War and many Indian articles are on display. At the American National Bank is exhibited a copy of a CRANMER BIBLE, a reprint of the famous edition issued in 1539–40 under authority of Henry VIII. This copy carries the date 1585 and the name of Christopher Baker, printer for Queen Elizabeth. It contains an almanac computing the special feast days and seasons for a period of fifty years (1580–1631). The first entry in the family records chronicles a birth in 1751 at "Port Glasgow, North Britain."

Left from Wagoner on graveled State 51 are (R) prehistoric INDIAN MOUNDS, 6.5 *m.,* which were excavated as a WPA project (1936) under the supervision of the Department of Anthropology of the University of Oklahoma. Two connected double-mound units, two single mounds, and traces of an ancient village were found. Digging exposed postholes indicating a fortification measuring about 150 feet square. Baked clay floors of the former dwellings, about twenty-five feet long and fifteen feet wide, revealed shallow, circular fire pits with raised brims and postholes in which the supports for the crossbeams of the thatched roofs stood. The articles unearthed include burial bundles, pottery, stone pipes, sheet-copper breastplates, solid copper and copper-coated ceremonial sticks, flint knives and scrapers, projectile points, shell beads, and fresh-water pearls; they are now on display at the University of Oklahoma.

BLUE MOUND, 98.7 *m.,* was so named because of the hue appearing over its summit (R) in the early morning light.

For a few months in 1871, while the Arkansas River to the south was being bridged, GIBSON, 102 *m.* (534 alt., 110 pop.), was the southern terminus of the Missouri-Kansas-Texas Railroad. Like other railroad outposts it acquired a wild and unsavory reputation. Even after the line built south to Muskogee, Gibson was an important shipping center, for prairie freighters and stagecoaches connected it with the Cherokee capital at Tahlequah and the army post at Fort Gibson. Its importance declined after the Arkansas

Valley and Kansas Railroad established a junction with the Missouri-Kansas-Texas at Wagoner in 1886.

OKAY, 105.2 *m.* (510 alt., 322 pop.), is approximately a half-mile north of the site of one of the oldest white settlements in Oklahoma. The firm of Brand and Barbour set up a trading post at this point in the first years of the nineteenth century and in 1819 sold their property to Colonel A. P. Chouteau, who had already established a post at Salina. Creole carpenters were brought from New Orleans and St. Louis to build the keelboats in which the French traders shipped their furs down the Arkansas and Mississippi rivers to New Orleans, where the boats and peltries were exchanged for supplies. The site was a busy shipping and trading point for it stood at the confluence of the Arkansas, the Grand (Neosho), and the Verdigris, whereby it gained the name Three Forks. At one time the Osage Indians claimed the section; later it was transferred by treaty to the Cherokees, and then the Creek Indians settled on a part of the area. In 1828, Chouteau's holdings were bought by the government for use as a Creek agency.

When Washington Irving made the trip described in his *Tour on the Prairies,* he stopped over night here; he wrote of the stern Osages, the gay Creeks, trappers, hunters, half-bloods, Creoles, Negroes, and frontiersmen, who made the place one of "complete bustle."

The busy little settlement was known by several names—Falls City, Verdigris Falls, Verdigris Landing, Three Forks, Creek Agency, and Sleepyville. The buildings were burned in whole or in part half a dozen times in the first half of the nineteenth century; and the bitter guerrilla fighting between the Northern and Southern factions that divided both the Creeks and Cherokees devastated the area during the Civil War. With the coming of the railroad in 1871, the settlement moved north to the present site and was known successively as Coretta Switch, North Muskogee, Rex, and finally Okay.

Blows of hard luck struck the town successively, one bringing about the last change of name by which the inhabitants attempted to create a boom. Discovery of natural gas near by shortly after the first World War led to the construction of a gas-stove factory, a native stone building at the eastern end of the bridge over which US 69 crosses the Verdigris. This is said to be on almost the exact site of the old Chouteau post. When the stove venture failed, the plant was sold to a designer and manufacturer of plows, who in turn went bankrupt and sold the factory to a company manufacturing OK trucks. The consequent employment of many laborers and skilled workmen increased the population, and the town enthusiastically changed its name to Okay. This enterprise, too, failed as did the airplane factory that took its place. A hardwood planing mill and a packing plant met the same fate. Even the elements have done their share to down Okay; in 1911 the town was swept by a devastating tornado, in 1927 by wind and flood, in 1936 by fire.

On the east side of the Verdigris River Bridge, 106 *m.,* the Daughters of the American Revolution have erected a THREE FORKS MARKER (R), commemorating "the important and ancient trail," the Texas Road, which crossed at this spot; the old trading post and the Three Forks landing; the

Osage and Creek agencies; the arrival of the first party of emigrating Creek Indians in February, 1828; Washington Irving's visit in 1832; and the near-by home of Sam Houston *(see Tour 2)*, who lived in this area in 1829–32.

South of the bridge US 69 parallels the Verdigris River where, before the Civil War, numerous trading posts stood on both banks. The old Texas Road followed almost the exact route of US 69 for a few miles north of the Arkansas River crossing. A branch, however, went southeasterly six miles to Fort Gibson. Midway on this road was the SITE OF WIGWAM NEOSHO, the log house built by Sam Houston in 1830 and occupied by him until 1832, when he started on his Texas adventure. It was here that he lived with his Cherokee wife, Tiana Rogers.

South of the Arkansas River crossing, 109.8 *m.*, is the site (L) of the council which Bernard de la Harpe, the French explorer, held on September 3, 1719, with some seven thousand Indians, representing the Tawakonis and the Wichitas and allied tribes. In his report of the expedition, which crossed from the southeastern section of what is now Oklahoma to this point, he stated that he gave fifteen hundred pounds of gifts to the assembled Indians on that day.

At 111.0 *m.* is the northern junction with US 62 *(see Tour 3)*, which unites briefly with US 69.

At 113.1 *m.* is the junction with an oiled asphalt road.

Left on this road through the college gateway to BACONE COLLEGE, 0.7 *m.*, a junior college maintained exclusively for Indians. The school was named for Professor Almon C. Bacone, the founder, who came to Indian Territory to teach in the Cherokee Male Seminary at Tahlequah *(see Tour 3)*. In 1879, he received permission to establish a university for Indians of all tribes under the supervision of the American Baptist Home Mission Society; the Baptist Mission House at the Cherokee capital served as the first home of this Indian university.

This society, the Woman's American Home Mission Society, and individual donors support the institution. In 1885, with the consent of the Creek tribal council, the school was moved to its present location, strategic because of its proximity to Muskogee, the governmental center for the Five Civilized Tribes. The junior college curriculum was instituted in 1927.

Bacone occupies a unique place in state education, for in addition to the regular curriculum, it strives to keep alive the ancient Indian arts. Patrick J. Hurley, Secretary of War (1929–33) under President Hoover, graduated here in 1905.

The plant is on a campus of 166 acres, eighty of which are under cultivation. The eleven college buildings *(open during school hours)* include SAMUEL RICHARDS MEMORIAL HALL, a three-story brick building of Norman design, erected in 1921 by an oil-rich Creek; the SALLY JOURNEYCAKE MEMORIAL, constructed of native stone by student labor and named for a famous Delaware Indian woman; the native-stone ARTS AND CRAFTS building; MEMORIAL HALL (now under construction, 1941), on the site of the first school structure; the INDIAN COTTAGE, a typical modern log cabin of the type recently built by many Indians on their rural holdings and used as a unit of the home economics department of the college; and the ART LODGE *(open to visitors only on the first Sunday of the month)*, which serves as the school recreational center. The lodge is built of native stone and lumber and is furnished throughout with handmade Indian furniture and rugs. In the Museum Room, relics, beadwork, wood carvings, and pottery are displayed. The fireplace was constructed of hundreds of stones gathered from various Indian reservations and places of historical interest.

The MILLY FRANCIS MONUMENT, in front of the Art Lodge, was erected in 1933 by the faculty and students of Bacone in honor of "Oklahoma's Pocahontas," the Indian woman who was awarded the first Congressional medal ever granted to a woman. Milly saved the life of Duncan McKrimmon, a Georgia militiaman stationed at Fort Gadsden, Georgia, during the border warfare between the United States and Spanish Florida in 1817–18. Captain McKrimmon had been captured by Seminole Indians and was about to be killed when Milly's eloquent pleading saved him, on condition that he shave his head and live among his captors. Two years later he was sold to Spanish traders for a barrel of whisky. It is said that the young soldier returned shortly thereafter and asked Milly to become his wife, but she refused. Later Milly Francis was captured along with a number of Seminoles and finally came west to live in the vicinity of Fort Gibson, where Colonel Ethan Allen Hitchcock learned her story. He petitioned Congress to recognize her deed, and an act was passed on June 17, 1844, granting her an annual pension of $96. The act further provided for a medal, but official Washington did not push the matter and Milly died in 1848 without having received it. Her heirs, however, later were given the award.

The MURROW INDIAN ORPHANS' HOME, on the campus, is a group of modern stone and brick buildings where homeless Indian children are cared for. The institution was moved here from Atoka where it was known as the Atoka Baptist Academy.

The SITE OF FORT DAVIS, a Confederate fort established for a short time during the Civil War, is also on the college grounds. A tract approximately 550 feet square has been given to the Fort Davis Memorial Association, which plans to restore the site. At the top of a mound is the place where the flagstaff stood, and near by is an old well which served the fortification.

MUSKOGEE, 114.2 *m.* (617 alt., 32,332 pop.) *(see Muskogee),* is at the junction with US 64 *(see Tour 2),* and the southern junction with US 62 *(see Tour 3).*

Section b. MUSKOGEE *to* TEXAS LINE, *159 m. US 69*

South of MUSKOGEE, 0 *m.,* the route passes through towns and counties bearing the names of chieftains and leaders of the Creek Indians who peopled this area after their removal from the East. Just east of the railroad tracks the ruts of the old Texas Road are still discernible. Herds of cattle being driven north from Texas along this route had to make way frequently for the long lines of emigrants' wagons headed south.

OKTAHA, 15.6 *m.* (591 alt., 233 pop.), is a small farming center (L) named after Oktarharsars Harjo, leader of a conservative faction among the Creeks. The town began as a station on the Missouri-Kansas-Texas Railroad in 1872.

On the banks of ELK CREEK, 18 *m.,* is the SITE OF THE BATTLE OF HONEY SPRINGS (L), the most important Civil War battle in Indian Territory. In the summer of 1863, several thousand Confederates under the command of Gen. Douglas H. Cooper were stationed at Honey Springs, a stop on the Texas Road, from which point they planned to attack Fort Gibson, key to the whole of Indian Territory. Union scouts, however, reported the proposed movement to Fort Gibson, and on the morning of July 17 the Union forces, under General James G. Blunt, marched from the fort and met the Confederates at Honey Springs. Outclassed in equipment and ammunition by the Federal troops, the Confederates retreated down the Texas Road, leaving two hundred dead and wounded lying amid the smoking ruins of their warehouses, which they fired to facilitate retreat. This turning point in the Indian Territory theater of war occurred only a few days after the fall of Gettysburg and Vicksburg, completing the geographical line of defeat resulting in the dissolution of the Confederacy.

The remains (L) of the abutments of an old bridge over which the Texas Road crossed are still discernible. The bridge was the focal point of the battlefield on the day of the Honey Springs rout. This and other bridges on near-by streams were built by citizens of the Creek Nation, who then levied tolls on travelers and freighters using the Texas Road.

CHECOTAH, 24.2 *m.* (638 alt., 2,126 pop.), the trade center for an agricultural and stock-raising area, was named for Samuel Checote, a great fullblood statesman. Checote, who had been educated in a Methodist mission school in Alabama, was elected principal chief of the Creeks when a new constitution was adopted by the tribe in 1867. But the conservatives objected to his introduction of constitutional procedures modeled after those of the white man, and under the leadership of Oktarharsars Harjo they carried on a series of insurrections against the tribal government. Although sinister and grasping whites fanned the flame, the leaders entered into a harmonious agreement in the fall of 1871. The settlement proved to be transitory—the difficulty finally culminated in the Green Peach War *(see Tour 3)*—but the railroad building through the Creek country during the temporary peace named the stations of Oktaha and Checotah in honor of the two leaders.

The ODD FELLOWS' HOME, for old people of that order, is a two-story, brick structure on a 160-acre tract, given to the lodge by William Gentry, a mixed-blood Creek citizen.

US 69 crosses the NORTH CANADIAN RIVER, 35.7 *m.,* where Alexander Lawrence Posey (1873–1908), well-known Creek writer and poet *(see Literature),* was drowned. Posey, the son of a Scotch-Irish father and a fullblood Creek mother, spoke only the Creek language until he was twelve. After attending Bacone College, he started on a career of leadership among his people and literary achievement in the white man's language. He held a number of tribal offices, and after the dissolution of the Creek government by the Dawes Commission he became city editor of the *Muskogee Times (see Newspapers).* He is best known for his published poems and for the "Fuss Fixico" newspaper column where in Indian-English dialect he loosed his satirical arrows at members of the Dawes Commission and other Federal office-holders of the Indian Territory.

EUFAULA, 37.2 *m.* (613 alt., 2,355 pop.), the seat of McIntosh County, is a few miles west of the confluence of the North and South Canadian rivers. The development of the present-day town began with the coming of the railroad in 1872, when residents of NORTH FORK TOWN, a thriving Creek center approximately two miles east, moved there to be near transportation facilities.

North Fork Town, taking its name from the North Fork of the Canadian, had been settled by the Creeks shortly after their migration from the East in 1836 and had become an important tribal community. It was the scene of the treaty-making between the Confederates and the Creeks, Choctaws, and Chickasaws in 1861. Two important trails, the Texas Road and a branch of the California Road, crossed at North Fork Town, making it a center of industry and traffic. In 1853 a post office was established under the name Micco, the Creek word for chief.

Northeast of Eufaula is the site of Asbury Mission, a boarding school established by the Methodist Episcopal Church in 1849 under a contract with the Creek Council. It was housed in a large brick building accommodating one hundred pupils, and during its existence made a definite contribution to the culture and progress of the tribe.

Another early Creek school, the EUFAULA INDIAN GIRLS' BOARDING SCHOOL, was opened in Eufaula in 1892 and is still active. First established by the Creeks as a part of the tribal educational system, it was taken over by the Federal government in 1899. The plant is owned by the Indians, but the United States pays for the maintenance. The school now has an enrollment of two hundred. The vocational department, in an imposing two-story building, offers courses in interior decorating, handicraft, and the household arts.

The oldest surviving newspaper in the state, the *Indian Journal (see Newspapers),* is published here. It was founded at Muskogee as a tribal organ in 1876.

A BOY SCOUT CAMP, 40.3 *m.,* is on the bank (R) of a bend in the South Canadian River. The wide, sandy stream formerly served as the boundary between the old Choctaw Nation on the south and the Creek Nation on the north.

McALESTER, 66.3 *m.* (718 alt., 12,401 pop.), *(see Tour 5),* is at the junction with US 270 *(see Tour 5).*

Between McAlester and the Texas Line the route traverses country cut by many streams and rivers; the towns are small and agriculture is the main occupation. Throughout the region are sites where events of historical importance took place when the land belonged to the Choctaw Nation.

At 71.8 *m.* is the junction with an improved dirt road.

Right on this road to the SITE OF PERRYVILLE, 0.3 *m.,* a trading post and stage station established on the Texas Road about 1838 by James Perry, member of a prominent Choctaw-Chickasaw family. A post office was opened here in 1841; and in 1858, when John Butterfield was awarded the contract to carry mail in stagecoaches across the continent, the route intersected the Texas Road at this station. Colbert Institute, a Chickasaw school, was founded here by the Methodist Church in 1852, but when the boundary line between the two tribes was fixed a few years later, the place fell on the Choctaw side; consequently the school was moved about fifty miles southeast where it was re-established as Collins Institute. Perryville became the seat of Tobucksy County of the Choctaw Nation in 1855.

During the Civil War the Confederates used Perryville as a military post and supply depot, and it was to this refuge that General Douglas H. Cooper retreated from the Honey Springs rout fifty miles north. Brigadier General William Steele met him here with additional forces, but despite the combination they were again beaten by Union forces under Major General James G. Blunt in August, 1863. After several men had been killed in the Battle of Perryville, Cooper realized the futility of resistance and evacuated the town, first dumping salt in the water wells. The Union soldiers confiscated what they could and then completed the destruction of Perryville by burning the buildings.

A reproduction of THE OLD STAGE STAND *(adm. free)* has been erected on the site; many relics of the Battle of Perryville are on display.

In 1880, SAVANNA, 75.4 *m.* (679 alt., 525 pop.), was a thriving coal-mining town with approximately eight times its present-day population. But after a disastrous explosion in 1887, when a number of miners were killed, the operators, blaming the great quantity of gas in the mines for the accident, moved their machinery and buildings to another location. Savanna never again reached its early-day size.

KIOWA, 83.7 *m.* (650 alt., 802 pop.), was founded in 1872 when the Missouri-Kansas-Texas Railroad was extended southward; it was known then as Kiowa Switch.

Left from Kiowa on a dirt road to WHITE'S CAVE, 5.9 *m.*, where, according to local legend, bullion was sealed in the walls many years ago by Spaniards who mined in this area. The cave was named for a pioneer settler.

A break in the limestone ridge at this point was responsible for the naming of LIMESTONE GAP. 93.2 *m.* (642 alt., 15 pop.), a settlement through which the old Texas Road passed before swinging to the southwest. Buck Creek (L) was spanned by a toll bridge at that time, operated by Captain Charles LeFlore, a member of the prominent Choctaw family. LeFlore's old home (R), a white frame two-story structure inclosed in a plank-fenced and flower-filled yard, is still standing.

CHOCKIE, 95.6 *m.* (669 alt., 59 pop.), an old Choctaw village, was first named Chickiechockie in honor of Captain LeFlore's daughters, who had in turn been named for the respective Chickasaw and Choctaw nationalities of their mother and father. Chickie, who became the wife of Lee Cruce, Oklahoma's second governor, died early in the twentieth century and her name was removed from the depot sign—but "Chockie" has remained to the present day.

First a stage stop on the Fort Smith to Red River Road, later an important lumber-shipping point when the railroad was built through, STRINGTOWN, 104.1 *m.* (596 alt., 718 pop.), is today (1941) an agricultural community.

ATOKA, 111.3 *m.* (582 alt., 2,548 pop.), is the seat of the county of the same name, both of which were named for a subchief of the Choctaw Nation. He is buried about twenty miles east of town near the little settlement of Farris. When the section was surveyed, the chief's resting place was found to be in the middle of the road, but the body was never moved.

Rev. J. S. Murrow, a Baptist missionary, founded Atoka in 1867. Shortly afterwards, he established the Atoka Baptist Academy, which eventually was absorbed into the Murrow Indian Orphans' Home on the Bacone College campus north of Muskogee.

The Atoka Agreement, between the Choctaw and Chickasaw nations and the Dawes Commission, providing for the surrender of tribal government and the allotment of lands, was signed at Atoka in 1897.

Atoka is at the junction with US 75 *(see Tour 9)*.

At 112.5 *m.* is the junction with an unimproved dirt road.

Right on this road to the junction with a second dirt road, 4.6 *m.;* L. here to SITE OF BOGGY DEPOT, 9.7 *m.*, an important old Choctaw-Chickasaw town which grew from an Indian log cabin built in 1837 to a flourishing trade center and Civil War army post. The name of the town comes from that of Clear Boggy Creek about one mile west; the Clear Boggy, Muddy Boggy, and North Boggy streams seem to have been given their names by early French traders who called them *Vazzures (vaseuse,* miry or boggy). Americans adopted the translation probably about the time of the exploratory expedition made in 1805 by Dr. John Sibley, who wrote in his report, "... we arrived at the mouth of the *Vazzures*, or Boggy River ..." "Depot" was added after the Choctaw-Chickasaw treaty of 1837, when the Chickasaws emigrated from the East and were paid annuities at the "depot on the Boggy." The Post Office Department officially named the town in 1849; a boundary treaty in 1855 placed it in the Choctaw Nation.

When a post route was established in 1850, Boggy Depot became an important town and several large two-story residences were erected. The settlement was at the junction of the Texas Road and one of the trails from Fort Smith, Arkansas, to the West and did a thriving business. The town church, built by Rev. Cyrus Kingsbury in 1840, served as the Choctaw capitol in 1858 when Chief Basil LeFlore ordered the national council to meet there temporarily during a factional dispute. The Confederates made Boggy Depot a military post during the Civil War, and the Confederate banner floated from a flagpole in the center of the town for four years. Incongruously, the Indian troops fighting for the South would gallop at high speed around the flag whooping and yelling and singing the Choctaw war song. One of the first Masonic lodges to be established in what is now Oklahoma was started there by Rev. J. S. Murrow about 1872. When the Missouri-Kansas-Texas Railroad was built through the area, the route missed Boggy Depot, and the town declined.

Today (1941) traces of the main streets of the old town are still visible, as are the tree-choked foundations of some of the houses; fallen sandstone markers with dates indicate early graves in the old cemetery; and abandoned wells and cement cisterns show the locations of former residences. The HOME OF CHIEF ALLEN WRIGHT *(open by appointment)*, built in 1860 out of wood from the great oaks growing about the place, is still standing and in good repair. Wright (1826–95) served two terms as principal chief of the Choctaw Nation and translated several books into the Choctaw language. It was he who named Oklahoma, for in 1866 he suggested the name for the proposed Indian territory. The word is a Choctaw phrase meaning "Red People" and had occurred frequently in the Treaty of Dancing Rabbit Creek when reference was made to the Choctaws. After that the name was in common use and was finally officially given to Oklahoma Territory and the state. Chief Wright, Rev. Cyrus Kingsbury, and other prominent pioneers are buried in the abandoned cemetery here.

CADDO, 131.8 *m.* (591 alt., 954 pop.), located on a small branch of the Blue River, is named for the Caddo Indians who occupied this region before the coming of the Choctaws. It then became a Choctaw court town, and was filled on the first Monday of each month with many tribal members who came to air their grievances or to stand trial. Caddo was later an important station on the trail between Fort Smith and Fort Sill but declined when the railroads offered a more convenient routing.

At MAYTUBBY SPRINGS (R) in Caddo three different kinds of mineral water flow from separate outlets only three feet apart. The springs were named for Captain Peter Maytubby, a Choctaw leader who settled near the town.

South of Caddo is a hilly region where a battle was fought in 1806 between the Caddoes, who occupied the territory at the time, and the Choctaws, who were then living in Mississippi. The latter tribe hunted on the plains of the present Oklahoma long before the nineteenth century, and on one occasion a hunting party of the eastern Indians was surprised by the resident Caddoes. Many bones and arrows were later found in the hills. It was from these hunting trips that the Choctaws learned much of the land which they selected here before Removal. Pushmataha, one of the Choctaw chiefs who consummated the exchange of territory with General Andrew Jackson at Doak's Stand, boasted that though the western land was supposed to have been unknown to him at the time, actually he knew it well for on "big hunts" he had been chased by Comanches from one end of the country to the other. The Washita River gained its name from these early expeditions, for the Choctaw words *owa chito* mean "big hunt."

At the STATE FISH HATCHERY *(visitors welcome)*, 138.8 *m.*, on the Blue River (R), 126 acres of water are used as spawning grounds. Many streams of this and other Oklahoma districts are stocked from the game fish propagated here. Channel catfish have been successfully bred as have "Texas strawberry bream," a species of game fish new to Oklahoma.

At 139.3 *m.* is the junction with a graveled road.

Right here to a junction with graveled State 22, 1.2 *m.;* R. on State 22 to a junction with a third graveled road, 2.6 *m.*

Right (N) here to NAIL'S CROSSING, 1.6 *m.*, where the Texas Road crossed the Blue River, named for a prominent Choctaw family. The Nail house is still standing—its logs held together firmly by the wooden pegs used in the original construction about 1847. Near by is a family cemetery that has been well kept through the years.

On the south bank of the Blue is the SITE OF FORT MCCULLOCH (L), established in 1862 by General Albert Pike and named for Brigadier General McCulloch, who commanded the Confederate forces in Indian Territory the first year of the Civil War. The complicated intrigues that distracted the military command of this region soon brought about Pike's resignation and the abandonment of the fort, but the places where the bastions and redoubts were erected are still plainly visible. Some remnants of a bridge built across the Blue at that time also remain.

State 22 continues to a junction with an improved dirt road, 9.6 *m.;* L. here to a junction, with a graveled road, 9.9 *m.;* R. to the junction with an improved dirt road, 13.4 *m.* and R. to the SITE OF FORT WASHITA, 14.9 *m.* This important military outpost, the first of a series of forts on the Washita River *(see Tours 3 and 10)*, was established in 1842 by General Zachary Taylor, later to become President of the United States. The purpose of Fort Washita was to protect the Chickasaws and Choctaws from border raids by the wild tribes of the Southwest. The Marcy Trail to California ran through this point, and the site became a refuge where emigrants might gather to await fellow travelers before starting on the more dangerous portion of their trip. The United States abandoned the fortification in 1861, however, and it was never again occupied except by the Confederates for a short time during the Civil War.

Today (1941), Fort Washita is a ghost fortress overgrown with post oaks, but the well-preserved remains of many of the buildings and sites clearly show the plan of the former stronghold. The ruins of massive-chimneyed barracks are still here, for the Goodland limestone quarried near the site has successfully withstood the elements; the straight chimneys of the old tavern built just outside the quadrangle rise like silent sentries; and water still flows from the stone springhouse.

North of the fort is the old MILITARY CEMETERY, used partly now as a community burying ground. The marker placed at the grave of General William Belknap, former commander of the southwestern forces of the United States Army who died there in 1851, is still erect; the body, however, was moved to the Fort Gibson National Cemetery *(see Tour 3)* and later to Washington, D.C.

DURANT, 144.2 *m.* (643 alt., 10,027 pop.) *(see Tour 6)*, is at the junction with US 70 *(see Tour 6)*.

CALERA, 149.8 *m.* (643 alt., 597 pop.), an agricultural center, was one of the first townsites in which white men could purchase lots and get titles for the land directly from the Indian tribes. The lot sale there took place in September, 1899.

In the fertile Red River valley area, COLBERT, 156.8 *m.* (661 alt., 602 pop.), serves as a trade center for the surrounding farm lands.

Right from Colbert on a graveled road to the DENISON DAM, 5 *m.*, a structure three miles long and 140 feet high, planned for completion in 1944. Approximately at the confluence of the Washita with Red River, the dam when full will impound water covering some 120,000 acres in Oklahoma and 22,000 in Texas. The primary purpose of the $50,000,000 project is flood control in Oklahoma, Texas, Arkansas, and Louisiana. Army engineers estimate that more than 138,000 acres of rich farm land would have been saved from flooding when the Red River went out of its banks in 1935 if there had been such a reservoir. In addition, hydroelectric power, generated at the dam, will be available for a large area.

The free bridge over the Red River, 159 *m.,* was the cause of the so-called Red River Bridge War in 1931. For many years previously the Texas Toll Bridge Company had operated a toll bridge at this crossing, but in 1929 Texas and Oklahoma, with the consent of Congress, began the construction of a free bridge. The company stockholders then secured an injunction from the Federal District Court to prevent the opening of the free bridge, and the Lone Star governor thereupon ordered barricades erected at its south end. On July 23, 1931, however, Oklahoma's governor, William H. ("Alfalfa Bill") Murray, ordered the State National Guard to clear the bridge and let traffic flow undisturbed; he had discovered a previous Supreme Court decision placing both banks of the river under the jurisdiction of Oklahoma. He also ordered the highway approaching the north end of the toll bridge plowed up and the paving removed. A judgment against Oklahoma was granted the company, but the Federal Circuit Court of Appeals reversed the decision, and the Red River Bridge War was ended.

US 69 crosses the TEXAS LINE, 159 *m.,* at a point five miles north of Denison, Texas *(see Texas Guide.)*

Tour 9

(Independence, Kans.)—Bartlesville—Tulsa—Okmulgee—Calvin—Atoka; US 75
Kansas Line to Atoka, 231.2 m.

Roadbed alternately concrete-paved and graveled.
The Atchison, Topeka, and Santa Fe Railway parallels the route between the Kansas Line and Tulsa; the St. Louis–San Francisco between Tulsa and Wetumka; the Missouri-Kansas-Texas between Coalgate and Atoka.
Good accommodations available at convenient distances.

This north-south road through eastern Oklahoma crosses rich range country in northern Oklahoma, skirts the eastern border of the earliest and most extensive shallow oil-field development in the state, bisects the old Creek Nation, and ends in the heart of the former Choctaw Nation. In this region are coal diggings that began as early as 1880 and declined almost to the vanishing point after the development of Oklahoma's rich fields of oil and fuel gas.

Almost at the route's halfway mark is the region in which the first gusher oil field of the state, the Glenn Pool, was developed; there, in the sandy, blackjack-studded hill country, illiterate Creek Indian full bloods were made millionaires by chance and oil-boom towns provided a melodramatic chapter in the state's history.

With its view of livestock, general and cotton farming, peanuts, pecans, oil, and coal, and its dip into cosmopolitan Tulsa, US 75 offers a rather complete summary of Oklahoma's resources, occupations, and landscapes.

US 75 crosses the KANSAS LINE, 0 *m.,* two miles south of Caney, Kansas *(see Kansas Guide).*

COPAN, 8.1 *m.* (776 alt., 549 pop.), in the northwestern corner of the old Cherokee Nation, was settled in the 1880's, growing up on the prairie around a store built to serve the Cherokee, Delaware, and Osage Indian trade. With the coming of the railroad, in 1898, the place gained some population; and the later development of an extensive shallow oil field toward the east caused it to experience a mild boom. With the decline of oil in the region, Copan became the trading point of a farming community.

DEWEY, 15.3 *m.* (700 alt., 2,114 pop.), was founded in 1898 by J. H. (Jake) Bartles, who had previously founded Bartlesville *(see Bartlesville),* and named in honor of Admiral George Dewey, whose victory at Manila Bay was fresh in everyone's mind.

When the Santa Fe purchased the grade of the projected Kansas, Oklahoma and Southwestern Railroad, which Bartles had surveyed and constructed from Caney, and began laying rails, this enterprising trader undertook to move a store from Silver Lake *(see below)* to the site of the new town. In order to do this, he built a road north from Bartlesville. Because of mud in the Caney River bottoms, through which his oxen could only with the utmost difficulty drag the store building, constructed of heavy walnut lumber, the removal required five months. Meanwhile, however, business went on in the store as it rested on log rollers in the road or was inched forward by the struggling oxen. The building, on West 8th Street, is used as a café, and the furniture, of heavy walnut also, was made out of lumber from a mill built by Bartles at Bartlesville and torn down in 1915.

The DEWEY PORTLAND CEMENT COMPANY PLANT at the northeastern edge of the town, one of the largest in the state, employs some five hundred workers, many of whom—Negroes and Mexicans—live in a close-packed group near by.

Dewey's annual round up (rodeo), which occurs in Fourth of July week, is one of the oldest, most popular, and interesting exhibitions of its kind in Oklahoma. There is also an annual Free Fair at the Dewey fairgrounds in September.

Right from Dewey on an improved dirt road to junction with another dirt road, 3 *m.;* R. to junction with a third dirt road, 4.2 *m.;* and L. to BAR DEW LAKE, 5 *m.,* a 212-acre reservoir made by damming a branch of the Caney River. At the dam is a ten-acre recreational area, developed by the WPA, which is popular not only with residents of Dewey but also with those of Bartlesville. The State Game and Fish Commission has a fish hatchery here.

BARTLESVILLE, 18.7 *m.* (694 alt., 16,267 pop.) *(see Bartlesville).*

At 21.7 *m.* is the junction with US 60 *(see Tour 4).*

The original Jake Bartles trading post, 23.3 *m.,* called SILVER LAKE, was also the site of the former Osage Indian Agency. When an accurate survey of the tract bought by the United States government from the Cherokees for occupation of the Osages, removed from Kansas in 1872, showed that Silver Lake was outside the boundaries, the Osage agent was required to remove as near to the center of the reservation as feasible. It was then that the agency was established at Pawhuska *(see Tour 4).* As a settlement, Silver Lake survived until Bartles started his store on its five months' journey to Dewey.

OCHELATA, 31.4 *m.* (570 alt., 333 pop.), was given the Indian name of Charles Thompson, principal chief of the Cherokees, 1875–79, when the Santa Fe Railway built a station there in 1899. The town is a supply point for farmers and ranchmen.

Left from Ochelata on a dirt road to the ELLEN HOWARD MILLER BIRD SANCTUARY, 7 *m.,* on an island formed by the branching of Caney River. It was founded by a former resident of the town, Mrs. Howard Miller, under whose supervision practically all species of birds native to Oklahoma were gathered. The limits of the refuge are plainly marked by signs warning visitors against disturbing the birds or their nests.

RAMONA, 38.9 *m.* (703 alt., 574 pop.), grew from the depot erected there in 1900 by the Santa Fe Railway and was named for the heroine of Helen Hunt Jackson's widely read novel about the Indians of California, *Ramona.* Later three older trading posts—Old Ringo, Austin, and Hillside Mission—merged with the town.

Like other settlements of this region, Ramona had a temporary boom due to the discovery and development of oil in the Verdigris shallow field; and like them became merely a farm and ranch trading place after this activity died down.

VERA, 45.8 *m.* (645 alt., 208 pop.), occupies a site which was once a part of the allotment of W. C. Rogers, the last elected principal chief of the Cherokee Nation. He donated the land to the Santa Fe Railway when a station was established in 1900, and earlier town-builders moved there from a site they had occupied two miles north. Vera now serves the people of an area given over largely to cattle pastures.

At 47.6 *m.* is the junction with an improved dirt road.

Right on this road is the SITE OF HILLSIDE MISSION, 6 *m.,* where a mission was opened in 1884 by John Murdock, a missionary sent out by the Society of Friends (Quakers) of Philadelphia to work among the Osages, Cherokees, and Delawares who lived within driving distance of the place. Substantial buildings of walnut lumber were erected, one of which, a house of twenty-four rooms, is standing. When John Watson was sent to relieve Murdock at the mission, he carried with him a shoot from the ancient elm under which William Penn signed the treaty with the Delaware Indians in 1682. It was planted in the mission grounds and is now a big tree.

In the cemetery across the road from the mission site a stone marks the grave of Chief Rogers *(see above)*.

COLLINSVILLE, 53.9 *m.* (621 alt., 1,927 pop.) *(see Tour 9A)*, is at the junction with US 169 *(see Tour 9A)*, which unites with US 75 for 21.3 miles.

In TULSA, 73.2 *m.* (700 alt., 142,157 pop.) *(see Tulsa)*, are junctions with US 64 *(see Tour 2)*, and US 66 *(see Tour 1)*, which unites southward with US 75 to SAPULPA, 90.9 *m.* (712 alt., 12,249 pop.) *(see Tour 1)*.

South of Sapulpa is the region in which the first spectacularly productive oil field in the state was developed in 1905–06. The discovery well came in —December 1, 1905—on land southeast of Sapulpa owned by Ida E. Glenn, a Creek citizen, and the field became known as Glenn Pool. Initial production was from a depth of 1,475 feet and amounted to seventy-five barrels a day. The second well drilled was a dry hole, but the third well was a thousand-barrels-a-day gusher; and the fourth went up to 2,500 barrels a day. The wells drew national attention to Indian Territory as a possible new center of oil production; and because Tulsa had already become the headquarters of the companies and individuals who were exploiting the Red Fork field *(see Tulsa)*, that city rather than the near-by Sapulpa benefitted by the rush of thousands to the new field. Interest was stimulated by the mystery surrounding the drilling of the discovery well; it was so well guarded that only the men working on it were allowed to approach the rig.

As more gushers came into production, there were neither facilities for shipping the oil to refineries nor sufficient steel-tank storage for it, and in desperation operators began damming ravines to hold the flood from the wells which they did not then know how to control. Millions of barrels, of course, were wasted before adequate tank storage could be built or pipe lines laid in to connect with refineries.

Many of the most productive wells of the old Creek Nation were drilled on the land of Indians who, resisting allotment of the communal lands of the tribe, had refused to select allotments themselves and had been arbitrarily given acreage in the worthless blackjack covered hills which other tribesmen did not want. One of these, whose name became known nationally because of the long drawn out litigation following his marriage to a white woman, was Jackson Barnett, an illiterate full blood who was declared incompetent, and whose millions (literally) of income from oil were controlled by the Indian Bureau and doled out as his appointed guardian willed. Others, like Katie Fixico, another incompetent whose money built the new County Courthouse at Okmulgee, and Enos Wilson, were examples of Creeks made rich from the Glenn Pool. Guardianship of these illiterate full bloods, declared by local courts to be incompetent, became rich plums eagerly sought by enterprising lawyers and sometimes led to scandals and prolonged litigation.

Producers, too, became principals in true stories of quick wealth, men like Robert McFarlin and James E. Chapman, the first a small-town banker and the other a small-ranch cattleman. From an investment of $700 in a first lease, these partners ran their holdings up within eleven years to an aggregate of leases, wells, stored oil, and pipe lines which they sold to a major company for $35,000,000; and it was said that the stock they received in payment immediately rose in value.

KIEFER, 98.3 *m.* (686 alt., 330 pop.), before the opening of Glenn Pool, was only a siding on the Frisco. Then, because it was the nearest unloading point for machinery needed in the oil field, houses and stores were built; and one of the first casing-head gas-treating plants—for extracting gasoline from wet gas—was located here.

In the semilegendary history of Kiefer it is recorded that it became one of the toughest of all tough oil towns; and that a near-by creek whose waters were covered by a thick film of waste oil and whose bottom was deep mud was the secret graveyard of many victims of the town's pistoleers.

BEGGS, 112.6 *m.* (690 alt., 1,283 pop.), gave its name to one of the richest oil fields ever opened up in the state. As development spread from the Glenn Pool area west and south, in the period from 1910 to 1915, this town began to boom, and by 1920 was an important supply point and residence center for oilmen. Production in the Beggs field is still (1941) heavy.

OKMULGEE, 124.1 *m.* (670 alt., 16,051 pop.) *(see Okmulgee),* is at the junction with US 62 *(see Tour 3),* which unites southwestward with US 75 for 24.7 miles.

At 128.2 *m.* are (R) the FIDELITY LABORATORIES *(open during working hours),* a link in an interesting process for the treatment of hog cholera. In the neighborhood are a number of fine swine farms and a packing plant. Blood from hogs butchered at the packing plant is utilized at the laboratories in making the anticholera serum, which is marketed throughout the world.

HENRYETTA, 138.9 *m.* (691 alt., 6,905 pop.) *(see Tour 3).*

WELEETKA, 154.2 *m.* (690 alt., 1,904 pop.), trade center of a good farming section, contains many Creek families and serves many others. In watermelon time, the streets are crowded with wagons and trucks of the Indian and white growers, and by buyers of the fine melons produced near by. At other seasons, Saturday, market day for the farmers of the countryside, is the time to see the town and the people who support it.

On the banks of Coal Creek, fifteen miles east of Weleetka, is the site of the Old Hickory Stomp Grounds, where in 1901 the fullblood Creek leader Chitto Harjo (known to the whites as Crazy Snake) gathered his numerous fullblood faction in a rump session of the tribal council to legislate against division of the Creek Nation by allotment. In justifying his action, he said: "He [the Federal Government] told me [the Creek Nation] that as long as the sun shone and the sky is up yonder these agreements will be kept . . . He said, 'Just as long as you see light here, just as long as you see this light glimmering over us, shall these agreements be kept, and not until all these things cease and pass away shall our agreement pass away.' That is what he said, and we believed it."

Not until United States Marshal Leo Bennett came with an armed force and haled Chitto Harjo and a number of his followers to the white man's court (where they received suspended sentences for obstructing allotment) was the full blood's faith in treaties completely destroyed. Eight years later, in an attempt to arrest him by authorities of McIntosh County, Chitto Harjo was shot through the hips and died at the home of a Choctaw Indian who was sheltering him from the white man's law that had declared him to be an outlaw rebel.

WETUMKA, 164.8 *m.* (770 alt., 2,340 pop.), in the Creek Indian language means noisy or sounding water. The town was settled by a band of the tribe soon after their removal from the town of the same name they had occupied in Alabama. To Wetumka the exiles brought not only the name but living fire from the old communal hearth. On the long road of banishment, two men were entrusted with the duty of keeping the fire. At each camping place, the coals were blown up anew, cooking done, and when the march was resumed new coals were carried forward. At the site of this western Wetumka, a new communal hearth was dedicated, and the head man of the band said, "Here is our town, we shall go no farther west."

Some 20 per cent of the town's people are Indian.

CALVIN, 184.8 *m.* (716 alt., 589 pop.), *(see Tour 5),* is at the junction with US 270 *(see Tour 5).*

South of Calvin, the highway curves, dips, and rises among scrub-forested hills, follows briefly narrow valleys, and passes by occasional small farmhouses and two or three more pretentious dwellings belonging to ranchmen whose livestock range the hill pastures. In this region, too, hidden from sight of the traveler on US 75, live numbers of fullblood Choctaws described as "conservatives" by the whites and mixed bloods because they like the old way of life.

COALGATE, 217 *m.* (622 alt., 2,118 pop.), was once a thriving, prosperous coal-mining center but began to decline to its present status as a supply point for the surrounding farming area when oil and fuel gas developments made extensive coal mining unprofitable. Under lease from the Choctaw Nation, the first coal mine was opened in 1882 within one hundred feet of what is now Main Street. The first vein tapped was so close to the surface that it was stripped by the miners with plows and scrapers and removed with sledges, steel coal pins, and shovels.

LEHIGH, 222.3 *m.* (599 alt. 519 pop.), is another mining center in the old Choctaw Nation, where coal was first mined in 1880. The settlement was named for Pennsylvania's coal-mining city. It was hardly more than a company commissary and a huddle of shacks until 1887, when a mine disaster at Savanna *(see Tour 8)* caused the closing of mines there and the removal to Lehigh of mining equipment and 135 houses.

In 1912, a destructive fire swept the town; and today (1941) gray-black ruins, including a large heat-distorted bank vault, are evidences of Lehigh's palmy days when its population was three thousand, and the miners' pay rolls amounted to $75,000 a month. A few small mines are still operating, and some four thousand tons of coal were mined and shipped out by truck in the year 1939.

Right from Lehigh on a dirt road to the junction with another dirt road, 2.5 *m.;* L. here, 4.3 *m.,* to the BIRTHPLACE OF PATRICK J. HURLEY, Secretary of War (1929–33) under President Hoover. His father was a coal miner and farmer of this district, and young Hurley satisfied his early thirst for books at the home of a neighbor, Ben Smallwood, a cultivated mixed blood who was for a time principal chief of the Choctaw Nation. The old Hurley home was burned some years ago, and a tenant house stands on the site.

ATOKA, 231.2 *m.* (582 alt., 2,548 pop.) *(see Tour 8)*, is at the junction with US 69 *(see Tour 8)*.

Tour 9A

(Coffeyville, Kans.)—Collinsville—Tulsa; 72.2 m., US 169

Intermittently paved roadbed of various types; also graveled.
Missouri Pacific R.R. parallels route between Kansas Line and Oologah; the Santa Fe between Collinsville and Owasso.

Good accommodations at frequent intervals.

This route passes through an area originally largely settled by the Delaware Indians who in 1867 used tribal funds to purchase equal rights with the Cherokees in the Cherokee Nation. Now (1941) mainly occupied by white farmers and ranchmen, this upland prairie region is dotted with small power plants, housed in galvanized iron shacks; each plant operates five or more pump jacks at shallow "stripper" oil wells. The route bisects an extensive shallow oil field, one of the first to be developed in the state; many of the wells have been on the pump for more than thirty years, producing from half a barrel to two or three barrels a day.

US 169 crosses the KANSAS LINE, 0 *m.*, 3.8 miles south of Coffeyville, Kansas *(see Kansas Guide)*.

SOUTH COFFEYVILLE, 0.6 *m.* (740 alt., 364 pop.), with its scattering of homes, beer, pool, and dance halls, garages, and stores, was once a notoriously wild border town where bootleggers flourished since both Indian Territory and Kansas were dry. When United States marshals arrived to raid the whisky joints, their proprietors hastily moved the stock of liquor out of the back doors a few yards across the Kansas Line. At times, outraged Kansans disregarded legal barriers to burn saloons and destroy whisky, but South Coffeyville's defiant bootleggers always restocked and carried on under brush arbors until they could rebuild.

The name of LENAPAH, 10.7 *m.* (759 alt., 395 pop.), is a variation of the ancient name of the Delaware Indian tribe, Lenape. The town is the center of a district formerly occupied by these Indians and by their ex-slaves.

East from the town lie productive cotton fields; many of the Negroes of Lenapah and the surrounding district work either as tenants or hired hands. West of the highway in this region pastures predominate.

Lenapah's population is roughly divided by its one east and west business street, with the Negroes on the north side and the whites on the south. In sharp contrast with the general appearance of the town are its two modern consolidated schools.

DELAWARE, 15.8 *m.* (716 alt., 542 pop.), named for the original Indian settlers, is a livestock shipping and trading point for the ranchmen west of town and the cotton and corn farmers of the region to the east, between the town and the Verdigris River. Its small business district (R) lies between the highway and the Missouri Pacific tracks.

At the height of the boom in the extensive shallow oil field surrounding Delaware, after 1907, the little town became a highly congested resort for drillers, roustabouts, pipe-line workers, pumpers, lease hounds, gamblers, bootleggers, and "entertainers" attracted by the prospect of easy money. In one block were fourteen saloons and gambling joints—all, of course, illegal—where brawls were common and killings not unknown.

From this era of Delaware's history dates the story of the teamster who went into an explosives magazine near the town to get nitroglycerine with which to "shoot" an oil well. There was a terrific explosion, and no trace whatever of the man or team was found until, months later, they turned up in New Mexico; and the teller of the tale may say solemnly, "him an' his team both was blown clean across Oklahoma an' the Panhandle of Texas!"

NOWATA, 21.7 *m.* (707 alt., 3,904 pop.) *(see Tour 4)*, is at the junction with US 60 *(see Tour 4)*.

At 39.6 *m.* is the junction with a graveled road.

A marker (L) in the shape of a cowskin framed by poles bears the inscription, "Two miles east is the birthplace of Will Rogers, the Oklahoma cowboy, who by way of Broadway, Hollywood, and the public press won his way to the hearts of the American people."

Left on the graveled road is WILL ROGERS' BIRTHPLACE *(open)*, 2.6 *m.* His father, Clem V. Rogers, a blood citizen of the Cherokee Nation and a prosperous cattleman prominent in tribal affairs, was one of the pioneer settlers in this region. He built his house at the foot of an oak-crowned sandstone bluff and could overlook, from its south windows, the broad expanse of Verdigris bottom farm land that he put under fence. Later, as open range ceased to exist, the Rogers pastures were fenced on the prairie that spreads westward.

The house was originally built of logs which later were covered with weatherboarding, painted white. With slight additions, it stands (1941) as it was when Will was born in 1879, a commodious, dignified, two-story ranch dwelling dominating the group of outbuildings—smokehouse, blacksmith shop and toolhouse, cribs, machinery sheds, and barn—and stock corrals to the east and south.

OOLOGAH, 40.7 *m.* (658 alt., 236 pop.), is Will Rogers' authentic home town and the post office address of the Rogers ranch, although Claremore *(see Tour 1)* is commonly referred to as Rogers' home. Oologah is merely a half dozen or so one-story business buildings and a scattering of modest residences that grew up around the depot of the Kansas and Arkansas Valley Railroad (now the Missouri Pacific) when the road built through in 1887. A miniature REPLICA (L) of the Rogers ranch house is near the railway station. Another memorial to Will is a granite marker also near the little station on the site of the baseball diamond where he used to play.

COLLINSVILLE, 50.9 *m.* (621 alt., 1,927 pop.), took its name from a Dr. Collins, who in anticipation of the building of the Santa Fe Railway through the region in 1900 gave land for a townsite. The railroad, however, passed a mile to the west, whereupon the town moved over to its present site. Demand for zinc in the first World War led to the erection of one of the largest zinc smelters in the country, but the postwar business depression caused it to close down. The town is mainly dependent on the farm and ranch population of the surrounding territory. A few oil and gas wells, however, are still producing at the southern edge of the big shallow field that extends southward almost from the Kansas Line.

Collinsville is at the northern junction with US 75 *(see Tour 9)*, which unites with US 169 for 21.3 miles.

A trading center for a farm community, OWASSO, 58.4 *m.* (592 alt., 371 pop.), lies like a fringe on both sides of the highway east of the Santa Fe station.

At 61.2 *m.* is the southern junction with US 75.

At 61.8 *m.* is the northern entrance to MOHAWK PARK, Tulsa's 2,400-acre recreational area through which Bird Creek flows between high banks overhung by thick tree growths.

At 62.3 *m.* is the junction with a graveled road which leads to the principal attractions of Mohawk Park.

Left on the gravel road 0.7 *m.*, to MOHAWK PARK POLO FIELD (L).

MOHAWK BOATHOUSE *(boats, recreational facilities)*, 1.1 *m.*, a building (R) of native brown sandstone and big beams, is in a grove beside a canoe lagoon. North of the boathouse is RECREATION LAKE *(swimming, boating, fishing; free)*.

The Zoo (Refectory) 1.7 *m.*, is a closely grouped series of exhibits; some of the animals are shown in rough stone structures with heavy hewn beams and some in small paddocks. The outstanding attraction of the zoo is MONKEY ISLAND, a large artificial hill of rocks surrounded by a moat whose outer walls slope inward to prevent the escape of the monkeys. In the rocks of the island are the dens for the animals. Adjoining the zoo on the south are the birdhouses, the lake refuge for wild fowl, botanical display and greenhouse.

The road, keeping to the north side of the canoe lagoons, enters the main PICNICKING AREA *(stone shelter houses, tables and ovens)*, 3.3 *m.*

The old buildings (R) of the MASHED-O RANCH *(private)*, 64.5 *m.*, are across Bird Creek in a bend of the stream. This ranch once included a large part of the range northward to Bartlesville and eastward from the border of the Osage reservation to the Verdigris River. It was W. E. Halsell, of Vinita *(see Tour 1)*, an intermarried citizen of the Cherokee Nation, who came up from Texas about 1880 with his first herd of longhorns and turned them out on the good grass of this region. The Bird Creek ranch, which includes a modern dairy, is still (1941) an important part of the extensive pasture holdings in Oklahoma, Kansas, and Texas of the Halsell family.

At 65.8 *m.* US 169 crosses a lagoon. On both sides of the highway are free picnicking areas.

At 66.6 *m.* is the junction with a graveled road.

Left on this road is the well-kept eighteen-hole MOHAWK MUNICIPAL GOLF COURSE *(grass greens; fee, $1)*, 0.6 *m.*

MOHAWK LAKE AND SEQUOYAH LAKE *(boating, fishing)*, 66.7 *m.*, are auxiliary reservoirs (R) for Tulsa's water supply.

In TULSA, 72.2 *m.* (700 alt., 142,157 pop.) *(see Tulsa)*, are junctions with US 66 *(see Tour 1)*, US 75 *(see Tour 9)*, US 64 *(see Tour 2)*, and State 33 *(see Tour 2A)*.

Tour 10

(Arkansas City, Kans.)—Ponca City—Oklahoma City—Ardmore—(Gainesville, Tex.); US 77.
Kansas Line to Texas Line, 266.6 m.

Roadbed paved throughout.
The Santa Fe Ry. parallels the route.
Tourist accommodations at short intervals.

Dividing the state almost exactly in half from north to south, US 77 crosses a greatly varied country. From the farm and range land of the old Cherokee Outlet, it passes into the red orchard land surrounding the first Oklahoma Territory capital, crosses the rich bottoms of the Canadian and Washita rivers where it is said locally—and proudly—that the biggest alfalfa fields in the world are to be seen. It taps areas of wild pecan groves, rises to rounded heights in the Arbuckle Mountains' cattle-raising region. Then, in its last fifty miles in Oklahoma, it dips across pastures, farm lands, and the sandy, timbered approach to Red River.

Over stretches in the north, now paved with concrete, the white settlers of Oklahoma Territory made their frenzied races for homesteads, first in 1889 and again in 1893; and out of that varied, adventurous population emerged men and women who in unusual and sometimes bizarre fashion left their imprint on the nation's life—showmen, a temperance crusader, an art collector, politicians, movie stars, and outlaw-catchers.

Within the limits of Oklahoma City, US 77 skirts the greatest gusher oil field ever developed in the state; at other points also, north and south of the capital, oil touches the highway and has to some extent affected the lives of communities and individuals. The University of Oklahoma, at Norman, and one of the state's teachers' training colleges, at Edmond, are also on this route. US 77 is, in fact, a chief artery through which flows almost all that is most Oklahoman in setting and population—Indian, Negro, and white; farmer, ranchman, oilman, politician, educator, and sportsman have contributed to the history of the region. Its story is compressed into a few years and admirably epitomizes the young state.

Section a. KANSAS LINE *to* OKLAHOMA CITY, *130.2 m.*

Where US 77 crosses the KANSAS LINE, 0 *m.* 4 miles south of Arkansas City *(see Kansas Guide)*, a large granite MONUMENT (R) commemorates the opening to settlement in 1893 of the Cherokee Outlet.

CHILOCCO, 1 *m.* (1,147 alt.) is only a railroad station and two houses for employees.

At 1.4 *m.* is the junction with an asphalt road.

Right on this road is CHILOCCO INDIAN SCHOOL *(open: guide on request at superintendent's office)*, 1.6 *m.*, established by an act of Congress in 1882 as a nonreservation boarding school for children of the Plains tribes in the western part of Indian Territory. After the breakup of the tribal governments preceding statehood and the dissolution of their educational system, the Five Tribes began sending many students to Chilocco. They now contribute more than two-thirds of the total enrollment of seven hundred; the remaining students come from thirty other tribes, practically all living in Oklahoma.

Chilocco—called "the School of Opportunity"—is perhaps the outstanding educational institution for Indians in the country. The girls are taught cooking, dressmaking, and other branches of home economics, as well as subjects of junior college grade. The boys have thorough training on the more than eight thousand acres of the school's good prairie land in general farming, dairying, livestock breeding and care, experimental work in agriculture, fruit growing, the breeding and care of poultry; they are also taught trades.

Six modern dormitories, known as "Homes," house the students. Set about a quadrangle, the buildings range from the three-story, gabled, turreted and ivied types of the nineties to the plain but impressive gray of Home Five for girls. All the main buildings are of light limestone. The plant also includes a modern four-unit shop building, gymnasiums, music studios, an auditorium, and a library containing four thousand books—in fact every facility for the operation of a well-equipped school of this size. Enormous horse, cattle, sheep, and dairy barns, machinery sheds, and a big poultry plant are part of the school's equipment. All expenses of the students are met by the government both during the school term and in the summer vacations.

NEWKIRK, 7.6 *m.* (1,149 alt., 2,283 pop.), seat of Kay County, came into existence after the opening of the Outlet. It profited considerably from the development of a shallow oil field south of town in 1923; today (1941) the red-clay soil is still spotted with oil-black, and pump jacks dip and rise in the cornfields and wheat fields near by.

At 19.5 *m.* is the junction with an asphalt-paved road.

Left on this road to WENTZ EDUCATION CAMP *(20 cabins; mess hall)* and POOL, 2.5 *m.* Given to the people, with the children especially in mind, by Lew Wentz *(see Ponca City)*, this 160-acre tract has become a popular resort used by the YMCA and YWCA, the Boy Scouts, the Camp Fire Girls and Girl Scouts, and the general public. There is a small, well-stocked game preserve.

The Pool, one hundred by fifty feet, has electric lights at the bottom, elaborate diving tower, dressing quarters, and wide tiers of stone and marble seats rising from one side and flanked by towers—all brilliantly lighted at night. From the top of one of the eighty-foot towers, reached by ladders, the visitor gets a long view of Ponca City and of the valley of the Arkansas River beyond. Wentz had artesian wells sunk in the bed of the river, five miles away, and water pumped to the pool.

With its lights and seating arrangements, this is a favorite place for water sports, races, and exhibition diving. Here, too, is held the yearly bathing beauty revue for "young ladies under the age of five," and another for those under twelve—the donor's ironic comment on other, and different, much publicized bathing beauty contests.

In KAW CITY, 12.5 *m.* (1,009 alt., 809 pop.), is the LAURA A. CLUBB ART COLLECTION *(open at all hours; free)*, housed in the Clubb Hotel, a plain red-brick, three-story structure. The collection includes many excellent canvases, exquisite old laces, and rare books.

Among the two hundred or more paintings hung in the lobby and the hallways are a Titian, a Sully, a Sir Peter Lely, a Gainsborough, a Sir Joshua Reynolds, a Hoppner, a Constable, two Corots, two Daubignys, two Bouguereaus, a Seignac, a Benjamin West, a Gilbert Stuart portrait of Washington, a Winslow Homer, a Wyant, two canvases by Inness, and what is perhaps the best extant collection of Thomas Moran's paintings.

For unsophisticated visitors the star of the exhibition is Kirchbach's "Christ and the Children," an enormous canvas, twelve by fifteen feet, that covers almost the whole of one wall of the hotel lobby; it was at one time assessed in England for taxation purposes at $125,000 and received an honorable mention at the Paris Salon exhibition in 1895.

A former school teacher who married a cattleman, Mrs. Clubb began buying paintings after oil came, in 1922, to enrich the family. When she bought her first painting, Van Marke's, "In the Pastures," for $12,500, it is said that her husband protested, "I could have bought a trainload of cattle for that!"

At 20.5 *m.* is the junction with a graveled road.

Left on this road to the AMERICAN LEGION HOME, 1.6 *m.*, the only institution of its kind in the country, a home for the children of deceased and disabled veterans of the first World War. They are cared for in a main administration building and three billets, all of Spanish design, set in a 120-acre tract that has been beautifully landscaped. In these quarters one hundred children are given general and vocational education under the supervision of the Oklahoma Department of the Legion.

At 21.3 *m.* is the entrance (L) to the former ESTATE OF E. W. MARLAND. Near by, at the center of a landscaped circle from which a tree-bordered avenue leads to the former Marland home, is the heroic bronze statue of the PIONEER WOMAN, standing on a broad base of native limestone. In the period of his greatest prosperity as an oilman *(see Ponca City)*, Marland conceived the idea of this memorial to the pioneer women of the West, provided for its financing, and asked for models from sculptors throughout the country. Bryant Baker's was selected by popular vote, and the statute was dedicated on April 22, 1930.

At 22.5 *m.* is the junction with an asphalt-paved road.

Left on this road to LAKE PONCA *(fishing, boating, picnicking)*, 4 *m.* Built as a WPA project at a cost of $560,000, Ponca City's source of water supply has become a popular resort for fishermen, speedboat drivers, and one-day visitors from the region.

West of PONCA CITY, 23 *m.* (1,003 alt., 16,794 pop.) *(see Ponca City)*, US 60 *(see Tour 4)* unites with US 77 for 4.2 miles.

At 33 *m.* is the 101 RANCH (R), a striking symbol of that changing West which brought fortune to men and took it away with no more than a shrug of regret.

In the early seventies, a shrewd trader named George W. Miller left Kansas with twenty thousand pounds of bacon to exchange for whatever could be sold at a profit. He arrived in San Saba County, Texas, in the spring with enough bacon to trade for four hundred longhorn steers. These he herded back over the good-grass trail to a range in the northeastern corner of Indian Territory belonging to the Quapaw Indians and sold them when fat at a handsome profit. In order to obtain more range for the enlarged herds he meant to own, he went out to the Cherokee Outlet and found grassland in plenty. His first lease was sixty thousand acres. Then, going back to Texas, he found that he could buy a steer for $3.00 in gold instead of for $6.00 in bacon.

Miller's next step was to induce the small tribe of Ponca Indians, then living temporarily with the Quapaws, to accept a reservation near his leased land and allow him to graze his cattle on it for one cent per acre annually. He was a good friend to the Indians, an excellent cattleman, a tireless hustler; and the earnings of his ranch grew enormously. When it became possible to buy Indian land, he acquired more and more; and when his sons, Joe, George Jr., and Zack, grew up, they too joined in pushing forward the enterprise.

George Miller died in 1903, in the dugout that had been ranch headquarters, just before the first "White House"—three stories and a basement —was completed. Before his death, he saw thirteen thousand acres of the ranch sown to wheat, three thousand planted in corn, and three thousand acres devoted to forage crops; he was paying $32,500 annually in rentals to the Indians, and running expenses amounted to $75,000 a year. But income ranged from $400,000 to $500,000 a year, and the problem was how to employ these earnings profitably. Then, to make the story better, oil was found on the 101 Ranch holdings.

It was the Miller sons who thought of the 101 Ranch Wild West Circus; and the first tryout was staged at Ponca City on April 14, 1908, with two hundred performers. For eight years the show made money, and the Miller sons devoted more and more time to it, and therefore less time to the legitimate business of the ranch. After 1916, the tide turned; in 1921, owing to losses and extravagance, it became necessary to reorganize. Then, in 1927, Joe Miller died of monoxide gas poisoning; two years later his brother George was killed in an automobile accident. Oil prices dropped, the show failed and closed; and Zack Miller found himself facing an indebtedness of $700,000. In August, 1931, the ranch was placed in receivership, and against the roared protests—backed by a loaded shotgun—of Zack, a man from the Federal courts was placed in charge. The guest register at the "White House," with its scores of names of the well-advertised in almost every line of endeavor, reflects the Miller sons' absorbing passion for publicity. Under the management of the receiver, much of the ranch has been cut up into small subsistence holdings, in a rehabilitation project.

At 35 *m.* is the WHITE EAGLE MONUMENT, erected by the Miller brothers in the former reservation of the Ponca Indians to the memory of a chief of that tribe whom their father induced to select this place as a reservation in 1879. On a hill which was once a signal station of the Indians, the monument of native red stone stands twenty feet high, twelve feet in diameter, bearing a huge white figure of an eagle at the top.

This Ponca chief was a principal figure in a drama of tribal exile quite as tragic though not as well known as the removal of the Five Tribes over what has come to be known as "The Trail of Tears."

In 1868, after the Federal government had induced the Poncas to make two cessions of land along the Missouri River in Dakota and had solemnly confirmed them in the possession of what remained, a treaty with the Sioux included a clause giving them every acre of the Ponca reservation. The Poncas refused to give up their ancient homes, and warfare between the tribes followed, in which the more powerful Sioux killed a fourth of the Poncas.

Nine years later, the government acted to save the Poncas, not by giving back their land and otherwise satisfying the Sioux, but by ordering them off. They still objected to removal, whereupon an official from Washington came to escort ten Ponca chiefs to Kansas and Indian Territory so that they could select a new home. They reached the country of the Osages in the fall of 1876, and, as one of the chiefs said, "We . . . found it stony and broken and not a country that we thought we could make a living in. We saw the Osages . . . without shirts, their skin burned, and their hair stood up as if it had not been combed since they were little children."

Arriving at Arkansas City, Kansas, without having induced the Poncas to choose a new location, the government man lost patience with the chiefs and deserted them. So they went back, five hundred miles, on foot. Then, in the summer of 1877, soldiers came to gather them up and march them to the Quapaw reservation in the northeastern corner of Indian Territory. It was here that George Miller found them, and from that region induced them to remove to land adjoining his lease.

In their new reservation—optimistically described by the Commissioner of Indian Affairs as "in all respects . . . far superior to their old location in Dakota"—158 of the tribe died within a short time. To make their situation more bearable, the government gave help in building homes and establishing schools, but in the winter of 1879 Standing Bear led a party back to the reservation of the Omahas, their kinsmen, in Nebraska, who gave them refuge and supplied them with seed to plant in the spring. But before they could plant, soldiers came to arrest Standing Bear; and he and thirty of his followers were imprisoned at Fort Omaha.

Through the intervention of citizens of Omaha, led by a newspaperman, the case of the Poncas came to trial on a writ of habeas corpus sworn out to secure their release. They were successful and returned to the Omaha reservation, where they were joined later by some two hundred others who came up from Indian Territory. The greater number of the Poncas, some seven hundred, remained on the land assigned to them in the Cherokee Outlet.

At the trial of Standing Bear, in which government attorneys contended that an Indian was not entitled to a writ of habeas corpus because he was not a "person within the meaning of the law," the old chief said, "The people of the devil . . . have tried to make me believe that God tells them what to do, as though God would put a man where he would be destroyed! . . . They have destroyed many already, but they cannot deceive me. God put me here, and intends for me to live on the land they are trying to cheat me out of."

MARLAND, 35.6 *m.* (1,001 alt., 257 pop.), was named for E. W. Marland, whose extensive oil leases covered the site, and who served as governor of Oklahoma from 1935 to 1939.

CERES, 48.6 *m.* (1,036 alt., 10 pop.), is a settlement of two stores and a filling station. Named for the Greek goddess of harvest, it is in the center of a farming and fruit-growing area. Peaches do especially well here.

In PERRY, 61.3 *m.* (1,005 alt., 5,045 pop.) *(see Tour 2),* is the junction with US 64 *(see Tour 2),* which unites westward with US 77 for 5.6 miles.

At 75.7 *m.* a Geological Survey post marks the line from which settlers made the Run into "Old Oklahoma" from the north when it was opened in 1889, and from the south into the Cherokee Outlet in 1893.

ORLANDO, 76.6 *m.* (1,078 alt., 332 pop.), though near an oil field, has not experienced the usual oil-field town boom. It has remained since its founding in 1889 a trade center for the substantial, progressive farmers who settled in the neighborhood. Twice, however, its calm has been broken, when the mad race into the Cherokee Strip took place on September 16, 1893, and again in 1896 when swindlers by salting a diggings with ore that assayed $185 to the ton duped a number of Orlando men into believing that gold had been found on a farm southwest of town.

MULHALL, 83.2 *m.* (936 alt., 406 pop.), named for "Uncle Zack" Mulhall, a showman who came into the country in 1889 as a rancher and livestock agent for the Santa Fe Railway, is now (1941) a supply point for farmers. In the prosperous days of "Uncle Zack" it was headquarters for eighty thousand acres of ranch land in "Old Oklahoma" and across the line in the Cherokee Outlet, the home of his rodeo, and a notable center of hospitality. Out of the Mulhall rodeo forces emerged two well-known figures in the entertainment world, his own daughter Lucille, who starred as the world's first "cowgirl," and the even better known Will Rogers.

Like the Millers *(see above),* the Mulhalls failed in ranching, the family scattered, and the last to occupy the old house was Lucille, who died just after Christmas in 1940.

The 489 remaining acres of the MULHALL RANCH *(open),* immediately west of the little town, lie around the low, spreading ranch house (R) near the highway. Its wide porches are characteristic of early Oklahoma homes.

South of 89.2 *m.,* the highway parallels the Cimarron River (L) for four miles where it breaks through the red sandstone region known as the Palisades. Huge moss-covered boulders, young trees, and a tangle of shrubbery make an interesting background for the wide, and usually almost completely sand-covered bed of the river.

GUTHRIE, 96.5 *m.* (1,021 alt., 10,018 pop.), described by its citizens both as "the Birthplace of Oklahoma" and "the Fraternal Capital of the Southwest," with its broad streets, wide walks, and the residential area merging easily into the business section, was the capital of Oklahoma from the time of the organization of the Territory in 1890 to 1910, when it was removed to Oklahoma City. In appearance and population, Guthrie has changed little in the thirty years since its loss.

The city came into existence overnight, attracting some fifteen thousand persons to the site on the day of opening. Within three weeks, what had been only a brown-painted Santa Fe depot had developed into a prairie metropolis with a functioning chamber of commerce and three newspapers. A waterworks system was operating in two months; the streets were electrically lighted within four months; and schools, churches, and hospitals were soon established.

Among those who have claimed Guthrie as home were such well-known early residents as General J. B. Weaver, candidate for President on the Greenback ticket in 1880; General J. C. Jamieson, who fought with Walker in Nicaragua; Fred G. Bonfils, later publisher of the *Denver Post;* Cassius M. Barnes, a Territorial governor of Oklahoma; John I. Dille, Chancellor of Iowa State University; Cora V. Diehl, first woman to be elected to office in Oklahoma; and Will Rogers, Lon Chaney, and Tom Mix, movie stars. William Wrigley made his first package of chewing gum at 113 North Division Street. Bill Tilghman, the marshal who ruled Dodge City, Bill Fossett, secret service operator and the Southwest's first G-man, and Chris Madsen, soldier of fortune and Indian fighter, were all early-day settlers in Guthrie; and Edward P. Kelly, later vice-president of the Rock Island railway, was first city marshal. Guthrie was also for a time the home of hatchet-wielding Carry (the family's spelling) Nation. She began her magazine-publishing experience at Guthrie in July, 1905, with *The Hatchet,* after being divorced on the ground of desertion by her husband, David Nation (lawyer, preacher, and editor). From Guthrie, Carry sallied out to smash saloon bars, attain wide notoriety, and tour Europe with the announced intention of suppressing liquor, beer, narcotics, and tobacco in all foreign countries.

As a trade center for a large farming district, and a pleasant residence city, Guthrie has maintained itself well and has become in a sense the state capital of Masonry. The SCOTTISH RITE TEMPLE *(open 8–5 weekdays: 10–5 Sun.),* is the largest structure of its type in Oklahoma and is said to be the largest in the world devoted exclusively to Masonic uses. Designed by J. C. Parr, Oklahoma City, and built at a cost of $2,500,000, this light-yellow brick structure of Greek Doric design is set in a ten-acre park near the eastern edge of the city. Its auditorium, with a stage sixty-two feet wide and ninety feet deep, has seats for 3,500; the dining room accommodates fifteen hundred; and the lobby is 52 by 190 feet.

In Guthrie, too, are the GRAND LODGE TEMPLE, the STATE MASONIC HOME FOR THE AGED, Harrison Avenue between Broad and Ash Streets, and the STATE MASONIC CHILDREN'S HOME, Elm and College Streets.

The CITY HALL, 304 W. Oklahoma Avenue, is a red-brick, three-story structure designed by J. A. Foquart, erected in 1902. The hall on the second floor was the meeting place of the Constitutional Convention of 1906–07; and in the time when the Territorial and the state capital was at Guthrie, was the scene of many official balls and banquets.

The old FEDERAL JAIL, corner of Warner Avenue and Second Street, was built as a private investment and rented to the government. It has been remodeled and is used by the Nazarenes as a church building.

The CARNEGIE LIBRARY, 402 E. Oklahoma Avenue, constructed of brick, stone, and marble, with a silver dome to draw the eye, was a gift from Andrew

Carnegie. Inside, golden oak paneling and pillars supporting the dome are set on plates of Bedford limestone, with bases of green and maroon tile. In the building also are clubrooms and a gymnasium.

On the library's front steps, C. N. Haskell, the state's first governor, took the oath of office, and there a symbolic marriage ceremony uniting Oklahoma and Indian Territories took place.

JELSMA FIELD AND CITY STADIUM, Harrison Avenue and E. Springer Street, is the largest municipal athletic field and stadium in the state. The grounds cover an area of four hundred by seven hundred feet, and the stadium seats five thousand.

MINERAL WELLS PARK, 0.5 *m.,* at the southern border of the city (R), is notable for several artesian mineral wells. Here, in 1893, when the park was only a grove of trees, Jacob S. Coxey, who later led "Coxey's Army" in a march to Washington, made one of his vehement speeches; here, too, William Jennings Bryan twice addressed large audiences.

At the entrance to the park is the rectangular SHAKESPEARE GARDEN, a gift to the city from the Guthrie Shakespeare Club. Three sides are bordered by privet hedges; the west end is bordered by a hedge of spirea that is, in turn, banked with flowering masses of crape myrtle, mock orange, redbud, Japanese quinces, forsythia, red hollyhocks, and five varieties of juniper. The waterlily pool, lined with red and white brick, has a white stone bench on each side, and climbing roses, beds of hyacinths, chrysanthemums, and verbenas are a mass of red and white when in bloom. In the pergola is a reproduction of Roubiliac's bust of Shakespeare.

Guthrie is at the junction with State 33 *(see Tour 2A).*

Right from Guthrie on State 33 to CATHOLIC COLLEGE OF OKLAHOMA, 2 *m.,* a Benedictine institution for women. Housed in a commodious four-story red-brick building set in the midst of a pleasant tree-shaded campus of seventy acres, this affiliate of the Catholic University of America offers the usual cultural courses. The college is an outgrowth of St. Joseph Academy, established at Guthrie in 1892.

At 112.9 *m.* is the junction with US 66 *(see Tour 1),* which unites with US 77 for 17.9 miles.

EDMOND, 116.3 *m.* (1,200 alt., 4,002 pop.) *(see Tour 1).*

MEMORIAL PARK, 120.1 *m.,* is a cemetery (L) of 135 acres, surrounded by brick walls. The TOWER OF MEMORIES (Chimes), near the center of the cemetery, is approached by a flower-bordered boulevard and is the park's outstanding feature; it is built of dressed limestone and rises to a height of seventy-two feet. The bells are usually rung on Sundays and holidays. Near the tower are a fountain and a pool. Wiley Post, noted aviator, who made a record round the world flight and a nonstop flight from Brooklyn to Berlin, is buried in the park.

OKLAHOMA CITY, 130.2 *m.* (1,194 alt., 204,424 pop.) *(see Oklahoma City).*

Left from Oklahoma City on S. Robinson and S.E. 29th Streets to the new AIR CORPS SERVICE DEPOT, 4.5 *m.* There, on a tract of 1,440 acres, 960 acres of which were given by Oklahoma City, the United States War Department is planning (1941) to spend some

$16,000,000 for storage and other facilities for air operations. When completed, the depot will accommodate a total personnel of 60 officers, 170 enlisted men, and approximately 2,500 skilled civilian workers, and will have facilities for overhauling three hundred airplane motors per month.

Section b. OKLAHOMA CITY *to* TEXAS LINE, *136.4 m.*

South of OKLAHOMA CITY, 0 *m.,* the route crosses the southern portion of old Oklahoma Territory and continues through the former Chickasaw Nation. The region through which it passes becomes increasingly productive, gives way for a time to mountain pastures, then to an area producing such widely varying staples as cotton and crude oil.

Established in 1887, MOORE, 10 *m.* (1,250 alt., 499 pop.), was named for an engineer of the Santa Fe Railway. On the grounds of the consolidated school is a monument to Washington Irving who, it is said, camped on the spot when he visited this region in 1832.

NORMAN, 19.2 *m.* (1,160 alt., 11,429 pop.) *(see Norman).*

LEXINGTON, 35.2 *m.* (1,030 alt., 1,084 pop.), on the north side of the South Canadian River and almost in the shadow of Purcell, is a local supply point for the fine farms of the river valley.

Historically, the neighborhood is interesting as the site of one of the first military camps and trading posts established so far west in the Indian Territory. Here, in the late summer of 1835 at a place called Camp Mason, was held the great council between the Five Civilized Tribes and the Plains Indians to agree on terms of peace. Five thousand met together and worked out a treaty which lasted until the Civil War. Nothing remains of either the camp or the trading post which the Chouteaus established after the great council of 1835.

In 1889, after the opening, the Sand Bar Saloon was built on stilts as near as possible to the Indian Territory (prohibition) side, and a long footbridge led to dry territory. At flood stages, the saloon was washed away, but was, of course, rebuilt time after time.

US 77 crosses the Canadian River into PURCELL, 36.4 *m.* (1,029 alt., 3,116 pop.), on a bridge built in 1938. The first bridge, put across in 1910, was a toll bridge and for a time the toll was $10. With increased traffic, it was lowered finally to $1; in 1931, when the operating company's charter expired, the legislature refused to renew it; the state took over and the toll was abolished.

The town tops the steep red bluff beside the river, and its streets, shaded by fine mistletoe-hung maples, elms, and gnarled cottonwoods, slope toward Walnut Creek on the south. At its southern edge are cotton gins.

At this point, the river marks the northern boundary of the old Chickasaw Nation. Few Indians, however, lived in this portion of the nation, and even before statehood the country was occupied mainly by white men and their families who leased land from the Chickasaws. The town was settled in 1887, when the Santa Fe came through, and was named for the engineer who surveyed the railroad's right of way through the region.

At 57 *m.* the route crosses the Washita River; near here freighters on the old Boggy Depot–Fort Sill road, over which great quantities of supplies for the western Plains Indians were transported by wagon train, forded the stream.

PAULS VALLEY, 59 *m.* (880 alt., 5,104 pop.), is the center of the region described as the garden spot of the Washita Valley. When the town was incorporated in 1899, it was named for Smith Paul, on whose land it was laid out. In the midst of fine fields of alfalfa, cotton, broomcorn, grain sorghums, corn; with fine orchards of pecans; and with an alfalfa mill for reducing that excellent fodder to meal, Pauls Valley is a solid, tree-embowered town of well-built residences and old fashioned business structures.

The STATE TRAINING SCHOOL (Reformatory) FOR BOYS *(visited by appointment)*, 62.6 *m.*, on a tract (L) four hundred acres making up the school's plant, is supplemented by the leasing of four hundred additional acres used by the 225 boys in training here. The thirty-one red-brick buildings of the school are set wide apart on a rather bare campus.

WYNNEWOOD, 67.9 *m.* (847 alt., 2,318 pop.), is the center of a farming region in which are produced excellent cotton, alfalfa, and the wild crop for which southern Oklahoma is noted—pecans. It is also a shipping point for livestock and poultry. At the southern border of town is a large cottonseed-oil mill and a small oil refinery. For the enjoyment of the citizens who live along its well-shaded streets there is a spacious city park, a municipal swimming pool, and a baseball park. At the northern edge of the town is a CCC camp.

DAVIS, 78.1 *m.* (838 alt., 1,698 pop.), on the east bank of the Washita River, was born when the Santa Fe came through in 1887. It is set at the foot of the rocky northern foothills of the Arbuckle Mountains and is the center of a good range country. The two-story NELSON CHIGLEY HOUSE is a fine example of the best dwellings built by prosperous Chickasaws in Territorial days.

In Davis is the junction with State 22 *(see Tour 10A)*

Right on State 22 to the ARBUCKLE STORE, 7 *m.*, where a cement marker (R) indicates the location (one mile south) of the INITIAL POINT, the spot from which all surveys of Oklahoma after the Civil War, except the three Panhandle counties, were made. The north and south line through that point is called the Indian Meridian. A marker at the point proper is only a large boulder, difficult to find without a guide.

Right from the store on an improved dirt road, 7.1 *m.*, to the SITE OF FORT ARBUCKLE *(visitors permitted upon request)*. This fort was established to keep order among the Plains Indians, to protect the immigrant Chickasaws from their raids, and to provide assistance to California-bound travelers. Its construction was supervised by Captain Randolph B. Marcy, who had escorted parties of California gold-seekers. Completed in 1851, the fort was named for General Matthew Arbuckle, who commanded in the Indian country for many years, and for whom the low mountain range south of the fort was also named. Somewhat later, the troops from Fort Towson *(see Tour 6)* were sent to Fort Arbuckle.

One of the log buildings (L) of the fort has been covered with siding and now (1941) forms a portion of the residence of C. W. Grant. The old quartermaster building, of rough-sawed boards, is used as the Grant barn. A quarter of a mile west on GARRISON CREEK is the never-failing spring that once supplied water for the fort.

South of Davis, US 77 winds across the Arbuckle Mountains, a low range of rounded limestone hills, rather sparsely covered with red cedar, soapberry, and blackjack oak trees, and supplying excellent short-grass pasturage. The section was a part of the former Chickasaw Nation, and its earliest white settlers were cattlemen who leased pastures from the Indian owners.

To geologists the Arbuckles are exceptionally interesting. They are one of the oldest ranges in the country and provide a chance to study the type of rock formations encountered in drilling for oil in other parts of Oklahoma and in Kansas and Texas.

At 82.6 *m.* is the junction with a graveled road.

Right on this road to YOUNG MEN'S CHRISTIAN ASSOCIATION CAMP, 1.5 *m.*, first opened in 1941 and built by Oklahoma City funds on a tract of 220 acres in the midst of the Arbuckle Mountain region. A lake covering thirty-five acres has been created by damming Lick Creek; and here swimming, boating, fishing, and water sports are provided. Marked trails for hikers lead off northward, westward, and southward through the hills.

Twenty cabins built of native stone, each with room for ten boys, are grouped about a central dining hall, which has a wide screened porch along its front. Inside, two enormous fireplaces have been constructed of geological specimens, fossils, and petrified wood from the Arbuckle Mountains region.

The camp takes two hundred boys at a time for two weeks; and when not in use by the boys, it is available for leadership training conferences and other men's religious groups.

Left on the graveled road to a Y junction 0.1 *m.*; R. here to PRICE'S FALLS *(camping and picnicking facilities; fishing; cabins)*, 2.7 *m.*, a popular resort from which such other points of interest as Seven Sisters Falls, Burning Mountain, White Mound, and Oil Springs may be visited *(road directions from caretaker at Price's Falls.)*

Right from Price's Falls on an improved dirt road to SWIMMING POOL, 3.7 *m.*, a clear basin in the rock bed of a small stream, sixty feet long and about fourteen feet wide. Below the pool is a lake created by a group of sportsmen. Certain small feeders of this lake are called spouting springs.

At 4 *m.* is the BAPTIST ASSEMBLY GROUNDS *(cabins, tents, lots for rent; tennis courts; swimming pool; office building; post office)*, a tract of 180 acres containing an open tabernacle for summer meetings.

CEDARVALE, 84.4 *m.*, is a popular camp *(cabins, swimming pool, store)* under the shadow of the high sheer bluff (L) of Honey Creek.

The METHODIST ASSEMBLY GROUNDS (L) *(cabins, dining hall, pavilion, swimming pool)*, 84.9 *m.*, a gift to the church by a citizen of Davis, are used by various religious groups during the summer. Hiking trails lead out over the Arbuckles toward the east. VESPER HILL, on the summit of which a cross has been erected, is the site of many out-of-doors religious services.

At 85.3 *m.* is the junction with a graveled road.

Right on this road into TURNER FALLS PARK *(free camp sites, ovens, tables, wood)*, owned by the city of Davis and maintained in part by the State Park Service. CCC workers finished the road through the area which had been begun by convicts in 1926 and constructed trails.

BLUE HOLE, 0.1 *m.*, has been blasted from the rock in the bed of Honey Creek and is filled by the cool water of that stream.

The road continues along the creek between high steep cliffs dotted with cedars to a parking place (L), 0.4 *m.* From this point a footpath with steps cut in the rocks leads to TURNER FALLS, 0.6 *m.*, where the water of Honey Creek tumbles through a rock gorge into a clear deep pool.

From another parking place, 0.9 *m.*, above the falls, there is a fine view of the surrounding mountain country.

At OBSERVATION HOUSE *(cafe, filling station)*, (1,389 alt.), 86.2 *m,* also overlooking Turner Falls, may be seen the peculiar striped effect of hillsides due to uneven weathering of the upthrust strata of rocks characteristic of this region. South from this point, roadside signs placed by the Lions Club of Ardmore indicate the geological formations, from the Mississippian to the Ordovician and Cambrian, that have been exposed to study by the ancient upthrust.

AT 91.9 *m.,* US 77 leaves the rough mountain country to descend to rolling pastures, grazing Hereford cattle, loading pens, branding chutes, and windmills. For three miles the highway runs through one ranch, the Lazy S.

SPRINGER, 93.5 *m.,* is a farm center.

Right from Springer on a graveled road to WOODFORD, 8.1 *m.* (1,014 alt., 100 pop.); R. from Woodford on a mountain road to ARDMORE MOUNTAIN LAKE *(boats; overnight or week-end camping not allowed),* locally called Hickory Creek Lake, 9.3 *m.,* which covers 215 acres and supplies water for the city of Ardmore *(see Ardmore)*. The State Game and Fish Commission keeps the lake stocked with largemouthed and smallmouthed bass, bream, crappie, and perch.

At 101.9 *m.* on the main route is the junction with a graveled road.

Left on this road is CARTER ACADEMY, 0.6 *m.,* a group of gray stone buildings. Founded near Durant *(see Tour 6)* in 1852 by the Chickasaws, it was originally known as Bloomfield, a name suggested by a Chickasaw ex-chief because of the profusion of flowers in the surrounding fields. The school might well have been named for George Washington, however, for at one time it annually received $1,000, a portion of the interest derived from funds appropriated by the First Congress of the United States to pay General Washington for his Revolutionary War services. Washington refused to accept the money and had it set aside for educational purposes.

In the fall of 1852 the school was officially opened, and twenty-five girls were enrolled. They were taught English, botany, spelling, reading, and history during the regular school hours, and in the afternoons, sewing, mending, cooking, baking, housework, drawing, painting, and singing. During the Civil War, Chickasaw soldiers camped near by, using the schoolroom as a hospital and a small building in the yard as a doctor's office. The academy was closed in May, 1863; reopened in 1876 as a girl's school of high-school rank, the government took it over along with all other Chickasaw tribal schools in 1906. After a fire had destroyed most of the buildings, Bloomfield was removed to its present site in 1914. Supported by Federal funds, the school is quartered in sixteen buildings and has a student enrollment of 150.

ARDMORE, 102.2 *m.* (872 alt., 16,886 pop.) *(see Ardmore),* is at the junction with US 70 *(see Tour 6).*

Right from the corner of Main and Washington Streets, in Ardmore, south on Washington Street, to LAKE MURRAY STATE PARK *(cabins, swimming, boating, fishing, camp sites),* 3.9 *m.,* an area of about twenty thousand acres including a reservoir which when full will cover 5,600 acres. The park is a center for fishing, swimming, and water sports of all kinds. It is the largest park in the State Parks system. The residence cabins are built of sandstone, with shingled roofs and steel casement windows, paneled inside with pine and walnut, with massive stone fireplaces in which are placed swinging iron cranes. The rangers' cabins are furnished with hand-rubbed walnut, some of the pieces being antiques and the others reproductions. The cabins are set back in clearings, almost hidden by growths of pine and hickory. One area, including a model camp, is reserved for Negroes.

At the entrance gate lodge is a Y-junction of the park circulation road.

Right to a Civilian Conservation Corps camp, 10.2 *m.;* a second camp, 11.7 *m.;* and

TUCKER TOWER, 13.7 *m.,* set on the top of a rocky crag that juts into the lake, is one of the most beautiful spots in the park. When the lake is filled (probably in 1942), eighty-five feet of water will lie directly under the long porch of the tower building. South of the tower, and northeast of the LAKE MURRAY DAM, 15.2 *m.,* is the lake area where motorboat races are held.

The CONFEDERATE HOME, 105.8 *m.,* was established (R) in Territorial days at McAlester, under the sponsorship of Dr. D. M. Hailey, founder of Haileyville *(see Tour 5),* and J. J. McAlester, founder of McAlester *(see Tour 5).* Public subscriptions were received by the Confederate Association, but shortly after statehood it was found that the donations were inadequate. It was made a state-supported institution and was moved to its present site in 1910. A broad, tree-lined drive leads across the well-improved grounds to the home. It was closed in 1941.

MARIETTA, 121.1 *m.* (846 alt., 1,837 pop.), a farm center, is the seat of Love County. The nucleus of the town was a little shack that served as the station of the Santa Fe Railway, which built its tracks through in 1887. The site of Marietta, and the surrounding area, was then in the possession of two Chickasaws, Jerry and Bill Washington; Jerry Washington's wife was named Marietta, and it was in her honor that the Santa Fe named the town.

At 134.5 *m.* is the junction with a paved road.

Right on this road is the old REFUGE SPRING, 1.2 *m.,* the burial ground of early Texas outlaws. The white cedar trees, set out about 1840, formed an approximate boundary between Texas and Oklahoma. When an outlaw, fleeing from Texas, reached this spot he was safe; but for many of them, especially those who had been severely wounded by pursuing posses, it proved only a temporary sanctuary.

US 77 crosses Red River to the TEXAS LINE, 136.4 *m.*, on a long bridge, eight miles north of Gainesville, Tex. *(see Texas Guide).*

Tour 10A

Davis—Sulphur—Platt National Park—Junction with US 70; 43.2 m. State 22, State 18, Perimeter Blvd.

Roadbed asphalt-paved and graveled.
Oklahoma Transportation Co. Bus Line follows route between Davis and Sulphur.
Excellent accommodations at Sulphur; free campgrounds in park, but no cabins.

East of DAVIS, 0 *m.* (838 alt., 1,698 pop.) *(see Tour 10),* State 22 proceeds eastward from its junction with US 77 *(see Tour 10)* and passes through rolling hilly country to SULPHUR, 9 *m.* (976 alt., 4,970 pop.), a pleasure and health resort with something of the appearance of a continental spa. Rock Creek flows through the town and divides it into East and West Sulphur, each section having its own business and residential sections. In East Sulphur are the city hall and many of the large hotels; in West Sulphur are the courthouse and county offices. The streets in both sections are paved with crushed rock, principally chert from near-by quarries. Mineral water, with sulphur and iron content, is plentiful and is used in many of the numerous swimming pools. The town's entire water supply comes from deep, flowing wells.

At 9.4 *m.* is the junction with State 18, which the tour follows south (R) through PLATT NATIONAL PARK *(free camping)*. The park, lying south of the junction, covers an area of 848 acres. There are thirty-one large springs *(faucets; water is free)*—eighteen sulphur, four iron, three bromide, and six fresh water—and several smaller ones. The tract was formerly included in the territory of the Chickasaw Nation, and a large part of it was purchased from the Indians by the Federal government in 1902, the year in which the park was established. First named Sulphur Springs Reservation, it was renamed in 1906 for U.S. Senator Orville Hitchcock Platt, of Connecticut, member of the Senate Committee on Indian Affairs (1879–1905).

From early spring to late fall colorful wild flowers are abundant here—Spanish larkspur, Virginia creeper, primrose, blue salvia, goldenrod, redbud, and the pink-flowered brier or cat's claw, locally known as gander's teeth. Five or six varieties of cactus, native to the state and the Southwest, grow among the rocks on the hillsides, and in the creek valleys are numerous trees. Wrens, herons, cardinals, meadow larks, horned larks, sparrow hawks, brown thrashers, and many other birds frequent the region seasonally, and raccoons, opossums, skunks, rabbits, and squirrels are found in or near the park.

TRAVERTINE CREEK, 9.6 *m.,* is crossed on a stone bridge.

At 9.7 *m.* is the junction with Perimeter Boulevard, over which the route continues due west (R) making an elongated circle through the park and returning to this junction.

Travertine Creek (R), which parallels Perimeter Boulevard for a short distance, is spanned by LINCOLN BRIDGE, 9.8 *m.,* a footbridge constructed of white limestone blocks, with turrets at each end. Across the bridge is FLOWER PARK, comprising five acres of cleared land; a small, shallow stream, formed by diverting the overflow from Vendome Plunge, a swimming pool near by, flows through the area.

The boulevard crosses ROCK CREEK, 9.9 *m.,* the largest stream in the park; it has been stocked by the State Game and Fish Commission with bass, catfish, perch, crappie, and bream. On the summit of a small knoll (R), just west of the Rock Creek bridge, are BLACK SULPHUR SPRINGS, which have an extremely strong sulphur content. The spring's pavilion, constructed of stone covered with rough stucco, is hexagonal in shape, with open sides and slender pillars supporting the sloping roof.

A large open pavilion (L) at BROMIDE SPRINGS AREA, 10.7 *m.,* houses medicinal springs. CCC workers built the red-brick structure surrounded by a flagged terrace. The varieties of mineral water obtainable here are indicated by labels on the faucets.

The BROMIDE CAMP GROUNDS *(trailer and tent accommodations, picnicking facilities)*, within the area (R), are well shaded.

South of the pavilion, a trail leads across a long steel footbridge over Rock Creek to the bottom of BROMIDE CLIFF (1,050 alt.), which rises 140 feet above the creek. CCC workers have built banked trails, with bridges and retaining walls from this point along the sides and to the summit of the cliff. At the foot, temporary structures are erected each year to seat the thousands of visitors who come to view the Easter Pageant. Near by are three springs that supply water to the pavilion; a larger spring boils up in the center of Rock Creek.

Perimeter Boulevard again crosses Rock Creek, 10.8 *m.*, winds around the western side of the cliff, and ascends to the top of the hill forming the precipice.

At 11.1 *m.* is a junction with a graveled road.

Right on this road to VETERANS LAKE *(state fishing license; no fee)* 0.1 *m.*, which covers 115 acres and has a maximum depth of eighty feet; the lake is stocked yearly with thousands of fingerlings.

A PARKING AREA (L) 11.2 *m.*, is near the highest point in the park. Several foot trails lead from here across the summit of Bromide Cliff to COUNCIL ROCK, locally called Robbers' Roost, offering a wide view of the park and the town of Sulphur. Here various Indian tribes lighted their signal fires or held councils of war or peace. A hiking trail leads from the rock down the cliff to Bromide Springs Pavilion.

The BUFFALO PASTURE *(no trespassing)*, 12.2 *m.*, is a large area (L) where a small herd of buffalo is maintained.

At 12.4 *m.* is the junction with State 18. The route continues east on Perimeter Boulevard and climbs a ridge. At the top, 12.7 *m.*, is a view of the OKLAHOMA SOLDIERS' TUBERCULAR SANITARIUM (R), a group of brick, cottage-like buildings trimmed with white, except the administration building, which is a square limestone structure. The grounds are landscaped, with well-kept lawns, and cedars.

The road descends a slope to Travertine Creek (L), which it parallels for two miles. Wild flowers grow in profusion and dense growths of oak and elm trees shade the valleys.

TRAVERTINE ISLAND (L), 14.1 *m.*, was formed by the "looping" of Travertine Creek. At the eastern end of the island is LITTLE NIAGARA, a waterfall over a rock formation in the creek.

BUFFALO SPRINGS *(picnicking facilities)*, 15 *m.*, is one of the two sources of Travertine Creek. The springs (L) boil up through a bed of sand, flecked with patches of green moss. Curving to the left in a hairpin turn, Perimeter Boulevard rounds the springs to parallel the north side of the creek and continues westward. ANTELOPE SPRINGS, 15.4 *m.*, the other source of Travertine Creek, flows from a small hill (L). Both Antelope and Buffalo Springs are fresh water sources and are often dry.

Travertine Island, 16.1 *m.,* is passed again (L) as the road proceeds southwestward.

Two adjoining SWIMMING POOLS, 16.5 *m.,* have been made by damming the creek. The near-by COLD SPRINGS CAMPGROUNDS, 15.6 *m.,* has floodlight illumination at night.

In the bend of the creek (L) is the NEGRO AREA *(campgrounds),* 17.2 *m.*

At 17.5 *m.* is the junction with State 18, which now again becomes the route.

Left on State 18 to PAVILION SPRINGS, 17.7 *m.,* where there is a pavilion (L) of native stone and handhewn timbers used for community gatherings. The ADMINISTRATION BUILDING (R) houses an extensive herbarium where some six hundred species of eighty-four families of plants found in the park have been identified. North of the winding, flagged walk leading to the building are HILLSIDE SPRINGS, from which a large volume of water flows.

South of the South Gate, 18.3 *m.,* of Platt National Park, State 18 continues to a junction with US 70 *(see Tour 6)* at 43.2 *m.*

Tour 11

(Caldwell, Kans.)—Enid—El Reno—Chickasha—(Ringgold, Tex.); US 81. Kansas Line to Texas Line, 233.2 m.

Roadbed concrete-paved.
The Rock Island Ry. parallels the route.
Good accommodations at short intervals.

Throughout its course in Oklahoma, US 81 has for historical background the old Chisholm Trail, the best known of the several trails beaten out by the millions of Texas longhorns driven to Kansas railroads and more northern Indian reservations in the two and one-half decades following the Civil War. Beginning with a mere thirty-five thousand head of cattle sent up the trails in 1867, the number rose year by year to a peak, in the eighties, of more than five hundred thousand a season.

First laid out by a trader named Jesse Chisholm who, in 1865, conducted a trading expedition from Wichita, Kansas, to the Indians living in the vicinity of the Wichita Mountains of Indian Territory, the Chisholm Trail proved to be the most feasible for drivers who sought plentiful water and good grazing for their northbound herds. Also as an advertisement printed in 1871 pointed out, it was shorter than others; the streams were "narrow and more easily forded than other trails; . . . and as the trail is through thinly settled country, drovers are not subject to molestation by settlers, have no taxes to pay, and . . . no ferriage is necessary."

So long was this trail used that a great body of tradition grew up around it and there was hot controversy, after trail driving had become history, as to its exact route and the man for whom it was named. That favorite cowboy song which opens with the couplet,

> Come along, boys, and listen to my tale,
> I'll tell you a story of the old Chisholm Trail,

is known wherever cowboy lore is known and loved—and that is throughout the country. Two other couplets of that endless jog-trot classic express the ambition of the tired cowboy after the herd had been loaded on the cars in Kansas,

> I'm goin' down south, not a-jokin' nor a-lyin'
> I'm goin' down south just a-whoopin' an' a-flyin'
>
> I'm goin' down south for to marry me a squaw,
> An' live on the bank of the Little Washitaw.

With the opening of old Oklahoma to settlement, in 1889, and the southward building of the Rock Island Railway, which reached Texas in 1892, the trail ceased to function as a cattle highway. Today, few traces of the widespreading and rutted paths made by the longhorns are anywhere visible.

US 81 serves a varied and prosperous section of Oklahoma. In the north are the broad, level wheat fields in the old Cherokee Outlet that justify the description of the area around Enid as the state's breadbasket. Farther south is the territory in which many of the border disputes between white pioneers and Indians led to battles and skirmishes, and where the farmer gained foothold against the ranchman and finally supplanted him. Somewhere in the neighborhood of Chickasha, wheat gives way to cotton, corn, sorghum grains, orchards, alfalfa, and vineyards. There is rough country between the Arbuckles and the Wichitas. Then, as the route comes nearer to the Red River bottom, the land is again well adapted to cotton.

Less than half a century has sufficed to change completely the character of the country and of the people along US 81. The Indian-Pioneer phase has passed and is already only a dramatic memory.

US 81 crosses the KANSAS LINE, 0 *m.,* 2.7 miles south of Caldwell, Kansas *(see Kansas Guide),* and continues south through the west central portion of the state.

MEDFORD, 15.1 *m.* (1,087 alt., 1,121 pop.), seat of Grant County, is at the northern edge of the most productive wheat-growing region in the state.

Out of the town and into national prominence as fliers came the brothers Apollo and Zeus Soucek; as lads of ten and twelve, about 1918, they constructed a homemade glider plane and started it in flight by mule power. In 1930, as an officer of the naval air force, Apollo established an American record for altitude, 43,165 feet. His brother Zeus, also a navy flier, designed some of the equipment used in his flights.

The small farming center of JEFFERSON, 22.1 *m.* (1,047 alt., 299 pop.), when first laid out was given the name of Pond Creek. The name was changed when the settlement four miles south proved its claim to being the site of Pond Creek station on the old stage route from Kansas to Fort Sill.

At 22.6 *m.* is the junction with an improved dirt road.

Left on this road to ROCK ISLAND PARK, 0.2 *m.,* marked by tall elm and cottonwood trees. Originally it was an eighty-acre allotment taken by a Cherokee in the Outlet and later turned over to a townsite company. When the railroad came, however, the station was built too far away to make the townsite valuable, and its few residents moved to Jefferson.

A marker, 22.8 *m.,* indicates the SITE OF SEWELL'S STOCKADE (L), three-fourths of a mile, which was one of the stopping places for trail drivers. In the early seventies, Sewell built the stockade for protection against Osage Indian mourning parties and war raiders; the Osage Black Dog war trail crossed the Salt Fork of the Arkansas one mile south.

It was an Osage custom to bury with a tribesman the scalps he had taken; and to send a warrior to the next world without at least one scalp was considered a tragedy. However, as intertribal warfare waned, the problem of getting a scalp to bury with a dead man became more and more acute and the custom arose of sending out secretly what were called mourning parties to bring in a scalp. To waylay and kill a Pawnee or other Indian might lead to war; and so scalps of isolated white men were in demand.

US 81 crosses the Salt Fork of the ARKANSAS RIVER, 24 *m.,* which drains the Great Salt Plains *(see Tour 2).*

At 25.3 *m.* is the junction with an improved dirt road.

Left on this road, across the railroad tracks, 0.3 *m.;* in a field (L) is the SITE OF THE POND CREEK STAGE STATION on the Chisholm Trail. In the days of the cattle drives there was a broad, deep lake here, but a short time before the opening of the Cherokee Outlet (1893) to settlement cattlemen who had the area under lease drained the lake. Still later, it was filled in.

On a little knoll about two hundred yards R. from the stage station site are the GRAVES OF TWO PIONEERS. One of them, Tom Best, was slain by an Osage funeral party in 1872; the other, Chambers, was an Osage victim in 1874. Their graves were marked in 1889.

POND CREEK, 26.3 *m.* (1,050 alt., 1,019 pop.), at the time of the opening of Old Oklahoma to settlement in 1889 was the southern terminus of the Rock Island Railway and was known as Round Pond. As the day of the opening, April 22, drew near, the Rock Island engaged D. R. Green, owner of a half-dozen rickety old stagecoaches, to carry those who meant to make the Run to the border. One of the last trains to arrive before the opening was from Chicago, and Green, in his "Leadville Cannon Ball' stagecoach, with a long caravan of coaches, wagons, hacks, buggies, and buckboards drawn up behind him, awaited the unloading of the train. Then came the rush to the border, nearly forty miles away. Though railway workers had repaired somewhat the rutted prairie road, that ride was a memorable experience.

In Pond Creek is the northern junction with US 60 *(see Tour 4),* which unites with US 81 for twenty-two miles.

South of Pond Creek the highway crosses a long stretch of undulant territory in the center of a great wheat-growing district. On these nearly level, deep-loam acres, the stretches of wheat are like a vast carpet of green through the winter; with the coming of spring they grow quickly to a knee-deep luxuriance of green; and by June harvest time they are a tapestry of golden yellow. Only around the farmhouses are there any trees. To the south, the great gray concrete towers of grain elevators and three city skyscrapers at Enid rise impressively out of the flat landscape.

At 30.7 *m.* is the northern junction with US 64 *(see Tour 2),* which unites with US 81–60 for 17.9 miles.

ENID, 48.3 *m.* (1,246 alt., 28,081 pop.) *(see Enid)* is at the southern junction with US 60 *(see Tour 4)* and US 64 *(see Tour 2).*

WAUKOMIS, 57.7 *m.* (1,264 alt., 397 pop.), lies in the center of the wide wheat-growing belt and is a farm trading point.

HENNESSEY, 70.1 *m.* (1,162 alt., 1,342 pop.), was laid out in 1889 and named for a freighter on the Chisholm Trail. On July 2, 1874, Patrick Hennessey's two-wagon outfit was attacked by Indians at Bullfoot Springs, at the southern edge of the present town. Hennessey was killed and his wagons, loaded with oats for cavalry mounts at Fort Sill, were burned. His grave (R), three blocks from the highway, is enclosed by an iron fence, and a rough-stone memorial in the form of a lighthouse twenty-four feet high has been erected. One block L. is the SITE OF THE OLD STAGE STATION; the building was burned on the day Hennessey was killed, and another was erected near by.

Roy Cashion, of Hennessey, a trooper in the First United States Volunteer Cavalry (Rough Riders) in the Spanish-American War of 1898 who was killed at San Juan Hill, is said to have been the first Oklahoma youth to give his life for his country on foreign soil.

Known for a time during the trail drives as Red Fork Ranch, DOVER, 79.4 *m.* (1,033 alt., 390 pop.), was a stage station where freighters on the Chisholm Trail changed teams. It was then no more than a stockade inside of which lived a stock tender named Chapin. Among those who stopped here was General Philip H. Sheridan on his way to Fort Supply *(see Tour 12).*

Freighters hauling supplies to Indian Territory forts over the Chisholm Trail route were compelled so often to detour to avoid the herds being driven north that a separate freight trail was beaten out which branched southwest at Red Fork Ranch for some miles, then turned south to forts Reno, Cobb, and Sill.

Near the spot where US 81 crosses the CIMARRON RIVER, 81.5 *m.,* occurred in September, 1906, one of Oklahoma's most serious railroad wrecks. A Rock Island passenger train, with the exception of the sleeping cars, plunged through a wooden bridge into the river; some of the train crew, passengers, and the train itself were lost. Ordinarily almost dry, with its wide bed little more than a stretch of blowing sand, the Cimarron is like most western Oklahoma rivers, treacherous with quicksands and apt to become a devastating torrent after heavy rainfalls. The bridge which replaced the wrecked one is of steel construction and its piers are sunk to bedrock.

The parents of the notorious Dalton Boys, outlaws whose exploits have been widely publicized in print and on the screen, were among the homesteaders near Dover; the mother was living on the farm at the time two of her sons were killed and another seriously wounded during an attempted bank robbery at Coffeyville, Kansas, on October 5, 1892.

A cattleman named King Fisher gave his name to KINGFISHER, 88.4 *m.*, (1,060 alt., 3,352 pop.), where he also operated a stage line and maintained a stage station. The name was also selected for one of the five original counties comprising old Oklahoma. Locally, the town is known as "the buckle of the wheat belt."

In the neighborhood of Kingfisher the Chisholm Trail was deeply rutted through the level prairie. At the time of the Run, April 22, 1889, these ruts were still so deep and narrow that, overgrown with grass as they were, vehicles engaged in the race for homesteads were wrecked and many horses' legs were broken. An old-timer, describing some of the biggest herds that made such ruts, has said that more than once as a boy he watched one herd passing his father's home from sunrise to sunset.

Between Kingfisher and the Texas Line curves on US 81 are sharply banked.

At 113.1 *m.* is the junction with an asphalt-paved road.

Right on this road to CONCHO, 2.2 *m.*, the administrative center of the Cheyenne and Arapaho Indian reservation of 5,280 acres. The twenty-six frame and brick buildings comprising the CHEYENNE AND ARAPAHO AGENCY form a rectangular group overlooking a wooded canyon which was once a favorite camping place for freighters because of its springs. First established in 1869 at a point 2.5 miles southeast of the present location near the North Canadian River, the place was known as the DARLINGTON AGENCY, so named for Brinton Darlington, a Quaker appointed to administer the affairs of the combined tribes. Darlington also opened a school there for the Arapahoes.

Although the Cheyenne and Arapaho Indians had been associated in war together, they desired separate schools; hence an institution expressly for the Cheyennes was founded in 1879. It was located at Caddo Springs (now Concho).

In 1909 the Darlington Agency was abandoned and the office moved to Concho, which had been named by the railroad in establishing a switch there. Its site is now the STATE GAME FARM *(visitors admitted)*, of 125 acres on which quail and wild turkey are propagated. In 1935 an electric hatchery, with a capacity of twenty thousand quail eggs, and a smaller hatchery and incubator for the turkey eggs, was installed. The fowl are used to restock Oklahoma's hunting areas.

The CHEYENNE AND ARAPAHO BOARDING SCHOOL, near the agency, is reached by following a winding road which crosses the deepest part of the canyon by means of an elevated footbridge. The canyon valley *(not open to visitors except by special permission of superintendent)* has been developed into a park and recreation area.

This is the only Cheyenne and Arapaho educational institution operating today. A faculty of twenty-nine teachers, all civil service employees, instruct the two hundred Indian boys and girls enrolled there. In addition to the regular school curriculum, trades, home economics, and farming are taught; a large experimental farm is maintained. Help offered to the adult Indians by the agency includes conservation and farming aid to the men, and domestic science and nursing for the women. There is a hospital which, in addition to the one at Clinton, serves all members of the two tribes.

Approximately five thousand Indians assemble at Concho for two annual events, the May Day Celebration and the Labor Day Festival *(visitors admitted to both events)*. On May Day a pageant, depicting tribal history, is staged by the school. The Labor Day Festival, sponsored by the superintendent of the agency, is centered about a feast for which whole beeves are barbecued. Baseball games and speeches are scheduled for the afternoon, with the night reserved for the dances, in which the weird Owl Dance, the gay Rabbit

Dance, and the light and fast Kick Ball Dance are featured. Painted bodies and vivid costumes make the performance a colorful display of rhythm and grace, effectively done to the throbbing beat of the tom-toms and the clapping of hands. Other dances are held during July and August at various points near the agency *(advance information from superintendent)*.

The legendary Sun Dance, a symbolic religious ritual, has been practiced in various forms by most of the Plains tribes, but because of the self-mutilation which was a part of the original ceremony, its presentation was prohibited by the government. As done today *(adm. 50c, inquire at agency for time and place)*, the Sun Dance retains the religious significance but not the torture of the former rite in which volunteer warriors inserted sticks through open gashes in their skin and dragged behind them heavy burdens tied to the sticks with lariat ropes. The purpose of the self-sacrifice was to display to the Great Spirit the willingness of the brave young warriors to bear the burdens and sorrows for the weaker and older members of the tribe. The chief's call upon the Great Spirit to watch the proceeding was directed to the sun, which served as an intercessor. The Cheyennes and Arapahoes have never performed the dance at a set time; but only as the fulfillment of a vow, or at a time when the need of a spiritual reawakening was apparent.

EL RENO, 117.7 *m.* (1,363 alt., 10,078 pop.) *(see Tour 1)*, is at the junction with US 66–270 *(see Tours 1 and 5)*.

South of El Reno, the country is somewhat more broken; and, instead of wheat, livestock and cotton are staple products.

Set on the tree-studded slope (R), UNION, 122.4 *m.* (1,321 alt., 400 pop.), seems to nestle between a tall sheet-metal grain elevator and a cotton gin. The town is a trading point for farmers and small ranchmen.

At 123.7 *m.* the route crosses the curving red-banked South Canadian River into the old Chickasaw Nation, then skirts its extreme western edge. Few of the tribe ever lived so far west, however, and the region was occupied before allotment by cattlemen; a few of the latter had married Chickasaw wives and thus became adopted citizens, but most of them operated ranches on leases or were intruders brazenly defying tribal laws intended to regulate white intercourse with Indians.

MINCO, 128.6 *m.* (1,538 alt., 921 pop.), lies in the valley of a small stream and spreads fanlike on either side of the highway. Upland pastures alternating with prairie farms suggest the neighborhood's range-land past.

Left from Minco on asphalt-paved and graveled State 37 is TUTTLE, 8.6 *m.* (1,296 alt., 940 pop.), where, at the eastern edge of town, stands the huge twelve-ton boulder marking the course of the Chisholm Trail and the SITE OF SILVER CITY TRADING POST. A bronze tablet states that the community's first school and burying ground were two miles north. "Dedicated to ranchmen, cowboys, early settlers, and their descendants," the tablet bears the names of 112 pioneers; it was placed there by the Daughters of the American Revolution.

Left from Tuttle on an improved dirt road to a store, 1.6 *m.*, near the south bank of the South Canadian River; here is the SITE OF SILVER CITY, one of the important halts and trading points on the old cattle trail. Early ranchmen in the neighborhood found it necessary to herd their cattle and horses, and pen them at night, to prevent them from being drifted away by grazing buffalo herds. It is said that they also employed Negro or Indian herders rather then white cowboys because white scalps were preferred by the raiding Comanche and Kiowa Indians.

Named for a village in Massachusetts, POCASSET, 137.3 *m.* (1,197 alt., 128 pop.), was the point at which Al Jennings—successively lawyer, train robber, convict, candidate for governor of Oklahoma, amateur evangelist, and author—once led his gang in the holdup of a train. In attempting to blow open the safe in the baggage and express car, the job was bungled and the whole car blown up. Not wanting to go away empty handed, Al and his fellows robbed the passengers of jewelry and some $400 in cash; then, salvaging from the wrecked car a bunch of bananas and a two-gallon jug of whisky, they rode away.

Where US 81 crosses the WASHITA RIVER, 146 *m.,* the stream is narrow and the valley is forested with oaks, elms, cottonwoods, and other trees.

At 146.5 *m.* is the junction with US 62 *(see Tour 3).*

CHICKASHA, 148.2 *m.* (1,116 alt., 14,111 pop.) *(see Tour 3).*

At 152 *m.* is the junction with State 19, an improved earth highway.

Left on this road is the SITE OF THE STAGE STATION, 1 *m.,* where the Boggy Depot–Fort Sill road crossed the Chisholm Trail. This stand, known as Fred, was a trading point and an overnight stop; it was at first located on the Washita River at the Trail crossing *(see Tour 3).*

A favorite camping place for trail drivers, RUSH SPRINGS, 168 *m.* (1,291 alt., 1,422 pop.), got its name from the springs which form the source of Rush Creek near-by. One of these fine springs is at the center of the MUNICIPAL PARK. The town is the market place for a farming district in which watermelons are a principal crop.

Five miles southeast of Rush Springs, on October 1, 1858, occurred one of the tragedies of the conflict between the whites and the Indians. At the urging of Wichita Indians, who were friendly with the whites, a considerable body of Comanches were on the way to Fort Arbuckle to discuss peace terms with the whites. While in camp, the Comanches were attacked at dawn by a force of cavalry under Captain Van Dorn from Fort Belknap, Texas, supported by one hundred friendly Indian scouts. Surprised and outnumbered, the Comanches lost practically all of their warriors, ninety in number. Five of Van Dorn's command were killed and a number wounded. In the Captain's defense it was said that he knew nothing of the mission on which the Comanches were bound; and that he was under orders to find and exterminate these tribesmen who had been raiding in Texas.

Although MARLOW, 176.9 *m.* (1,308 alt., 2,899 pop.), is now a peaceful law-abiding center for a prosperous farming community, with wide streets, a municipal power plant, light, and water system, pleasant parks, good homes, and modern schools, it was named for a family of outlaws.

In the early 1880's five Marlow brothers lived in a dugout in the brush on Wildhorse Creek in what is now the townsite, near the Chisholm Trail. It was the nocturnal custom of the Marlow boys to raid the herds being driven up from Texas and drive off longhorns to the timber twelve or fifteen miles east of the trail, then in a day or two drive the cattle back to the herd pretending to have found them straying or in possession of cattle thieves. For a long time they were successful in collecting rewards, but the cattlemen, victimized too often, became suspicious, set a trap for them, and wiped out the band .

With the coming of the Rock Island railroad, about 1892, a station was established here, and at the request of men living near by it was called Marlow.

Some Oklahomans

E : FSA

AT EASE

OIL FIELD DITCH DIGGER

LEE : FSA

A RELIGIOUS RALLY

LEE :

E : FSA

AN OIL FIELD WORKER AT HOME

LEE : F

BEHIND THE EBB OF THE FRONTIER

PLAY AFTER WORK

LEE : F

LEE : FSA

A PIE SUPPER; COOK AND GUEST

FARM BOYS AT A PLAY PARTY

LEE : FSA

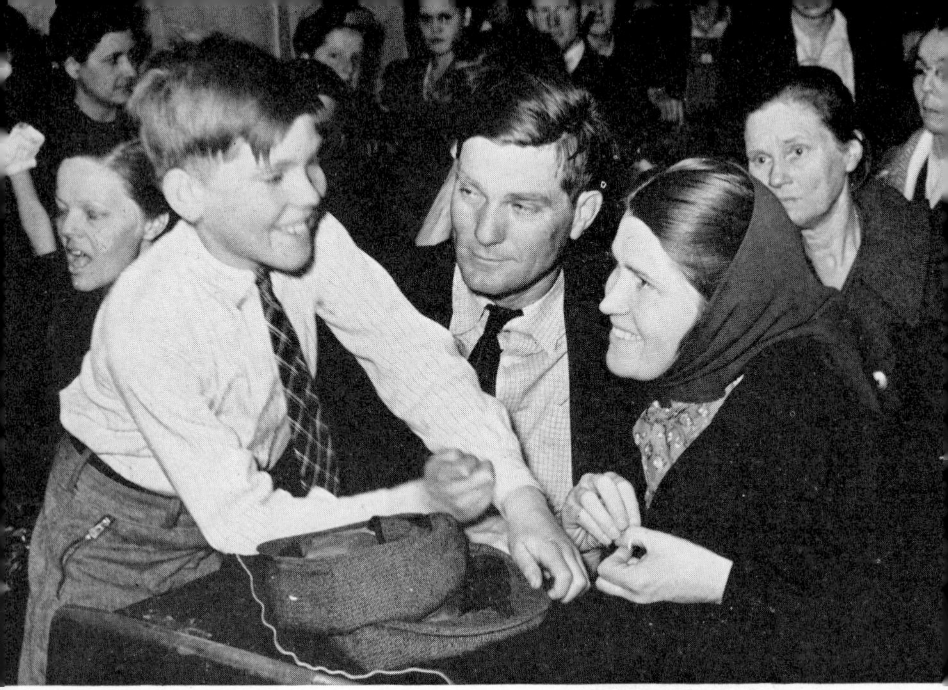

LEE : FS

FARM FAMILIES AT A COMMUNITY GATHERING

INDIAN TRIBAL MEETING

U. S. INDIAN SERVIC

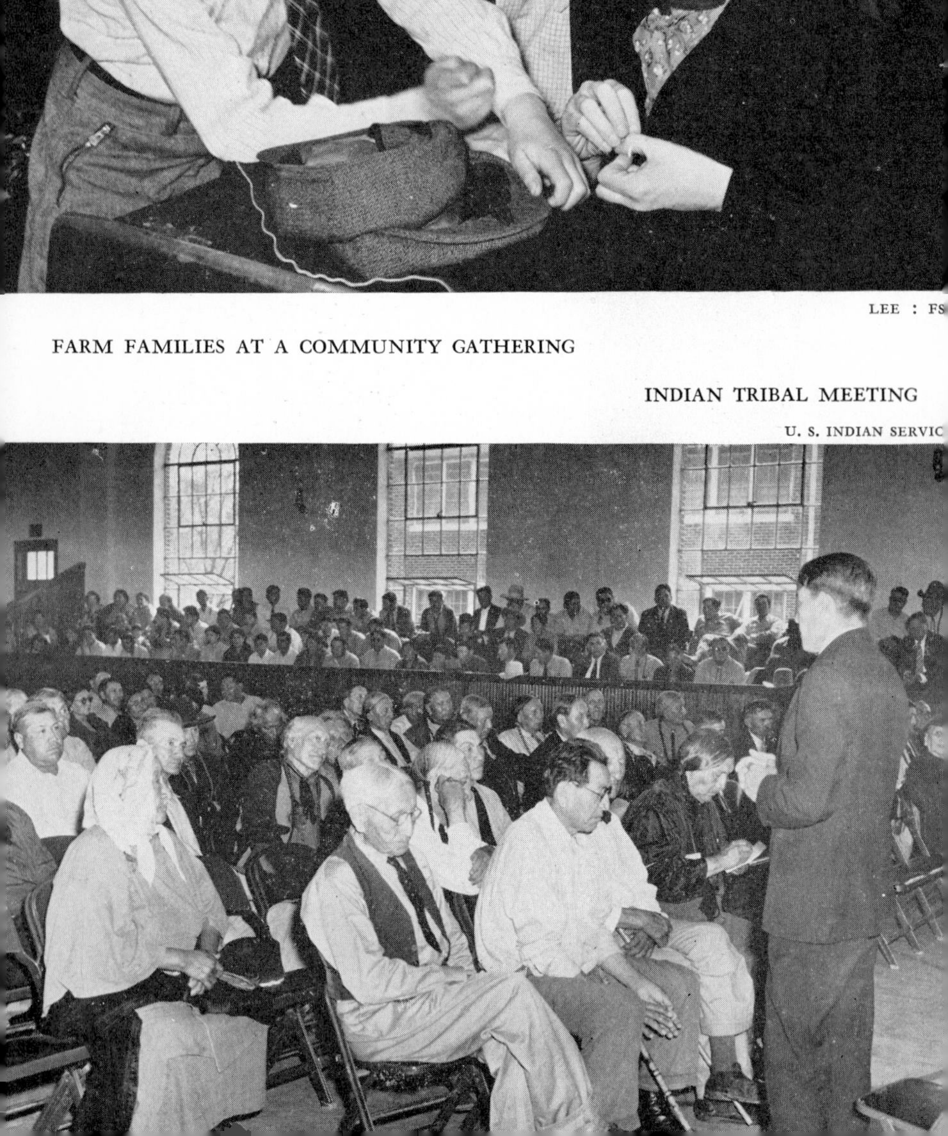

ASSOCIATED PRESS WIREPHOTO

WILL ROGERS AND WILEY POST

A PIONEER OF "TERRACING": J. J. BROWN (AT RIGHT)

LEE : FS

"A WOMAN'S PLACE"

"A MAN'S WORLD"

LEE : FS

At 177 *m.,* in a triangle formed by the junction of the highway with State 29, is a MONUMENT TO ALL OKLAHOMA PEACE OFFICERS. Its erection was inspired by the killing of Sheriff W. A. Williams near the spot in 1930. The pear-shaped memorial was cut from pink granite quarried in the Wichita Mountains *(see Tour 3B).*

DUNCAN, 187.8 *m.* (1,131 alt., 9,207 pop.), was named for a trader, Willian Duncan, once a tailor at Fort Sill, who settled near by in 1879 after marrying a citizen of the Chickasaw Nation. In 1889, when it became known that the Rock Island Railway was coming through from the north, Mrs. Duncan, acting under her tribal rights, selected as a farm a five-hundred-acre tract in the path of the rails. Three years later, with the depot built and the townsite laid out, Mrs. Duncan sold lots on the understanding that when it became possible to give title legally she would do so. The promise was carried out after allotment, and when the Kiowa-Comanche reservation was opened to settlement in 1901 an additional tract of 540 acres was added to the original townsite.

The business section of the city lies on a small plateau, from which the residence streets drop off toward the north, west, and south and end in the somewhat rough red land out of which Stephens County pastures and farms have been carved.

Duncan's growth has been based on stock-raising, agriculture, and oil. It is one of the largest primary markets for cream in the state, buying more than two million pounds annually; its cotton gins turn out from twenty-five to thirty thousand bales a year, and there are two cottonseed oil mills. The city is the central supply point for an area in which more than nineteen hundred producing oil wells have been drilled since the first one came in, on March 10, 1918, for two hundred barrels a day. Some $6,000,000 annually passes into the hands of stockmen and farmers in exchange for products marketed in Duncan.

To serve the oil industry, six supply houses have quarters in the city, and there is a refinery with a daily capacity of 6,500 barrels. The Halliburton oil well cementing process for safeguarding wells, which is used throughout the world, was originated and developed here. The processing plant employs an average of 340 workers, with an annual payroll of more than $600,000. Branches are operated in eleven other oil-producing states, in South America, and in several European countries.

A new and modern high school is the apex of a system of district schools whose attendance exceeds 2,500, with a teaching staff of fifty-six. There are, also, a high school and an elementary school for Negroes, and a privately operated business college. The city light and power plant and its water supply system are municipally owned. FUQUA PARK, named for Duncan's first mayor, is a tract of thirty-two acres at the northern edge of the city. There is a municipal swimming pool in the park, and also—at the southwestern corner facing US 81—Duncan's recently erected (1941) armory.

COMANCHE, 197.4 *m.* (983 alt., 1,533 pop.), is a wide-spreading town that grew up in the midst of an oil field in which may still be seen (1941) the pump jacks which serve the wells. Before the coming of the railroad in 1892 it was called Wilson Town in honor of a member of the Chickasaw tribe. The town originated as a trade center for a large area of ranch territory in both the old Chickasaw Nation and the Kiowa-Comanche reservation in which cattlemen leased range at the rate of twenty-five cents per head of cattle. After allotment, settlers came in, and the region became primarily one of farms.

A market town for farmers, ADDINGTON, 206.2 *m.* (915 alt., 250 pop.), is made up of one block of brick business buildings and scattered residences.

At 212.6 *m.* is the Y-junction with US 70 *(see Tour 6).*

An old town fighting stubbornly for existence is the way RYAN, 222.8 *m.* (833 alt., 1,115 pop.), has been described. Many of its residences and business buildings present a dilapidated appearance; and perhaps the largest structure in town is an abandoned chicken hatchery. In 1908 Ryan lost its year-long fight with Waurika *(see Tour 6)* for the seat of Jefferson County.

TERRAL, 231.5 *m.* (849 alt., 521 pop.), was named for a preacher who was responsible for laying out the townsite when the railroad came through in 1892.

At 233.2 *m.* US 81 crosses Red River, the Oklahoma-Texas Line, four miles north of Ringgold, Texas *(see Texas Guide).*

Tour 12

(Ashland, Kan.)—Woodward—Seiling—Frederick—(Vernon, Tex.); US 183.

Kansas Line to Texas Line, 222.2 m.

Roadbed alternately asphalt- and concrete-paved and graveled.
No train service between Kansas Line and Arapaho; between Arapaho and Texas Line the route is paralleled by the Frisco Railway.
Accommodations limited to larger towns.

South of the Kansas Line, US 183 passes through the old Cherokee Outlet, a thinly settled area of rolling country dotted with sagebrush and soapweed, and broken by deep gullies. The soil is loose and sandy, and dunes lie like rough windrows along the road and in the wide stream beds. A few of the largest cattle ranches in the state here produce the finest grade of beef cattle. On scattered farms some grain is grown but forage and broomcorn are the principal crops. Where cultivation is careless, much of the land is badly eroded.

The long section of the route between Seiling and the Texas Line roughly parallels the old Western Trail, the cattle trail which was beaten out by Texas herds after conditions on the Chisholm Trail *(see Tour 11)* made that route too difficult. Fences across the old trail built by white cattlemen who leased from the Chickasaw Nation, and a tax of ten cents per head levied for a time on all cattle driven through that nation, led to the establishment of this more western trail. How many cattle went to market over it no one knows. One estimate is that in 1882, the peak year, four hundred thousand were driven up to Kansas, and that during the nineteen years it was used the total was seven million. Other historians cut the total to fewer than two million. Whatever the truth is, certain settlements along this route began life as "cow towns."

The region between the southern edge of the former Cherokee Outlet, near the present-day Seiling, and the Texas Line comprised both the old Cheyenne and Arapaho reservation, opened to whites in 1892, and that of the Kiowas and Comanches, opened in 1901. It is highlighted historically by echoes of border warfare and tales of hidden Spanish treasure.

Along its southern Oklahoma section, US 183 serves small cities and towns—some of them outgrowths of Indian trading posts—that thrive on abundant cotton crops, dairying, and the quarrying of high-grade granite. It crosses upland country where the air is dry, healthful, exhilarating, and where the people, somewhat hard hit by the dry years in the 1930's, maintain their belief in the excellence of their heritage.

US 183 crosses the KANSAS LINE, 0 *m.,* twenty miles southeast of Ashland, Kansas *(see Kansas Guide).*

At 10.5 *m.* is the junction with US 64 *(see Tour 2),* which unites with US 183 to Buffalo.

Seat of Harper County, BUFFALO, 12.3 *m.,* (1,791 alt., 1,209 pop.), was founded in 1907 when Oklahoma became a state. Surrounding the town is an area devoted to farms along the creeks, and to ranches on the upland on which are raised high-grade Hereford cattle that find markets among breeders in other states. The county has been certified by the United States Department of Agriculture as free from bovine tuberculosis.

The area is well known to sportsmen for small game, quail, prairie chickens, and especially doves; and Buffalo is headquarters for many hunters in season. At the southern edge of town is a park and a municipal swimming pool *(10c).*

SUPPLY, 31.4 *m.* (1,994 alt., 414 pop.), first came into existence as Fort Supply in 1867. It was an army base of operations against the Plains Indians, especially the Cheyennes and Arapahoes. At different times it was field headquarters for generals Miles, Sheridan, Custer, and Sully, all well-known commanders in the protracted border warfare following the Civil War.

In 1894, the United States gave the old military reservation to the Territory of Oklahoma; and in 1903 the Territory authorized the establishment there of the WESTERN OKLAHOMA HOSPITAL, an institution for the mentally deficient. A granite marker on the hospital grounds commemorates the officers and troop units that were stationed at Fort Supply.

The town, true to its name, is still the supply point for neighboring farms and the hospital.

At WOLF CREEK, 33.7 *m.,* the Cheyennes and Arapahoes were defeated in 1837 by the allied forces of the Kiowas, Comanches, and Apaches. Two years later permanent peace was made among these tribes.

WOODWARD, 45.1 *m.* (1,916 alt., 5,406 pop.), is the seat of Woodward County, which was carved out of the Cherokee Outlet, and is the metropolis of a wide area of ranch and farm lands.

An upland plains city, its wide streets, trim brick business buildings, and the solid residences built by its citizens and by ranchmen who have established homes in town because of school facilities for their children, give Woodward a neat and substantial appearance. In CENTRAL PARK, one of four city parks, are the city hall, Community House, American Legion Hall, and the Carnegie Library with some twelve thousand volumes. A new and modern COURT HOUSE, constructed at a cost of $100,000, is the outstanding feature of West Park.

WOODWARD JUNIOR COLLEGE, part of the public school system, has a sixty-piece band that participates in contests throughout the state, and a strong debating team.

One daily newspaper, the *Daily Press,* and three weeklies, survive from this breeding ground for western Oklahoma journalists. Pioneering in the newspaper field, the *Woodward Jeffersonian* appeared seven days after the opening and reported that "the first man to arrive ... was David Jones, one of the good men from the Panhandle of Texas whose horse had more wind than the average newspaper man." In the first year another paper, the *Woodward Advocate,* was launched. Then came the *Woodward Democrat,* the *Dispatch,* and the *News.* This last became the *News-Bulletin,* which is published weekly.

Like other cities created overnight in the Outlet, Woodward acquired between noon and sunset of September 16, 1893, a population of five thousand; and that night a voluntary committee on law and order sent around the warning, "if you must shoot, shoot straight up!" While all lots on the townsite were staked instantly by the swarming invaders, 160-acre homesteads in the new county were less in demand because the land was thought to be too arid for farming. A week after the Opening, contrary to previous experience, many homesteads had not been staked—including some that turned out to be excellent farms.

Woodward is an important market for livestock and agricultural and dairy products. From the county come milo, kaffir, broomcorn, hay, vegetables, and certain small fruits. Among the city's industries are a chicken hatchery, a packing plant, an ice manufacturing plant, an ice cream factory, a cotton gin to handle the product of some fifteen hundred acres of fine cotton land, and a factory where fifty dozen brooms are turned out daily. In the big LIVESTOCK SALES PAVILION, an average of $86,000 monthly is paid for the cattle, horses, mules, and hogs placed on sale.

At the northwestern edge of the city is the THURBER EARTHEN PRODUCTS PLANT, where clay is mined by steam shovels, dried, crushed, and shipped as

Fuller's Earth to oil refineries for clarifying purposes. Average output is forty carloads a month.

Adjoining the town on the southwest is the U.S. GREAT PLAINS FIELD AND EXPERIMENT STATION, where on a tract of nine hundred acres United States Department of Agriculture workers are engaged in studying the problem of range rehabilitation and suitable crops for the region.

Notable among the pioneer citizens of Woodward was Temple Houston, son of Sam Houston who won Texas from Mexico, was its first president, and, when Texas became a state of the Union, its first governor. Temple Houston was a lawyer specializing in criminal practice and a flamboyant orator, who wore his hair long, dressed spectacularly, and left a memory of his talents and idiosyncracies so vivid that he served as a principal character in Edna Ferber's well-known Oklahoma story, *Cimarron.*

Right from Woodward on a graveled road to CRYSTAL BEACH PARK *(swimming, boating)*, 1.7 *m.*, a tract of 246 acres, which includes a modern airport, a stand for band concerts, a race track, the scene of an American Legion race meet held July 2–4 annually, and a lake supplied from an artesian well that spouts mineral water. Adjoining the airport is the RODEO ARENA, where, about the middle of September each year, the widely known Elk's rodeo is held. A concrete grandstand seats six thousand persons.

Contestants and visitors come to the rodeo from nearly every western state. Nowhere in Oklahoma are such rodeo events as steer-roping, bronco-riding, steer-bulldogging, and calf-roping more expertly performed; nowhere will the visitor see better-trained horses.

Left from Woodward on a graveled road to a junction with a second graveled road, 1.5 *m.;* R. to BOILING SPRINGS PARK *(swimming, cabins, picnicking)*, 6 *m.*, a 720-acre tract of woods and hills on the north bank of the North Canadian River. The park, named for a large spring that surges up through sand, was a well-known watering place in pioneer days. Springs provide water for a four-acre lake where a commodious bathhouse has been erected. Reforestation work, started here by CCC workers under the National Forest Service, will be carried on; a wildlife sanctuary has the greatest concentration of quail of any place in the state. There is a community meeting house for tourists and neighborhood groups.

In the thirty miles southeast of Woodward the route passes through the range area south of the North Canadian River and enters a region where broomcorn is a valuable crop.

In SEILING, 80.2 *m.* (1,760 alt., 629 pop.) *(see Tour 4)*, are junctions with US 270 *(see Tour 5)* and US 60 *(see Tour 4)*, which unites westward with the route for two miles. At 82 *m.*, US 183 turns sharply south.

A bridge, 89.3 *m.*, spans the South Canadian River, one of the quicksand-trapped streams of western Oklahoma that becomes treacherous in times of flood. Before the day of bridges, travelers were often forced to make long detours in order to find safe fords, and many tales are told of horses and wagons that were lost in the five to eight feet of quicksand in the river bed. All but one of the twenty-one spans—each sixty feet in length—of an earlier bridge were washed from their foundation piers by a flood and now lie beneath the smooth surface of the sand.

Right from the bridge on a dirt road that parallels the south bank, to the WAGON-ROAD CROSSING, 12 *m.*, used by early-day freighters from Fort Supply to Fort Sill and as a ford for cattle driven over the Western Trail.

South for about forty miles, the soil is sandy and shows evidences on the slopes of serious erosion.

TALOGA, 89.8 *m.* (1,708 alt., 533 pop.), was made seat of "D" County after the United States government survey of the Cheyenne and Arapaho reservation in 1891 prior to its opening in 1892 to settlement. The county did not acquire the name Dewey until after the battle of Manila Bay in 1898.

On the south bank of the South Canadian River, Taloga is the central point of a considerable stock-farming area. In the neighborhood, too, are fields that lie in shallow valleys sheltered from the dry, blowing winds of this edge of the dust bowl. Here is grown much of the broomcorn that makes the region rank second in the state in the production of this staple.

PUTNAM, 102.6 *m.* (1,959 alt., 142 pop.), is a trading point for farmers and stockmen whose fields and pastures lie on the high backbone between the South Canadian and Washita rivers.

Seat of Custer County, ARAPAHO, 122.4 *m.* (1,540 alt., 401 pop.), is known locally for its success in the long-drawn fight made by Clinton *(see Tour 1),* the metropolis of the county with a population more than sixteen times as great, to gain the county seat. A new and modern county courthouse, erected as a WPA project, a new school building, and a new municipal building testify to the optimism of the town's citizens in the face of a 7.5 per cent loss in population between 1930 and 1940. Stock-raising, wheat farming, and scattered fields of alfalfa represent the resources of the region surrounding the town.

In Clinton, 126.5 *m.* (1,564 alt., 6,736 pop.), *(see Tour 1),* is the junction with US 66 *(see Tour 1).*

At 131 *m.* is a junction with a dirt road.

Left on this road to MOHAWK LODGE, 4 *m.,* where a practical and successful experiment in preserving the distinctive Indian arts and crafts of the Cheyennes, Arapahoes, and other western Plains tribes is being carried on. Authentic Indian art work is for sale here.

Established in 1898 with funds obtained by Mr. and Mrs. Walter C. Roe, missionaries, working on the Cheyenne and Arapaho reservation, as a center for domestic instruction of Indian women, the commodious Lodge building developed into a workshop and a market center for the Indians' buckskin work, beadwork, blankets, and basketry. Now (1941) on a self-supporting basis, the Lodge provides a market outlet not only for the Cheyennes and Arapahoes, but for the Apaches of the Fort Sill and Mescalero, New Mexico, bands; the Northern Cheyennes of Montana; the Navahos of Arizona; and the Rocky Boy band of Crees and Chippewas of Minnesota.

CORDELL, 143.1 *m.,* (1,565 alt., 2,776 pop.), the center of a good farming area, is the seat of Washita County, with its business district close about Courthouse Square. For ten years after the opening of the Cheyenne and Arapaho lands to settlement, Cloud Chief, some eight miles east of Cordell, was the county seat, but when the Frisco Railway built through the region, old Cordell, a mile east of the present city, moved to the rails and soon became the county seat.

Three banks, four cotton gins, a flour mill and three grain elevators; a well-attended weekly community auction; a $10,000 Carnegie Library, built in 1911; a weekly newspaper, the *Beacon*—these summarize the activities of this center of a good cotton-growing region.

ROCKY, 153.5 *m.* (1,560 alt., 442 pop.), grew from a store building made of rocks hauled to the railroad by a trader among the Kiowas. The town, named when a post office was opened in the store, is a trading point for a diversified farming region.

At 162.7 *m.* is the junction with asphalt-paved State 9.

Right here to HOBART, 1.7 *m.* (1,550 alt., 5,177 pop.), named for Vice-President Garrett A. Hobart (1897–99). The seat of Kiowa County, and known locally as "The City of Iris," Hobart serves a rich and highly diversified farming area, especially along Elk Creek, two miles west. Here, on the opening to settlement of the Kiowa-Comanche lands in 1901, many Kiowa Indians took their allotments, which are mostly farmed by white men. The valley lands produce heavy crops of alfalfa, cotton, and forage grains of different varieties; dairying and poultry-raising are also important. On the uplands small grains, kaffir and sorghum crops are raised; and the pastures support many cattle and sheep. Initial development of a shallow (1,000 to 1,100 feet) oil field near Hobart has indicated a considerable productive area.

The city centers around COURTHOUSE SQUARE, on which face a modern Federal Building and the Carnegie Library; and four blocks north is the KIOWA COUNTY HIGH SCHOOL–JUNIOR COLLEGE BUILDING, with its attractive campus and athletic field. At the southeastern corner of the city, where the tracks of the Rock Island and Frisco railroads cross, are cotton gins, compresses, and an oil mill. Near by are stock feeding pens.

Named in honor of Colonel Theodore Roosevelt by a man who served with the Rough Riders in the Spanish-American War, ROOSEVELT, 174.6 *m.* (1,460 alt., 744 pop.). is a farm supply point on a branch of Otter Creek.

MOUNTAIN PARK, 186.8 *m.* (1,376 alt., 441 pop.), is dependent on granite quarrying and farm crops from the near-by Otter Creek valley. Here, in the shade of the trees fringing the creek, "singing conventions" are held in summer by settlers from Kansas and Texas. These are all-day Sunday meetings at which only religious songs are sung. Picnic lunches are brought along, and if the weather is bad the meeting is held in a near-by church.

At Mountain Park is told the story of Anton Sarekup, a Bohemian-born citizen, who arrived in 1915 and bought 160 acres of land ostensibly for farming, though most of it lay on the rugged slopes of Mount Radziminski and was fit only for goat-raising. Anton, therefore, acquired goats; and from time to time bought more of the mountain—as he said, for pasture. When he had title to the whole mountain, he wired a fellow Bohemian, Frank Svobada, a granite-finisher of Omaha, Nebraska, who had financed the purchase. Svobada soon began extensive exploitation of the enormous granite pile that is Mount Radziminski; as many as five hundred granite-cutters have been employed.

A thirty-acre municipal park, containing a swimming pool *(free)* made by damming Otter Creek, offers fine picnic and recreational facilities.

Right from Mountain Park on a series of unimproved roads: R. at 4 *m.*, L. at 5 *m.*, R. at 6 *m.*, L. at 7 *m.*, L. at 12 *m.*, and R. at 13 *m.*, a short distance to the Wilbur Miller farmhouse (L). Left here on a road through the farmyard to a GIANT PECAN TREE, 13.5 *m.* on the north bank of the North Fork of Red River. So far as is known, this pecan tree is the largest of its kind in the world; it is thirty feet in circumference six inches above the ground and more than 130 feet high.

The SITE OF CAMP RADZIMINSKI (R) is on the southeast bank of Otter Creek between Mountain Park and Snyder. The camp was established in 1858 by Captain Earl Van Dorn and named for a lieutenant of his regiment who had lately died. It was from this palisaded camp that Van Dorn moved his troops to attack the Comanches near the site of Rush Springs *(see Tour 11).* With the construction of Fort Cobb *(see Tour 3)* in 1859, Camp Radziminski was abandoned by the United States troops and occupied immediately by a body of Texas Rangers, who remained there for more than a year patrolling the border and indulging in skirmishes with the Indians. In recent years, many hundreds of credulous visitors have come to the site of the camp seeking for buried Spanish treasure.

SNYDER, 189.3 *m.* (1,360 alt., 1,278 pop.) *(see Tour 3),* is at the junction with US 62 *(see Tour 3).*

In MANITOU, 200.5 *m.* (1,254 alt., 258 pop.) is a ten-acre park with a swimming pool *(free).*

At 207.8 *m.* is the junction with a dirt road.

Right on this road to the HOLLOMAN GRAVEL PIT, 0.3 *m.,* on the Holloman Farm. The pit covers three acres, but the formation is far more extensive. Here have been found clay balls inside of which, say local reporters, were living frogs. Bones of prehistoric animals and stone age implements have also been taken from the pit.

FREDERICK, 208.4 *m.* (1,289 alt., 5,109 pop.), seat of Tillman County, was one of the towns that came into existence when the Kiowa-Comanche reservation was opened to settlement in 1901. Hard durum wheat and cotton are the staples of the good farming region surrounding Frederick. Two cotton compresses with a combined capacity of forty-five thousand bales a season; a cottonseed oil mill that operates ten months in the year; seven gins; and a cottonseed delinting plant help to account for the city's aspect of prosperity. Wide, well-kept streets, substantial homes, churches, and excellent schools characterize the city. A Carnegie Library, with more than eight thousand volumes, a business college, a floodlighted football stadium, and a swimming pool are in the town. Near the city is Burts Lake *(fishing, swimming, boating, and picnicking).*

In November, Frederick is host to an annual Cotton Carnival, to which visitors from all the big southwestern cotton-growing areas come.

The city points with pride to a sixteen-year record of no ad valorem taxes for municipal purposes. It is supported by revenues from city-owned public utilities which maintain lower rates for light and power than the Federal Power Commission's average for the state.

It was from Frederick that President Theodore Roosevelt started on April 8, 1905, on a wolf hunt that became famous because Jack Abernathy, a young ranchman of the region, caught a coyote with his bare hands and Roosevelt wrote about the feat. Later, after leaving his job as United States marshal, Abernathy repeated his coyote-catching stunt for the movies.

In the A. H. Holloman home, 421 North 12th Street, is a COLLECTION OF FOSSILS AND STONE IMPLEMENTS *(open by appointment)* taken from the Holloman Gravel Pit.

DAVIDSON, 220.5 *m.* (1,160 alt., 507 pop.), called Texawa at its founding on the opening of the Kiowa-Comanche reservation, is a farm community.

At 222.2 *m.,* US 183 crosses a bridge over the Red River, the Texas Line, sixteen miles northeast of Vernon, Texas *(see Texas Guide).*

Tour 13

(Englewood, Kans.)—Arnett—Sayre—Altus—(Vernon, Tex.), US 283. Kansas Line to Texas Line, 204.9 m.

Roadbed mostly graveled; intermittent stretches of paving and improved dirt.
No railway parallels this route; busses between Mangum and Altus, and between Altus and Vernon, Texas.
Accommodations in the larger towns.

Except for a small area toward the southern end, US 283 crosses high level upland. It serves a "dust bowl" area, where the hot winds blow and the light soil is carried away. It penetrates the former Cheyenne and Arapaho country and comes near the timbered breaks of the Washita where the massacre of Black Kettle's band in the dawn of a freezing winter day helped to establish the military glory of General Custer. In its southern section, US 283 crosses the once-disputed Greer County, which was joined to Oklahoma after the United States Supreme Court decided it was not in Texas.

With the boundary dispute settled, this arid section of the state is intent on the greater problems of water supply and reforestation; and generous Federal help is promised. Among a number of irrigation projects planned for the western half of Oklahoma is the Altus-Lugert reservoir, which will cover some fifteen thousand acres and supply water for seventy thousand acres of semiarid land.

More general, and less costly, are the shelter-belt plantings in the region through which US 283 passes. Here, in the five years 1935–40, an aggregate of 2,500 miles of ten-row belts were planted on more than four thousand farms. As worked out in this area, a cross section of a ten-row shelter belt shows successive rows of shrubs, cedars, pines; then larger semipermanent growths like nut trees, hackberry, ash, catalpa, American elm; and finally four rows of fast growing trees for early protection, such as honey locust and black locust, Chinese elm, coffee trees, cottonwood, Osage orange, and Russian olive. Sometimes flowering willow, walnut, and other varieties are used. The species chosen is determined by the soil, and no planting is done in soil where there is slight chance for the trees to survive.

In the agreement between the United States Forest Service and the farmer, it is required that the trees be cultivated until they grow big enough to shade-kill weeds. The percentage of survivals of planted trees in the Oklahoma section of the shelter belt has exceeded 65, even in the drought years 1935-37. Under favorable conditions, fast-growing trees reach a height of ten feet within a year, and twenty-four feet in three years. At that stage, they serve effectively to lift most of the searing winds above the level of planted crops.

Three miles south of Englewood, Kansas, US 283 crosses the KANSAS LINE, 0 *m.*

At 12.2 *m.* is the junction with US 64 *(see Tour 2),* which unites eastward with the route for 4.5 miles.

ROSSTON, 14 *m.* (2,139 alt., 143 pop.), a small farming community, lies entirely to the right of the highway.

At 16.7 *m.* is the eastern junction with US 64; US 283 turns sharply south.

LAVERNE, 23.8 *m.* (2,104 alt., 816 pop.), is in the productive valley of the Beaver River, the trading point for ranchmen, and for farmers who harvest wheat, alfalfa, wild hay, broomcorn, and sorghum crops. A beginning has been made in this region in irrigation from underground water sources that lie only a little way beneath the surface.

At 29.9 *m.* is the junction with US 270 *(see Tour 5).*

SHATTUCK, 54.1 *m.* (2,237 alt., 1,275 pop.), was settled in 1904 by descendants of German-Russians who first came to the United States in the 1870's and settled chiefly in Nebraska. Originally German, the group lived for a century in Russia where it enjoyed freedom from taxation and military service. When these advantages ended, the German-Russians emigrated to America. The Shattuck pioneers first engaged in general farming, but more recently broomcorn has been a principal crop.

At 63.9 *m.* is the junction with US 60 *(see Tour 4),* which unites eastward with US 283 for 6.6 miles.

ARNETT, 69.9 *m.* (2,560 alt., 529 pop.) *(see Tour 4).*

At 70.5 *m.,* US 283 again turns abruptly south.

At 82.1 *m.* is the junction with a dirt road.

Right on this road is GRAND, 1.5 *m.,* a ghost town whose broad unpaved main street was once busy with the traffic of farmers and merchants. In the first World War, when the price of wheat rose to $2.00 and more per bushel, the land around Grand was broken and seeded, and a prosperous community grew up. But as wheat prices declined and the soil blew away, farmers were starved out, and the town ceased to have any reason for existence. Its vacant buildings are weather-beaten, and their foundations banked with great drifts of sand.

South of Grand, across the South Canadian River, are the ANTELOPE HILLS, six conspicuous, irregular gypsum peaks that rise out of the level plain. The river loops around the northern edge of the hills, and on its bank grow scattered trees and sparse vegetation. From the top of the hills there is a panoramic view of the countryside.

CHEYENNE, 108 *m.* (1,932 alt., 1,070 pop.), came into existence when the Federal government established a Cheyenne Indian agency there in 1891, a year before the reservation was opened to settlement.

Right from Cheyenne on a road extending from Main Street to a junction with an improved dirt road, 1 *m.;* R. to a second junction at 1.5 *m.;* R. here to a granite marker (R), 1.8 *m.,* which commemorates the BATTLE OF THE WASHITA. In the bitter winter of 1868, General George A. Custer *(see Tour 3A),* later killed by the Sioux in the Custer Massacre, led his cavalry some seventy miles from Fort Supply *(see Tour 12)* to the Washita River, and in the night closed in on three sides of a Cheyenne Indian encampment under Chief Black Kettle. At dawn he charged and scattered the totally unprepared Indians; his troopers killed and wounded some two hundred men, women, and children, with negligible losses to his own command.

SAYRE, 130.3 *m.* (1,810 alt., 3,037 pop.) *(see Tour 1),* is at the junction with US 66 *(see Tour 1),* which unites southward briefly with US 283.

WILLOW, 151.4 *m.* (1,735 alt., 248 pop.), was named for Will O'Connell, the town's first settler and postmaster. It lies within a cotton producing area, and some four thousand bales are ginned here annually.

BRINKMAN, 154.4 *m.* (1,694 alt., 164 pop.), established in 1910 on the line of the Wichita Falls and Northwestern Railway (now the Missouri-Kansas-Texas) and first named Kell, for an official of the road, changed its name to honor a man who helped to finance the townsite. It is said that more wheat is shipped from Brinkman than from all the other markets in Greer County combined, and that from three to five thousand bales of cotton are ginned yearly.

Right from Brinkman on an unimproved dirt road to the town of Jester, 12 *m.* (pop. 550); L. here, through a pasture, to a NATURAL CAVE, 15.5 *m.,* on a creek bank. Only partially explored, the cave is believed to extend for miles. A few hundred feet from the entrance the ceiling is low, and water prevents further advance. The cave is a refuge for rabbits and other small animals, and at dusk myriads of bats fly out on their nightly quest for insects.

At 159.7 *m.* on the main route is the northern junction with asphalt-paved State 9.

Left on State 9 in GRANITE, 7 *m.* (1,618 alt., 1,058 pop.), the center of a quarrying industry. The main streets of the town end abruptly against a towering cliff of granite.

The STATE REFORMATORY, 8.2 *m.*, is for first offenders who, because of their youth, are not confined to a penitentiary. Inside the sixteen-foot walls of rough-hewn granite is the ten-acre tract on which the five large buildings of the prison stand—cell blocks, workshops, and offices. Outside the walls near the highway are cottages and a two-story lodging house for the accommodation of officials and employees. An adjoining farm of twelve hundred acres is worked by the inmates.

State 9 unites southward with US 283 to 161.9 *m.*

Right on State 9, a graveled road, is REED, 11 *m.* (1,744 alt., 125 pop.); L. from Reed on an unimproved dirt road to CAVE CREEK, 2.5 m. Along the banks are many tunnels and grottoes known locally as the BAT CAVES because of the thousands of bats that emerge after sunset. One cavern with a six-foot high ceiling can be penetrated for half a mile. It is necessary, of course, to carry a lantern or flashlight in the cave.

JAY BUCKLE SPRINGS, 14 *m.,* was an early-day camp site of the Kiowa Indians; and after statehood became a watering place for ranchmen. The springs supply people living within a radius of five miles.

At 23 *m.* is VINSON, (1,883 alt., 188 pop.), a small back-roads town; R. from Vinson on a dirt road is the NATURAL BRIDGE, 26.4 *m.,* a great rock formation nearly one hundred feet high, that overlooks an area pitted with rock caves. Many of the caves contain springs, and the water keeps the interior cool on the hottest day.

MANGUM, 162.9 *m.* (1,588 alt., 4,193 pop.), was named for Captain A. S. Mangum, one of the organizers of the townsite in what was then known as Greer County, Texas.

Greer County, so long a disputed territory, was reorganized in 1860 under an act of the Texas legislature signed by Governor Sam Houston. In 1881, after the lands of Greer County had been apportioned, one-half to the schools of Texas and the rest to the service of the state debt, certain veterans of the war for Texas independence were given land here. By 1884, Mangum, H. C. Sweet, and J. R. Crouch had come in against the wishes of cattlemen who used the ranges. The issue was raised that the county was not Texas land, but was in fact a part of Indian Territory. When Oklahoma Territory was created in 1890, however, Greer County was not included; not until 1896 was the issue finally settled by a decision of the United States Supreme Court. Meanwhile, the governor of Texas succeeded in getting the Federal government to recognize the titles of the Texas veterans to the townsite of Mangum.

The city is the center of a large farming district lying between the Red River and the North Fork of the Red River.

At 175.2 *m.* is the junction with graveled State 44.

Left on State 44, across the North Fork of Red River, 1.7 *m.*

Left at this point, 0.5 *m.*, on a graveled road is the entrance to QUARTZ MOUNTAIN STATE PARK *(fishing, swimming and picnicking facilities, overnight cabins)*, closed temporarily, under lease (1941) to the United States Reclamation Service for the building of a $5,500,000 dam south of the present Lake Altus dam across the North Fork. The new construction will impound water for irrigation.

This park is a 3,300-acre tract broken by red granite and quartz hills and ledges varying in height from six hundred to eight hundred feet; the slopes are covered with great lichen-crusted boulders. There are five miles of graveled roads, and the hillsides are covered with live oak, white oak, pin oak, mesquite, and cedar. In early spring, redbud trees make a fine showing. The park is a bird refuge and shelters quail, blue jays, redbirds, mockingbirds, and many other species native to the state.

LAKE ALTUS and LUGERT DAM, within the park, provide the water supply for the city of Altus *(see Tour 3)*. The dam is 458 feet long, and 37 feet high. A tunnel under it runs from bank to bank of the North Fork.

At 4 *m.* on State 44 is LUGERT, a town with only a half-dozen houses and a grain elevator clustered about the small red station of the Santa Fe. South of Lugert, at the mouth of DEVIL'S CANYON, early Spanish explorers, according to legend, established a settlement from which they carried on extensive gold-mining operations in the Wichita Mountains. The story is that they were driven out by hostile Indians, who herded them all into a near-by canyon and slaughtered them. Ruins of the adobe houses and copper and iron implements and artifacts tend to confirm the tale of Spanish gold diggers. Quantities of human bones have been uncovered in the valley.

BLAIR, 180.3 *m.* (1,462 alt., 570 pop.), is known as the little town in the Oklahoma cotton and alfalfa belt that survived a tornado in 1928 and eleven subsequent years of depression caused by ruinously low prices for cotton and crop failures, and then came back stronger than ever. This recovery has been due to intelligent diversification of crops and improvements of livestock on the surrounding farms. Blair's modern brick schoolhouse has a capacity of four hundred grade and high school students, and the school district is almost free of debt. The town is in the newly formed Lugert-Altus irrigation district to be supplied from the new dam across the North Fork.

ALTUS, 189.9 *m.* (1,389 alt., 8,593 pop.) *(see Tour 3)*, is at the junction with US 62 *(see Tour 3)*.

South of Altus, US 283 traverses an almost level plain for ten miles. Here the fields are plowed along contour lines to prevent excessive washing away of the soil; and the distant ends of the contour ridges meet the horizon. South of these fields lie sandy, badly eroded bottom lands. Just before Red River is reached, are irregular mounds (L) of blown sand on which grow scrub cedar and desert weeds.

US 283 crosses Red River, 204.9 *m.*, which at this point is a narrow stream formerly called Prairie Dog Town Fork, over a bridge twenty miles north of Vernon, Texas *(see Texas Guide)*.

Tour 14

(Sedan, Kans.) — Hominy — Drumright — Ada — Tishomingo (Denison, Tex.); State 99.
Kansas Line to Texas Line, 246.2 m.

Roadbed alternately paved and graveled.
The Santa Fe Railway parallels the route between Bigheart and Pawhuska, and between Madill and Woodville; the Missouri-Kansas-Texas Railroad between Wynona and Hallet; the Oklahoma City-Ada-Atoka Railway between Konawa and Ada.
Accommodations at frequent intervals.

Starting in the Osage Indian country and touching every phase of that tribe's comparatively brief experience in their present location, this route passes successively through the former Creek, Sac and Fox, Shawnee, Potawatomi, Seminole, and Chickasaw reservations. It is edged by missions and churches, some still existent and some merely ruins and sites, erected by zealous friends of the exiled races for their consolation and education.

Agriculturally, this highway from Kansas to Texas is typically Oklahoman. First, pasture and livestock, then corn and wheat, then orchards and wild pecan groves and fields of peanuts; then cotton. It is oil-smeared at intervals throughout its course in Oklahoma. In the northern third of State 99's course, it splits the first large-area oil pool developed in Oklahoma, beginning in 1912, and toward its southern extremity bisects the last of such extensive fields to be opened up (1934).

From rolling bluestem upland pasture land, State 99 passes to fertile river bottoms, mounts again to prairie ridges, winds through wooded hills where the traveler may still see little log cabins built by Indians, and emerges on the bank of Red River (1941) at a point that will be many feet under water when the Denison Dam project *(see Tour 6)* is completed (perhaps in 1944).

This tour might be termed a panoramic view of Oklahoma at work.

State 99 crosses the KANSAS LINE, 0 *m.,* 8.2 miles south of Sedan, Kansas *(see Kansas Guide).*

CANEY RIVER, 2.2 *m,* drains broad rich bottoms that produce abundant crops of corn.

At 4.5 *m.* the route crosses Pond Creek, a small tributary of the Caney; local legend has it that one of the last funeral parties sent out by the Osages in search of a scalp to bury with a dead warrior came upon two loggers in camp here, Jack Wimberly and Al Gifford. The Osages were not interested in Wimberly's red hair but craved a bit of Gifford's scalp, and offered him twenty ponies for a narrow strip just above the forehead. Gifford, of course, refused to deal with them, whereupon they took the strip by force—and next morning the twenty ponies were duly delivered.

The settlement of BIGHEART, 10.2 *m.* (832 alt., 13 pop.), once an Indian trading center, was named for an Osage chief, James Bigheart. Only three or four houses and a small store remain. This is a region of upland limetsone where grass is good; and in the big summer pastures of ranchmen who lease from the Osages range herds of graded Hereford cattle.

Beyond ROCK CREEK, 13.2 *m.,* the rounded hills rise beside the highway in rugged ledges sparsely clothed by scrub oaks. This nearly worthless timber and the scant grass coverage have caused this section to be called the "strip range."

At 20.2 *m.* the highway begins its descent to the Sand Creek bottoms that lie under the shadow of a range of hills. Among the pecan and persimmon trees that flourish in the sandy loam were camps of the old "Thieves Path," overnight stopping places in the 1890's for men who had stolen horses in Texas and were driving them to Kansas for sale.

At 20.8 *m.* is the junction with US 60 *(see Tour 4),* with which State 99 unites southward to PAWHUSKA, 26.5 *m.* (885 alt., 5,443 pop.) *(see Tour 4).*

The center of a shallow oil field, WYNONA, 35.9 *m.* (887 alt., 810 pop.), is one of the smaller boom towns that shrank after the peak of development had passed.

Wynona is at the approximate center of the old Osage Indian culture, and for a long time ancient customs and rites could best be studied there. One of these, the "Sending Away the Spirit," was held the fourth day after the death of a warrior at a selected tree, the bark of which was cut away by the master of ceremonies and the surviving warriors. When the tree trunk stood bare it was stained red and, as a symbol of the spirit of the dead man, was bidden to travel with the God of Day on its endless journey.

Another ceremony for the dead warrior took place on the return of the war party to the town. Within sight and sound of the tepees, they sat down in a circle and began to wail for their lost companion. Then from the town came the master of ceremonies and the people; and in the smoke of fragrant cedar boughs the warriors, their cast-aside clothes, weapons, saddles—even their horses—were purified. All their discarded property was then distributed to those of the three clans of the Osages who took part in the rites. As a final precaution, the returning warriors marched in procession around the encampment in order to establish a line across which the spirit of death could not pass.

Near Wynona, at the end of October or the beginning of November, usually occurs the annual wolf hunt, which lasts four or five days. Organized by dog owners, it is primarily a field trial for wolf dogs, and from seventy-five to one hundred owners enter an average of 125 contestants. Five mounted judges follow the dogs, which are sent out to start a wolf at three o'clock in the morning. Dog owners and visitors camp out during the trials, and at night bench shows, fiddlers' tourneys, and cow-horn blowing contests are held. About the same time of year a country-wide hunt, starting from a point ten miles west of Wynona, is undertaken by ranchmen and farmers to rid the ranges and pastures of coyotes that kill calves and sheep.

At 45.4 *m.* is an OSAGE INDIAN GRAVEYARD (R), where American flags wave on tall poles set up at the graves. It is said that this custom dates from the death in 1845 of a leader called Tom Big Chief, who wished to be so honored; it was generally adopted after 1873, when the custom of raising the scalp of an enemy on a pole was renounced. According to local history, the last scalp so exhibited was that of a Wichita Indian chief, and its taking all but precipitated war between the tribes. Gifts by the government of flags to be displayed at the graves of tribal members who fell in the Spanish-American War and the first World War further encouraged the flag practice. Tattered flags are replaced on the Fourth of July. After the coming of oil riches to the tribe, many pretentious monuments were placed in this cemetery.

Established as a subagency for the Osages in 1874, HOMINY, 46.5 *m.* (780 alt., 3,267 pop.), became a trading point for the Indians who lived in the southern part of the reservation. These, according to legend, are descendants of the Dwellers in the Upland Forest; that is, the people who fled into a forest a long time ago from a great flood. Others sought safety on a hill, and became known as Dwellers on the Hilltop, whose modern center is Gray Horse *(see Tour 4),* in the western part of Osage County; a third band, caught in flight among thorn trees, earned the title of Dwellers in the Thorny Thickets, and Pawhuska *(see Tour 4)* is their central town.

Oil wealth is almost wholly responsible for this modern, predominantly Indian town, with its municipal hospital, twenty-acre recreational park, municipally owned power, light, and water plants, country club and nine-hole golf course, floodlighted baseball park, eleven-acre athletic field, National Guard Armory for Battery D, 160th Field Artillery, and good schools. A cottonseed-oil plant, gin, feed mill, hatchery, poultry farm, stockyards, and feeding pens for fattening beef animals indicate its industrial status.

Veterans of the first World War observe Armistice Day at the ceremonial ROUNDHOUSE in the old Indian section of Hominy with a ceremony called the Feast of Peace. In deference to the elders of the tribe, it is conducted in the Osage tongue. The roundhouse is also the scene of various other tribal rites, dances, and feasts during the year.

Between Hominy and Cleveland, State 99 winds among rugged wooded hills, though nowhere is the grade of the highway steep.

CLEVELAND, 56.3 *m.,* (740 alt., 2,510 pop.) *(see Tour 2),* is at the junction with US 64 *(see Tour 2),* with which State 99 is united for six miles westward.

At 63.3 *m.,* State 99 turns sharply south (L).

A small town that had a brief boom due to oil, HALLETT, 66.3 *m.* (740 alt., 159 pop.), is a trading point for a farm community.

On the GEORGE FLEMING FARM, 68.2 *m.,* are hundreds of evergreen trees fantastically trimmed to simulate dogs, horses, deer, household and other objects.

JENNINGS, 69.7 *m.* (918 alt., 453 pop.), in the former Cherokee Outlet, is near the northern edge of the old Creek Nation and was named for the allotee on whose land the town was built.

In the triangle formed by State 99 and the Arkansas and Cimarron rivers, which unite twenty miles east of Jennings, lie heavily wooded, rugged hills, steep gullies, creek bottoms, and natural caves that became the refuge of such bank-robbing outlaws as the Daltons, the Doolins, Matt Kimes, Wilbur Underhill, and Ray Terrill, well known to the people who lived there. As a matter of policy the outlaws refrained from committing local robberies.

The Cimarron River is crossed just north of OILTON, 77 *m.* (818 alt., 1,225 pop.). This town marks the approximate northern limit of the famous Cushing Field that in 1912 and for a number of years thereafter made this the richest field in the world. It is still (1941) an important gasoline shipping point, some two thousand cars annually being sent out. The first river-bed oil well in Oklahoma was drilled in the near-by Cimarron.

The site of Oilton was a cornfield in 1915 when it was platted as the oil boom was reaching its crest. Lots sold at first for $500 each, and within a week one hundred houses had been erected. Owners of lots on Main Street boosted their asking price to $4,000, which seemed excessive even to the most optimistic businessmen. So buyers sought lots a block north, and there further development centered. On what was meant to be the principal street there remains only one crumbling stone business building that once housed a drugstore.

South of Oilton, State 99 climbs to the backbone of a low ridge through a forest of oil derricks; under most of them well-pump beams dip and rise.

At 77.6 *m.* is the eastern junction with State 33 *(see Tour 2A),* which unites with State 99 southward for 10.5 miles.

DRUMRIGHT, 85.1 *m.* (866 alt., 4,303 pop.), began its career as Fulkerson, but was renamed for the owner of the land on which the townsite was laid out in 1913. For nearly three years its tents, lean-tos, and ramshackle wooden buildings, set amid three hundred or more oil derricks over richly producing wells, sheltered bootleggers, highjackers, gamblers, and nearly every other variety of boom-town outlaw along with the decent population. Then, in 1916, the town made "Fighting Jack" Ary chief of police. He promptly moved against the leader of the criminal element, a half-blood Creek Indian named Creekmore; and after he was in prison the other bad boys either left town or followed him to jail.

Drumright's principal street runs over steep Tiger Hill, on which in the early period of the neighboring oil field's development many spectacular wrecks of mule-drawn trucks loaded with heavy equipment furnished thrills for the people of the town.

A municipal swimming pool, built by WPA labor, was opened to the public in 1940.

Immediately west of Drumright on the route, is the former Sac and Fox reservation.

At 88.1 *m.,* the western junction with State 33, the route turns sharply south.

STROUD, 105 *m.* (905 alt., 1,917 pop.) *(see Tour 1),* is at the junction with US 66 *(see Tour 1).*

At 110.5 *m.* is the SITE OF THE SAC AND FOX INDIAN SCHOOL. Established by the Quakers in 1872 with tribal funds, the school was closed in 1919, when the affairs of the tribe began to be administered jointly with those of the Shawnees, Kickapoos, Potawatomis, and Iowas from the combined agency at Shawnee *(see Shawnee).*

At 111 *m.* is the abandoned SAC AND FOX AGENCY, where the business affairs of the tribe were cared for from 1872 until the closing of the agency.

This small remnant of a powerful Indian tribe that once occupied an extensive territory in northern Illinois and southern Wisconsin was removed from the neighborhood of Lawrence, Kansas, making the nineteen-day journey in the middle of the winter and arriving at the new location December 14, 1869. The rest of the winter they lived in tents supplied by the government and worked at erecting permanent homes and putting land under the plow.

PRAGUE, 123.4 *m.* (992 alt., 1,422 pop.) *(see Tour 3),* is at the junction with US 62 *(see Tour 3).*

In the neighborhood of the NORTH CANADIAN RIVER, 129.9 *m.,* a number of Caddoan Indian mounds *(see Early Oklahomans)* have been found.

South of the river, State 99 leaves the Sac and Fox country and enters the former Seminole Indian Nation.

SEMINOLE, 141.9 *m.* (863 alt., 11,547 pop.), *(see Tour 5),* is at the junction with US 270 *(see Tour 5).*

BOWLEGS, 146.9 *m.* (840 alt., 500 pop.), was named for a member of the Seminole tribe on whose allotment the town was built. The first oil well drilled in the Seminole Field in 1924 was also on land owned by a Bowlegs, a grandson, according to local report, of that tribal chief, Billy Bowlegs, who fought against the removal of the tribe from Florida.

KONAWA, 157.7 *m.,* (962 alt., 2,205 pop.), is an active trading center and shipping point for a fertile and productive farming area.

Right from Konawa on a graveled road, 4 *m.;* R. on an improved dirt road is St. Mary's Academy, 6 *m.,* a convent school for Indian girls. Founded in 1884 by four Sisters of Mercy from Illinois, who came at the invitation of Benedictine Fathers to teach white and Indian girls in day and boarding school, it has received students from practically all of the Five Tribes and from many of the Plains tribes. Enrollment (1941) is 110.

Established in 1876 by Father Isidore Robot, of the Benedictine Order, Sacred Heart Mission, which sponsored St. Mary's Academy, occupied a tract of 640 acres in this locality given by the Potawatomi and Shawnee tribes *(see Tour 5).* The Abbey, a two-story building surmounted by a cross, is still in use, as are the stables, a bakery, and other utility structures now (1941) under the care of St. Gregory's College at Shawnee *(see Tour 5).*

At 163 *m.* on the main route is the junction with asphalt-surfaced State 56.

Left at this point to the old John F. Brown Home, 8 *m.,* a huge two-story frame building painted dark yellow erected by a rich Seminole chief when there was a settlement and trading post near by called Sasakwa. Across perhaps one hundred feet of the house's L-shaped front, a first-floor porch and a second story veranda, both with ornamental balustrades, suggest a strange opulence in the midst of a bleak sand-hill and scrub-oak region.

On the Seminole Indian Church and Camp-Meeting Grounds, 8.4 *m.,* are a score or more large brush arbors under which families and groups camp during the summer religious meetings. In good weather, the meetings, which last for several days, are held out of doors; the small, well-built, frame meeting house is used when it rains.

SASAKWA, 10.2 *m.,* (839 alt., 532 pop.), superseded the older settlement of the same name near the old Brown home; L. here on a dirt road to SPEARS HILL 12.1 *m.,* site of the encampment of one hundred or more tenant farmer participants in the so-called Green Corn Rebellion of 1917.

Syndicalist propaganda, and agitation to resist the first World War draft in this neighborhood and in adjoining counties, led to the formation of the Working Class Union. In August some five hundred members armed themselves and, as a protest against the draft, began damaging railroad bridges, cutting fences, and turning livestock into the fields. In camp, this mixed force of whites, Indians, and Negroes lived largely on barbecued beef and the old Indian green-corn dish called "tomfuller." This item of their diet, plus the fact that it was the season of the annual green-corn dance of the neighboring Shawnees, fixed the name on this abortive effort to take over the government of the United States.

The movement was of so little importance that local authorities were able to stop the aimless destruction and disperse the rebels. Only three men lost their lives, and two of these deaths were accidental. Eighty-six men were tried and sentenced to serve prison terms ranging from one to five years.

At 163.6 *m.,* State 99 crosses the South Canadian River and enters the old Chickasaw Nation, which extended southward to the Texas border.

Seat of Pontotoc County, ADA, 175 *m.* (1,027 alt., 15,143 pop.), was named for the daughter of Jeff Reed, pioneer mail carrier, who in 1889 erected the first building on the site, a combination log store and dwelling. A post office was located here in 1891; and the first railroad into Ada came in December, 1900.

The city grew rapidly as the industrial and trading center of an extensive territory. Its population was 4,349 in 1910; it almost doubled by 1920 and again almost doubled by 1940. This increase was due only in part to the opening of a number of very productive oil fields near by in 1934; Ada's citizens are apt to say that the city was bound to forge ahead because of its natural advantages, material and educational.

This attitude of self-assurance is illustrated by modern Ada's reaction to a descriptive piece by a "humorous" reporter in a New York magazine. The writer drew upon his imagination to picture a banner strung across a little town's main street saying," This is Ada. Ada's not a lady, but . . ." As an added "Oklahoma touch," he went on to describe the town residence of a mythical fullblood Seminole Indian woman, to whom seven million dollars in oil money had been paid, as overrun with pigs, chickens, dogs, and goats. When newsmen asked Ada's Chamber of Commerce for a statement refuting the wise-cracking New York reporter, they were told, "We have nothing to say. Why dignify such nonsense by comment?"

The city is an excellent example of a community based on a healthy balance of resources—industrial, commercial, agricultural, and educational. Its flouring mills find an exceptionally wide market and in the city, too, is one of the largest cement plants in the country. Near Ada are some of the best fine-stock ranches in the state, and the farms of Pontotoc County, mostly carved out of forested land, yield generously. Cotton is the principal crop, but corn, wheat, oats, sorghum cane, and hay are important farm products.

Negroes, who make up about 4 per cent of the population, live in a well-kept section at the northern edge of the city, where a consolidated school, which also takes students from the surrounding countryside, has an enrollment (1941) of 286. The Negroes support four churches in Ada.

The *Ada News,* which began publication as a tiny weekly in 1900, the first year of Ada's existence, became a small daily in 1903 and passed into the control of a stock company in 1910. By 1941, the *News* owned its own building, was issuing both a morning and an afternoon edition, with a combined circulation of more than seven thousand, and a weekly edition for farm readers. Its editor (1941) has served the paper since 1914. Another weekly, the *Bulletin,* has both city and country circulation.

Largest and most interesting of the oil fields near Ada is the Fitts, ten miles southeast of the city, where the deepest wells, approximately 5,200 feet, penetrate nine oil horizons. At its peak, around 1936, this field had more than one thousand producing wells. In five and one-half years the Fitts Field produced eighty-seven million barrels of crude oil. Less extensive but highly profitable are the Bebee, Jesse, and Allen fields that extend in a sort of arc from northeast to southwest of the city.

Radio station KADA, 1,230 kc., has the distinction (1941) of being the only one in the United States located in a city as small as Ada that receives broadcasts from two national chains (NBC and MBS).

EAST CENTRAL STATE COLLEGE, Main Street and Francis Avenue, forms a solid and impressive eastern border to the city, with seven commodious buildings dotted about its forty-one-acre campus, and its expanding athletic plant lying under the slope beyond. It is the third largest college in the state, with an average enrollment of about one thousand during the regular term and more than that number in its summer session. Its teaching staff of sixty-five is augmented by twelve administrative officers.

Created by an act of the state legislature in 1909, the school began as a teachers' training institution and was known as East Central State Normal School. In 1919, the course of study was increased to four years of college work, the granting of degrees was authorized, and the name was changed to

East Central State Teachers College. In 1939, with a shift of emphasis from normal to general college work, its present (1941) title was assumed. However to quote the current catalog, "the primary purpose for which the East Central College exists is the education of teachers." Special instruction is offered to teachers in the summer sessions, and in the Horace Mann Training School and senior and junior high schools that are maintained as departments of the college.

At the entrance to the college grounds, Main Street and Francis Avenue, is a giant CALLIXYLON, the fossilized stump of a tree that dates back to the Devonian period. It was found by John Fitts, for whom the Fitts oil field was named, placed in its present position by him, and dedicated to the memory of David White, noted plant paleontologist and at one time chief geologist of the United States Geological Survey. When found, this enormous stump was somewhat shattered, but practically all the pieces were recovered and cemented together to form one of the most impressive exhibits of fossilized wood in the United States.

East Central's plant centers about old SCIENCE HALL, facing the entrance, a spacious buff-brick, four-story building with a wide white-pillared front erected in 1909. South of it is the burnt-brick, three-story utilitarian ADMINISTRATION BUILDING, the HEALTH BUILDING, the president's comfortable two-story residence, and six concrete-surfaced tennis courts. East of the tennis courts, overlooking the athletic area, are KNIGHT HALL, where 175 women students live, and FENTEM HALL, for men students. Dining facilities for both women and men students are in Knight Hall. The modern and spacious EDUCATION BUILDING, of red brick, is at the north end of the campus.

The CITY LIBRARY, E. 14th Street and Rennie Avenue, is a small Colonial-type brick building, noticeably different from the usual "Carnegie" style of structure in Oklahoma cities. Although the city charter authorized the establishment of a city library in 1912, it was not until 1935 that quarters and an appropriation of $4,500 were provided. Then the old city hall was remodeled, and an annual budget of $4,000 was assigned. Since then, more space has been added, and the collection of books has grown well past the point where the borrowers' register showed more names than there were volumes in the library. A popular feature is the childrens' room. Another is the growing collection of exhibits, including paintings of native Oklahoma flowers by Mrs. C. O. Barton, and material concerning the early history of Ada and of Pontotoc County.

The UNITED STATES POST OFFICE AND COURTHOUSE, E. 12th and Constant Streets, is a modern massive building of limestone; from the third story sun deck the visitor gets a long view westward across the city and hills.

The CENTRAL FIRE STATION, E. 12th Street and Broadway, is a striking small, modern building. Monolithic in appearance and simple in line, it houses the city's up-to-date fire-fighting equipment.

Left from Ada on State 12 to the VALLEY VIEW HOSPITAL, 0.2 *m.,* a community institution erected in 1936–37 on a ten-acre tract that overlooks a broad valley. It was made possible by joint contributions of the city and the Commonwealth Fund of New York. This well-equipped hospital offers free service to needy patients within a radius of twenty-five miles up to 25 per cent of its capacity. Postgraduate fellowships have been provided for ten medical students, and for students of hospital administration, nursing, laboratory, X-ray technique, and related services. A NURSES' HOME is part of the institution's plant.

Right from Ada on State 12 to ROY TURNER RANCH *(visitors welcome)*, 24 *m.*, a million-dollar plant (L), occupying some ten thousand acres, on which are bred registered Hereford cattle. At the ranch's last sale (1941), one of its show herd bulls sold for $10,000. Maintained at the utmost limit of efficiency, the ranch plant, as well as its purebred stock, is worth visiting.

Just beyond the southern edge of Ada is WINTERSMITH PARK *(swimming, boating, fishing)* a rugged tract (L) of 137 acres surrounding a lake that provided Ada's water supply before Byrd's Mill Spring was acquired. Bridle paths, hiking trails, a large and luxuriously outfitted native-stone bathhouse, and a tree-shaded amphitheater seating three thousand persons are the park's outstanding features.

At 186.5 *m.* is the junction with an improved road.

Right on this road to BYRD'S MILL SPRING, 2.7 *m.*, the source of Ada's water supply. Out of this enormous natural spring, protected by a covering of concrete, spouts an almost unbelievable volume of clear, sweet water—from ten to twenty million gallons a day. The spring was a favorite meeting and camping place for the Indians and was named for a former chief of the Chickasaws who operated a gristmill there with water power supplied from the spring.

FITTSTOWN, 187.4 *m.* (990 alt., 150 pop.), is composed almost wholly of corrugated iron or frame houses occupied by oil-field workers. It was named for John Fitts, the geologist who was responsible for the development of the rich Fitts oil pool.

PONTOTOC, 196 *m.* (976 alt., 325 pop.), once a widely known Indian trading post, is the center of a good cotton-growing region, and its main industry is ginning.

At 205 *m.* is the junction with State 61, a graveled road.

Left on State 61 to WAPANUCKA, 12.6 *m.*, (620 alt., 730 pop.), where one of the first schools in the Chickasaw Nation was opened in 1852. It was first called the Wapanucka Female Manual Labor School. Its limestone building was condemned, and the school closed, in 1901. Reopened in 1903 as a boys' school, after the building was repaired, it was again closed in 1907. The building stands in a ruinous condition on the bank of Delaware Creek.

Near Wapanucka, in June of 1865, occurred a little-known battle between Comanches and Chickasaws. The Comanches, 350 strong, swept in from the west and for four days raided farms and ranches and rounded up a big herd of stolen horses. Before they could get back to their own territory, however, the Chickasaws, armed with rifles and pistols, overtook them. The Comanches, with only bows and arrows, were severely punished and many were killed, including a chief. The Chickasaws, having recovered their horses, took no prisoners and permitted the Comanches to go home. No report was made of the fight.

At 208.7 *m.* on the main tour is the junction with an improved dirt road.

Right on this road to BALLARD'S PARK *(swimming, cabins, recreational facilities)*, 5 *m.*, the site of former Chickasaw summer gatherings for sport and amusement. It lies in a wooded area threaded by small streams. Adjoining the park is a U.S. FISH HATCHERY.

At 210.8 *m.* on State 99 is the junction with an improved dirt road.

Right here to a natural park called DEVIL'S DEN *(private, adm. 25c, fishing, camping, cabins), 2 m.,* through which Pennington Creek flows in a series of rapids, cataracts, and falls. It is a rugged, boulder-strewn area, in which the Devil's Den proper—a cave-like recess—is formed by the overhead joining of two enormous rocks. Other features of the park are a great balanced rock known as the Devil's Chair; Dead Man's Cave, a cavern in the rocks containing grotesque formations; and, high up on the one of the canyon walls is a curiously shaped rock known both as the Devil's Coffin and the Witch's Tomb. One and one-half miles down Pennington Creek is the old site of Harley's Institute, Chickasaw Boys' Boarding School, now the site of the Tishomingo Golf Club.

TISHOMINGO, 214.6 *m.* (670 alt., 1,951 pop.), seat of Johnston County, was named for a beloved Chickasaw leader and was capital of the Chickasaw Nation from its formation as an independent nation in 1856 until statehood. It is now (1941) a trade center for a productive farming region lying along the bends of Pennington Creek and the Washita River, and for the ranch country to the north and northwest.

After the Chickasaws effected their formal separation from the Choctaws by treaty in 1855, their own government was organized and the tribal capitol installed in a small log building, which still stands in the northwestern part of the town. The second capitol was built of brick hauled from Paris, Texas. After being gutted by fire, this brick building was torn down and replaced by a two-story structure of native granite, which has been used as the JOHNSTON COUNTY COURTHOUSE since 1907.

Before the Chickasaw capital was located here, the place was known by the Indians as a fine camp site and was called Good Springs. In 1850, a residence was built near the springs by Jackson Frazier, an Indian, and soon afterwards two stores began business. Tishomingo, the name given in 1856, became a post office in 1857. One of Oklahoma's governors, William H. ("Alfalfa Bill") Murray *(see History),* came to the town when a young man, married the niece of a Chickasaw governor, Douglas Johnston (for whom the county was named), and started his career as a lawyer-politician. He presided over the Constitutional Convention in 1906–07.

At one time, Tishomingo's population was more than twice the 1940 figure. After 1920, it began to decline because of drought, depression, and fires.

The first Oklahoma state legislature, in 1908, authorized the establishment at Tishomingo of the MURRAY STATE SCHOOL OF AGRICULTURE, which attained junior college rank in 1924. The two-year college course emphasizes agriculture, dairying, animal husbandry, science, mechanical arts, home economics, and education.

On a twenty-acre campus at the southern corner of the city, and on 270 acres of farm land owned by the school plus 260 acres leased, the 450 students receive practical instruction and experience. Fifteen acres, of which ten are irrigated, are given over to truck farming. With the planting of trees and shrubs, the campus has become an interesting setting for the wide-spaced buildings which include nine major units and a number of other small utility structures. The two men's dormitories, DOUGLAS JOHNSTON and CHICKASAW HALLS, which together accommodate 155 students, are almost identical three-story brick and stucco structures of attractive southern mansion design. Haskell Lucas Hall, another men's dormitory, was opened for the school year 1941–42.

In BETTY FULTON HALL, a solid brick building erected in 1924, live more than one hundred women students. A two-story brick building approximately at the center of the campus houses the manual arts department. One of the newest buildings (1941) is the ARMORY-GYMNASIUM, of roughly dressed stone, with quarters for one National Guard unit, drill space, rifle range, locker rooms, and classrooms. The drill floor is also used as the school's gymnasium. The three-story brick ADMINISTRATION BUILDING is largely used for academic work and also houses the library of more than eight thousand volumes.

When the Denison Dam Project, on the Red River, is completed and the reservoir is full, the water will come to within a quarter of a mile of Tishomingo's southern limit, with one arm reaching up Pennington Creek through the city.

MADILL, 227.3 *m.* (775 alt., 2,594 pop.) *(see Tour 6),* is at the junction with US 70 *(see Tour 6),* with which State 99 unites briefly.

Established as a trading post in 1883, WOODVILLE, 246.2 *m.* (598 alt., 364 pop.), was named for a Federal judge in pre-statehood days and serves an area of Red River bottom farm land.

At 246.2 *m.,* State 99 crosses over Red River thirteen miles north of Denison, Texas *(see Texas Guide).*

Tour 15

Junction with US 66–69—Jay—Westville—Sallisaw—Heavener—(Mena, Ark.); US 59; 198 m.

Roadbed graveled throughout.
The Kansas City Southern Ry. roughly parallels the highway between Watts and the Arkansas Line.
Accommodations at convenient intervals.

This route passes through country that is, in effect, a visual summary of a century of Cherokee Indian history and a seventy-five-mile glimpse of old Choctaw backgrounds. Except for a few miles of flat farm land south of Afton and occasional short stretches across timber-encircled grassland areas which the Indians used to call "old fields," US 59 in Oklahoma threads the narrow valleys and winds across the ridges of one of the most eye-filling sections of the state. Caves, waterfalls, a natural bridge; the Spavinaw and Grand River lakes; ruins and still-standing buildings of the first missions established in the West by those valiant soldiers of the Lord who came out of New England early in the 1800's; a one-hundred-mile April trail of dogwood, wild plum blossoms, and redbud—these are some of the features the traveler over US 59 will remember.

It is a comparatively poor region, where farms are small and far apart. Much of the way the timber is all but worthless commercially; and where there were once fine stands of pine the problem of reforestation is more pressing than that of marketing the sawmills' output.

Almost from end to end, US 59 in Oklahoma provides for the fisherman, the squirrel hunter, the history scout, and folklore collector; the plain vacationist has access here to beautifully clear streams, rugged hills, ancient cabins, and good camp sites. Toward its southern end, the tour penetrates the northern border of the Winding Stair and Kiamichi Mountains *(see Tour 15A)*, where the United States Forest Service, the CCC camps, and the state are co-operating to open the region to visitors.

Against its attractions, for some, will be set the inevitable dust of this highway and the chiggers and wood ticks that can make summer picnicking and camping miserable for those not provided with preventive lotions or powders.

US 59 branches south from its junction with US 66-69 *(see Tours 1 and 8)*, 0 *m.*, one mile east of Afton *(see Tour 1)*, and then trends southeastward across an area of prairie farms to a crossing of GRAND RIVER, 8.5 *m.*, where it is widened by the waters backed up from Grand Lake *(see Tour 1)*. The route then enters wooded country which grows more and more rugged.

Roughly at the northern edge of the old Cherokee Indian country, GROVE, 13.1 *m.* (757 alt., 1,093 pop.), is a trading center for scattered farms and a shipping point for locally grown apples, peaches, grapes, and berries. Southward, the route crosses clear, fish-stocked streams and cuts through oak woods covering the flint-rock hills.

Eight miles northeast of Grove are the ruins of a town called Cayuga, promoted and almost entirely built by a Wyandotte Indian named Mathias Splitlog. The site of Kansas City, Kansas, and other land near by, was in possession of the Wyandottes before they were removed to the small reservation they now (1941) occupy in northeastern Oklahoma. While still in Kansas, Splitlog, born in Canada in 1813, developed a keen business sense and acquired considerable wealth as a flour miller, builder, and real estate dealer. After coming to the Indian Territory, he resumed his building operations on the banks of Cowskin Creek, and his creation, Cayuga, became the first town in Delaware County. Extending his operations to Missouri, he built a railroad *(see below)* to serve his own flour and saw mills, his wagon-building works, and his mines.

Splitlog died in 1893, and his creations have practically disappeared; only the ruins of a three-story millhouse mark the site of Cayuga. That and Splitlog Street in Kansas City, Kansas, and a small Missouri town named Splitlog are the only reminders of this pioneer Indian tycoon.

At 18 *m.* is the junction with a graded road.

Left on this road to POLSON CEMETERY, 6 *m.,* where the Cherokee Confederate Brigadier General Stand Watie is buried. In Cherokee history, this part-Indian loomed large as one among the insignificant minority of the tribe who signed the spurious "treaty" under which the Federal government acted in removing them from Georgia and Tennessee in 1838. Three other signers—Elias Boudinot, Watie's brother; Major Ridge; and his son John—were killed, after the removal, by Cherokees who regarded them as traitors. From that time on Stand Watie became a bitter opponent of Chief John Ross, titular head of the tribe for almost forty years, whom he accused on no better evidence than unfriendly gossip of instigating the killings. Many other killings followed, and at one time Watie gathered a force to overthrow the Ross government.

Committing himself and his adherents to the Confederate cause at the outbreak of the Civil War, Watie recruited a regiment of Cherokees, took part in the battle of Pea Ridge, Arkansas, was made brigadier general and put in command of an Indian brigade. According to local history, he was the last Confederate officer to surrender, two months and more after Appomattox. At one time during the Civil War he laid claim to the office of chief of the Cherokees, but his right to the office was recognized only by his own limited following.

Immediately north of the STAND WATIE GRAVE are those of members of the Ridge family, including Major Ridge.

Named for Jay Washburn, a nephew of Stand Watie, JAY, 29.6 *m.* (1,035 alt., 741 pop.), is the seat of Delaware County, having won that distinction from Grove in a special county-seat election on December 8, 1908. The removal of the county seat to Jay was followed by a comic opera war between two factions of the little town's promotors, each of whom strove to have the county records stored in its own courthouse. From their sketchy entrenchments, the forces of old and new Jay faced each other for several days, some wild firing was done (the only casualty a stray mule), and then the war was called off.

Built on land cleared of forest growth, the town is supported by the trade of farmers and fruit and berry growers. Undeveloped deposits of lead, zinc, and iron are believed to exist near by; and gray limestone is quarried. There are several churches and a CHEROKEE INDIAN COMMUNITY HOUSE. Jay is one of the three county-seat towns in Oklahoma which has never been served by a railroad.

At 31.4 *m.* is the junction with State 20, a graveled road.

Right at this point to SPAVINAW, 15 *m.* (668 alt., 255 pop.), once one of the northern towns of the Cherokee Nation and the center of a region broken by flint-rock hills and gorges through which clear streams plunge. The original town was purchased by Tulsa in 1922, when Spavinaw Creek was dammed to provide a water supply for that city, and moved to higher ground. LAKE SPAVINAW *(boats and tackle for hire)* now covers the old site, where once a five-story gristmill and a sawmill served the needs of the Indians.

Surrounding Lake Spavinaw is SPAVINAW HILLS PARK (cabins, picnic facilities) a sixteen-hundred-acre tract acquired by Tulsa to protect the lake from pollution and as a refuge for wildlife. If he is lucky, the visitor who tramps the trails of this park may see wild turkeys *(no open season)* and he is almost sure to see squirrels, rabbits, and quail. Fishermen take bass, channel catfish, crappie, and bream from the lake, which is periodically restocked from the hatcheries of the State Game and Fish Commission and those maintained by the city of Tulsa. CCC workers have improved the southern shore of the lake for public recreation. Two private clubs, the Tulsa Ozark and the Tulsa Spavinaw, are on the northern and southern sides of the lake.

FORT WAYNE STORE (R) was named for an outpost of old Fort Wayne, the actual site of which is now at the bottom of the lake.

SALINA, 28 *m.* (618 alt., 687 pop.)*(see Tour 8).*

At 34.2 *m.* is the house (R) which, it is said, was occupied by Stand Watie's family during the Civil War. Behind it is a steep-walled ravine which, some three hundred yards below, is spanned by a natural bridge.

At 34.5 *m.* is the junction with an unimproved dirt road.

Left on this road, on the north bank of Spavinaw Creek almost at the Arkansas Line, is the SITE OF FORT WAYNE, 9.3 *m.* The founding of this border outpost dates back to 1832; it was from this headquarters that Captain Nathan Boone, a son of Daniel Boone, conducted some of the early Indian Territory boundary surveys. In 1842, its importance as a military post having passed, the garrison was removed. Until 1846 the fort stood unoccupied. Then the old buildings became the rendezvous for the force of malcontents whom Stand Watie gathered and proposed to lead against John Ross, chief of the Cherokees; and again, in 1861, Watie used Fort Wayne as a recruiting base for his Confederate Indian troops.

Now (1941) there is hardly a trace of the old fort, even the foundation stones having been taken away—as so often has happened at historic sites—for use as building material by neighborhood residents.

At 51 *m.* on the main route is the junction with graveled State 33.

Right on State 33 to KANSAS, 1.4 *m.* (1,000 alt., 163 pop.), a trading point for a restricted farming area, and to the junction with a graveled road, 4 *m.*

Left here to OAKS, 6.6 *m.* (800 alt., 93 pop.), a Cherokee settlement that grew out of the establishment of a Danish Lutheran school in 1902. Right from Oaks on an unimproved dirt road to the SITE OF NEW SPRINGPLACE MORAVIAN MISSION, 7.1 *m.* There, in 1842, Moravian missionaries to the Cherokees erected a combination log schoolhouse and church. Situated at a ford on the beautifully clear Spring Creek, crossed by a branch of the old military road from Fort Gibson *(see Tour 3)* to Jefferson Barracks, at St. Louis, Missouri, the mission grew and prospered until the fierce sectional strife of the Civil War compelled its closing. After the war, the Moravians reopened the school and mission and continued the work until 1898, when the allotment of the Cherokee Nation in severalty deprived them of the land they had used.

A pastor of the Danish Lutheran church, Rev. N. L. Nielson, took over in part the mission's preaching, and the establishment of the school followed. It has been built up to an enrollment of more than sixty Cherokee boys and girls.

What remains of the solidly built old mission are a stone chimney and foundation sills. The rest was taken, with the approval of the Indian agent, to repair the barn of the Cherokee who owned the land on which it stood.

In the neighborhood, beadwork, bows and arrows, and bright-hued baskets of Indian design and making may be purchased at a number of Cherokee homes.

At its junction with State 33, US 59 makes a right-angle turn and proceeds eastward.

A ROADSIDE PARK *(picnic facilities),* 53.1 *m.,* is maintained by the State Highway Department.

At the summit of a hill, 57.4 *m.,* is a fine view of some thirty miles of timbered hills and fertile, farm-dotted valleys.

FLINT, 56.2 *m.* (1,197 alt., 25 pop.), now (1941) only a tiny settlement, was important in the first years of Cherokee occupancy of the neighborhood. Here in 1838 a water-wheel gristmill and a sawmill were set up. Millstones for the gristmill were sent from France, coming by water to Van Buren, Arkansas, and from that landing on the Arkansas River by ox team. The mill was long ago moved from its original site; it is said that the original French "burrs" are still in use.

In 1872, Polly Chesterton, wife of the miller, was killed by an Indian named Ezekiel Proctor, who meant the shot for her husband. Proctor's trial led to the so-called Goingsnake District Courthouse massacre *(see Tour 3)*.

A welcome refuge from summer dust and heat, DRIPPING SPRINGS *(adm. 10c, cabins)*, 60.6 *m.*, is a compact resort area (R) centered about a descending series of falls over which a small stream sometimes sends a rushing flow of water but which usually is so scant that visitors may enter the recesses of the rock behind the dripping waterfalls without getting wet.

A first waterfall drops seventy-five feet, the second, thirty feet; and finally there is a cascade of fifteen feet. In order to reach the bottom of this, where greenery and coolness and seats await, the visitor crosses a deep gorge on a swinging footbridge some 175 feet in length. Then from the wooded grove in which the resort's rustic cabins are set and where picnic facilities are provided, steep but safe paths descend to the canyon floor and the pools in which grow many water plants.

At 63 *m.*, US 59 turns sharply southward to the junction with an unimproved dirt road, 68.8 *m.*

Left on this road is LAKE FRANCIS *(boats for fishing, and for trips down the Illinois* River, $1 per day) *(see Tour 16)*, 0.3 *m.*, extending southward along the border between Oklahoma and Arkansas for five miles.

South of the Illinois River, US 59 passes through Watts, 69 *m.* (958 alt., 307 pop.), a rendezvous for hunters and for fishermen, many of whom obtain from the town boats and guides for the Illinois River float.

At 73.8 *m.* is the junction with a graveled road.

Right on this road to SITE OF CHEROKEE BAPTIST MISSION ("Breadtown"), 0.9 *m.*, established in 1839 by Rev. Evan Jones, a missionary who had been active among the Cherokees of North Carolina for years before their removal. So closely had Jones become identified with the tribe that he was chosen by Chief John Ross in 1838 to lead one contingent of emigrants to the new home of the Cherokees in Indian Territory. It was with the help of another leader, the Cherokee Bushyhead who was afterwards chief justice of the Cherokee Nation, that the missionary established the new Baptist Mission.

The site of this mission was called "Breadtown" because it was one of the places at which rations to the newly arrived exiles were issued by contractors, most of them white men who cheated shamelessly and were never checked by the Federal government that hired them to feed the Indians.

Generally known for years simply as "Baptist," this mission under the vigorous and militant Evan Jones and his son, John B. Jones, became the center of education and Christianization; and the roll of twelve hundred members, practically all full bloods, of the six Baptist churches and four branches in the Cherokee Nation closely rivaled the Methodists' membership at six missions.

The second printing press set up in the Cherokee Nation was at "Baptist," and here in 1844 appeared the first issue of *The Cherokee Messenger*—printed, of course, in the Cherokee characters invented by Sequoyah *(see Newspapers and History)*.

An aggressive Unionist, Evan Jones was driven out of the Cherokee country during the Civil War by Stand Watie's Confederate forces.

In WESTVILLE, 78.9 *m.* (1,128 alt., 716 pop.) *(see Tour 3)*, is the junction with US 62 *(see Tour 3)*, which unites westward with US 59 for two miles; US 59 now turns sharply south.

A charcoal-burning kiln at BARON, 87.9 *m.* (904 alt., 150 pop.), is said to be the only one in the state. A tomato-canning establishment, four stores, a crack sandlot baseball team, fine fishing in Baron Fork Creek *(bait provided for fishermen, if requested in advance of arrival, address postmaster),* and a cluster of modest residences make up the town.

Baron Creek, in the old days, was a favorite fishing resort for the Cherokees, who sometimes took great numbers of fish by stupefying them with the juice of certain roots. The roots were bruised and thrown into the water; the drugged fish were caught with the hands, with gigs, or shot with arrows, and the fish that were not taken soon recovered completely from the effects of the juice.

STILWELL, 94.3 *m.* (1,108 alt., 1,717 pop.), is the seat of Adair County and the center of a district that contains a higher percentage of Indian population than any other in the state. Here is, in fact, the heart of the district first settled by the immigrant Cherokees in 1839 and earlier.

The town is largely dependent upon farming, fruit-growing, and lumbering for its growth. It has a five-acre town park and a county fairgrounds. Two churches maintained by Cherokees are near by, the Fairfield Baptist, northwest, and the Cherry Tree Baptist, south, of town.

Annually in June, the Cherokees meet at Stillwell for a cornstalk shoot. In this tournament, bundles of cornstalks are set up at a certain distance from the shooters armed with bows and arrows; and the winner is the bowman whose arrow has pierced most stalks in a bundle. The game is one of the most ancient played by the men of the tribe.

Right from Stilwell on graveled State 51 to BIDDING MILL, 12.4 *m.,* one of the very few remaining gristmills run by water power. The first mill here, with a crude undershot wheel, was built in the late sixties or early seventies. About a decade later it was acquired by Doctor Nicholas Bitting, who rebuilt the old wheel; this in turn gave way, under a later ownership, to the more modern overshot wheel of steel which is still (1941) in operation. The name Bitting, applied to the mill, has become corrupted to Bidding, the spelling used by the United States postal authorities for the tiny settlement.

Along this eastern fringe of Oklahoma—especially from Stilwell to the Arkansas River—US 59 is called "The Dogwood Trail." It should, if possible, be traveled in the last three weeks of April, when not only the white blaze of the large-petaled dogwood under the tall oaks can be seen, but the pink of the redbud trees and the fragrant wild plum blooms along the small streams are at their best.

At 117.4 *m.* is the junction with a graveled road.

Right on this road to MARBLE CITY, 6.1 *m.* (628 alt., 214 pop.), site of DWIGHT MISSION, which is still in operation. Along with old "Baptist," this Presbyterian center of education, of religious teaching, and of humanitarian interest in the Indians was outstanding. First established in Arkansas about 1820, when a minority of the Cherokees emigrated voluntarily to lands in that Territory—as usual "guaranteed" by the Federal government for their occupation as long as grass grows and water runs—it was removed to its present site in 1829 when the United States forced the Cherokees out of Arkansas. As conceived and administered by Rev. Cephas Washburn, the mission was both a school for boys and girls and a church for everybody. In the 1840's, the mission occupied some thirteen commodious log buildings; there were a dozen workers and more than sixty students lived, studied, and worked there. It became a notable training school for native Cherokee teachers and gave great impetus to education in the Cherokee Nation.

Right from Marble City on an unimproved dirt road to a Y-junction, 7.1 *m.;* L. here to a junction with a county dirt road, 11.2 *m.;* R. here to CRYSTAL CAVES *(open June-September; adm. $1),* 28.2 *m.,* at the head of a glen in which are picnic grounds and a swimming pool. Studded with stalactites and stalagmites, and with formations of white, yellow, and brown, the caverns extend more than a mile under the hills, but only one-half mile can be seen by visitors.

US 59, proceeding southward, descends from the hills and emerges upon flat, sticky land which is apt to become troublesome to the motorist after hard rains. Here it skirts the western edge of a hill, south of the Cookson Hills, which is known locally as Wildhorse Mountain.

SALLISAW, 124.2 *m.* (513 alt., 2,140 pop.) *(see Tour 2),* is at the junction with US 64 *(see Tour 2).*

US 59 crosses the ARKANSAS RIVER, 134.9 *m.,* into the old Choctaw Nation. South for some miles the route is likely to be difficult after heavy rains.

At 146.1 *m.* is the junction with US 271 *(see Tour 7),* which unites with US 59 for 17.2 miles.

POTEAU, 160.2 *m.* (483 alt., 4,020 pop.) *(see Tour 7).*

Between Poteau and the Arkansas Line, US 59 passes through rough country; though the route is constantly being graded and cleared, rains cause falls of rocks and other debris, and the driver is advised to be careful. In places, the roadbed is elevated, and there is danger of skidding into the ditches. Also, loggers use the road, and their trucks must be watched for.

In the valley of the Poteau River, HEAVENER, 172.4 *m.* (561 alt., 2,215 pop.), lies at the northern limit of the Ouachita mountain range. Fertile farms and fine pastures are near by; the immediate area was known to the Choctaw Indians as the Prairie of the Tall Grass. The town was named for Joe Heavener, a white man who had lived among the Choctaws a long time and owned the land on which it was laid out. So well liked by the Indians was Heavener that at times he served as arbitrator of disputes and as peacemaker among them.

The town is a division point on the Kansas City Southern Railway, a part of which was built by the wealthy Wyandotte Indian, Mathias Splitlog *(see above),* and for some years the road was known as "The Splitlog."

Looming over Heavener to the northeast is the mass of a hogback ridge called POTEAU MOUNTAIN, with an elevation above the town of some twelve hundred feet. Under it lie undeveloped veins of coal, and on its slopes are stands of hardwood timber.

The Heavener chapter of the Isaak Walton League has been successful in getting a FISH HATCHERY built on the bank of the nearby Black Fork River. Here, on a 196-acre tract, thirty-six acres have been set aside for propagating ponds; and six of the ponds have been stocked with black bass, bluegill, bream, and crappie. A dam across the river 250 feet long and 80 feet high provides water for the hatchery ponds.

At 190.4 *m.* is the junction with an improved dirt road *(see Tour 15A).*

PAGE, 191.9 *m.* (922 alt., 698 pop.), is in the heart of the OUACHITA NATIONAL FOREST, which takes in parts of the Winding Stair Mountains to the west and the Kiamichi Mountains to the south. Page is a well-known outfitting point for campers and fishermen who follow the trails and streams, and for the many hunters who invade the Kiamichis annually in the brief open season on deer.

The summit (R) of RICH MOUNTAIN, 194.2 *m.,* is on the Oklahoma-Arkansas Line. On this mountain, it is said by naturalists and timber experts, may be found forty-seven varieties of trees, twenty-seven species of wild fruit, seventeen kinds of medicinal plants, and more than one hundred different flowers besides many mosses and ferns, some of which are subtropical. At the top of the mountain, at an elevation of two thousand feet above the valley floor, is a small farm and an abandoned inn.

US 59 crosses the ARKANSAS LINE, 198 *m.,* fifteen miles northwest of Mena, Arkansas *(see Arkansas Guide).*

Tour 15A

Junction with US 59—Big Cedar—Bethel—Broken Bow—Junction with US 70; 73.3 m.; unnumbered road. State 21.

Roadbed natural gravel; steepest gradient 12 per cent. After flooding rain, advisable to wait a few hours for the run off.
Accommodations limited to Smithville and Broken Bow.

The route crosses the southern half of the Ouachita National Forest, then enters the equally rugged and interesting area which has been included by the Division of Forestry of the Oklahoma Planning and Resources Board in a fire protection unit. This means that the whole region is under special care by either the Federal or state government, that the CCC-built roads are well maintained, that game is properly protected, that the streams are stocked with fish, and that the visitor is provided with every reasonable facility for his convenience and enjoyment. In return the hunter, fisherman, camper, or passing tourist is urged to co-operate wholeheartedly in the effort to prevent fires. From strategically placed lookout towers, to which visitors are generally welcome, rangers keep the entire area under observation at all times.

This is essentially a route for sportsmen and experienced campers. It penetrates the best hunting and fishing region in the state, which is also the roughest and most trying to the driver unused to mountain roads. In the woods and valleys of the Winding Stair and Kiamichi Mountains are found deer, ducks, quail, and squirrels; and there are open seasons on all. Here, too, the wild turkey may be seen, but there is no open season on this game bird. Beautiful natural swimming pools are plentiful, and camp sites easy to reach. From such streams as the Kiamichi, Mountain Fork, Glover, Big Eagle, Eagle Fork, and smaller creeks fishermen take smallmouthed and rock bass, channel catfish, sunfish, goggle-eyed perch, drum, and buffalo; and in doing so they pass down shadowed canyons, scramble through cliffside underbrush and over high-piled rocks that give character to this southeastern corner of the state.

The timber resources of this area are still considerable, and lumbering is a principal industry, though far less important than it once was. The operations of lumber companies, and destruction due to fires over more than a generation, have almost exhausted the fine stands of pine and radically depleted the hardwoods—oaks, hickories, elms, hard maples, and sycamores. The problem faced in the Ouachita National Forest is one of reforestation; and here, as well as in the state fire protection unit, the lumbering interests now co-operate intelligently and wholeheartedly in fire prevention by adopting modern practices in the disposal of waste.

In the valleys are farms whose owners generally supplement their income from crops by work in the logging camps, at the "groundhog" (small local) sawmills, and in the cooperage plants and shingle mills of the region. Out of the timber of these mountains, too, come such other varied forest products as crossties, telephone poles, fence posts, mine timbers, ax handles, and firewood.

Westward from its junction with US 59, 0 *m.* *(see Tour 15),* 0.7 miles northeast of PAGE (922 alt., 698 pop.) *(see Tour 15),* the route proceeds along an unnumbered road built by the CCC to a junction with a second natural gravel road, 4.5 *m.*

Straight ahead on this road to WINDING STAIR TOWER *(visitors welcome)*, 1.5 *m.*, one of the lookout towers of the Ouachita National Forest that affords a long view of the northern reaches of forests and crags of the Ouachita and Winding Stair ranges.

The main route turns sharply south (L) and skirts the western edge of the Rich Mountain hogback, a part of the Ouachita system.

A supply point, BIG CEDAR, 10.8 *m.* (964 alt., 30 pop.), has two stores at which groceries, fishing tackle, and useful local information may be obtained.

The KIAMICHI RIVER, 12.8 *m.*, is the most important stream of the southeastern Oklahoma mountain region. South of the river, the route climbs up the main range of the Kiamichis, reaching the SUMMIT, 14.8 *m.* From this point can be seen miles of timbered ridges and valleys spotted with small farms and pocked by smoke from scattered "groundhog" sawmills.

At 15.2 *m.* is the junction with a CCC-built skyline drive.

Left on this drive to CROW'S NEST, 7 *m.*, another lookout tower of the Forest Service, from which there is a fine view of the Lynn, Blue Bouncer, Pine, Rich, and Walnut mountains, Turkey Snout Ridge, and some of the Arkansas Ouachita range.

South of the summit is the valley through which flows Cucumber Creek, and a second valley drained by the united Big Eagle and Eagle Fork creeks. Here, close to the McCurtain County northern border, near Boktukola Mountain and in the rough breaks at the head of Eagle Fork in the old Choctaw Nashoba (Wolf) County, the Kiamichis are at their wildest. Deer are most plentiful here. Bait-casting fishermen seek the deep pools and sinkholes, and shotgun hunters find squirrels, quail, and ducks in season.

CUCUMBER CREEK, crossed at 20.1 *m.,* is a stream that has been generously stocked with smallmouthed bass. The name of this creek comes from the curiously curved and thickened branch-ends of the magnolia trees on its banks.

SMITHVILLE, 30.2 *m.* (700 alt., 290 pop.), is a favorite outfitting and starting place for sportsmen, campers, and those who make a floating trip down the Mountain Fork River to and on Little River. According to pioneers, it was in this region that in the old days the Choctaws found game and fish most plentiful, fishing when "the rabbit hollered" or "the Peter bird sang," using as bait almost anything from bread dough to foot-long fishworms, one of which was judged ample for catching twenty fish.

It was the Indian squirrel-shooter, too, who established the vogue of the "still hunt," still popular in the Kiamichis. With the idea of obtaining game with the least amount of effort, the still hunter goes out at daybreak, when no breeze is blowing to ruffle the leaves of the trees. Finding a likely spot, he halts and stands immobile watching the tree-tops, where any movement of a squirrel will attract the eye. Then the shot, which must be quick and accurate.

At Smithville is the junction with State 21, a graveled highway, over which the tour continues.

On the bank of one branch of Glover Creek, BETHEL, 44.7 *m.* (750 alt., 37 pop.), is a trading point for scattered farm families and mill workers, and a favorite rendezvous for deer hunters in the short open season. More than twelve hundred deer hunters come to the Kiamichis each year; some three-thousand deer are reported, with perhaps six hundred bucks of an age to shoot. An average bag for all hunters is three hundred bucks, many with twelve to sixteen points, that weigh from 150 to 200 pounds.

Glover Creek is one of the best streams in the state for buffalo fishing. To take the buffalo, it is suggested that a gallon or so of cornmeal or shorts be tied in a bag, and the bag sunk in a large hole six to seven feet deep a few days before the hole is to be fished. The recommended bait is a marble-size pinch of this soaked cornmeal, mixed with flour dough, pressed on the hook. The buffalo does not swallow the bait, but nibbles at it, and the fisherman snags the fish in the gills when he feels the nibbling. The buffalo is a big fish, ranging in weight from thirty to ninety pounds.

At 47.2 *m.* is the junction with an improved, CCC-built road.

Left on this road to a STATE GAME PRESERVE, 8.1 *m.,* comprising 14,720 acres of densely wooded land lying across, and adjacent to, the Mountain Fork River, which has been stocked with perch, bass, sunfish, drum, buffalo, and other species of fish. Behind the fence which (1941) is under repair are many deer.

In this section the route twists and turns, dips downhill and rises abruptly, and the driver is advised to keep his car in gear on the grades.

Topping the highest peak (L) of the southern Kiamichis, CARTER MOUNTAIN TOWER *(visitors welcome)*, 53.6 *m.*, is a lookout for state fire wardens. From an elevation of 1,974 feet, plus the height of the tower, the visitor who climbs the tower stairs is rewarded by a view extending fifteen miles and more in every direction.

The route makes a sharp turn, 55.2 *m.*, to the top of a bluff over which, in the old days, Indians used to run deer to their destruction.

At 60.1 *m.* is the junction with a CCC-built natural gravel road.

Left on this road to MOUNTAIN FORK RIVER, 4 *m.*, where it is feasible to launch a boat or a float, and where there is good fishing. Across the river at HOCHATOWN, a country school marks the site of the old Choctaw settlement.

At 64.1 *m.* on the main route is the junction with an improved CCC-built road.

Left on this road to BEAVERS BEND STATE PARK, 3 *m.*, a 1,250-acre tract of wild beauty. The clear, fast-flowing Mountain Fork River bisects the park, running between high and rugged banks. There are deep canyons down the sides of which water cataracts; great masses of tumble rocks; a great variety of trees and wild flowers; and squirrels, some deer, quail, wild turkeys, and the gone-wild "razorback" hogs of more or less distant farmers. Trails lead through the park.

From Mountain Fork River the fisherman may take channel cat, white perch, bass, and crappie; a low-water dam across the river backs the water up to form a mile-long lake *(boats, camp site, picnicking)*.

The park area, it is said, contains the greatest variety of birds to be found in the state. Among the wild flowers are bird-foot and dogtooth violets, wild hyacinth, iris, plum, trillium, bloodroot, honeysuckle, trumpet creeper, and the profusely growing wild rose.

State 21 descends gradually from this point to BROKEN BOW, 73.3 *m.* (467 alt., 2,367 pop.) *(see Tour 6)*, at the junction with US 70 *(see Tour 6)*.

Tour 16

Lake Francis Dam (Watts)—Tahlequah—Cookson—Junction with US 64; Illinois River, approximately 107. m. *(all mileages are approximate)*.

Accommodations limited to towns near the river banks; cabins and camping facilities at various points on the river. Between Watts and Tahlequah, vegetables may be purchased from farmers; between Tahlequah and Gore, the region is thinly settled, and the small farms are at considerable distances from the stream. A state fishing license *(nonresident, 10 days $1.25; resident, $1.25 per yr.)* may be obtained at Lake Francis Dam, at Tahlequah, or at the large camps along the river.

This Tour is a drifting voyage down the Illinois, a picturesque stream that twists its way in a southerly and slightly westerly direction through the hills of the old Cherokee country at the eastern edge of Oklahoma. The river penetrates a region known as the last retreat of the full bloods. At places it is broken by portages that vary from a few feet to a mile, though none is difficult under ordinary conditions. Throughout almost the length of the tour, the river runs between rugged flint-rock bluffs that range in height from 50 to 150 feet. The water is generally deep, and the stream bed either rock or coarse gravel; occasionally it is covered with silt washed in from upland farms. Those who choose the fall to drift down the Illinois will find rich color among the trees and shrubs that cling to the steep bluffs and crowd to the water's edge, with brilliant reds and yellows predominating.

Fishermen may make the tour at any time, though it is least advisable at the midsummer low-water stage. The best seasons are early spring and late fall. The river and its tributaries are stocked annually from the fish hatcheries maintained by the State Game and Fish Commission, which has also constructed more than three hundred low-water dams in feeder streams in order to regulate the volume of the Illinois and to provide year-round fishing.

The Illinois is free of rapids, whirlpools, and undertows, flowing swiftly, but always smoothly except during brief periods following heavy rains. The entire "float" may occupy the leisurely fishermen for nine days, but for one with fewer days to spend on the water it can be done rather easily in four; and a still more hurried floater may arrange to take either the upper section from Lake Francis to Tahlequah, or the lower from Tahlequah to Gore.

At the western end, 0 *m.,* of LAKE FRANCIS DAM, 1.6 miles north of WATTS (958 alt. 307 pop.) *(see Tour 15),* filling station attendants will supply boats, with the services of the necessary guide included, for approximately $10 per week. Here the voyager gets into fishing clothes—commonly shirt and trousers of denim, sneakers, and a battered hat, with an old coat to wear in the cool of the evening; he stows in the boat the blankets needed at night, and changes of clothing. Also he checks such necessary camping equipment as a frying pan, coffee pot, tin plates, and a large all-purpose pocket knife. Luxury equipment on the river are such items as tent, wading boots, and rifles. Dry fly fishermen and plug casters are outnumbered two to one by those who cut willow switch poles and bait their hooks with live bait obtainable along the stream. Signs along the way offering minnows for sale are frequent. Below the mouth of Baron Fork Creek, southeast of Tahlequah, however, it is well to have a minnow seine in the boat.

Most commonly taken in the Illinois are crappie, largemouthed and spotted bass, blue channel catfish (which sometimes attain enormous size), mountain and black perch. Red horse, a delicious, hard-fighting fish, varying in size from three to eight pounds, is seldom taken except during "shoalings."

The floater fortunate enough to be on the river just after a period of high water and just before it has subsided to the normal stage may see a shoaling, a local term used to describe the taking of red horse. The flood carries them downstream over shoals to the deep pools, and as the water subsides they (like salmon) fight back upstream. In that period, a stretch of shoal water will sometimes seem to be choked with them. Then local shoaling parties rush to the scene with long heavy lines to which large hooks are attached at intervals of about six inches. The lines are thrown into the water in big loops and, though the hooks are not baited, the red horse take them or are caught by the gills as the lines are pulled in.

For practically all of the entire trip, the fly caster will stick to the boat because the banks are too rugged and thicket-covered to permit fishing from the land. Recommended to the bass fishermen are dark flies and live minnows; the water is so clear that brilliantly colored flies and spinners are not required. Good flies to use on this water are the black gnat, Nez Perces, black hackle, black spider, a fly known locally as "yellow Sally," and other small yellow or brown varieties. For casting, experienced fishermen choose the small dark river runt, the Al Foos, or similar shimmy wigglers.

At 25 *m.*, downstream, is SULLIVAN'S CAMP, with four cabins and ample camping space. A store here is stocked with fishing equipment and groceries. Adjoining the camp on the south is a RECREATION GROUND *(free water, picnic facilities)*, maintained by the State Game and Fish Commission.

Northwest of the camp are the buildings and grounds of the NORTHEAST OUTING CLUB *(private)*.

At 27. *m.* is HANGING ROCK CAMP *(private)*; and near it is a ROADSIDE PARK *(open to tourists)* (R) extending from the west bank of the river to State 10.

NORTHEASTERN TEACHERS CAMP, 39 *m.*, is privately owned, but floaters are usually permitted to camp here. A mile downstream is the little town of ELLERVILLE, and at 41 *m.* is MARTIN'S CAMP *(open to the public)*. In this section the river banks offer good camp sites, and at near-by farmhouses country produce may be bought.

At MAC'S CAMP, 43 *m.*, in the great bend of the river, where it turns to flow northeast for several miles, are six cabins, a store, and a café and dance hall. Immediately west of it, and near State 10, is a tourist camp.

At 54 *m.* is the BRIDGE over which US 62 *(see Tour 3)* crosses the river; Tahlequah (864 alt., 3, 027 pop.) *(see Tour 3)* is 3.2 miles west. North of the bridge, at the highway, is RIVERSIDE PARK, owned and maintained by the city of Tahlequah, equipped with complete facilities for floaters.

For the floater who wishes to vary his voyage by leaving the river to hunt *(State license, $1.25, and land owners' permission required)*, the Cookson Hills south of Tahlequah offer the best opportunity. Here, cottontail rabbits *(no closed season)* and red and gray squirrels *(closed season Jan. 1 to May 1)* are fairly plentiful in the woods. The country is too thickly wooded and has too few clearings to tempt the quail hunter; and the only wild ducks seen are occasional teal that linger for a time after early October.

On this section of the river it is unprofitable for the fishermen to explore the small tributary streams, for they are uniformly shallow, clear, and devoid of large rocks or sunken logs to provide hiding places for the fish.

However, BARON FORK CREEK, 59 *m.*, is a good fishing stream (L), accessible by boat for twenty miles or more from its mouth. Besides the varieties found in the Illinois, the fisherman in this beautiful, canyon-confined stream may take excellent miniature brown bass, a game fish that prefers the cold spring-fed creek to the warmer expanses of the river. The creek, varying in width and depth, has cut its way through rugged hills, has a rock-and-gravel bottom, and is shaded for most of the day by the high, nearly sheer cliffs that for the greater part of the distance rise on either side.

HUBBARD'S CAMP and SHARON'S CAMP, both on Baron Fork close to the Illinois, are well equipped to care for the floater. Sharon's consists of a twenty-acre tract on which are eight cabins and adequate facilities for campers.

At 66 *m.* the river makes a wide horseshoe bend, flowing rather swiftly under the shadow of a limestone bluff (L) that rises some one hundred feet above the water. At the middle of the bend is a similar cliff (R), its sheer surface bare and deeply eroded. Trees at the tops of these cliffs grow so near the edge that their shadows are cast upon the water.

At 69 *m.* the bluff slopes so gradually that near-by farmers have cut a road down to the river (L) over which they haul water for livestock.

Left on this road to BARBER, 2.5 *m.,* a tiny country settlement grouped about a small church in which services are conducted in the Cherokee language; the Sunday sermon is usually (1941) preached by Jackson Standing Deer Larvin, a North Carolina–born Cherokee who came to Indian Territory at the age of nine. The Indian congregation gives the church good support and resort to such white country people's devices as pie suppers and cake sales to raise money to pay the preacher.

The CHEROKEE CEMETERY, 3 *m.,* is worth a visit on Decoration Day. The evening before, Indians come from miles around on foot, on horseback, by wagon and automobile and camp at TOM FIXON'S PLACE near by. Here the evening is spent in singing songs in Cherokee. In the morning they march in procession to the burying ground and hold a service, after which they re-form to march slowly among the graves scattering flowers indiscriminately upon all graves. Most of the flowers are made of crepe paper, but some are gathered from roadsides and pastures. At noon a communal meal is spread on plank trestle tables, in which the characteristic Cherokee dishes of *conutchcie* (a hominy made of corn and nuts), bean bread, and lye-treated hominy are served.

Many white residents of Barber and the surrounding neighborhood belong to a religious sect called the True Followers of Christ. They have no church building and no ordained minister, but meet on Sunday afternoons at the home of a member, where services are conducted by various adherents. The True Followers' faith teaches them to rely upon "the power of the Word," and to refuse all medical aid when ill. Instead, the elders of the congregation assemble at the home of the patient and pray for his recovery.

Members of the sect habitually greet one another with the "holy kiss" and observe the feet-washing ritual at Sunday services. Women members are forbidden to bob their hair, use cosmetics, or wear beads, rings, and other ornaments. Severe simplicity of dress is demanded, though no uniform has been adopted. They profess to be in constant communication with God and declare that messages come from Him directing each small detail of their lives.

COOKSON, 77 *m.* (592 alt., 50 pop.), is the old Cherokee settlement (L) from which the Cookson Hills were named. Here, at STATTON'S STORE and CAMP, the floater may secure supplies and accommodations. In this region there is a striking succession of bloom from early spring to late fall beginning with dogwood and redbud and extending to wild asters and goldenrod. In between come the clumps of Cherokee wild rose, wild ginger, honeysuckle, dogfennel, and horehound.

Along this part of the river the water flows swiftly between high and precipitous banks, and there are few landing places. In the deep water here are found the best of the big blue channel catfish. Local fishermen put out trotlines, usually at night, but in any case weighted to a depth to prevent being caught by a passing boat. The floater is advised to seek a quiet deep pool and use chicken liver or dough soaked with chicken blood for bait.

At 107 *m.* is a bridge over which US 64 *(see Tour 2)* crosses the Illinois River.

Congress has authorized the construction of a dam across the Illinois River at this point (approximately three miles above its confluence with the Arkansas River). It is a part of the projected $44,000,000 Mississippi River flood control project and will be known as the TENKILLER FERRY RESERVOIR. When completed, it will have a capacity of some nine hundred thousand acre feet and storage for more than 11 per cent of the waters from the Illinois River drainage area. The importance of the proposed project is indicated by army engineers' estimate that about 30 per cent of the waters which caused the disastrous Mississippi floods in 1927 came from three Oklahoma rivers—the Illinois, the Grand, and the Verdigris.

Right from the bridge on US 64 is GORE, 1.7 m. (480 alt., 334 pop.) *(see Tour 2).*

PART IV
Appendices

Chronology

1541 Francisco Vásquez de Coronado crosses western Oklahoma in search of the golden city of Quivira; claims land for Spain but makes no permanent settlement.

Hernando de Soto explores along present eastern border of Oklahoma.

1650 Don Diego del Castillo spends six months in the Wichita Mountains prospecting for gold and silver.

1682 Robert-René Cavelier, Sieur de La Salle claims for the King of France all lands drained by the Mississippi River (including Oklahoma) under the name of Louisiana.

1719 Bernard de la Harpe crosses southeastern Oklahoma from the Red River to the vicinity of the present Muskogee.

Claud Charles de Tisné visits Pawnee villages near the present site of Chelsea.

1762 Louisiana (including Oklahoma) is ceded to Spain by France.

1800 Louisiana is retroceded to France by Spain.

1802 United States makes a compact with Georgia to remove the Creeks and Cherokees from the state as soon as it can be done "peaceably and on favorable terms."

Pierre Chouteau induces some of the Osages to remove from Missouri to northeastern Oklahoma and opens up a profitable trade with them.

1803 United States purchases Louisiana from France.

President Thomas Jefferson draws up a proposal for exchanging land occupied by Indians in the eastern states for "equivalent portions" in Louisiana.

1804 All of Louisiana north of the thirty-third parallel is designated as the District of Louisiana and placed under the administration of Indiana Territory; William Henry Harrison thus becomes the first American governor of Oklahoma.

1805 District of Louisiana is organized as the Territory of Louisiana with the seat of government at St. Louis.

1806 Lieutenant James B. Wilkinson descends the Arkansas River crossing northeastern Oklahoma.

1808 Several Cherokee chiefs and headmen inform President Jefferson that a portion of the tribe wishes to emigrate to the West.

1811 Territory of Louisiana is organized as the Territory of Missouri.
George C. Sibley, United States Indian agent, explores the Great Salt Plains near the present Cherokee.

1817 Cherokees sign the first removal treaty obtaining land in the present state of Arkansas, and the movement of one-third of the tribe to the new location begins.
Fort Smith is established on the present border of Oklahoma to protect the immigrant Indians.

1819 That portion of the Territory of Missouri south of 36°30′ is organized as the Territory of Arkansas, including all of Oklahoma except a strip along the present northern boundary.
Thomas Nuttall, English naturalist, visits Oklahoma studying flora and fauna.
Boundary between the United States and the Spanish possessions is fixed at the Red River and the one-hundredth meridian, thus establishing the southern and western limits of Oklahoma.

1820 Choctaws purchase the area south of the Canadian and Arkansas rivers—the first eastern Indian tribe to acquire land in Oklahoma—but few remove to the new location.
Arkansas legislature passes an act creating Miller County in southeastern Oklahoma and establishing the Miller Courthouse, the first court within the present state.

1821 Rev. Epaphras Chapman founds Union Mission on Grand River among the Osages—the first Protestant mission in Oklahoma.
Sequoyah completes the Cherokee alphabet.

1824 First post office in Oklahoma is opened at Miller Courthouse.
Fort Gibson—the first fort in Oklahoma—is established on the Grand River; Fort Towson is established on the Red River near the mouth of the Kiamichi.

1825 Treaty with the Choctaws fixes the present eastern boundary of Oklahoma from Fort Smith to the Red River.

1826 Creeks purchase a tract of land in Oklahoma, and a portion of the tribe prepares to emigrate.
Military road is constructed from Fort Gibson to Fort Smith, the first road established in Oklahoma.

1828 First immigrant Creeks arrive in Oklahoma and begin to lay out farms in the Arkansas valley.
Cherokees in Arkansas exchange their land for a tract in Oklahoma; the boundary established by this treaty fixes the remainder of the present eastern boundary of the state.

1829 Arkansas Cherokees begin their removal to Oklahoma; Sequoyah settles in the present Sequoyah County; Dwight Mission, established by the Presbyterians for the Arkansas Cherokees, is removed to Oklahoma.
Sam Houston, after resigning as governor of Tennessee, settles near Fort Gibson and is granted full citizenship rights by the Cherokee Council.

President Andrew Jackson in his message to Congress advises removal of all Indians remaining in the East.

1830 Indian Removal Act is passed by Congress.

Choctaws cede the remainder of their land in Mississippi and prepare to remove to Oklahoma, the main removals taking place during the succeeding three years.

A Presbyterian church is organized among the Creeks in the Arkansas valley.

1832 Cherokee Council provides for the opening of five schools, the first school law enacted in the present state of Oklahoma.

Washington Irving accompanies United States rangers on an expedition from Fort Gibson to the present site of Norman, recording his experiences in *A Tour on the Prairies*.

Creeks cede the remainder of their land in the East, thus paving the way for the removal of the succeeding four years.

A Presbyterian church is organized among the immigrant Choctaws at Wheelock, and a Baptist church among the Creeks.

1833 Seminoles are tricked into signing a removal treaty, which is followed by the long and exhausting Seminole War and the final colonization of the tribe in Oklahoma.

1834 United States Commissioners draw up a territorial form of government for the immigrant Indians, the first of many futile attempts to create an Indian state of Oklahoma.

Leavenworth-Dodge Expedition from Fort Gibson visits southwestern Oklahoma and establishes friendly relations with the wild tribes.

1835 Comanche and Wichita Indians enter into treaty relations with the United States at a council held near the present site of Lexington.

Criminal jurisdiction of the Federal courts of Arkansas is extended over Oklahoma.

Cherokees remaining in the East cede their land to the United States, thus paving the way for the removals of the succeeding three years.

Samuel A. Worcester installs a printing press at Union Mission and publishes the first book printed in Oklahoma.

1837 Chickasaws surrender their lands in the East and begin their removal to Oklahoma.

1838 Choctaws complete a council house of hewn logs near the present site of Tuskahoma, the first capitol built in Oklahoma.

1839 Newly arrived Cherokees and "Old Settler Cherokees" adopt a new constitution and establish a council ground at Tahlequah.

1842 Fort Washita is established to protect the Chickasaw settlements from the wild tribes of the Southwest.

Choctaw congregation at Wheelock builds a stone church, which still stands as the oldest church building in Oklahoma.

1843 A great council of eighteen Indian tribes is held at Tahlequah, and a code of intertribal law is drawn up and adopted by the Cherokees, Creeks, and Osages.

1844 *The Cherokee Messenger*—the first newspaper published in Oklahoma —is issued at a Baptist missionary station north of the present Westville; it is followed a month later by *The Cherokee Advocate,* published at Tahlequah.

First cotton gin in the Cherokee Nation—probably the first in Oklahoma—is constructed on the Arkansas fifteen miles above Fort Smith.

1849 First Masonic Lodge established in an Indian tribe is organized at Tahlequah.

Hordes of California gold-seekers follow a well-defined trail across Oklahoma.

1850 Texas relinquishes the land north of 36°30′, thus forming the southern boundary of the Oklahoma Panhandle.

1851 Fort Arbuckle is established.

1852 Tahlequah is incorporated under Cherokee law—the first incorporated town in Oklahoma.

1854 Kansas-Nebraska Act defines the southern boundary of Kansas at 37°, thus fixing the northern boundary of Oklahoma.

1856 Seminoles separate from the Creeks and form their own government.

Chickasaws set up a tribal government, adopt a constitution, and establish Tishomingo as their capital.

1858 Butterfield stage and mail route is laid out, crossing Oklahoma from Fort Smith west and south to the Red River.

1859 An intertribal law code is drawn up by the Five Civilized Tribes (Cherokees, Choctaws, Chickasaws, Creeks, and Seminoles) at North Fork Town.

Fort Cobb is established on the western frontier of civilized Indian settlement.

1860 Choctaws adopt the constitution under which their government functions until the end of the tribal period.

1861 United States abandons the forts in Oklahoma; most of the Indian tribes align with the Confederates; thousands of Union Indians flee to Kansas.

1862 A Union military expedition from Kansas penetrates to Fort Gibson.

1863 Union forces defeat the Confederates at Honey Springs, the most important battle fought in Oklahoma during the Civil War.

1865 Confederate Indians surrender to Union forces more than two months after Appomatox; United States officials hold a council with the Indians and lay down terms for the resumption of treaty relations.

1866 Five Civilized Tribes sign treaties with the United States freeing their slaves, ceding the western half of Oklahoma for the settlement of other Indians, and agreeing to a tentative intertribal organization.

The name Oklahoma is first suggested by Allen Wright, member of the Choctaw treaty delegation.

Congress grants franchises for the construction of the first two railroads across Oklahoma.

1867 United States makes the first of a series of treaties, assigning reservations to Indian tribes in the ceded territory.
Creeks adopt their final constitution.

1869 Fort Sill is established as the base of operations against the Plains Indians.

1870 Construction is started on the Missouri-Kansas-Texas Railroad—the first to enter the Oklahoma area.
Federal government begins the survey of the Chickasaw district, establishing the initial point from which all of Oklahoma except the Panhandle is eventually surveyed.
First meeting of the intertribal council is convened at Okmulgee.

1872 First coal mining on a commercial scale begins at McAlester in the Choctaw Nation.

1874 Fort Reno is established.

1875 Resistance of the Plains Indians to white encroachment is finally crushed.
Intertribal council at Okmulgee holds its last session.

1876 Last buffalo herd is reported in Oklahoma.

1879 First telephone in Oklahoma is set up, connecting Fort Sill and Fort Reno.
"Boomers" begin their attempts to settle on the "Oklahoma Lands."
Will Rogers is born in the Cherokee Nation near Oologah.
Population of the Indian Territory is estimated at 81,381; this includes Indians, a few white residents, and ex-slaves of the Indians.

1882 Isparhecher begins the rebellion against the Creek government known as the Green Peach War.
Atlantic and Pacific Railroad establishes a station in the Creek Nation at a place called "Tulsey Town" by the Indians.

1883 Isparhecher faction makes peace with the constitutional Creek government.
Cherokee Strip Live Stock Association leases the "Outlet" from the Cherokee Nation.

1884 A company of Choctaw citizens drills for oil near Atoka.

1887 Congress passes the Dawes Act, providing for breaking up the Indian reservations into individual allotments and opening the surplus land to white settlement.

1889 First Federal court in Oklahoma is established in Muskogee.
Oklahoma's first producing oil well is drilled near Chelsea.
First Run opens an area in Oklahoma to white settlement; Oklahoma City, Guthrie, Norman, and other cities and towns are established.

1890 Congress creates a Territorial government for the settlers in the "Oklahoma Lands"; Guthrie becomes the capital; George W. Steele is appointed governor; the First Territorial Legislature adopts a code of laws and establishes a school system.

Panhandle is joined to the Territory of Oklahoma.

First Federal census shows a population of 78,475 in Oklahoma Territory and 180,182 in the area of the Five Civilized Tribes.

1891 First statehood convention is held in Oklahoma City.

First Territorial college—later the Central State College—is opened at Edmond; the Oklahoma Agricultural and Mechanical College is opened at Stillwater.

The Sac and Fox, Iowa, Shawnee, and Potawatomi reservations are opened for settlement, adding two new counties.

1892 University of Oklahoma is opened at Norman.

The Cheyenne and Arapaho country is opened for settlement, adding six new counties.

1893 Dawes Commission is created for the purpose of liquidating the affairs of the Five Civilized Tribes.

Oklahoma Historical Society is founded at Kingfisher.

Cherokee Outlet is opened to white settlement by the greatest of all the Runs in Oklahoma.

1896 Greer County is awarded to the United States by a Supreme Court decision and joined to the Territory of Oklahoma.

1897 Choctaws, Chickasaws, and Seminoles make agreements with the Dawes Commission.

1898 Congress passes the Curtis Act providing for compulsory liquidation of the Five Civilized Tribes.

Many Oklahoma and Indian frontiersmen serve with Roosevelt's Rough Riders in the Spanish-American War.

1899 United States takes over the schools, the Dawes Commission starts allotting the lands, and the first townsites are platted for the Five Civilized Tribes.

1900 First course in geology is taught at the University of Oklahoma.

Federal census shows a population of 398,331 in the Territory of Oklahoma and 392,060 in the Five Civilized Tribes area.

1901 Kiowa-Comanche and Wichita reservations are opened to settlement, the last opening in Oklahoma.

1905 Inhabitants of the Five Tribes area hold a convention and draw up a constitution for a state to be named Sequoyah.

Glenn Oil Pool is discovered.

1906 Congress passes the Enabling Act providing statehood for Oklahoma; the constitutional convention meets at Guthrie.

1907 November 16. Oklahoma is admitted to the Union, the forty-sixth state; the first election reveals overwhelming Democratic majority; Charles N. Haskell, the first governor, is inaugurated at Guthrie.

Special Federal census enumerates a population of 1,414,177 for the new state.

1910 State capital is removed to Oklahoma City.

Population, 1,657,155.

1911 State legislature provides for placing a statue of Sequoyah in Statuary Hall in the national Capitol.
Lee Cruce is inaugurated as governor.

1912 Cushing Oil Pool is discovered.

1913 Healdton Oil Field is discovered.

1915 Robert L. Williams is inaugurated as governor.

1916 Oklahoma National Guard sees service on the Mexican Border.

1917 United States declares war on Germany; in the first draft Oklahoma registers 173,744; the sporadic "Green Corn Rebellion" breaks out against conscription.

1918 End of first World War, for which Oklahoma furnished 88,496 men in uniform and purchased $116,368,045 worth of Liberty Bonds.

1919 J. B. A. Robertson is inaugurated as governor of Oklahoma.

1920 Oklahoma for the first time in its history votes Republican.
Oil fields in Osage County begin spectacular production.
Population, 2,028,283.

1923 John Calloway (Jack) Walton becomes governor, is impeached and removed from office, and is succeeded by Martin Edwin Trapp.

1926 Greater Seminole Oil Field is developed, bringing serious overproduction in the oil industry.

1927 Henry S. Johnston becomes governor.

1928 Oklahoma City Oil Field is opened.

1929 Governor Johnston is impeached and removed from office; William J. Holloway becomes governor.

1930 Population, 2,396,040.

1931 William H. ("Alfalfa Bill") Murray is inaugurated as governor.
Governor Murray closes Oklahoma oil wells in an effort to stabilize prices.
Wiley Post, noted Oklahoma air pilot, completes round-the-world flight of 16,474 miles in 8 days, 15 hours, 51 minutes.

1935 E. W. Marland is inaugurated as governor.
Will Rogers and Wiley Post die in airplane crash in Alaska.

1937 Construction begins on $22,750,000 Grand River Dam in eastern Oklahoma.

1939 Leon C. ("Red") Phillips becomes governor.

1940 Population, 2,336,434, a loss of 59,606 since census of 1930.

Selected Reading List

This list is not designed as an exhaustive or scholarly bibliography, but as a guide to the general reader seeking further information about Oklahoma.

Alford, Thomas Wildcat. *Civilization* (Florence Drake, editor). University of Oklahoma Press, Norman, Oklahoma, 1936. Life on the Shawnee reservation as told by a great-grandson of Tecumseh; a firsthand account of Indian life and customs and the adjustment to the white man's institutions.

Allen, C. M. *The Sequoyah Convention.* Harlow Publishing Company, Oklahoma City, Oklahoma, 1925. A history of the movement which resulted in the formation of the state of Oklahoma.

Alley, John. *City Beginnings in Oklahoma Territory.* University of Oklahoma Press, Norman, Oklahoma, 1939. Shows how the cities of Guthrie, Oklahoma City, Kingfisher, El Reno, Norman, and Stillwater sprang up at the time of the first Run.

Ball, Max W. *This Fascinating Oil Business.* Bobbs-Merrill Company, Indianapolis and New York, 1940. A nontechnical book, giving a complete description of the oil industry from prospecting to the finished product; not confined to Oklahoma, but presenting an adequate background of oil development in the state.

Barnard, Evan G. *A Rider of the Cherokee Strip.* Houghton Mifflin Company, Boston and New York, 1936. A firsthand account in vivid, narrative style of ranching and homesteading in Oklahoma.

Bass, Althea. *Cherokee Messenger.* University of Oklahoma Press, Norman, Oklahoma, 1936. A readable biography of Samuel Austin Worcester; an account of the missionary work of the Worcester family, and the early educational progress of the Cherokees.

Brookings Institution. *Organization and Administration of Oklahoma.* Harlow Publishing Company, Oklahoma City, 1935. A critical study of the functioning of Oklahoma government with recommendations for improvement. Since its publication, of course, much has transpired which could not have been anticipated in the report itself.

Buchanan, James Shannon, and Dale, Edward Everett. *A History of Oklahoma.* Row, Peterson and Company, New York, 1935. Designed for a school textbook and told in simple language; historically sound, and one of the best brief surveys of Oklahoma history.

Buck, Solon J. *The Settlement of Oklahoma.* A reprint from Volume XV, Part II, of the transactions of the Wisconsin Academy of Science, Arts and Letters, Madison, Wisconsin, 1907. A research project, well annotated.

Canton, Frank M. *Frontier Trails* (Edward Everett Dale, editor). Houghton Mifflin Company, Boston and New York, 1930. An autobiography of a colorful Oklahoma pioneer.

Collings, Ellsworth, and England, Alma Miller. *The 101 Ranch.* University of Oklahoma Press, Norman, Oklahoma, 1937. An account of the manifold activities of this famous ranch near Ponca City; traces the development from range cattle industry to agriculture, oil production, rodeos, and Wild West shows.

Dale, Edward Everett. *The Range Cattle Industry.* University of Oklahoma Press, Norman, Oklahoma, 1930. A vivid and authentic history of ranching on the Great Plains, including the area now comprising the state of Oklahoma.

———, and Litton, Gaston, editors. *Cherokee Cavaliers.* University of Oklahoma Press, Norman, Oklahoma, 1939. Forty years of Cherokee history, graphically told in the correspondence of the Ridge-Watie-Boudinot family.

———, and Rader, Jesse L. *Readings in Oklahoma History.* Row, Peterson, and Company, New York, 1930. A collection of nontechnical source material, illustrating phases of Oklahoma history.

Debo, Angie. *And Still the Waters Run.* Princeton University Press, Princeton, New Jersey, 1940. The liquidation of the Five Civilized Tribes in preparation for statehood, and the picture of the Indians as citizens of Oklahoma.

———. *The Rise and Fall of the Choctaw Republic.* University of Oklahoma Press, Norman, Oklahoma, 1934. A political, social, and economic history of the Choctaw Indians.

———. *The Road to Disappearance.* University of Oklahoma Press, Norman, Oklahoma, 1941. A scholarly study of the Creek Indians to the dissolution of their tribal government in Oklahoma.

Ferguson, Mrs. Tom B. *They Carried the Torch.* Burton Publishing Company, Kansas City, 1937. The spirited reminiscences of a pioneer newspaper woman; almost a social history of the development of Oklahoma Territory.

Foreman, Carolyn Thomas. *Oklahoma Imprints.* University of Oklahoma Press, Norman, Oklahoma, 1936. A comprehensive history of printing in the area forming the present state of Oklahoma, from the establishment of the first press in 1835 to the time of statehood. Useful as a reference book, presenting in its newspaper history a complete cross section of Indian and pioneer life.

Foreman, Grant. *Down the Texas Road.* University of Oklahoma Press, Norman, Oklahoma, 1936. A handy little booklet, giving an authentic description of historical places along Highway 69 through Oklahoma.

———. *Fort Gibson.* University of Oklahoma Press, Norman, Oklahoma, 1936. A readable pamphlet describing the active life that centered around this frontier post.

———. *Marcy and the Gold Seekers.* University of Oklahoma Press, Norman, Oklahoma, 1939. The journal of Captain Randolph B. Marcy with an account of the gold rush over the "California Trail" across Oklahoma.

———. *Sequoyah.* University of Oklahoma Press, Norman, Oklahoma, 1938. The definitive biography of this Indian genius.

———. *The Five Civilized Tribes.* University of Oklahoma Press, Norman, Oklahoma, 1934. Probably the most interesting of this historian's many books; an authentic picture of life in what is now Oklahoma before the Civil War.

———, editor. *Adventure on Red River.* University of Oklahoma Press, Norman, Oklahoma, 1937. Report on the exploration of the headwaters of the Red River by Captain Randolph B. Marcy and Captain G. B. McClellan.

———. *Indians and Pioneers.* University of Oklahoma Press, Norman, Oklahoma, 1936. The story of the American Southwest before 1830.

———. *Advancing the Frontier.* University of Oklahoma Press, Norman, Oklahoma, 1933. A well-told and documented story of the immigrant Indians and their problems from 1770 to 1830.

———. *Indian Removal.* University of Oklahoma Press, Norman, Oklahoma, 1932. A readable and authentic account of the emigration of the Five Civilized Tribes.

Gittinger, Roy. *The Formation of the State of Oklahoma.* University of Oklahoma Press, Norman, Oklahoma, 1939. A scholarly history of events leading to the creation of the state.

Glasscock, C. B. *Then Came Oil.* Bobbs-Merrill Company, Indianapolis and New York, 1938. Oklahoma history as affected by the discovery and development of the oil industry of the state.

Gould, Charles N. *Oklahoma Place Names.* University of Oklahoma Press, Norman, Oklahoma, 1933. Explains the origin of numerous names of rivers, cities, towns, and mountains of Oklahoma.

Hill, Luther B. *A History of the State of Oklahoma.* The Lewis Publishing Company, Chicago and New York, 1908. An early attempt to tell the story of Oklahoma from the date of the Louisiana Purchase, through the formation of the state.

Hitchcock, Ethan Allen. *A Traveler in Indian Territory* (Grant Foreman, editor). The Torch Press, Cedar Rapids, Iowa, 1930. An extremely interesting journal of Hitchcock's visit to the Indian Territory in 1842. It is especially rich in Creek material, showing how that recently transplanted tribe was establishing its institutions upon a remote frontier.

Irving, Washington. *A Tour on the Prairies* (George C. Wells and Joseph B. Thoburn, editors). Harlow Publishing Company, Oklahoma City, 1926. The well-known classic tracing Irving's route across Oklahoma, edited with reference to present-day landmarks.

Lewis, Anna. *Along the Arkansas.* The Southwest Press, Dallas, Texas, 1932. Early history of the Arkansas River region in Oklahoma; also the Cimarron and Canadian.

Marable, Mary Hays, and Boylan, Elaine. *A Handbook of Oklahoma Writers.* University of Oklahoma Press, Norman, Oklahoma, 1939.

Mathews, John Joseph. *Wah'Kon-Tah.* University of Oklahoma Press, Norman, Oklahoma, 1932. A beautifully written interpretation of the Osage spirit, based on notes kept by Laban J. Miles, United States Agent to the tribe.

Morrison, William Brown. *Military Posts and Camps in Oklahoma.* Harlow Publishing Company, Oklahoma City, 1936. An account of the military posts established at different times in Oklahoma.

Nye, W. S. *Carbine and Lance.* University of Oklahoma Press, Norman, Oklahoma, 1937. A popular and accurate account of Indian campaigns in western Oklahoma, centered about the history of Fort Sill.

Oklahoma Historical Society. *Chronicles of Oklahoma.* Oklahoma City, 1921— A quarterly publication containing scholarly articles by historians and colorful reminiscences by pioneers.

Oklahoma Writers' Program. *Tulsa, a Guide to the Oil Capital.* Mid-West Printing Company, Tulsa, Oklahoma, 1938. Contains information about the history, industry, and cultural institutions of Tulsa with directions to its points of interest. Brief and factual.

Rainey, George. *The Cherokee Strip.* The Co-operative Publishing Company, Guthrie, Oklahoma, 1933. An intimate, readable history of the Cherokee Outlet from the date of its acquisition by the Cherokees to the opening in 1893.

———. *No Man's Land.* Enid, Oklahoma, 1937. A story of the Oklahoma Panhandle beginning with the first white man's visit to the region. Contains many human-interest stories peculiar to the section.

Ridings, Sam P. *The Chisholm Trail.* Co-operative Publishing Company, Guthrie, Oklahoma, 1936. A comprehensive and entertaining account of the drives, personalities, and places along the trail in the period of its greatest use.

Rister, Carl Coke. *Southern Plainsmen.* University of Oklahoma Press, Norman, Oklahoma, 1938. A history of the southern half of the Great Plains, especially noting the characteristics of the short-grass country which includes western Oklahoma.

Ryan, Frederick Lynne. *A History of Labor Legislation in Oklahoma.* University of Oklahoma Press, Norman, Oklahoma, 1932. A scholarly book, which traces the important developments in labor legislation since the opening of the Choctaw coal fields in 1872.

———. *The Rehabilitation of Oklahoma Coal Mining Communities.* University of Oklahoma Press, Norman, Oklahoma, 1935. A systematic study showing the condition of a typical modern mining area and submitting constructive proposals for social betterment.

Sears, Paul B. *Deserts on the March.* University of Oklahoma Press, Norman, Oklahoma, 1935. A brilliant study of soil erosion; not limited to Oklahoma, but inspired by Oklahoma problems.

Seger, John H. *Early Days Among the Cheyenne and Arapahoe Indians* (Stanley Vestal, editor). University of Oklahoma Press, Norman, Oklahoma, 1934. The memoirs of a great educator among Plains Indians; an intimate, informal account written with grace and charm.

Snider, Luther Crocker. *Geography of Oklahoma.* Oklahoma Geological Survey, Norman, Oklahoma, 1917. Describes the geology, physical features, mineral resources, plant and animal life, agriculture, and political and social institutions of Oklahoma. Encyclopedic in style but nontechnical. Not seriously outdated.

Starr, Emmet. *History of the Cherokee Indians.* The Warden Company, Oklahoma City, Oklahoma, 1921. In this genealogical history of the Cherokees is included much of the tribe's legends and folklore.

Stewart, Dora Ann. *Government and Development of Oklahoma Territory.* Harlow Publishing Company, Oklahoma City, 1933. An account of the building of a commonwealth in the seventeen years from 1890 to 1907, with special emphasis on the Federal government's program of Indian education.

Thoburn, Joseph B., and Wright, Muriel H. *Oklahoma, a History of the State and Its People,* Vols. I-IV. Lewis Historical Publishing Company, New York, 1929. A convenient set that may be found in most public libraries of the state.

Wardell, Morris L. *A Political History of the Cherokee Nation.* University of Oklahoma Press, Norman, Oklahoma, 1938. The political story of the Cherokees from the Removal in 1838 to the breakup of tribal government.

Weaver, Findley. *Oklahoma's Deficit.* University of Oklahoma Press, Norman, Oklahoma, 1940. A thorough study of state finance. It discusses the basic causes of the recurring deficit, the revenues and expenditures, the lack of adequate financial accounting, the nullification of the constitutional debt limitations, and recommended reforms.

Weidman, Samuel. *The Miami-Picher Zinc-Lead District.* University of Oklahoma Press, Norman, Oklahoma, 1932. A technical study dealing with the history, geography, geology, mining and milling methods, and production statistics of the Oklahoma portion of the Tri-State Mining Region.

Wright, Muriel H. *Our Oklahoma.* Co-operative Publishing Company, Guthrie, Oklahoma, 1939. A school text on Oklahoma history, profusely illustrated, readable, accurate.

Index

UNIVERSITY OF OKLAHOMA PRESS

NORMAN